IFIP Advances in Information and Communication Technology 685

IFIP Advances in Information and Communication Technology

The IFIP AICT series publishes state-of-the-art results in the sciences and technologies of information and communication. The scope of the series includes: foundations of computer science; software theory and practice; education; computer applications in technology; communication systems; systems modeling and optimization; information systems; ICT and society; computer systems technology; security and protection in information processing systems; artificial intelligence; and human-computer interaction.

Edited volumes and proceedings of refereed international conferences in computer science and interdisciplinary fields are featured. These results often precede journal publication and represent the most current research.

The principal aim of the IFIP AICT series is to encourage education and the dissemination and exchange of information about all aspects of computing.

More information about this series at https://link.springer.com/bookseries/6102

Therese Keane · Cathy Lewin ·
Torsten Brinda · Rosa Bottino
Editors

Towards a Collaborative Society Through Creative Learning

IFIP World Conference on Computers in Education, WCCE 2022
Hiroshima, Japan, August 20–24, 2022
Revised Selected Papers

Springer

Editors
Therese Keane
School of Education
La Trobe University
Deepdene, VIC, Australia

Torsten Brinda
University of Duisburg-Essen
Essen, Germany

Cathy Lewin
Education and Social Research Institute
Manchester Metropolitan University
Manchester, UK

Rosa Bottino
Istituto Tecnologie Didattiche
Consiglio Nazioanale delle Ricerche
Genoa, Genova, Italy

ISSN 1868-4238 ISSN 1868-422X (electronic)
IFIP Advances in Information and Communication Technology
ISBN 978-3-031-43392-4 ISBN 978-3-031-43393-1 (eBook)
https://doi.org/10.1007/978-3-031-43393-1

This Springer imprint is published by the registered company Springer Nature Switzerland AG
The registered company address is: Gewerbestrasse 11, 6330 Cham, Switzerland

Paper in this product is recyclable.

Preface

Every four years, Technical Committee 3 (Education) of the International Federation for Information Processing (IFIP) has presented a major international conference: the World Conference on Computers in Education (WCCE). WCCE 2022 was held at the International Conference Center in Hiroshima, Japan. WCCE was originally due to take place in 2021 but the conference was postponed by a year due to the COVID pandemic. The conference was hosted from August 20–24, 2022 and for the first time in IFIP TC3 history was organized in a hybrid format, which also allowed participation via the Internet. The decision for a hybrid format was mainly caused by the worldwide impact of the COVID pandemic on international travel and conference participation.

WCCE was established as the main event of IFIP TC3 and a central place to share current interests in research and practice in learning and technology. WCCE creates a unique exchange place for educational excellence from all over the world, in a multidisciplinary and inter-professional spirit.

This book contains revised selected papers from the IFIP World Conference on Computers in Education (WCCE 2022), organized by Technical Committee 3: Education (TC3) and its working groups in collaboration with the Information Processing Society of Japan (IPSJ). WCCE 2022 provided a forum for new research results, practical experiences, developments, ideas, and national perspectives related to the conference focus and the themes listed below for all levels of education (preschool, primary, secondary, higher, vocational, and lifelong learning), including the professional development of educators (teachers, trainers, and academic and support staff at other educational institutions) and related questions on educational management.

The special focus of the WCCE 2022 conference was *Towards a Collaborative Society Through Creative Learning*, which has also been selected as the title of this book. As the world is increasingly interconnected and complex, the need for more critical and creative thinkers as well as for people to be able to fruitfully collaborate with others is increasing. Creative strategies must be implemented in education so that citizens in general, and students at all levels in particular, are better prepared to create new and meaningful forms of ideas, take risks, and be flexible and cooperative.

Submissions to the conference were invited to address one or more of the following *four key themes*:

- Digital education in schools, universities, and other educational institutions.
- National policies and plans for digital competence.
- Learning with digital technologies.
- Learning about digital technologies and computing.

Altogether, 174 submissions of full and short papers, symposia, posters, demonstrations, workshops, panel sessions, and national sessions were received and reviewed by reviewers in a double-blind peer-review process. Among these submissions were 91 full papers (12 pages in length) and 40 short papers (six pages in length), totalling 131.

Each of these academic papers was initially reviewed by three reviewers. Five further academic papers resulting from the Symposia at the conference were submitted after the conference had taken place, which were also reviewed by three reviewers each. Altogether, there was a total of 136 papers (96 full papers, 40 short papers). Sixty-one papers (54 full papers and 7 short papers) were accepted for publication in the volume at hand. The overall acceptance rate was 44.9%. The initial reviewing period lasted for approximately 30 days and successful manuscripts that were accepted for the book were then revised again. Manuscripts that were evaluated to need major revision were subjected to a further round of reviews that lasted for a further 30 days. In the initial round of reviews, the average number of submissions assigned to a reviewer was 5.7 papers.

The revised selected papers in this book arise from contributions from (in alphabetical order) Australia, China, Estonia, France, Germany, Greece, Indonesia, Ireland, Israel, Italy, Japan, Kenya, Malaysia, Morocco, New Zealand, Norway, Portugal, Serbia, Slovakia, South Africa, South Korea, Switzerland, Taiwan, the United Kingdom, and the United States of America, which reflects the conference's success in bringing together and networking experts from many countries worldwide.

This book selects a range of research papers that focus on the ways that digital applications and computing education have, are, and will help to develop a collaborative society. It includes papers that concern new and developing uses of digital applications and computing in professional practice, and long-term implications and effects on society and creativity. This book brings together papers that illustrate and detail these forms of digital and computing education, across a wide range of countries, in different contexts. The text focuses on the need for more critical and creative thinkers as well as for people able to fruitfully collaborate with others as the world becomes more and more interconnected and complex. Creative strategies must be implemented in education so that citizens in general, and students at all levels in particular, are better prepared to create new and meaningful forms of ideas, take risks, and be flexible and cooperative.

The book is organized into the following sections:

- Digital education and computing in schools
  - Digital education in schools
  - Computing in schools
- Digital education and computing in higher education
  - Digital education in higher education
  - Computing in higher education
- National policies and plans for digital competence

Digital Education

Digital education has revolutionized the way schools, universities, and other educational institutions approach teaching and learning. In innovative institutions, it has provided a platform for nurturing creativity by encouraging students to explore new ideas, engage in collaborative projects, and think critically. Integrating technologies into teaching practices has enabled educators to develop effective and creative pedagogies, making learning more engaging and interactive. Digital tools have also facilitated assessment, evaluation, and certification processes, ensuring a comprehensive and efficient approach to tracking students' progress. Moreover, educational institutions have focused on empowering educators through training and professional development programs, equipping them with the necessary skills to leverage digital resources effectively.

Recent phenomena such as virtual education and haptic technologies have opened up new avenues for learning and engagement. These technologies have not only enhanced the accessibility of education but have also provided opportunities for students to actively participate in their learning processes. With the emergence of digital tools supporting collaboration and practice, students and teachers have assumed new roles, transforming traditional classroom dynamics. Students now have the ability to collaborate globally, engage in project-based learning, and develop critical thinking skills through online discussions and collaborative platforms. Furthermore, the use of digital technologies has extended beyond formal learning environments, connecting informal learning situations with formal contexts. This integration promotes lifelong learning, as individuals can access educational resources, tutorials, and interactive platforms outside of the traditional classroom setting. Learning with digital technologies has undoubtedly enriched the educational experience, fostering a dynamic and interactive approach that prepares students for a rapidly evolving digital world.

Learning about computing has become increasingly important in today's digital age. Exploring computational thinking lays the foundation for understanding the logic and problem-solving skills necessary for effective engagement with digital technologies. Computing and computer science education provide students with the knowledge and skills to navigate the ever-evolving digital landscape. Programming languages tailored for education offer an accessible entry point for students to develop coding proficiency and computational skills. By embracing learning about digital technologies and computing, students gain the necessary skills and knowledge to thrive in the digital era and contribute meaningfully to the advancement of technology.

National Policies and Plans for Digital Competence

National policies and plans for digital competence play a pivotal role in shaping the educational landscape. Through the analysis of national cases and comparisons of different plans and policies in various countries, it becomes evident that a strategic approach is essential for fostering digital competence among students. These policies guide the development of curricula that integrate digital skills into the core subjects, ensuring that students are equipped with the necessary knowledge and capabilities to thrive in the digital era. By establishing clear guidelines and goals, national policies provide a framework for curriculum development that aligns with the evolving needs of society. Furthermore, they encourage the inclusion of digital literacy, coding, and computational thinking across disciplines, enabling students to develop a comprehensive understanding of digital technologies.

We would like to thank everyone who was involved in the organization of the WCCE 2022 conference – as a member of either the program committee or the local organizing committee, as a reviewer, or in any other role for the substantial work they did to make this conference a success! Regarding the book-editing process, we would also like to thank the working group "Informatische Bildung NRW" of the German Informatics Society (GI) for providing their ShareLaTeX server for collaborative editing of LaTeX papers.

We hope that the choice of papers in this volume will be of interest to you and further inspire your own work. 'Towards a collaborative society through creative learning' is a development that is of central importance to all countries and communities; we thank the authors of the included papers for offering important, new, and contemporary perspectives that lead the discussion in this field.

July 2023

Therese Keane
Cathy Lewin
Torsten Brinda
Rosa Bottino

Organization

International Program Committee

Rosa Bottino (Co-chair of the IPC)	Institute for Educational Technologies of the Italian National Research Council, Italy
Torsten Brinda (Co-chair of the IPC)	University of Duisburg-Essen, Germany
Jaana Holvikivi (WG 3.4 Representative)	Samtaim Oy, Finland
Cathy Lewin (Editor, WG 3.3 Representative)	Manchester Metropolitan University, UK
Javier Osorio (WG 3.7 Representative)	Las Palmas de Gran Canaria University, Spain
Don Passey (Chair of TC3)	Lancaster University, UK
Toshinori Saito (LOC Representative)	Seisa University, Japan

Local Organizing Committee Members

Masami Hagiya (Chair of the LOC)	University of Tokyo, Japan
Toshinori Saito (Vice-chair of the LOC)	Seisa University, Japan
Masahiko Inami	University of Tokyo, Japan
Akihiro Kashihara	University of Electro-Communications, Japan
Mika Kumahira	Showa Women's University, Japan
Noyuri Mima	Future University Hakodate, Japan
Jun Murai	Keio University, Japan
Hajime Oiwa	ex. Keio University, Japan
Kan Suzuki	University of Tokyo, Japan
Naoko Takahashi	Kokugakuin University, Japan
Ikuo Takeuchi	ex. University of Tokyo, Japan
Eriko Uematsu	Niigata University of Rehabilitation, Japan

Additional Reviewers

Monica Banzato	Università Ca' Foscari Venezia, Italy
Mike Barkmin	University of Duisburg-Essen, Germany
Fatma Batur	University Duisburg-Essen, Germany
Christine Bescherer	Pädagogische Hochschule Ludwigsburg, Germany
Rakesh Mohan Bhatt	Institute of Technology and Management, Dehradun, India

Ana Amélia Carvalho	University of Coimbra, Portugal
Miroslava Cernochova	Charles University in Prague, Czech Republic
Marie Collins	City of Dublin Education and Training Board, Ireland
Muhammed Dağlı	Amasya University, Turkey
Nadine Dittert	University of Potsdam, Germany
Birgit Eickelmann	University of Paderborn, Germany
Andrew Fluck	Independent Educator, Australia
Gerald Futschek	Vienna University of Technology, Austria
Monique Grandbastien	LORIA, Université de Lorraine, France
Mareen Grillenberger	Pädagogische Hochschule Schwyz, Switzerland
Louise Hayes	Manchester Metropolitan University, UK
Claudia Hildebrandt	University of Oldenburg, Germany
Pieter Hogenbirk	Projectbureau Odino BV, The Netherlands
Angela Lee Siew Hoong	Sunway University, Malaysia
Maryam Jaffar Ismail	State University of Zanzibar, Tanzania
Tetsuro Kakeshita	Saga University, Japan
Djordje Kadijevich	Institute for Educational Research, Serbia
Francesca Coin	Università Ca' Foscari Venezia
Ivan Kalas	Comenius University, Slovakia
Mehmet Kara	Amasya University, Turkey
Steve Kennewell	Cardiff Metropolitan University, UK
Shizuka Shirai	Osaka University, Japan
Farhana Khurshid	Fatima Jinnah Women University, Pakistan
Anton Knierzinger	University College of Education Linz, Austria
Matthias Kramer	University of Duisburg-Essen, Germany
Volkan Kukul	Gazi University, Turkey
Mart Laanpere	Tallinn University, Estonia
Margaret Leahy	Dublin City University, Ireland
Elizaphan Maina	Kenyatta University, Kenya
Gioko Maina	Aga Khan Academy Mombasa, Kenya
Nicholas Mavengere	Bournemouth University, UK
Peter Micheuz	Alpen-Adria-Universität Klagenfurt, Austria
Izabela Mrochen	MultiAccess Centre, Poland
Wolfgang Mueller	University of Education Weingarten, Germany
Robert Munro	University of Strathclyde, UK
Simone Opel	FernUniversität in Hagen, Germany
Gabriel Parriaux	University of Teacher Education (HEP Vaud) — Media, Switzerland
Stefan Pasterk	University of Klagenfurt, Austria
Martynas Patasius	Kaunas University of Technology, Lithuania
Maria Teresa Ribeiro Pereira	Instituto Superior de Engenharia do Porto, Portugal
Marcelo Brites Pereira	University of Minho, Portugal
Shephard Pondiwa	Midlands State University, Zimbabwe
Barry Quinn	University of Liverpool, UK
Christophe Reffay	Université de Franche-Comté, France

Paolo Rocchi	Luiss University, Italy
Ralf Romeike	Freie Universität Berlin, Germany
Sindre Røsvik	Giske Kommune, Norway
Eric Sanchez	University of Geneva, Switzerland
Andreas Schwill	University of Potsdam, Germany
Atsushi Shimada	Kyushu University, Japan
Bernadette Spieler	Zurich University of Teacher Education, Switzerland
Riana Steyn	University of Pretoria, South Africa
Alan Strickley	CRIA Technologies, UK
Takeo Tatsumi	Open University of Japan, Japan
Marta Turcsanyi-Szabo	Eötvös Loránd Tudományegyetem, Hungary
Arthur Tatnall	Victoria University, Australia
Sayaka Tohyama	Shizuoka University, Japan
Mary Webb	King's College London, UK
Michael Weigend	WWU Münster, Germany
Lawrence Williams	Technology, Pedagogy and Education Association, UK
David Wooff	BPP University, UK
Soonja Yeom	University of Tasmania, Australia
Sarah Younie	De Montfort University, UK

Contents

Computing in Higher Education

Digital Education in Schools

Digital Education in the Post-Covid Era: Challenges and Opportunities to Explore

Kleopatra Nikolopoulou(✉)

National and Kapodistrian University of Athens, Athens, Greece
klnikolop@ecd.uoa.gr

Abstract. The COVID-19 pandemic (from mid-March 2020) took most educational systems by surprise, forcing million educators and students to radically change how they teach and learn. Online teaching was forced for about 1.5 years and, during this period, digital technology played a major role in enabling teachers to teach students at a distance using various digital platforms and tools. The purpose of this paper is to explore the challenges and opportunities that come with online-digital education, in the post-COVID era. Opportunities to explore include the integration of digital education in the educational system, adoption of appropriate (mobile) pedagogies, more flexible and mobile forms of teaching and learning, reconsideration of National policies, redesign of curricula, improvement of institutional infrastructure, creation of educational resources, and enhancement of students' and teachers' digital technology (and online pedagogy) skills. With regard to learning from the crisis and moving forward in the post-pandemic normal, some recommendations are finally addressed.

Keywords: Digital Education · Post-Covid · Challenges · Opportunities

1 Introduction

Overnight, the educational process became virtual; schools, universities, and other education institutions had to adapt quickly and moved entirely online. Covid-19 outbreak was declared, by the World Health Organization to be a global pandemic on March 2020 [1]. Educational institutions were forced to close and there was a sudden switch to online teaching and learning in many countries worldwide [2]. The pandemic, with the consecutive lockdowns, affected all levels of education, while digital technology played an important role in enabling teachers to teach students at a distance using digital platforms, tools for synchronous and asynchronous communication, accessing learning materials, and interactive collaborative activities [3, 4]. The pandemic crisis may have had more impact on the adoption of digital technologies than many previous research projects together. The rapid and forced transition from face-to-face to online teaching has revealed problems/barriers, has posed challenges, but it is also associated with opportunities worth being investigated.

Published by Springer Nature Switzerland AG 2023
T. Keane et al. (Eds.): WCCE 2022, IFIP AICT 685, pp. 3–14, 2023.
https://doi.org/10.1007/978-3-031-43393-1_1

The purpose of this paper is to investigate challenges and opportunities that come with digital online education, in the post-COVID era. It first describes the digital learning from a pedagogical perspective, challenges/barriers, followed by the identification of opportunities to explore in the post-pandemic era. Finally, considering aspects of digital education that had been advantageously delivered during the pandemic, it summarizes major recommendations. For the purpose of this paper, some clarifications are presented: (i) the term 'digital technology' is used as synonymous to 'ICT' (Information and Communication Technology). Digital education/learning refers to the educational process that includes digital technology in any form (e.g., online courses or use of digital tools in class), (ii) 'mobile learning' (m-learning) is defined as the process of learning mediated by mobile devices, anytime and anywhere with no restrictions on time and location [5]; considering the mobility of technology, learners and learning, (iii) 'online learning' (e-learning) is conducted via the internet and is distinct from distance learning, although these terms are increasingly used interchangeably. Also, 'online teaching' and 'emergency remote teaching' (a new concept proposed by Hodges et al. [6]) are different concepts; however, both terms refer to the spatial distance between students and teachers, and they include the use of technology to provide education. Finally, hybrid/blended education takes place partially on the internet; this may include some students being in class while others are online or all students meeting part of the time online and part of the time face-to-face [7].

2 Digital (Mobile) Learning from a Pedagogical Perspective

Since mobile technology was extensively used during the pandemic [8] it is argued that digital learning, in many cases, can be considered as equivalent to digital mobile learning. M-learning has many benefits: continuous, ongoing, flexible learning; it enables time for reflection; it facilitates informal and formal learning; it supports personalization; it is readily available; ubiquitous; contextual and relevant [9, 10]. Traxler, Read, Kukulska-Hulme, & Barcena [11] reported that personal digital mobile technologies have permeated societies; consequently, affecting education. The pedagogical potential of mobile learning is essential because this could be utilized-exploited when teachers implement innovative pedagogical practices. Earlier research [12] presented a pedagogical perspective of m-learning, which highlighted three central and distinctive pedagogical features of m-learning: authenticity (highlights opportunities for contextualised and participatory learning), collaboration (relates to connected aspects of m-learning), and personalization (it has implications for ownership and autonomous learning). How learners experience these features is influenced by the organization of m-learning environment, including face-to-face strategies. That is, teachers' m-learning practices in the classroom strongly affect students' experiences.

Later on, Schuck, Kearney, and Burden [13] explored mobile technologies as facilitators of learning in the Third Space (a site where formal and informal learning may occur, a transition of learning across contexts – often between formal and informal learning spaces). Implications of learning in the Third Space include new roles for teachers (e.g., as learners themselves) and students, teacher dispositions (openness to change) and possible broadening of the curriculum (more flexibility). Mobile pedagogies for innovative teaching and learning (innovative mobile pedagogies) employ the features/functions and educational affordances of mobile technology to enhance learning [14]. Effective-innovative m-learning is expected to impact positively on learners. Burden, Kearney, Schuck, and Hall [15] investigated innovative m-learning pedagogies for school-aged learners, by adopting a systematic literature review. They found low to medium degrees of innovation in most studies. Intrinsic values of online pedagogy mean that digital technologies can be used to create distinctive learning environments, increase inclusion, and help improve learning experiences, making them more personalized and better tailored to the needs of individual learners [16].

3 Challenges and Opportunities to Explore in the Post-Covid Era

The switch to online learning has had consequences for the accessibility, quality, and equity of education. Countries and education sectors were affected differently due to a variety of factors, such as the age of learners and their ability to learn independently, the nature of pedagogies used at each particular level, and the extent of the integration of distance and online learning into usual education provision [17]. Different problems-barriers were revealed during the two waves of the pandemic [18–23], indicatively: technical and organizational obstacles such as infrastructure, bad internet connection, and inadequate interactive resources; limited or decreased levels of interactions/communication between students – students/teachers; low student engagement and participation; insufficient school/institutional support (e.g., guidelines on acceptable means of communication or platform use); lack of practical or laboratory sessions; negative feelings of anxiety and isolation; concerns about equity issues; health problems, for both students and teachers. Most of the barriers were identified across all educational levels and, in particular, those related to technical obstacles and institutional support. A barrier linked to young students was the low student engagement-participation due to lack of support at home [22]. In parallel, the lack of practical or laboratory sessions is predominantly linked to practical academic fields/specializations in the higher education sector [21, 24]. For example, university students' perceived challenges regarding adaptability issues, lack of practical work, and time-management issues [24]. Many teachers were unprepared for online education/practices, indicated limited readiness to engage with mobile technologies, and lacked appropriate pedagogical or digital skills; many teachers expressed concerns about students' learning progress. School/institutional support was often informal, self-organized, or insufficient. Lack of funding/infrastructure, lack of time (to prepare/plan/design learning activities), and limited student participation, were also reported as barriers. Researchers reported on the digital gap between students during the pandemic, and stressed the sustainability of learners' education into education systems to ensure educational continuity for all learners in times of disruption [25]. According to Longman and Younie [26], social inequality in the UK has been negatively affected, with disadvantaged students gaining much less benefit from online provision. In parallel, a review on research trends indicated issues such as developing new online resources, providing free access to online resources, and enhancing teachers' and students' digital skills as future possibilities for education [27]. Taken into account the barriers identified during the pandemic, potential opportunities noteworthy to be explored are discussed below.

3.1 Digital Education Integrated in the Educational System

Digital teaching and learning, by applying appropriate pedagogical practices, is a core part of the educational process, rather than a novelty add-on. There are different ways for incorporating digital education into everyday teaching and learning processes [28]; and this depends on various factors such as the educational level, the school context/policy, teachers' skills, subject taught, learning objectives, etc. Integration of digital tools is a challenge for all student age groups and, in particular, for the younger ones. Is means that pedagogical approaches need to consider adopting age-appropriate digital/virtual tools of interaction and learning. It is essential to (continue to) investigate the effectiveness of technology-mediated activities and, broadly, the impact of the digital technologies on teaching and learning. For example, Ross [29] indicated that digital technology is most effective when it provides students with opportunities to engage in activities focused on higher-order thinking.

A survey across the European Union [30] found that 67% of teachers provided distance education for the first time in the spring of 2020; not all teachers possessed sufficient digital skills to provide distance online education. Thus, an opportunity arises for online learning approaches to be integrated into education as a cohesive component of learning and teaching. Of course, the degree and the way of integration will differ among different educational sectors. More specifically, this approach is more suitable for older students (higher education sector) rather than for young children who learn via hands-on experiences (experiential learning). Pedagogical practices are essential; such practices might include creation of lesson resources, presentation of information, provision of learning support, and application of inquiry-based learning practices.

3.2 Opportunities to Engage in More Flexible and Mobile Forms of Teaching and Learning

Another opportunity to be explored is the engagement with more flexible forms of teaching and learning. The rapid worldwide adoption of affordable personal mobile devices (e.g., tablets and smartphones) should be exploited for access to quality educational material. Technology or investment in mobile technology, might lead to a more flexible-resilient educational system. Learning via mobile devices allows for learning to occur anytime and anywhere, and across contexts (e.g., formal, semi-formal and informal), while there are encouraging research results for mobile technology utilization in schools and universities [3, 31, 32]. During the pandemic, mobile learning enabled learners to continue their education from any location [8], while students and teachers could access online learning resources and communicate via (mobile) technology. Mobile technology supported teaching-learning is recommended in the post-pandemic era.

3.3 National Policies Reconsideration – Digital Mobile Technology Utilization

Adequate policy responses facilitate the management of education in times of crises. After the pandemic, an opportunity arises for national policies to be re-considered and evaluated, and develop guidelines, so as to cope more efficiently in future crises; i.e., for stronger public educational systems. Such policies should become more favorable towards the utilization of digital mobile technologies for educational purposes; mobile technology was used during the pandemic and many students are familiar with it [33]. Educational policy makers are suggested to plan in-service training programs that support online education, stress the role of mobile technologies, and emphasize the pedagogy of online education [22]. School leaders/principals can set directions for using m-learning; e.g., to actively monitor and evaluate implementation of pedagogical changes [23]. Communication among stakeholders, exchange of good educational (digital) practices, and support for teachers implementing digital innovative practices/pedagogies (including mobile pedagogies) are important. Changes and re-design of curricula could incorporate the concept of online/blended education as part of the institution's developmental strategy. Improvement of curricula need to assure resilience and sustainability in the future. Effective remote learning policies need to be reconsidered.

3.4 Improvement of Institutional/School Infrastructure – Creation of Educational Resources

Another opportunity linked to the pandemic concerns the up-to-date equipment and educational resources, and the provision of tablet/laptop vouchers for socially disadvantaged students. Appropriate and reliable learning devices, and digital citizenship tools that keep families and teachers connected are essential to the future of education [34]. Funding and investment in technological infrastructure could minimize the digital divide to ensure access to education for all students (irrespective of gender, age, or background). Inclusive and forward-looking digital education and training that support all learners is related to financial resources to optimize students' internet use.

Currently, most compulsory education materials are designed for classroom use and classroom pedagogies. Saikat et al. [8] indicated that during the pandemic some of the learning materials presented via m-learning were well organized and useful to the students. Thus, it is useful to develop tools to facilitate video collaboration, discussion and communication (e.g., student-student/-teacher collaboration). Online, open-access and high quality educational resources (e.g., virtual experiments, worksheets) could facilitate communication. Indicatively, virtual laboratories enable learners to create and conduct experiments remotely (experiments that would otherwise be dangerous, or time consuming to access), while among the benefits are flexibility of access, and cost reduction [35]. It is noted that an evaluation of digital platforms and their characteristics [36] is necessary, before their usage by teachers or students.

3.5 Enhancement of Students' and Teachers' Digital Technology Skills

The switch to online education and reliance on digital technology during the pandemic did not find all students and teachers with the necessary technology skills. However, as many teachers and students have further developed skills in using digital devices [37, 38], the enhancement of their digital skills is another opportunity. Students need such skills in order, for example, to access appropriate material and use efficiently the online platforms. Digital skills, in combination with other factors (such as access to digital technology, the internet and ability to contribute to knowledge production), are expected to minimize the digital divide-gap between students. Studies indicated that even experienced teachers struggled with making the switch to online education and, in particular, on how to use platforms/tools in pedagogically effective ways [39]. For teachers, technology skills are useful for creation of teaching materials (e.g., multimedia) and for familiarization with synchronous and asynchronous tools for teaching. Teacher training can empower teachers to maintain and enhance their online teaching presence [22], while in online environments the teachers must be more explicit regarding the design-structure of the course [40]. Among others, training may help teachers develop/exercise skills to design, adapt and implement interactive online content-activities, to organize the online learning environment, to manage the virtual classroom (e.g. using resources, monitoring activities and students), and to facilitate communication (e.g. by encouraging students' participation). Advanced digital skills, as well as online meetings or digital engagements will be useful for future crises.

4 Recommendations – Suggestions

Strengths-benefits and barriers, identified during the pandemic, can lead to opportunities. Specific aspects of digital education that had been advantageously delivered during the pandemic include mobile devices' utilization for educational purposes [8], students' and teachers' exercise-development of digital skills [38], creation/adaptation of educational material for online lessons and opportunities for teachers' professional development [8, 36, 41]. Suggestions as to how these might be capitalized on, with opportunities for digital education are summarized in the subsequent sub-sections.

4.1 Digital Learning should be Integral to Good Teaching: Pedagogy is Essential

Digital teaching and learning should be integral with good pedagogical practices, rather than a novelty add-on. Examples of activities which were deployed during the pandemic include: (i) collaborative activities among university students such as group-work with the aim to produce a group result [21], by using the platform of the online courses; e.g., students have a common file in MS Teams and they can make changes online, and (ii) environmental activities for young children; e.g., to find flowers, photograph them and send/share their photos via the computer. The planning of in-service training programs that support online/blended teaching and learning is suggested. The development of such programs needs to emphasize the pedagogy of online education, so as to enhance online teaching presence. Flexible online learning should include mobile learning. Policy makers could also modify the existing ban of smartphones and tablets within classrooms. Mobile learning played a role during the pandemic, and there is a potential for mobile technology to support learning goals in different subjects [3]. Future research is suggested to explore how teachers use digital technology tools and improve pedagogy to support online environments that are inclusive of social interaction, and collaboration.

Opportunities that come with online education were often not realized by educational institutions; e.g., better quality and accessible digital education for all students. When the pandemic sent everyone home in mid-March 2020, families with school-age children, teachers, and lower-income households without internet access were hit especially hard

[34]. Sometimes students did not have appropriate technology and internet connectivity available at home (or the necessary technological skills) to work online. The issue of equal access for all students is important.

4.2 Support for Teachers and Students

Formal support and in-service training, regarding online teaching, are critical. The forced use of online platforms and tools contributed to the exercise/development of digital skills. Teacher professional development will facilitate teachers, for example, to improve digital teaching and learning skills, plan activities for specific groups of students, set operational learning objectives, provide feedback, and create age-appropriate online resources. Educational institutions should provide opportunities for teachers to further develop their digital skills, as well as their online pedagogical competencies. Teachers are facing new challenges by having to work in new ways (e.g., blended and online environments), and also in new contexts with much reduced control of their students' learning experiences [37]. The socio-emotional wellbeing of teachers and students, the exchange of good practices and resources, as well as facilitation of communication between school and families (in particular, those with a disadvantaged background), are all issues to be considered. In parallel, digital technology skills will aid students to access online/virtual learning environments outside of school location. Students will need extra support to be motivated and engaged with online learning activities, since there is a lack of face-to-face personal contact.

4.3 Sufficient Cooperation among Stakeholders and Teachers

Education systems and, in particular, stakeholders (policy makers, curricula developers, school/faculty principals, consultants, etc.) need to develop strategies to adjust to future crises. The role of school principals was indicated as important during the pandemic as, for example, they contribute to the establishment of a digital learning culture in their schools [37, 42]. School principals-leaders need to support teachers for online teaching practices. One suggestion is collaboration and cooperation among stakeholders, since learning from colleagues is important for the continuity of education. Innovative teaching practices and pedagogies should be shared within the educational community. Cooperation between policy makers and teachers is also important to understand how schools and institutions work.

Recognition from leadership and fair expectations are important for teachers. School leaders can play a role in strengthening digital teaching-learning, in supporting staff and student wellbeing, and in communicating objectives among stakeholders. School principals' experiences during the pandemic are expected to impact on school policy and practice [23]. It is interesting to identify and support existing educational networks, to encourage/promote cooperation and exchange beyond national contexts; e.g., exchange of experiences among different educational communities of practice.

4.4 Ensure Funding and Digitalization – Transformation of Education

A core principle of real education is adaptability. Resilient education systems should be responsive and adaptive to future crises; digitalization-transformation of education is a relevant aspect. Digital learning may cover a variety of situations, and digital tools can be used differently in different education levels and contexts, both within and outside of classrooms. For example, online tasks/assignments may complement face-to-face learning or replace it entirely. Online assessment is probably complementary to traditional forms of assessment and more suitable for university students; In many countries worldwide, the K-12 sector was (and still is) less digitalized in comparison to the higher education sector. Funding is important to ensure the development of appropriate technology infrastructure and (online) learning resources. Recommendations reported by a systematic review on K-12 research during the pandemic [43], included provision of funding for professional development and equipment, designing collaborative activities, as well as clear policy and direct guidance for schools. Rubene et al. [44] explored how the COVID-19 crisis contributed to the digital transformation of education in Latvia; their recommendations for policy-makers include the digital transformation of education in relation to the digitalization and use of digital solutions at all levels of education.

The design of educational computer systems and apps is suggested to incorporate features that support online teaching and learning; e.g. clear teacher-student communication, one-to-one feedback-support, multitasks (online tests, forum, chat, etc.), and multiple student assessment. More open design of online tools and platforms could allow teachers make their own decisions on how to utilize the system during online teaching. Online teaching-learning tools are particularly useful when these support and encourage interactions, engagement, communication and collaboration [45]; these tools could be designed for different devices including smartphones and tablets.

4.5 Hybrid/Blended Education in the Post-Covid Era

After the pandemic and the forced full application of online education the way is paved for the hybrid-blended learning mode, in particular, in universities [21, 24, 37]; it is a practical solution and a viable option for providing education in times of disruption and crises, when face-to-face engagements are difficult. Blended learning approaches combine the convenience and flexibility of online courses with face-to-face interactions, and are associated with benefits such as flexible learning [24] and improved student self-directed learning [40]. As hybrid learning environments are challenging and under-researched [46], future research is suggested to explore their potential in teaching and learning.

5 Future Research

The COVID-19 pandemic can be considered as a turning point for many dimensions, including digital education [47]. Shutting down educational institutions was an unprecedented occurrence and it is possible that there might be circumstances in the future that will necessitate a similar situation. Limitations and possibilities of online education differ among different educational levels (i.e., from school to university level), so future research is useful to identify specific issues corresponding to different educational sectors/levels. Future research is suggested to explore the opportunities that digital technologies afford for online collaboration. Also, research is needed on recent educational technology issues such as bring-your-own-device (BYOD) policy, artificial intelligence, and the cultural differences in the conceptualization and delivery of digital technology. These issues relate to policy makers' interests in harnessing educational technologies to address national and international concerns such as improving attainment, supporting inclusive pedagogies, and skilling the workforce to meet the demands for digital expertise [48].

Online education (e-learning) cannot replace formal face-to-face classroom-based education, but it could be considered as a viable alternative for crises situations in the post-pandemic normal/era. Researchers suggest that blended and online learning environments are becoming the new norm for education worldwide after the pandemic [24, 49, 50]. In particular, these are suitable for the higher education sector where students are adults and more independent learners. As a consequence, the identification and exploration of opportunities of digital education is an ongoing research issue. Indicative research questions include: How effective can be the hybrid teaching and learning experiences, within the different educational levels? How are we moving to the age of online/blended teaching and learning?

References

1. Cucinotta, D., Vanelli, M.: WHO declares covid-19 a pandemic. Acta. Bio.-Med. Atenei. Parm. **91**(1), 157–160 (2020)
2. UNESCO: 10 recommendations to ensure that learning remains uninterrupted. https://en.unesco.org/news/covid-19-10-recommendations-plan-distance-learningsolutions (2020). Last accessed 5 Sep 2021
3. Nikolopoulou, K.: Students' mobile phone practices for academic purposes: strengthening post-pandemic university digitalization. Sustainability **14**(22), 14958 (2022)
4. Starkey, L., Shonfeld, M., Prestridge, S., Cervera, M.G.: Special issue: Covid-19 and the role of technology and pedagogy on school education during a pandemic. Technol. Pedagog. Educ. **30**(1), 1–5 (2021)
5. Schuler, C., Winters, N., West, M.: The Future of Mobile Learning: Implications for Policy Makers and Planners. UNESCO, Paris (2012)
6. Hodges, C., Moore, S., Lockee, B., Torrey, T., Bond, A.: The difference between emergency remote teaching and online learning. EduCause Review. https://er.educause.edu/articles/2020/3/the-difference-between-emergency-remote-teaching-and-online-learning (2020). Last accessed 5 Sep 2021
7. Sullivan, P.M.: From the student perspective: An analysis of in-person, hybrid, and online learning during the pandemic. In: Sullivan, P., Sullivan, B., Lantz, J. (eds.) Cases on Innovative and Successful Uses of Digital Resources for Online Learning, pp. 80–95. IGI Global (2022)
8. Saikat, S., Dhillon, J.S., Wan Ahmad, W.F., Jamaluddin, R.A.: A systematic review of the benefits and challenges of mobile learning during the COVID-19 pandemic. Educ. Sci. **11**(9), 459 (2021)
9. Sullivan, T., Slater, B., Phan, J., Tan, A., Davis, J.: M-learning: exploring mobile technologies for secondary and primary school science inquiry. Teach. Sci. **65**(1), 13–16 (2019)
10. Zhang, Y. (ed.): Handbook of Mobile Teaching and Learning. Springer, Heidelberg (2015). https://doi.org/10.1007/978-3-642-54146-9
11. Traxler, J., Read, T., Kukulska-Hulme, A., Barcena, E.: Paradoxical paradigm proposals – Learning languages in mobile societies. Argentinian J. Appl. Linguist. **7**(2), 89–109 (2019)

12. Kearney, M., Schuck, S., Burden, P., Aubusson, P.: Viewing mobile learning from a pedagogical perspective. J. Res. Learn. Technol. **20**(3), 1–17 (2012)
13. Schuck, S., Kearney, M, Burden, K: Exploring mobile learning in the Third Space. Technol. Pedagog. Educ. **26**(2), 121–137 (2017)
14. Burden, K., Kearney, M, Schuck, S., Burke, P.: Principles underpinning innovative mobile learning: stakeholders' priorities. TechTrends **63**, 659–668 (2019)
15. Burden, K., Kearney, M, Schuck, S., Hall, T.: Investigating the use of innovative mobile pedagogies for school-aged students: a systematic literature review. Comput. Educ. **138**, 83–100 (2019). https://doi.org/10.1016/j.compedu.2019.04.008
16. Rapanta, C., Botturi, L., Goodyear, P., Guardia, L., Koole, M.: Online university teaching during and after the covid-19 crisis: refocusing teacher presence and learning activity. Postdigit. Sci. Educ. **2**, 923–945 (2020)
17. Van der Graaf, L., Dunajeva, J., Siarova, H., Bankauskaite, R.: Research for CULT Committee – Education and Youth in Post-COVID-19 Europe – Crisis Effects and Policy Recommendations. European Parliament, Policy Department for Structural and Cohesion Policies, Brussels (2021)
18. Howard, S.K., Tondeur, J., Siddiq, F., Scherer, R.: Ready, set, go! Profiling teachers' readiness for online teaching in secondary education. Technol. Pedagog. Educ. **30**(1), 137–154 (2020)
19. Judd, J., Rember, B.A., Pellegrini, T., Ludlow, B., Meisn, J.: "This is Not Teaching": The Effects of Covid-19 on Teachers. https://www.socialpublishersfoundation.org/knowledge_base/this-is-not-teaching-the-effects-of-covid-19-on-teachers/ (2020). Last accessed 9 Sep 2021
20. Nikolopoulou, K.: University students' online learning experiences in context of COVID-19: study in Greece. Educ. Innov. Emerg. Technol. **2**(2), 17–27 (2022)
21. Nikolopoulou, K.: Face-to-face, online and hybrid education: University students' opinions and preferences. J. Dig. Educ. Technol. **2**(2), ep2206 (2022)
22. Nikolopoulou, K.: Online education in early primary years: teachers' practices and experiences during the Covid-19 pandemic. Educ. Sci. **12**(2), 76 (2022)
23. Scully, D., Lehane, P., Scully, C.: 'It is no longer scary': digital learning before and during the Covid-19 pandemic in Irish secondary schools. Technol. Pedagog. Educ. **30**(1), 159–181 (2021)
24. Li, D.: The shift to online classes during the Covid-19 pandemic: Benefits, challenges, and required improvements from the students' perspective. Electronic J. e-Learn. **20**(1), pp1-18 (2022). https://doi.org/10.34190/ejel.20.1.2106
25. Leask, M., Younie, S.: Education for all in Times of Crisis: Lessons from Covid-19, 1st edn. Routledge, UK (2021)
26. Longman, D., Younie, S.: A critical review of emerging pedagogical perspectives on mobile learning. In: Marcus-Quinn, A., Hourigan, T. (eds.) Handbook for Online Learning Contexts: Digital, Mobile and Open: Policy and Practice, pp. 183–199. Springer, Cham (2021)
27. Karakose, Y., Demirkol, M.: Exploring the emerging COVID-19 research trends and current status in the field of education: a bibliometric analysis and knowledge mapping. Educ. Proc. Int. J. **10**(2), 7–27 (2021)
28. Sangeeta, Tandon, U.: Factors influencing adoption of online teaching by school teachers: a study during COVID-19 pandemic. J. Public Affairs **21**, e2503 (2020)
29. Ross, S.M.: Technology infusion in K-12 classrooms: a retrospective look at three decades of challenges and advancements in research and practice. Educ. Tech. Res. Dev. **68**(5), 2003–2020 (2020)
30. Di Pietro, G., Biagi, F., Costa, P., Karpinski, Z., Mazza, J.: The Likely Impact of COVID-19 on Education: Reflections based on the Existing Literature and Recent International Datasets. Publications Office of the European Union, Luxembourg (2020)

31. Nikolopoulou, K.: Mobile devices in early childhood education: teachers' views on benefits and barriers. Educ. Inf. Technol. **26**(3), 3279–3292 (2021). https://doi.org/10.1007/s10639-020-10400-3
32. Nikolopoulou, K.: Secondary education teachers' perceptions of mobile phone and tablet use in classrooms: benefits, constraints and concerns. J. Comput. Educ. **7**(2), 257–275 (2020). https://doi.org/10.1007/s40692-020-00156-7
33. Nikolopoulou, K.: Mobile learning usage and acceptance: perceptions of secondary school students. J. Comput. Educ. **5**(4), 499–519 (2018). https://doi.org/10.1007/s40692-018-0127-8
34. Common Sense: Common Sense Media 2020 Annual Report (2021). www.commonsense.org. Last accessed 5 Sep 2021
35. Kukulska-Hulme, A., et al.: Innovating Pedagogy 2020: Open University Innovation Report 8. The Open University, Milton Keynes (2020)
36. Daniela, L., Rūdolfa, A., Rubene, Z.: Results of the evaluation of learning platforms and digital learning materials. In: Daniela, L., Visvizi, A. (eds.) Remote Learning in Times of Pandemic: Issues, Implications and Best Practice, pp. 1–15. Routledge (2021)
37. Cox, M., Quinn, B.: Learning leaders: teaching and learning frameworks in flux impacted by the global pandemic. Can. J. Learn. Technol. **47**(4), 1–20 (2021)
38. Lee, S.J., Ward, K.P., Chang, O.D., Downing, K.M.: Parenting activities and the transition to home-based education during the COVID-19 pandemic. Child. Youth Serv. Rev. **122**, 105585 (2021). https://doi.org/10.1016/j.childyouth.2020.105585. Last accessed 5 Sep 2021
39. Trust, T., Whalen, J.: Should teachers be trained in emergency remote teaching? lessons learned from the COVID-19 pandemic. J. Technol. Teach. Educ. **28**(2), 189–199 (2020)
40. Van Dorresteijn, C.M., et al.: What factors contribute to effective online and blended education? (Summary): Research group 'Online education during Covid-19'. Universiteit van Amsterdam (2020)
41. Wang, Z., Jiang, Q., Li, Z.: How to promote online education through educational software—an analytical study of factor analysis and structural equation modeling with Chinese users as an example. Systems **10**(4), 100 (2022)
42. Karakose, T., Polat, H., Papadakis, S.: Examining teachers' perspectives on school principals' digital leadership roles and technology capabilities during the COVID-19 pandemic. Sustainability **13**, 13448 (2021)
43. Bond, M.: Schools and emergency remote education during the Covid-19 pandemic: a living rapid systematic review. Asian J. Distance Educ. **15**(2), 191–247 (2020)
44. Rubene, Z., Daniela, L., Sarva, E., Rūdolfa, A.: Digital transformation of education: envisioning post-COVID education in Latvia. In: Daniela, L. (ed.) Human, Technologies and Quality of Education, pp. 180–196. University of Latvia, Rīga (2021)
45. Leary, H., Lee, V.R., Recker, M.: It's more than just technology adoption: understanding variations in teachers' use of an online planning tool. TechTrends **65**(3), 269–277 (2021)
46. Norgard, R.: Theorising hybrid lifelong learning. Br. J. Edu. Technol. **52**, 1709–1723 (2021)
47. Zawacki-Richter, O., Bozkurt, A.: Research trends in open, distance, and digital education. In: Zawacki-Richter, O., Jung, I. (eds.) Handbook of Open, Distance and Digital Education. Springer, Singapore (2022)
48. Passey, D., et al.: Computers and education – recognising opportunities and managing challenges. In: Goedicke, M., Neuhold, E., Rannenberg, K. (eds.) Advancing Research in Information and Communication Technology: IFIP AICT 600, pp. 129–152. Springer, Cham, Switzerland (2021)

49. Amitabh, U.: How technology will transform learning in the COVID-19 era. https://www.weforum.org/agenda/2020/08/how-edtech-will-transform-learning-in-the-covid-19-era/ (2020). Last accessed 19 Sep 2021
50. Chattaraj, D., Vijayaraghavan, A.P.: Why learning space matters: a script approach to the phenomena of learning in the emergency remote learning scenario. J. Comput. Educ. **8**, 343–364 (2021)

A Study of Measurement of Mentoring Activities Using Text Mining Technology

Kaori Namba[1(✉)], Toshiyuki Sanuki[1], Tetsuo Fukuzaki[1], and Kazuhiko Terashima[2]

[1] IBM Japan, Ltd., Tokyo 103-8510, Japan
{Knamba,fukuzak}@jp.ibm.com, toshiyuki.sanuki1@ibm.com
[2] Machida Technical High School, Tokyo 194-0035, Japan
terashima@machidath.ed.jp

Abstract. P-TECH is a pioneering education reform initiative to prepare young people with the academic, technical, and professional skills required for 21st-century jobs and ongoing education. Mentoring is one of the key activities of P-TECH for students to think about their pathways and build engineering attitudes. After each mentoring session, we take surveys to evaluate how the sessions affected the students and we achieved our objectives. In addition to conventional method, we executed systematic analysis of the responses to the open-ended questions using text mining technology. The subjects of this paper were 30 high school sophomores in 2019. We mentored them eight times in 2019 and 2020 and took surveys after each session. We gathered 1784 documents in total as the responses to open-ended questions and analyzed them with a text mining tool. The tool showed the top three frequent nouns were synonyms for "myself", and the top three correlated nouns of "myself" were "future", "thought", and "way". This indicates many students considered their pathways during the mentoring sessions and discussed them in their surveys. The tool also showed that the top correlated noun/verb phrases were "build… Plan", "obtain… Advice", and "have… Interest". This indicates that students correctly received the messages intended by the mentoring. Our results showed that the mentoring activities helped students consider their future. Text mining was a useful technique to analyze answers to open-ended survey questions.

Keywords: P-TECH · Survey · Measurement · Mentoring · Text mining

1 Introduction

The social demand for career planning and development of high school students is growing as they prepare to succeed in new occupations [1]. Mentoring, the act of helping and giving advice to a younger or less experienced person, is well recognized as an effective method for working people or students to develop their career or skills. In the business field, the progress of a mentee is measured by tracking their individual development plan since mentee's development objective and goal are clear, and each mentee has some level of maturity to describe own plan.

Published by Springer Nature Switzerland AG 2023
T. Keane et al. (Eds.): WCCE 2022, IFIP AICT 685, pp. 15–20, 2023.
https://doi.org/10.1007/978-3-031-43393-1_2

In the case of high school students, mentoring is a relatively new approach to develop their career or skills and the method to measure the efficacy of mentoring activities is not well established. It is usually measured by the analysis of student's responses to a predefined questionnaire at each mentoring activity. However, this is not sufficient for a schoolteacher to identify insights regarding the effects on student's thinking or motivation under personal conversation between mentor and mentee [2].

We propose a new method to analyze the efficacy of mentoring activities for students by using text mining technology to investigate effects on student's thinking through mentoring. As a part of the P-TECH pilot program in the Tokyo Metropolitan Government [3], we conducted a two-year mentoring program for high school students, and we applied this method with a prototype system based on the IBM Watson Discovery platform, to analyze the text data of student's responses during this period. We successfully identified effects in student thinking through the mentoring.

2 Conventional Method

Mentoring is well recognized as an effective approach for working people and there are activities to apply mentoring into career development for students [4]. The experiences of working adults in actual fields are useful student mentees in high school to help them plan and decide their future career.

Evaluation of mentoring is mainly performed through self-evaluation. It is suitable for a mentee to evaluate their growth by themselves. Objective-based evaluation is also required to measure effectiveness of mentoring activities, and surveys are often used [5]. A survey usually consists of two types of questions: quantitative questions and opened ended questions. Evaluation of quantitative questions is often performed with statistical analysis, requestion analysis, and so on. On the other hand, evaluation methods for open-ended questions are not well established yet. In most cases, the teacher or mentor needs to read through the text of the response of each question, requiring careful understand and insight of what each student is thinking. This analysis approach is subjective and takes efforts, especially with large volumes of data from multi-year mentoring activities.

The answer to an open-ended question is considered *text data*, i.e., natural language. It used to be challenging for a computer to analyze text data. With recent progress in artificial intelligence (AI) technology, a computer can now analyze text such as student's responses regarding their mentoring activities. This paper introduces and discusses the usefulness of text analysis technique, known as *text mining*, to analyze qualitative changes in student's thoughts about mentoring activities.

3 Proposed Method

3.1 Text Mining

Text mining is a process to extract useful information from text data with Natural Language Processing (NLP) technology. Using NLP, sentences are divided into parts-of-speech (nouns, verbs, adjectives, etc.) and useful information is extracted by analyzing the frequency of word occurrence and correlation. Text data is a typical case of qualitative data, and the goal of text mining is to collect high value-added information from qualitative data.

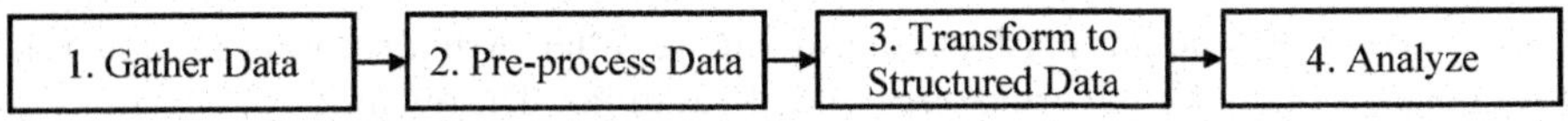

Fig. 1. Analysis steps of text mining

Text mining steps are shown in Fig. 1 Significant effort is generally required to manually gather, pre-process, and transform data. This is one reason why text mining is not commonly used by non-experts.

3.2 IBM Watson Discovery

IBM Watson Discovery (IWD) [6] is a platform that enables intelligent search and text mining for large volumes of text data. IWD can gather text data from independent sources within a company and/or from the internet and extract hidden meaning from this data. IWD provides many useful features. We used the following:

- **Frequency:** indicates how many documents contain a given word.
- **Trend:** indicates a trend of the frequency of a word.
- **Collocation:** indicates simultaneous occurrence of certain words in a sentence.
- **Correlation:** indicates how relevant a word is to documents that match a search condition. The correlation value measures the level of uniqueness of the high frequency as compared to other documents.

IWD almost automates Step 1 to 3 from Fig. 1. It also provides an easy and intuitive analysis tool for Step 4. IWD brings the power of text mining to non-experts.

4 Tokyo P-TECH

P-TECH stands for Pathways in Technology Early College High Schools. P-TECH 9–14 School Model is a pioneering education reform initiative to prepare young people with the academic, technical, and professional skills required for 21st century jobs and ongoing education [7]. To provide a holistic approach to education and workforce development, IBM, the New York City Department of Education, and The City University of New York designed and launched the first P-TECH school in Brooklyn, New York, in September 2011—and the first class graduated in June 2015.

In Japan, there are three P-TECHs in 2022. Tokyo P-TECH [8] is the first P-TECH in Japan for Machida Technical High School and Nihon Kogakuin College Hachioji Campus, started in April 2021. Three IT companies partner with the two schools to help students with three years of Information Technology courses at the high school, and with two years of Network & Security courses at the college.

Starting in April 2019, we conducted a trial run prior to the official Tokyo P-TECH for Machida Technical High School. Several volunteers from the partner company gave IT lectures, and provided job shadowing, on-site teaching, and mentoring.

We conducted eight mentoring sessions for 30 students by ten mentors from IBM Japan. We visited the school for the first four sessions and the remaining sessions were conducted remotely due to the COVID-19 pandemic.

We asked all 30 students to fill out questionnaires after each mentoring session. Each survey consists of quantitative and open-ended questions. The quantitative questions ask about student satisfaction and/or enjoyment on a 5-point scale. The open-ended questions ask the students to describe knowledge acquired in the session, future challenges, and so on. This paper analyzes student answers to these open-ended questions.

5 Analysis and Result

5.1 Data

Each survey has multiple open-ended questions. We treated each answer as one *document*. We collected 2,021 documents from eight mentor surveys and entered them into Watson Discovery. Then, we excluded 237 trivial documents that essentially meant "Not Applicable" as this could introduce noise into the results. The following results are based on an analysis of the remaining 1784 documents.

5.2 Analysis Result

The top ten nouns are shown in Fig. 2 (a). The word "myself" is the most frequent and prominent noun. Runner-ups are nouns related to a pathway ("pathway", "job") and studying ("study", "qualification"). It means many students wrote in the surveys about themselves and their future. The top ten verbs are shown in Fig. 2 (b). "think" is the most frequent and prominent verb, and "consider" is the third place. We consider this reflects that both the teachers and the mentors repeatedly insisted on the importance of thinking at both mentoring sessions and usual classes.

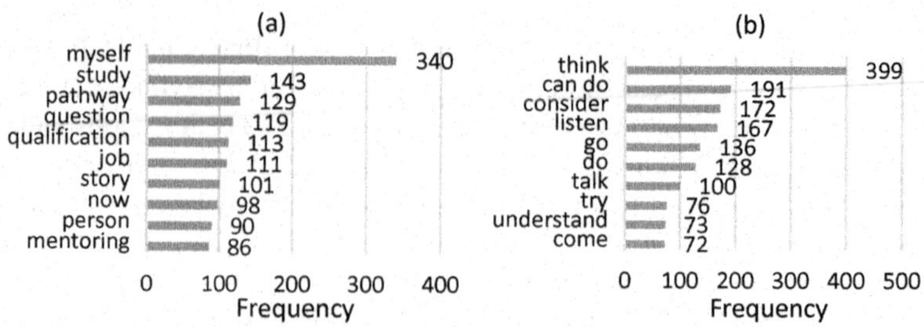

Fig. 2. The frequency of (a) nouns and (b) verbs

Then, we focused on the most frequent noun, "myself." Fig. 3 shows the top ten collocated (a) nouns and (b) verbs with "myself", sorted by correlation. The nouns "future", "way", "pathway", and "job" have the highest correlation, and all indicate future pathways. This along with the high correlations of "consider" and "think in Fig. 3 (b) show that many students considered their pathways during the mentoring sessions and discussed them in their surveys.

(a) Collocated nouns with "myself"

Noun	Frequency	Correlation
future	25	1.8
thought	18	1.7
way	12	1.6
pathway	52	1.5
job	13	1.2
mentoring	29	1.1
this time	27	1.1
mentor	26	1.1
opinion	10	1.0
objective	13	1.0

(b) Collocated verbs with myself

Verb	Frequency	Correlation
consider	[illegible]	1.6
find	16	1.5
do	[illegible]	1.5
decide	20	1.3
speak	25	1.3
think	[illegible]	1.2
go	45	1.2
understand	16	1.2
have	16	1.1
learn	21	1.1

Fig. 3. Collocated (a) nouns and (b) verbs with "myself", sorted by correlation

Noun	Verb	Frequency	Correlation
plan	build	14	[illegible]
advice	obtain	10	[illegible]
interest	have	12	11.5
qualification	get	42	10.0
workforce	enter	10	9.4
vacation	have	22	8.8
way	go	5	6.0
actual	build	4	3.9
hereafter	go	13	3.7
school	go	8	3.6

Fig. 4. Collocation between nouns and verbs, sorted by correlation

Figure 4 shows collocation between general nouns and verbs, sorted by correlation. High correlation combinations indicate goals of mentoring, like "build… Plan", "obtain… Advice", "have… Interest", etc. This indicates that students correctly received the messages intended by the mentoring.

We applied trend analysis from various perspectives to understand student growth over time though the mentor sessions. We did not identify any clear trends. For example, Fig. 5 shows the trend of mentoring keywords, i.e., Career ("pathway", "job", "college", etc.), Study (includes "study", "class", "programming", etc.), and Future (includes "future", "objective", "dream", etc.). We expected that these words would be mentioned more in later sessions, but this is not what the data show. The word "pathway" is the most frequent in the sixth mentoring session, since it was the time for the students to decide their pathway whether entering further education or taking a job. It may be that the current set of questions is not suited for the investigation of student growth. We are considering future enhancements to our surveys.

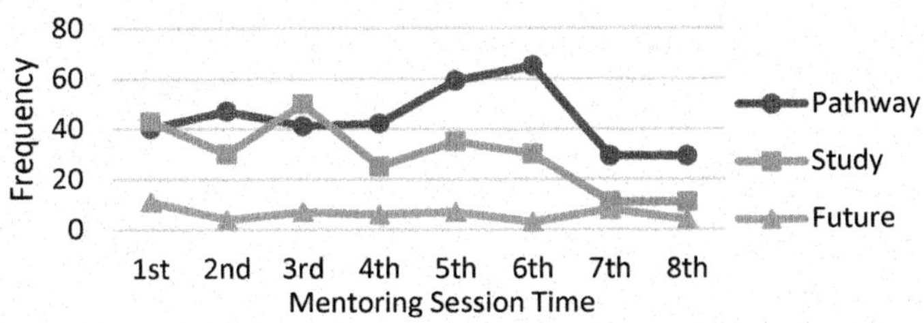

Fig. 5. Trend of mentoring keywords

6 Conclusion

We used text mining to analyze the responses of open-ended survey questions after Tokyo P-TECH mentoring activities. As predicted, our results show that the mentoring activities helped students consider their future. Text mining was a useful technique to analyze answers to open-ended survey questions.

In future work, we would like to identify the relationship between numeric indices and the answers to open-ended survey questions. Additionally, we plan to modify the survey questions to better clarify student growth though mentoring.

References

1. U.S. Bureau of Labor Statistics: "Career Outlook", https://www.bls.gov/careeroutlook/2015/article/career-planning-for-high-schoolers.htm. Last accessed 28 Feb 2022
2. Heppen, J.B., Zeiser, K., Holtzman, D.J., O'Cummings, M., Christenson, S., Pohl, A.: Efficacy of the check & connect mentoring program for at-risk general education high school students. J. Res. Educ. Effect. **11**(1), 56–82 (2017)
3. Tokyo Metropolitan Government: Press Release https://www.metro.tokyo.lg.jp/tosei/hodohappyo/press/2019/04/23/18.html
4. Akili, W.: Mentoring engineering students: challenges and potential rewards. In: 121st ASEE Annual Conference & Exposition, pp. 1–13. Indianapolis, Indiana (2014)
5. Akerele, O., Vermeulen, A., Marnewick, A.: Determining the benefits of the engineering mentoring programmes for graduates. In: Proceedings of the International Conference on Industrial Engineering and Operations Management (2019)
6. Watson Discovery: https://cloud.ibm.com/docs/discovery-data?topic=discovery-data-about. Last accessed 28 Feb 2022
7. Learn about P-TECH schools: https://www.ptech.org/about/. Last accessed 18 Feb 2022
8. Tokyo P-TECH: https://www.mext.go.jp/content/20210210-mxt_syogai01-100003289_4.pdf. Last accessed 18 Feb 2022

Development Plan and Trial of Japanese Language e-Learning System Focusing on Content and Language Integrated Learning (CLIL) Suitable for Digital Education

Shizuka Nakamura[1(✉)] and Katsumi Wasaki[2(✉)]

[1] Graduate School of Medicine, Science and Technology, Shinshu University, Nagano, Japan
21hs206b@shinshu-u.ac.jp

[2] Faculty of Engineering, Shinshu University, Nagano, Japan
wasaki@cs.shinshu-u.ac.jp

Abstract. In the field of Japanese language education, even though it is very important to solidify the foundation of a student's pronunciation ability, this area is sometimes neglected due to a bias towards grammar lecturing and vocabulary building. In addition, although audio materials are commonly included in teaching materials, few students use them for self-learning. However, for non-kanji-reading learners, learning the Japanese writing systems (hiragana, katakana, and kanji) can be a major obstacle, which means audio materials increase in importance by providing an effective alternative way to learn the Japanese language. With those points in mind, this paper examines the development of digital education (DX) e-learning materials that can provide non-kanji-reading learners with authentic contexts and serve as a bridge to learning correct speech without causing them to feel psychologically intimidated by the intricacies of Japanese writing systems. We then report on the use of the first teaching materials developed for Japanese language education using neural speech based on a pedagogical method known as Content and Language Integrated Learning (CLIL). This material was developed as courseware on Moodle.

Keywords: Distance learning · Text-to-speech · Moodle · Neural voice · CLIL

1 Introduction

1.1 Current Status of Japanese Language Education

While the number of Japanese language learners is increasing rapidly both in Japan and abroad, the number of teachers can only support about 17% of the total number of learners in Japan [1] and about 2% abroad [2]. Therefore, online learning has become indispensable in the field of Japanese language education, and there is an urgent ongoing need to develop digital education (DX) e-learning materials to address the imbalance

Published by Springer Nature Switzerland AG 2023
T. Keane et al. (Eds.): WCCE 2022, IFIP AICT 685, pp. 21–26, 2023.
https://doi.org/10.1007/978-3-031-43393-1_3

caused both by the shortage of teachers and the increasing number of learners. In addition, even though it is very important to solidify the foundation of students' pronunciation abilities, this area is sometimes neglected due to a bias toward grammar learning and vocabulary building [3]. However, even though a learner's spoken Japanese may be grammatically correct, incorrect pronunciation may lead to misunderstandings. Therefore, as has been stated in numerous learner objectives, simply learning correct Japanese grammar is insufficient for meeting professional job requirements.

In addition, for learners who are unable to read kanji, mastering the Japanese writing systems (hiragana, katakana, and kanji) is a major barrier [4] that has the potential to cause language anxiety (i.e., angst and tension caused by difficulties when learning a foreign language), which is one of the factors that can affect learning efforts [5]. Furthermore, focusing excessively on reading materials, particularly kanji, can lead to learning based predominantly on visual information, which can interfere with listening and speaking studies. Considering these issues, we believe developing e-learning curricula that utilize text-to-speech (TTS) and speech-to-text (STT) resources is necessary.

Furthermore, numerous words should only be used when they properly reflect the background of Japanese culture, and these concepts and contents are difficult to impart simply by memorizing literal vocabulary translations. From the earliest learning stages, the learners need to learn Japanese cultural awareness for advanced communication.

To resolve these problems in the field of Japanese language education, this paper describes the status of a learning management system (LMS) that was developed using audio learning materials and the method of Content and Language Integrated Learning (CLIL) for non-kanji-reading learners and published on Moodle, as well as ongoing efforts to develop more effective DX learning methods.

1.2 Literature Review

A previous study on Japanese speech materials has included the development of a system that automatically outputs a "prosody graph", which is an easy-to-understand visualization of the prosodic features (prosody) that visually correct the rhythm of input Japanese speech using speech synthesis and speech recognition technology [6]. This system allows students to learn Japanese pronunciation comprehensively and easily with the proper accent, intonation, pauses, prominence, and voiceless vowels, along with proper syllable sense, rhythm, speech rate, and sentence-level voice affirmation.

Participants who used the system developed by Matsuzaki [6] rated it positively. However, most of those participants were Chinese language speakers, and the method has not been applied to students who were unable to read kanji. Accordingly, a method that provides useful learning content while taking into consideration the difficulty of providing teaching materials that do not rely entirely on visual information needs to be carefully considered.

In addition, CLIL pedagogy has become recognized internationally, including in Europe, and there are numerous examples of its application in the English as a second language (ESL) field. However, only a few studies have applied the CLIL approach to teaching Japanese as a second language, and there are no reports of its application to speech education.

2 Methods

2.1 Teaching Materials on Moodle

The teaching materials used in our system were developed based on courseware deployed on Moodle. This LMS has numerous features aimed at improving user management and efficiency that can be used to centralize learner progress reports and relieve instructor burdens.

Trial materials for basic, beginner and intermediate classes have been released, and improvements were made based on instructor and learner feedback. In addition, we have developed a variety of subjects that touch on Japanese culture and use discussions, which are ideal for student-instructor interactions, to share experiences and teach them about Japanese culture.

2.2 Text-to-Speech and Speech-to-Text

We used TTS speech synthesis technology, which vocalizes text via an artificial voice; and STT, which displays voice data input by the learner in text form, to present learning content and facilitate practice sessions. The use of TTS allows learners to advance their studies without being bound by the Japanese writing systems (hiragana, katakana, and kanji).

In contrast, by using STT to practice speaking as part of their self-study efforts, students can work on their pronunciation skills as often as they desire, without embarrassment, and thus gain confidence via repeat learning.

In the trial materials, non-neural voices were used, but both learners and instructors pointed out that the voice was monotonous, and the intonation was unnatural. Therefore, a switch was made to neural voices, and other improvements were implemented. In addition, the pitch and intonation of the neural voices were carefully adjusted to achieve more human-like enunciations.

2.3 Content and Language Integrated Learning

CLIL is a pedagogy in which students acquire both content and language by learning specific content (subjects, themes, and topics) through the target language [7]. CLIL is characterized by a method that follows the four concepts of content (applied to cultural studies), communication (applied to language acquisition), cognition (applied to cultural comparisons), and community/culture (applied to presentations/discussions). Therefore, we could avoid the introduction of vocabulary that relies on translations and instead provide a curriculum aligned with learners at all levels. In addition, the grammar introduction exercise, materials could introduce many interesting aspects of Japanese culture to the learners.

3 Trial for Japanese Learners

3.1 The Target Learner

To evaluate TTS, one non-kanji-reading intermediate learner was tasked with role-playing the receipt of a complaint over the telephone.

Furthermore, 19 beginner-level learners of Japanese were randomly divided into two groups to evaluate the learning effects in the TTS-based learning group (10 learners) and the conventional learning group (9 learners).

3.2 Implementation Details

We practiced a role-playing scenario that involved making/receiving a complaint over the phone and evaluated the learner's progress after two weeks of practice. For five days, we presented a standard neural voice to the learner to encourage self-learning of the role of conveying complaints. Then, on Day 7, the neural voice was presented with an adjusted tone and pitch, and the learner was again encouraged to self-learn for an additional five days. The adjusted neural voices are shown in the following Table 1.

Furthermore, in the evaluation involving beginners, the learners were required to complete weekly homework assignments such as reviewing grammar, memorizing vocabulary, researching Japanese culture, etc. during the eight-week course.

Table 1. Adjusted neural voices.

Adjusted voices	Speaker A	Speaker B
Emotions	Voice somewhat remorseful Voice somewhat panicked	Voice somewhat angry
Voice rate	1.0	0.9
Voice pitch	1.0	0.8
Voice intonation	Adjust intonation to be more human-like	Adjust intonation to be more human-like

3.3 Intonation Adjustment

There is a wide variety of Japanese language education audio files that are available on compact disks (CDs) or for downloading from the Internet. However, those audio materials are recordings of human voices because no materials are currently available using neural voices. The problem with human voices is that there are many areas where the audio cannot be adjusted sufficiently to create different senses of emotion or realism, which means intonations need to be carefully adjusted to make speech sounds natural enough for effective use in repeated practice sessions. In this study, we attempted to fine-tune an unadjusted neutral voice to make it more closely resemble a human voice.

3.4 The Results

The target learner was asked to complete a five-point self-assessment survey (see Table 2), the results of which showed that self-learning using neural speech made the students more confident about their speech and increased the frequency of their practice sessions. In addition, by adjusting the audio, we could see that the learner was learning while imagining more realistic scenes. In other words, the target learner was able to produce smoother and more natural speech because of practicing with adjusted voices compared to practicing with unadjusted voices.

In addition, the following Table 3 shows the main results of interviews with beginning learners. In Group 1, we found that the learners were confident in their speech and enjoyed the conversation. On the other hand, Group 2 was found to be nervous about speaking.

Table 2. Target learner assessment of standard neural voices week 1, adjusted neural voices week 2 (five-point scale)

Assessment Items	Day 1	Day 7	Day 14
1. Language skills are growing	2	2	4
2. The audio material is interesting	5	5	5
3. The content is interesting	3	3	4
4. Self-learning is interesting	3	3	4
5. I have more confidence in my speech	3	3	4
6. I was able to understand the audio	1	3	5

Table 3. Main results of interviews with beginning learners

Group 1: Learners with TTS	Group 2: Learners without TTS
1. I gained confidence in my speech	1. I want to take the next classes
2. I enjoyed interacting with my classmates and accessing the materials daily	2. I was nervous when my name was called first in the online class
3. The breakout exercises were lively	3. The pace of the class was fast
4. There was a lot of content, and the pace of the class was fast	4. I was nervous when my classmates asked me questions in Japanese

Development Plans

As explained in Sect. 3.3, a wide variety of Japanese language education audio files are available on CDs or for downloading from the Internet. However, they use human voices, while the material used in this study is neural speech to improve the efficiency of the learning process. Looking to the future, we intend to implement a Moodle plugin that will allow easy generation of neural speech and free adjustment of the speech. This implementation is expected to further improve the quality of our teaching materials.

4 Discussion and Conclusions

In this paper, we reported on the development of a Japanese e-learning system focusing on CLIL that is suitable for DX. To accomplish this, we developed an e-learning material using neural speech and evaluated it with one intermediate and 19 beginner students. As a result, using TTS, the learners enjoyed learning, were more confident in their speech, and showed higher self-evaluation. In addition, they also reported being more absorbed in learning about Japanese culture and the Japanese language and it was the success of our system by a survey in which 90% of the responses were positive.

However, improvements to neural speech materials based on the questionnaire results were made to enhance the speech ability of target learners, but the expression of emotion was still found to be weak compared to human voices, so further improvements will be needed.

Our future work will consider TTS and STT function enhancements as well as additional APIs as part of efforts to improve the quality of Japanese pronunciation to a level equivalent to that of native Japanese speakers. In addition, as mentioned above, a Moodle plugin using neural voices will be implemented so that the audio can be adjusted in that API.

Although the CLIL approach was found to be a suitable pedagogical method for fast content learning, motivating learners, keeping them interested in learning, and helping them learn authentic Japanese language skills, we also intend to continue to analyze conventional and advanced learning with this system.

References

1. Japan Foundation: Survey Report on Japanese-Language Education Abroad 2018. pp. 10–11, 25–26 (2020)
2. Agency for Cultural Affairs: Government of Japan: Overview of Japanese Language Education in Japan in 2019, p. 5 (2020)
3. Byrne, M.: Teaching Japanese with High and Low Accents. Japanese Language and Culture Training Program Training Reports, vol. 27, pp. 44–63 (2012)
4. Nakamura, M.: Proposal of kanji learning to reduce the burden on non-kanji learners. J. Res. Teach. Jpn. Lang. **4**, 31–54 (2019)
5. Nishitani, M., Matsuda, T.: The development of e-learning teaching materials for teaching Japanese based on the interpretation of language anxiety. Jpn. Soc. Inform. Syst. Educ. **29**(3), 140–151 (2012)
6. Matsuzaki, H.: Development of a system outputting "prosody graph" using an automatic speech recognition engine. Jpn. Lang. Educ. Methods **19**(1), 72–73 (2012)
7. Okuno, Y., Kobayashi, A., Sato, R., Motoda, S., Watanabe, T.: Introduction to CLIL (Content-Integrated Learning) for Japanese Language Teachers, 2nd edn. Bonjinsha, Tokyo (2020)

STEM Programs at Primary School: Teachers Views and Concerns About Teaching "Digital Technologies"

Tanya Linden[1](✉), Therese Keane[2], Anie Sharma[3], and Andreea Molnar[3]

[1] The University of Melbourne, Melbourne, Victoria 3010, Australia
lindent@unimelb.edu.au

[2] La Trobe University, Melbourne, Victoria 3086, Australia
t.keane@latrobe.edu.au

[3] Swinburne University of Technology, Melbourne, Victoria 3122, Australia
{aniesharma,amolnar}@swin.edu.au

Abstract. Modern technology is ubiquitous across all facets of life. The continuously evolving STEM (Science, Technology, Engineering and Mathematics) education landscape has provided an excellent opportunity to integrate the knowledge of digital technology to solve STEM-based project problems. However, there is no consistency in how STEM programs are taught across Australian primary schools. Whilst primary school teachers have integrated technology into their classroom, the teaching of the Technology discipline has been very patchy. Moreover, using technology such as computers is not the same as learning about computer hardware or about writing software to make it function. To achieve effective integration of technology in teaching and learning, we need to educate and encourage students to become creators of digital solutions rather than consumers, which in turn requires primary school teachers to have the confidence and capacity to teach students this specialized discipline. To address this gap, this study focuses on primary school teachers' intentions, beliefs, and perspectives on teaching Technology, as well as teaching STEM subjects overall. Understanding these beliefs and perspectives will help in building teachers' capacity and ultimately improving learning processes for primary school children. The paper reports on one phase of the project – a pilot study investigating the attitudes of primary school teachers towards meaningful integration of digital technologies in primary school programs conducted through the lens of the conceptual framework for the Dimensions of Attitudes towards Science (DAS). The preliminary findings demonstrate an urgency in addressing primary school teachers needs in getting access to knowledge and resources to build their capacity in the Technology discipline.

Keywords: Digital Technologies · STEM · Teachers Attitudes

T. Keane et al. (Eds.): WCCE 2022, IFIP AICT 685, pp. 27–38, 2023.
https://doi.org/10.1007/978-3-031-43393-1_4

1 Introduction

As the teaching of computing became prevalent in the 1990s, the Australian Education Council [1] declared Technology as one of the eight key learning areas identified in the school curriculum. However, the teaching of Technology across schools has been ad-hoc and some schools are doing this better than others. With the introduction of the Adelaide Declaration on National Goals for Schooling at the turn of the 21st Century [2], Australian State and Commonwealth governments collaborated to produce a declaration stating that students will "be confident, creative and productive users of new technologies, particularly information and communication technologies, and understand the impact of those technologies on society" [2, p. 229].

Almost a decade later, the Melbourne Declaration was produced and replaced the Adelaide Declaration. The main findings of the Melbourne Declaration [3] were that successful learners for the 21st century needed:

- To have the essential skills in literacy and numeracy and be creative and productive users of technology, especially ICT, as a foundation for success in all learning areas;
- To be able to think deeply and logically, and obtain and evaluate evidence in a disciplined way as the result of studying fundamental disciplines;
- To be creative, innovative and resourceful, and be able to solve problems in ways that draw upon a range of learning areas and disciplines;
- To be able to plan activities independently, collaborate, work in teams and communicate ideas.

The Melbourne Declaration was an important document that explicitly stated the significance of the use of Technology and ways it could be used in the classroom. Similar recognitions of the importance of teaching and learning technology were identified in Europe and the United States [4].

In response to the disparate teaching of Technology across Australian primary schools in the six states and two territories, a national curriculum (named Australian Curriculum) was developed that addressed the teaching of Digital Technologies [5]. The compulsory Digital Technologies curriculum from the Foundation Year (age 5) to Grade 6 (age 12) was designed to assist in ensuring that the goals from the Melbourne Declaration were met.

Whilst the curriculum works well for teaching of individual subjects which is particularly suited at secondary school levels, teaching Digital Technology in primary school subjects is problematic as many primary school teachers prefer to teach subjects in an integrated manner [6]. The current three-dimensional design of the Australian Curriculum recognizes that learning does not fit neatly into a curriculum solely organized by learning areas or subjects that reflect the disciplines [7]. The curriculum authorities expect teachers and schools to plan integrated STEM projects and lessons according to their resources and expertise through an interdisciplinary approach addressing the deeper integration between these subjects [6].

Whilst STEM is largely an integrated approach to teaching of the four subject areas, the Technology subject is the glue connecting Science, Mathematics and Engineering. It has been suggested that STEM activities should include meaningful learning objectives of the Technologies learning area rather than acting as a tool to integrate Science and

Mathematics [8]. However, often the integration of Technology is treated as merely using a laptop, downloading information from the internet, or using software such as a word-processor, a spreadsheet, or a presentation tool to display information. For true transformation of the use of technology to occur, students need to be encouraged to be active knowledge developers rather than simply consumers of information [8, 9]. That is, students will be required to develop programs through programming, and creating digital solutions to problems. This will require teachers to develop capacity in their students and they too will need to have the required knowledge to be able to confidently teach these complex concepts.

With primary school teachers being generalist in nature, that is many of them have completed a teaching degree without having studied another degree prior to teaching, many have very little experience in teaching highly complex concepts that are often found in STEM [10, 11]. Fewer than one in three primary teachers has completed any tertiary study in computing or information technology [11]. Therefore, teaching Technologies has been noted as difficult for teachers who do not have any background in this field [12, 13].

For the past two decades, Information and Communication Technologies (ICT) has been adopted in the classroom to support teaching and learning practices such as finding information on the internet or typing up documents. Teaching highly sophisticated and complex concepts which is now required by the Digital Technologies curriculum such as programming, algorithms and breaking down problems using computational thinking skills requires a level of understanding that most teachers do not possess.

1.1 Teachers' Attitudes Towards Integrating Digital Technologies Learning Areas into STEM Subjects

Teachers' attitudes towards technology integration in instructions and students' learning, i.e. use of digital technology to support teaching and learning, have been widely studied in the research literature [14, 15]. However, there is a lack of studies, especially in Australia, investigating primary teachers' attitudes and capabilities in integrating Technology into STEM lessons. There have been reports on teachers' lack of technical knowledge and skills, low confidence, and self-efficacy and the ability to integrate technology in classroom instructions to stimulate students to learn successfully [16–18]. However, very few studies discuss challenges in integrating technology in STEM disciplines and how teachers struggle to add more content knowledge of technologies in their STEM programs for meaningful integration [8, 19]. There have been many focused programs run by the Australian Government, such as summer school for STEM students and national competitions, the ICT Summer Schools initiative (digIT), and Curious Minds, to encourage robotics, coding and other aspects of digital education in Australia [18]. Researchers and policymakers call for greater focus on the digital technologies learning area [8, 9]. Notably, integrating various aspects of digital technologies into STEM subjects by primary school teachers is unmapped in Australia.

Teaching quality greatly depends on the teachers' expertise, experience and general attitudes towards the subject [20]. Studies have shown that, in addition to the curriculum, teachers' attitudes are significant determinants affecting students' attitudes towards a subject [21, 22]. An attitude can be defined as a complex and multidimensional construct shaped by knowledge, values, feelings, motivation, and self-esteem [23]. Attitudes are commonly grouped into humans' cognitive, affective, and behavioral attributes [24]. The different subdimensions of attitudes have often been studied separately in literature with respect to individual science, mathematics, technology, or engineering subjects [25–27].

Research shows that enjoyment, confidence, anxiety, and teachers' position towards technology integration in the classroom are the most common constructs contributing to the success of integrating technology into students' learning experiences [12, 28]. Also, the research literature identifies perceived control, comprising self-efficacy beliefs and context factors as essential in forming teachers' attitudes towards any subject [23, 29].

1.2 Research Context and Research Question

To address the research gap in studying problems associated with integrating Technology topics in STEM subjects, this study seeks to answer the following research question:

What are the attitudes of primary school teachers towards meaningful integration of digital technologies in primary school programs?

The investigation into the attitudes of primary school teachers towards teaching of STEM subjects and the integration process was conducted through the lens of the conceptual framework for the Dimensions of Attitudes towards Science (DAS) [23]. The framework identified three constructs of Cognitive, Affective and Perceived Control attitudes which are further described by several subdimensions (Fig. 1). The DAS instrument is applied to teachers' perceptions, intentions, and beliefs towards teaching and integrating concepts and practical experiences of Digital Technologies in students' learning.

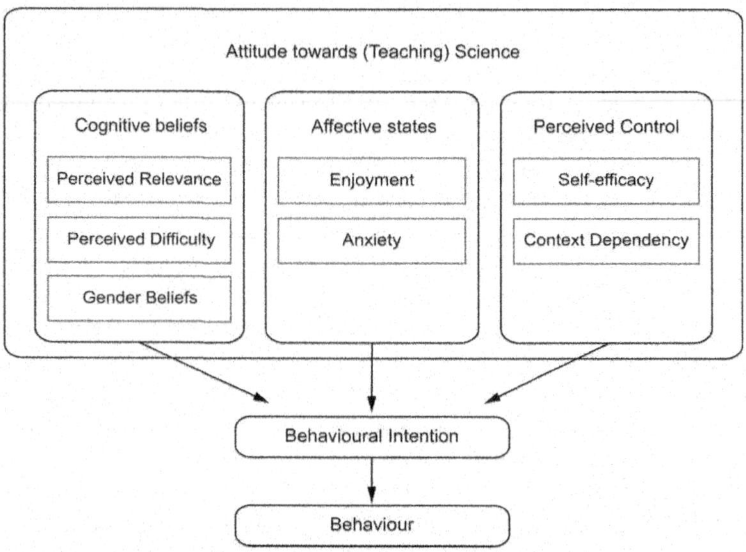

Fig. 1. A conceptual framework for DAS (Dimensions of attitudes towards science) [22]

2 Methodology

The reported study is a part of the larger project that aims to gain understanding into primary teachers' attitudes towards the successful implementation of STEM programs. Teachers' attitudes towards teaching STEM are influenced by several characteristics, including demographic variables such as gender, educational background and length of teaching experience, as well as access to training and resources. The project adopted a mixed-method sequential explanatory design, which comprises two distinct phases: the quantitative phase followed by the qualitative one [30]. This type of study enables a policy researcher to explain the phenomena through numbers, charts, and basic statistical analyses followed by gaining deeper insights into the issues identified through a quantitative study [31]. However, this paper reports on the pilot part of the quantitative phase only, further quantitative investigations and the qualitative phase of the study are beyond its scope.

In the quantitative phase, to develop a questionnaire for assessing teachers' attitudes towards integrating Technology in primary school programs, the researchers adapted items from the DAS instrument. Additional questions had to be written to identify the critical factors impacting teachers' attitudes in integrating various key elements of digital technologies, design and technologies learning area, science, mathematics and engineering subjects.

Most of the items in the questionnaire were graded using a Likert scale from one (strongly disagree) to five (strongly agree). There were also some open-ended questions to get clarifications on Likert-scale choices and some multiple-choice questions The main theme of the questions focusing on the Digital Technologies learning area were:

- Frequency of teaching key areas like ICT tools, data collection, presentation and creating solutions to problems, examining the main components of digital systems, studying networks for data transmission, and designing and following simple algorithms;
- Questions targeting perceived relevance, perceived difficulty, gender beliefs, enjoyment, anxiety, context factors and self-efficacy constructs as per the DAS instrument's conceptual framework (Fig. 1).

The validity and reliability of the questionnaire was assessed through a pilot study.

2.1 Establishing Validity and Reliability of the Questionnaire

To establish content validity, the researchers contacted ten primary school teachers from different schools with a range of teaching backgrounds in science, technology, engineering, mathematics and non-STEM backgrounds, with the request to respond to the questionnaire and provide feedback on the items. The feedback was collected using the Table of Specifications (ToS) feedback form. This ToS feedback form requested that teachers assess each question in the questionnaire in terms of the conceptual framework for DAS.

Only five out of the ten invited teachers attempted the questionnaire. They assessed each of the items for comprehensibility and accuracy, as well as checked whether each item was a true representative of the subdimension of the DAS instrument dimensions, i.e. perceived difficulty, perceived relevance, gender beliefs, anxiety, self-efficacy, and context factors. The checkmarks were counted, and it was deemed that for every subdimension the tally of checkmarks was sufficient. The percentage of respondents' agreement on the suitability of questions to measure the subdimensions of DAS was 80% and 100%. Thus, the questionnaire was accepted as valid.

Reliability analysis was conducted using the internal consistency method through Cronbach's Alpha coefficients. The reliability coefficient was calculated for Likert-type items subscale-wise. The subscale wise and overall instrument's Cronbach's alpha coefficients are reported in Table 1.

Table 1. Cronbach's Alpha Coefficient of Overall scale and Subscales

Subscale	No. of Items	Cronbach's Alpha
Planning Integrated STEM lessons	5	0.75
Technology Role in STEM lessons	5	0.79
Teaching Integrated STEM Lessons	5	0.83
STEM Teaching support	4	0.91

For the estimation of reliability, Cronbach's alpha coefficient was applied to ascertain the internal consistency of the research tool [32]. Usually, a Cronbach Alpha coefficient above 0.75 is considered to indicate good reliability. As shown in Table 1, Cronbach's alpha coefficients were in the range of 0.75 to 0.91. Hence, the research instrument was deemed significantly reliable for data collection.

3 Findings From the Pilot Study

The updated questionnaire was used to conduct a wider pilot study. 36 participants responded to the questionnaire, however three sets of responses had to be discarded because they were incomplete. Thus, a total of 33 teachers' responses were used to assess the instrument's suitability for actual data collection. Eight teacher participants were teaching students at early year levels (5- to 8-year-olds), four at middle year levels (8 to 10 year-olds), eight were teaching at upper year levels (10 to 12 year-olds), four teachers were teaching all year levels as STEM specialists, six teachers and three casual teachers identified themselves as other.

The data was analyzed using SPSS (Statistical Program for Social Sciences). Due to the small sample size, T-tests, non-parametric analysis tools, Cronbach's alpha test and descriptive statistics were used to analyze data. These tests are considered suitable in cases where the sample size is less than 50. The data analysis showed that there were 22 participants with science, mathematics, technology, or STEM background, while 11 came from a non-STEM background.

The teacher respondents were asked to self-report their skill levels as related to planning and teaching the STEM areas in the primary year levels, using a Likert scale from 'Not at all confident' to 'Moderately confident'. The mean was calculated to be between 2 to 3 scale points (Table 2); therefore, it can be judged that among generalist primary teachers, technology and engineering are the most challenging learning areas to teach, and they expressed the need for training and support in both areas.

Table 2. Confidence levels as related to different STEM fields

Descriptive Statistics					
How confident do you feel about planning and teaching the following in the primary year levels?	N	Minimum	Maximum	Mean	Std. Deviation
Digital Technologies	33	1	4	2.55	.869
Design and Technology	33	2	5	3.03	.918
Engineering	33	1	5	2.88	1.023
Valid N (listwise)	33				

The Kruskal-Wallis test was conducted to find the anxiety levels in teachers from all education backgrounds (Table 3). The accepted significance level for the test is 0.05. Our data shows a significance level of 0.589, which indicates that regardless of the background, all teachers felt anxious teaching digital technologies and design and technology subjects.

Table 3. Hypothesis for Kruskal-Wallis test to assess anxiety levels

Hypothesis Test Summary				
	Null Hypothesis	Test	Sig.^{a,b}	Decision
1	The distribution of A is the same across categories of Education	Independent-Samples Kruskal-Wallis Test	.589	Retain the null hypothesis

Based on the descriptive analysis, in the Digital Technologies learning area, on average only 6% of teachers integrate or teach different key areas of digital technologies in primary classrooms on a daily basis (Table 4). The learning areas showing highest levels of teachers' capabilities and integration is information and communication technologies (ICT) which is depicted in the first two rows in Table 4. The second most integrated learning area is 'design, modify, and follow simple algorithms' in specialist STEM lessons. Teachers' responses demonstrate that digital technologies areas depicted in rows 3–6 are more challenging with less than 25% of respondents integrating them frequently and not on the daily basis.

Teachers were asked to provide answers to the question "Technology plays an important role in STEM lessons. Please select how your STEM lessons often include the following components of Digital Technology or Information Communication Technology?" where different groups of technologies were listed. Descriptive statistics were used to analyze responses (Table 5). The results on the Likert scale from 'Almost Never' to 'Very Frequently' fall in only three scale categories of 'Almost Never', 'Rarely', or

Table 4. Integration of key areas as noted by teachers

Digital Technologies areas	Percentage (%) of teachers stating integration of key areas in other subjects				
	Almost Never	Rarely	Sometimes	Daily	Frequently
Technology tools like MS word, PowerPoint, Blogs, search engines, Video filming etc	0	10.38	30.77	7.69	51.16
Collect, access and present different types of data using range of software to create information and solve problems	15.38	15.38	38.46	4.31	26.47
Examine the main components of common digital systems (hardware and software components) for a purpose	23.36	7.69	46.15	0	22.8
Creating digital solutions	14.29	21.43	42.86	0	21.42
Design, modify and follow simple algorithms represented diagrammatically and in English, involving sequences of steps, branching, and iteration	46.15	23.08	7.69	0	23.08
Study of networks to transmit data	46.15	7.69	30.77	0	15.39

'Sometimes'. Most generalist primary teachers admitted that they have rarely or almost never integrated the key learning concepts of digital technologies, including the main components of digital systems, creation of digital solutions using the range of software and transmission of data using the range of networks.

According to the pilot data, participants believe that different technologies play a vital role in STEM lessons. As far as teaching integrated STEM lessons are concerned, most teachers are not confident in teaching engineering concepts, digital technology, design and technology in STEM programs at primary year level. Their responses demonstrate that urgent actions are needed to address lack of teachers' knowledge and lack of training and ongoing support in incorporating Technology topics in integrated STEM lessons. Therefore, the following recommendations were proposed.

- To address teachers' lack of knowledge, it is recommended to make additional training available. The training can be face-to-face where teachers require substantial assistance. Online interactive materials could be helpful as micro-modules. For the benefit of teachers, access to these materials should be available through a blended learning option. This is in line with previous research (e.g. [6]).
- To reduce lack of confidence and anxiety issues, communities of practice need to focus on the aspects of sharing best practices on running activities for students [33].
- To complement best practices from the previous point, a repository of materials needs to be created with associated lesson plans and curriculum mapping. Teachers should

Table 5. Descriptive analysis of responses on of Digital Technology and/or Information Communication Technology

Design Technologies	N	Minimum	Maximum	Mean	Std. Deviation
Technology plays an important role in STEM lessons. Please select how your STEM lessons often include the following components of Digital Technology or Information Communication Technology?					
Technology tools like MS Word, PowerPoint, Blogs, search engines, Video filming etc	33	1	3	2.12	0.87
Collect, access and present different types of data using range of software to create information and solve problems	33	1	3	1.7	0.57
Examine the main components of common digital systems (hardware and software components) for a purpose	33	1	3	1.7	0.51
Creating digital solutions	33	1	2	1.6	0.49
Study of networks to transmit data	33	1	3	1.69	0.68
Design, modify and follow simple algorithms represented diagrammatically and in English, involving sequences of steps, branching, and iteration	33	1	2	1.5	0.5

be able to keep populating this repository, sharing their successfully used lesson plans, activities and teaching advice. Although this recommendation does not stem directly from the teacher responses to the questionnaire, it is a known fact that having access to quality teaching materials helps in boosting confidence of teachers and improving efficacy as well as addresses the issue of overload and time pressure for lessons development [6, 34]

4 Conclusion

Although past research studies investigated teachers' attitudes towards digital technologies at length, they focused on using digital technologies to improve the teaching process and students' learning experience. However, analysis of research literature and educational policy documents identified the need to study teachers' attitudes towards integrating the content of Technology topics into STEM lessons, i.e. teachers' confidence and capabilities to facilitate students activities in creating digital solutions to problems.

To address this gap, the reported phase of this research study used a quantitative approach to assess primary school teachers' attitudes towards integrating digital technology with various levels of difficulty into subjects. The conducted pilot study identified technology and engineering as most challenging for primary school teachers. Regardless of their background, teachers felt anxious when it came to teaching highly specialized areas, such as digital technologies and design and technology subjects. The deficiency of knowledge creates lack of confidence and causes anxiety, which prevent teachers from implementing and sustaining digital technologies integration into STEM subjects. Although further data collection and analysis are needed for sound validity of findings, these preliminary results demonstrate that teachers need practical support in having access to knowledge bases, lesson plans, teaching activities, professional development, and capacity building.

This study has some limitations. In the quantitative phase, only a small number of teachers provided responses to the questionnaire. Although for the pilot study this number of responses was acceptable, it needs to be followed by further data collection and analysis to address the limitations of the sample size. A qualitative phase to further investigate reasons behind lack of capabilities to integrate Technology into STEM teaching needs to be conducted. This additional investigation could analyze the current support available to teachers at primary schools and offer a set of practical suggestions as a response to primary teachers' needs.

References

1. Australian Education Council: A Statement on Technology for Australian Schools. Curriculum Corporation, Carlton (1994)
2. MCEETYA: The Adelaide Declaration on National Goals for Schooling in the Twenty-First Century. Ministerial Council on Education, Employment, Training and Youth Affairs, Carlton South, Victoria, Australia (1999)
3. MCEETYA: Melbourne Declaration on Educational Goals for Young Australians. Ministerial Council on Education, Employment, Training and Youth Affairs (MCEETYA), Carlton South, Victoria, Australia (2008)
4. Keane, T., Keane, W.: A vision of the digital future-government funding as a catalyst for 1 to 1 computing in schools. Educ. Inf. Technol. **25**(2), 845–861 (2020)
5. Australian Curriculum: Australian Curriculum Assessment and Reporting Authority (ACARA), Digital Technologies – Aims. https://www.australiancurriculum.edu.au/f-10-curriculum/technologies/digital-technologies/aims/. Last accessed 12 Apr 2023
6. Keane, T., Linden, T., Snead, S.: Engaging Primary Girls in STEM: Best Practice Implementation, Innovations, and Gaps in Victorian Classrooms. Swinburne University of Technology. Swinburne University of Technology, Melbourne, Australia (2022)

7. Australian Curriculum Assessment and Reporting Authority (ACARA): Curriculum review process paper. ACARA, Sydney, Australia (2020)
8. Fitzgerald, M., Danaia, L., McKinnon, D.: Barriers inhibiting inquiry-based science teaching and potential solutions: perceptions of positively inclined early adopters. Res. Sci. Educ. **49**(2), 543–566 (2019)
9. Birzina, R., Pigozne, T.: Technology as a Tool in STEM Teaching and Learning. In: Rural Environment. Education. Personality. Proceedings of the 13th International Scientific Conference, vol. 13, pp. 219–227. Latvia University of Agriculture, Latvia (2020)
10. MacDonald, A., Danaia, L., Sikder, S., Huser, C.: Early childhood educators' beliefs and confidence regarding STEM education. Int. J. Early Childhood **53**, 241–259 (2021)
11. McKenzie, P., Weldon, P.R, Rowley, G., Murphy, M., McMillan, J.: Staff in Australia's Schools 2013: Main report on the survey. Australian Council for Educational Research (2014)
12. Romeo, G., Lloyd, M., Downes, T.: Teaching teachers for the future (TTF): Building the ICT in education capacity of the next generation of teachers in Australia. Australas. J. Educ. Technol. **28**, 949–964 (2012)
13. Williams, P.J., Kierl, S.: The status of teaching and learning of technology in primary and secondary schools in Australia. In: Proceedings of the IDATER 2001 Conference. Loughborough University, Loughborough, UK (2001)
14. Eickelmann, B., Vennemann, M.: Teachers' attitudes and beliefs regarding ICT in teaching and learning in European countries. Eur. Educ. Res. J. **16**(6), 733–761 (2017)
15. Petko, D., Prasse, D., Cantieni, A.: The interplay of school readiness and teacher readiness for educational technology integration: a structural equation model. Comput. Sch. **35**(1), 1–18 (2018)
16. Powers, S., Mehlinger, H.: Guiding principles for technology and teacher education. In: Willis, D., Price, J., Davis, N. (eds.) Proceedings of SITE 2002 – Society for Information Technology & Teacher Education International Conference, pp. 1414–1417. Association for the Advancement of Computing in Education (AACE), Nashville, Tennessee, USA (2002)
17. Rosicka, C.: Translating STEM education research into practice. Australian Council for Educational Research, Camberwell, Victoria, Australia (2016)
18. Timms, M.J., Moyle, K., Weldon, P.R., Mitchell, P.: Challenges in STEM learning in Australian schools: Literature and policy review. Australian Council for Educational Research (ACER), Melbourne, Australia (2018)
19. Wang, H.-H., Moore, T.J., Roehrig, G.H.: STEM integration: teacher perceptions and practice. J. Pre-College Eng. Educ. Res. **1**(2), 1–13 (2011)
20. Jones, M.G., Legon, M.: Teacher attitudes and beliefs: reforming practice. In: Lederman, N., Abell, S. (eds.) Handbook of Research on Science Teaching, pp. 830–847. Routledge, NY (2014)
21. Guskey, T.R.: Teacher efficacy, self-concept, and attitudes toward the implementation of instructional innovation. Teach. Teach. Educ. **4**(1), 63–69 (1988)
22. Osborne, J., Simon, S., Collins, S.: Attitudes towards science: a review of the literature and its implications. Int. J. Sci. Educ. **25**(9), 1049–1079 (2003)
23. van Aalderen-Smeets, S.I., Walma van der Molen, J.H., Asma, L.J.F.: Primary teachers' attitudes toward science: a new theoretical framework. Sci. Educ. **96**(1), 158–182 (2012)
24. Rosenberg, M.J., Hovland, C.I.: Cognitive, affective and behavioral components of attitudes. In: Rosenberg, M.J., Hovland, C.I. (eds.) Attitude Organization and Change: An Analysis of Consistency among Attitude Components. Yale University Press, New Haven (1960)
25. Albion, P.R., Spence, K.G.: Primary connections" in a provincial queensland school system: relationships to science teaching self-efficacy and practices. Int. J. Env. Sci. Educ. **8**(3), 501–520 (2013)
26. Beswick, K., Fraser, S.: Developing mathematics teachers' 21st century competence for teaching in STEM contexts. Math. Educ. **51**(6), 955–965 (2019)

27. Kearney, M., Schuck, S., Aubusson, P., Burke, P.F.: Teachers' technology adoption and practices: lessons learned from the IWB phenomenon. Teacher Development **22**(4), 481–496 (2018)
28. Njiku, J., Maniraho, J.F., Mutarutinya, V.: Understanding teachers' attitude towards computer technology integration in education: a review of literature. Educ. Inf. Technol. **24**, 3041–3052 (2019)
29. Ajzen, I.: The theory of planned behavior. Organ. Behav. Hum. Decis. Process. **50**(2), 179–211 (1991)
30. Leech, N., Onwuegbuzie, A.: A typology of mixed-methods research designs. Qual. Quant. **43**, 265–275 (2009)
31. Creswell, J.W.: Chapter 18 - mixed-method research: introduction and application. In: Cizek, G.J. (ed.) Handbook of Educational Policy, pp. 455–472. Academic Press, San Diego (1999)
32. Tavakol, M., Dennick, R.: Making sense of Cronbach's alpha. Int. J. Med. Educ. **2**, 53–55 (2011)
33. Keane, T., Seemann, K.: Towards a Thriving Digital Resource Ecology with Teachers. Government of Victoria and Swinburne University of Technology, Melbourne, Australia (2020)
34. Caplan, S., Baxendale, H., Le Feuvre, P.: Making STEM a primary priority: Practical steps to improve the quality of science and mathematics teaching in Australian primary schools. PwC, Australia (2016)

Fostering Students' Resilience. Analyses Towards Factors of Individual Resilience in the Computer and Information Literacy Domain

Kerstin Drossel(✉), Birgit Eickelmann, Mario Vennemann, and Nadine Fröhlich

Paderborn University, Technologiepark 21, 33100 Paderborn, Germany
{kdrossel,birgit.eickelmann,mario.vennemann, nadine.froehlich}@mail.uni-paderborn.de

Abstract. In this contribution the resilience of students in the *computer and information literacy* (CIL) domain is focused. In this context, research towards individual student resilience is of relevance in order to examine characteristics from the student level that can be used as setscrews by educators and other educational stakeholders to minimize or overcome social issues in the CIL domain. Taking advantage of the representative cross-sections of students from the *International Computer and Information Literacy Study 2018* (ICILS 2018), the question of the prevalence of resilient students (research question 1), differences between educational systems in international comparison (research question 2), and students' related antecedents and process factors from the ICILS 2018 contextual model (research question 3) have been focused via using a logistic regression approach. The sample consisted of 46,561 students aged 14 from 14 countries. Cross country analyses revealed that student's sex and their cultural capital are the strongest predictors for resilience in the CIL domain. However, including family's process characteristics shows that students' self-efficacy toward the use of *information and communication technology* (ICT), their use of ICT for information-related activities itself and the use of ICT for basic and advanced purposes have been identified as significantly related to student resilience.

Keywords: Student Resilience · Computer and Information Literacy · Logistic Regression · UneS-ICILS 2018

1 Introduction and Theoretical Framework

In this part of the contribution, an introduction (Sect. 1.1) is complemented by an allocation of the research presented in this paper onto a relevant theoretical framework (Sect. 1.2). Further, insights into already existing research towards resilience in the context of the competent use of ICT (Sect. 1.3) are given and corresponding research questions are developed (Sect. 1.4).

Published by Springer Nature Switzerland AG 2023
T. Keane et al. (Eds.): WCCE 2022, IFIP AICT 685, pp. 39–50, 2023.
https://doi.org/10.1007/978-3-031-43393-1_5

1.1 Introduction

The use of *information and communication technology* (ICT) has become an important part of our lives, which not only contributes to personal private life but also has a tremendous relevance for professional carriers in the present and in the future. In the light of on-going developments toward knowledge and information societies, the relevance of being able to use ICT in a competent manner is increasing on a global scale [1]. In this context, international organizations and initiatives started to conduct empirical studies in order to evaluate and monitor students' achievement in that domain [2]. Aside from providing researchers and educational stakeholders with recent information about the functioning of their educational systems, mentioned studies also aim on indications of how educational systems could be improved on different levels and what prerequisites can support (or hinder) student achievement in the aforementioned domain. In this context, it has been shown that the competent use of ICT is affected by partly substantial social inequality; often referred to as the so-called digital divide [3].

Having a focus on the socio-economic status (SES), research has shown that students aged about 14 years old with a high SES significantly outperform those students, whose families are regarded to have a low socio-economic profile [2, 4]. However, laying a focus on the SES profile of entire schools, researchers were also able to identify schools, where exactly the opposite pattern emerges: Here, at schools that have on average a challenging SES-related student body composition (*low* SES profile) students showed a *high* level of ICT-related proficiency. These schools were regarded as being organizationally resilient and school factors contributing to the resilience of entire schools (such as principal's leadership or teachers' attitudes towards teaching and learning with ICT) were stressed [5].

Although the concept of resilience stems from the field of psychology, the topic of resilience has not yet been focused with regard to the question of which student characteristics make students resilient in their proficiency of using computers and other digital media in a competent manner. For other educational domains (such as reading, mathematics or science), research has already examined the phenomenon of students' individual resilience and was able to show that resilient students in those educational domains share common characteristics that could be used by teachers or other educational stakeholders as a setscrew to overcome educational inequalities [6]. Acknowledging the increasing relevance of the use of ICT for students' future careers and private life, the question of which individual characteristics contribute to or hinder students' resilience in the use of ICT has only been addressed by identifying resilient *schools* as a whole.

Therefore, this contribution aims to identify resilient *students* in the context of competent ICT use and further aims to examine student characteristics that contribute to or hinder individual resilience by applying secondary analyses to the latest database from international large-scale assessments in this domain: The *International Computer and Information Literacy Study* (ICILS 2018) of the *International Association for the Evaluation of Educational Achievement* (IEA). Because of their fully computer-based assessment methodology, representative cross-sections from multiple educational systems and benchmarking participants and because of a rich body of student background information gathered by the study, this database can be regarded highly relevant for addressing previously mentioned research questions.

However, the research presented in this contribution is the first analytical step in a larger project that aims to generate deeper insights into teaching and learning with ICT at those schools who were identified as being organizationally resilient in the aforementioned study: *Unexpected successful schools in the digital age* (UneS-ICILS 2018). Due to the quantitative methodological approach of ICILS 2018, findings towards the educational use of ICT and its relation to students' achievement can only be drawn from the *frequency* of ICT use for teaching and learning. Hence, qualitative insights into what exactly students and teachers do with ICT to support achievement in the CIL domain is not a desiderate of ICILS 2018 and is investigated with the national follow-up study UneS-ICILS 2018 in Germany. The study is supported by the German Federal Ministry of Education and Research for the duration of about three years (10/2020 to 09/2023) and utilizes a qualitative methodology (lesson observation, interviews with agents of teaching and learning with ICT, document analyses) to answer the overarching question on *what* is done with ICT in those schools that showed to be somehow special with regard to their challenging SES-related student body composition and high average CIL.

Because of the fact that individual characteristics can be regarded as tremendously important for student learning in the CIL domain, a first step of the UneS project is to identify resilient students in ICILS 2018 and to conduct secondary analyses in order to evaluate covariates of students' resilience in the domain of CIL and to prepare an interpretative framework for those qualitative analyses previously mentioned.

1.2 Theoretical Framework

In order to theoretically allocate the research conducted in this contribution, the contextual framework of ICILS 2018 is used since it acknowledges for the fact that student learning is influenced not only by prerequisites of the family but also by factors on multiple levels of education (e.g., school and system level). Further, ICILS 2018 is the first international large-scale assessment which assesses the *computer and information literacy* (CIL) of eight graders utilizing a fully computer-based approach for outcome measurement in this domain. Both aspects lead the authors to believe that the contextual model (and the corresponding outcome) is suitable to answer previously mentioned research questions.

The contextual model in ICILS 2018 differentiates four educational levels and emphasizes so-called *antecedents* and *processes* as structural elements on each level [2, 7]. Antecedents are external factors that are regarded as central prerequisites for CIL learning [8]. They are contextual factors that are not directly influenced by learning-process variables or outcomes. Processes are in contrast those factors that directly influence CIL learning.

The *individual (student) level* comprises individual characteristics of the student, their learning processes, and their performance in CIL. While students' age, their gender and aspirations are regarded as antecedents of learning in the CIL domain, their computer-related self-efficacy, the use of information and communication technologies (ICT) or students' attitudes towards learning with ICT are modelled as processes that are regarded as being important to student learning in the CIL domain.

The *level of the home environment* comprises students' background characteristics, especially in terms of the learning processes associated with family, home, and other immediate out-of-schools contexts. Examples for home environment antecedents are the provision with and access to ICT equipment at home. At this point in the model, the social background, and the migration background (immigration background and family language) of the students and their families are also located as individual student characteristics. In these family and extracurricular contexts, the theoretical model of the study also identifies the use of digital media and the acquisition of knowledge and skills with and about digital media as process factors.

However, although there are other levels conceptualized in the ICILS 2018 contextual framework such as the school and classroom level (e.g. ICT equipment of the schools, digitalization-related cooperation or measures to promote digital skills for teachers) or the level of the wider community (remoteness and access to internet facilities), these are not directly relevant to the research presented in this contribution and interested readers are referred to the Assessment Framework of ICILS 2018 [7].

With regard to the research presented in this contribution, it is important that from a theoretical point of view, all levels refer to each other and student achievement is related to student variables as well as to other variables, e.g., on the school or wider community level.

1.3 Research Findings towards the Phenomenon of Resilience in the CIL Domain

As reported in the previous paragraphs, the phenomenon of educational resilience in the CIL domain has only been explored with whole schools as a focus. Content wise this means that researchers were interested in the prevalence of so called organizationally resilient schools and their common characteristics. Here, Eickelmann, Gerick and Vennemann [9] were able to show that the number of resilient schools among those countries and regions participating in the ICILS 2013 study is subject to considerable variation. On average 7.7 percent of the schools focused could be regarded as being organizationally resilient. While for example in Poland about a fifth of the participating schools could be identified as resilient the lowest proportion of resilient schools was observed in the Czech Republic (ibid.). However, the authors were not only interested in the sheer prevalence of resilient schools but also focused on what school characteristics may foster (or hinder) organizationally resilience in the CIL domain. As a result, authors conclude that principal's school leadership and especially a high priority on developing a shared vision of using ICT in teaching and learning among teachers can be regarded as a necessary prerequisite for the resilience of whole schools in the CIL domain.

Similar findings were also part of the latest cycle of the ICILS 2018 study. Here researchers also focused on organizationally resilient schools and conducted in depth analyses in order to identify shared characteristics of resilient schools. Results towards the prevalence of organizationally resilient schools in the second ICILS cycle showed now that about a twentieth of the focused schools in 14 participating countries and regions could be regarded as "overcoming the digital divide" [5] and that teachers' positive attitudes towards ICT and their high self-efficacy towards teaching and learning with ICT can be regarded as the "motor" (ibid., p. 16) for organizationally resilience in the CIL domain. Although both cycles cannot be directly compared due to a different number of countries participating the studies these results show that school specific resilience is a dynamic phenomenon and that there are also countries where none of the schools could be identified as being resilient.

In contrast to the CIL domain in other educational domains such as reading [10] or mathematics [11] the phenomenon of resilience including its predictors were focused on the student level and researchers were interested in factors that contribute or hinder achievement. In this context, positive attitudes towards the educational domain have been found to be the strongest predictor for student resilience. However, in the CIL domain research towards student resilience is not readily available and will therefore be focused in this contribution.

1.4 Research Questions

As proposed, empirical research findings toward factors contributing to student resilience in the CIL domain are not available. Therefore, in this contribution, the following three research objectives will be addressed:

1. What is the proportion of students that show high achievement in the CIL domain and have a low SES (resilient students)?
2. Are differences observable between educational systems when an international comparison is focused?
3. Which student-level factors (antecedents and process variables) are related to student resilience in the CIL domain?

2 Data Sources, Methods, and Statistical Techniques

In this section of the contribution the technical prerequisites and constraints of the analyses are reported. Hence, the subsequent paragraph focus on the data source of ICILS 2018 (Sect. 2.1), the approach utilized in order to identify resilient students in the CIL domain (Sect. 2.2), on the method of logistic regression to determine the relation of predictor variables and the probability of being resilient (Sect. 2.3) and on those instruments and materials used (Sect. 2.4).

2.1 Data Source: Representative Samples from the ICILS 2018 Database

In order to answer the previously stated research questions and following the methodological rationale of UneS-ICILS 2018 secondary analyses of the ICILS 2018 database were used. In ICILS 2018 – as well as in other IEA studies – a multi-staged clustered sampling approach was administered [7]. This means that in a first step, a representative randomly selected cross-section of schools was sampled within the respective educational system or benchmark participants. In a second step, students of grade eight are sampled within the sampled schools [12]. With this approach, some sources of statistical uncertainty can be found but can be addressed by weighting and jackknifing [13]. Both are considered in this paper in order to ensure proper estimates. For this contribution, all students of the ICILS 2018 study (N = 46,561) and schools (N = 2,226) from 14 educational systems and benchmarking participants were included.

2.2 Identifying Resilient Students

In order to identify the resilient students in the CIL domain, their scores in the computer-based CIL test and information regarding their SES were taken into account. The Highest International Socio-Economic Index of Occupational Status (HISEI; [14]) was divided by percentile splits resulting in variable identifying students with low, medium, and high SES. The same procedure has been conducted to students' test scores in the CIL domain (5 plausible values) resulting in a variable that distinguishes a low, a medium, and a high performing group of students. In this contribution, a student is regarded as being resilient in the CIL domain when she or he originates from the lowest 33.3 percent of the HISEI spectrum of their educational system and simultaneously belongs to the 33.3 percent of highest scoring students in their country. This procedure is in line with already existing research of resilience in other educational domains such as reading, mathematics and science [6].

2.3 Statistical Techniques Explaining the Probability of being Resilient in the CIL Domain: Logistic Regression

In educational research and especially in educational large-scale assessments mostly so-called ordinary least square (OLS) linear regression techniques are used to determine the relation between an outcome variable and one or more predictor variables [15]. This method, however, is only valid when the outcome variable is continuous and in educational research other non-continuous nominal variables are also of interest. Here, for example it could be of researcher's interest what influences the likelihood of being allocated to one group or another. In this case the outcome variable has a binary nominal scale and corresponding analyses have to acknowledge this. Therefore, in this contribution the determinants of being resilient in the CIL domain are analyzed using a so-called logistic regression approach which accounts for the binary dependent variable distinguishing between non-resilient (0) and resilient students (1) in the CIL domain. The underlying model of the logistic regression approach utilized in this contribution could be summarized as follows:

$$\mathrm{P}(\mathrm{Y}=1|\mathrm{X}=x_i)=\frac{1}{1+\exp(-x_i\beta)}$$

Another difference compared to linear regression analysis is the method of obtaining proper estimates for the best fitting regression curve since logistic regression models use the iterative algorithm of Maximum-Likelihood-Estimation (MLE, [16]). Further, the model-fit of logistic regression models is also based on R^2 coefficients. But unfortunately, they cannot be interpreted as R^2 from OLS regression approaches since these determine the proportion of the explained variance in the total variance of the dependent variable. The R^2 in the context of logistic regressions are not based on variance decomposition or the ratio of two variances, but on the ratio of two probabilities, the likelihood of a Null-model and that of the fully specified model. These often results in lower R^2 coefficients compared to OLS regression approaches.

Further, in the case of analyzing data from large-scale assessments further statistical pitfalls have to be taken into account. Because of the complex sampling approach in

ICILS 2018 the regression analyses have to account for weighting and the so-called Jackknife-Repeated Replication Technique (JRR; [13]) in order to correct standard errors of respective estimates for the clustered sampling in ICILS. Further, in ICILS 2018 – as in other studies of the IEA – student achievement in the CIL domain is operationalized by 5 plausible values. This means, that every regression model presented in this paper was calculated with each of the plausible values and have been averaged afterwards [17].

2.4 Instruments and Materials

In contrast to the dependent variable of the subsequent analysis, the variables used as predictors of educational resilience in the CIL domain could either have ordinal and continuous scales and were selected according to the ICILS theoretical framework (cf. Section 1.2). Hence, students' sex, an indicator of their family's cultural capital (both regarded to be antecedents), one indicator of students' self-efficacy towards using ICT and three dimensions of their use of ICT in teaching and learning with different focuses were selected for the analyses in this paper. Table 1 summarizes those predictor variables and gives example questions in case an internationally scaled index [12] has been included.

Table 1. Summary of predictor variables used in the logistic regression analyses of this contribution and examples of corresponding item wordings

Variable	Description	Item example wording
S_SEX[1]	Student's sex	Are you a girl or a boy?
S_BOOKS[2]	Student family's cultural capital	About how many books are there in your home?
S_BASEFF[3]	ICT self-efficacy regarding the use of general applications	How well can you do each of these tasks when using ICT? – Write or edit text for a school assignment
S_USEINF[3]	Use of ICT for exchanging information	How often do you use ICT to do each of the following communication activities? – Ask questions on forums or question and answer websites
S_ADVTOOL[3]	Use of specialist applications for activities	When studying throughout this school year, how often did you use the following tools during class? – Multimedia production tools
S_BASTOOL[3]	Use of general applications for activities	When studying throughout this school year, how often did you use the following tools during class? – Word-processing software

[1] 0 – girl; 1 – boy
[2] 0 – maximum of 100 books; 1 – more than 100 books
[3] Internationally scaled index (M = 50; SD = 10; cf. [12])

3 Results, Summary, and Conclusion

In the subsequent paragraphs of this paper the results towards the research questions are reported. While Sect. 3.1 focuses on the identification of resilient eight graders Sect. 3.2 is subdivided into cross-country analyses (Sect. 3.2.1) and within-country analyses (Sect. 3.2.2).

3.1 Results Towards the Proportion of Resilient Students in the CIL Domain (Research Question 1)

As described in the previous section of this paper, one main aim of research question 1 is to identify resilient students in the CIL domain by considering their SES (HISEI) and CIL test scores in the participating countries (cf. Section 2.1). The results show that there are partly tremendous differences in the proportion of resilient students and that three country groups can be distinguished: Those countries where the proportion of resilient students in the CIL domain is significantly higher than the ICILS 2018 average, countries where the mentioned proportion of resilient students does not significantly differ from the ICILS 2018 average and countries where the proportion of resilient students is significantly lower than the ICILS 2018 average (Table 2). In this context, it could be observed that in the Republic of Korea (33.1%), in Kazakhstan (28.2%) and in Finland (26.3%) the amount of low SES students with high test scores in the CIL achievement test (so-called resilient students) is significantly higher than in all other participating countries of ICILS 2018. However, in most countries the focused proportion does not significantly differ from the ICILS 2018 average (23.3%). In this group of countries Italy (25.7%), Portugal (25.5%), Denmark (25.3%), Russian Federation (24.4%), Germany (24.3%), Uruguay (24.2%), United States (23.9%), North-Rhine Westphalia (21.8%), and France (21.2%) can be found. In Chile (17.1%) and in Luxembourg (5.7%), the proportion of resilient students is significantly lower than the respective ICILS average.

3.2 Results Towards Determinants of Students' Resilience in the CIL Domain (Research Question 2)

As stated in the previous section, logistic regression is used in order to identify antecedent and process factors that are related to the phenomenon of eight graders resilience in the domain of CIL. Table 3 summarizes the results for two different regression models. While in model 1 only the *antecedent* variables are included model 2 additionally accounts for *those process factors* regarded as relevant for student learning in the contextual model of ICILS 2018 (cf. Section 1.2). As can be obtained from model 1 in Table 3 students' sex ($B = 0.34$; $p < .05$) and students' family's cultural capital ($B = 0.36$; $p < .05$) show a positive relation to the phenomenon of resilience in the CIL domain when other process variables are not controlled for. Without controlling for any other variable that means that boys and students with more than hundred books in their home (student families with a high cultural capital) have a better chance to be resilient than girls or students whose families possess a maximum of 100 books. Interestingly, when process factors from the student- and the home environment-level are included in the logistic model, the relation between students' sex ($B = -0.27$; $p < .05$) and their family's cultural capital (B

Table 2. Proportion of resilient students in those educational systems and benchmarking participants of ICILS 2018 (N = 14)

Participating country	%	(SE)	
Republic of Korea	33.1	(1.7)	▲
Kazakhstan	28.2	(2.1)	▲
Finland	26.3	(1.9)	▲
Italy	25.7	(1.7)	■
Portugal	25.5	(2.0)	■
Denmark	25.3	(1.6)	■
Russian Federation	24.4	(2.5)	■
Germany	24.3	(2.4)	■
Uruguay	24.2	(1.9)	■
United States	23.9	(0.9)	■
ICILS 2018 Average	**23.3**	**(0.5)**	■
North-Rhine Westphalia	21.8	(1.8)	■
France	21.2	(1.3)	■
Chile	17.1	(1.5)	▼
Luxembourg	5.7	(2.0)	▼

▲ Proportion of resilient students from the lower third of the HISEI spectrum is significantly larger than the ICILS 2018 average ($p < .05$).
■ Proportion of resilient students from the lower third of the HISEI spectrum is not significantly larger than the ICILS 2018 average
▼ Proportion of resilient students from the lower third of the HISEI spectrum is significantly lower than the ICILS 2018 average ($p < .05$).

= -0.52; $p < .05$) are now significantly and negatively related to the probability of being a resilient student in the CIL domain. Further, students' self-efficacy regarding the use of basic ICT applications (0.04; $p < .05$) and the use of those basic tools (0.03; $p < .05$) are the only constructs that positively related to student resilience in the CIL domain.

Table 3. Results of the logistic regression analysis towards student resilience in the CIL domain in all participating countries and benchmark participants of ICILS 2018 (N = 14)

	Model 1				Model 2			
	B	(SE)	Exp	(SE)	B	(SE)	Exp	(SE)
Antecedent factors								
S_SEX	0.34**	0.08	1.53	0.37	−0.27**	0.07	0.81	0.05
S_BOOKS[1]	0.36**	0.08	1.59	0.15	−0.52**	0.09	0.65	0.09
Process factors								
S_BASEFF					0.04**	0.00	1.04	0.00
S_USEINF	-	-	-	-	−0.01**	0.00	0.99	0.00
S_ADVTOOL	-	-	-	-	−0.03**	0.00	0.97	0.00
S_BASTOOL	-	-	-	-	0.03**	0.00	1.03	0.00
Intercept	−2.93**	0.10	0.06	0.00	−3.63**	0.49	0.06	0.04
Nagelkerke R^2	.02				.06			

Notes: [1] 0 – girl; 1 – boy. [2] 0 – maximum of 100 books; 1 – more than 100 books. [3] Internationally scaled index (M = 50; SD = 10) ** p < .05

4 Summary and Conclusion

In this contribution, the resilience of *students* in the CIL domain is focused since analyses towards student resilience and its covariates can be regarded as the first analytical step of the UneS-ICILS 2018 project in order to establish an interpretative framework for the qualitative in-depth analyses. In this context research towards individual student resilience is of relevance in order to examine characteristics from the student level that can be used as setscrews by educators and other educational stakeholder to minimize or overcome social in the CIL domain. Taking advantage of the representative cross-sections of students from the ICILS 2018 study the question of the prevalence of resilient students (research question 1) and their related antecedents and process factors from the ICILS 2018 contextual model (research question 2) have been focused via using a logistic regression approach.

Analyses toward the prevalence of resilient students in the CIL domain show that there is considerable variation in the proportion of resilient students among those 14 countries and benchmark participants focused in this paper. While for example in the Republic of Korea, Kazakhstan, Finland, and Italy more than a quarter of sampled eight graders were identified as resilient, in Chile and Luxembourg the smallest proportion of resilient students was observed. The rest of the ICILS-countries and the ICILS 2018 average can be located in between of those both poles. In order to identify characteristics that foster or hinder students of being educationally resilient in the CIL domain (in terms of those antecedents and process variables distinguished by the ICILS 2018 contextual model) logistic regression analyses have been utilized. Cross country analyses revealed that students' sex and their cultural capital are the strongest predictors for resilience in the CIL domain. However, including family's process characteristics shows that students' *self-efficacy* toward the use of ICT, their *use of ICT* for information-related activities itself and the use of ICT for *basic and advanced purposes* have been identified as significantly related to student resilience.

Although student background characteristics are quite stable and cannot be altered by teacher initiatives or school measures, results towards student antecedents have practical relevance since they imply the implementation of supporting measures for disadvantaged students in respective educational systems (e.g., for students with low cultural capital). Further, from the authors' perspective initiatives and measures supporting students' resilience in the CIL domain should influence those process characteristics mentioned in the previous paragraph. For example, teachers could support students' use of ICT for different purposes by applying individual tasks (for example in the context of homework) that need the use of ICT to be solved. However, this would also be a chance to foster students' self-efficacy in using ICT since this factor has also shown to be positively related to resilience in the CIL domain.

However, having in mind the cross-sectional nature of ICILS 2018 and the quantitative approach of the study some limitations also apply. First, with the cross-sectional design of ICILS only interrelations between students' resilience and predictor variables can be revealed. For causal inference, however, longitudinal studies are strongly recommended. Secondly, the study assesses e.g., the use of ICT for teaching and learning based on quantitative methodology. This means that the study can draw inference on quantitative measures but what is done in detail with ICT in teaching and learning is still a blind spot of the study. Hence, those qualitative approaches applied by the follow-up study UneS-ICILS 2018 are regarded to initiate new insights into the topic of students' resilience in the CIL domain and in its consequence reveal further setscrews for educators to foster students CIL achievement and in turn encourage creative learning for all students.

References

1. Shinohara, M., Horoiwa, A.: Information literacy: Japan's challenge to measure skills beyond subjects. Educ. Res. **63**(1), 95–113 (2021)
2. Fraillon, J., Ainley, J., Schulz, W., Duckworth, D., Friedman, T.: Preparing for Life in a Digital World: IEA International Computer and Information Literacy Study 2018 International Report. International Association for the Evaluation of Educational Achievement (IEA), Amsterdam (2019)
3. Otani, S.: Social and cultural issues: social, cultural and economic issues in the digital divide – Literature review and case study of Japan. Online J. Space Commun. **2**(5), 1–9 (2021)
4. Gougeon, L., Cross J.S.: Computational fluency and the digital divide in Japanese higher education. In: Rodrigo, M.M.T., et al. (eds.) Proceedings of the 29th International Conference on Computers in Education, pp. 672–674. Asia-Pacific Society for Computers in Education (2021)
5. Drossel, K., Eickelmann, B., Vennemann, M.: Schools overcoming the digital divide – In depth analyses towards organizational resilience in the computer and information literacy domain. Large-Scale Assess. Educ. **8**, 1–19 (2020)
6. Agasisti, T., Avvisati, F., Borgonovi, F., Longobardi, S.: What school factors are associated with the success of socio-economically disadvantaged students? An empirical investigation using PISA data. Soc. Indic. Res. **154**(3), 1–33 (2021)

7. Fraillon, J., Ainley, J., Schulz, W., Duckworth, D., Friedman, T.: IEA International Computer and Information Literacy Study 2018: Assessment Framework. International Association for the Evaluation of Educational Achievement (IEA), Amsterdam (2019)
8. Fraillon, J., Ainley, J., Schulz, W., Friedman, T., Gebhardt, E.: Preparing for Life in a Digital Age: The IEA International Computer and Information Literacy Study International Report. Springer, Melbourne (2014)
9. Eickelmann, B, Gerick, J.,Vennemann, M.: Unerwartet erfolgreiche Schulen im digitalen Zeitalter – Eine Analyse von Schulmerkmalen resilienter Schultypen auf Grundlage der IEA-Studie ICILS 2013 [Unexpectedly successful schools in the digital age – An analysis of school characteristics of resilient school types based on the IEA study ICILS 2013]. J. Educ. Res. Online (JERO), Empirische Bildungsforschung – eine Standortbestimmung'**11**(1), 118–144 (2019)
10. Cheung, K., Sit, P.S., Kaycheng, S., Ieong, M., Mak, S.: Predicting academic resilience with reading engagement and demographic variables: comparing Shanghai, Hong Kong, Korea, and Singapore from the PISA Perspective. Asia Pac. Educ. Res. **23**, 895–909 (2013)
11. Chirkina, T., Khavenson, T., Pinskaya, M., Zvyagintsev, R.: Factors of student resilience obtained from TIMSS and PISA longitudinal studies. Issues Educ. Res. **30**, 12–45 (2020)
12. Fraillon, J., Ainley, J., Schulz, W., Friedman, T., Duckworth, D.: IEA International Computer and Information Literacy Study 2018 Technical Report. International Association for the Evaluation of Educational Achievement (IEA), Amsterdam (2019)
13. Johnson, E.G., Rust, K.F.: Population inferences and variance estimation for NAEP data. J. Educ. Stat. **17**(2), 175–190 (1992)
14. Ganzeboom, H.B.G., de Graaf, P.M., Treiman, D.J., de Leeuw, J.: A standard international socio-economic index of occupational status. Soc. Sci. Res. **21**(1), 1–56 (1992)
15. Long, J.S.: Regression Models for Categorical and Limited Dependent Variables. Sage, Thousand Oaks, CA (1997)
16. Scott, M.W.: Applied Logistic Regression. SAGE, Thousand Oaks (2002)
17. Wu, M.: The role of plausible values in large-scale surveys. Stud. Educ. Eval. **21**(2–3), 114–128 (2005)

A Workshop of a Digital *Kamishibai* System for Children and Analysis of Children's Works

Masataka Murata[1], Keita Ushida[2](✉), Yoshie Abe[2], and Qiu Chen[2]

[1] Digital Arts Inc., 1-5-1 Otemachi, Chiyoda-ku, Tokyo, Japan
[2] Kogakuin University, 1-24-2 Nishi-shinjuku, Shinjuku-ku, Tokyo, Japan
{ushida,Abeyoshie,chen}@cc.kogakuin.ac.jp

Abstract. The authors have developed a digital *kamishibai* system, for authoring and performing *kamishibai* is said to have good educational effects on children. The system is implemented so that even children can operate it easily. The characteristics of the system are authoring with drag-and-drop operation and performance with ad-lib animation. Through the experiment, the authors made sure that children over six years old could handle the system. In this paper, the authors carried out a workshop in which children authored and performed digital *kamishibai*. Forty-eight groups participated. From the questionnaire, both children and their parents were mostly favorable to the system. The effects mentioned above were observed. Through the workshop, various *kamishibai* works were made. The authors showed these works to a staff of a children's hall (an expert of *kamishibai*) and had review them. He pointed out children's comprehension of stories, characteristics and style of representation, and structures and originality of the works. One of the future works is a detailed analysis of the works.

Keywords: Picture Story · Kamishibai · Storytelling

1 Introduction

It has been said that making and telling a story by children themselves is effective for education [1]. However, it has rarely been practiced. Although there are several digitally-supported systems for story making and telling for education are found [2–4], the target users of these systems are teachers and educators, not children.

The authors focused on *kamishibai*, one of the storytelling styles in Japan, and have developed a digitally-supported *kamishibai* system [5]. It is carefully implemented in terms of usability so that even children can author and perform *kamishibai*. Its interface is simple, and the users can author *kamishibai* by combining picture materials with drag-and-drop operations. The system also has functions for performing *kamishibai*. In addition to conventional performance, the user can move the characters on the canvas ad-lib (without prior settings) with touch operation. This feature is unique for digital-supported systems. The authors carried out a pilot experiment to evaluate the usability of the system [6]. Children over the age of six were able to handle the system without

Published by Springer Nature Switzerland AG 2023
T. Keane et al. (Eds.): WCCE 2022, IFIP AICT 685, pp. 51–56, 2023.
https://doi.org/10.1007/978-3-031-43393-1_6

difficulty. And, the effects of children's authoring and performing *kamishibai* mentioned in [1] were observed.

In this paper, the authors report on a digital *kamishibai* workshop for children and an analysis of the *kamishibai* works.

2 A Digital *Kamishibai* Workshop for Children

2.1 Overview of the Workshop

The authors carried out a digital *kamishibai* workshop as a part of a science education event for children. The workshop aimed to investigate the behavior of the participants (children) and to collect their works for analysis. The children participated in the workshop in groups of one to four. Each group authored and performed digital *kamishibai*.

The total time for authoring and performing *kamishibai* was 50 min. The authors prepared two stories for the theme of *kamishibai*: *Cinderella* and *Urashima Taro*. The authors collected picture materials related to the stories beforehand so that the participants could use the materials instantly and so that the time for authoring could be saved. Each group chooses a theme from the two stories. After authoring and performing *kamishibai*, one child from each group and his/her parent answered a questionnaire.

Forty-eight groups participated in the workshop.

2.2 Questionnaire for Children

Profiles of the Participants. The age range of the respondents was 2–12 years. The average was 8.3, and the median was 9. The ratio of males to females was 6:4.

In terms of computer experience, about 60% of the respondents used PCs less than once a month, while about half of the respondents used tablets or smartphones more than ten times a month. This indicates that the participants were familiar with and could handle them, but that they were not so familiar with PCs.

In terms of experience with *kamishibai*, 76% of the respondents had seen *kamishibai* performance.

About the Kamishibai System and Participants' Works. About half of the respondents answered that it was easy to both author and perform *kamishibai* with the system. About 60% of the respondents answered that they were able to author *kamishibai* as they desired. Respondents over the age of five tended to be favorably impressed. This tendency is thought to be the same as that observed in [6], along with the fact that children over the age of six were able to use the *kamishibai* system easily.

Over 70% of the respondents answered that they wanted more time to author *kamishibai*. Although the participants would be able to author more satisfying *kamishibai* with more time, too much time might decrease children's concentration (the 50 min was set based on a school hour).

The respondent's comments were mostly positive. Many of them responded that the workshop was interesting. Other comments included the following: I was able to author my favorite *kamishibai.* I was able to make an original (different from the given theme) story. I was satisfied that I was able to handle a computer well. However, some respondents commented that they did not have enough time (the same as in the questionnaire).

2.3 Participants at the Workshop

The participants' approach to the work was different depending on whether the group consisted of one person or more.

Groups of Multiple Children. In authoring, they discussed the content of the *kamishibai* and exchanged ideas. Some parents joined the discussion and commented. In some groups, they changed the main creator for each page. In other groups, one of the members operated the PC and the others gave their opinions on the work.

In performing, almost all the participants animated the characters on the canvas with touch operation. This function was naturally accepted by the participants. In detail, three main performance styles were observed. 1) Performance with storytelling. In this case, in some groups, one child was the storyteller and animator, and in the other groups, one child was the storyteller and others were the animators. In the latter case, active collaboration and communication among the participants were observed. 2) Performance with sound effects (without storytelling). In this case, the participants animated the characters collaboratively. 3) Silent performance. In this case, in most groups, the parents asked the children about the situation they performed. Active communication between children and parents was observed.

Groups of One Child. In authoring, some were obsessed with their work. Some enjoyed authoring with talking with their parents. In performing, their performance style was mostly like 3) described above.

Issues in Infant Participants' Operation. In the digital *kamishibai* system, a mouse is mainly used for authoring, while touch operation is used for performing. Infant (under six years old) participants tended to author *kamishibai* with touch operation (unsupported, however). This would result in the impression that infant participants had difficulty in operation. To improve operability for infants, authoring with touch operation should also be supported.

Summary of Participants' Behavior. Most of the participants enjoyed the workshop. Every group continued to make *kamishibai* after the time was up. This is consistent with the responses to the questionnaire described above. Overall, also in this workshop, the effects of making and telling stories by children mentioned in [1] (communication is promoted and various works are created) were also observed in this workshop.

2.4 Questionnaire for Parents

In the questionnaire for the parents, more than half of them answered that both authoring and performing (digital) *kamishibai* were good for the education of children.

The parents' comments included the following: It was easy to use and allowed for trial-and-error, because of the advantages of computers. It would be more creative than just reading books. The children seemed to enjoy considering the structure of the story to compose scenes.

Overall, the parents seemed to believe that digital *kamishibai* would provide valuable experiences for children. Some parents wanted the system to be more expressive.

3 Review of *Kamishibai* Works

The authors had the staff of children's hall review the *kamishibai* works authored in the workshop described in Sect. 2.

The staff of children's halls often perform *kamishibai*. Therefore, they are well informed not only about *kamishibai* performance but also about *kamishibai* works. The authors showed the staff of children's hall the kamishibai works and the video recording of the workshop and had them review the works.

Stories of the Work. Children were able to reorganize the story into *kamishibai*. In some works, the details of the story were modified. For example, in Fig. 1, *Urashima Taro* was not a man but an octopus. However, the climax of the story was expressed in almost all the works. In the works by older children, the detail of the story was also represented.

Fig. 1. Modified *Urashima Taro*: Taro is represented as an octopus in the scene

Composition of the Stage and Selection of the Material. In the arrangement of the characters in the background, in some works, they were adjusted to the background (Fig. 2 left), while in other works they were not (Fig. 2 right). The impression of each type was different. As for the positioning of the characters, their feet tended to adjust to the bottom of the canvas. The children would assume that the bottom of the stage was the ground.

In the picture materials, there were two pictures of an old man: one pleased and one disappointed. In the last scene of *Urashima Taro*, some works adopted the former, while others adopted the latter. This reflected the children's impression of the story.

The Originality of the Works. Even in the limited condition, originality was found in every work. It was because the children represented the impression of the story after

Fig. 2. Two types of arrangement of the characters in the background: Adjusted to the background (left), enlarged as the foreground (right)

they understood it. In other words, the works made in the workshop reflected the story that the children had internalized. In contrast, it would also be interesting to instruct to make *kamishibai* for others, i.e., for performing and telling the story to others.

The Task of the Workshop. In this workshop, since the theme of *kamishibai* was given and the picture materials were limited, the range of expression was not so wide. However, this limitation made the children's work easy. This task would help them express their feelings and organize the stories they experienced. In addition, the children would learn the structure of stories by analyzing existing stories.

Performing Kamishibai and Animation. One of the differences between books and *kamishibai* is whether the performer exists. The reader of a book understands it with his/her imagination. The audience of *kamishibai* receives the performer's intent in addition to the content. The digital *kamishibai* system will help performers express intent more richly with animation.

4 Discussion

Based on the children's behavior and the questionnaire, most of the participants were able to author their original *kamishibai* by understanding and reorganizing the given theme.

In terms of operability, children over six years old were able to handle the system enough. However, children under six years of age preferred to touch operation and had some difficulty in operating the current system. Supporting touch operation in authoring will make it easier for infants to use the system.

Although the picture materials prepared for the workshop were limited, various *kamishibai* works were created. In other words, the children created the work's originality by devising combinations and arrangements of materials under limited conditions.

The staff at the children's hall pointed out that authoring *kamishibai* with a given theme would promote the ability to understand the structure of stories. In addition, other abilities could be promoted through well-designed conditions and tasks.

The function of the animation seemed to work effectively in performance in the workshop. The performer seemed to devise the motion of the character. S/he can tell the story not only with words but also with images.

5 Conclusion and Future Works

In this paper, the authors reported on a digital *kamishibai* workshop for children and a review of the works made in the workshop. The digital *kamishibai* (authoring and performing) system was developed by the authors, for children.

The impression of digital *kamishibai* was good for both the children and their parents. The children enjoyed the digital *kamishibai* and created various *kamishibai* works.

The works were reviewed by a *kamishibai* expert. He pointed out children's comprehension of the stories, the characteristics and style of representation, and the structure and originality of the works.

A more detailed analysis of the *kamishibai* works is one of the future works. Through the analysis, appropriate conditions (preparation, task, etc.) for utilizing the system will be found. To analyze and evaluate digital *kamishibai*, other experts' reviews are needed. After analysis and consideration, the authors plan to hold a workshop and contribute to children's education.

References

1. Bingushi, K., Nozaki, M., Kojima, C.: The Effect of Making "Kamishibai." Nagoya Ryujo Junior College annual report of studies **34**, 77–86 (2012). (in Japanese)
2. Koyama, Y., Miyaji, I., Miyake, S., Namimoto, M., Shimoda, M., Yokota, K.: Development and evaluation of the hands-on 3D digital picture-card show system. Trans. Japanese Soc. Info. Sys. Edu. **26**(1), 119–128 (2009). (in Japanese)
3. Takase, S.: Utilization of information and communications technology for an educational tool: creation of a three-dimensional digital picture-story show. Nagoya Ryujo Junior College Annual Report of Studies **32**, 147–150 (2010). (in Japanese)
4. Kato, T.: Picture-story show with interactive whiteboard for infants. Bulletin of Nagoya Uni. Arts **35**, 77–87 (2014). (in Japanese)
5. Murata, M., Ushida, K., Chen, Q.: Development of a digital picture-story system with touch operation. IEICE Technical Report, MVE2018–7 (2018). (in Japanese)
6. Murata, M., Ushida, K., Chen, Q.: A digital picture story system with touch operation —development and evaluation via workshop—. IEEE GCCE **2019**, 1082–1083 (2019)

ELSI (Ethical, Legal, and Social Issues) Education on Digital Technologies: In the Field of Elementary and Secondary Education

Nagayoshi Nakazono(✉)

Faculty of Global Studies, Reitaku University, Kashiwa, Chiba, Japan
nnakazon@reitaku-u.ac.jp

Abstract. This study proposes the need to introduce ELSI (Ethical, Legal, and Social Issues) education on digital technologies in school education, particularly primary and secondary education. Currently, various advanced technologies such as artificial intelligence and data science, are being used in our daily lives. New ethical, legal, and social issues arise with the use of such new technologies, and the concept of ELSI, which examines these issues, is gaining popularity. To properly utilize advanced technologies, it is necessary to involve the general public in ELSI, and education regarding ELSI is necessary to obtain basic knowledge and understanding for this purpose. This paper defines ELSI education as "Learning with ELSI" and emphasizes the necessity of introducing ELSI education in primary and secondary education. To implement ELSI education, teachers must have sufficient knowledge of ethics, law, and society, and be up-to-date regarding the changes in the information society. ELSI education should not be introduced as an entirely new education but as a new concept assimilated in existing education. This paper introduces a practical example of using a chatbot as a subject and presents a practical form of ELSI education. In this age of advancing technologies, it is important to incorporate ELSI education in the curriculum at the elementary and secondary levels based on the developmental stage of learners.

Keywords: ELSI education · Ethics · Elementary and secondary education · Artificial intelligence · Advanced technologies

1 Introduction

1.1 Research Background

This paper proposes the need to introduce ELSI education on digital technologies in school education, such as elementary and secondary education. ELSI is an acronym for Ethical, Legal, and Social Issues.

In recent years, various digital technologies have been developed with which our lives have become deeply involved. For example, home appliances equipped with artificial intelligence (AI) are now common and can be easily purchased by

Published by Springer Nature Switzerland AG 2023
T. Keane et al. (Eds.): WCCE 2022, IFIP AICT 685, pp. 57–68, 2023.
https://doi.org/10.1007/978-3-031-43393-1_7

electronics retailers. Robots are widely being used in factories and stores. Various new technologies are being utilized not only in hardware, such as robots, but also in software, such as big data.

As new technologies and products are developed and become available for use in our daily life, we must use them "correctly." However, new technologies sometimes cannot be explained by conventional "correctness." To utilize new technologies, it is necessary to define "correctness" suited to those technologies and apply it to actual utilization. Although the abstract expression "correctness" was used here, in terms of more concrete definition, it is a matter of ethics, law, and society. ELSI is a framework for discussing these implications. The consideration of ELSI has been emphasized when developing and applying new technologies.

In recent years, school education, including elementary and secondary education, has increasingly been dealing with digital and advanced technologies such as AI [1] and data science [2]. However, simply introducing digital and advanced technologies is not sufficient to understand their essence. To properly understand and appropriately utilize advanced technologies, it is necessary to correctly understand their essence. This means that ELSI of digital and advanced technologies must be addressed in school education.

1.2 Purpose and Significance of This Study

The purpose of this study is to define ELSI education and clarify the significance of introducing ELSI education in elementary and secondary education. To set the background, we will identify the relationship between advanced technologies, such as digital technologies and ethics, and examine how these are dealt with in school education in the digital age.

ELSI education has not been extensively discussed in the context of school education. Although there are references to the concept of ELSI in the literature, including the CS Standards by the Computer Science Teachers Association [3], its practice in schools is insufficient. This study introduces the concept of ELSI to the educational community and lays the groundwork for enabling ELSI-aware practices in the education of digital technologies. This research will make the education of digital technologies in school education more important and will help to develop human resources who can "correctly" utilize various advanced technologies.

2 What is ELSI?

2.1 Origin and Overview of ELSI

Though ELSI is an acronym for "Ethical, Legal and Social Issues," in some contexts, it may also stand for "Ethical, Legal and Social Implications." In Europe, it is also synonymously termed ELSA, an acronym for "Ethical, Legal and Social Aspects."

The National Institutes of Health (NIH) of the United States (US) established the Office for Human Genome Research in 1988 to conduct full-scale research on the human genome [4,5]. J. D. Watson, the director of this organization, decided that a portion of the project budget should be allocated for research on ethical and social issues, which is commonly understood as the beginning of ELSI. Thus, it is a concept that has spread from life sciences to other fields, and research on ELSI has been active in the life sciences, medical, and pharmaceutical fields.

Science and society have many points of contact [6]. ELSI is an examination of the ethical, legal, and social issues and implications of science, technology, and research. As technology advances and research proceeds, examining its ethical, legal, and social aspects is an important perspective in the social implementation of technology and research. Zwart and Nelis stated that ELSI is characterized by "proximity," "early anticipation," "interactivity," and "interdisciplinarity" [7].

- proximity: embeddedness in scientific programmes
- early anticipation: of issues, publics and those responsible for dealing with these issues
- interactivity: to encourage stakeholders and publics to assume a more active role in co-designing research agendas
- interdisciplinarity: to bridge the boundaries between research communities such as bioethics and STS (science and technology studies)

2.2 Relationship Between Ethics, Law, and Society

Although ethics (E), law (L), and society (S) are closely related to each other, they are different concepts. Here is a summary of these relationships, with reference to Kishimoto's explanation [8]. Ethics (E) are the norms on which people should rely in society. Though they change in the long term, in the short term they are stable. Ethics serve as the foundation of law. Law (L) is influenced by both ethics and society. Society (S), also known as public opinion, is changeable and unstable.

Ethical, legal, and social issues are related to each other, and each may have a different opinion. For example, consider the act of a student asking a friend to let them copy the homework. This act is not a legal problem if the friend agrees (L). However, from an ethical standpoint, the value that "homework should be done on one's own" is expressed, and this behavior is judged to be inappropriate (E). If this action is posted on social networking sites, it could be at risk of social criticism (S). Thus, ELSI should be considered from multiple perspectives, taking ethics, law, and society into account.

2.3 RRI: Responsible Research and Innovation

ELSI is a concept that has developed mainly in the US, whereas Responsible Research and Innovation (RRI) has been proposed as a similar concept in Europe. RRI is defined as follows (cited from page 3 of [9]):

> Responsible Research and Innovation (RRI) refers to the comprehensive approach of proceeding in research and innovation in ways that allow all stakeholders that are involved in the processes of research and innovation at an early stage (A) to obtain relevant knowledge on the consequences of the outcomes of their actions and on the range of options open to them and (B) to effectively evaluate both outcomes and options in terms of societal needs and moral values and (C) to use these considerations (under A and B) as functional requirements for design and development of new research, products and services.

One of the characteristics of RRI is that it is future-oriented as opposed to the self-reflective aspects of ELSI. In fact, it is an extension and development of the concept of ELSI. The RRI approach has been incorporated into the EU's research and innovation program, Horizon 2020 [10], and its follow-up, Horizon Europe [11].

2.4 Recent Trends in ELSI: Examples from the Field of Artificial Intelligence

Although ELSI started in the field of life sciences, in recent years, with the diverse development of advanced technologies, it is being increasingly recognized in a variety of fields. As a specific case study, this section presents the trends in ELSI in the field of AI.

In recent years, ample research on ethics in AI, robotics, and the information age have been published [12–14]. It would be meaningful to consider ELSI with respect to these advanced technologies.

Several guidelines have been developed for ELSI in the field of AI.

"Ethically Aligned Design" by IEEE [15] is an ethical guideline for autonomous and intelligent systems. It outlines eight principles: Human Rights, Well-being, Data Agency, Effectiveness, Transparency, Accountability, Awareness of Misuse, and Competence. It is unique in that it was developed by researchers and focuses primarily on ethics in the development and implementation of systems.

The G20 meeting, held in Osaka, Japan in 2019, formulated the "AI Principles" [16]. The five principles are "inclusive growth, sustainable development and well-being," "human-centered values and fairness," "transparency and explainability," "robustness, security and safety," and "accountability." It is meaningful that many countries have agreed on the value of "human-centered AI."

Academic attempts have also been made to pursue ELSI in AI. Ikkatai et al. proposed a method called "Octagon measurement" to quantify society's attitude toward AI technology and attempted to measure AI ethics [17].

2.5 Necessity of Public Participation in ELSI

ELSI is an attempt to examine advanced technologies such as life sciences in a professional manner. However, in this experiment, the participation of experts and the general public was necessary.

In discussions on science technologies, the general public is often excluded. However, science and technology are not only utilized in the laboratory (*in vitro*), but also applied in everyday life (*in vivo*). Thus, the viewpoint of the general public, who actually use technologies, is also necessary for science technologies. Soneryd terms this idea the "Technologies of Participation" [18]. For example, in the field of medical genetics, patient support groups have been reported to have a significant influence over both research and clinical services [19].

Based on the concept of "Technologies of Participation," ELSI on advanced technologies also requires the participation of the general public. To effectively participate in ELSI discussions, it is crucial for the public to have a basic understanding of ELSI. To enable everyone to learn about ELSI, it is considered that ELSI education should be implemented in school education.

3 ELSI Education in Elementary and Secondary Education

3.1 Definition of ELSI Education

Until now, ELSI has not been adequately discussed in the context of education. Thus, this paper first defines ELSI education.

The role of Information and Communication Technology (ICT) in the curriculum is referenced in defining ELSI Education. UNESCO organizes the role of ICT in the curriculum into the following three categories [20]:

- Learning about ICT: which refers to ICT as a subject of learning in the school curriculum
- Learning with ICT: which refers to the use of ICT
- Learning through ICT: which refers to the integration of ICT as an essential tool in a course/curriculum

With reference to the organization of ICT, the following classifications can be made for ELSI:

- Learning about ELSI: which refers to ELSI as a subject of learning in the school curriculum
- Learning with ELSI: which refers to the use of ELSI
- Learning through ELSI: which refers to the integration of ELSI as an essential tool in a course/curriculum

In this paper, "ELSI education" is defined as "Learning with ELSI," that is, "education practiced based on the ELSI concept."

"Learning about ELSI" is education about ELSI itself. As ethics, law, and society, which make up the ELSI, are covered in social studies and other subjects, thus they are not included in ELSI education.

"Learning through ELSI" is an education in which ELSI is an important part of the learning object. Although there are disciplines in which ELSI forms the core of learning, such as the life sciences in higher education, it is not realistic to treat ELSI as a requirement at the primary and secondary levels.

"Learning with ELSI" includes an education in learning something through the ELSI approach. In primary and secondary education, students study a variety of subjects, such as language and mathematics, and their goals are explicit. "Learning with ELSI" does not change those goals, but introduces ELSI as one of the ways to learn to achieve them. In other words, it positions ELSI as a "tool" for learning. This type of education is referred to as ELSI education.

3.2 Introduction of ELSI Education

This paper proposes the introduction of ELSI education in primary and secondary education.

In the education systems of most countries, the subject of primary and secondary education includes "social studies." Although the name of the subject varies in different countries, it generally covers history, geography, economics, civics, philosophy, ethics, and sociology, among others. Thus, in many countries, ethics, law, and society are already part of the school curriculum.

However, most social-studies content is not ELSI education. This is because social studies is about ethics, law, and society *themselves*. After learning about ethics, law, and society, ELSI education focuses on how it relates to things that happen around us.

In previous educational research and practice, ELSI education in primary and secondary education has rarely been discussed. This study proposes the necessity of ELSI education in a country-independent manner, referring to previous studies in Japan [21,22].

3.3 Why ELSI Education Is Needed?

Primary and secondary education is studied by all or most citizens in many countries. This means that it requires general learning for the many, rather than specialized learning for the few.

However, the world continues to change dramatically with the development of science and technology. For example, AI has become commonplace for many people in recent years, and many home appliances and other products equipped with AI are now popular in the market. With the spread of ICT, including computers and the Internet, the information people handle has become big data, and people are now expected to process it using knowledge from data science. In school education as well, various advanced technologies have been introduced, including AI and big data.

Furthermore, the introduction of advanced technology requires people to generate a paradigm shift. What humanity has taken for granted in the past will no longer be applicable, and a new common sense will be born. Traditional learning content is of course important, but in addition to that, school education must also deal with new learning content and provide learning adapted to the common sense of the new world.

ELSI education is important to support these new kinds of learning. The paradigm shift caused by the introduction of advanced technology will transform our values. Will the ethical values of the past continue to apply in the future? Are current laws appropriate for the new generation? How is our society changing? To answer these questions, it is necessary to introduce an ELSI perspective to school education.

3.4 Ethics, Morality, and Digital Citizenship

Ethics, an element of ELSI education, is a concept that is difficult to interpret.

Morality is a synonym for ethics. Although ethics and morality are recognized as words with the same meaning, they are sometimes distinguished by context. When distinguishing between them, morality is considered personal and normative, whereas ethics is the standard of "good and bad" distinguished by a particular community or social setting [23].

The relationship between morality and ethics in education varies across countries. For example, the US education system differs in each of the states in the country, but "Character Education" is promoted by the federal government in general. Character Education intends to develop virtues based on Eleven Principles that are good for the individual and the society [24]. It is not a concept unique to the US; various studies on it have been conducted around the world, and there is literature discussing it from a philosophical perspective [25]. In recent years, a new definition has been proposed, that focuses on constructing a moral identity within a life narrative [26]. Another example is moral education (*doutoku kyouiku*), which is being promoted in Japan [27]. Moral education in Japan is characterized by its emphasis on morality rather than ethics.

The distinction between ethics and morality in education is sometimes ambiguous. Especially in primary and secondary education, it may be more desirable for students who do not have specialized knowledge to have ambiguous definitions that fit the everyday context than to seek academically rigorous definitions. However, it is advisable for teachers to be aware of the differences between these concepts to promote ELSI education more appropriately.

Digital citizenship education has also become popular in recent years. Digital citizenship appeared in the 2007 edition of the National Educational Technology Standards (NETS) [28] developed by the International Society for Technology in Education (ISTE) in the United States, and was defined later in the 2016 edition of the ISTE Standards [29] as follows (cited from page 3 of [30]):

> Students recognize the rights, responsibilities and opportunities of living, learning and working in an interconnected digital world, and they act and model in ways that are safe, legal and ethical.

The definition of digital citizenship includes "ethics," and education in the future will also be required to include ELSI education from the standpoint of digital citizenship. From the perspective of the educational community, ELSI education and digital citizenship are relatively new concepts. It will be interesting to see how these concepts can be combined to create a new type of education.

4 Perspectives on Promoting ELSI Education

4.1 Directions for ELSI Education on Digital Technologies

To implement ELSI education, it is necessary to understand not only ethics, law, and society, but also the background of advanced technologies such as digital technologies. In particular, legal issues (L) are often set by following technological innovations, and it is essential to consider society and ethics from the aspect of technology to predict and examine legal trends.

In contrast, in many countries, school education covers so much content that there is not enough scope to introduce new aspects of learning. Therefore, it is important to consciously develop ELSI education in primary and secondary education based on the existing content on social studies and advanced technology, rather than education that is constructed from full scratch.

Figure 1 illustrates the relationship between existing studies and ELSI education. The latter is not to be added as an entirely new education, but rather introduced as a new concept within the existing education. In other words, teachers can implement ELSI education by introducing the ELSI concept while maintaining their existing curriculum.

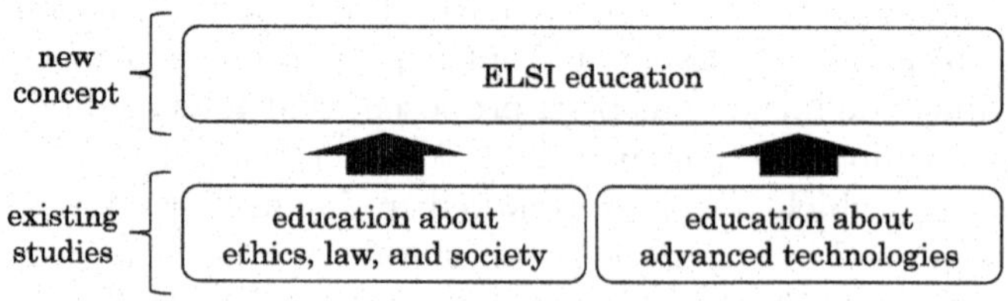

Fig. 1. Positioning of ELSI Education

4.2 Preparation for Teachers to Implement ELSI Education

To implement ELSI education, it is necessary for teachers who teach it to have sufficient knowledge of it. In particular, they must consider teaching materials for ELSI education from the perspective of each of the ELSI elements: ethics, law, and society.

In addition, in order to implement ELSI education, teachers must be equipped with the qualities to deal with "questions for which there are no right answers." Many of the issues that school education has dealt with in the past have had clear answers. Nevertheless, there are many ELSI-related subjects for which the correct answer is unclear, and many of them pose dilemmas. For example, the "trolley problem" [31], a well-known ethical and moral problem, is one in which no matter which decision is chosen, it is difficult to say that it is the "right" answer. ELSI education needs to address these questions for which there are no "right" answers. Of course, this trend is not only common in ELSI education, but also in all education in recent years.

ELSI education on advanced technologies also needs to keep pace with changes in the information society. Teachers should keep up-to-date with not only the ELSI elements of ethics, law, and society, but also the advanced technologies to which they are applied.

Some teachers who teach subjects related to the humanities and social sciences may have little knowledge of computing. However, today and in the future, society will be driven by digital technologies. Therefore, faculties in any discipline must have the minimum knowledge of digital technologies, including computing. ELSI education in the new era will involve teachers' knowledge of their field of expertise as well as digital technologies.

4.3 Example of ELSI Education in Practice

As a specific example of ELSI education, this paper examines a case study of the topic of machine-learning chatbot statements. In this case, the chatbot is assumed to be a bot that replies to the text it receives on social networking services such as Twitter with an answer obtained through machine learning such as deep learning.

Chatbots are used in a variety of places, including social networking services and corporate websites. They are also likely to be familiar among students. In recent years, chatbots have come to be able to respond as naturally as if they were real people, powered by AI (machine learning, such as deep learning), which inputs a large number of sentences as training data.

However, some chatbots have learned inappropriately, whereas others have come to give answers that make their communication partners uncomfortable. A representative example is "Tay" by Microsoft Corporation[1]. Tay, which appeared on Twitter in 2016, was equipped with AI that learned from users' mentions (conversations). However a few hours after its release, Tay began making discriminatory and inappropriate comments, and it was finally shut down.

What if we examine the incident of Tay from the perspective of ELSI? While it is possible to judge that discriminatory remarks are wrong, even if they are made by an artifact, the question remains as to whether Tay, which does not think for itself, is responsible for its own words. If there is no responsibility, there is no rational reason to suspend Tay because of human selfishness. Where does responsibility lie in such cases? Thus, when learning about AI, it is necessary to consider the concept of responsibility, which reinforces the importance of ELSI education. Alternatively, it may be argued that such details are no longer an issue and that only the fact that discriminatory statements were released into the public domain should be discussed. Some are alarmed by the technologies on which Tay is based. This may be an opportunity for young people to become interested in machine learning.

ELSI education on Tay can be implemented at the elementary education level. Although Tay is an AI, its statements of right and wrong currently follow the same standards as those of humans. In elementary school, for example, students

[1] TayTweets (@TayandYou) on Twitter https://twitter.com/tayandyou.

could be asked to think morally about the good and bad of Tay's statements, and after making them aware of the difference between good and bad statements, they could be asked to think about the case where the statement was made by a non-human. In this context, the "non-human" entity could be thought of as an AI or pet, which would be easier for children to think about.

Thus, there is no uniform point of view regarding the ELSI perspective. As a case in which a chatbot "failed" is being discussed, there may be a lot of negative opinions about chatbots. However, from the viewpoint of "Does the chatbot have responsibility?", there will be opinions that sympathize with them, which are pushed around for human convenience. Of course, it is necessary to carefully consider whether these opinions are based on universal principles (ethics) or individual moral values (morality).

The situation in which AI (machine learning) makes such biased decisions is called "algorithmic bias" [32]. If learners' knowledge and motivation are sufficient, it may be important to explain such technical issues in ELSI education from an ELSI perspective.

5 Conclusion

This paper presents an overview of ELSI (Ethical, Legal, and Social Issues), which is becoming increasingly important with the development of advanced technologies, and discusses the necessity of introducing ELSI education in primary and secondary education. The three categories of how ELSI is treated in education are "Learning about ELSI," "Learning with ELSI," and "Learning through ELSI." "Learning with ELSI" education is defined as ELSI education in elementary and secondary education. We suggest that ELSI education should not be added as an entirely new education, but rather introduced as a new concept in existing curriculum.

This study provides only a superficial description of ELSI education and a general framework for its implementation. In actual ELSI education, each teacher is required to deepen their understanding of ELSI and examine various teaching materials carefully from various perspectives.

Ethics, law, and society have a long history as disciplines and educational subjects. However, it has not been sufficiently practiced to examine various technological innovations while relating them to each other. In the future, advancing technologies innovations will be born one after another, and the technologies will be commercialized and made available to the general public, including children. Rather than failing to use consciously, promoting ELSI education while keeping pace with the speed of technological innovation will allow advanced technologies to be used more appropriately and effectively, and will be the driving force behind the creation of the next advanced technologies. For this purpose, it is important to promote ELSI education that is appropriate for the developmental stage of learners from the early stage of primary and secondary education, without waiting for later stages of education or professional life. ELSI should be regarded as a "handle" for realizing better education and promoting its practice.

Acknowledgements. This work was supported by JSPS KAKENHI Grant Numbers 17K14048, 21K02864, and JST RISTEX Grant Number JPMJRX17H3, Japan.

References

1. Barakina, E.Y., Popova, A.V., Gorokhova, S.S., Voskovskaya, A.S.: Digital technologies and artificial intelligence technologies in education. Eur. J. Contemp. Educ. **10**(2), 285–296 (2021)
2. Engel, J.: Statistical literacy for active citizenship: A call for data science education. Stat. Educ. Res. J. **16**(1), 44–49 (2017)
3. Computer Science Teachers Association: CS Standards. https://www.csteachers.org/page/standards. Accessed 2 Oct 2022
4. National Human Genome Research Institute: Report of the working group on ethical, legal, and social issues related to mapping and sequencing the human genome. https://www.genome.gov/Pages/Research/DER/ELSI/ELSI_Working_Group_1st_Report.pdf. Accessed 2 Oct 2022
5. Watson, J.D.: The human genome project: past, present, and future. Science **248**(4951), 44–49 (1990)
6. Okamura, A., Nishijo, K.: Constructing vision-driven indicators to enhance the interaction between science and society. Scientometrics **125**, 1575–1589 (2020)
7. Zwart, H., Nelis, A.: What is ELSA genomics? EMBO Rep. **10**(6), 540–544 (2009)
8. Kishimoto, A.: What is ELSI?. https://elsi.osaka-u.ac.jp/en/what-is-elsi. Accessed 2 Oct 2022
9. European Commission Directorate-General for Research and Innovation: Options for strengthening responsible research and innovation: report of the Expert Group on the State of Art in Europe on Responsible Research and Innovation. Publications Office of the European Union, Luxembourg (2013)
10. European Commission Directorate-General for Research and Innovation: Horizon 2020 in brief: the EU framework programme for research & innovation. Publications Office of the European Union, Luxembourg (2014)
11. European Commission Directorate-General for Research and Innovation: Horizon Europe, the EU research and innovation programme (2021–27): for a green, healthy, digital and inclusive Europe. Publications Office of the European Union, Luxembourg (2021)
12. Coeckelbergh, M.: AI Ethics. MIT Press, Cambridge (2020)
13. Wallach, W., Allen, C.: Moral Machines: Teaching Robots Right from Wrong. Oxford University Press, Oxford (2009)
14. Floridi, L.: Information: A Very Short Introduction. Oxford University Press, Oxford (2010)
15. IEEE: Ethically Aligned Design. Institute of Electrical and Electronics Engineers (IEEE), Piscataway, 1st edn. (2019)
16. G20: G20 AI Principle. https://www.mofa.go.jp/mofaj/gaiko/g20/osaka19/pdf/documents/en/annex_08.pdf. Accessed 2 Oct 2022
17. Ikkatai, Y., Hartwig, T., Takanashi, N., Yokoyama, H.M.: Octagon measurement: Public attitudes toward AI ethics. Int. J. Hum. Comput. Interact. **38**(17), 1589–1606 (2022)
18. Soneryd, L.: Technologies of participation and the making of technologized futures. In: Chilvers, J., Kearnes, M. (eds.) Remaking Participation: Science, Environment and Emergent Publics, pp. 144–161. Routledge, Abingdon (2016)

19. Mikami, K.: Citizens under the umbrella: citizenship projects and the development of genetic umbrella organizations in the USA and the UK. New Genet. Soc. **39**(2), 148–172 (2020)
20. Pelgrum, W.J., Law, N.: ICT in Education Around The World: Trends, Problems and Prospects. UNESCO, International Institute for Educational Planning, Paris (2003)
21. Nakazono, N.: Artificial intelligence, data science and ELSI education in primary and secondary education. IEICE Technical Report, SITE2021-45 121(283), 19–26 (2021). (in Japanese)
22. Nakazono, N.: Education of ethical, legal, and social issues (ELSI education) in primary and secondary education: A study from the perspective of information education. IPSJ SIG Technical Report 2022-CE-163(13), 1–9 (2022). (in Japanese)
23. Grannan, C.: What's the difference between morality and ethics?, Encyclopedia Britannica. https://www.britannica.com/story/whats-the-difference-between-morality-and-ethics. Accessed 2 Oct 2022
24. Lickona, T.: Eleven principles of effective character education. J. Moral Educ. **25**(1), 93–100 (1996)
25. Kristjánsson, K.: Aristotelian Character Education. Routledge, London (2015)
26. McGrath, R.E.: What is character education?: development of a prototype. J. Charact. Educ. **14**(2), 23–35 (2018)
27. Maruyama, H.: Moral education in japan. https://www.nier.go.jp/English/educationjapan/pdf/201303MED.pdf. Accessed 2 Oct 2022
28. NETS Project: National Educational Technology Standards for Students. International Society for Technology in Education, Washington, D.C. (2007)
29. Brooks-Young, S.: ISTE Standards for Students: A Practical Guide for Learning with Technology. International Society for Technology in Education, Portland (2016)
30. International Society for Technology in Education: ISTE Standards: Students. International Society for Technology in Education (2016). https://www.iste.org/standards/iste-standards-for-students. Accessed 2 Oct 2022
31. Foot, P.: The problem of abortion and the doctrine of the double effect. Oxford Rev. **5**, 5–15 (1967)
32. Baer, T.: Understand, Manage, and Prevent Algorithmic Bias: A Guide for Business Users and Data Scientists. Apress, Berkely (2019)

EdTech as an Empowering Tool: Designing Digital Learning Environments to Extend the Action Space for Learning and Foster Digital Agency

Sadaqat Mulla[1(✉)] and G. Nagarjuna[2]

[1] Tata Institute of Social Sciences, Mumbai, India
sadaqat.mulla@tiss.edu
[2] Tata Institute of Fundamental Research, Mumbai, India
nagarjun@gnowledge.org

Abstract. Educational Technology (EdTech) can be both empowering or constraining depending upon the underpinning design. Drawing from the experiments conducted as part of a large scale EdTech intervention in India, this paper shares qualitative findings on designing digital learning environments (DLE) as tools that empower the learner. Building upon the literature on digital agency and microworlds, the first section propounds that for EdTech to become an empowering tool the design of EdTech should expressly cultivate a learner's digital agency and extend the action space for learning. While digital agency encompasses aspects of competence, confidence and accountability; the action space for learning (ASL) is defined as a cognitive-pedagogic construct where learners operate. Subsequently, the paper outlines the key characteristics of EdTech that empowers, and shares research findings. It was found that when DLEs are thoughtfully designed to provide a manipulable action space in a microworld where learners can own the dynamics of the environment through variables and controls, then a learner's digital agency is fostered through the extended possibilities of ASL.

Keywords: Action Space for Learning · Digital Agency · Digital Learning Environment · DOER

1 Introduction

Digital learning environments (DLEs) are digital technology-based applications that provide a virtual environment for the teaching-learning process [1, 2]. These DLEs, also referred to as educational technology (EdTech) solutions, can be both empowering or inhibiting depending upon the underpinning design [3–5]. There is a plethora of research on the affective role of design in the efficacy and usability of DLE [1, 2, 4]. However, more often than not DLEs get developed for limited passive instructional purposes that encourage a transmission model of pedagogy where teachers direct learners

Published by Springer Nature Switzerland AG 2023
T. Keane et al. (Eds.): WCCE 2022, IFIP AICT 685, pp. 69–74, 2023.
https://doi.org/10.1007/978-3-031-43393-1_8

to progress linearly through different subject content. This kind of a design on the one hand undermines the possible transformative potential of technology [5–7] and on the other hand reinforces the perils and pitfalls of conventional didactic pedagogy. In order to meaningfully harness digital technologies for education it is imperative to consider the learning design aspects [3]. Because, the power of EdTech lies not in device but in design. Based on the ideas of manipulable "microworlds" [6, p. 120] and constructivist learning environments [7] we make a case for a learner-centered design of EdTech that empowers learners by providing a manipulation space and tools to extend the action space for learning. Subsequently, through the exemplar artefacts and research evidence from a large-scale multi-state, multi-partner EdTech intervention in India we demonstrate and argue that such an empowering EdTech design would foster learners' digital agency - an emerging 21st century capability. Finally, the paper concludes with recommendations for further research and a call to investigate potential of EdTech as an empowering tool by employing an action-oriented approach for teaching and learning.

2 Methodology

The objective of this article is to contribute first steps toward developing an eclectic model of EdTech as a tool to empower learners by drawing complementarity from the fields of learning design, learning sciences and educational technology. Situating the arguments for active and constructivist learning within the ideas of manipulable "microworlds" [6, 7] we seek to extrapolate the discourse in learning sciences literature on action-oriented peripersonal space [8] and "field of promoted action" [9] to construct a case for an action space for learning. Subsequently, drawing from the qualitative and quantitative research evidence generated from a large-scale EdTech intervention in India, we employ inductive reasoning to develop a case for an EdTech that empowers learners by fostering digital agency [10].

The design experiments were conducted by authors along with a team while designing the EdTech applications between the years 2016 and 2019. Qualitative findings are drawn from design-based research studies with teachers and students.

3 Towards an Action Space for Learning

3.1 What is Action Space for Learning?

Seymour Papert was an optimist, almost a utopian, about the transformative potential of computers and technology for education. However, he was categorical in how technology should and should not be designed for education. He offers the microworld as an interactive technology enabled learning environment where learners "become the active, constructing architects of their own learning" [6, p. 122]. He argues that in order to make a microworld an "incubator for knowledge" it is essential to provide a manipulable space which offers opportunities for "personal appropriation" and "owning the dynamics". Similarly, Jonassen [7] considers a manipulable space to be an essential characteristic of constructivist learning environments (CLE) where learners can conduct meaningful activities by manipulating the environment through objects, signs, and tools.

In the cognitive science literature on the action-oriented learning, Abrahamson and Sánchez-García [9] present field of promoted action as a social microecology in which a novice learner is presented with a specific motor problem as well as constraints. Such a field of promoted action can be used by educators to design and implement a non-linear pedagogy through ecological conditions, tasks, and resources to facilitate students' self-exploratory activity. Similarly, the literature [8] defines peripersonal space as a set of spaces/fields manifesting physiological or perceptual actions between objects and the body.

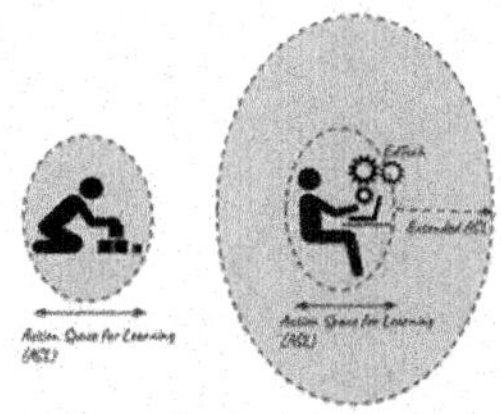

Fig. 1. Action Space for Learning – a cognitive-pedagogic construct which gets extended by an empowering EdTech

Thus, we propose (see Fig. 1) that the eclectic blend of manipulable microworlds and field of promoted action/peripersonal space leads to the conception of an action space for learning (ASL). The ASL is hence characterized by three features:

(1) manipulands - objects, variables, controls and tools
(2) action - an interactive learning activity
(3) action space – a field and boundary to operate within

Apropos to above, we suggest that such an action space for learning fosters digital agency. Provisioning of equitable opportunities to cultivate digital competence, confidence and accountability are essential elements of digital agency [10]. Consequently, in a DLE designed as an ASL, manipulands and opportunities for action help foster competence and confidence whereas the action space with controls and constraints compels learners to be accountable of their actions.

4 Empirical Context

This section discusses the salient features of design experiments towards an empowering EdTech.

4.1 The DOER Microworld – Lego Modelled Distributed Decentralised Open Educational Resources

While embarking on the initiative of the Connected Learning Initiative (CLIx) to demonstrate a model of "quality at scale" by leveraging EdTech, we wanted to learn from the history of EdTech – what worked/not worked, when and why. The literature tells us that more often EdTech solutions take little cognizance of pedagogical nuances and continue to reinforce transmissive pedagogies and passive learning [5–7]. Papert [6] calls these as 'technocentric' approaches where *tech* drives the *ed*. Therefore, we began with *ed* i.e. educational considerations and developed a framework of three pedagogical pillars - authentic learning, collaboration and learning from mistakes - around which the entire intervention including the EdTech enterprise solutions were to revolve. These pedagogical pillars were rooted in the literature of active and constructivist theories of learning [3, 6, 7].

Grounded with the educational aspects of the proposed EdTech solutions, we adopted a lego approach of designing EdTech solutions [2, 11]. We analysed and borrowed the existing open-license solutions which complied with the pedagogical pillars. Consider these as *lego blocks*. Subsequently, we developed a flexible digital learning environment as a *lego board* which allowed us to create a mashup of various open-license, open-standards compliant learning tools. The resultant federated EdTech solutions stack is called a DOER - Distributed Decentralized Open Educational Resources which worked both online and offline to serve even in the internet-scarce regions. Importantly, following Papert's concept of microworlds, we introduced several manipulable affordances in the DOER such as - collaborative story making, sharable e-Notes, and Gallery to showcase artefacts. The federated DOER had dynamic math tools such as GeoGebra and Turtle logo, integrated SugarLab tools and a number of digital interactives such as Open Story Tool and simulations. Further, structured course modules were designed to leverage affordances of platform to achieve the pedagogical goals. Therefore, by design, the DOER encouraged interactivity, creation, collaboration and allowed learners to make mistakes in a manipulation space.

4.2 EdTech as an Empowering Tool - Extending the Action Space for Learning and Fostering Digital Agency

With thoughtfully designed EdTech and consciously provided affordances to extend the action space for learning we deployed the EdTech solutions stack i.e., DOER platform in more than 500 intervention schools between 2016 and 2019. What emerged was just phenomenal. Most of the students in the intervention were first generation learners and digital novices in secondary schools [12]. However, the design considerations that embodied the DOER platform and learner-centric features of buddy login, built-in mechanisms for feedback and multimodal content that encouraged a culture of sharing, seeking, giving feedback through a civilized digital discourse engendered an extended action space for learning where learner agency came to the fore (see Fig. 2).

The exemplar design features presented above demonstrate that thoughtfully designed EdTech can extend the action space for learning (ASL) and cultivate digital agency (DA) – an emergent 21st century capability. The ASL and DA are arguably peculiar to a digital learning environment (DLE) as against a physical learning environment (PLE). This is because the DLE posits unique affordances for teaching and learning due to its distinct media through which it operates [5]. Therefore, it becomes important to understand and perhaps redefine the notions of learning and action space for learning in this media and examine how a learner engages in this virtual space. Through the above examples we argue that DLE provides affordances for teaching and learning that are unthinkable in a PLE thereby engendering a digital agency that operates in a DLE. Similarly, DLE could provide a field of promoted action which we call as action space for learning where a learner engages in perceptual and meaningful educational activities.

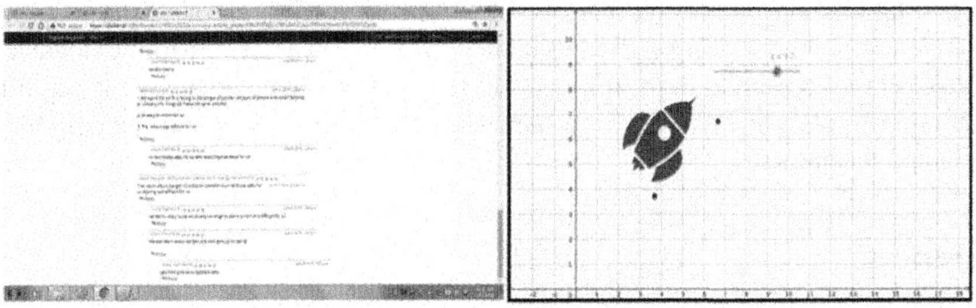

Fig. 2. (Left) First generation digital learners engaged in a civilized digital discourse through threaded discussion moderated by teachers; (Right) A young learner from disadvantaged background of slum created a rocket propellant using GeoGebra and exclaimed "Madam, you made me a scientist!", an exemplary case of EdTech as an empowering tool.

In the next section we present research findings of overall CLIx offerings including the aforementioned aspects of design and features of EdTech solutions.

5 Research Findings

The CLIx intervention used a design-based research framework [1] to analyse the efficacy and impact of EdTech interventions through base-line, mid-line and end-line surveys as well as a DOER platform data during phase-I of the intervention (2015–2019). The research findings [12] indicate that students made significant gains in basic and intermediate technical skills (significant at the 5% level) and application based technological skills (significant at the 5% level). Findings from a learning outcome study have shown significant gains among students in Mathematics (avg 7.16 points gain), Science (avg 13 points gain) and English (avg 2.12 gain in listening and avg 8.51 gain in speaking).

The opportunity to use the DOER platform in a computer lab has produced significant shifts in students' knowledge and competencies of basic digital skills (such as turning on a computer) and specific digital skills pertaining to the DOER action space of learning (ASL) and hence indicates fostering the digital agency (DA). Significant improvements were observed with respect to students' digital skills relating to extended ASL in the case of the student group that received engagement opportunities with the DOER platform compared to the external control group that did not have access to it.

6 Conclusion

Drawing complementarity from the fields of learning design, learning sciences and educational technology, we proposed first steps toward developing an eclectic model of designing EdTech as a tool to empower learners. Extrapolating the concepts of digital learning environments as manipulable microworlds, we have propounded the notion of action space for learning (ASL) to foster learners' digital agency - an emergent 21st century skill. We argued that the design underpinnings of EdTech solutions make these tools as empowering or constraining. Through design-based research experiments we presented initial evidence to substantiate these profferings. In times of mushrooming EdTech solutions and platforms there is an urgent need to foreground the essentiality of considerations about design, digital agency and empowerment. More extensive and inter-disciplinary research and framing is needed to generate evidence that can inform educators and policy makers to more meaningfully leverage EdTech for empowering learners and teachers.

References

1. Wang, F., Hannafin, M.J.: Design-based research and technology-enhanced learning environments. Educ. Technol. Res. Dev. **53**(4), 5–23 (2005)
2. Brown, M., Dehoney, J., Millichap, N.: The Next Generation Digital Learning Environment: A Report on Research. EDUCAUSE (2015)
3. Sawyer, K.: The new science of learning. In: Sawyer, K. (ed.) The Cambridge Handbook of the Learning Sciences, pp. 1–18. Cambridge University Press, UK (2010)
4. Anderson, T., Shattuck, J.: Design-based research: a decade of progress in education research? Educ. Res. **41**(1), 16–25 (2012)
5. UNESCO-MGIEP: Rethinking Pedagogy: Exploring the Potential of Digital Technology in Achieving Quality Education. UNESCO-MGIEP, New Delhi (2019)
6. Papert, S.: Mindstorms: Children, computers and powerful ideas, vol. 1. Basic Books Inc, New York (1980)
7. Jonassen, D.: Designing constructivist learning environments. In: Reigeluth, C. (ed.) Instructional-design theories and models: A new paradigm of instructional theory, pp. 215–239. Pennsylvania State University, University Park (1999)
8. Bufacchi, R.J., Iannetti, G.D.: An action field theory of peripersonal space. Trends Cogn. Sci. **22**(12), 1076–1090 (2018)
9. Abrahamson, D., Sánchez-García, R.: Learning is moving in new ways: the ecological dynamics of mathematics education. J. Learn. Sci. **25**(2), 203–239 (2016)
10. Passey, D., Shonfeld, M., Appleby, L., Judge, M., Saito, T., Smits, A.: Digital agency: empowering equity in and through education. Technol. Knowl. Learn. **23**(3), 425–439 (2018)
11. Mulla, S., Shende, S., Nagarjuna, G.: Including the excluded, connecting the disconnected: lessons from a large scale experiment in India of designing open educational technologies that work for all. Working paper presented in Open Education Global Conference 2019, Milan, Italy. https://clix.tiss.edu/wp-content/uploads/2019/12/Mulla2019-OEGlobal.pdf, last accessed 12 June 2023
12. TISS: Making EdTech Work for Secondary School Students & their Teachers: A Report of Research Findings from CLIx Phase I. Tata Institute of Social Sciences, Mumbai (2020)

Educational Support to Develop Socially Disadvantaged Young People's Digital Skills and Competencies: The Contribution of Collaborative Relationships Toward Young People's Empowerment

Toshinori Saito(✉)

Seisa University, Yokohama, Kanagawa, Japan
t-saito@gred.seisa.ac.jp

Abstract. Digital skills and competencies are necessary for thriving in the coming digital society, and it is important for youths to gain these competencies as well as to become empowered as actors in the digital environment. This paper contends that collaborative relationships established as part of an educational support group to develop socially disadvantaged young people's digital skills and competencies positively impact their empowerment. We discuss the findings of four years of action research among a support group for socially disadvantaged youths in a provincial city in Japan. The results suggest that the collaborative relationships established within an educational support group can create a rich learning context and foster collaborative agency for youths. Moreover, computer programming carried out in the context of these relationships may generate cooperation and a unique programming culture shared among the youths.

Keywords: Digital Skills · Collaboration · Empowerment · Programming

1 Introduction

Digital literacy and competency are now fundamental to forming civil society. In recent years, several frameworks have pointed to the importance of knowledge, skills, competencies, and attitudes toward digital technologies. These frameworks provide a perspective on simple digital technology use and complex activities such as "communication and collaboration" or "problem-solving." For example, the European Commission's Digital Competence Framework for Citizens (DigComp 2.0) [1] and UNESCO's Digital Literacy Global Framework [2], based on a review of DigComp 2.0 and other global examples of digital skill frameworks, both refer to a comprehensive, synthesized competence model for digital technology use and for activities emerging from its use by defining several competence areas as targets for improving citizens' digital skills.

However, few studies provide insight into the specific processes through which citizens acquire digital literacy and competency. Several have focused on linking computing

Published by Springer Nature Switzerland AG 2023
T. Keane et al. (Eds.): WCCE 2022, IFIP AICT 685, pp. 75–86, 2023.
https://doi.org/10.1007/978-3-031-43393-1_9

to social participation. For example, Wagh, Cook-Whitt, and Wilensky [3] demonstrated the potential for inquiry-based learning through interaction with program code, using the concept of computational engagement in a K-12 science education case study. They showed that the acquisition of programming as a component of digital literacy and competency not only involves learning computing skills but also has the potential to elicit an inquisitive attitude in learners. A case study by Yu, Ruppert, Roque, and Kirshner [4] addressed youth participation in civic activities as promoted through computer programming projects based on a conceptual framework of critical computational literacy. The study demonstrated, based on observations of after-school activities, that creation through computer programming can lead to young people's social participation. In presenting the concept of computational participation, Fields, Kafai, and Giang's studies [5, 6] analyzed the influence of social aspects (e.g., gender gap) on children's participation in programming in the Scratch community. They argued for the need to understand the sociological and cultural aspects of learning to code. Further, a study on computational empowerment by Iversen, Smith, and Dindler [7] suggested that support projects should aim not only to help children acquire digital literacy but also to enable them to make critical decisions about the role of technology in their lives.

Like these studies, this paper assumes digital literacy and competency acquisition as a learning goal for children and all citizens. In contrast, however, the focus is explicitly on educational support as part of social participation support for young people in socially difficult situations. Further, the research is about the empowerment of the young people in the support group, including lay supporters who do not have expertise in digital technology, conducted by university educators in computing education.

Correspondingly, this paper discusses the contribution of participants' collaborative relationships toward empowerment in the context of a program for Educational Support for Digital Skills and Competencies (ESDC) for socially disadvantaged youths [8]. The aim is to develop a better understanding of the benefits of having young people participate in an ESDC program as members of a voluntary group rather than as isolated individuals. For this purpose, the study views empowerment as a regaining of people's ability to choose to engage in digital technology in a way that they cannot in isolation. This idea takes over the sociological understanding of empowerment as a reciprocal change in an individual and their surrounding circumstances through the restoration of the denied possibility of choice, which is integral to human agency (see [9, 10]).

Thus, this paper investigates the contributions of collaborative relationships within the context of ESDC for socially disadvantaged youths living in a mid-sized provincial city in Japan. For this purpose, the author conducted a participatory study to help youths learn about computing. The following two research questions are addressed:

RQ1. How can collaborative relationships among participants contribute to the empowerment of young people in the context of ESDC?

RQ2. What educational significance can be ascribed to computer programming carried out in collaborative relationships within an ESDC program?

2 Relevant Literature

Findings from collaborative learning research provide implications for the type of collaborative relationships investigated here. Anderson [11] pointed out the importance of evaluation equality among participants in collaborative work. Baker [12] described collaborative situations as characterized by members with different qualities but equal status and rights in the interaction, problems requiring collaboration, a high degree of joint attention and synchronous interaction, certain problem-solving procedures, a purpose of understanding collaboration beyond reaching a correct answer, and support through Vygotskian scaffolding. Both studies highlight equality-based interrelationships and respect for diversity in capacities among members of support groups.

To understand the contribution of collaborative relationships in the ESDC group, the author focuses on shared culture, mutual trust and interdependence, and agency, following the previous studies. Kucharska [13] pointed out that collaborative culture and trust shared among project members coexist and support each other in a project setting facing external conditions of cooperation, complexity, the uncertainty of environmental conditions, time, and budget pressures. Yoda [14], in discussing collaborative relationships between physicians and engineers in medical device development settings, noted the importance of education, geographic proximity, good leadership, and individuality of members to create collaboration across cognitive, organizational, social, and institutional barriers. Meirink, Imants, Meijer, and Verloop [15], in their research on teacher development settings, found the important of balancing two seemingly conflicting elements: a high level of interdependence and autonomy of each member.

This research continues the focus of previous studies that have revealed the importance of collaborative culture and methods in creative activities, including computer programming. Kucharska and Kowalczyk [16] found that a collaborative culture in team project management, along with trust and shared tacit knowledge, is deeply involved in value creation in projects. Sawyer's [17] investigation of creativity-driven design education found that collaborative and interactive processes are essential for improving performance in knowledge construction. In computer programming, from the viewpoint of productivity and quality improvement, cooperative programming methods and systems have been developed to support software creation (see [18, 19]).

Expanding on the previous works, this paper emphasizes the emergence of social participation rather than the quality of the programs produced or the improvement of the participants' programming skills. Studies that are closer to the present research are Peppler and Kafai [20] and Kong, Chiu, and Lai [21]. The former focused on the importance of collaboration in media art production in design studios, reporting that young people learned computer programming from the perspective of social participation and were motivated by working with peers and mentors to create and share their work. It also noted that collaboration is an indicator of higher membership in the community. The latter revealed that students with better attitudes toward collaboration had higher creative self-efficacy but not programming self-efficacy. It also noted that students might view collaboration positively as a means of enhancing creativity to solve programming challenges when they cannot generate sufficient ideas on their own.

3 Methodologies

Action research (AR) was adopted as a participatory research method. In the AR approach, participants seek positive social changes based on democratic values [22] by exploring solutions to problems [23]. AR requires a shared vision among researchers and other participants concerning the process and problem-solving goals, and in this process, learning through shared reflection among participants is highly valued [24].

AR was implemented in a support group for disadvantaged young people. The author and group members worked together to establish ESDC as a new option for supporting young people's social participation. This paper describes the findings of reflective exercises conducted within the group, from the perspective of youth empowerment.

For the participatory study, the author engaged in the group's activity, aiding the youths' rehabilitation and social participation. The youths in the support group were experiencing social withdrawal or school absenteeism. The group met in a mid-sized provincial city in Japan and varied in size during the study period from one to ten young people with two to five staff members, either full-time or part-time. The author acted as a part-time supporter, assisting the young people in learning computing and informatics.

The study commenced in May 2015, following a similar pilot study from December 2013 to January 2014, and finished in March 2020. The findings are based on an analysis of field notes written for eight days every Thursday from June to August 2016. During this period, the author and youths were involved mainly in computing and informatics learning through a project to construct a programmable robot called Mugbot, which is an open-source social robot.[1]

Data were collected in the form of field notes, text descriptions with some pictures and videos, observations of events and occurrences, dialogues with the participants, and reflections on every session during the study period from June 23, 2016 to March 9, 2020, which constituted a 147-day record[2] written originally in Japanese. Interviews were not used as the pilot study showed that they may cause tension in young people.

The data were coded by thematic analysis [25, 26] using NVivo. First, the author scrutinized the field notes to identify themes related to the research questions [26] and concepts relevant to each theme. Because the only academic member in this study was the author, peer review did not verify the coding. Instead, at the end of each day in the support group, the author disclosed the interpretation of the day's events to the participants (i.e., young people and support members), asked for their opinions on its validity, and incorporated their ideas into the field note descriptions. Initially, 43 subcodes emerged from the field notes. Then, by inductive categorization, these codes were classified into nine abstract code categories as Table 1 shows. The author then reinterpreted the coding results to determine themes and issues essential to the research questions. Full ethics approval was obtained from the Research Ethics Committee of Seisa University (No. 1613).

---

[1] Mugbot was initially designed by the Koike Laboratory in Tokyo Metropolitan University http://www.mugbot.com.

[2] The typical length of a day's field notes was approximately 1,000 to 2,000 words in English.

Table 1. Code from thematic analysis.

Code name	N.E.S[3]	N.R.F.D[4]
Foundations of autonomy in community culture	8	39
Opportunities to acquire digital competencies associated with coding	7	16
Two values that programming involves (instrumental value, intrinsic value)	2	6
Learning in the local community	5	10
Watching over as moral support	3	14
Life fulfillment of participants arising in the support	4	23
Agency of participants at the center of the support	4	43
Intervention with participants by supporters	6	20
Transformation of participants through group activities	4	12

4 Findings

Based on the data analysis, four thematic topics emerged: (1) Role identities formed among the young people in collaborative relationships within the ESDC group added the meaning that programming was an activity leading to social participation; (2) In the programming projects, the participants' voluntary group contributions and resulting learning drove their acquisition and proficiency in digital literacy and competency; (3) Programming became a proactive learning experience for the young people due to their trial-and-error attempts to solve issues; and (4) Programming changed its status in the group from an individual practice to the group's culture when group members' active engagement with programming became part of their collaborative relationships.

4.1 Role Identity Adding Meaning to Programming as Social Participation

Role identity, or the imaginative view of oneself as being and acting as an occupant of a certain position [27], seemed to add meaning to computer programming as an activity leading to the young people's social participation. The young people helped facilitate the projects they engaged in, forming their role identities in a collaborative relationship. For example, two participants who were both in their late 20s and had experienced school drop-out and social withdrawal ("Y1" and "Y2") started their Mugbot production project after they happened to see a demonstration of Mugbot programming at "Scratch Day in Tokyo," a significant event for Scratch programmers. They naturally established a division of tasks based on their respective areas of expertise and helped each other, and this task division later became established as their role identities. For them, mutual assistance based on their role identity in the project seemed to be virtual social participation in that it involved responsibility for others. Tables 2 and 3 show excerpts from the field notes suggesting the task division.

[3] Number of Encapsulated Subcodes.

[4] Number of References to Field notes Description.

Table 2. Excerpt from field notes, June 23, 2016.

Although Y1 maintains the attitude that he has no idea about hardware, he is happily inputting programs on his PC (Y1 is rather talkative when he is having fun). This attitude suggests that he takes pride in his role as the software developer while Y2 takes care of the hardware. (June 23, 2016)

During the project, a role identity emerged for Y1 and Y2, where Y1 was in charge of software implementation and Y2, hardware assembly. Y1 learned to program first and took the lead in dealing with complex issues that arose when controlling the Mugbot in collaboration with the author. Y2 worked to understand the program with the help of Y1 while assembling the hardware. This role-identity-based assignment drove their participation in the project for over two months.

Table 3. Excerpt from field notes, August 24, 2016 (1).

Y1 and Y2 are proceeding with Mugbot production with some degree of autonomy. >> Y1 has been working on the software part of Mugbot's production by himself, reading texts and making full use of search engines. Recently, Y1 has voluntarily submitted progress reports and meeting requests to the author. >> Y2 supports Y1's work, mainly by wiring Mugbot. This role division was decided based on Y2's wishes. (August 24, 2016)

Y1 and Y2 seemed to give programming different meanings based on their role identities, while programming was the common foundation of their collaborative relationship. For Y1, learning and practicing programming was participation in the collaborative relationship by contributing to the shared goal of facilitating the Mugbot production. For Y2, assembling the Mugbot hardware was his role in the project. In addition, Y2's programming learning was a sincere response to Y1's help and preparation for participating more deeply in the project within the collaborative relationship.

4.2 Active Group Contributions and Resulting Learning as Drivers of Digital Literacy and Competency Acquisition

In projects such as making Mugbot or teaching programming classes for kids, which included programming opportunities, the participants' active group contributions and resulting learning drove their acquisition and proficiency in digital literacy and competency. On many occasions, the participants, including the staff, contributed to the projects' progress according to their interests. Their contributions to the group inevitably required more digital literacy and competency than they held, and to meet the requirements, they had many opportunities to develop greater digital literacy and competency.

Table 4 presents a scene in which the organizer of the support group (S1) and Y2 spontaneously introduced Scratch programming to group members who were less familiar with it. This demonstrates that teaching programming to each other had become an established culture within the group. In support of this culture, Y2 and S1 learned to program in order to teach it to others.

Table 4. Excerpt from field notes, August 24, 2016 (2).

Below is how the support staff (S1, the support group organizer) came up with the idea of introducing Scratch to a teacher in training in the group (T1), a high school student who had come to observe (H1), and a former group member (H2) who had come for a conversation, and how Y2 was able to help them do so immediately (with no specific request or advice from the author). > > S1 approached T1 and H1, who were in the meeting room, and encouraged them to gather in the learning space. S1 then approached Y2 to set up a laptop computer (purchased with a local government grant) on a table in the study space. > > In addition, S1 introduced Scratch programming to H2, who came later, and encouraged him to try building something. At that time, H2 was reluctant, saying that he was not very good with computers, but S1 encouraged his participation by saying, "This [Scratch] is for people who are not good at it." (August 24, 2016)

Table 5 presents a situation in which Y1 attempted to pass on the knowledge he had just learned to other members in the process of building Mugbot. As a member who had a relatively better understanding of programming, he wanted to share the knowledge he had gained with other members rather than keeping it to himself. This is a typical occasion of learning through contribution in the group.

Table 5. Excerpt from field notes, July 14, 2016.

Y1 stated that he did not understand an operation using ASCII codes (an expression that reads a string reflecting an input string, i.e., a value entered by the user, one digit at a time and converts it to a number) and asked the author to explain it. The author explained to him the meaning of the formula, and Y1 immediately explained it to S1 and Y2. Y1 generally seemed to understand the behavior of the variable due to the operations in the formula. Then S1 seemed to have understood most of the explanation by Y1 and the author's additional explanation. Y2 did not react well, perhaps because Y2 seemed a little confused. (July 14, 2016)

4.3 Programming as a Proactive Learning Experience Through Trial-and-Error Attempts Without Sufficient Information or Knowledge

Programming became a proactive learning experience for the ESDC group due to inevitable trial-and-error attempts. The projects were initiated under an approach of "learn what you need on the fly," and accordingly, the young people had to overcome various challenges without sufficient prior knowledge, which made their programming learning proactive because they had to experiment. The author saw that this situation stimulated the young people's initiative in learning and, in response, stayed out of it as much as possible to watch them learn on their own.

In particular, Y1 showed significant growth in programming skills. Table 6 shows is an excerpt from the field notes on Y1's trial-and-error attempts in the Mugbot production, in which he gradually showed initiative in dealing with garbled characters caused by a misconfiguration of the Raspberry pi.

Table 6. Excerpt from field notes, July 21, 2016.

1:31 p.m. Mugbot production continued. Garbled characters when starting up Raspberry pi Coping with Y2 and Y1 >> (The author's comments) How far can they go on their own? 1:33 p.m. S1 said to Y1, "You can see the Raspberry pi setup here [in the book], Sect. 2." S1 also seemed to be able to read the material 1:56 p.m. S1, Y1, and Y2 continued to deal with the garbled characters with the author. The author looked up some countermeasures on the Internet and advised Y1 on how to solve the problem, which Y1 then implemented. Y1 was also thinking about the cause on his own: he went back to the initial settings of the Raspberry pi and asked Y2 what settings he had made (or to what extent he had made them). (July 21, 2016)

Below, Table 7 shows a description of Y1's later growth in digital skills and competencies. Y1 behaved more autonomously in problem-solving.

Table 7. Excerpt from field notes, August 4, 2016.

On the positive side, Y1 found a solution to the Raspberry pi network connection on his own (by running the dhclient command). Here we see Y1's autonomy in problem-solving behavior (he had been searching for the cause of the ssh connection problem with his reasoning since last week when the author was absent) and his expanding knowledge of ICT (enough knowledge to be able to proceed with his research). (August 4, 2016)

4.4 Active Involvement with Programming as the People's Cultural Identity

The group members came to view their involvement with programming as part of their group identity. After they had accumulated active involvement with programming in various situations, it went beyond personal practice and became a part of the group's culture as a commonly shared practice and value oriented to creativity. For instance, as Table 3 shows, S1 and the youths began to suggest and support the introduction of programming to people who visited the group for reasons such as considering joining. Table 8 depicts a scene in which S1 invited a visitor (H2) to play with Scratch.

The group members' involvement in programming was an outcome of their latent culture of creativity. For example, they (especially S1, Y1, and Y2) worked together to introduce programming to group newcomers. Their introduction generally emphasized the pleasure of creation and even the pleasure of discovering oneself capable of creation rather than acquiring practical digital skills. The programming language used was usually Scratch because of the ease of use and its capacity for prompting creative thinking.

Table 8. Excerpt from field notes, August 24, 2016 (3).

H2 was very vocal: "I'm not the best with computers. I'm not very good at using a computer. I'm too busy looking up maps. Programming definitely makes my head dizzy. [Looking at S1's work] It would take me ten years to make something like that." *S1 responded moderately to H2's appeal that he was not good at using computers ("Not good at it? This [Scratch] is for people who aren't good at it, so it's perfect for you...") and encouraged H2 to write some programs in Scratch. Eventually, the instruction to H2 progressed to the point of drawing polygonal shapes using repetition while resembling turtle graphics in content. (August 24, 2016)*

5 Discussion

What understanding do the above observations bring about concerning RQ1 and RQ2? Regarding RQ1, collaborative relationships in the ESDC group contributed to the young people's empowerment by (a) providing a rich context in which programming was experienced as discovery-learning-opportunities and (b) helping nurture collaborative agency based on contributions and challenges involved in programming projects. Then, regarding RQ2, the educational significance of programming in the context of ESDC can be found in (c) creating a collaborative membership essential for social participation through contributions to others and (d) developing a cultural basis for participants' human development as actors in a digital society.

Point (a) is based on Finding (1) regarding computer programming's meaning in the ESDC group as a role identity that also encouraged young people's social participation, as well as Finding (3) that trial-and-error attempts made programming a proactive learning experience. The rich context refers to the overall influence that invests participants with both meaning and inevitability of their activities in collaborative relationships with shared responsibility. In the author's observation, such context can generate a mutually supportive role identity among participants, enhancing responsible learning (see [20]). The youths in the ESDC group seemed to learn and challenge themselves because they were responsible members, not isolated individuals. Thus, they contributed to re-create their collaborative relationships within the support group. Further, this role identity allowed them to recognize trials and errors in programming as discovery-learning opportunities even in situations where they lacked sufficient knowledge and information.

Point (b) focuses on empowerment through the nurturing of collaborative agency supported by collaborative relationships in ESDC. This argument is derived from Finding (2) on the acquisition of digital literacy and competencies through voluntary contributions of the members, as well as Finding (3) on the educational aspects of trial-and-error attempts in programming. Collaborative agency in this context refers to the ability to take on roles and responsibilities in a collaborative relationship. The collaborative relationships in the ESDC group helped participants develop collaborative agency in programming projects that necessitated a trial-and-error process and ultimately pushed them toward social participation. The argument comes from the young people's behavior in the support group: At first, they saw themselves as passive learners. However, they eventually overcame programming difficulties by actively offering what they were good at—a demonstration of collaborative agency. This seemed largely due to their inclusion in collaborative relationships, which gave them the foundation to exercise their independence and supported the autonomous learning necessary for their contributions to the group (see [13]).

Point (c) is derived from Finding (1) on the participants' role identity that added programming as an activity leading to social participation, as well as Finding (2) on the participants' active contributions and resulting learning that drove their digital literacy and competency. Collaborative membership in this argument signifies mutual acknowledgment as members of a programming culture, which gave the participants an identity basis deriving their active contributions. Learning and utilizing programming skills in ESDC projects generated collaborative membership supported by their mutual contribution to the projects. Such membership can be the first step toward social participation, especially among young people seeking support (see [16, 20]), and this kind of membership indeed emerged in the ESDC group. For example, Y1, with his relatively advanced programming skills, was acknowledged as a leading contributor by other members, especially when their project reached a critical juncture. Y2, who was not particularly good at programming, was appreciated for his willing contribution in introducing Scratch programming to newcomers.

Point (d) is an assertion concerning programming as a cultural basis of the participants' human development. This assertion is derived from Finding (1) regarding role identity and Finding (4) on the status of programming as part of the group's culture and collaborative relationships. Human development, a term that comes from Sen's capability approach [28], represents the substantiation of physical and cognitive conditions under which people can enjoy their freedom to lead a life worth living. Digital technology as the physical condition of digital society is deemed to disclose its potential to help people's realization of purpose corresponding to their ability to utilize technology.

ESDC, on the other hand, facilitated the youths' adaptation to computer programming, namely, their voluntary participation. Behind the ESDC's facilitation was its inclusion into the programming culture as well as the young peoples' group identities and their continuous efforts that emerged from role identities. They could take programming-related challenges for granted, expanding their digital skills and competencies and thus increasing the probability of benefiting from digital technologies, because their engagement with programming had become part of the group culture.

6 Conclusion and Limitations

The findings of this paper affirm that ESDC characterized by cooperative relationships among participants and projects that require computer programming, is effective as a method of empowerment for young learners. Through the lens of sociological concepts such as role identity and cultural inclusion, the study found the contribution of cooperative relationships in ESDC for empowerment purposes lies in the creation of a rich learning context and cooperative agency with group contribution and responsibility as its core. In contrast, the educational significance of computer programming based on participants' cooperative relationships exists in these features: First, it provides participants with cooperative memberships that serve as a basis for their social participation. Second, it provides the groundwork for forming a culture that makes it inevitable for the participants to participate in digital society through their involvement in programming. Further hypothetical synthesis of these findings is that the interaction between the projects requiring programming and collaborative relationships among participants in ESDC will work to create a context within which agency and membership, supported by collaboration, will be generated among participants. Besides, the accumulation of their practices creates their own digital culture, and their mutual inclusion in it enables them to participate in the digital society while maintaining collaborative relationships.

It must nonetheless be emphasized that since this qualitative study is based on a small sample, one should be cautious about generalizing the research results. The findings must be read critically, especially in light of sociocultural factors, diffusion of digital technologies, and educational circumstances surrounding digital skills and competencies.

Acknowledgments. The author would like to thank all of the members of the support group who kindly offered the opportunity for this study to be conducted. This study was supported by JSPS KAKENHI Grant Number 16K01136.

References

1. Vuorikari, R., Punie, Y., Carretero, S., Van Den Brande, L.: DigComp 2.0: The digital competence framework for citizens. update phase 1: the conceptual reference model. Publications Office of the European Union, Luxembourg (2016)
2. Law, N., Woo, D., Torre, J. de la, Wong, G.: A global framework of reference on digital literacy skills for indicator 4.4.2. UNESCO Institute for Statistics, Canada (2018)
3. Wagh, A., Cook-Whitt, K., Wilensky, U.: Bridging inquiry-based science and constructionism: Exploring the alignment between students tinkering with code of computational models and goals of inquiry. J. Res. Sci. Teach. **54**(5), 615–641 (2017)
4. Yu, J., Ruppert, J., Roque, R., Kirshner, B.: Youth civic engagement through computing: cases and implications. ACM Inroads. **11**, 42–51 (2020)
5. Fields, D.A., Giang, M., Kafai, Y.: Programming in the wild: trends in youth computational participation in the online scratch community. In: Proceedings of the 9th Work. Primary Secondary Computing Education - WiPSCE '14, pp. 2–11. New York (2014)
6. Fields, D.A., Kafai, Y.B., Giang, M.T.: Youth computational participation in the wild: understanding experience and equity in participating and programming in the online scratch community. ACM Transactions on Computing Education **17**(3), 1–22 (2017)
7. Iversen, O.S., Smith, R.C., Dindler, C.: From computational thinking to computational empowerment: A 21st century PD agenda. In: PDC '18 Proceedings of the 15th Participatory Design Conference, pp. 1–7 and 11 (2018)
8. Saito, T.: Advocating for educational support to develop socially disadvantaged young people's digital skills and competencies: can support encourage their human development as digital citizens?. In: Digital Transformation of Education and Learning - Past, Present and Future. OCCE 2021. IFIP Advances in Information and Communication Technology, vol. 642, , 54–66. Springer, Cham (2022)
9. Kabeer, N.: Resources, agency, achievements: Reflections on the measurement of women's empowerment. Dev. Chang. **30**(3), 435–464 (1999)
10. Lyons, M., Smuts, C., Stephens, A.: Participation, empowerment and sustainability: (How) Do the links work? Urban Studies **38**(8), 1233–1251 (2001)

11. Anderson, H.: Collaborative relationships and dialogic conversations: Ideas for a relationally responsive practice. Fam. Process **51**(1), 8–24 (2012)
12. Baker, M.J.: Collaboration in collaborative learning. Interact. Stud. **16**(3), 451–473 (2015)
13. Kucharska, W.: Relationships between trust and collaborative culture in the context of tacit knowledge sharing. J. Entrepreneu. Manage. Innov. **13**, 61–78 (2017)
14. Yoda, T.: The effect of collaborative relationship between medical doctors and engineers on the productivity of developing medical devices. R&D Management **46**, 193–206 (2016)
15. Meirink, J.A., Imants, J., Meijer, P.C., Verloop, N.: Teacher learning and collaboration in innovative teams. Camb. J. Educ. **40**, 161–181 (2010)
16. Kucharska, W., Kowalczyk, R.: Trust, collaborative culture and tacit knowledge sharing in project management – a relationship model. In: Proceedings of the 13th International Conference on Intellectual Capital, Knowledge Management & Organisational Learning: ICICKM 2016, pp. 159–166 (2016)
17. Sawyer, R.K.: Dialogic status in design education: Authority and peer relations in studio class conversations. Social Psychology Quarterly **82**, 407–430 (2019)
18. Kropp, M., Meier, A., Mateescu, M., Zahn, C.: Teaching and learning agile collaboration. In: Conference: IEEE 27th Conference on Software Engineering Education and Training - (CSEE&T), pp. 139–148. Austria (2014)
19. Tissenbaum, M., Sheldon, J.: Computational action in app inventor: Developing theoretical and technological frameworks for collaboration and empowerment. In: Lund, K., Niccolai, G.P., Lavoué, E., Hmelo-Silver, C., Gweon, G., Baker, M. (eds.) A Wide Lens: Combining Embodied, Enactive, Extended, and Embedded Learning in Collaborative Settings, 13th International Conference on Computer Supported Collaborative Learning (CSCL) 2019, Vol. 2, pp. 985–988. Lyon, France: International Society of the Learning Sciences (2019)
20. Peppler, K.A., Kafai, Y.B.: Collaboration, computation, and creativity: Media arts practices in urban youth culture. Proceedings of the 8th international conference on Computer supported Collaborative Learning, pp. 590–592. International Society of the Learning Sciences, New Jersey USA (2007)
21. Kong, S.C., Chiu, M.M., Lai, M.: A study of primary school students' interest, collaboration attitude, and programming empowerment in computational thinking education. Comput. Educ. **127**, 178–189 (2018)
22. Stringer, E.T.: Action research, p. 1. Sage Publications, Thousand Oaks (2013)
23. Brydon-Miller, M., Greenwood, D., Maguire, P.: Why action research? Action Research **1**(1), 9–28 (2003)
24. Järvinen, P.: Improving Guidelines and Developing a Taxonomy of Methodologies for Research in Information Systems. JYU dissertations (2021)
25. Braun, V., Clarke, V.: Using thematic analysis in psychology. Qual. Res. Psychol. **3**(2), 77–101 (2006)
26. Carter, M.J., Mangum, H.: Role identities: Measurement and outcomes of conventional vs. idiosyncratic balance. Current Psychology **41**, 2586–2597 (2020)
27. Fukuda-Parr, S.: The human development paradigm: Operationalizing sen's ideas on capabilities. Fem. Econ. **9**(2–3), 301–317 (2003)

Development and Evaluation of a Field Environment Digest System for Agricultural Education

Kanu Shiga, Tsubasa Minematsu(✉), Yuta Taniguchi, Fumiya Okubo, Atsushi Shimada, and Rin-ichiro Taniguchi

Kyushu University, Fukuoka, Japan
{shiga,minematsu}@limu.ait.kyushu-u.ac.jp, taniguchi.yuta.941@m.kyushu-u.ac.jp, {fokubo,atsushi}@ait.kyushu-u.ac.jp, rin@kyudai.jp

Abstract. Smart agriculture has assumed increasing importance due to the growing age of farmers and a shortage of farm leaders. In response, it is crucial to provide more opportunities to learn about smart agriculture at agricultural colleges and high schools, where new farmers are trained. In agricultural education, a system is used for managing environmental information, such as temperature and humidity, obtained from sensors installed in the field. However, it is difficult to make effective use of this system due to the time required to detect changes in the field interfering with class time and the problem of oversight. In this study, we proposed a field environment digest system that will help learners by providing the summarized field sensing information, and support them in analyzing the data. In addition, to examine the potential for using field sensing information in agricultural education, we investigated the usefulness of the summarized sensor information and students' usage of this information. In this paper, we outline the contents of the developed system and the results of the digest evaluation experiments.

Keywords: smart agriculture · agricultural education · educational support system

1 Introduction

Smart agriculture has grown rapidly because of improvements to the Internet-of-Things (IoT), such as drones and sensor networks. Farmers obtain agricultural sensing information, such as the temperature and humidity in farm fields [1], with which they can manage the fields effectively [2]. Additionally, a wide range of practical applications are being implemented, including growth diagnosis using drones [3] and production management using satellite imagery [4]. It is important for young farmers and students in agriculture courses to develop decision-making skills based on such information. In recent agricultural education, field management systems [5] have also been used for managing farm based on field sensing

T. Keane et al. (Eds.): WCCE 2022, IFIP AICT 685, pp. 87–99, 2023.
https://doi.org/10.1007/978-3-031-43393-1_10

information in addition to traditional e-Learning systems, such as e-book systems and learning management systems [6].

In agricultural education, it is necessary to train farmers who can utilize this kind of smart agriculture in the future. Toward this goal, IoT infrastructures are being built to support agricultural education [5]. Various web-based applications, cell phone applications, and learning modules are also being developed to utilize the real-time sensing data obtained through such IoT infrastructure [7]. To utilize field sensing information such as temperatures and humidity on farms, data visualization approaches are proposed, such as graphs of time series data or heat maps of field temperatures. In current agricultural pedagogy, the visualization system is used to provide field sensing information to the learner [8].

As mentioned above, systems and applications for smart agricultural education have been developed, but the effective use of such visualized data for agricultural education remains unclear. It has been pointed out that training programs for teachers are needed in order to motivate learners to use sensing data [9]; teachers are not familiar with sensing data and therefore need additional training. Moreover, a lecture on data analytics was provided to experts who were already engaged in agriculture [10]. However, the targets of smart agriculture education may not only be experts who have agricultural know-how, but also include the learners who have less agricultural knowledge, such as students in agricultural high schools. These students have a variety of tasks, such as acquiring knowledge and growing crops, and they cannot devote their time solely to studying sensing information analysis.

Although such field sensing information is represented by graphs and heat maps in conventional systems, it is difficult for students to find relevant information from these formats as they need to possess the necessary knowledge of agriculture and field sensing information. With these problems, it is difficult to effectively utilize field sensing information within a limited lecture time. We believe that students' learning can be supplemented with summarized sensor information in order to facilitate their studies. However, it is not clear whether the summarized sensor information would be useful. In addition, since the utilization of field sensing information agricultural education lacks clarity, we need to ascertain its effective usage for agricultural education. For the investigation, we need to track how learners use the field sensing information. Therefore, our research questions are as follows:

(RQ1) Is the use of summarized sensor information useful?

(RQ2) How do learners utilize the summarized sensor information?

In this study, we proposed a field environment digest system to help learners by providing the summarized field sensing information and to support them in analyzing sensing data, such as time series data of temperature and humidity. This system can provide a digest as a candidate for sensor values to focus on. To investigate how learners use the system, it was equipped with a mechanism for collecting their operation logs, such as switching sensors, changing time periods, manipulating charts, selecting list elements, and selecting table elements. As a specific summary method in this system, we prepared two methods: a table digest and a list digest. The table digest is for summarizing and visualizing the field sensing information as statistical information, and the list digest is for extracting and visualizing the period considered important from the field sensing information based on change detection. Sudden changes in temperature and humidity can lead to the deterioration of crop quality, and therefore it is expected that changes in the condition of crops can be captured by monitoring changes in the field. In extracting the periods representing the changes, we used ChangeFinder [11] for change detection in time series data.

2 Related Work

To resolve the issues of reduction in the labor force and increased production costs in rural areas, there is growing demand for smart agriculture processes such as drone breeding diagnostics [3], rice paddy management [4], and visualization of temperature and humidity information on maps [12]. Such progress in smart agriculture technology has made it necessary to increase opportunities to learn about them in agricultural education. According to Ejifor et al. [9], a curriculum for smart agriculture education is being developed. In addition, Bryceson [1] has shown that there is actually a movement for the use of smart agriculture in agricultural education.

There are several cases of smart agriculture education being conducted. Takemura et al. [10] conducted a course on data analysis for agriculture at a university. Research on building IoT infrastructure to support education has also been conducted by Gunasekera et al. [5], who have also developed various web-based applications, cell phone applications, and learning modules to leverage the real-time sensing data obtained through such IoT infrastructure. There are various examples of such monitoring systems as IoT infrastructure. SALATA [2], developed by Akayama et al., is a system that collects and shares field sensing and farm operation information collected in the field, before relating them to each other in a time series. In addition, research has been conducted by Taniguchi et al. utilizing SALATA in the field of agricultural education [8]. Field sensors that collect field sensing information include MIHARAS[1] and Midori Cloud. Both are aimed at reducing the labor required for patrolling and increasing productivity. There are various types of sensors, including those for fields and weather. SALATA provides users with a simple graphical representation of the time series in the visualization.

However, it is difficult for students to analyze the sensor values in a simple graphical visualization, and there is no research to assist them in doing so. In addition, it is not clearly defined how field sensing information should be utilized in agricultural education, so it is necessary to clarify what kind of utilization is effective for agricultural education. Therefore, in this study, we obtained the learners' operation logs and tracked students' activities. Notably, all of the research cases mentioned above were conducted involving university students and experts with some knowledge. It is still unclear what effect these

[1] https://www.nishimu-products.jp/miharas/en. Last accessed 25 Feb. 2022.

studies have on beginners, such as agricultural high school students, which is thus an issue that should be investigated.

3 Field Environment Digest System

The field environment digest system provides digests of several field sensing information sources, in addition to visualizing time series data. As shown in Fig. 1(a), our system provides three types of information: chart visualization, table digest, and list digest. This system also has the capability to collect operation logs. By investigating how learners use the system, we aimed to make the summarized field sensing information provided by the system useful.

The configuration of this system is shown in Fig. 1(b). The blue arrows represent field sensing information, and the red arrows represent operation logs. Since the field sensing data from the MIHARAS field sensors are stored in a database on AWS (Amazon Web Services), the field environment digest system obtains the data from the database and provides the learner with the original field sensing information as well as the summarized field sensing information over the LMS (Learning Management System). Students using this system are assumed to be those who use e-Learning systems. In this system, temperature, humidity, saturation, solar radiation, rainfall data, electrical conductivity, and volumetric water content obtained from MIHARAS sensors are used as field sensing data. The field sensing information to be displayed is based on the data obtained from the application programming interface in SALATA API [2].

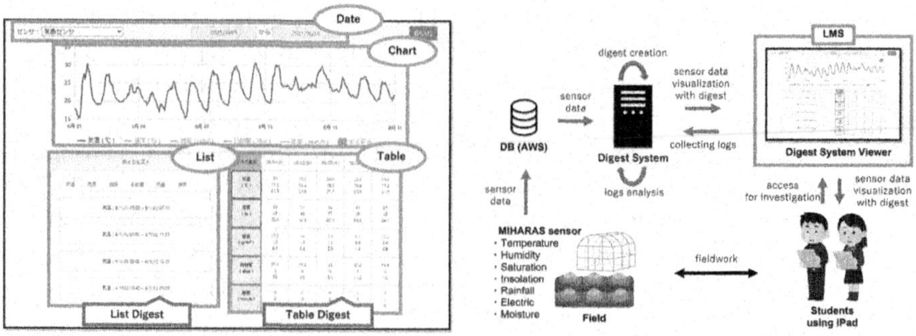

(a) The viewer (b) The configuration

Fig. 1. Field Environment Digest System

3.1 Chart-Based Visualization of Field Sensing Information

As in the previous system, time series data is visualized using charts. In the chart visualization, the user selects the period of time for displaying the field sensing information. In the upper part of the screen, in the date area of Fig. 1(a), the

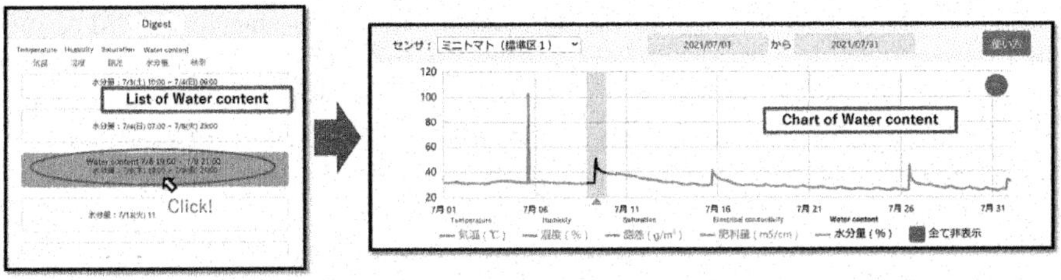

Fig. 2. Highlighting charts from a list item. Selecting an item in the list will highlight the corresponding period in the charts.

time period can be selected from the calendar. In the chart area at the center of the screen in Fig. 1(a), time series data are visualized using charts. The chart visualizes the field sensing information obtained from the field by dividing it into categories. These can be viewed by each category, or multiple categories can be viewed simultaneously. Users can view the charts in more detail, zoom in and out easily, and change the category of the charts.

3.2 Table Digest

In the table summarizing the field sensing information, the maximum, minimum, and average values of the data for each day are calculated and displayed, as illustrated in the table area of Fig. 1(a). The table digest provides statistical values, and users can grasp longer-term trends at a glance. When selecting an element in the table, the chart of the corresponding sensing information can be displayed in the corresponding period. The users can refer to detailed field sensing information from the table quickly.

3.3 List Digest

In the list digest, we extract and visualize the periods that are considered important from the field sensing information. This system provides change points in the sensing information as the important periods. The reason is that sudden changes in temperature and humidity affect the quality deterioration of crops, therefore it is possible to capture the changes in the condition of crops by detecting the changes in the sensing information.

To create this list, we used a change detection method called ChangeFinder [11]. ChangeFinder can detect change points from time-series data by computing change scores for each time period. For further information on ChangeFinder, refer to [11]. When detecting change points from time series data, we used each category of the field sensing information separately.

We apply ChangeFinder to the time series data $\{x_t\}$ $(t = 1, 2, \cdots, n)$ for computing the change scores. The change scores are normalized for all periods for determining the change point as a percentage of change scores $\mathrm{Score}(x_t)$. The point x_t is detected as a change point when $\mathrm{Score}(x_t) > p$, where p is a threshold value. Since the change scores are normalized, the threshold value is set as a percentage. In addition, there is a forgetting parameter o as a parameter of ChangeFinder. The smaller this forgetting parameter o is set to, the more the change score will be calculated considering the influence of past data. We adjust p and o based on the time series data of the field sensing information. We describe the details in Sect. 4.1.

The periods extracted as change points are displayed in the form of a list. The list of each category of the field sensing information is generated, and the users can change the displayed list by selecting category tabs on the list area. As shown in the Fig. 2, the users can select an item in the list to highlight the corresponding part of the charts. By highlighting the change points on the chart area, the points become clearer when users need to focus on the points. This makes the sensing information of the field useful, as it reduces the need to find the periods that represent the changes in the field.

3.4 Collecting Operation Logs

The field environment digest system can collect the user's operation logs and timestamps such as switching sensors, changing time periods, operations on charts, elements in selected lists, and elements in selected tables. We collected operation logs in the date, chart, list, and table areas in Fig. 1(a). In the date area, by collecting logs related to switching sensors and changing the display period, it is possible to check which sensor and period the user viewed the field sensing information of. In the chart area, by collecting operation logs about chart operations, we can check categories and time periods users have viewed in detail by manipulating the charts. In the list area, by collecting operation logs related to lists, we can check what kind of digests are viewed by users. In the table area, by collecting operation logs related to tables, we can check what categories and time periods users have browsed in detail by manipulating the tables. In short, by collecting these logs in detail, we can track the usage history of learners. For example, by tracking the logs, we can see that a user has used the list and then used the chart to see the period highlighted by the list.

4 Experiment

4.1 Experimental Setting

As an evaluation of the field environment digest system, a questionnaire with nine questions scored on a five-point scale and a free-description questionnaire with three questions were administered to students at an agricultural high school. The 37 students attended a twice-weekly lecture on agricultural economics at an agricultural high school, and we instructed them to use our digest system in four lectures from July 15 to August 26, 2021. First we showed the students how to use our digest system. Specifically, we created and displayed a video explaining how we expected them to use the system (e.g., using charts after using lists).

Moreover, we set up questions on Moodle, and instructed students to answer the evaluation questionnaire and free-description questionnaire while using the system on August 30. In this experiment, each student used this system with an iPad provided by the school, and they started to use e-Learning systems and the table devised in April 2021. At the agricultural high school, we installed MIHARAS sensor poles to measure the farm field where the students study. The students observed the sensor values from the sensor poles via our digest systems.

In the field environment digest system, the list digest was created using Change-Finder. We set the parameters of ChangeFinder to detect 40% of the points when the temperature difference was more than 10 °C in one hour. Although it is possible to increase the detection rate, doing so would increase the total number of detection points and worsen the visibility. As the results of the parameter adjustment, our system presented two types of digests to the users: one with the forgetting parameter o and the threshold p set to $o = 0.01$ and $p = 15$, and the other with $o = 0.05$ and $p = 35$. The digest with the forgetting parameter o and threshold p set to $o = 0.01$ and $p = 15$ makes it easier to capture the changes over a long time period in the time series; for example, a digest that captures the different changes that occurred after three consecutive days of changes in temperature. The digest with forgetting parameter o and threshold p set to $o = 0.05$ and $p = 35$ makes it easier to capture the changes over a short period in the time series; for example, the digest captures changes in moisture content, such as a sudden increase in moisture content due to rainfall. We also set the other ChangeFinder parameters, the order of the autoregressive model was set to 1, and the range of smoothing was set to 10. To create the digest, we normalized the change point scores for the period (September 1, 2019 to July 1, 2021), excluding the change point scores for the training data (August 1-31, 2019).

4.2 Experimental Results

Results of the Questionnaire. The questions and results of the questionnaire are shown in Table 1. The number of the respondents was 37. On a five-point scale, 1 is not at all applicable, 2 is not applicable, 3 is undecided, 4 is applicable, and 5 is very applicable.

Between Q1 "the table improves your understanding of the sensor values" and Q2 "the list improves your understanding of the sensor values", the percentage of respondents who gave a score of 5 in Q1 was lower than in Q2. The table digest can be more effective for learners than the list digest; however, most of the learners accepted both digests. This implied that digests can be useful for learners. In Q3 "the main points of the sensor values became clearer", about 80% of the students responded positively. This showed that learners felt our system was able to help students find points of interest in sensor values. In the responses to Q4 "you were able to efficiently check your field environment during periods when there was no class" and Q5 "became easier to think about why the sensor values are changing", about 80% of the students answered affirmatively. This implied that checking the simplified field sensing information helped the

Table 1. Questionnaire Results

Questions	1	2	3	4	5
Q1. The table improves your understanding of the sensor values	0	0	6	28	3
Q2. The list improves your understanding of the sensor values	0	2	4	24	7
Q3. The main points of the sensor values became clearer	0	0	6	24	7
Q4. You were able to efficiently check your field environment during periods when there was no class	0	2	5	21	9
Q5. Became easier to think about why the sensor values are changing	0	2	4	23	8
Q6. You became more aware of the weather sensor values	0	1	11	18	7
Q7. You became more aware of the field sensor values	0	1	9	23	4
Q8. It is useful for understanding the course content	0	1	2	21	13
Q9. You became more motivated in class	0	0	13	14	10

students to consider the sensor values and the field environment. However, about 15% of the students gave a not positive response, with score lower than 3 in Q5. This indicated that it was difficult for them to interpret the sensor values and understand the field environment. In Q6 "you became more aware of the weather sensor values" and Q7 "you became more aware of the field sensor values", about 70% of the students answered positively, which indicates that the awareness of the sensor values improved. About 90% of the students answered positively in Q8 "it is useful for understanding the course content" and about 65% in Q9 "you became more motivated in class", respectively, which indicated that this system was useful for understanding and engaging in the class. From this result, we can conclude that almost all of the responses to the questionnaire were relatively positive. However, as the results of Q4 and Q5 show, it was still difficult to interpret the sensor values and evaluate the field environment. In addition, among the additional comments, we received positive responses such as "Was able to establish and improve a habit of examining data" and "Was able to establish and improve a habit of connecting data to the field environment."

Regarding RQ1, based on the results of these questionnaire responses, it was found that learners are positively affected by the provision summarized field sensing information to them. Therefore, we believe that our system will enhance the usefulness of field sensing information. In addition, when we asked learners to write freely about this system, many commented that the system was easy to use and that they became more aware of sensor values, suggesting that the system was user-friendly.

Results of the Free Description Type Questionnaire. This section describes the results of the experiment and the relationship between the charac-

Table 2. Results of K-means clustering

Cluster	Description	Students
0	mainly used charts	7
1	mainly used lists	3
2	mainly used tables	5
3	used a combination of charts and lists	2
4	used a combination of charts and tables, the charts more frequently	7
5	a combination of charts and tables, the tables more frequently	4
6	a combination of lists and tables	5

teristics of each student's operation obtained from the operation log. The three questions asked in the free description type questionnaire are as follows:

1. Choose a date and time to focus on from the list of water content and answer why you focused on that date and time.
2. Consider the causes of the increase in water content on July 9, 2021 and July 25, 2021, respectively.
3. Choose a date and time to focus on and discuss the change in moisture content during that period.

The number of respondents was 34. For all questions, respondents were instructed to answer freely using the survey form on the learning platform Moodle. The questions are for the sensor values of volume moisture content from July 1, 2021 to July 31, 2021. In answering the questions, the students were instructed to answer for the sensors in their own field while they use this system. The average response time was about 16 min. One student, who answered without using this system, was excluded from this evaluation.

For analysis of students' operation logs, we focused on three components: chart, list, and table components. These components correspond to the chart, list, and table areas in Fig. 1(a), respectively. We counted the number of the transitions between their two components and self-loops. In other words, we computed a nine-dimensional vector representing activities of each student in this experiment. Each nine-dimensional vector was normalized by its maximum value. K-means was applied to their nine-dimensional vectors to categorize the features of each student. In this experiment, we set a hyper-parameter K of K-means to 7 based on the elbow diagram.

Figure 3(a) shows the calculated center vectors of each cluster. Each clustering vector was normalized by its maximum value and signified a representative pattern showing how the students in the cluster used our system. Based on each large feature, we manually categorized the clusters. A description of each cluster and the number of students to which it belongs is shown in Table 2.

The results of these categorizations indicate that we were able to provide multiple uses for the learners. The usage was categorized into 15 students who

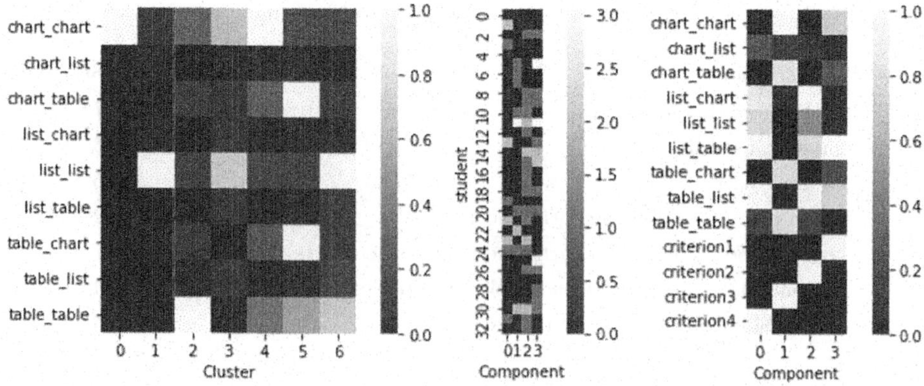

(a) Center vectors by K-means. (b) NMF score of the students. (c) NMF scores of usages and description evaluation.

Fig. 3. Results of K-means clustering and NMF for analyzing student usages. In (a), the color means the ratio of operation transitions, where the brighter the color, the more the operation transition occurs. In (b) and (c), the color indicates the NMF scores, where the brighter the color, the higher the scores. Note that the usage and description evaluation in (c) are normalized for visualization.

mainly used a single element and 18 students who used a combination of multiple elements, with more students using a combination of multiple elements.

From the results, we found that there were various ways to use the information, and it might be necessary to include other summarized field sensing information. In addition, students used the multiple elements provided by our system. Thus, even if the learners were beginners, they could combine various types of the summarized sensing information. However, since it is not clear what kind of use would be more effective, we need to evaluate how to use it.

We also examined the relationship between the responses to the questionnaire and the characteristics of the operation. In this study, we investigated the descriptions based on the following four criteria. These criteria were based on interviews with teachers at an agricultural high school.

1. Does it describes the specific sensor values?
2. Were multiple sensors considered in the description?
3. Were multiple time zones considered in the description?
4. Does it describes a discussion of the field environment?

We evaluated the three responses of the free description type questionnaire using binary values based on four evaluation criteria. We conducted Non-negative Matrix Factorization (NMF) [13] on the matrix that concatenates the 4-dimensional vector that is the sum of each evaluation and the 9-dimensional vector described above. For each student's 9-dimensional vector, each element of the vector was normalized by the maximum value of the same element in all students. In this experiment, we set the number of components of NMF to four based on the elbow diagram.

In NMF, a matrix is approximated by the product of two small matrices. In this study, the small matrices represent the features of the students and the patterns of usage and scores. For example, Component 0 of Student 1 in Fig. 3(b) had a large value, meaning Student 1 had the pattern of Component 0 column in Fig. 3(c); the Component 0 column represents patterns for Criterion 4 and the list usage. Since each component is associated with each evaluation criterion, we examined which operations are associated.

According to Fig. 3(c), there is a relationship between usage and each evaluation criterion. Evaluation Criterion 1 is related to students who used a combination of lists and tables, and used charts by themselves, Evaluation Criterion 2 to students who used a combination of lists and tables, and used charts from lists, Evaluation Criterion 3 to students who used a combination of charts and tables but not lists, and Evaluation Criterion 4 to students who used a combination of lists and tables, used charts from lists, and used lists by themselves.

These results indicate that the students who used multiple elements wrote descriptions that met the above evaluation criteria. The students who used the lists and tables in combination were more likely to consider multiple sensors and dates. In addition, they were more likely to describe their thoughts about the field environment. Therefore, we suggest that a system needs to provide multiple field sensing information, not just singular ones. In this investigation, we found that there was a relationship between usage and each evaluation criteria. Therefore, we believe that we can support the students who did not describe the criterion.

Regarding RQ2, the results of categorizations by K-means indicate that learners used our system in various ways. From the questionnaire results, we understand that providing the summarized field sensing information could encourage the students to use the data. In addition, the results of the NMF indicate that there was a relationship between the usage of our system and the evaluation of the description content. In particular, we found that students who used the summarized field sensing information such as lists and tables were more likely to write descriptions that satisfied the evaluation criteria prepared by the teacher. Therefore, these findings suggest that providing multiple elements, rather than just a single element, can improve the effectiveness of students' use of data.

To support the students who received low evaluations, it is possible to advise them on how to effectively use the system. For example, showing them ways in which students with higher ratings use the system might enable them to write descriptions with high ratings. In addition, as a support for teachers, by analyzing the logs, it is possible to find out how the highly evaluated students are using the system, and thus design their lectures based on this information.

5 Conclusion

In this paper, we proposed a field environment digest system to help learners by providing summarized field sensing information and to support learners in analyzing the sensing data. To evaluate the potential for agricultural education using field sensing information, we investigated whether the summarized sensor information would be useful, and how students would use the summarized field sensing information. In the experiment, an evaluation questionnaire and a free-description questionnaire were administered at an agricultural high school in order to find out the effectiveness of providing summarized field sensor information to help the learners and determine what kind of summary would be appropriate. From the results of our experiments, we believe that summarizing field sensing information and providing it to learners can help them analyze the field sensing information. In addition, we were able to provide multiple uses to the learners. We found that students using multiple digests were likely to describe more details, such as specific sensor values. However, even though it was easier for students to understand the focus of the sensor values, it is still difficult to analyze and consider the environment of the field.

A limitation of our study was the short duration of this experiment. Consequently, we could not evaluate the use of the system in the entire process of growing crops. Therefore, we could not evaluate the effectiveness for skill required in agricultural education. In addition, this system was not implemented in the other classes in the high school. In the future, systems should be developed that encourage students' activities according to their usage status, and be evaluated for longer periods. In addition, we did not analyze the contents of the agricultural information used by the students in this system. From our experiments, we found that there are several ways of using the system, but we believe that students who use this system in the same way may check different categories and for different periods of time. In future work, we consider investigating the time and categories students checked through the system to provide more detailed feedback to students and teachers.

Acknowledgements. This work was supported by JSPS KAKENHI Grant Number JP18H04117.

References

1. Bryceson, K.: Disruptive technologies supporting agricultural education (2019)
2. Akayama, N., Arita, D., Shimada, A., Taniguchi, R.: SALATA: a web application for visualizing sensor information in farm fields. In: 9th International Conference on Sensor Networks (SENSORNETS 2020) (2020)
3. Inoue, Y.: Satellite-and drone-based remote sensing of crops and soils for smart farming-a review. Soil Sci. Plant Nutr. **66**(6), 798–810 (2020)
4. Nguyen, T.T., et al.: Monitoring agriculture areas with satellite images and deep learning. Appl. Soft Comput. **95**, 106565 (2020)
5. Gunasekera, K., Borrero, A.N., Vasuian, F., Bryceson, K.P.: Experiences in building an IoT infrastructure for agriculture education. Procedia Comput. Sci. **135**, 155–162 (2018). the 3rd International Conference on Computer Science and Computational Intelligence (ICCSCI 2018) : Empowering Smart Technology in Digital Era for a Better Life

6. Ogata, H., et al.: Learning analytics for e-book-based educational big data in higher education. In: Yasuura, H., Kyung, C.-M., Liu, Y., Lin, Y.-L. (eds.) Smart Sensors at the IoT Frontier, pp. 327–350. Springer, Cham (2017). https://doi.org/10.1007/978-3-319-55345-0_13
7. Bryceson, K.P., Navas Borrero, A., Gunasekera, K.: The internet of things (IoT)-smart agriculture education at the university of Queensland. In: Proceedings of Edulearn 16, 8th International Conference on Education and New Learning Technologies, pp. 8036–8044 (2016)
8. Taniguchi, R.I., et al.: Integrated contextual learning environments with sensor network for crop cultivation education: concept and design. In: Proceedings of the IADIS International Conference Cognition and Exploratory Learning in the Digital Age, pp. 242–248 (2019)
9. Ejiofor, T., Bassey, N.: Integration of ICT tools in agricultural education curriculum for quality instructional delivery (2021)
10. Takemura, Y., Kamei, K., Sanada, A., Ishii, K.: Smart agriculture IoT education course in enPiT-everi (education network for practical information technologies - evolving and empowering regional industries). In: Proceedings of International Conference on Artificial Life & Robotics (ICAROB2021), pp. 401–404. ALife Robotics (jan 2021)
11. Takeuchi, J., Yamanishi, K.: A unifying framework for detecting outliers and change points from time series. IEEE Trans. Knowl. Data Eng. **18**(4), 482–492 (2006)
12. Kubicek, P., Kozel, J., Stampach, R., Lukas, V.: Prototyping the visualization of geographic and sensor data for agriculture. Comput. Electron. Agric. **97**, 83–91 (2013)
13. Lee, D.D., Seung, H.S.: Algorithms for non-negative matrix factorization. In: Proceedings of the 13th International Conference on Neural Information Processing Systems, pp. 535–541. NIPS 2000, MIT Press, Cambridge, MA, USA (2000)

Predictive Evaluation of Artificial Intelligence Functionalities of Software: A Study of Apps for Children's Learning of English Pronunciation

Mengqi Fang(✉) and Mary Webb

King's College London, London, UK
{mengqi.fang,mary.webb}@kcl.ac.uk

Abstract. This paper is based on a study that developed and used a predictive evaluation method to evaluate educational software with embedded Artificial Intelligence (AI) functionalities for children's learning of English pronunciation. The approach built on Squires and Preece's [1] heuristics which used a social constructivist view of learning but were developed before AI functionalities were commonplace in educational software. Three AI-powered English learning apps were selected for the predictive evaluation. The evaluation enabled a comparison between the AI-powered English-learning apps based on their potential for learning. The study is the first to predictively evaluate pedagogical values of AI functionalities for improving ESL pronunciation and may provide an approach to developing predictive evaluation more widely for educational software that embeds AI functionalities.

Keywords: AI Functionalities · Software Evaluation · Predictive Evaluation · English Learning · English Pronunciation

1 Introduction

AI functionalities have been incorporated into educational software for some years [2] but recent developments have greatly increased the potential of AI in education [3] and the range of AI functionalities that may be incorporated into software. Earlier explanations [2] of the potential of AI to support learning focused on: 1) the system being knowledgeable in the domain to be taught; 2) the modelled expertise enabling the system to conduct interactions; 3) natural language processing enabling improved interaction; 4) planning for the learner or inferring learners' plans from their behaviour; 5) self-improving systems that learn from the effects of their behaviour. These functionalities are still prevalent in AI-enabled educational software but they have been further improved by developments especially in machine learning [3]. Machine learning (ML) is the underlying driver of most recent AI applications. ML uses a range of different algorithms that can "learn" from data and therefore they learn and adapt to students' behaviour in real-time. Furthermore, significant research has focused on embedding AI functionalities into intelligent

Published by Springer Nature Switzerland AG 2023
T. Keane et al. (Eds.): WCCE 2022, IFIP AICT 685, pp. 100–112, 2023.
https://doi.org/10.1007/978-3-031-43393-1_11

agents (bots) that can perform various roles in educational software including tutor, mentor or co-learner. AI functionalities currently being embedded in educational software include: automatic evaluation of students' skills and understanding; personalised feedback; expert systems; intelligent human-computer interaction including identifying students' emotional responses, visualisation, intelligent agents, teachable agents, adaptive instruction and tracking learning activities [3, 4].

The rapid development and incorporation of AI into education have led to concerns about insufficient teacher preparation and teachers' limited understanding of AI and its potential for learning [5]. In order to make effective decisions about the use of software with students, all educators including parents as well as teachers need to be able to predictively evaluate [6] the pedagogical potential of software. However, approaches to predictive evaluation of educational software were developed prior to incorporation of significant AI functionalities [1] and little recent research exists in this area. Therefore, there is a need to examine how software with AI functionalities can be evaluated and whether previous approaches can be applied or adapted.

The study on which this paper is based focused on AI functionalities in English language learning software for young Chinese learners to develop their pronunciation. This context was chosen because AI is becoming used extensively in such software for two main reasons. First the Chinese government has made a massive investment, issued tax breaks and policies to facilitate the use of AI in education [7]. Secondly as English has become a global lingua franca, speaking English is increasingly important and pronunciation is a basic element in building speaking skills and enhancing intelligible communication [8]. However, young Chinese ESL learners inevitably face challenges of learning pronunciation owing to the lack of exposure to English and limited professional and personal guidance for English pronunciation in China [9, 10]. These actions and concerns have been an impetus for the design of AI-powered language learning tools (such as English Liulishuo, Tencent English, Open Language, Zebra English, Squirrel AI learning, Whales Love, etc.), and stimulated tens of millions of students to use AI-powered language learning applications [7]. AI functionalities currently available in such software typically include automatic evaluation of pronunciation, personalised feedback, intelligent human-computer interaction, adaptive instruction and tracking of learning activities [11]. However, the support for using AI-powered English learning apps seems to have been driven by development of technologies rather than considerations of learning [12]. Limited evidence about the effectiveness of AI in supporting language learning, particularly the pedagogical value of AI functionalities for children's learning of English pronunciation has been provided.

In this paper we begin with a review of developments and challenges of predictive evaluation especially social constructivist approaches which are particularly relevant to language learning but are also relevant to most areas of learning. Based on this review, we adopt Squires and Preece's [1] social constructivist evaluation approach. We explain our procedure for identifying and selecting AI-powered English-learning apps for the evaluation. We then discuss our adaptation of Squires and Preece's approach for predictive evaluation and present the results of our evaluation of three selected apps. We conclude with implications for practice and further research.

2 Literature Review

2.1 What Is Predictive Evaluation?

Predictive evaluation is an assessment of the quality and potential of a software application performed before its intended use with students [6]. Teachers typically conduct such an evaluation when planning lessons or purchasing educational software [6] and parents also need to be able to make informed choices. There are two types of predictive evaluation: informal and formal [1]. Informal predictive evaluation depends on previous experiences to make a judgement concerning the potential and quality of an application before using it [1]. However, such an evaluation could be challenging when teachers and parents have limited experience and face new and innovative educational software applications. Therefore, a formal approach that enables educators to review software and make initial decisions about which software to use is needed [1]. The typical approach of formal predictive evaluation is to use a checklist which provides a set of questions addressing both educational and usability issues. Usability typically refers to the degree of ease and effectiveness of use [13]. However, checklists have been criticized by Squires and Preece [6] who argued that typically checklists fail to: 1) encompass a consideration of learning issues [1] and 2) consider the interaction between learning and usability in relation to how, for example, technologies are used for pedagogical purposes or how usability issues relate to learning outcomes. Similar problems were also identified more recently in Dimitrijević and Devedžić's study [14] which systematically reviewed 45 papers regarding methods used to select educational technologies. McDougall and Squires [15] maintained that the problems associated with using checklists are symptomatic of the failure to adopt a situated perspective on the evaluation of educational software. Since learning is situated in a specific context and influenced by environments, people and artefacts, evaluations of educational software need to be conducted according to the educational settings in which they will be used [15]. Therefore, scholars have developed social constructivist guidelines with consideration of both learning and contexts [1].

2.2 A Social Constructivist Approach to Predictive Evaluation of Software

Social constructivism is often used to explain the nature of learning and is frequently applied to language learning [16]. According to Vygotsky [17], the learning process is affected and mediated by external factors such as cultural, historical and social interactions. Vygotsky [17] believed that children first obtain knowledge and develop their skills in a social context and then internalise and use those skills as individuals. Therefore, the construction of their knowledge is not independent of the social and cultural contexts in which learners exist.

Vygotsky [17] further proposed that a child's learning occurs in their zone of proximal development (ZPD), which is defined as 'the distance between the child's actual developmental level as determined by independent problem-solving and the level of potential development as determined through problem-solving under adult guidance, or in collaboration with more capable peers' [17]. Thus, a learner is better able to learn through social interaction with more capable people, such as teachers, tutors and peers who can act as knowledgeable others and help the learner by providing guidance, suitable tasks, feedback and support [18]. Traditional collaborative learning happens in small human groups. However, recently collaboration has been extended to involve non-human agents such as virtual agents or robots with AI technologies [19].

In Vygotskian theory, artefacts are also important for learners to construct knowledge or accomplish their goals [17]. Artefacts can be physical (pen and paper), symbolic (music, numbers, arithmetic systems and languages) or cultural (technologies, portfolios and tasks) tools which can be used for learning a second language (L2). Vygotsky [17] argued that humans do not act on the world directly but rather rely on artefacts and activities to mediate or regulate their relationships with others and themselves. Lantolf [16] who pioneered the application of Vygotsky's theories in second language learning agreed that, through mediational tools, learners can strengthen their control over their behaviours externally and regulate their minds internally.

An AI-powered English-learning app can be regarded as a cultural artefact that mediates learning of ESL pronunciation. Learners can initially use the AI functionalities to accomplish activities with the assistance of intelligent tutors, interact with others and co-construct knowledge. They then internalise that knowledge individually.

Squires and Preece [1] claimed that adopting a socio-constructivist approach can help provide insights into the interaction between usability and learning in the context in which the software is used. From the social constructivist perspective, constructing knowledge is both a social and cognitive process [20]. Squires and Preece [1] identified the importance of learning being authentic and described cognitive and contextual authenticity—as key perspectives for predictively evaluating educational software.

According to Squires and Preece [1], cognitive authenticity consists of three concepts: credibility, complexity and ownership. Credibility refers to the plausible opportunities that the environment (educational software) offers to learners for exploration and learning. The environment featured in the software should be a simulation of a real learning context; learners should be provided with a channel to express their opinions or ideas and to actively construct their knowledge. In an authentic learning environment, learners are provided with feedback about their actions, reflecting the influence of their actions on the system, artefacts or environment. The feedback can also allow users to correct their responses, test their ideas and attempt different solutions to their problems. In addition, credibility refers to the activities offered by an environment that support multiple knowledge representations, thus allowing learners to gain multiple perspectives and experience various contexts.

Complexity refers to the intricacy of learners and the environment [1]. As suggested by social constructivism, diversity in terms of learners' prior knowledge or experience can account for their different learning goals or processes, thus influencing their construction of knowledge. To manage such complexity, learners need help or scaffolding. Educational software, which functions as a kind of cultural artefact, is expected to offer this help by addressing learners' differences and specific problems.

As learning is supposed to be actively constructed and internalised by learners in a social constructivist learning environment, a sense of ownership is important. The software can provide strategies that encourage learners to take control of and be responsible for their individual learning. Therefore, strategies that promote intentional learning and motivation are important to consider when evaluating educational software.

In line with a situated perspective and social constructivism, Squires and Preece [1] also characterised contextual authenticity, which concerns two components of the learning environment: the real curriculum and collaboration. Contextual authenticity emphasises that the curriculum and skills provided in an app need to meet learners' goals and needs. Furthermore, the quality of a curriculum's content is also critical; for example, determining whether the content relates to learners' prior knowledge. Finally, regarding social interactions, collaborative learning such as peer discussions and group work must be considered when evaluating software.

The feasibility of applying the concepts of cognitive and contextual authenticity proposed by Squires and Preece [1] in predictive evaluation of language learning software is supported by drawing parallels with more recent studies that used social constructivism to evaluate traditional language learning software. Simina and Hamel [21] presented the characteristics of an ideal socio-constructivist language learning software environment for second language acquisition. According to Simina and Hamel [21], the characteristics of the language learning software environment should be centred on learners and provide a space in which learners are free to form their own interpretations, which corresponds to the credibility concept proposed by Squires and Preece [1]. Moreover, the software environment should promote the authenticity of learning through providing context-related activities for learners to connect both new and prior knowledge, which corresponds to the contextual authenticity proposed by Squires and Preece [1]. Simina and Hamel [21] added that the ideal language learning software environment should embed assistance for learners in constructing knowledge and learners should be able to interact with others and share multiple representations to reflect and monitor their learning progress. The opportunities for learners to interact with others and share multiple representations are in line with the collaboration and credibility concepts proposed by Squires and Preece [1].

Overall, the elements of the ideal socio-constructivist language learning software proposed by Simina and Hamel [21] closely correspond with Squires and Preece's [1] emphasis on cognitive and contextual authenticity thus lending support for evaluation of language learning software that focuses on these elements.

While Squires and Preece [1] developed a tentative set of heuristics incorporating learning and usability considerations for evaluating the types of software available at that time, our analysis suggested that the nature of AI-functionalities was changing usability considerations. Therefore, we developed a framework that characterised the intersection between the elements of Squires and Preece's [1] analysis of cognitive and contextual authenticity and AI functionalities. First we identified the AI functionalities of English language apps for ESL pronunciation.

3 Predictive Evaluation of the AI Functionalities of English Learning Apps for ESL Pronunciation

3.1 Selection of AI-Powered English Learning Apps for Pronunciation

To identify the AI-powered English-learning apps available to Chinese children, we searched for the keywords 'ESL pronunciation' and 'AI' in the App Store. We then filtered these apps according to their reviews and ratings and chose apps designed for ESL learners aged under 16. To ensure the apps had embedded AI features, we reviewed the apps' websites and explored the apps. We selected the three most well-known AI-powered English-learning apps which feature free content that is facilitated by AI functionalities for learning ESL pronunciation (see Table 1).

Table 1. Selected Apps

App name		English Liulishuo	Open Language	Tencent English
URL		https://www.liulishuo.com/liulishuo.html	https://www.openlanguage.com/p/index/	https://study.qq.com
App store rating		4.5; 130,000 ratings	4.9; 69,000 ratings	4.6; 25,000 ratings
Target age group		Age over 12	Age over 12	Age over 4
AI functionalities	Automatic evaluation	Mark pronunciation using a number score and a colour	Mark pronunciation using a number score and a colour	Rate pronunciation using the number of stars and a colour
	Personalised feedback	Implicit feedback; Audio of model pronunciation accompanied by a score	Implicit feedback; Audio of model pronunciation accompanied by a score	Explicit instruction on mispronunciation in forms of video and text
	Intelligent communication	A casual chat with a humanoid chatbot	Fixed conversation with a chatbot that has no appearance	Fixed conversation with a chatbot that has no appearance
	Adaptive instruction	Adaptive feedback provided by the chatbot on learners' output	Test learners' competence and promote courses based on individual levels	Adaptive feedback and instruction on mispronunciation

(continued)

Table 1. (*continued*)

App name		English Liulishuo	Open Language	Tencent English
	Tracking learning activities	Record the number of learning days in a week, average scores and average duration of learning	Record the courses that have been followed	Record the duration of engagement, the number of vocabulary words and sentences learned, and the learning score

Note: all data about ratings and downloads were obtained on 15 December 2021

3.2 AI Functionalities for English Pronunciation

The selected AI-powered learning apps have multiple AI functionalities that can support learning ESL pronunciation. We analysed the AI functionalities of the selected learning apps to determine how they support social constructivist heuristics (see Table 2 for a summary).

Table 2. The Relationships Between AI Functionalities and Social Constructivist Heuristics

AI functionalities	Cognitive authenticity			Contextual authenticity	
	Credibility	Complexity	Ownership	Collaboration	Curriculum
Automatic evaluation	Help learners monitor and test ideas; Guide learners to solve problems				
Personalized feedback	Provide multiple forms of feedback and multiple ways for learners to learn				

(*continued*)

Table 2. (*continued*)

AI functionalities	Cognitive authenticity			Contextual authenticity	
	Credibility	Complexity	Ownership	Collaboration	Curriculum
Intelligent communication	Act as knowledgeable others and simulate teacher-student interaction		Motivate learners to control and be responsible for individual learning	Act as peers to practise pronunciation with	Provide contextualised input and authentic learning materials
Adaptive instruction		Adaptive feedback or instruction that is consistent with learners' performance			Consider learners' ZPD; promote courses related to a learners' individual level
Tracking learning activities	Help learners monitor their learning process and make improvement			Share learning reports with others; extend authentic learning	

Automatic Evaluation of Pronunciation. All three selected learning apps feature AI-enabled automatic scoring to evaluate pronunciation quality and provide real-time scoring or feedback regarding learners' pronunciation of individual words. Open Language evaluates learners' pronunciation and provides a score based on the criteria of fluency, accuracy and integrity. Tencent English assesses learners' pronunciation based on the three abovementioned criteria but does not provide a score to mark learners' performance; instead, it rates learners' pronunciation using one to five stars, which represents implicit feedback. Similarly, English Liulishuo also assesses learners' pronunciation with regard to accuracy, fluency, integrity and intonation and gives a score for each of these elements. The fluency, accuracy, integrity (i.e. wholeness and completeness of the utterance) and intonation are all important elements that should be considered when assessing pronunciation.

The three apps all allow learners to practise their pronunciation by speaking into a microphone. The apps then record, recognise and analyse English speech by using sophisticated integrated algorithms to compute scores (in the form of values ranging from 0 to 100) or a number of stars thus providing immediate feedback. Furthermore, when learners practise their pronunciation, their performance is highlighted by a colour in all three apps—poor pronunciation is normally highlighted in red, whereas correct pronunciation is highlighted in green. This visualisation can help learners become aware of their mispronunciation. Thus, learners can adjust their pronunciation learning plans or repeatedly practise pronunciation to achieve a higher score over time.

Automatic evaluation simulates pronunciation tutoring, in which learners can obtain an immediate evaluation of their performance and have their pronunciation automatically corrected. The intelligent evaluation function of AI is similar to an English teacher who has the patience to constantly offer feedback to learners. Learners who are provided with such immediate feedback can monitor their progress. This functionality, which simulates a real learning context, is consistent with the ideal social constructivist language learning suggested by Simina and Hamel [21]. Furthermore, in line with the notion of credibility proposed by Squires and Preece [1], the feedback can help learners test their ideas and guide learners to solve their problems and improve their performances.

Personalised Feedback. The three mobile learning apps provide personalised feedback based on individual learners' mispronunciations or problems. The Tencent English app offers personalised feedback for particular sounds a learner has mispronounced by highlighting their errors in red. When they press the red-coloured word or phoneme (unit of sound), the learner receives specific instructions for further practice such as making the sound, understanding words that contain the specific phonemes and studying sentences that contain the words a learner has mispronounced. The instructions are accompanied by visual or textual aids, such as a video that features a model speaker correctly pronouncing a word. Providing feedback in multiple forms enables learners to explore and learn to choose the types of feedback they prefer in order to construct their knowledge actively. In Open Language, when learners press their mispronounced words, they only receive feedback on the word in the text, accompanied by an audio of model pronunciation. Similarly, English Liulishuo only displays learners' scores and colours learners' mispronunciations with limited textual instructions concerning how learners can correct their pronunciation. Learners need to press mispronounced words to obtain hyperlinks to the model pronunciation, which they then imitate and rerecord their pronunciation. It seems that in these two apps, learners follow automatic speech evaluation-based imitation-speaking methods with immediate feedback. Such feedback provides little information about errors in pronunciation or the causes thereof, which may impede learners' attempts to correct their pronunciation. Furthermore, the representation of the feedback is limited to text and audio elements, which means that these two apps cannot provide alternative ways for learners to explore pronunciation correction and limit multiple interpretations. This more limited range of feedback could further the fossilisation of errors and might lead to frustration.

Intelligent Communication. Intelligent communication refers to human-computer interactions in which learners speak English to chatbots on mobile phones or computers and receive a response. This functionality is supported by natural language processing (NLP) and machine learning (ML) techniques, which create a natural language communication environment. All three apps have a chatbot functionality. In Tencent English and Open Language, learners can roleplay with a chatbot to practise speaking. The roleplay creates a supportive speaking environment for students who are reluctant to speak in front of other people. Learners are provided with various speaking tasks to complete whenever they choose. In accordance with social constructivist principles, the chatbot can act as a peer for learners to practise and collaborate with. The chatbot also acts as a teacher or knowledgeable other for learners, as it incorporates machine learning to detect learners' pronunciation, provides personalised feedback for individual learning and promotes learners' interactions with it.

However, the chatbots in Tencent English and Open Language are not trained to respond to casual conversations. The human-chatbot communication seems to be based on drill practices that resemble a traditional pronunciation-training approach [22]. Unlike the predetermined chatbots in Tencent English and Open Language, English Liulishuo incorporates an AI foreign teacher chatbot. The chatbot can have a casual chat with learners, which creates an immersive and authentic learning environment that enables learners to explore and express their ideas actively. Furthermore, the chatbot provides contextualised input by using multimedia, such as pictures and videos, which corresponds to contextual authenticity from the perspective of social constructivism.

Previous studies have claimed that incorporating chatbots into apps could motivate learners to practise pronunciation [23, 24]. According to Zhang [25], who analysed the advantages and disadvantages of AI technology-assisted English learning from the perspectives of Krashen's second language acquisition theory, communicating with AI-powered chatbots can reduce the anxiety caused by face-to-face communication, lessen the degree of learners' emotional filtering and create a relaxing input and output environment. A relaxing environment can promote positive attitudes towards and motivation for speaking English. From the perspective of social constructivism, motivated and intentional learning can help learners to control and take responsibility for their learning.

Adaptive Instruction. According to Aleven [26], adaptivity is the most important feature of AI because it allows an app to study individual differences, provides different guidance for different learners and adapts to learners' needs. In order to enable adaptive instruction, Open Language assesses learners' English level following the Common European Framework of Reference (CEFR). The app identifies a learner's issues in terms of comprehension, listening, pronunciation, vocabulary, grammar, speaking and fluency and then automatically offers courses that are consistent with that learner's level. The chatbot in English Liulishuo can understand learners' output and provide adaptive feedback on their actions. The Tencent English-learning app also provides both adaptive feedback and instruction according to learners' performances and regarding particular mispronunciation to help increase awareness and promote progress. Aligned with social constructivism, the adaptive learning materials provided by the apps can manage the complexity of both learners and their environments by taking into account both differences of needs, goals and levels faced by an individual learner.

Tracking Learning Activities. All three apps can also supervise and track learners' learning activities and learners can view their learning records. In Tencent English, once a learner completes a training session, the app produces a learning profile for them. The profile is presented in the form of a card that displays the number of vocabulary words and sentences learned, the learner's average score, the phrases practised, the length of time the learner spent on the app and the quality of his or her performance. Open Language and Liulishuo can also record the time that a learner spends on each app and how many times a week they have engaged with the app. However, the report reveals nothing regarding learners' pronunciation improvements or progress, which means that the apps cannot help learners monitor how their pronunciation has improved. However, learners can share the tracking results of the three apps with others via links to Wechat or QQ, which are the largest social media platforms in China. Sharing with other people can increase learners' social interaction with peers or teachers, which extends their authentic learning experiences.

4 Conclusion

All three of the AI-powered English-learning apps that we analysed have elements of the AI functionalities of automatic evaluation, personalised feedback, intelligent communication, adaptive instruction and tracking learning activities that can support a socio-constructivist approach to language learning. The analysis of the details of their functionalities revealed many similarities but also some differences that would be likely to affect their value for a socio-constructivist approach to language learning. In relation to automatic evaluation and adaptive instruction there are no important differences between the apps from a socio-constructivist perspective. However personalised feedback in Tencent English was more supportive of a socio-constructivist approach than the other two apps as it provides multiple forms of feedback which could allow learners to choose types of feedback that suit them best in order to construct their knowledge actively. Furthermore, Tencent English has more sophisticated tracking of learning activities which would enable learners to monitor their progress more effectively. In relation to intelligent communication, however, English Liulishuo, unlike the other two apps, provides a chatbot capable of a casual chat with learners. This casual chat capability can create a more immersive and authentic learning environment and contextual authenticity is further enhanced by its use of multimedia. Therefore, we can conclude that all of these apps have different advantages and limitations from a socio-constructive perspective at the present time. Their different strengths and limitations will affect their potential for supporting language learning across different learning contexts and for different learners. For learners who need more explicit feedback on the correction of mispronunciation, for example, Tencent English may be the most appropriate app as it provides feedback in visual, textual and audio forms that enable learners to explore and choose the types of feedback they prefer to construct their knowledge actively. Learners who have a low motivation for English speaking may find chatting with the chatbot incorporated in English Liulishuo interesting and immersive. Open Language may be more appropriate for those who want to develop their skills in relation to specific levels of English and prefer to receive instruction designed for their particular levels.

The use of social constructivist theory for the evaluation helps to determine whether the apps support the general rules of foreign-language learning in the process of assisting learning of ESL pronunciation. Such evaluations provide a means for teachers, parents and learners to make informed choices regarding the use of AI-powered technologies. While this study focused only on apps for supporting pronunciation by young Chinese learners, the approach may be valuable for other educational software that incorporates AI functionalities since social constructivist approaches to learning are applicable across many fields. However, it should be noted that for some types of software, for example creative and problem-solving apps where more open-ended opportunities are needed, further usability considerations may be needed because AI functionalities may not yet be as effective.

Predictive evaluations are a useful first step in examining the potential of software but are insufficient to indicate the value of AI for English learning. Empirical studies of the apps in use will be needed to determine to what extent and how the AI functionalities can enable the learning of English pronunciation. Comparing the outcomes of such studies with the predictions made by the earlier evaluations are also needed to validate the quality of the predictive evaluation approach. However, studies of software in use are time-consuming and the rapid developments in AI functionalities mean that predictive evaluations will continue to be important ways for teachers, parents and learners to select software and decide how to use it.

References

1. Squires, D., Preece, J.: Predicting quality in educational software: evaluating for learning, usability and the synergy between them. Interact. Comput. **11**(5), 467–483 (1999)
2. Dillenbourg, P.: The role of artificial intelligence techniques in training software. In: Proceedings of LEARNTEC. Karlsruhe (1994)
3. Schiff, D.: Out of the laboratory and into the classroom: the future of artificial intelligence in education. AI & Soc. **36**(1), 331–348 (2020). https://doi.org/10.1007/s00146-020-01033-8
4. Zhang, K., Aslan, A.B.: AI technologies for education: recent research & future directions. Comp. Educ. Artif. Intell. **2**, 100025 (2021)
5. Woo, J.H., Choi, H.: Systematic review for AI-based language learning tools (2021). https://arxiv.org/abs/2111.0445
6. Squires, D., Preece, J.: Usability and learning: evaluating the potential of educational software. Comp. Educ. **27**(1), 15–22 (1996)
7. Hao, K.: China has started a grand experiment in AI education. It could reshape how the world learns. MIT Technol. Rev. 1–9 (2019)
8. Mahdi, H.S., Al-Khateeb, A.A.: The effectiveness of computer-assisted pronunciation training: a meta-analysis. Rev. Educ. **7**(3), 733–753 (2019)
9. Gao, Y., Hanna, B.: Exploring optimal pronunciation teaching: integrating instructional software into intermediate-level EFL classes in China. CALICO J. **33**(2), 201–230 (2016)
10. Wang, Y., Yang, S.: A study of the design and implementation of the ASR-based iCASL system with corrective feedback to facilitate English learning. Educ. Technol. Soc. **17**(2), 219–233 (2014)
11. Biswas, G., Leelawong, K., Schwartz, D., Vye, N.: The teachable agents group at vanderbilt.: learning by teaching: a new agent paradigm for educational software. Appl. Artif. Intell. **19**(3–4), 363–392 (2005)
12. Rogerson-Revell, P.M.: Computer-Assisted pronunciation training (CAPT): current issues and future directions. RELC J. **52**(1), 1–17 (2021)
13. Shackel, B.: The concept of usability. In: Visual Display Terminals: Usability Issues and Health Concerns, pp. 45–87. Prentice Hall (1984)
14. Dimitrije, S., Devedžić, V.: Usability evaluation in selecting educational technology. In: Proceedings of the 11th Conference of Information Technology and Development of Education, pp. 208–214. ITRO, Zrenjanin (2020)
15. McDougall, A., Squires, D.: A critical examination of the checklist approach in software selection. J. Educ. Comp. Res. **12**(3), 263–274 (1995)

16. Lantolf, J.P.: Language emergence: Implications for applied linguistics - A sociocultural perspective. Appl. Linguis. **27**(4), 717–728 (2006)
17. Vygotsky, L.S.: Mind in society: The Development of Higher Psychological Process. Harvard University Press, Cambridge (1978)
18. Salomon, G., Perkins, D.N.: Individual and social aspects of learning. Rev. Res. Educ. **23**(1), 1–24 (1998)
19. Leelawong, K., Biswas, G.: Designing learning by teaching agents: the Betty's brain system. Int. J. Artif. Intell. Educ. **18**, 181–208 (2008)
20. Li, J.: English pronunciation curriculum model on reading assistant SRS: constructivism view. Educ. Sci. Theory Pract. **18**(5), 1246–1254 (2018)
21. Simina, V., Hamel, M.J.: CASLA through a social constructivist perspective: WebQuest in project-driven language learning. ReCALL **17**(2), 217–228 (2005)
22. Pokrivcakova, S.: Preparing teachers for the application of AI-powered technologies in foreign language education. J. Lang. Cult. Educ. **7**(3), 135–153 (2019)
23. Fryer, L.K., Ainley, M., Thompson, A., Gibson, A., Sherlock, Z.: Stimulating and sustaining interest in a language course: an experimental comparison of chatbot and human task partners. Comput. Hum. Behav. **75**, 461–468 (2017)
24. Fryer, L.K., Nakao, K., Thompson, A.: Chatbot learning partners: connecting learning experiences, interest and competence. Comput. Hum. Behav. **93**, 279–289 (2019)
25. Zhang, Y.: An analysis of AI technology assisted English learning from the perspective of SLA theory. In: 2019 3rd International Conference on Economics, Management Engineering and Education Technology, pp. 885–890. ICEMEET, Nantong (2019)
26. Aleven, V.: A is for adaptivity, but what is adaptivity? Re-defining the field of AIED. In: CEUR Workshop Proceedings, pp. 11–20 (2015)

Computing in Schools

Curriculum Development and Practice of Application Creation Incorporating AI Functions; Learning During After-School Hours

Kimihito Takeno[1](✉), Keiji Yoko[2], and Hirotaka Mori[3]

[1] Shiga University, 2-5-1 Hiratsu, Otsu Shiga, Japan
kimi@edu.shiga-u.ac.jp

[2] Soran Elementary School, 76-1, Doizumi-cho, Seto-shi, Aichi, Japan
kyokoo@seto-solan.ed.jp

[3] Kyoto Municipal Saikyo High School, 1 Nishinokyo-Higashinakaaicho Nakagyo-Ku, Kyoto, Japan

Abstract. There is an urgent need to develop human resources which can utilize the power of AI and data in order to enrich society through technological innovation and value creation. On the other hand, in school education, due to the framework of each subject and time limitation, it is difficult to implement a curriculum to work on application creation. Therefore, in this study, we attempted to develop and evaluate teaching materials for developing iOS applications for junior high and high school students in order to provide opportunities for interested students to learn independently during after-school hours. As a result, the students' responses on programming showed no significant change for the experienced students, but "surprise" and "feeling that I can do it" were meaningful learning opportunities for the beginners. Looking at the responses of the students regarding AI, although they knew the term AI, their perceptions varied from "humanistic", "familiar", and "coexistence with AI".

Keywords: Curriculum Development · Application Creation · AI · After-School Hours

1 Introduction

1.1 Background

In recent years, with the development of science and technology, AI (Artificial Intelligence) has had a great impact on our society [1, 2], and we are seeing more and more services with AI functions in all aspects of our lives. In the field of image recognition, the accuracy of AI is increasing every year, and by using deep learning, AI will surpass human recognition rate in 2015 [3]. In the school education sector, the technological development of AI will affect human activities, and therefore the learning that students acquire in school will need to change. Furthermore, with the development of technologies such as IoT and Big Data, it has become possible to incorporate highly accurate AI

Published by Springer Nature Switzerland AG 2023
T. Keane et al. (Eds.): WCCE 2022, IFIP AICT 685, pp. 115–123, 2023.
https://doi.org/10.1007/978-3-031-43393-1_12

into the machines around us based on large amounts of data, and AI is spreading into our society and industries.

There are claims of a sense of crisis regarding these developments in science and technology, including AI. Michael Osborne has predicted that nearly half of all jobs can be replaced in the next 10–20 years due to AI [4]. Ray Kurzweil has also predicted that AI will surpass human intelligence by 2045, and that the singularity will arrive, which will drastically change the nature of society [5]. At the same time, Japan's policy is also based on Society 5.0, which aims to incorporate advanced technologies such as AI, IoT, robotics, and big data into industry and social life to achieve economic development and solve social problems [6]. Society 5.0 calls for the development of human resources who can drive a new society, specifically those who can make creative discoveries and imaginations that will be the source of technological innovation and value creation, and those who can make the most of the power of AI and data in various fields. Therefore, there is an urgent need to develop human resources who can utilize AI.

1.2 Current Status and Issues of Education on AI

Against this background, in Japan, programming education has become compulsory at the elementary school level, and programming content is increasing in junior high and high schools as well [7–9]. In particular, the high school subject Information II includes learning content about AI in the area "Information and Data Science.

In the previous study, we identified practical examples of education on various AI topics. Nakamura and Yamamoto [10] implemented a course on regression algorithms using Python in a high school industrial course. Akiyama, Hanada, et al. and Zama, Yamamoto, et al. attempted to deepen understanding of AI through programming to create chatbots for middle school technology classes [11, 12]. Others such as Itagaki and Asamizu also provide classroom practices to deepen understanding of AI [13]. From these previous studies, it is clear that students have positive impressions of AI, a deeper understanding of AI, and a sense of the usefulness of AI and the need to learn about it through the class. At the same time, in all the studies, securing sufficient study time and setting tasks for students to work on are issues that need to be addressed.

In this way, AI-related classes are being conducted, but the number of examples is still small, and it can be pointed out that a wider variety of teaching materials is needed. One of the problems with AI-related education, in particular, is that the content is not continued in elementary, middle, and high schools. Even if a class on AI is conducted, it is completed only in that class, and it is difficult to imagine how to learn more about it and how the content learned can be connected to society. Particularly in Japan, because it is connected to university entrance examinations, students may end up superficially acquiring knowledge rather than being interested in AI development and programming development for social needs and problem solving. It has also been proven that AI can pass university entrance exams in Japan [14]. In addition, although the promotion of programming education is expected from elementary school, it is difficult to implement a curriculum by working on application creation due to the framework and time limitation of each subject in school education.

1.3 Purpose and Significance of this Study

Therefore, the purpose of this study was to develop a curriculum that enables students to create iOS applications that incorporate AI for image recognition using after-school hours so that they can learn independently without relying on time-constrained subject learning. iOS applications are pervasive in our lives, and it is easy to imagine their connection to society. The iOS application is written in a programming language called Swift. This Swift is an application for the iPad called Swift playgrounds, where you can learn basic grammar and programming concepts. This application enables elementary and junior high school students to learn programming because it is intuitive like visual programming. These materials are based on Swift, so there is a high possibility of consistent learning in elementary, middle, and high school.

In addition, since it is not possible to spend enough time on application creation in the regular curriculum practice, this study decided to use after-school hours to provide opportunities for interested students to learn independently. Also, we attempted to provide learning opportunities for students who are interested in programming by using the online environment.

2 Method

2.1 Overview of Research Methods: Development of Teaching Materials, Practice, Pedagogical Methods and Evaluation

In this study, we created four programming assignments that serve as teaching materials for novice learners to be able to create iOS applications that incorporate AI. In addition, about 10 junior high school and senior high school students who voluntarily participated in the study were asked to answer the post-survey. The participating junior and senior high school students were from high schools in Hokkaido and Kyoto, and the educational practice was conducted in an online, simultaneous interactive manner between junior and senior high school students from the two schools. The participating students were approached by teachers from the two schools and voluntarily participated in this class. The students were diverse in grade level and had varying degrees of existing knowledge and experience, but all were interested in learning more about programming. All students had no experience in creating applications.

After the instructor's explanation, the learners were encouraged to work on their own in pairs [15]. If they could not solve the problem by themselves, they would ask questions to the instructor. Two teachers and one university teacher were involved in the project. In November 2021, four 120-min sessions were held after school.

2.2 Overview of the Developed Curriculum

The goal of this study was to create an iOS application that incorporates AI for image recognition through the creation of a self-introduction application in four sessions. Topics 1 and 2 had the same learning content, and students learned how to use Xcode through the creation of a business card app. In Topic 3, students tried to learn about AI functionality in an animal book app. In Topic 4, students created a self-introduction app and presented it to each other. For the AI functions, we used CoreML, a framework released by Apple in 2017 that allows users to handle machine learning without any specialized knowledge.

In the first session, we set up an elementary explanation, "Touching Xcode", assuming that the students were using Swift for the first time (Fig. 1). Xcode is an application for working with Swift on a Mac. In the second session, students learned about button functions and screen transition functions. In the third session, the students decided to implement the AI function in the self-introduction application they were creating, and in the fourth session, they presented the application they had created (Fig. 2).

Since programming was a challenge that could not be done continuously during regular school hours, we decided to use after-school hours and set each session to 120 min, guaranteeing 480 min of programming experience over four sessions.

Fig. 1. Example code for business card application

Fig. 2. Example code for an animal picture book application

3 Educational Practices and Student Responses

3.1 Practice: Overview, Production, Examples of Work

The educational practice was carried out during after-school hours in November and December of 2021, connecting the two schools online. The students used their personal Macs and school loaned Macs to work on the curriculum for this study using Xcode (Fig. 3). Learners naturally shared information with their friends, making pair work highly effective for learning programming. In addition, through the activity of introducing themselves with the application, each student is trying to create an original application (Fig. 4).

Fig. 3. Educational Practice

3.2 Results of the Survey

After the practice, the students were asked to respond online, but not all students responded, so the results for six students are shown. Students answered that they enjoyed

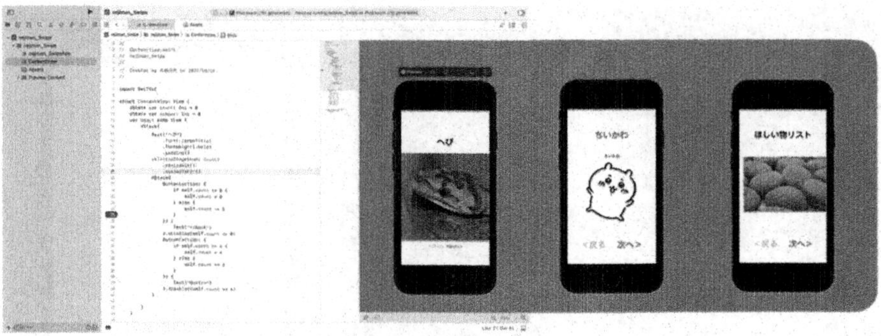

Fig. 4. Examples of students' work

the curriculum, and 30% of the students answered that it was difficult and 60% answered that it was not difficult. In addition, the students were asked to write freely about the curriculum they had developed.

They were asked to respond to the changes in their perception of programming and AI after participating in the educational practice (Table 1). For those who have experience in programming, there were no significant changes, but "surprise" and "feeling that I can do it too" seemed to be meaningful learning opportunities for the beginners. Looking at the responses of the students regarding AI, it seems that although they knew the term AI, their perceptions of it changed from "humanistic" to "familiar" to "coexistence with AI".

They were also asked to respond to any difficulties or pleasures they had in educational practice (Table 2). Looking at the responses regarding the difficulties, "differences in speed of progress" and "preparation for the necessary knowledge and skills" were the most common. These are issues that need to be addressed in the future, but it may be

Table 1. Changing perceptions of programming and AI

	What were your perceptions of programming before and after your participation?	**What were your perceptions of AI before and after your participation?**
A	I was surprised to find that what I thought was all about creating something from scratch was about incorporating other people's work to create something new!	I felt that the AI was a little human, but not too human, because it could make mistakes in some simple things, and could be very accurate in some difficult things.
B	When I was in junior high school, I studied drawing circles and coloring in technology classes, and I thought it was difficult to do calculations and such, but this time, the range of things I could do became even wider, and I was surprised to find that I could do them too.	I had thought that only professional engineers could handle it, but listening to the explanation and trying it myself made me feel closer to it.
C	Before participating in this event, I thought it would be easy to do as long as I could speak English, but I was surprised to find out that there was a lot more to it than I thought, including mathematics, so I thought it was very profound.	Before participating, I thought it would be very difficult to make, but even though the base was provided, it was surprisingly easy to make!
D	I realized that programming technology is a process and not a result. I found it interesting that it is similar to music notation and mathematics in that it proceeds from top to bottom.	Even if you don't understand how AI works, you can use what's available on the Internet as it is, and you don't need to be a professional to make use of it.
E	Of course, I can do a lot of things, but I was able to learn and experience the detailed steps of writing the code, thinking about the procedure and confirming that it works one by one, such as what is necessary for each operation and actually attaching the buttons. It will take time, but I think I can do it, and I will be motivated to try to make it myself because I am interested in it.	I had heard about AI even before I participated in the workshop, and it did not change my perception that much. However, it was a good opportunity for me to seriously think about how I would like to live in harmony with AI.
F	I do this on a regular basis, so there is no change.	Not particularly.

possible to prepare contents that allow students to study at home or on their own. Looking at the responses about enjoyment, "immersion in the process of creation" and "sharing and working together on the creation" are some of the most popular. Although immersion can be achieved through self-learning, sharing and creating together are important learning opportunities that can be gained at school.

Table 2. Free description of problems and enjoyable experiences

	Please tell me what kind of problems you had.	Tell us what you enjoyed about it.	Please tell us what you would like to learn (or create) in the future.
A	I couldn't go once, so I fell a little behind the others and had a hard time catching up.	It was interesting to see how the code was struck and how the backstage was assembled.	This time I was using an Apple-specific language, but now I'd like to learn a language that can be used on a variety of platforms!
B	Errors and not knowing how to use the computer.	We showed each other our work.	Now I'm thinking it would be interesting to be able to register the bugs and other creatures I've caught or encountered, like in a Pokemon illustrated book.
C	The fact that there were English words I didn't know.	To be able to create more and more work as I type on the keyboard.	I want to create and publish Java and games.
D	When I tried to add a sound, it went crazy and I couldn't do it in the end. I ended up just copying and pasting the instructions. I think it is difficult to write with the previous and following sentences in mind, even if you just follow the instructions on the Internet. Also, I thought it was hard to learn because there are different versions from the ones on the Internet.	It was fun to make business cards and present them to each other. It was also fun to add images to the AI.	The AI was mostly a copy and paste, so I would like to understand what it is up to.
E	When there were many experienced people around, the speed became faster and it was hard to keep up. Also, there were a lot of unfamiliar commands that I couldn't use, and I had to do a lot of work around them, which took a lot of time.	As the number of times I developed apps increased, I felt a sense of accomplishment in that even if my work didn't work well in the latter half of this workshop, I was able to guess the reason and fix it on my own, and I was able to help others who seemed to be having trouble for the same reason. It was fun to actually play with what I had created on the actual machine!	I want to make something that can do more than just add buttons and change pages, and make something that I like. I would also like to be able to use my experience to help people around me who are in trouble.
F	How to operate a Mac	Writing and running code.	Algorithms for left over calculations, something that combines IoT and AI.

4 Conclusion

In this study, we tried to provide practical learning opportunities for AI human resource development, which has been attracting attention in recent years, in school education beyond the framework of existing subject instruction. Therefore, we attempted to develop teaching materials and educational practices for developing iOS applications for junior high and high school students in order to provide opportunities for interested students to learn independently using the online environment and after-school hours. The results of the study showed the following.

1. In order to enable novice learners to create iOS applications that incorporate AI, we have created programming assignments that serve as teaching materials for all four sessions.
2. By using the developed curriculum in an online environment and after-school hours, we were able to provide students with meaningful learning opportunities.
3. The results of the teaching practice also showed that preparing content that allows students to study on their own is important in order to provide more fulfilling learning opportunities.

In 2021, Swift programming will be available on the iPad, as announced by Apple. It can be predicted that the GIGA school initiative will make programming and app development more accessible. Therefore, we would like to propose an integrated Swift learning system for elementary, middle, and high school students. The GIGA initiative is the Japanese government's policy to give one tablet to every child in grades 1 through 9. Looking at the share of each company's tablets in Japan, 1/3 of the role is occupied by Apple's iPad. In high schools, a similar policy will begin in 2022, but the share of Apple may expand. Apple Swift also has an advantage in the ease with which you can publish your own applications to the world.

Acknowledgement. This work was supported by JSPS KAKENHI Grant Numbers 20K02910, 22K02629.

References

1. Wu, Y., et al.: Google's neural machine translation system: bridging the gap between human and machine translation. arXiv:1609.08144. Cornell University (2016)
2. Mohri, M., Rostamizadeh, A., Talwalkar, A.: Foundations of Machine Learning, second edn. MIT Press (2018)
3. NikkeiXTECH. Nikkei Robo CNN makes great progress in image recognition; classification error rate drops by nearly half per year. https://xtech.nikkei.com/dm/atcl/mag/15/00144/00014/. Last accessed 22 Feb 2022
4. Frey, C.B., Osborne, M.: The future of employment. https://www.oxfordmartin.ox.ac.uk/downloads/academic/future-of-employment.pdf. Last accessed 22 Feb 2022
5. Kurzweil, R.: Singularity is Near [Essence Version] When Humanity Transcends Life. NHK Publishing, Tokyo (2016)
6. Cabinet Office: What is Society 5.0. Science and technology policy, in Japanese. https://www8.cao.go.jp/cstp/society5_0/. Last accessed 22 Feb 2022
7. Ministry of education, culture, sports, science and technology: the course of study for elementary school. Government of Japan, in Japanese. https://www.mext.go.jp/a_menu/shotou/new-cs/1387014.htm. Last accessed 22 Feb 2022
8. Ministry of education, culture, sports, science and technology: the course of study for lower secondary school and technology. Government of Japan, in Japanese. https://www.mext.go.jp/component/a_menu/education/micro_detail/__icsFiles/afieldfile/2019/03/18/1387018_009.pdf. Last accessed 22 Feb 2022
9. Ministry of education, culture, sports, science and technology: the course of study for high school and information. Government of Japan, in Japanese. https://www.mext.go.jp/content/1407073_11_1_2.pdf. Last accessed 22 Feb 2022
10. Nakamura, M., Yamamoto, T.: Examination of the teaching process on the subject of artificial intelligence in high school industrial department. J. Integr. Cent. Clin. Educ. Pract. **18**, 39–46 (2020)
11. Akiyama, M., Hanada, M., Kanke, H., Honda, M.:Development of programming classes for technology subject in junior high school to promote understanding of AI: using distributed automatic conversation system as the teaching materials. Bulletin of the Center for Educational Research and Practice, Faculty of Education and Human Studies, Akita University, vol. 42, pp. 55-64 (2020).

12. Zama, T., Yamamoto, T., Nakamura, M.: Lesson practice of "programming interactive contents" in junior high school technology education with chatbot using natural language processing of artificial intelligence. Japan Soc. Educ. Inf., Study Educ. Inform. **35**(3), 45–53 (2019)
13. Itagaki, S., Asamizu, T., Sato, K., Nakagawa, T., Ando, A., Horita, T.: Development and practice of technology education class at junior high school to understand about AI through problem based learning with programming research report of JSET conferences **19**(5), 129-136 (2019)
14. Arai, N., Ozaki, K.: Why does it matter whether or not ai is able to pass university entrance examinations? 8. Why were high school students outperformed by "Artificial Unintelligence"? Jouhoushori 613–615 (2017)
15. Uchida, K., Oya, Y., Okuda, T.: A relationship between the amount of utterances and the learner characteristics at pair work in computer literacy education. J. Inf. Process. **55**(5) (2014)

Assessing Engagement of Students with Intellectual Disabilities in Educational Robotics Activities

Francesca Coin and Monica Banzato(✉)

Ca' Foscari University, Venice, Italy
{francescacoin.psi,banzato}@unive.it

Abstract. Engagement is a multi-componential construct, difficult to measure in its general form as in the typical development but even more in the atypical development. Currently, there are no instruments in the literature to measure engagement in its different dimensions (behavioural, affective, social and cognitive) for students with intellectual disabilities involved in creative robotics activities. With this aim, we tried to apply a survey system based on the triangulation of three ad hoc tools: an observation grid, analysis of verbal productions and a questionnaire. This triple system of application allowed us to understand whether the creative robotics activity proposed to children with intellectual disabilities aroused their interest and involvement, and to what extent.

Keywords: Engagement · Student with intellectual disability · Educational Robotics

1 Introduction

Following the EU educational policies, the last Education Reform in Italy (2016) introduced computational thinking at all school levels. Regrettably, in the Italian school reality, students with intellectual disabilities (ID) appear to be excluded from programming activities with educational robotics (ER) [1]. The research literature confirmed the same gap: there are very few publications on educational ER programming activities with students with ID [2]; most research is focused on humanoid robotics, the role of assistive devices or the effectiveness of computer-assisted instruction. The range of publications narrows dramatically when examining the age of students: the few existing studies focus mainly on children between 6 and 12, while adolescents aged 15 to 20, in high school, appear decidedly under-represented [2]. Therefore, this exploratory study aimed to measure the engagement of 8 high school students with ID, aged between 16 and 22, in ER programming activities (with Arduino as base), in a school in the North-East of Italy. In this work, considering the target students, we considered very simple activities of programming and coding: for example, students lifting flashcards (paper or digital) to make the robot perform the specific action displayed in the flashcards.

Published by Springer Nature Switzerland AG 2023
T. Keane et al. (Eds.): WCCE 2022, IFIP AICT 685, pp. 124–136, 2023.
https://doi.org/10.1007/978-3-031-43393-1_13

Engagement is considered a key construct to identify the educational potential of ER activities, at behavioral, cognitive, affective, and social levels. Although there is a conspicuous amount of research on this construct in the educational field for typical development, the study of engagement for atypical development is still limited to the use of robotics in therapeutic and clinical settings (particularly with the use of humanoid robotics). Thus, there is a gap in the literature on the educational dimension of engagement of ER programming activities for students with ID [2]. To measure the engagement of these students, we constructed and applied three ad hoc research instruments: an observation instrument, a verbal interaction analysis instrument and a questionnaire. In the next paragraphs, the definition and measurement of engagement will be analyzed, the tools of our proposal will be described, and finally the tools will be applied to a case study of 8 students with ID engaged in basic robotics activities.

2 Engagement and Its Measurement

The meaning and measurement of engagement has evolved over time "to represent increasingly complex understandings of the relationships between desired outcomes of college and the amount of time and effort students invest in their studies and other educationally purposeful activities" (pp.683) [3]. Engagement is generally described as a multi-componential construct and over time several models have been constructed to define it. For example, Finn's [4] model includes two components: behavioural (participation) and affective (identification, belonging, evaluation). The same categories are considered by Skinner et al. [5] in their comparison between Engagement vs. Disaffection, both involving a behavioural and an affective aspect. Other authors add a further component, cognitive, linked to self-regulation goals and the amount of investment [6]. Gunuc & Kuzu [7] recall the importance of the social aspect, which is mutually dependent with engagement, especially in school and learning contexts.

The measurement of engagement levels is one of the most challenging issues for researchers in the field. Until the late 1990s this issue had been placed on the back burner [8]. However, over the last two decades a number of scholars have focused on the variety of data collection techniques most suitable for measuring engagement. The most common are self-report measures. Among the earliest are Jacques' [9] 13-item interview containing questions about attention, perceived time, motivation, needs, control, attitudes and general engagement and Webster and Ho's [10] seven-item questionnaire with questions about attention, challenge, intrinsic interest, and variety. They are followed by more recent instruments such as the User Engagement Scale by O'Brien & Toms [11], the Motivation and Engagement Scale by Liem & Martin [12] and the UTAUT model by Heerink et al. [13].

Despite the increase in research on this subject, there seem to be considerable difficulties in measuring cognitive and psychological engagement. Frequently, the same questions can be used to represent different subtypes of engagement, while the subtypes are often examined separately, precluding further levels of comparison [6].

Some researchers have used performance indicators, not as direct measures of engagement, but as its correlates. For example, Konradt and Sultz [14] used pre- and post-activity measures to examine changes in users' affective and cognitive states during interaction with an educational application. However, even metrics such as interaction analysis, number of eye fixations, heart rate, etc., have limitations: they explain what is happening during a user's interaction with a given activity, but do not address the cognitive or emotional state of users, which are crucial for engagement [10].

There is also the problem of generalizability of the results: often a tool is valid for the precise domain or activity it was constructed for, but these results are not applicable to other domains. Moreover, the elements contained in each of these tools represent a small part of the engagement attributes indicated so far.

Champion [15] hypothesized that multiple measures (self-report, participant observation, biometrics) are needed to study engagement, but did not offer any empirical results or describe how these measures could be triangulated to say anything meaningful about engagement. Therefore, for our purposes, we decided to build ad hoc tools, to measure engagement of student with cognitive disability, which will be outlined in the following sections.

3 Tools Developed to Measure Engagement

3.1 Observation Grid

The observation grid included the analysis of non-verbal expressive behaviour. We were inspired by the work of Mehrabian [16], making appropriate modifications for our activity, as we will explain below. The behaviours were divided into three categories: Posture and stance, and Movements and Facial expressions. The first category includes: Touch, Distance, Stretching, Eye contact, Body orientation. Since most of the robotics activities were carried out in a sitting position, only touch and eye contact were analysed.

In the second category are: Trunk movements, Swinging, Nodding, Gesturing, Self-manipulation, Foot and leg movements. For the same issue of seated positioning, some categories were excluded; we selected nodding, gesturing and self-manipulations or stimming (i.e., repeatedly touching a part of one's own body, finger-flicking and so on). In relation to trunk and arm movements, the asymmetrical position of the arms is interpreted as a sign of relaxation.

The third category is devoted to Facial expressions and is divided into Positive and Negative expressions. We chose to analyse the most frequent and explicit expressions: smiling and laughter as positive interactions, and yawning indicating boredom and disengagement.

The following criteria were used to compile the observation grid:

1. *Duration of eye contact* with the different objects: duration is expressed in seconds of fixations towards the interlocutor and the objects selected for each activity: robot, paper and digital flashcards with arrow, carpet, interactive whiteboard.
2. *Number of eye contacts* with different objects: the number of direct fixations of eye contact towards the interlocutor and the objects selected for each task are counted: robot, paper and digital flashcards with arrow, carpet, interactive whiteboard (IWB).
3. *Number and duration of facial expressions*: smiling, laughing, yawning, etc. are counted.

4. *Number and duration of body movements*: gesturing, nodding, self-manipulations, standing up and sitting, relaxation, stimming are counted.
5. *Number and duration of physical distance from objects*: spontaneous touching, touching on command, hesitation to respond are counted.

In relation to the above classifications, it can be noted that eye contact refers to the behavioural aspect of engagement, as it involves physical movement, therefore it is related to the factors Time on task [6], Focused attention [8], Persistence [12], Use [13] and Effort [5].

The *number of ocular occurrences* signals interest and attraction and is therefore related to the factors Novelty [8] and Interest [5].

Facial expressions represent the emotions felt towards the object or activity; therefore, they are related to the factors Attitude and Perceived enjoyment [13], Felt Involvement [8] and Enjoyment [5].

Body movements can be interpreted as emotional signals of nervousness or relaxation; therefore, they are related to Anxiety [13], Uncertain control [12], Self-regulation [6] and Perceived usability [8].

The *physical distance from the objects*, in particular in the meaning of *spontaneous touching*, indicates Perceived ease of use [13], Participation [6], Self-efficacy [12], Aesthetic [8], Enthusiasm and Exertion [5].

Time indicates the duration of each work phase, including some, not many, moments of relaxation and those dedicated to the actual activity. The category *Eye contact* reports a continuous event, as it indicates the duration of eye fixation and is expressed in seconds. The other categories indicate punctual events and are expressed in number of times per minute.

3.2 Verbal Expressions

Also, via video recording, it was possible to transcribe the verbal comments of the pupils. They were classified into two categories according to the extent of verbal production: *short interjections* and *complete words or sentences*. Subsequently, the spontaneity of these productions was assessed: "*Completely spontaneous*", "*In response to a question*" or "*Completion/repetition of portions of sentences*" produced by the interlocutor. Spontaneous productions indicate a greater involvement and state of well-being on the part of the pupil, while responses to questions and completion of sentences indicate a high degree of participation but less ease in the situation. In addition to these, the category "*Avoidance of answer*" was added to indicate the condition of discomfort and low willingness to participate [17].

3.3 The Questionnaire

The questionnaire (see Table 1) was composed of the most frequent factors mentioned in the literature. In particular, we selected questions with a direct correspondence in the classifications of the five mentioned authors. The aim was to create an instrument lean and quick to complete (19 items), with questions presented in lexically and syntactically simple formulations. The questions are posed in the affirmative form and the participants are asked to mark their agreement with the proposed statements in a 5-level Likert scale. The answers are accompanied by a verbal label (5 = Completely agree, 4 = Agree, 3 = Uncertain, 2 = Disagree, 1 = Do not agree at all) and a graphic representation (a smiley more or less smiling).

Table 1. RE engagement questionnaire for students with ID

Item	Heerink [13]	Appelton et al. [6]	Liem et al. [12]	O'Brien et al. [8]	Skinner et al. [5]
It's nice to use the robot	Attitude	Participation	Self-efficacy	Aesthetic	Enthusiasm
I like working with the robot	Perceived enjoyment	Participation	Self-efficacy	Felt involvement	Enjoyment
I like giving commands to the robot	Perceived Enjoyment	Participation	Self-efficacy	Felt Involvement	Enjoyment
I want to know more about robots	Perceived usefulness	Aspiration	Mastery orientation	Novelty	Interest
I want to continue the activity now	Intention to use	Time on task	Persistence	Endurability	Persistence
I am afraid of making mistakes*	Anxiety	Self-regulating	Anxiety	Perceived Usability	Exertion
I'm afraid of breaking the robot*	Anxiety	Self-regulating	Anxiety	Perceived Usability	Exertion
It is easy to command the robot	Perceived ease to use	Strategizing	Self-efficacy	Perceived Usability	Exertion
I'm scared of the robot*	Anxiety	Self-regulating	Anxiety	Perceived Usability	Enthusiasm
The robot is difficult to use*	Perceived ease to use	Strategizing	Uncertain control	Perceived Usability	Exertion
Papers flashcards with arrow are easy to use	Facilitating Condition	Strategizing	Self-efficacy	Perceived Usability	Effort

(*continued*)

Table 1. (*continued*)

Item	Heerink [13]	Appelton et al. [6]	Liem et al. [12]	O'Brien et al. [8]	Skinner et al. [5]
Digital flashcards with arrow are easy to use	Facilitating Condition	Strategizing	Self-efficacy	Perceived Usability	Effort
I'd spend my free time playing with robots	Intention to use	Value	Persistence	Endurability	Interest
I'm not interested in this activity with robots*	Perceived usefulness	Value	Disengagement	Felt Involvement	Interest
I got bored*	Attitude	Participation	Disengagement	Felt Involvement	Interest
It made me angry*	Attitude	Self-regulating	Disengagement	Felt Involvement	Enjoyment
I want to continue using the robot at school	Intention to use	Completion	Persistence	Endurability	Interest
I want to take the robot home	Intention to use	Completion	Persistence	Endurability	Interest
I want to use it with my schoolmate	Social influence	Participation	Valuing	Endurability	Enthusiasm

There are 13 questions concerning positive conditions (e.g., "It is easy to control the robot") and 6 questions are reported in the opposite form, marked with asterisks (*) in the table (e.g., "The robot is difficult to use"). Despite the adjustments and simplifications, several pupils were not able to read and fill in the questionnaire independently. It was therefore necessary to read the questionnaire and simplify the way of answering. The questionnaire took the form of a structured interview. The adaptations necessary show that the questionnaire is not the easiest or most reliable tool to use in ID contexts. Hence, we suggest turning it into a more interactive conversation and to accompany it with observation.

4 Case Study

4.1 The Educational Activity with Creative Robotics

The classroom activity was carried out individually by the pupils. After a brief presentation, a researcher began with a recited tale of Aesop's The Mouse and the Frog, to introduce the protagonists of the activity. Then the robot, called Rospino© [18], was presented and the pupils were asked to complete it by assembling some of its parts, in-volving them in the simplest stages of its construction. The robot represented the frog in the story and it had to replicate some of the character's actions or movements (e.g., reaching his friend the mouse, entering the pond, reaching the den while avoiding the kite, etc.), moving on a decorated carpet.

The aim was to program the robot's movements (coding), so it would reach the target object or character, through four paths of increasing difficulty. The movement could be programmed in three ways with increasing levels of abstraction: low, physically moving oneself and the robot along the path; intermediate, selecting the directional paper flashcards with arrow, representing arrows, needing to show the robot the path; and high, clicking the digital flashcards with arrows directly through the interactive whiteboard (IWB).

Not knowing the abilities of the pupils, who had very different intellectual levels and coding experiences, it was decided to start the activities at the intermediate level. If the pupil proved to be particularly good at selecting the instructions on paper, he or she went directly to programming software; if he or she had difficulties, the activity could be simplified further with manipulable materials. The total duration of the activity was about 45 min.

4.2 The Participants

Eight young students aged between 15 and 20 years, attending a high school in north-eastern Italy, participated in the case study. Among them were seven males and one female. All of them presented certified ID of various degrees, from mild to moderate. The nature of the disability was different: Down's Syndrome, Autism Spectrum Disor-der, premature birth, and other undefined aetiologies. Only children whose parents gave their permission and willingness to accompany them during extracurricular hours participated. The students were asked if they were interested in participating in the activity. They were given time to see the setting and the materials. They could stop the activity at any time according to their wishes and needs. The pupil's support teacher was present at the activities.

4.3 The Method

The entire activity was video-recorded, and the observation grid was applied retrospectively, using the ELAN coding software to note the number and duration of the behaviours observed. Some indices were transformed into percentages and number of events per minute to make them comparable despite the different duration of the overall recording.

The questionnaire was submitted at the end of the activity, reading support was provided, or the structured interview method was used. It was not possible to administer the instrument to a pupil who, due to excessive fatigue, did not show his willingness. The small number of participants made it impossible to apply inferential statistical analyses, nor to compare the responses of males and females.

5 Results

5.1 Questionnaire and Interview

The pupils declared their involvement in the ER activity, in fact the questions "Is it nice to use the robot?" and "Do I like working with the robot?" obtained the highest score (5) among all respondents, as well as their reciprocal in the negative "Did I get bored with during the activity with the robot?" and "Did this activity with the robot make me angry?" obtained the lowest score (0).

A slight difficulty in the use of the tools (e.g., paper, and digital flashcards) was perceived, as the related questions received slightly lower average scores "Do you like giving commands to the robot?" (4.86), "Is it easy to command the robot?" (4.57), "Is it difficult to use the robot?" (4.43), "Are the digital flashcards with arrows easy to use?" (4.50), but not "Are paper flashcards with arrows easy to use?" which gets full marks (5). The question is explained by the fears that emerge regarding possible mistakes, "Are you afraid of making mistakes?" (3.86) and damage, "Are you afraid of breaking the robot? (4.43).

The boys declared that they wanted to continue the activity immediately (4.29), in their free time (4.57), at school (4.86) and at home (4.43). Some more doubts arose about the possible involvement of their companions in the activity (3.86).

5.2 Observation Grid

The eye contact showed that the pupils were able to focus their attention correctly on the object of each activity: during the narration phase, they observed the interlocutor 67.27% of the time; during the presentation and assembly phase of the robot, their gaze was directed 59.14% of the time to the robot; during the coding phase with paper flashcards, attention was directed to the arrow flashcards for an average of 62.6% of the time among the four proposed exercises; the interactive whiteboard (IWB) received attention 44.72% of the time it was used; and their gaze returned to the robot 51.08% of the time it was moving on the carpet (see Table 2).

The glances directed at other objects are, however, quite relevant to the activity: during the narration phase 11.42% of the time, they directed their gaze at the paper flashcards representing the characters in the story.

During the different phases, eye contact with the interlocutor remained constant, on average 13.71% of the time, as he continued to give explanations or phrases of encouragement to the pupil.

The other object that seems to have attracted their attention, even when it was not at the centre of the activity, is the robot, at 12.63% of the time on average, which is a good sign for an educational robotics workshop.

Table 2. Eye Contact: occurrences in % per activity sections (stage)

Stage	Robot	Flashcard	Speaker	IWB
Narration	02.80	11.42	67.27	00.00
Robot	59.14	00.29	10.70	00.00
Paper Flashcard 1	16.24	58.78	09.94	00.00
Paper Flashcard 2	16.27	66.77	10.54	01.10
Paper Flashcard 3	16.83	62.48	12.54	00.00
Paper Flashcard 4	09.98	62.43	22.83	00.00
Digital Flashcard (IWB)	14.39	07.97	16.97	44.72
Movement (carpet)	51.08	00.16	12.32	00.85

The moment in which eye contact appeared less focused, i.e., the only phase in which attention was directed to the key object less than half the time, was the programming phase on the interactive whiteboard, as the pupils frequently directed their eyes to the digital flashcard and the robot to remember the sequence of commands to be entered.

As regards the occurrences, i.e., the number of glances directed at each object, the pupils shifted the direction of their gaze on average 10 times per phase. Most of the glances were directed at the interlocutor (10.63/min) alternating with the target object of the activity of the moment (see Table 3).

Table 3. Eye Contact: occurrences of the number of glances in minute

Stage	Robot	Flashcard	Speaker	IWB
Narration	01.93	01.73	06.28	00.00
Robot	03.75	00.13	10.42	00.00
Paper Flashcard 1	03.54	05.29	09.66	00.00
Paper Flashcard 2	02.74	04.87	09.71	00.68
Paper Flashcard 3	02.44	04.86	11.77	00.08
Paper Flashcard 4	02.08	04.57	19.33	00.00
Digital Flashcard (IWB)	01.61	01.35	05.92	04.14
Movement (carpet)	03.89	00.09	11.96	00.18

Concerning Facial expressions, smiling was the most frequent, occurring an average of 5 times per phase, approximately 1.4 times per minute. The phases that produced the most smiles were the narration (2.12/min) and the assembly of the robot (2.37/min). The phases that produced fewer smiles were the initial programming activities with the paper flashcards (between 1.16 and 1/min), which probably required more concentration.

Real laughter arose only during the comic moments of the narration (0.32/min), rare in the moments of work with robots (0.09/min) and the interactive whiteboard (0.10/min).

Laughter was completely absent in the phases of work with flashcards which, as already noted, required more effort.

Yawns were only produced by one boy, who left the activity prematurely, stating that he did not feel well due to irregular sleep the night before. Other expressions, including expressions of perplexity, thought and concentration or looks of agreement were produced by only three pupils, the most sociable and least shy of the group.

With regard to Movements, the most frequent was the movement of the head indicating consent, i.e., nodding (2.56/min), followed by significantly less frequent gestures indicating participation in the dialogue and attempts at explanation (1.1/min). Self-handling gestures indicating discomfort were scarce (0.73/min) and body movements to stand up or sit down when not requested were very rare (0.23/min).

Concerning Physical contact with objects, the pupils often tried to touch the objects of the activity spontaneously, on average 4.41 times per phase, or 1.4 times per minute. This occurred especially in the last phases of programming with the digital flashcards (2.5/min), a sign that they had become familiar with the activity, and during the movement of the robot (1.57/min). There were practically no Hesitations in responding (0.15/min), except the few that occurred during the programming phase with the interactive whiteboard (0.30/min), in fact it was the only phase in which it was necessary to give more precise commands on what to touch (0.85/min). The interactive whiteboard is a tool that pupils have in class and daily use. It is possible, however, that during curricular activities teachers explicitly limit contact between pupils and the interactive whiteboard for fear of damage and that this attitude has inhibited pupils from using it spontaneously.

5.3 Verbal Expressions

The pupils produced an average of 14.72 verbal comments per phase, i.e., approximately 6.27 comments per minute. Most of them were whole words or sentences (78%) and only a minority were short interjections (22%). Of these, 51% were produced spontaneously, 37.25% in response to a question and 11.43% in completion or repetition of parts of the interlocutor's sentence. As is normal, there were some boys who were more talkative than others: the maximum verbal exchange was reached by a boy who produced 11.10 comments per minute, 56% of which were whole sentences and 43% short interjections. Of these, 60% were spontaneous, 30% in response and 11% in completion. The smallest interaction was with the girl, evidently more shy, who produced 1.74 comments per minute, of which, however, 98% were words and 2% interjections, thus demonstrating a certain communicative effort. Only 27% were related to spontaneous productions, while 50% were provided in response to questions and 21% to complete sentences.

Response avoidance was almost nil. Even in the rare cases in which the verbal response was late in arriving at the interlocutor's input, it was replaced by eye contact and facial expressions.

6 Discussion

The results that emerged from observation matched the answers in the interviews.

The pupils declared a high involvement in the ER activity and in fact the direction of their gaze, directed more than half of the time to-wards the key object of the activity, confirmed this finding. Facial expressions and body posture also showed conditions of ease and well-being, while the frequency of spontaneous tactile contact with the objects demonstrated their confidence and interest. Expressions of boredom or discomfort were minimal.

The pupils expressed a slight difficulty in using the tools, particularly in the initial phases of programming with the paper flashcards: this was detected by the pupils' constant glances at the interlocutor in search of confirmation, the number of gestures to implement their explanations and the difference in the frequency of smiling expressions and tactile contact with the objects. This clumsiness often tended to diminish in the later stages, a sign that the children were now familiar with the tool. As pointed out, the most difficult device to use was the interactive whiteboard, which required more direct instructions (e.g. "to take a step forward, click on this icon with the forward arrow"). The problem turned out to be related to the fear of making mistakes, breaking something, or causing damage.

The pupils declared they wanted to continue the activity, and the behavioural feedback to this statement can be seen by counting the small number of times the participants tried to get up or sit down to move away from the activity in progress. The fact that they were focused on maintaining visual and tactile contact with objects and inter-locutors is a clear indication of their involvement. It is of course not possible to verify the truth regarding their intentions to continue the activity at other times of the day.

Eye contact, number of occurrences and facial expressions were found to be the most useful indicators: relatively easy to measure, applicable in any context and strongly predictive of the degree of interest and involvement. Particular attention should be paid to the subcategories of facial expressions. Only the more extroverted and higher cognitive level pupils indulged in more complex expressions; for the others the range of expressions was limited to selected basic expressions.

Body movements are more difficult to assess, as they are limited by the type of setting and activity performed. In the design phase of the instruments, it was decided to select only some of the categories listed by Mehrabian [16]. Distance, Stretching and Body Movements were not assessable in a sitting position, as well as Trunk Movements, Swinging and Foot and Leg Movements, which may, however, be interesting to measure in another work context. Also, the category Relaxation/Arm symmetry, although included in the measurement, proved difficult to assess in a sitting position and not very significant with respect to the real perception of well-being of the children. Motor stereotypes were only performed by the boy with autism spectrum syndrome at the end of the activity, indicating emerging fatigue.

Verbal interactions showed a high degree of participation and comfort in the workshop situation, as most of the comments were spontaneously produced and composed of whole words and/or sentences. There was almost no response avoidance. The analysis of verbal comments, however, turned out to be a partial instrument for the measurement of engagement: it is too subject to pupil's differences, linked to cognitive level and pathology. Moreover, it is extremely limited if not combined with the recording of facial expressions and gestures accompanying verbal production.

7 Limits and Conclusions

The triangulation of the instruments proved to be an indispensable method of detection. Each of the three devices proved to be useful for measuring the level of engagement but limited when taken individually.

A major limitation remains the impossibility of establishing standardised parameters that can be used as thresholds to indicate a sufficient range of attention. Eye contact maintained for more than half of the time on the object of interest is a clear sign of engagement in the activity in progress. However, this, and especially the other parameters are very sensitive to personal, setting- and activity-related variations. For example, a high percentage of spontaneously produced words and sentences is a good indicator of social engagement, but a more introverted person will tend to produce fewer verbal comments than a more sociable person, without their engagement being lower. This variability increases further in the presence of syndromes or diseases of different aetiology, as in this case.

Replicating the research in different contexts, it will be possible to refine the tools in order to make them each time more suitable to the setting (e.g., sitting or standing), to the activity (with more or fewer objects used in sequence or at the same time), as well as to different syndromes causing disability (different intellectual levels, socialisation disorders etc.).

From the data, it can be considered that the triad of tools used showed characteristics of completeness, as it covers the four components of engagement; and of ductility as it can be easily modified to make it more suitable to one's own setting; and of practicality, as it can be applied to various contexts, even by teachers.

Note: for reasons of national assessment of Italian university research, the authors must declare which sections each has written, in spite of the fact that work is entirely the result of continuous and intensive collaboration. Sections 2, 3, 4 and 7 are by F. Coin. Sections 1, 5 and 6 are by M. Banzato. Our thanks to P. Tosato, G. Riello and M. Hoffman.

References

1. Indire: Gli snodi dell'inclusione. Monitoraggio dei centri territoriali di supporto (2020). http://www.indire.it. Last accessed 17 Aug 2022
2. Pivetti, M., Di Battista, S., Agatolio, F., Simaku, B., Moro, M., Menegatti, E.: Educational robotics for children with neurodevelopmental disorders: a systematic review. Heliyon **6**(10), e05160 (2020)
3. Kuh, G.D.: What student affairs professionals need to know about student engagement. J. Coll. Stud. Dev. **50**(6), 683–706 (2009)
4. Finn, J.D.: Withdrawing from school. Rev. Educ. Res. **59**(2), 117–142 (1989)
5. Skinner, E.A., Kindermann, T.A., Furrer, C.J.: A motivational perspective on engagement and disaffection: conceptualization and assessment of children's behavioral and emotional participation in academic activities in the classroom. Educ. Psychol. Measur. **69**(3), 493–525 (2009)
6. Appleton, J.J., Christenson, S.L., Kim, D., Reschly, A.L.: Measuring cognitive and psychological engagement: validation of the student engagement instrument. J. Sch. Psychol. **44**(5), 427–445 (2006)

7. Gunuc, S., Kuzu, A.: Student engagement scale: development, reliability and validity. Assess. Eval. High. Educ. **40**(4), 587–610 (2015)
8. O'Brien, H.L., Toms, E.G.: The development and evaluation of a survey to measure user engagement. J. Am. Soc. Inform. Sci. Technol. **61**(1), 50–69 (2010)
9. Jacques, R.D.: The nature of engagement and its role in hypermedia evaluation and design. Unpublished doctoral dissertation, South Bank University, London (1996)
10. Webster, J., Ho, H.: Audience engagement in multimedia presentations. ACM SIGMIS database: the DATABASE for Adv. Inf. Syst. **28**(2), 63–77 (1997)
11. O'Brien, H.L., Toms, E.G.: What is user engagement? A conceptual framework for defining user engagement with technology. J. Am. Soc. Inform. Sci. Technol. **59**(6), 938–955 (2008)
12. Liem, G.A.D., Martin, A.J.: The motivation and engagement scale: theoretical framework, psychometric properties, and applied yields. Aust. Psychol. **47**(1), 3–13 (2012)
13. Heerink, M., Krose, B., Evers, V., Wielinga, B.: Measuring acceptance of an assistive social robot: a suggested toolkit. In: RO-MAN 2009-The 18th IEEE International Symposium on Robot and Human Interactive Communication, pp. 528–533. IEEE, Cambridge (2009)
14. Konradt, U., Sulz, K.: The experience of flow in interacting with a hypermedia learning environment. J. Educ. Multimedia Hypermedia **10**(1), 69–84 (2001)
15. Champion, E.: Applying game design theory to virtual heritage environments. In: Proceedings of the 1st International Conference on Computer Graphics and Interactive Techniques in Australasia and Southeast Asia, pp. 273–274. ACM, New York (2003)
16. Mehrabian, A.: Some referents and measures of nonverbal behavior. Behav. Res. Meth. Instru. **1**(6), 203–207 (1968)
17. Flanders, N.: Analyzing Teacher Behavior. Addison-Wesley, New York (1970)
18. Rospino© Homepage, http://www.projectschool.it. Last accessed 17 Aug 2022

Arguing for a Quantum Computing Curriculum: Lessons from Australian Schools

Andrew E. Fluck(✉)

Carrick, Tasmania, Australia
Andrew.Fluck@utas.edu.au

Abstract. This chapter makes an argument for the development of a quantum computing curriculum. Building from a general look at innovation adoption, it presents survey data from 307 schools on the implementation of a new *Digital Technologies* subject in Australia. It was found that states and territories were taking 6–11 years to report student learning in the subject to parents. On a national basis, the analysis finds implementation is taking nearly 10 years from when the subject was framed, until full delivery. Despite this trajectory, the curriculum was radically revised after only 7 years. This rate of revision makes it difficult for schools to keep up with curriculum policy. With binary digit (bit) storage sizes predicted to fall to atomic levels in the next three decades, it is argued that quantum computing will become increasingly important. A future curriculum for this new computing paradigm therefore needs to be developed as a matter of urgency, so schools can anticipate innovation instead of lagging behind it. The chapter proposes a quantum curriculum for schools be developed as part of an international effort with the scope of recent Informatics frameworks.

Keywords: informatics · computing curricula · case study · quantum computing

1 Introduction

1.1 Technological Innovations

Historians have labelled technological innovations with descriptions such as 'Stone Age', 'Bronze Age', 'Iron Age', '"Agrarian Revolution', 'Industrial Revolution' and 'Information Age'. Each of these pertains to a period of time or a turning point in human thought.

Although many societies and geographic regions passed through these Ages in sequence, they did not all do so at uniform times. Additionally, some societies skipped Ages. For instance, the Bronze Age ended in Africa in 1200 BCE, while it lasted until 600 BCE in Europe (600 years later). Technological discrepancies can lead to friction between societies (e.g., Iron-Age Spaniards in 1532 used steel weapons to defeat Bronze-Age Incas in Peru). Sometimes these technological differences emanate from physical

A. E. Fluck—Independent Educator.

Published by Springer Nature Switzerland AG 2023
T. Keane et al. (Eds.): WCCE 2022, IFIP AICT 685, pp. 137–148, 2023.
https://doi.org/10.1007/978-3-031-43393-1_14

properties, abundance and associated techniques. Thus, to melt Bronze at 913 °C is easier than Iron (1,538 °C) which requires a bloomery or forced-air furnace.

Specific theories have been developed to illustrate the spread of technological innovations. These include Diffusion of Innovations [1], Technology Acceptance Model version 2 [2] and the Unified Theory of Acceptance and Use of Technology [3]. Common to all of these is user perception or expectancy, facilitated by communication, or knowledge of the impact of the technology. In today's world (the Age of the Internet), communication is at close to the speed of light and virtually without cost. Given this convenience, how quickly might we expect innovations to spread across society and into schools?

1.2 Educational Transformations

Although Einstein is credited with the general theory of Relativity from 1915, it is not yet taught in most Australian Primary/Elementary schools. An exception is the 'Einstein-First project' from 2013 [4]. Thus, the time between new knowledge generation and educational adoption can be over a century.

One might only speculate how long it was before flint knapping tuition was discontinued as metals began to be smelted. The pace of educational transformation appears to be only loosely connected with the adoption of technological innovations in society more broadly. One argument would be that education is more about mind-tools like language, mathematics, emotions and culture than specific physical devices.

Hattie [5] and others have found ways to gauge the effectiveness of educational innovations, using effect sizes, effectiveness ratings or improvement indices [6]. The Brookings Institute uses a 'leapfrog potential' model, one component of which is the Substitution, Augmentation, Modification, and Redefinition (SAMR) framework for technology [7]. However, many of these metrics only provide a comparison between a control/traditional learning and teaching process, and a new pedagogical approach.

It could be said that numeracy is a subset of Mathematics, and Literacy is congruent to Literature (but not identical). Technological transformations can lead to curriculum upheaval, and the teaching of new, different content, skills, attitudes. So, it is difficult to find a comparison for efficacy metrication if the educational transformation pertains to Mathematics when the only comparator is a Numeracy skill. Still harder, when the new skill is the use of very advanced Mathematics for the student age-range under consideration [8] or any other similar technology-mediated educational transformation. There seems to be a research gap in determining the time it takes for technological innovations to be implemented in school classrooms.

These concepts of technological innovation and educational transformation are now explored in a case study emerging from developments in Australia.

2 Australian Case Study

2.1 Background

Within Australia, there is considerable regional autonomy for school curricula, but the nationally developed Australian Curriculum is used by most institutions. Variations occur by state/territory and school funding arrangements. Approximately 30% of schools operate independent of sole government funding. In 2015 Ministers of Education endorsed the Digital Technologies curriculum, making it available to all schools nationally for the first time [9]. Within the overarching Australian Curriculum, computer use in schools is divided into 'ICT' and 'Digital Technologies'. ICT involves Digital Literacy and learning with a computer (as a consumer). This is the pedagogical adaptation to student computer use. Digital Technologies (elsewhere known as Computer Science, Informatics or Computing) involves computational thinking, programming and learning about computers (as a creator). This chapter now examines the introduction of this new subject.

2.2 Australian Computer Society Survey of Schools

The Educator's Committee of the Australian Computer Society decided to inform policy advice by collecting data on this situation. A national survey was conducted in November 2020–April 2021 and received data from 307 schools. These included primary, high school and senior colleges (covering students aged from 5–18). Responses came from government schools, independent and Catholic schools. It focused on the Digital Technologies subject in the Australian Curriculum. The representativeness of the sample differed by state and territory, with X^2 (7, n = 243) = 131.4, $p = .000$. Four states/territories (ACT, NSW, NT & VIC) were under-represented. The other four (QLD, SA, WA and TAS) were over-represented.

Looking at the veracity of the survey respondents, there was some confusion about this distinction between ICT (as a general capability) and Digital Technologies (as a discrete subject). One of the survey questions asked:

> *List three software programs/tools (or websites) students use most in their learning of Digital Technologies/IT over the entire year.*

The answers to the question were analysed to determine which tools were strictly relevant to Digital Technologies, and thus the accuracy of respondent knowledge. Programming tools/sites such as Scratch, Minecraft, Code.org and robotics were clearly relevant to the Digital Technologies subject. However, online literacy learning apps, for example, focused on literacy reading/writing/inferencing skills. Therefore, this second kind of tool was not classified as strictly relevant to the Digital Technologies subject. Khan Academy was also a popular response, but its popularity for programming/coding videos put it into the 'relevant' category (Table 1).

This failure of teacher-respondents to accurately identify Digital Technologies/Information Technologies tools was worrying.

The average time spent teaching Digital Technologies closely matched the design time in the Australian Curriculum. The time spent per week ranged from 1.1 h for students aged 4–10 years to 1.9 h for students aged 13–14 years.

Table 1. Proportion of teacher-selected tools strictly relevant to Digital Technologies/Information Technology.

Student Year levels	Percentage
F – Year 2	30%
Years 3–4	36%
Years 5–6	60%
Years 7–8	70%
Years 9–10	60%

Less than half (46%) of responding schools reported operating a bring-your-own-device policy. Where such policies operated, they tended to focus on tablets for students aged less than 10 years, and laptops for older students.

In half the schools, Digital Technologies was reported as taught in an integrated fashion with other subjects for students in Primary/Elementary schools (aged up to 12). However, it was taught as a separate subject in the majority of Secondary/High schools with older students.

Once again, about half the teachers of Digital Technologies in Primary schools were untrained in the subject. However, in High schools, this out-of-area proportion dropped to 20% when they were teaching students 15–16 years old (Table 2).

Table 2. Proportion of teachers of Digital Technologies working outside their area of expertise (109 to 136 schools responded, according to year-group) [10]

Student Year	Proportion of schools where more than half the teachers do not have Digital Technologies expertise
P/K/F – Year 2	56%
Years 3–4	57%
Years 5–6	54%
Years 7–8	31%
Years 9–10	20%
Years 11–12	12%

Finally, a comment from one teacher-respondent read as follows:

The Digital Technologies curriculum is very heavy on jargon which makes it really hard for teachers with no formal expertise in that area to teach comfortably – it does in fact almost scare them away from teaching it. It would be good to have a curriculum in plain language (all key terms explained) and have links to places where teachers can find more information before they have to teach something [10]

This lack of confidence was echoed by many, emphasizing the gap between current schooling requirements and their own education when they were younger. It is also a comment reflective of the rapid change of the technology from niche to society-wide entitlement over the span of a generation.

The data were interrogated further to see if reporting to parents had any relation to the time spent teaching Digital Technologies (DT), time spent on professional learning and proportion of teachers out of area. There was a weak, but significant, correlation between mean extent of reporting Digital Technologies from Kindergarten to Year 10 to parents, and the mean time devoted to teaching the subject, r (198) = .199, p = .005. Also, there was a weak but significant correlation between mean reporting of Digital Technologies K-10 and mean time spent on teacher professional learning for the subject, r (196) = .225, p = .001. However, no significant correlation was found between mean reporting of Digital Technologies K-10 and mean proportion of teachers out of area, r (200) = −.064, p = .364.

Therefore, increased professional learning and more time spent teaching Digital Technologies are associated with a greater proportion of schools reporting student achievements in the subject to parents/guardians. That teaching 'out of area' made little impact on the proportion of schools reporting student progress, is either a testament to the generic ability of teachers to master any subject, or to their leadership for insisting the subject be taught and reported despite this missing background in their staff.

3 Time from Innovation to Educational Implementation

Figure 1 shows how the proportion of respondent schools reporting student progress with Digital Technologies varied by state/territory within Australia. The report used this question to capture where the subject was taught, assessed and student progress monitored. All of those would have to occur for a report on learning to be sent to parents/guardians. Answers in each school were by year-level bands, so up to seven responses per school were possible (for a K-12 school).

In Western Australia, 95% of schools stated they report student achievements in the Digital Technologies subject to parents. In New South Wales (the most populous state), only 54% of schools stated this reporting to parents occurred. This could be explained by the variation of the Australian Curriculum used in that state, where the subject is taught integrated with the Science subject. In Tasmania, only 56% of schools reported Digital Technologies learnings to parents (Table 3).

So, after six years of the Digital Technologies subject being available, actual implementation in schools was patchy. About 21% of schools were yet to deliver the subject. This could be explained by the lack of obligation imposed by government guidelines. In Tasmania, these guidelines only mandated reporting for English/Literacy and Mathematics/Numeracy. Using the standard S-curve for adoption growth, full reporting (including Digital Technologies) is expected to begin in 2024 [11 p. 3]. That will make it nearly 10 years between when the subject was framed, and actual nationwide delivery.

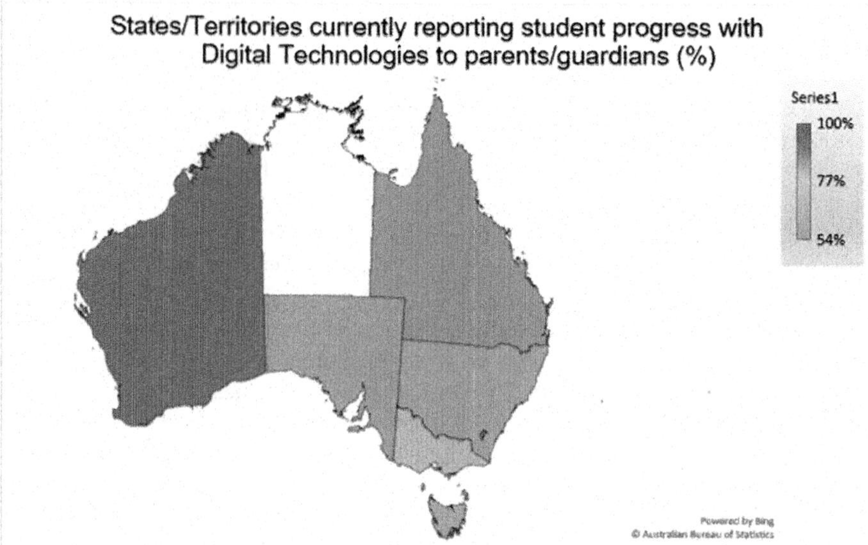

Fig. 1. Extent of Digital Technologies reporting to parents/guardians [10]

Table 3. Regional reporting of learning achievement for Digital Technologies to parents – and expected year for full implementation [10]

State/territory	Proportion of schools reporting Digital Technologies learning achievements to parents by end of 2020	N (year level bands)	Implementation progress rate over 6 years (% per year since 2015)	Expected year for 100% implementation (linear extrapolation)
Northern Territory	100%	3	17%	2021
Western Australia	95%	106	16%	2021
Australian Capital Territory	93%	15	16%	2021
Queensland	86%	205	14%	2022
South Australia	85%	142	14%	2022
Victoria	66%	99	11%	2024
Tasmania	56%	52	9%	2026
New South Wales	54%	80	9%	2026

To complicate matters, a substantial review of the subject curriculum will become available for schools to use from the start of 2023. In the revised subject, the number of content descriptors for Digital Technologies will grow by 65% (from 43 to 71). This reflects some advances in the field, but also responds to the teacher-respondent quoted above. Thus, this fragmentation makes learning outcomes more accessible to teachers, turning complex outcomes into two simpler outcomes. The proportion of learning outcomes related to coding/programming will decrease from 14% to 8% [12]. This is much less than in other jurisdictions, ranging from 17% (Singapore) to 28% (New Zealand).

Although the period from publication of the initial Australian Curriculum in 2015 to the revision in 2023 was eight years, this was less than the expected implementation period of ten years. The curriculum is being revised at a faster pace than many schools can implement it. Schools are finding it difficult to keep pace with technological innovation.

4 Future Innovations and Transformations

4.1 Arguing for a Quantum Computing Curriculum

Given this conclusion, what can be done about it? It is now argued that schools cannot continue to lag innovation, but educational leaders need to anticipate change to remain relevant in current society.

In many ways, the Digital Technologies subject is evolving faster than government agencies can revise the guiding curriculum documents. The current curriculum is largely based on digital computers using binary digits (bits) and procedural programming. The rise of Quantum Computing challenges these fundamental concepts.

Australia has nurtured some promising technology innovations in quantum computing. These include room-temperature qubits from nitrogen vacancies in diamond [13, 14] and work at Michelle Simmons' group at the University of New South Wales with qubits made from Phosphorous atoms in Silicon [15]. Therefore, it is relevant to illustrate how some of these technological innovations can become educational transformations.

While some universities are actively engaging in this area of study [16, 17], few schools were found doing so. There is scant evidence of quantum computing curricula for schools. A search of the Education Resources Information Center (ERIC) database for *quantum computing* in 2022 revealed only 18 items (in a library of 1.7 million records, dating back to 1966). Another search for "*quantum computing*" *curric** in the IEEE Xplore database found only 13 articles. In both databases, the results mostly related to higher, rather than school education or focused on quantum mechanics instead. Those that were school-centred focused on teaching approaches rather than curriculum structures.

Among the teaching approaches, gamification is popular to engage and stimulate student learning. Nita et al. [18] analysed this using their *Quantum Odyssey* puzzle game software with 50 UK high school students, and found visual understanding of quantum computing topics was improved.

Entanglement is a key quantum computing concept for students to understand, and was the focus of two reports. Satanassi [19] described an early international project and compared Finnish with Italian approaches which were evaluated with 26 upper secondary school students. That used a teleportation example to engage students with entanglement via narrative and technical methods. In so doing, they blended elements of quantum communication with quantum computing. Marckwordt et al. [20] describe how high school students (ages 13 to 18) can be taught about the quantum concept of "entanglement" through dodgeball.

Further empirical evidence that quantum computing can be taught in schools comes from Hughes et al. [21]. They describe their experience with the IBM quantum computers and 45 high school students who accessed an online course with interactive problem sets and simulation-based labs. Salehi et al. [22] gathered data in 10 countries from 317 students, most of whom were aged over 18. They introduced students to quantum computing concepts through linear algebra and IBM Qiskit. Outside Europe, Angara et al. [23] took a wider view of USA and Canadian year 9–12 students. That team examined the learning materials supporting the IBM Qiskit language and IBM online quantum computers. They commented that the "Computer Science Teachers Association (CSTA), the preeminent American Computer Science education association behind initiatives like the K–12 CS Standards,19 has demonstrated limited engagement in the area of Quantum Computing Education preuniversity" (p. 13). In short, the literature is scant on school quantum computing curricula in the broader sense.

4.2 Other Teaching Approaches

As a teaching stimulus, students can calculate the storage volume required for a single binary digit (bit) from the dimensions of historical storage devices. For instance, the mercury delay line in 1951 measured 110 × 880 × 80 mm and held 12,800 bits (605 mm^3 per bit). By 2018, a micro-Secure Digital (SD) card measured 15 × 11 × 1 mm and held 64 GB bits (2.58×10^{-9} mm^3 per bit). Figure 2 shows how this plot can be diagrammed and extended.

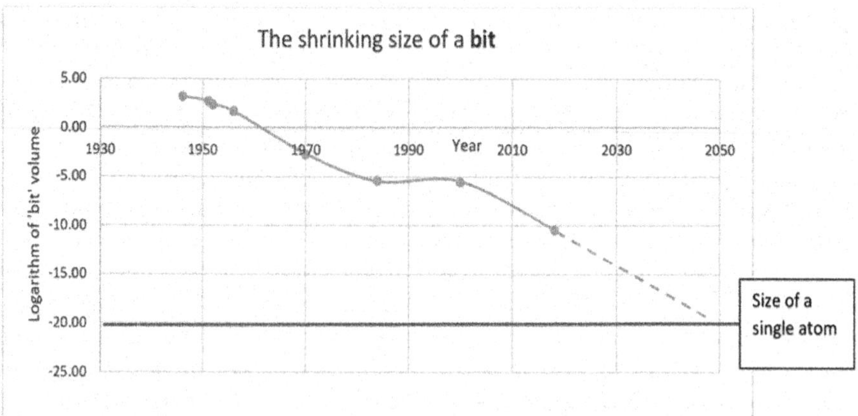

Fig. 2. Size v. date plot of computer memory capacity

From this information, students can predict the year when the storage space for a single bit will become as small as an atom. Facing this date, they can be introduced to the probabilistic features of qubits, entanglement and superposition.

Various resources are available for schools to explain this transition from the defined procedural use of bits to the non-deterministic use of qubits. These include [24]:

- Michael Nielsen - Quantum computing for the determined [video lectures] (https://michaelnielsen.org/blog/quantum-computing-for-the-determined)
- IBM - Qiskit Textbook (beta) https://qiskit.org/textbook-beta/; Quantum Composer (https://quantum-computing.ibm.com/composer/files/new)
- Microsoft - Quantum Katas (https://github.com/Microsoft/QuantumKatas); with Brilliant - Quantum Computing (course) (https://brilliant.org/courses/quantum-computing/)
- Jack Ceroni – Quantum Computing resources for high school students (https://unitary.fund/posts/high_school_resources.html)
- Cirq 1.0 on Google's Quantum Virtual Machine using a qubit grid. (https://quantumai.google/education)

Despite the availability of these educational resources, it remains to be seen how long it will take for Australian curricula to include Quantum Computing, or for schools to report on student learning achievement.

4.3 The Role of Informatics Frameworks

Other jurisdictions are recognizing the importance of being responsive to technological innovations and agile with consequent educational transformations. The K–12 Computer Science Framework [25] was designed by some USA states and national stakeholder associations such as the Association for Computing Machinery (ACM). That framework is grounded in algorithmic digital computing. It has great advice for adopters regarding teacher professional development (which the case study above identified as important). Also, there is good regard for early childhood education. The writers look at future research, and particularly implementation. However, there is no mention of quantum techniques or non-deterministic computing such as machine learning.

There was no such omission from the CC2020 Report [26]. Aimed at undergraduate programs rather than schools, this curriculum identified quantum computing as an emerging area. Deloitte had nominated quantum computers as a 'macro force' (p. 89).

More recently, *Informatics for All* (<informaticsforall.org> [27] is a broader, international coalition aiming to provide a framework for national curricula. It follows on from the Rome declaration [28], which called on nations to ensure every child is taught the basics of information technology. The Framework is quite effusive on Artificial Intelligence and Machine Learning, so one might hope this aspect will be adopted Europe-wide and further. However, quantum computing and communications are absent at this stage.

5 Future Moves

Childe, Bestwick, Yeomans et al. [29] have filed a UK patent application for a quantum key distribution protocol. This documents a method whereby a commercial enterprise can operate a satellite for quantum communication between two ground points. The commercial enterprise will be unable to intercept the secret messages being passed through the satellite, thus provide un-hackable communications as a service. Such technological advances have the potential to have massive impacts on financial, military and social spheres, both beneficial and evil. The question to ask, is how long will it take for the effects to be understood, and then how much longer for school students to be taught about them? Should quantum communications be considered as part of a school curriculum on quantum computing?

6 Conclusion

The imperatives of technological innovation and the implied need for educational transformation encourages us to reflect upon existing school curricula. There will continue to be tension between the old and the new. On one hand, it is valid to want new citizens to think for themselves, be adaptable in many future circumstances, and not rely upon technology to survive. In their younger years, they need to develop key mind-tools such as language, literacy and numeracy. On the other hand, increasing numbers of students acquire pocket-sized devices in their teens that can translate foreign languages in real time, provide instant global communications and provide other computing benefits. It would seem anachronistic to forbid them the opportunity to extend their personal capacities by not teaching how to access and beneficially use these devices. To transform education with computers requires a proactive stance for schools to keep pace with innovations. In this regard, an international effort to prepare a quantum computing curriculum for schools would be of great value.

Such a curriculum should articulate with emerging quantum computing curricula in higher education [17]. It should link the fundamental concepts for quantum computing to appropriate learning ages and look at visual, intellectual and attitudinal understandings for school students. Ideally, it will fit within a broader Informatics framework to be useful in schools right around the world. It is often useful to accompany such a niche curriculum document with practical teaching examples, but care should be taken not to link too strongly with any specific software development tool.

References

1. Rogers, E.: Diffusion of Innovations, 5th edn. Free Press (2003)
2. Venkatesh, V., Davis, F.D.: A theoretical extension of the technology acceptance model: four longitudinal field studies. Manage. Sci. **46**(2), 186–204 (2000). https://doi.org/10.1287/mnsc.46.2.186.11926
3. Venkatesh, V., Morris, M.G., Davis, G.B., Davis, F.D.: User acceptance of information technology: toward a unified view. MIS Q. **27**(3), 425–478 (2003)
4. Kaur, T., Blair, D., Moschilla, J., Stannard, W., Zadnik, M.: Teaching Einsteinian physics at schools: part 1, models and analogies for relativity. Phys. Educ. **52**(6), 065012 (2017). https://doi.org/10.1088/1361-6552/aa83e4
5. Hattie, J.: Visible Learning: A Synthesis of Over 800 Meta-analyses Relating to Achievement. Routledge (2009)
6. What works clearinghouse: Procedures Handbook v. 4.1 (2020). https://ies.ed.gov/ncee/wwc/Docs/referenceresources/WWC-Procedures-Handbook-v4-1-508.pdf

7. Winthrop, R.: We studied 3,000 new education ideas — here's how to choose the best. Apolitical (2018). https://apolitical.co/solution-articles/en/we-studied-3000-new-education-ideas-heres-how-to-choose-the-best
8. Fluck, A.E., et al.: Large effect size studies of computers in schools: calculus for kids and science-ercise. In: Tatnall, A., Webb, M. (eds.) Tomorrow's Learning: Involving Everyone, pp. 70–80, Springer Nature, Switzerland (2017)
9. Australian Curriculum, Assessment and Reporting Authority [ACARA]: The Australian Curriculum: Technology – Digital Technologies (v.8.4) (2022). https://www.australiancurriculum.edu.au/f-10-curriculum/technologies/digital-technologies/
10. Australian Computer Society [ACS]: ACS response to the 2020/21 Australian Curriculum Review (2021). https://www.acs.org.au/content/dam/acs/acs-public-policy/ACS%20response%20to%20F-10%20Australian%20Curriculum%20review.pdf
11. Department of Education, Tasmania (DoE): Communicating Learning Progress with Families Policy v.2 (2020). https://documentcentre.education.tas.gov.au/_layouts/15/DocIdRedir.aspx?ID=TASED-1060461114-3674
12. Fluck, A.E., Girgla, A.: Changing computer curricula in Australia. In: Passey, D., Leahy, D., Williams, L., Holvikivi, J., Ruohonen, M. (eds.) Digital Transformation of Education and Learning – Past, Present and Future. OCCE 2021. IFIP Advances in Information and Communication Technology, vol. 642. Springer, Cham (2022). https://doi.org/10.1007/978-3-030-97986-7_12
13. Hare, J.: Quantum computing leap puts ANU spin-off on $1b track. Australian Financial Review (2021). https://www.afr.com/technology/quantum-computing-leap-puts-anu-spin-off-on-1b-track-20210323-p57d6v
14. Náfrádi, B., Choucair, M., Dinse, K.P., et al.: Room temperature manipulation of long lifetime spins in metallic-like carbon nanospheres. Nat. Commun. **7**, 12232 (2016). https://doi.org/10.1038/ncomms12232
15. Kobayashi, T., Salfi, J., Chua, C., et al.: Engineering long spin coherence times of spin–orbit qubits in silicon. Nat. Mater. **20**, 38–42 (2021)
16. Friedrichs, C.L., et al.: An analysis of quantum computing courses world-wide. In: Proceedings of Seidenberg Student Faculty Research Day (2021). http://csis.pace.edu/~ctappert/srd/a5.pdf
17. Piattini, M.: Training Needs in Quantum Computing. In: Proceedings of the 1st International Workshop on the QuANtum SoftWare Engineering & pRogramming. Talavera de la Reina, Spain, 11–12 February 2020. http://ceur-ws.org/Vol-2561/paper2.pdf
18. Nita, L.: Inclusive learning for quantum computing: supporting the aims of quantum literacy using the puzzle game Quantum Odyssey (2021)
19. Satanassi, S.: Quantum computers for high school: design of activities for an ISEE teaching module. Master's Thesis. Universita di Bologna (2018)
20. Marckwordt, J., Muller, A., Harlow, D., Franklin, D., Landsberg, R.H.: Entanglement ball: using dodgeball to introduce quantum entanglement. Phys. Teach. **59**, 613–616 (2021)
21. Hughes, C., Isaacson, J., Turner, J., Perry, A., Sun, R.: Teaching quantum computing to high school students. Phys. Teach. **60**, 187–189 (2022)
22. Salehi, Ö., Seskir, Z., Tepe, İ: A computer science-oriented approach to introduce quantum computing to a new audience. IEEE Trans. Educ. **65**(1), 1–8 (2022)
23. Angara, P.P., Stege, U., MacLean, A., Müller, H.A., Markham, T.: Teaching Quantum Computing to High-School-Aged Youth: A Hands-On Approach. IEEE Trans. Quantum Eng. **3**, 3100115 (2022)
24. Quantum computing report: Education: Resources (2022). https://quantumcomputingreport.com/education/
25. K12CS: A Vision for K–12 Computer Science (2016). https://k12cs.org/wp-content/uploads/2016/09/K%E2%80%9312-Computer-Science-Framework.pdf

26. ACM & IEEE-CS: Computing Curricula 2020: CC2020 – Paradigms for Global Computing Education (2020)
27. I4ALL: The Informatics Reference Framework for Schools (2022). https://www.informaticsforall.org/wp-content/uploads/2022/03/Informatics-Reference-Framework-for-School-release-February-2022.pdf
28. I4ALL: The Rome Declaration (2019). https://www.informaticsforall.org/rome-declaration/
29. Childe, B., Bestwick, D., Williams, D., Iqbal, O., Yeomans, A.J.V.: Quantum key distribution protocol (GB2590064). Intellectual Property Office – UK (2019). https://patentimages.storage.googleapis.com/87/c0/c3/ed62a6fdf25490/GB2590064A.pdf

Characterization of Knowledge Transactions in Design-Based Research Workshops

Elsa Paukovics(✉)

University of Geneva, 1211 Geneva, Switzerland
elsa.paukovics@unige.ch

Abstract. PLAY is a design-based research project which gathers different communities of experts in collaborative workshops. Those latter are designed to create an educational game (Geome) to guide classroom visits to the Museum of Nature at Sion in Switzerland. Theoretical models in the sciences of education are tested through design, experimentation and evaluation of the game. In this paper, we investigate knowledge sharing during collaborative workshops. More specifically, processes of knowledge translation in verbal interactions are under our scope. We analyze the game Geome as a boundary object. We characterize uni- or multilateral transactions according to how reciprocally the meaning of knowledge is negotiated. We also note the explicitness dimension of translations. These transactions are finally addressed in the light (i) of the development of skills among actors and (ii) the creation of scientific knowledge.

Keywords: Knowledge Translation · Collaboration · Design-Based Research · Knowledge Co-Production · Boundary Object

1 Introduction

The implementation of a digital learning environment relies on the collaboration between different communities of experts. In particular, it lies at the intersection of computer science, design, and pedagogical skills. Bryk [1] reports on the need to develop the improvement paradigm in education. It involves recognizing "the complexity of the work of education and the wide variability in outcomes that our systems currently produce" [1, p. 467]. In this sense, design-based research is a method of conducting research aimed at the collaborative development of learning environments which integrate technologies as solutions to meet a practical need [1]. The solutions developed provide an opportunity to test theoretical models based on knowledge from educational practices and theories in educational sciences. Users and designers of the solution (teachers, learners, and other professionals in the educational field) are thus involved in the development and research activities with educational scientists. They participate together in meetings, design thinking workshops, research seminars, experimentation of prototypes, etc. It raises the issue of collaboration in the creation of knowledge. How do different professionals understand each other? What and how is the knowledge produced? Through which process? How does the involvement of different experts affect the creation of this knowledge?

T. Keane et al. (Eds.): WCCE 2022, IFIP AICT 685, pp. 149–159, 2023.
https://doi.org/10.1007/978-3-031-43393-1_15

Given that design-based research is in full expansion [2], this paper discusses the epistemic and methodological issues of this approach which supports the development of learning environments integrating technologies. Specifically, a case study is conducted about a particular design-based research (called PLAY) aimed at the design, experimentation and evaluation of a learning game. The collaboration and sharing of knowledge between professionals from different fields are studied. We aim at understanding the process of knowledge creation in the specific context.

2 Theoretical Framework: Knowledge Sharing Process in Design-Based Research

The nature, source, management, and ownership of knowledge are a non-exhaustive list of topics studied in a number of sectors of activity (economics, law, anthropology, education, etc.). Didactics theories define knowledge as "what allows us to train a capability" in a more or less conscious way [3, p. 61] in terms of "power to act in a situation". We raise these questions in regard to the framework of *meta-didactical transposition* [4]. This framework treats knowledge as a social construction which takes place in interactions. We study the construction of knowledge in design-based research where professionals with various skills are collaborating to develop technology-enhanced learning environments [5]. Knowledge co-construction requires the establishment of a shared interpretative space [6], in other words, a common background between researchers and practitioners which is built up as the collaboration evolves [6, 7].

Indeed, knowledge co-construction involves knowledge sharing. This sharing can be analyzed in exchanges during collaborative workshops [7–10]. Some knowledge, specific to the different communities involved in the collaboration, is shared and negotiated during the workshops [11, 12]. Knowledge from educational practices, knowledge from scientific educational theories, and computer knowledge are notably articulated in collaboration processes [13]. However, this knowledge should not be considered in a dichotomous way. Each actor, regardless of his or her field of activity, is mobilizing both practical and theoretical knowledge. Sanchez et al. [14] analyze the praxeologies, i.e., the theoretical arguments mobilized by actors to justify practices, of actors engaged in the collaboration of a design-based research. The co-construction of knowledge is based on the sharing of praxeologies, which means the establishment of common understandings regarding theories about professional practices [14].

2.1 Boundary Objects to Share Knowledge

Another way to study knowledge sharing consists in the analysis of boundary objects. The boundary object [15, 16] is a theoretical concept invoked to analyze collaboration between several communities working together, particularly in the field of education [12]. These are objects which can be abstract and/or concrete. These are both embedded in action, subject to reflection, located in a situation and in a temporality [12]. A boundary object embodies common and generic knowledge acquired by all professionals. However, the boundary object is also composed of specific knowledge, which is not shared by all, but remains specific to certain actors according to their expertise. The object's development relies on this knowledge both specifically and generically. Consider the example of an online educational platform: the platform can be studied as a boundary object (Fig. 1).

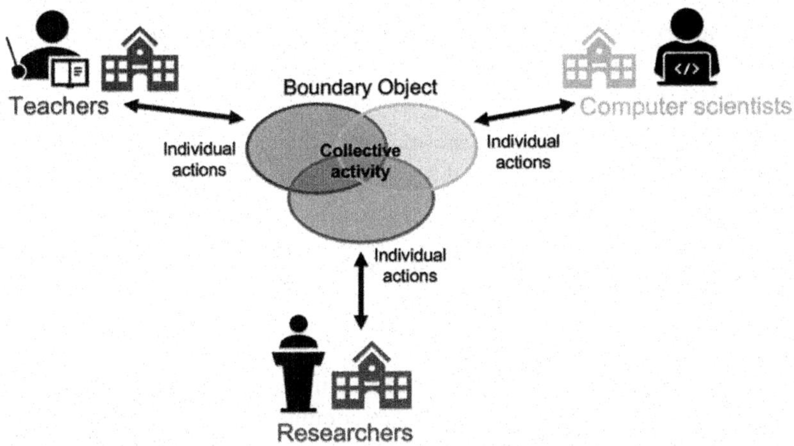

Fig. 1. Representation of boundary object shared by teachers, researchers and computer scientists

Computer scientists, teachers and educational researchers collaborate to develop this platform. Each actor has his own representation of this platform according to his field of expertise. The computer scientists may conceive the platform as a web interface with different functionalities, while the teachers will represent the platform as a learning environment based on the didactization of learning objectives. Since the platform is at the center of the collaboration, developers' work is interdependent with teachers' work.

2.2 Knowledge Transactions

Boundary objects are mobilized with the framework of *meta-didactical transposition* [4] to study the interactions between teachers and researchers involved in design-based research. The boundary object also allows the sharing of representations and knowledge between teachers and researchers. Carlile [17, 18] distinguishes three levels of knowledge sharing according to the degree of novelty of knowledge. By degree of novelty, it is implied: how familiar an actor is with the knowledge being shared, or in other words, to what degree knowledge is shared between two or more individuals. These three levels of knowledge sharing are represented in the Fig. 1. The bottom of the triangle represents the knowledge already known by both actors while the top shows what is not yet known (Fig. 2).

Carlile [17] thus identifies three levels of knowledge sharing: the syntactic level, the semantic level and the pragmatic level. The syntactic level assumes that the knowledge is known and shared by the individuals. It is then simply a matter of agreeing on the vocabulary which is used. There is no negotiation of meaning but only an agreement on the syntax. The semantic level involves a negotiation of the meaning of knowledge:

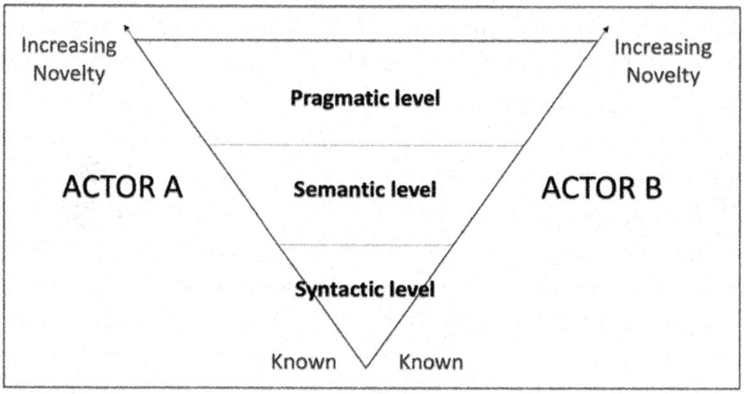

Fig. 2. An integrated Framework for Managing Knowledge Across Boundaries, taken from Carlile [17, p. 558]

"A semantic approach recognizes that even if a common syntax or language is present, interpretations are often different which makes communication and collaboration difficult." [17, p. 444]. The negotiation process at this semantic level is called translation. The third level is the pragmatic level: At this level, the question is not the vocabulary or the meaning of knowledge anymore but the interest in this knowledge. At the pragmatic level, there is a lack of common interest in knowledge. A transformation of the representations of the knowledge in question as specific knowledge to be shared is necessary. In the context of R&D, the transformation can be facilitated by the setup of workshops aiming at understanding the objectives of the project and creating common interests [19].

On the basis of these theoretical insights, this paper focuses on shared knowledge through boundary objects. More specifically, it raises questions about knowledge transaction processes [17] between the different professionals involved in the design of technology-enhanced learning environments.

3 Case Study of the PLAY Project

To address these questions, we conduct a comprehensive case study. The case study is a methodological approach that allows us to consider a multitude of variables in order to study a phenomenon in a complex and contextual manner [20]. This approach is inductive, in the sense that our object of study is specified as the research progresses [21]. Our study is in line with the constructivist paradigm conceptualized by Guba and Lincoln, considering that there is no single reality but that reality is socially constructed, multiple and relative [22]. Therefore, our study aims at building a comprehensive model of the observed phenomenon [23].

Our case of study is a research project supported by the Swiss National Science Foundation (SNF) which runs for over four years. This project is led by a researcher specialized in educational technologies and learning games. This project intends to develop an educational game (named Geome) in mixed reality (both digital and tangible) to be used in the context of school visits in a museum of nature. The main research purpose is to study the epistemic development of students through the game experience with Geome at the museum. The project was initiated following the expression of a specific need of the museum's director. Indeed, his wish was to sensitize and familiarize the students to the concept of the Anthropocene in a playful way during the classroom visits to the museum. The game is designed, tested and evaluated in a collaborative way by two graduate researchers, two PhD students, the museum director, three to four museum staff, one to two computer developers, three teachers and, one teacher trainer. Some actors come and others leave as the project progresses. Some professionals are also invited to intervene on an ad hoc basis (e.g., a graphic designer, researchers in computer science, etc.).

Researcher1 (Res1) is the lead researcher for the PLAY project. He oversees the creation of Geome and all research activities. Other researchers (e.g. PhD students) are involved in the research activities and in the design of the game-based learning situation. The computer developers are working mainly on the computer development of Geome (tablet application), its implementation in the museum, and the data collection and storage. The museum employees (e.g. Mus3) explain the learning needs of the museum related to the concept of the Anthropocene and the natural sciences. Teachers (e.g. Teacher2) bring their students to the museum to test Geome. All these actors participate in several workshops concerning Geome as a learning game. They are all involved in the development of this digital learning environment based on their own professional expertise and their field of activity. Workshops are organized to work collaboratively on the design, experimentation and evaluation of the game. These activities aim at testing and developing theoretical scientific models of what a game actually is, of gamification and of epistemic development.

We attend these collaborative workshops with the purpose of collecting data through participant observation. The data collected are (i) general project documentation and (ii) video recordings of the collaborative workshops. In total, 19 excerpts from 7 meetings were subjected to discourse analysis and thematic analysis, based on a shared object analysis model [9]. The workshops gather from 6 to 16 participants. Most of the time about 10 professionals are present. We thus identify shared objects with the characteristics of the boundary object and analyze the knowledge transactions [17].

4 Analyses

4.1 The Learning Game Geome as a Boundary Object

Our analysis leads us to identify the game Geome as a boundary object established through workshops along the project. Geome is the design-based research's product in the sense that it is the technology-enhanced learning solution which needs to be developed and tested. It is an object that is both concrete and abstract, anchored in time, in action and in reflection. The actors collaborate to design this product from their different expertise and competences.

The educational game Geome assumes the role of a boundary object as a product of design-based research. Geome is made up of several components more or less shared by the actors. Its components are based on different types of knowledge. The actors exchange some of this knowledge in order to contribute to Geome development. The "metaphor of the game" has been identified as one component of the boundary object (Geome) [9]. We define game metaphors as the symbols, images or stories used to gamify learning objectives [24]. The metaphor must ensure consistency between the mechanics of the game and, the meaning of the knowledge constructed by the students. The concept of metaphor [24] thus is an element of the gamification model. Several researchers participating in the workshop are simultaneously working to develop this model [24]. In that sense, the notion of metaphor is a scientific knowledge being conceptualized.

4.2 Verbatim Analyses

Based on the 19 excerpts analyzed (from 7 workshops), we have identified processes of translation as a negotiation of meaning [17] regarding some of the knowledge which constitute the game Geome. One of these translations relates to the metaphor of the game. Indeed, the word "metaphor" is mobilized by the actors to characterize and discuss the design choices of the game. The researcher (Res1) does not mention that the metaphor is a scientific notion that he is currently working on. Furthermore, no definition of the term is clearly formulated. In a first workshop (about 180 min with nine participants), the researcher (Res1) qualifies the proposals twice to one of the museum collaborators (Mus3) with the term "metaphor":

> "We could imagine that we have, for example, a possibility of capture and a possibility of (animal) domestication, and if we decide to domesticate the animal, it is a bit like those old Tamagotchi with which you decide to care, to feed, etc." (...) (Mus3)
>
> (...) "Yes that would indeed be a more interesting metaphor." (Res1)

However, Res1 does not define the notion "metaphor" or make the meaning given to it explicit. Nor does he specify that metaphor is a theoretical concept in the process of being conceptualized. He simply mobilizes the term to qualify Mus3 remarks. In a next workshop (about 120 min with eight participants), Mus3 expresses his concern about the design choices of the game by using the term "metaphor":

> "I'm ultimately coming to this metaphor of the Tree of Life (element of the game) which is actually a relationship, I mean a metaphor for our relationship to nature. But in fact, students will take this metaphor at face value " (...) (Mus3)
>
> "I think, in terms of the game, you shouldn't try to explain everything through the game, you know." (...) "Because if we try to make a game in which we will finally metaphorize things well, well, we won't succeed. Because the metaphor is always a bias (...)" (Res1)

Res1 answers Mus3 by explaining the meaning he gives to the term metaphor in order to counter-argument Mus3's remarks. He thus gives his point of view on what a game's metaphor is. He does not refer to literature, but uses the term metaphor in a decontextualized way. He describes a general characteristic of game's metaphor without relying directly on Geome: "metaphor is always a bias" (Res1). In this sense, the process of translation relates to the disambiguation of a knowledge that is worked out in a common way.

4.3 Towards Multilateral and Explicit Translation Processes

Our analysis allows us to identify many knowledge transactions processes concerning the notion of metaphor during the 7 workshops spread over a year. The same knowledge is thus translated several times as the work session progresses.

It leads us to characterize the translation process as more or less *explicit/implicit* and *unilateral/multilateral*. These are not distinct and watertight categories of translation, but gradients of explicitness and reciprocity that makes translation possible. The table below describes and illustrates these characteristics in four sharing configurations: (i) *implicit unilateral*, (ii) *explicit unilateral*, (iii) *implicit multilateral* and (iv) *explicit multilateral* (Table 1).

Table 1. Process leading to translation

	Implicit	Explicit
Unilateral	A single actor expresses the meaning he/she gives to knowledge without an explicit request being made. He/she does not formalize his/her statement as knowledge sharing *e.g., "In this part of the game, I guess an interesting metaphor for the impact of domestication." (Res1)*	A single actor expresses the meaning he/she gives to knowledge explicitly (e.g., following a request). He/she formalizes his/her statement as a knowledge sharing *e.g., "what do you mean by breaking down the metaphor" (Teacher2), "breaking down the metaphor is (...)" (Res1), "okay" (Teacher2)*
Multilateral	Two (or more) actors express themselves on different meanings they give to the same knowledge without it being explained *e.g., "it is the metaphor of our relationship with nature" (..) (Mus3), (...) "Metaphor is always a bias" (Res1), "in the metaphor of nature, it is not only mammals" (...) (Mus)*	Two (or more) actors express themselves explicitly on different meanings they give to the same knowledge *e.g., "what do you mean by breaking down the metaphor" (Teacher2), "breaking down the metaphor is (...) and you how did you understand it?" (Res1) "In this case breaking down the metaphor would be (...) " (Teacher2)*

We postulate that the more multilateral and explicit a transaction is, the stronger the translation process will be. By strong, we mean that the translation relates a clear and sustainable sharing of meaning. The multilateral dimension would be necessary to co-construct a shared meaning since it means that each actor has access to the representations of the other. Indeed, a unilateral transaction means that the sharing of a meaning is only in one direction. The sharing is not reciprocal as only one person expresses himself.

On this basis, translation could be instrumentalized in workshops with tools or activities which promote the clarification of meanings. For example, a summary tool could be set up. This would be a document on which the main concepts would be reported. The workshop's participants would be asked to express themselves on these concepts during a round table discussion at the end or beginning of the meeting. We could also imagine assigning the role of translation facilitators to one or more actors. Their role would be to encourage the clarification of ideas during the exchanges. They would encourage the multilateral exchange of meaning. For example, they would occasionally take the floor to reformulate or question the participants, e.g., by saying: "and you, how do you understand that?", "is that what you meant", etc. These techniques to support the translation process can be compared to brokering actions [12]. Indeed, brokering actions aim at facilitating the sharing between different professional cultures in a design-based research context [4, 12]. These actions may seem time-consuming, however, in the long term, it could assist the development of a shared interpretative space [6] and thus foster the co-production of knowledge.

Although [17] presents three levels of knowledge transaction, we essentially identify processes which are close to translation in the verbal exchanges of collaborative workshops. The transformation level is marked by a lack of common interest [17]. At this level, the actors negotiate their interest in knowledge [17, 19]. In the case studied, educational researchers and practitioners begin to settle common interests in a first phase of co-problematization in design-based research. This phase consists of negotiating a need for a field to be studied with regard to scientific questions. In the framework of the PLAY project, the first common interest is the design of a game to meet an educational need (raising awareness of the Anthropocene issue). The common interest is to create a metaphor to gamify the knowledge intended to be learned. The process of transforming the interests concerning the metaphor of the game would have been undertaken at the very beginning of the project, before the design workshops are analyzed in this contribution. This could be a reason why the transformations are not visible in our analysis. It is also possible that our analysis model [9] and the data collected do not allow to access the transformations. Specifically, it is possible that transformation processes occur e.g., in email exchanges or conversations outside of workshops. We plan to conduct interviews with project actors to query them about their representations and interests regarding the issue of the game metaphor.

5 Conclusion

In this paper, we examined the processes of knowledge transactions [18] between different professionals during 7 workshops of the PLAY project. Considering the educational game to be conceived as a boundary object, we identified processes of translation of the notion of metaphor which is a theoretical concept under development. We characterized these processes more or less explicit/implicit and uni-/multilateral. Considering the educational game conceived as a boundary object [15], we identify the "game metaphor" as an element that composes this boundary object. The metaphor is a theoretical concept which is currently being conceptualized by researchers. Nevertheless, this notion is not presented as a theoretical concept by one of the researchers (Res1) who, on several occasions, shares the meaning he gives it. Res1 does not refer to the scientific community. The term metaphor is mobilized in a common language. We identify the negotiation of the game's metaphor alongside the evolution of the meaning given to the term "metaphor". These negotiations can be observed as the actors interact with each other. Thus, the skill of "metaphorizing a game" is articulated with the theoretical concept of metaphor. We postulate that the actors develop skills related to the act of "metaphorizing the game".

Although the main objective of the design-based research is to produce scientific knowledge [25]. We emphasize that the collaboration seems to improve the professional skills of the actors involved, whether they are teachers, computer developers or educational researchers. Our research framework does not directly aim at investigating the professional development of the actors. However, the analysis of the transactions of knowledge which shapes the boundary object, leads us to postulate the acquisition of: (i) new theoretical knowledge (e.g., "what is a metaphor"), (ii) new skills related to the design of educational games (e.g., "how to construct and deconstruct a metaphor") and (iii) new collaborative skills related to the very capacity to share knowledge (e.g., "what information do I give to be understood and heard while expressing my point of view"). It is true that the collaboration between different actors, in view on the co-construction of knowledge, is not self-evident [26]. Transaction processes must be encouraged and instrumentalized. We therefore emphasize the need to study the instrumentation of design-based research, in particular to foster knowledge sharing and the emergence of co-constructed knowledge.

To continue this research, we are currently conducting a case study in another design-based research context by capitalizing on the same analysis model. We are collecting and analyzing data in the framework of the project. This second case study will allow us to bring the results presented in this paper in a different context.

References

1. Bryk, A.S.: 2014 AERA distinguished lecture: accelerating how we learn to improve. Educ. Res. **44**(9), 467–477 (2015). https://doi.org/10.3102/0013189X15621543
2. Cividatti, L.N., Moralles, V.A., Bego, A.M.: Incidence of design-based research methodology in science education articles: a bibliometric analysis. Revista Brasileira de Pesquisa Em Educação Em Ciências, e25369, 1–22 (2021). https://doi.org/10.28976/1984-2686rbpec2021u657678
3. Sensevy, G.: Le sens du savoir. Eléments pour une théorie de l'action conjointe en didactique. De Boeck, Belgium (2011)
4. Arzarello, F., Robutti, O., Sabena, C., Cusi, A., Garuti, R., Malara, N., Martignone, F.: Meta-didactical transposition: a theorical model for teacher education programmes. In: Clark-Wilson, A., Robutti, O., Sinclair (eds.) The Mathematics Teacher in the Digital Era, pp. 347–372. Springer, Dordrecht (2014)
5. Wang, F., Hannafin, M.J.: Design-based research and technology-enhanced learning environments. Educ. Tech. Research Dev. **53**(4), 5–23 (2005). https://doi.org/10.1007/BF02504682
6. Bednarz, N.: Recherche collaborative et pratique enseignante (Regarder ensemble autrement). L'Harmattan, Paris (2013)
7. Ligozat, F., Marlot, C.: Un espace interprétatif partagé entre l'enseignant et le didacticien est-il possible? Développement de séquences d'enseignement scientifique à Genève et en France. In: Müller, A. (ed.) Le partage de savoirs dans les processus de recherche en éducation, pp. 143–163. De Boeck, Belgium (2016)

8. Paukovics, E.: Éléments de la TACD pour comprendre le rapport aux savoirs co-construits dans une Ingénierie didactique coopérative. In: Goujon, C. (ed.) Actes du congrès: La TACD en question, questions à la didactique, vol. 5, pp. 207–217. CREAD, Rennes (2019). https://tacd-2019.sciencesconf.org/data/ACTES_Session5_Congres_TACD_Rennes_2019.pdf
9. Paukovics, E.: Comprendre la co-construction des savoirs en analysant les objets-frontière et objets bifaces dans une séance de travail de recherche orientée par la conception. Actes Du Congrès TACD. Nantes **4**, 144–155 (2021). https://tacd-2021.sciencesconf.org/data/pages/TACD_2021_Actes_volume_4_final.pdf
10. Aldon, G., Monod-Ansaldi, R., Nizet, I., Prieur, M., Vincent, C.: Modéliser les processus de collaboration entre acteurs de l'éducation et de la recherche pour la construction de savoirs. Nouveaux cahiers de la recherche en éducation **22**(3), 89 (2020). https://doi.org/10.7202/1081289ar
11. Marlot, C., Toullec-Théry, M., Daguzon, M.: Processus de co-construction et rôle de l'objet biface en recherche collaborative. Phronesis **6**(1–2), 21–34 (2017). https://www.cairn.info/revue-phronesis-2017-1-2-page-21.htm
12. Monod-Ansaldi, R., Vincent, C., Aldon, G.: Objets frontières et brokering dans les négociations en recherche orientée par la conception. Educ. Didactique **13**(2), 61–84, (2019). https://www.cairn.info/revue-education-et-didactique-2019-2-page-61.htm
13. Lapointe, P., Morrissette, J.: La conciliation des intérêts et enjeux entre chercheurs et professionnels lors de la phase initiale de recherches participatives en éducation. Phronesis **6**(1–2), 8–20 (2017). https://www.cairn.info/revue-phronesis-2017-1-page-8.htm
14. Sanchez, E., Monod Ansaldi, R., Vincent, C., Safadi-Katouzian, S.: A praxeological perspective for the design and implementation of a digital role-play game. Educ. Inf. Technol. **22**(6), 2805–2824 (2017). https://doi.org/10.1007/s10639-017-9624-z
15. Star, S.L., Griesemer, J.R.: Institutional ecology, 'translations' and boundary objects: amateurs and professionals in Berkeley's museum of vertebrate zoology, 1907–39. Soc. Stud. Sci. **19**(3), 387–420 (1989). https://doi.org/10.1177/030631289019003001
16. Leigh Star, S.: Ceci n'est pas un objet-frontière !: Réflexions sur l'origine d'un concept. Revue d'anthropologie des connaissances **4**(1), 18 (2010). https://doi.org/10.3917/rac.009.0018
17. Carlile, P.R.: A pragmatic view of knowledge and boundaries: boundary objects in new product development. Organ. Sci. **13**(4), 442–455 (2002). https://doi.org/10.1287/orsc.13.4.442.2953
18. Carlile, P.R.: Transferring, translating, and transforming: an integrative framework for managing knowledge across boundaries. Organ. Sci. **15**(5), 555–568 (2004). https://doi.org/10.1287/orsc.1040.0094
19. Canik, Y., Fain, N., Bohemia, E., Telalbasic, I., Tewes, V.: Intefrating individual knowledge into innovation process of R&D alliances 1805–1814 (2018). https://doi.org/10.21278/idc.2018.0238
20. Albarello, L.: Choisir l'étude de cas comme méthode de recherche. De Boeck, Belgium (2011)
21. Hlady Rispal, M.: La méthode des cas: Application à la recherche en gestion. De Boeck, Belgium (2002)
22. Dumez, H.: Faire une revue de littérature: Pourquoi et comment ? Le Libellio d'Aegis, **7**(2), 15–27 (2011). https://hal.archives-ouvertes.fr/hal-00657381
23. Avenier, M.: Les paradigmes épistémologiques constructivistes: post-modernisme ou pragmatisme? Manag. Avenir **43**(3), 372 (2011). https://doi.org/10.3917/mav.043.0372
24. Bonnat, C., Sanchez, E., Paukovics, E., Kramar, N.: Didactic transposition and learning game design. Proposal of a model integrating ludicization, and test in a school visit context in a museum. In: Ligozat, F., Klette, K., Almqvist, J. (eds.) Didactics in a Changing World: European Perspectives on Teaching, Learning and the Curriculum (Springer International Publishing AG). Springer (2023)

25. Monod Ansaldi, R., et al.: Un exemple de recherche collaborative orientée par la conception analysée au regard de la Théorie anthropologique du didactique. Atelier Méthodologies de Conception Collaborative Des EIAH: Vers Des Approches Pluridisciplinaires (2015). http://atief.fr/sitesConf/eiah2015/uploads/Atelier5_Monod-Ansaldi%20et%20al.pdf
26. Audoux, C., Gillet, A.: Recherche partenariale et co-construction de savoirs entre chercheurs et acteurs: L'épreuve de la traduction. Revue Interventions Économiques **43**, 1–8 (2011)

Developing Gender-Neutral Programming Materials: A Case Study of Children in Lower Grades of Primary School

Sayaka Tohyama[1](✉) and Masayuki Yamada[2]

[1] Shizuoka University, 3-5-1 Johoku, Naka-Ku, Hamamatsu, Shizuoka, Japan
tohyama@inf.shizuoka.ac.jp
[2] Kyushu Institute of Technology, 680-4 Kawazu, Iizuka, Fukuoka, Japan

Abstract. There is considerable literature on ways to increase the participation of girls in the programming or computer science domains. However, further efforts are needed to foster 'gendered innovations' in today's digitalized world. In this study, we focused on facilitating a gender-free image of programming among young children using two types of educational materials we developed. The learning materials have an opposite order of items from each other using Scratch based on materials provided from the Japanese Ministry of Education: 'general' material starts with introducing 'move X steps' while 'gender-neutral' material starts with 'say X' and 'when I receive X' (message passing). We conducted five rounds of afterschool programming lessons between November 2021 and January 2022 for two groups of four second graders (two boys and two girls) in primary schools using general and developed materials. The detailed analysis using transcripts from videotaped data of children's construction process suggests that the developed materials were more effective for both girls and boys to support their programming construction process. Additionally, boys seemed to be helped more than girls when using the developed materials.

Keywords: Programming Education · Gender · Lower Primary School · Scratch

1 Introduction

1.1 Programming and Gender in Primary Schools

Programming/coding education for children in primary schools is a growing trend around the world [1–3]. There are a variety of educational purposes and national/school curricula for programming education, including incorporating them as part of mathematics education [4] and positioning students for further education in computer science [5]. While several years have passed since new national curriculum for programming was introduced [6], more research is needed on how to balance gender in the programming or computer science domain. This is especially true for programming courses offered as part of primary education, which appear to be designed for both boys and girls; however, there is a need to increase girls' consecutive participation.

Published by Springer Nature Switzerland AG 2023
T. Keane et al. (Eds.): WCCE 2022, IFIP AICT 685, pp. 160–172, 2023.
https://doi.org/10.1007/978-3-031-43393-1_16

According to the theory of constructionism, children can think using their preferred externalized ideas [7]. During construction, the externalized ideas function as tangible artefacts for improvement of the children's learning [8]. Both boys and girls display the ability for construction of their ideas in programming and the way they display it differs somewhat [9]. The key to performance for both genders appears to be the ability to choose their 'objects to think with' [10]. This indicates the construction of each child differs because the children's preferences or specialities differ.

The difference in children's preferences may include gender-related differences. The OECD PISA 2018, a well-known method of international student assessment, revealed that girls' reading scores were 30 points greater than boys, while boys' mathematics scores were 5 points greater than girls, suggesting domain-specific gender differences are relevant to subjects in schools [11]. Another study suggested that boys' self-concept of mathematics is higher than girls' [12]. There is a possibility that both achievement and self-concept of mathematics influences girls' low occupation of ICT-related work because mathematics and programming are deeply related.

Based on these findings, there is a possibility for motivating students, including girls, in programming if they can use their abilities and create their own preferred works on programming. The idea does not oppose 'mathland' suggested by Papert [7]: the idea is to make introductions to programming more domain-free. After students' initial participation, they can be introduced to mathematical components during construction of their preferred works.

1.2 Previous Efforts to Eliminate the Gender Gap in Programming Education

There are very few women working in the programming and computer science domains [13] and therefore, there have been many global efforts to introduce a gender balance. The first approach is providing girls-only programming education. For example, Linda Liukas, author of *Hello Ruby* [14], started the 'Rails Girls' community to involve girls in the world of programming [15]. Similarly, in 2021, European Girls' Olympiad in Informatics was organized to encourage girls' participation in programming; only junior-high school and high school girls could apply [16].

Second, efforts have been made to identify and eliminate unconscious gender bias. It is suggested that female programming teachers are more effective at advancing the study of programming for girls than their male counterparts, especially from kindergarten to primary education [17]. In addition, the literature suggests that there are various tacit gender-related biases around computers. For example, providing a gender-neutral room, instead of a stereotypical computer science room with science fiction books, computer parts, and so forth, can eliminate biases and further stimulate girls' interest in programming [18, 19].

Third, efforts have been made to revise educational materials used for teaching programming. Existing educational materials may be unconsciously gender-biased because of the limited number of women who have published programming educational materials or participated in programming education. The above-mentioned *Hello Ruby* [14] is globally recognised as one of the few books on computer science written from a female perspective. Furthermore, as Medal and Pournaghshband pointed out, names and contexts in computer science educational materials should be gender neutral to make girls confident about the subject [20]. One such approach was suggested by Kafai et al. They used e-textiles, sewing strings of conductive fibres to connect sensors, actuators, and so forth, for gender-neutral constructive programming education. E-textiles can appeal to both genders, since interest in electric circuits are traditionally attributed to men and sewing to women. In activities using e-textiles, students can engage in their own construction regardless of gender [21].

To develop gender-neutral programming educational materials, studying gender preferences in the programming domain from the perspective of gendered innovations [22] is also effective. According to Kafai, female students prefer realistic situations and avoid violent expressions when creating video games, compared to male students [9]. The same tendency was captured in a previous study on programming workshops, where sixth-grade girls in a primary school attempted to externalise their experience of climbing Mt. Fuji very realistically. The girls even expressed that it had started raining during the climb, causing them to slip [23]. Spieler and Slany also reported on such a practice using 'pocket code' in 'No One Left Behind' from the European H2020 project. They suggested that the order of work and studying items influenced female students more than male students [24].

Although existing studies offer promising ideas, most of these participants were junior high to high school students, with the exception of Tohyama et al.'s study [23]. It may a promising venture to motivate younger girls than students in upper grades of primary school, junior high, and high school because younger students seem freer from gender biases. The field of programming can be analogically considered from the situation of mathematics education: mathematics as a subject meant for only males become stronger as students get older [25]. Moreover, to encourage lower-grade primary school girls to pursue programming, it is important to relate programming to their preferences from 'object-to-think-with' perspectives. As Kafai suggested [9], storytelling is a promising way to introduce young girls to programming. Further, the participation of both genders in programming activities is essential for ensuring students' conceptualisation of this domain in a gender-independent manner. There are great possibilities for young girls to engage in programming as a gender-free activity if we implement these points in an educational environment.

2 Purpose

Based on previous research, the purpose of this study is to develop programming learning materials which introduce storytelling, rather than movement of objects, to involve lower grades of boys and girls in programming. This study also aims to examine the effect of these materials from the viewpoint of gendered innovations. The research questions are as follows:

(1) Which of our materials is more appropriate from a gender-inclusive perspective?
(2) What is the difference in children's activities between two kinds of materials?

3 Method

3.1 Afterschool Programming Club

We organised a programming club for second graders from primary schools (7–8 years old). These students were appropriate participants because they could externalise and report their subjective perspectives and engage in programming activities that require some knowledge of mathematics. Second graders in Japan have experience in reporting their own impressions and feelings verbally in school activities, and they have also studied multiplication tables and double-digit addition/summation in mathematics.

We conducted five afterschool 90-min sessions (including rest time) on programming. These sessions were offered once a week, between November 2021 and January 2022 in a conference room of a national university. The club was designed from the viewpoint of constructionism [26], which helps children learn via the construction of objects they are personally interested in. The programming club was separated into two groups: 'G', with general educational materials, and 'N', with gender-neutral educational materials. Each group consisted of two girls and two boys. The teachers at the club included the first author (female) and an undergraduate student (male) as a teaching assistant (TA). Each child was assigned a laptop with touch screen function to construct programs on Scratch[1]. Scratch is a little difficult for lower grades in primary school, so schools often use Scratch Jr[2] instead [27]. However, we selected Scratch to enhance the children's construction without functional limitations.

From the applicants to our afterschool programming club, we randomly selected four boys (B1g, B2g, B3n, B4n) and four girls (G1g, G2g, G3n, G4n) who had almost no programming experience. Table 1 shows the design of the club. All children attended public primary schools in Japan near the institution to which the first author is affiliated. The selected children were randomly assigned to either group. Before the programming club, we explained our research direction, method of data collection, and compliance with the first author's university research ethics to their parents. We obtained written informed consent from all parents. All attendees wore face masks and worked in an airy meeting room to prevent the spread of COVID-19. The room had no objects stereotypically associated with computer science.

Table 1. Design of programming club.

Group	Duration of the club	Teaching type	Participants
G	2021/11/1–2021/12/6	General	Kids: B1g, B2g, G1g, G2g
N	2021/12/16–2022/1/20	Gender-Neutral	Kids: B3n, B4n, G3n, G4n

The first author developed two kinds of educational materials for teaching using Scratch: general and gender-neutral. The gender-neutral ones was developed from the

[1] https://scratch.mit.edu/.

[2] https://www.scratchjr.org.

perspective of supporting children's creation of their stories following Kafai [9], rather than the perspective of game-creation. They were reviewed by the second author. Both types of materials were based on the resource used for teaching programming in Japanese primary schools, provided by the Japanese Ministry of Education [28].

The materials used for both the G and N groups differed in the order of content but not the content itself (Table 2). The G-group material first introduced 'move X steps' block and the coordinate plane to move objects on Scratch, then explained loop and conditionals. After that, 'say X' block for the objects to say something and message passing using 'broadcast X' and 'when I receive X' blocks between objects were taught. Finally, variables and inequity signs were introduced. Meanwhile, the N-group material first introduced 'say X', 'when I receive X', and 'broadcast X' for enhancing children's creation without coordinate planes. After that, loop and conditionals were explained. Then, variables and inequality signs were introduced. Finally, 'move X steps' and the coordinate plane were explained.

A second-grade boy was asked to play the role of a student for a preliminary class to prepare for this workshop. We conducted the preliminary class using the 1st material (Table 2) from G group to check whether the difficulty was appropriate or not. No issues were noted in the preliminary class.

The participants attended an approximately 20-min lecture by the teacher at the start of each class to study new Scratch blocks and their usage, before proceeding to their own work. They were informed that they would have to present their work to their parents in the final class. They could create as many works as they desired and were informed that the teacher and TA would answer all their questions.

Table 2. Contents of educational materials.

club	general (G)	gender-neutral (N)
1st	'move X steps' coordinate plane	'say X' 'broadcast X', 'when I receive X'
2nd	conditional (if-then), loop (repeat)	
3rd	'say X' 'broadcast X', 'when I receive X'	variables inequality sign (<,>)
4th	variables inequality sign (<,>)	'move X steps' coordinate plane
5th	(no new materials provided)	

3.2 Data Collection

The children answered a questionnaire sheet created by the first author at the end of each class. In the questionnaire, they were first asked whether they enjoyed their programming activities, then asked whether they considered programming more of a male or female activity. Participants asked to choose one option from a 4-point Likert scale. Their work was saved on laptops they utilised. We recorded each participant with IC recorders and video cameras; we also recorded their laptop screens. All the classroom discourses were transcribed.

First, we analysed the 40 answered questionnaire sheets (five sheets per child) from the survey. The results are presented in 3.1. Second, we counted the number of works produced per child and extracted the theme of their first and final works from their explanations during the classes. These results are presented in 3.2. Finally, we conducted a detailed analysis using the transcripts of the two boys in each group to understand how they were able to engage in self-directed construction. We focused on boys from the gendered-innovation perspective [22] because the results from 3.2 showed almost no observed difference in girls between the G and N groups, and our developed educational material seem to be effective for boys.

In the detailed analysis, we counted the number of participants' questions based on the categories suggested by Miyake and Norman [29]. Miyake and Norman revealed an interaction between learners' knowledge levels and the material's levels: novice learners tend to ask more questions when they study with easier materials than with harder materials because they can understand the content. In our study, it was expected that participants would ask more questions when they understood what they needed to do to realise their objectives as compared to possessing a shallow understanding. If participants had a shallow understanding, they may have had difficulties in formulating questions, which may not have contained concrete plans to construct their ideas on Scratch. Based on this hypothesis, we counted two types of questions independently: 'without hypothesis or content (w/o H)' questions, which required the teacher or TA to teach them concretely about how to code and realise their ideas on Scratch, and 'with-hypothesis (w/ H)' questions, which dealt with simple things like telling them where to click or which blocks to choose on Scratch. For example, the question 'I don't know how but what should I do to create a baseball game?' was coded as the w/o H category. In that situation, the teacher or TA concretely explained ways to realise the participant's idea. On the contrary, the question 'Where should I click to start drawing?' was coded as the w/H category because the participant was engaging in self-directed programming, with a plan to realise their objectives on Scratch. For the analysis, the first author coded all the discourse, while the second author coded discourse from the two classes independently. After coding, the first and second authors reviewed each other's coding results and confirmed that there were no discrepancies. The results are presented in 3.3.

We expected that girls in the gender-neutral group would be more engaged in programming because they could experience non-game-creation programming. Furthermore, we expected that the girls would ask more 'w/H' than 'w/o H' questions because they could start constructing stories not only for game-creation; thus, they could be helped to choose their preferred blocks on Scratch.

4 Results

4.1 Questionnaire Survey

The completed questionnaires suggested that all participants enjoyed every programming club activity. Furthermore, regarding the programming impression question, none of the participants stated that they considered programming to be a male or female domain. Thus, contrary to adult impressions, the student participants had no gendered impressions of programming.

4.2 First and Final Works

In the first class, B1g, B2g, G1g and B4n created programs of character movement. Meanwhile, G2g and G4n created programs of talking characters. B3n and G3n drew characters without programs, and started inputting their programs into the characters in their second class. All participants completed their final work within club time and completed their presentations as shown in Table 3. As is evident, the themes of their works differed from each other based on their various preferences. Participants had constructed other works before their final one.

Table 3. Theme of final works and number of works including final works.

Child	Theme of the final work	Total # of works
B1g	A ball thrown to a batter in a baseball field	2
B2g	Game of get away from enemies	2
G1g	Girls in a balloon party	4
G2g	Story of getting a pocket monster	3
B3n	Story of battling dragons	4
B4n	Community of wizards	2
G3n	Story of a pocket monster and a Japanese character	2
G4n	Story of a birthday girl's room	3

4.3 Questions in the Construction

During the construction, participants questioned the teacher and TA frequently. Although the final works showed no clear qualitative gender and group differences as shown in 3.2, the characteristics of participants' questions differed between the two groups. In the analysis, we focused on B1g and G1g from G group and B3n and G3n from group N. B1g appeared to have only vague plans to realise his ideas using Scratch, so he asked the teacher and TA to realise his ideas instead. B3n, G1g, and G3n concentrated on their construction and rarely requested the teacher and TA's support to realise their ideas. G1g used 'move X steps' and some blocks of the coordinate plane, while G3n completed her work without the coordinate plane blocks and used a lot of 'when I receive' and 'broadcast X' blocks to tell her story.

The numbers of questions asked by B1g, G1g, B3n, and G3n are shown in Table 4. Compared to B1g, G1g's ratio of 'w/o H' questions was lower. B1g requested the teacher or TA complete his idea on Scratch in every class by asking 'w/o H' questions. In the fifth class, he repeatedly requested the teacher's help because he was in a hurry to complete his work for the final presentation. G1g also asked more 'w/o H' questions than 'w/ H' questions because she was also hurrying to complete her program.

Table 5 shows the total number of questions and the ratio of two questions. First, we focused on the G group. The ratio of B1g's 'w/o H' questions was the highest among the four children. Also, G1g's ratio of 'w/o H' questions was a little higher than B3n and G3n's ratios. Compared to B1g, G1g's ratio was lower. Second, we compared between both the G and N groups. B3n and G3n rarely asked 'w/o H' questions during the classes than B1g and G1g. From these analyses, B1g had more difficulty with his self-directive construction than G1g. Moreover, the N-group children seemed to have plans for realising their ideas and were more engaged in their programming activities than the G group.

Table 4. Number of questions in each class.

Kids	1st class		2nd class		3rd class		4th class		5th class	
	w/ H	w/o H	w/ H	w/o H	w/ H	w/o H	w/ H	w/o H	w/ H	w/o H
B1g	2	2	3	4	2	2	2	2	0	8
G1g	8	0	9	4	8	1	7	4	2	3
B3n	3	0	2	2	7	0	0	0	0	0
G3n	8	0	8	1	8	2	8	1	9	1

Table 5. Total number and ratio of questions.

Kids	Total # of questions		Ratio	
	w/ H	w/o H	w/ H	w/o H
B1g	9	18	33.3%	66.7%
G1g	34	12	73.9%	26.1%
B3n	12	2	85.7%	14.3%
G3n	41	5	89.1%	10.9%

The detailed stories of the children's construction are shown below. Until the fourth class, B1g's main activities were mimicking the sample code provided by the teacher. He had his 'baseball game on Scratch' idea during the second class, but did not proceed with his creation until the fifth class. He mimicked the teacher's code and tested it on his laptop in the first class. During the second class, he whispered, 'I want to construct my program, which shows the boy throwing the ball and the girl hitting the ball with her bat, but I can't…' The teacher responded by asking, 'So, where should the ball go?' and B1g answered 'Umm, to her bat…' The teacher said 'So, how many steps should the ball go towards the right?' to deconstruct his idea. However, he did not continue talking with the teacher and started talking with his classmate. Instead, B1g tried to realise pieces of his baseball idea by selecting a baseball image from the 'Background' menu on Scratch and used the 'move X steps' block on the ball. However, the ball only moved slightly towards the girl's bat. During the third class, he tried to draw some pictures, selected some sprites from the 'Choose a sprite' menu on Scratch, painted the selected sprites, and spoke to G1g and B2g (sitting next to B1g); there was no progress in his baseball game on Scratch. His baseball work, mainly coded by the teacher using 'move X steps', 'when I receive X', and 'broadcast X', was finally realised during the fifth class. In his work, the ball would first move towards the right from the boy to the girl, before 'HOME RUN!' would appear on the screen (the TA wrote the message). The number of sprites with any code was two: the ball and the message "HOME RUN!" (Fig. 1).

Contrastingly, B3n engaged in self-directed construction during all the classes. His final work was a story of some dragons. He used 'when I receive X' and 'broadcast X' blocks to eventually show the images and dialogues between the dragons (Fig. 2). His final work seemed to be based on his learning in the second class. He was confused about how to organise his characters in sequence and discussed this with the TA for a while. He eventually understood how to use the 'when I receive' block in relation to 'switch costume to X'. The default names of costumes in Scratch were in numerical order, so he was required to make the command using numbers if he wanted to change his characters' costumes. He created his characters with some costumes and finally succeeded in changing them if the character received messages.

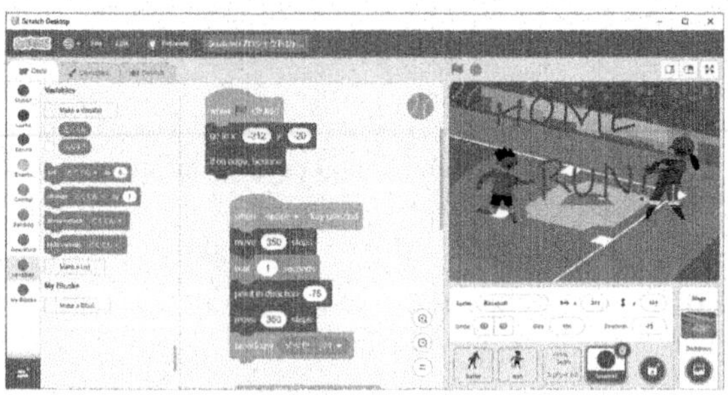

Fig. 1. B1g's final work.

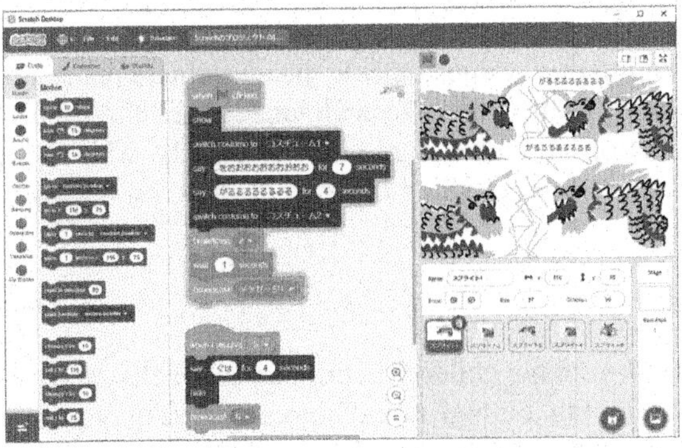

Fig. 2. B3n's final work.

5 Discussion

Unlike previous results derived from studies on adults, our study's participants had no gendered impression of programming. They engaged in their activities without being affected by gender biases. However, we should consider that only three girls had applied, compared to 16 boys, during the first recruitment of the programming club. Almost the same ratio of girls and boys had received the information about the recruitment for the programming club. One girl of the four was recruited after two extra recruitment drives. These results suggest that the four girls and their parents might have had a less gendered image of programming before the programming club started than the other girls and parents who did not apply to the club.

In our study, we noted that all the children had finished their final work and completed the final presentation. Additionally, the educational materials that we developed helped children engage with programming. Further, it can be suggested that girls who used materials developed by us may felt more supported in constructing their stories than those who used general educational material. This could be because of the order of our developed materials that first introduced storytelling-familiar blocks: 'say X', 'broadcast X' and 'when X receive'. As shown in Table 3, three of the four girls presented a story for the final presentation using the storytelling-familiar blocks. Interestingly, one of the girls used general materials which first introduced 'move X steps', created her program without 'move X steps', and used 'say X' in the first programming class. Kafai suggested that girls prefer storytelling in their programming [9], and three of the four girls in this study showed the same tendency.

According to the final works of B1g and B3n, both boys used 'when I receive X', 'broadcast X', and 'wait X seconds'. Only B1g used 'move X steps' and 'go to x:X y:Y'; moving these blocks required knowledge of the coordinate plane. The teacher explained the characteristics of the coordinate plane and how to locate sprites using X and Y metrics on Scratch to both classes. However, B1g had difficulty continuing his work using the metrics lecture from the first class. B3n engaged in his construction during class and finished his work without blocks on the coordinate plane. Although 'move X steps' is often introduced at the beginning of Scratch texts for novice programmers, it might have still proved difficult for B1g. B3n tacitly avoided using the blocks of the coordinate plane. However, this does not mean that B1g and B3n struggled with numerical values; both had dealt with numerical values outside the coordinate plane situation on Scratch. Additionally, both used 'wait X seconds' with numerical values. Further, B1g correctly calculated the summation of double-digit values mentally, while B3n used numbers to control the order of events in the 'when I receive X' and 'broadcast X' blocks.

6 Conclusion

This study suggests that younger children in primary school have no gendered impression of programming. In our club, both girls and boys engaged in programming and realised their ideas. However, contrary to previous findings on ways to involve girls in programming, we found that the gender-neutral educational materials we developed were more effective for the boys than general materials we developed. The gender-neutral educational material may have also supported the girls' programming requirements about storytelling; however, we were unable to suggest this effect clearly because of the limited number of children. Detailed analysis and additional practices of programming education are required to understand the effect of the material in girls.

Our results also suggest that girls naturally engaged in programming activities. In the activity, the girls were dedicated in their efforts to complete their constructions and rarely got stuck. On the contrary, the boys would get stuck using blocks of the coordinate plane and had difficulty finding other ways to realise their ideas.

The limitation of this study stems from being a case study. Hence, the universal applicability of the results must be further verified. We aim to revise the developed educational materials and use them in future practices of programming education. In our future studies, we will design our programming education considering boys and girls differ in developmental order at their earlier ages [30]. Furthermore, we should improve scaffold designs from a social support viewpoint [31] in our programming club.

Acknowledgments. We would like to express our sincere appreciation to the children and their parents who joined our club.

References

1. Means, B.M., Stephens, A. (eds.): Cultivating Interest and Competencies in Computing. National Academies Press, Washington, DC (2021)
2. European Schoolnet: Computing our future: Computer programming and coding – Priorities, school curricula and initiatives across Europe, http://www.eun.org/documents/411753/817341/Coding+initiative+report+Oct2014/2f9b35e7-c1f0-46e2-bf72-6315ccbaa754, last accessed 2022/02/11
3. Jitsuzumi, T., Tanaka, E., Aizawa, S., Tohyama, S., Uchiyama, Y.: Approaches to fostering 21st-century ICT capabilities for future generations in APT countries. Asia-Pacific Telecommunity Publishing (2018)
4. Benton, L., Saunders, P., Kalas, I., Hoyles, C., Noss, R.: Designing for learning mathematics through programming: a case study of pupils engaging with place value. Int. J. Child-Comput. Interact. **16**, 68–76 (2018)

5. Hubwieser, P., et al.: A global snapshot of computer science education in K-12 schools. In: ITiCSE-WGP 2015 – Proceedings of the 2015 ITiCSE Conference on Working Group Reports, (November), pp. 65–83 (2015)
6. Japanese Ministry of Education: Japanese curriculum standard for elementary schools. https://www.mext.go.jp/content/1413522_001.pdf. Last accessed 25 Sep 2022 (in Japanese)
7. Papert, S.: Mindstorms: Children, computers, and powerful ideas. Basic Books, NY (1980)
8. Akkerman, E.: Piaget's Constructivism, Papert's Constructionism: What's the difference? https://learning.media.mit.edu/content/publications/EA.Piaget%20_%20Papert.pdf. Last accessed 25 Sep 2022
9. Kafai, Y.B.: Video game designs by girls and boys: variability and consistency of gender differences. In: Cassell, J., Jenkins, H. (eds.) From Barbie to Mortal Kombat: Gender and Computer Games, pp. 90–114. The MIT Press, Cambridge (1998)
10. Kafai, Y.B.: Gender, games and computing. In: Kafai, Y.B., Richard, G.T., Tynes, B.M. (eds.) Diversifying Barbie and Mortal Kombat: Intersectional perspectives and inclusive designs in gaming, pp. 376–390. ETC Press, Pittsburgh (2016)
11. OECD PISA 2018 results: https://www.oecd.org/pisa/publications/pisa-2018-results.htm. Last accessed 11 Feb 2022
12. Manger, T., Eikeland, O.-J.: The effect of mathematics self-concept on girls' and boys' mathematical achievement. Sch. Psychol. Int. **19**(1), 5–18 (1998)
13. Ashcraft, C., Eger, E., Friend, M.: Girls in IT: The facts. https://wpassets.ncwit.org/wp-content/uploads/2021/05/13215545/girlsinit_report2012_final.pdf. Last accessed 12 Feb 2022
14. Liukas, L.: Hello Ruby: Adventures in coding. Feiwel & Friends (2015)
15. Rails Girls: http://railsgirls.com/events.html. Last accessed 11 Feb 2022
16. European Girls' Olympiad in Informatics. https://egoi.org. Last accessed 11 Feb 2022
17. Sullivan, A., Bers, M.U.: The impact of teacher gender on girls' performance on programming tasks in early elementary school. J. Inform. Technol. Educ.: Innov. Pract. **17**, 153–162 (2018)
18. Cheryan, S., Plaut, V.C., Davies, P.G., Steele, C.M.: Ambient belonging: how stereotypical cues impact gender participation in computer science. J. Pers. Soc. Psychol. **97**(6), 1045–1060 (2009)
19. Cheryan, S., Meltzoff, A.N., Kim, S.: Classrooms matter: the design of virtual classrooms influences gender disparities in computer science classes. Comput. Educ. **57**(2), 1825–1835 (2011)
20. Medel, P., Pournaghshband, V.: Eliminating gender bias in computer science education materials. In: Proceedings of the Conference on Integrating Technology into Computer Science Education (ITiCSE), pp. 411–416 (2017)
21. Kafai, Y.B., Fields, D., Searle, K.: Electronic textiles as disruptive designs: supporting and challenging maker activities in schools. Harv. Educ. Rev. **84**(4), 532–556 (2014)
22. Gendered Innovations Homepage. https://genderedinnovations.stanford.edu. Last accessed 12 Feb 2022
23. Tohyama, S., Matsuzawa, Y., Yokoyama, S., Koguchi, T., Takeuchi, Y.: Constructive interaction on collaborative programming: case study for grade 6 students group. In: Tatnall, A., Webb, M. (eds.) Tomorrow's learning: Involving everyone (IFIP AICT 515), pp. 589–598. Springer, Cham (2017)
24. Spieler, B., Slany, W.: Female teenagers and coding: Create gender sensitive and creative learning environments. In: Proceedings of the 5th Conference on Constructionism, pp. 644–655 (2018)
25. Cvencek, D., Meltzoff, A.N., Greenwald, A.G.: Math-gender stereotypes in elementary school children. Child Dev. **82**(3), 766–779 (2011)
26. Papert, S.: Situating constructionism. In: Harel, I., Papert, S. (eds.) Constructionism, pp. 1–12 (1991)

27. Rich, P.J., Browning, S.F., Perkins, M.K., Shoop, T., Yoshikawa, E., Belikov, O.M.: Coding in K-8: international trends in teaching elementary/primary computing. TechTrends **63**(3), 311–329 (2019)
28. Japanese Ministry of Education: Coding for get away from the cat part 2. https://www.mext.go.jp/a_menu/shotou/zyouhou/detail/1416408.htm. Last accessed 12 Feb 2022 (in Japanese)
29. Miyake, N., Norman, D.A.: To ask a question, one must know enough to know what is not known. J. Verbal Learn. Verbal Behav. **18**(3), 357–364 (1979)
30. Geist, E., King, M.: Different, not better: Gender differences in mathematics learning and achievement. J. Instr. Psychol. **35**, 43–52 (2008)
31. Vygotsky, L.S.: Thought and Language. The MIT Press, Cambridge (1962)

The Impact of Tolerance for Ambiguity on Algorithmic Problem Solving in Computer Science Lessons

Lisa Zapp[1], Matthias Matzner[2(✉)], and Claudia Hildebrandt[2]

[1] Studienseminar Leer Für das Lehramt an Gymnasien, Leer, Germany
[2] University of Education Heidelberg, Heidelberg, Germany
matthias.matzner@uni-oldenburg.de, hildebrandt@ph-heidelberg.de

Abstract. Learners can perceive algorithmic problem solving to be ambiguous, especially in computer science lessons. Tolerance to this individually perceived ambiguity is an internal factor that can influence the absorption and processing of knowledge both positively and negatively. Thus, it was examined whether there is a connection between tolerance for ambiguity and the performance of students such a task for algorithmic problem solving in computer science lessons. The results show that there is a significant correlation between tolerance for ambiguity and the number of points achieved in the test for algorithmic problem solving.

Keywords: Tolerance for Ambiguity · Algorithmic Problem Solving · Quantitative Research · Computer Science Lessons · Upper Secondary Education

1 Introduction

Algorithmic problem solving is one of the central competencies that students should learn during computer science lessons. This skill helps students to acquire more knowledge about computer science and is applicable in a plethora of professions. The authors have observed often how some students would be stumped by ambiguous algorithmic problem-solving tasks. On inquiry the students replied that they were irritated by the diversity of possible solutions or by the openness of the task itself.

This phenomenon can also occur when learning a foreign language and is theoretically associated with the factor of tolerance for ambiguity [1]. It is assumed that students can accept and endure ambiguous situations to varying degrees [2, 3]. The aim of the study at hand is to answer the question "To what extent are tolerance for ambiguity and solving ambiguous algorithmic problem-solving tasks connected?", which relates to the empirical findings in the field of foreign languages [4–6]. For this study, an ambiguous task for algorithmic problem solving was developed. Using a standardized test for tolerance for ambiguity [7] and the students' solutions on the task, the relationship between tolerance of ambiguity and performance in algorithmic problem solving is investigated. The performance measures include the number of points achieved and the time required for the task.

Published by Springer Nature Switzerland AG 2023
T. Keane et al. (Eds.): WCCE 2022, IFIP AICT 685, pp. 173–183, 2023.
https://doi.org/10.1007/978-3-031-43393-1_17

2 Theoretical Background

The first part of the study is comprised of definitions for tolerance for ambiguity and algorithmic problem solving. Since the factor of tolerance for ambiguity has not yet been investigated in the field of computer science education, related research about foreign language acquisition and mathematics education is processed. After that, the theoretical relationship between the variables is worked out, considering the definitions and categories according to Budner [8] and Norton [9].

2.1 Tolerance for Ambiguity

Tolerance for ambiguity describes how well or badly a person can deal with ambiguous situations and can influence the absorption and processing of knowledge and information [3]. Intolerance for ambiguity is a psychological factor which Budner (1962) defined as "[...] the tendency to perceive ambiguous situations as sources of threat" [[8], p. 29]. In reversal, the tolerance for ambiguity describes a tendency which either tolerates ambiguous situations or rejects their ambiguous nature.

Budner forgoes a determination of the valence of the factor of tolerance for ambiguity, although the wording of the definition seems to tend towards a negative valence of intolerance for ambiguity [8]. The more neutral definition of tolerance for ambiguity by Brown (2000) is chosen as the central definition for the study at hand: "The degree to which you are cognitively willing to tolerate ideas and propositions that run counter to your own belief system or structure of knowledge" [1, p. 118].

It should be noted that ambiguity is subjectively perceived – something may seem clear to one person and ambiguous to another. Also, ambiguity can arise in various situations and to varying degrees. Budner (1962) developed three categories to describe the varying degrees, while Norton (1975) added a fourth category. The four categories that a situation can be characterized as are:

1. In a completely new situation all the information is new and unknown [8].
2. In a complex situation a lot of information is available, but either the amount of information is too large or the information is too complex [8].
3. In a contradictory situation different approaches or solutions to a problem are possible [8].
4. In an unstructured situation the necessary information, desired beginning and end states may be available, but lack any order which would promote problem solving [9].

2.2 Algorithmic problem solving

The PISA-consortium defines problem-solving as follows: "Problem solving begins with recognizing that a problem situation exists and establishing an understanding of the nature of the situation. It requires the solver to identify the specific problem(s) to be solved and to plan and carry out a solution, along with monitoring and evaluating progress throughout the activity" [10, p. 123]. In more abstract terms, problem solving are the activities that translate the beginning state to a desired end state [11, 12]. First, the beginning and the desired end state must be identified. Then, necessary transitional states and transitional actions between the states must be determined. Finally, a definite sequence of clearly executable instructions must be formulated and implemented as an executable program that solves the given problem [13–15].

2.3 State of Research

The factor tolerance for ambiguity has been researched in foreign language acquisition since 1975, but the results in this area of research are quite controversial [7]. The controversy arises from disagreements between [1, 5] and [15] – among others – about whether tolerance for ambiguity has a positive or negative influence on the absorption and processing of knowledge. Brown [1] argues on a theoretical level that tolerance for ambiguity can be an advantage in foreign language acquisition, as students more tolerant towards ambiguity are better able to tolerate the irregularities in the foreign language. Intolerance can, however, also contribute to the fact that the students reject new knowledge, since this threatens the already existing knowledge [1]. Brown (2007) even argues that very high levels of intolerance could prevent language learning. Inversely, it could be concluded that a certain degree of tolerance for ambiguity can have a positive influence on students when learning a foreign language. However, a low tolerance for ambiguity can also have a positive effect, as this can protect the students' existing knowledge from doubts that could arise from new knowledge [1]. However, it is unclear how much tolerance for ambiguity there must be for this positive effect to occur [16].

In addition to these theoretical arguments, empirical findings are available as well. For example, Stark, Gruber, Renkl and Mandl (1997) have studied the connection between tolerance for ambiguity and the acquisition of transferable knowledge. They examined 60 vocational commerce school students with the help of a computer simulation [17]. The research design is a 2x2 factor correlational study, where ambiguous situations were developed through different learning contexts (uniform vs. multiple) with varying levels of support (unguided vs. guided) [17]. A statistically significant link was identified between close transfer and tolerance for ambiguity. Even if the connection between tolerance for ambiguity and transfer of learning varied greatly between the groups, the authors nevertheless concluded that a higher tolerance generally tends to indicate better transfer of learning [17]. Furthermore, Stark et al. (1997) found that solving simple tasks worked better when there was no support from the teacher. In contrast, the learning process for more complex tasks was more likely to be improved if the teacher provided guidance. A different study suggests that more ambiguity-tolerant students benefit from a more complex learning environment [18]. Additionally, the study by Buela and Joaquin (2018) found that tolerance for ambiguity can be a positive predictor of mathematical problem solving [2]. Furthermore, they were able to determine moderate positive associations between the ability to solve problems and the tolerance for ambiguity [2]. Summarizing, it seems that students with higher tolerance for ambiguity are better able to cope with more complex tasks, can transfer knowledge better and have a higher ability to solve problems.

While performing cognitively demanding tasks, the available amount of cognitive resources people invest in performing a task are also important in this context. According to the classical Cognitive Load Theory (CLT) extraneous, germane, and intrinsic cognitive load are three types of cognitive load which together make up total cognitive load [16, 17]. But this aspect is not part of investigation.

2.4 Tolerance for Ambiguity in Algorithmic Problem Solving

In the following section, we will illustrate the ambiguity of algorithmic problem-solving tasks through examples taken from recent computer science lessons. Imagine the following example task: implement a square with an edge length of 5 cm in the Scratch programming environment. This task defines the desired end state very clearly. The situation can still be classified as completely new [8] if the students have no prior knowledge of programming and the Scratch environment. For students that have prior knowledge, the task will have less or even no ambiguity at all. Imagine another example task: sort an uncertain quantity of numbers using a program. This task offers no information about the quantity of numbers that should be sorted, whether an application should be developed or found and used (such as currently available table calculation software) or which developing environment should be used for implementing an eventual application. This task can be classified as first, third and fourth category or completely new, contradictory and unstructured. The first category is applicable since the developing environment is unspecified. As no desired end state is specified, the students must determine it themselves which justifies numerous approaches and, thusly, the task can also be classified in the 3rd category [8]. As no structure for the solution is provided by the task description, the 4th category [9] applies here as well.

When solving problem tasks the application of meta-cognitive strategies can improve process and product. Metacognition is often defined as "thinking about thinking" [12, p. 188]. More fittingly meta-cognitive strategies should be described as the "focus on the selection and control of problem-solving strategies". Examples of meta-cognitive strategies are "planning how to approach a given learning task, evaluating progress, and monitoring comprehension" [12, p. 188]. With an effect size of $d = 0.69$, the meta-cognitive strategies factor is one of the most effective teaching interventions [12].

3 Research Method

A written two-part questionnaire was administered: the part was a tolerance for ambiguity test [7] and the second part was a test for algorithmic problem solving. The data of 23 German 12th and 13th grade students attending a computer science course in the school year of 2020/2021 were collected. The sample was split into students with high and low levels of tolerance for ambiguity and compared on their task performance using non-parametric procedures using SPSS.

3.1 Instrumentation

Tolerance for Ambiguity Test. The independent variable tolerance for ambiguity is assessed through the Multiple Stimulus Types Ambiguity Tolerance Scale-II, MSTAT-II [7]. The test does not use examples and is not tied to a specific context. Furthermore, McLain (2009) developed the questions in adherence to the definitions of tolerance for ambiguity by Budner [8] and Norton [9]. Additional advantages of this test are its demonstrated reliability and validity [7].

In addition, the test by McLain (2009) consists of 13 statements, which are rated on a five-digit scale ("does not apply" – "does apply") and is therefore very short and compact, making it very suitable for a written survey [7]. The 13 statements were translated into German. The translation attempts to preserve the original intentions of McLain (2009). The test – therefore – remains complex due to its abstract level, repetition and similarity between statements and reversely coded statements.

In the MSTAT-II test, a maximum of 65 and a minimum of 13 points can be achieved, whereby higher scores indicate higher tolerance for ambiguity [9]. Reversely coded statements are 1 through 6, 9, 11 and 12 (Table 1). The internal consistency was determined good to very good [19] with a Cronbach's alpha of 0.83.

Table 1. Statements of the tolerance for ambiguity test according to McLain [7].

Item	Reverse	Statement
1	√	I don't tolerate ambiguous situations well
2	√	I would rather avoid solving a problem that must be viewed from several different perspectives
3	√	I try to avoid situations that are ambiguous
4	√	I prefer familiar situations to new ones
5	√	Problems that cannot be considered from just one point of view are a little threatening
6	√	I avoid situations that are too complicated for me to easily understand
7		I am tolerant of ambiguous situations
8		I enjoy tackling problems that are complex enough to be ambiguous
9	√	I try to avoid problems that don't seem to have only one "best" solution
10		I generally prefer novelty over familiarity
11	√	I dislike ambiguous situations
12	√	I find it hard to make a choice when the outcome is uncertain
13		I prefer a situation in which there is some ambiguity

Test Items for Algorithmic Problem Solving. The students' algorithmic problem solving is assessed by an implementation task. The procedure for the survey is based on the research by Atef-Vahid et al. (2011) [4]. The performance of the students was reflected by two measures, namely the number of points earned and the processing time.

Tasks from the Society for Computer Science [20] were deemed too time intensive, while tasks from the Bebras Contest [21] would have to be altered too much to reflect an implementation task. Therefore, an ambiguous task of algorithmic problem-solving was designed by altering Lutz Kohl's (2009) telephone provider task dealing with the main concept of if-else statements and being solved with a block-based programming language

[14]. The alteration made consisted of converting telephone rates, originally presented in tabular form, into an unstructured text (cf. Test items for algorithmic problem solving).

Assignment: *Marco made too many phone calls in the last month. His parents have now decided to allow him a fixed amount of money for phone calls. Marco wants to make optimal use of his allowance and has therefore selected the minute rates from four different providers and the associated telephone numbers. The new provider Telefonus with the number 01357 would cost Marco 0.03 euros per minute for landline calls and 0.38 euros for calls to the mobile network. In the off-peak times, calls are cheaper, as the landline network costs only EUR 0.02 and the mobile network EUR 0.30. Mobilus (02368) is a provider that has particularly low mobile network prices. In this case, it would cost Marco 0.25 euros to make calls during peak hours and 0.20 euros during off-peak times. However, the prices with this provider for the fixed network are more expensive compared to the other providers. Peak hours for fixed network at Mobilus cost 0.07 euros and off-peak time 0.05 euros. His girlfriend Anna recommended the provider Genialio (096573) to Marco, because it costs only 0.01 euros for the fixed network during off-peak times and 0.04 euros during peak hours. For the mobile network, Marco would pay 0.32 euros (peak hours) and 0.27 euros (offpeak time). The name says it all for the provider Cheapus (016783), because it costs 0.05 euros per minute in the fixed network during peak times and 0.03 euros per minute in off-peak times. The prices for the mobile network are 0.03 euros for the main time and 0.27 euros in the off-peak time. Marco now asks you whether you can implement an operation for him which always selects the best rate.*

The task can be classified as 3rd category [8] due to the different approaches and solutions possible. The task is also classified in the 4th category since the information regarding the telephone provider is presented in an unstructured manner [9]. The ambiguity of the task is increased by having to solve the task on paper (i. e. programming on paper). Therefore, the structure and feedback provided by the interface of the block-based programming language is not available. The students noted the exact point of time before starting and after solving the task.

3.2 Participants

At the selected secondary school in Germany, a total of 27 students attended a computer science course at an increased level of difficulty in the school year of 2020/2021. Of these, 13 students attend a course in 12th grade and 14 students in 13th grade. A total of 23 students were interviewed as four students could not be interviewed due to quarantine. All students took computer science classes in 11th grade. During the course, the students implement programs with the block-based programming languages Snap! and Scratch. The students are used to record their syntax when programming on paper in exam situations. Furthermore, both courses are supervised by the same teacher and mainly dealt with implementation tasks for multi-dimensional lists in the lessons prior to the data collection. The students did not know the concept of algorithmic problem solving. The teacher explained in a preparatory meeting that all implementation tasks dealt with prior in the classroom relate to this task.

3.3 Data Collection and Processing

The 23 questionnaires were digitized and evaluated using Statistical Packages for the Social Sciences (SPSS). The sample was divided into two groups according to split-half method on their tolerance for ambiguity: rather low tolerance for ambiguity (TfA-low) and rather high tolerance for ambiguity (TfA-high). In the TfA-low and TfA-high group, were split at a value of higher than 47. Based on this classification, twelve of the students can be classified in the TfA-low group and eleven in TfA-high group.

The students' solutions to the implementation task were rated according to four different sample solutions. These sample solutions were prepared in advance by computer science and electrical engineering students. It should be noted that there are other solutions that solve the problem validly. The answers were rated with a minimum of zero to a maximum of 15 points. The Mann-Whitney U test was determined as most suitable to compare the score and the processing time of the two groups, since the sample is small, the groups are independent from one another, and normality of sample distribution is not required [22]. In addition, Spearman-Rho correlations were calculated for the independent variable tolerance for ambiguity and the dependent variables score and processing time. A correlation analysis according to Spearman-Rho is carried out, since this is a non-parametric statistic, which can reduce the influence of extreme values [22].

4 Results

For preliminary analyses, the composition of the sample was investigated including quitters and grade level. In total seven students quit the ambiguous task and did not record an end time. It was checked whether the quitters differed in their level of tolerance for ambiguity. A Mann-Test revealed no statistically significant difference in tolerance for ambiguity between the quitters and completers ($U = 32.0$, $p = 0.107$).

A Mann-Test revealed statistically significant difference in score on the algorithmic problem-solving task between the 12th and 13th grade students ($U = 33.5$, $p = 0.050$). With 12th (mean rank = 14.4) graders outperforming the 13th graders (mean rank = 8.9). This difference prompted a further check whether grade level was connected to placement in either group with a Chi^2 – Test. The result shows no statistical connection between grade level and the group placement (χ^2 (1) = 0.03, $p = 0.855$). Although this contradicts the expectation that higher grade is connected to higher performance, the grade level does not predict classification into tolerance for ambiguity groups. Grade level is therefore excluded from possible mitigating variables.

For the main analysis, the connection between the tolerance for ambiguity and the score on the algorithmic problem-solving task was investigated. Table 2 shows the mean ranks of the score on the algorithmic problem-solving task across the tolerance for ambiguity groups (TfA-low vs TfA-high). The statistical inference via Mann-Whitney U-test returns a statistically significant result. The direction of the difference can be determined by comparing the mean ranks of the groups, revealing the TfA-high group to have outperformed the TfA-low group. The effect size of group membership of .490 can be classified as medium according to Cohen (1992) [23], calculated via the formula [22]:

$$r = z\frac{z}{\sqrt{N}}.$$

Table 2. Mann-Whitney results on the comparison of score and processing time on algorithmic problem-solving task between tolerance of ambiguity groups.

		Score			Processing time	
TfA-groups	N	mean rank	rank sum	N	mean rank	rank sum
Low	12	8.83	106	7	8.50	59.50
High	11	15.45	170	9	8.50	76.50
Total	23			16		
Mann-Whitney		U = 28.0	p = 0.019		U = 31.5	p = 1.000

If no division into groups is made, a Spearman-Rho correlation returns similar results. Spearman-Rho correlation between tolerance for ambiguity and score on algorithmic problem solving was also found to be statistically significant (rho = 0.58; p = 0.004). The positive correlation coefficient indicates that higher levels of tolerance for ambiguity can be associated with a higher score on algorithmic problem solving. This correlation coefficient can be classified according to Cohen as a medium to strong correlation [23]. Spearman-Rho correlation between tolerance for ambiguity and processing time on algorithmic problem solving was found to be not statistically significant (rho = –0.06; p = 0.816).

5 Discussion and Conclusion

The research question of the paper at hand was based on previous research [4, 17]. The results presented above represent an extension of previous research. The question to what extent tolerance for ambiguity and solving ambiguous algorithmic problem-solving tasks are connected was investigated by group differences and correlations. The results clearly demonstrate that there is a positive relationship between level of tolerance for ambiguity or the sheer score on tolerance for ambiguity and the number of points achieved in ambiguous algorithmic problem-solving tasks. There was no connection between tolerance for ambiguity and processing time, which may have been due to the considerable number of quitters of the task. The quitting behavior was not connected to the level of tolerance for ambiguity of the students, leading to speculations about a mitigating variable, such as self-efficacy.

Based on the present results, the research question can be answered to the effect that there is a positive connection between tolerance for ambiguity and the solving of ambiguous algorithmic problem-solving tasks. However, in this context it should not be disregarded that a small and specific sample was examined, so that the representativeness of these results is limited. Nevertheless, these results extend the results from the foreign language research [4, 5] and that for problem-solving and transfer [2, 17]. Further analyses investigated the possible connection between time spent on the ambiguous task and the score. Neither a group comparison, nor a bivariate correlation indicated a connection between the two. However, as not all students finished the ambiguous task, the processing time for these quitters could not be recorded truthfully. However, tolerance for ambiguity did not seem to be the explanation for whether the students finished the ambiguous task or not. As the students may have not been fully engaged with the task yet, low self-efficacy could have played a role in the decision to quit [24]. Self-efficacy is the trust in one's own skills to be able to master difficult situations. Either the quitters did not know how to solve the ambiguous task, or they did not persevere enough to activate the necessary knowledge. To further corroborate this speculation, data on self-efficacy and an objective measure for the general problem-solving skill would be needed.

Furthermore, Atef-Vahid et al. [4] found that students less tolerant for ambiguity took longer to process the ambiguous task than the more tolerant students. However, the processing time was clearly limited by the school's given time, so that not all students had the opportunity to complete the task at their own pace. A connection between tolerance for ambiguity and processing time could have been found if the students had had unlimited time. It is therefore advisable to allow more time for processing when repeating such a test. When examining the processing time, it was also found that seven students abandoned the task. Of these seven, five came from the group AT-rather low and two from the group AT-rather high. The task abandonment could be due to low tolerance for ambiguity as Budner [8] stated that a low tolerance can lead to people being overwhelmed by ambiguity and thereby refusing the situation. The research at hand could nonetheless not confirm this suspicion.

When interpreting these results, however, it should be considered that the relationship between tolerance for ambiguity and performance on an ambiguous task was only demonstrated for the present sample [22]. The scores on the ambiguous task represent the performance of the students on the day of the survey under the given circumstances only, so the performance of the students could differ between days, under different circumstances and on different tasks. The research at hand does not take such variations into account. Stark et al [17] created various situations of ambiguity in problem solving and compared the results. With such an approach, it could also be checked whether students more tolerant for ambiguity perform better in algorithmic problem solving if they work in groups compared to working alone or depending on the amount of information they receive.

The small sample limits the meaningfulness of the presented results as it cannot be assumed that the results of this sample represent the entirety of all computer science students [22]. Due to the small sample, the students were divided into two equally sized groups. However, the value of tolerance for ambiguity of six of the students are very close to the cutoff between the two groups. The same question with any cut-off arises whether a point difference in the tolerance for ambiguity value can really be decisive for whether a person can be viewed as more intolerant or more tolerant. The research at hand corroborated the group comparison with a correlation.

Regarding the sample composition, possibly mitigating variables could be ruled out by preliminary analyses. Therein, the students' grade level did not seem to matter for the placement into either of the tolerance for ambiguity groups. However, it was discovered that the 12th graders outperformed the 13th graders on the algorithmic problem-solving task. Intuitively, one could expect that this should be reversed, and the 13th graders should have outperformed the 12th graders. The 12th graders may have had related subject matter more recently than the 13th graders and therefore an advantage on the algorithmic problem-solving task. Additionally, the 13th graders are closer to their final examinations and may therefore be less focused on such a research related task. The study at hand has neither the data nor the scope to explain this finding in depth.

The results of this investigation indicate that there is a positive connection between tolerance for ambiguity and the solving of ambiguous algorithmic problem-solving tasks. Ambiguity in tasks may reduce performance of some students and therefore skew results. Consequently, it is necessary to develop students' tolerance for ambiguity if a reduction of ambiguity is not desirable. Open-ended tasks seem promising in achieving this by defining a general goal without specifying a solution. Such a general goal could be formulated as developing an algorithm that automatically sorts a set of elements, for instance sorting by size. Different algorithms can be used to sort a set of elements.

Ambiguity may be used to adapt task difficulty. There are students whose performance is hampered by the ambiguity of the task. Offering additional material (pertaining to the content or the solution approach) could reduce the degree of ambiguity and mitigate its negative effect on these students. It could be reasonably considered devising "learning-to-learn" programs for such situations as the targeted strategies would be highly associated with the subject matter to be learnt [12]. Computer science concerns the acquisition and application of various solution strategies. Additionally, algorithmic problem solving has to be communicated as a skill that requires mental flexibility. Nonetheless, it must be clear to the students that some solutions can be less optimal than other or plainly wrong – especially when not achieving the set goal.

Furthermore, the study at hand hints at new avenues of research, such as the understanding of the subjectivity of the perception of ambiguity and the reasons for abandoning algorithmic problem-solving tasks. Investigating these routes could help to improve lesson material and methods in computer science and possibly other subjects as well.

References

1. Brown, H.D.: Principles of Language Learning and Teaching. Pearson Longman, Harlow (2007)

2. Buela, M., Beltran-Joaquin, N.: Student ambiguity tolerance as predictor of problem-solving ability in mathematics. In: The Asian Conference on Education 2018: Official Conference Proceedings (2018)
3. Liu, C.: Relevant researches on tolerance of ambiguity. Theor. Pract. Lang. Stud. **5**(9), 1874–1882 (2015)
4. Atef-Vahid, S., Alireza Fard Kashani, A.F., Haddadi, M.: The relationship between level of ambiguity tolerance and cloze test performance of Iranian EFL learners. Linguist. Literary Broad Res. Innov. **2**(2), 149–169 (2011)
5. Ely, C.M.: Tolerance of ambiguity and use of second language learning strategies. Foreign Lang. Ann. **22**(5), 437–445 (1989)
6. Husch, B.: Software-Entwicklung im Unterricht. Informatik als Schlüssel zur Qualifikation: GI-Fachtagung „Informatik und Schule 1993 "Koblenz, 11.–13. Oktober 1993, 101 (2013)
7. McLain, D.L.: Evidence of the properties of an ambiguity tolerance measure: the multiple stimulus types ambiguity tolerance scale-II (MSTAT-II). Psychol. Rep. **105**(3), 975–988 (2009)
8. Budner, S.: Intolerance of ambiguity as a personality variable. J. Pers. **30**(1), 29–50 (1962)
9. Norton, R.W.: Measurement of ambiguity tolerance. J. Pers. **39**(6), 607–619 (1975)
10. OECD: PISA 2012. Assessment and Analytical Framework: Mathematics, Reading, Science, Problem Solving and Financial Literacy. OECD, Paris, France (2013)
11. Betsch, T., Funke, J., Plessner, H.: Problemlösen: Denken – Urteilen, Entscheiden, Problemlösen. Springer, Berlin, Heidelberg (2011)
12. Hattie, J.A.C.: Visible Learning: A synthesis of Over 800 Meta-analyses Relating to Achievement. Routledge, Oxon (2009)
13. Barnes, D. J., Fincher, S., Thompson, S.: Introductory problem solving in computer science. In: Daughton, G., Magee, P. (eds.) 5th Annual Conference on the Teaching of Computing, pp. 36—39. Centre for Teaching Computing, Dublin City University, Dublin, Ireland (1997)
14. Kohl, L.: Kompetenzorientierter Informatikunterricht in der Sekundarstufe I unter Verwendung der visuellen Programmiersprache Puck. Friedrich-Schiller-Universität Jena, Jena (2009)
15. Erten, İH., Topkaya, E.Z.: Understanding tolerance of ambiguity of EFL learners in reading classes at tertiary level. Novatis-Royal **3**(1), 29–44 (2009)
16. Sweller, J., van Merriënboer, J.J.G., Paas, F.G.: Cognitive architecture and instructional design. Educ. Psychol. Rev. **10**(3), 251–296 (1998)
17. Stark, R., Gruber, H.H., Renkl, A., Mandl, H.: Wenn um mich herum alles drunter und drüber geht, fühle ich mich so richtig wohl – Ambiguitätstoleranz und Transfererfolg. Psychol. Erzieh. Unterr. **44**(3), 204–215 (1997)
18. Leiserson, C.E., Rivest, R.L., Stein, C.: Algorithmen – Eine Einführung. Oldenbourg Verlag, München (2010)
19. Grunwald, G., Hempelmann, B.: Angewandte Marktforschung: Eine praxisorientierte Einführung. Oldenbourg Wissenschaftsverlag GmbH, München (2012)
20. Gesellschaft für Informatik: Grundsätze und Standards für die Informatik in der Schule Bildungsstandards Informatik für die Sekundarstufe I. LOG IN 28, 150/151 (January 2008), Beilage, (2008)
21. Bundesweite Informatikwettbewerbe. Downloads 2019. https://bwinf.de/biber/downloads/ (2019). Retrieved 4 May 2021
22. Field, A.: Discovering Statistics Using IBM SPSS Statistics. Sage, Los Angeles (2018)
23. Cohen, J.: A power primer. Psychol. Bull. **112**(1), 155–159 (1992)
24. Albert Bandura, A.: Toward a psychology of human agency. Perspect. Psychol. Sci. **1**(2), 164–180 (2006)

Symbiotic Approach of Mathematical and Computational Thinking

Kristin Parve and Mart Laanpere(✉)

Tallinn University, Narva Road 25, 10120 Tallinn, Estonia
{kristin.parv,mart.laanpere}@tlu.ee

Abstract. Although CT is a rapidly expanding field of educational research, it is a relatively new concept in official national curricula. From the perspective of curriculum policy, CT is closest to two subjects taught in primary and secondary schools: computing/informatics and mathematics. Since informatics is not present as a separate subject in many countries, proponents of CT should find alternative routes for introducing this new body of knowledge in curricula. There are three main ways as to how it has been done in various countries: (A) adding CT into the existing informatics/computing curriculum, (B) integrating CT in the curriculum of some other subject – most likely, mathematics, and (C) introducing CT through cross-curriculum theme and interdisciplinary STEM/STEAM projects. This paper discusses the similarities and differences of computational and mathematical thinking that could potentially empower each other though meaningful integration in math lessons. Using the cases of Finland, Estonia, and Lithuania as examples, different approaches to integrating computational thinking into K-12 education will be contrasted and compared.

Keywords: Computational Thinking · Mathematical Thinking · informatics curriculum

1 Introduction

There is a well-known story about a philosophy professor who took an empty jar to his lecture. Standing in front of the class, he pulled some rocks out of his belongings and filled the jar with them. Everyone agreed that the jar was full. He then pulled out some pebbles and so filled the larger gaps between the rocks. The jar once again was full. Surprisingly, he then pulled out a box of sand and let it fill up the remaining spaces in the jar. The jar was full again. Even though this scene must have been unexpected, it proves the point that all the larger and smaller pieces you placed in the jar represent aspects of your life. It matters a lot if the jar is first filled with rocks or sand – if the sand, small unneccessary items are put in the jar first, you'll never have enough time for the big important things in your life.

This widely popular story has had its place as a reminder to set priorities in one's life and take time for important things. Yet, this paper won't try to argue or support that

Published by Springer Nature Switzerland AG 2023
T. Keane et al. (Eds.): WCCE 2022, IFIP AICT 685, pp. 184–195, 2023.
https://doi.org/10.1007/978-3-031-43393-1_18

matter. Computational thinking has been one of the most popular topics around computer science education in schools for more than 15 years, and many of the educators believe computational thinking to be one of those big rocks or at least some pebbles in the jar. But is it actually necessary or could we maybe solve the question of adding computational thinking teaching in K-12 differently?

First, we will provide an overview of two constructs – computational and mathematical thinking, then discuss the similarities and differences. Three cases from small European countries are used as examples to contrast and compare different approaches to introducing Computational Thinking in K-12 education. The metaphors of the rocks, pebbles and sand will help us to explain the challenges and solutions where identifying a suitable level of granularity of CT elements might avoid overwhelming the existing curricula.

2 Key Concepts

2.1 Computational Thinking

Computational Thinking (CT) as a term was coined by Wing [1], although it was not a totally new concept [2]. Its roots go back to the 1980s when Seymour Papert was first to mention it in his work about the LOGO programming language [3]. During the last 15 years, computational thinking has been at the centre of educational research as well as school innovations. Wing [1] described CT as a way of thinking that "*involves solving problems, designing systems, and understanding human behaviour, by drawing on the concepts fundamental to computer science*" [1, p. 33]. Over the years, there have been a number of attempts to operationalise the definition of CT, yet it has still remained a challenge. On a larger scale, proposed definitions of CT can be divided into two categories: ones that are more related to programming and computing concepts and the ones that see computational thinking as a broader problem solving skill [4]. First group of definitions value the computer science counterpart in them, adding skills like programming, debugging, computational models and solutions, and the use of software to them [2, 5–7]. The more universal definitions of computational thinking see it as a broader, transferable skill that could be addressed in the context of different subjects. Those definitions include CT components like problem identification, decomposition, algorithmic thinking, evaluation and generalisation as well as data practices [8–10].

Despite the ongoing discussion, studies mostly agree that integrating computational thinking in the school context will be beneficial. Weintrop *et al.* [6], who studied computational thinking in the context of mathematics and science, stated three main benefits of the integration. Firstly, it will develop the reciprocal relationship between learning mathematics, science and CT concepts; secondly, it will help to create a more accessible classroom environment; and finally, it keeps the mathematics and science classrooms aligned with current professional practices.

Integrating CT in the school context can be done on different levels. It can be 1) unplugged, meaning no computers are used, 2) include digital gadgets like programmable robots, or 3) be screen-based, with visual- or text-based programming environments [11]. Kotsopoulos *et al.* [12] proposed a four-phased Computational Thinking Pedagogical Framework (CTPF) that consisted of unplugged, tinkering, making and remixing stages. They stressed that a sequential approach may be helpful to understand the idea of computational thinking for novice learners.

From the perspective of policy makers, there are overall three different approaches to implement computational thinking to school education: 1) adding computational thinking across the curriculum in different subjects; 2) computational thinking is taught as a separate subject and 3) implementing computational thinking ideas into subjects that already exist in the school curricula [13].

2.2 Mathematical Thinking

Mathematical thinking does not refer solely to a specific subject, rather to a larger set of mathematical processes and operations that could generally be applied to any field [14]. As Polya [15] stated, the most important part of mathematical education is that it should teach students to think. Harel and Sower [16] stressed that mathematical understanding and thinking should be kept apart. Mathematical understanding refers to making sense of a particular mathematical problem, while mathematical thinking is something more universal, the key to understanding.

Habits of Mind were introduced by Cuoco, Goldenberg, and Mark in 1996 [17] for rethinking and reorganizing high school mathematics learning and teaching. They argued that high school mathematics teaching should provide students with real mathematical methods in order to help them think about mathematics in the way that mathematicians do. They suggested that those habits of mind could be divided into two: ones that are not limited to mathematics only, but cut across other disciplines, and the ones that are related to mathematics, so-called content specific habits. Mathematics related habits include skills like "thinking big and talking small" meaning generalizing and abstracting, thinking in ways of functions, using multiple points of view and mixing deduction and experiment. General habits include skills like finding patterns, experimenting, formulating written and oral descriptions, tinkering, inventing, using visualization, and conjecturing and guessing [17].

Mathematical literacy is defined in PISA as "*…an individual's capacity to formulate, employ and interpret mathematics in a variety of contexts. It includes reasoning mathematically and using mathematical concepts, procedures, facts and tools to describe, explain and predict phenomena. It assists individuals to recognise the role that mathematics plays in the world and to make the well-founded judgements and decisions needed by constructive, engaged and reflective citizens*" [18, p. 65]. This definition emphasises the need to use mathematics in context and to develop a deeper understanding of mathematics concepts because more and more daily-life situations and problems require some basic level of mathematical reasoning [19].

Mathematical literacy in the new PISA 2022 Mathematics Framework Draft [20] consists of the relationship between mathematical reasoning and problem solving skills (Fig. 1). Firstly, one has to be able to notice the mathematical nature in a (real life) situation and formulate it in the correct mathematical terms. The employment stage refers to the need to use the mathematical tools taught in school to solve the problem. Lastly, the outcome has to be evaluated in the context of the (real-life) problem. All those steps mentioned above are supported by mathematical reasoning skills.

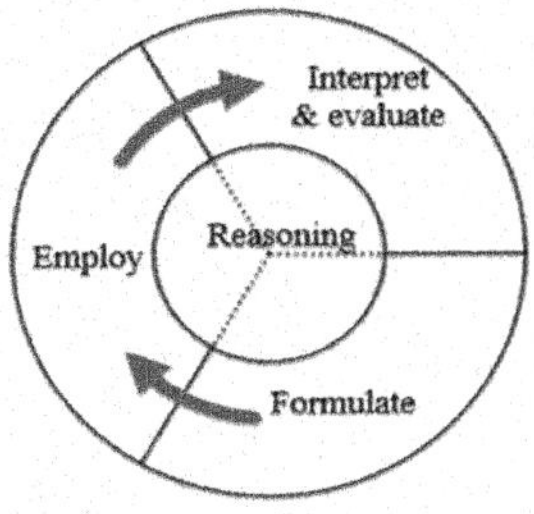

Fig. 1. Mathematical thinking process illustrated in PISA 2022 Mathematics Framework Draft [20]

2.3 Similarities between Computational and Mathematical Thinking

In the organising principle for mathematics curricula *Habits of Mind*, Couco and his colleagues stated that high school students should be helped to "learn and adopt some of the ways that mathematicians think about problems" [17]. About a decade later when teaching informatics was at a crossroad, Wing dreamed that everyone should be taught the basics of computational thinking – the ways and tools computer scientists use when solving problems [1]. Although those concepts differ from each other, they also share similar traits, not to mention the similarities in how the problems were addressed.

When trying to understand and compare the real heart of the two concepts, mathematical and computational thinking, one notices a similar aim of those two ways of thought processes. Going back to the 80's, Halmos [21] outlined that the existential reason for mathematics or as Stanic and Kilpatric [22] said – the real heart of it, is to solve problems. Winding 20 years ahead, similar ideas are used to describe the essence of computational thinking. Wing [1] said that "computational thinking involves solving problems" [1, p. 33], later computational thinking as an activity was seen as something "associated with, but not limited to, problem solving" [8]. Therefore, computational thinking not only shares ways with mathematical thinking [23], but also has similar overall aim. While going more in depth with the comparison of those concepts, several authors have made their statements about that.

Sneider and his colleagues [24] tried to describe the connection between mathematical and computational thinking using a Venn diagram (Fig. 2). Mathematical skills are related strictly to the subject, like counting, arithmetic, algebra, geometry and others. Computational thinking involves skills like simulation, algorithmic reasoning, gaming, programming and others. But these two ways of thinking also share a number of similar capabilities like problem solving, modeling, analyzing and interpreting data and statistics and probability.

Swedish researchers Bråting and Kilhamn [25] have studied the connections between algebraic and computational thinking in the context of changes in the local curriculum. Teaching mathematics includes fostering algebraic thinking. They stated that at least on the theoretical level, both algebraic and computational thinking value the process of problem-solving more than the result, although the domains themselves are rather different from each other [25, 26].

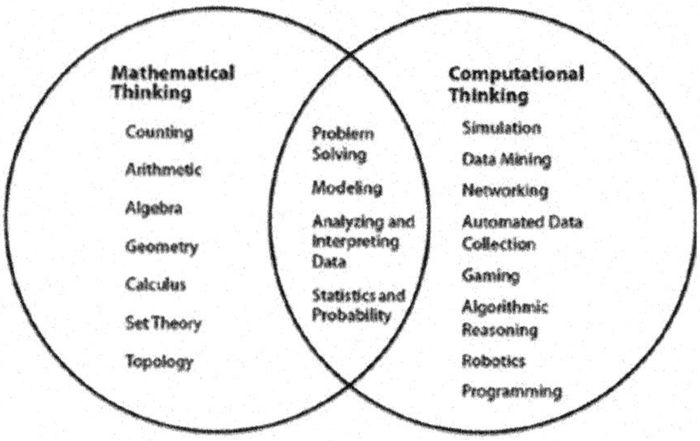

Fig. 2. The overlap of Computational and Mathematical thinking illustrated by a Venn diagramm [24]

Pei *et al.* [27] also see the overlap between computational and mathematical thinking. They describe how computational thinking and mathematical habits of mind are strongly related and mutually supportive. Therefore, adding a computational aspect to the mathematics classroom will create a larger and more meaningful mathematics learning experience. Weintrop and his colleagues [6] also saw computational thinking as a beneficial component of mathematics classrooms. They formulated a taxonomy where the integration of CT can be divided into four categories: data practices, modeling and simulation practices, computational problem-solving practices and systems-thinking practices [6]. More recent research on integrating computational thinking into mathematics education was conducted by Kallia and her colleagues [28], who described computational thinking as an'umbrella' concept that does not depend on the context, therefore, is adaptable to different situations. It was agreed that while talking about computational thinking in the context of mathematics education, three main aspects should be considered: *problem solving* as a fundamental part of mathematics education in which computational thinking can be taught, *cognitive process* meaning the different thinking processes that mathematical and computational thinking share, and *transposition* or the ability to phrase the solution of a mathematical problem [28].

The overlap between those concepts has been noticed and acted on already at a larger scale. The need to "encompass the synergistic and reciprocal relationship between mathematical thinking and computational thinking" is clearly stated in the draft of the PISA 2022 Mathematics framework [20, p.7]. Enriched with many examples, the main emphasis is on how those two concepts complement each other, giving out endless possibilities to deepen the understanding of mathematics while interacting more effectively with new technologies. More precisely, students should be able to show their computational thinking skills in the three parts of mathematical literacy described above [20]. In addition to the named benefits of integrating CT into mathematics classes, Stephens and Kadijevich [29] also described examples of integrating CT into mathematics classes in several countries. Since the integration of CT into mathematics is complex, countries have chosen different levels of integration (cross-curricular integration vs a separate subject) or fundamentally different approaches (more of a gradual introduction vs having a formal subject for everyone).

3 CT-Related Curriculum Policies in Three Countries

Computational thinking has been added to national curricula in various countries. While some of the countries have chosen to teach computational thinking as a separate discipline, other countries have divided it into several subjects as a cross-curricular approach or added it into the curricula of the subjects students are already familiar with [13]. An overview of the three different approaches in Lithuania, Finland and Estonia is introduced in the next sections.

3.1 Lithuania

The Lithuanian education system is free of charge and is compulsory until the student is 16 years of age. School education consists of mainly three parts: primary, basic and secondary education, all together 12 years. In addition to that, youth schools are an alternative to basic education that offer pre-vocational training during the studies. Secondary education curricula consist of compulsory and optional modules and this level of education can be acquired in either gymnasiums, pre-gymnasiums, full or short secondary, vocational or other schools [30].

Information technology (IT) courses are part of compulsory education in Lithuania. At primary level, informatics is taught as a part of other subjects. In the lower secondary school (grade 5–10) IT is taught for one hour a week, emphasising students to see the integrative nature of IT and how it benefits their overall study process. While IT is compulsory at the lower secondary level, it is an elective course at upper secondary school (grade 11–12). The level of IT studies in schools at both lower and upper secondary school level depends heavily on the level of skills and knowledge of the teachers [30–32].

Teaching and learning computational thinking (lithuanian "*informatinio mąstymo*") concepts are also part of the compulsory IT course. The subject includes five areas of knowledge: information; digital technologies; algorithms and programming; virtual communication; security, ethics and legal principles. The studies in upper secondary school include topics related to electronic publishing, database design and management, and programming [30, 31]. In 2023 a new curriculum will come into effect that will change the matter of IT education. More of a cross-curricular approach at the primary school level is being introduced, including studying CT components in other subjects [32]. The new curriculum, that is most probably going to be accepted in the summer of 2022, continues with a compulsory computer science education as a separate subject from the 5th grade, setting teaching computational thinking skills as one of the main learning outcomes in the basic school as well as secondary school level.

3.2 Finland

The Finnish educational system also consists of basic education (grades 1–9) and upper secondary education. Upper secondary education can be divided into two: more general and rather academically oriented education, and vocational education which aims is to prepare students for direct employment or further studies in the polytechnics [33]. Up until recently, only basic education was compulsory. Continuing studies in the upper secondary or vocational level was rather popular with more than 90% of young people electing to do so, but it was not officially compulsory. Starting from August 2021, the compulsory education was extended, now students have to complete an upper secondary qualification (either from the general or vocational education) or attend school until 18 years of age [34, 35].

	Years 1–2	Years 3–6	Years 7–9
Digital competence	using digital media, technological fluency	impact of technology, tech-integration	
Math	step-by-step instructions	visual programming	algorithmic thinking, good computing conventions
Crafts		robots, automation	embedded systems, own artifacts

Fig. 3. Computer Science related topics in Finnish basic school (Niemelä *et al.*, 2017)

Finland has approached teaching CT as a more cross-curricular activity. The division of computer science related topics in basic school level can be seen above (Fig. 3). Starting from 2016, they were one of the first countries in the European Union to set "algorithmic thinking" and programming as a mandatory part of the curriculum starting from the 1st grade [31]. In the basic education, *i.e.* grades 1–9, learning and teaching CT is integrated in different subjects from arts to environmental studies, but mainly in the mathematics lessons. Algorithmic thinking is stated as one of the 20 objectives for Maths. Later on in upper secondary education, different courses related to programming, computer science and CT are offered [32]. The introduction to CT skills is a continuous process where in every grade some additional skills are taught. It starts with learning to give step-by-step instructions in the first two school years that is followed by using visual programming tools. During the years in the basic education, they are gradually introduced to more and more complex concepts. In whatever subject the programming tasks are used, they always serve a higher purpose for the learning process and are also aligned with transversal competences in the national core curriculum [31].

3.3 Estonia

The Estonian education system also consists of nine years of basic education that can be followed by general upper secondary or vocational education. Education is provided free of charge and the studies are meant to support the lifelong learning process [36, 37].

The informatics related subject has been on and off the national curriculum in Estonia. From the mid 90s to the early 2000s, it was part of the national curriculum as an elective course named informatics. In the first decade of the 2000s, informatics was not a separate subject in the curriculum, but students had to be introduced to compulsory information and communications technology (ICT) skills by the end of basic school as a part of other subjects. From 2011, informatics or subjects related to the concept are back as elective subjects in basic as well as upper secondary education [38].

More of an holistic approach of informatics education throughout the twelve years of school has been offered to be in the new updated national curricula and is described in the figure above (Fig. 4). New versions of the syllabuses were sent to the government in January 2022 and hopefully will be in action from 2023. In the basic education curriculum, the central concepts that the curriculum is based on are 1) design thinking for

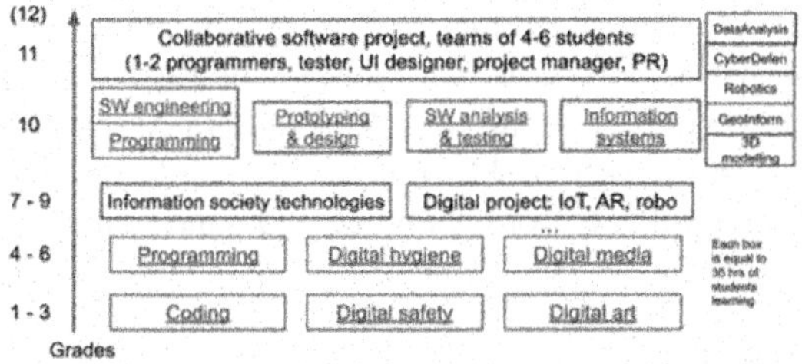

Fig. 4. Holistic view of K-12 informatics curriculum (Niemelä *et al.*, 2021)

creative and collaborative learning and 2) computational thinking for a more thorough way of solving real world problems. As seen in Fig. 4, during grades 1–6, students are introduced to basic concepts of different fields, whereas in grades 7–9 the knowledge will be brought together to solve real-life problems in a collaborative way. During the upper secondary school level, the informatics related subjects stress the importance of developing practical ICT, creative thinking and collaboration skills. Therefore, the outcomes of the elective courses can be put into action during the collaborative software project. Students in basic and in upper secondary school level have to conduct an empirical research or practical project to graduate, therefore adding digital project in the lower secondary school and collaborative software project in the upper secondary school level gives students more possibilities to pass the mandatory part of curriculum in more collaborative and 21st century self-directed learning ways.

4 Discussion

As shown above, there is no one way to integrate computational thinking ideas into school curriculum. Several examples of integrating CT into mathematics have been introduced by Stephens and Kadijevich [29], but in general three main ways of integration have been identified [13]: (1) CT as a cross-curricular theme; (2) CT as a separate subject; (3) selected CT ideas integrated in a few chosen subjects. As our study showed, often some kind of mix of these approaches is used. Lithuania has a long history of computer science education [38], therefore it is no surprise that the main way to bring computational thinking ideas to K-12 education is through a separate computer science curriculum, but pilot studies have already been conducted to introduce more of a cross-curriculum approach in primary schools in the future [32]. Finland has also worked on a mix of cross-curricular integration and single-subject model, although the main responsibility for teaching CT lies on mathematics teachers [13, 32]. Estonia falls somewhere between these two approaches. Computational thinking is mentioned in the "not yet official but already in use" documentation for the upcoming elective informatics subject both in basic and secondary school. Although elective courses have many benefits, such as having a wide range of topics to cover and an unlimited number of lessons that the school themself can agree on, it also brings up some problems. Dagiene and Stupuriene [30] mentioned that although informatics is a compulsory subject in Lithuania, the level of teaching depends heavily on the knowledge and skills of the teachers. Estonia is facing a similar problem – although teaching ICT skills is set as a priority in Estonia, there is a lack of competent IT teachers [39], and the actual level of IT education varies between schools. It has been calculated that only a quarter of teachers actually have qualifications to teach IT. Although having computational thinking skills integrated into the next curriculum is already a step ahead, it might still not be enough.

Now, imagine the jar full of rocks, pebbles and sand again. School curricula are mostly full and those already existing subjects like mathematics can be seen as rocks in the jar, filling biggest parts of the curricula. This also means that adding new courses or subjects automatically refers to the need to discard some of the existing learning outcomes. Therefore, the integration of CT or anything else new has to be thought through, adding them in smaller pieces, or as pebbles and sand to the jar.

Some countries see teaching computational thinking as a quite a pebble in the jar of curriculum – it has its place as a separate subject like Lithuania does. As shown before, they soon will have an additional way of cross-curricular approach at the primary level. This could be seen as some sand in the existing slots in the jar. Finland has taken another path, adding computational thinking as smaller pieces mainly in the context of mathematics to the curriculum. While trying to visualise it, mathematics could be seen as a bigger rock and the computational thinking counterpart as a sand to fill in the gaps around it. Estonian approach is more difficult to picture. Is computational thinking added as a sand to the learning outcomes of informatics lesson that could easily fill the voids or is it just adding additional pebbles to the jar that are already falling out of the jar?

As discussed above, computational thinking shares many similarities with mathematical thinking, sharing similar sub-skills [6, 24] and a ground-base [1, 17, 24, 25]. Using the same metaphor, the integration of CT into mathematics classes could also be illustrated with rocks, pebbles and sand. The smallest granularity of CT elements in the mathematics classroom could be computational tasks meant only for the gifted students as a way to enrich the school-level mathematics or prepare them for the mathematics competitions. The next level of granularity, pebbles, could address some specific learning outcomes of mathematics curricula and engage all students in widening their understanding of abstract mathematical concepts in computational context that might be more interesting, closer to real life. The largest granularity level of CT elements would bring in another "rock" in the jar by introducing CT as a separate course – if the existing curriculum allows it. On the other hand, the "CT rock" could be also introduced as a cross-curricular theme, in the form of interdisciplinary project-based learning as it is done in Finnish case of phenomenon-based learning.

5 Conclusions

This paper considers the similarities and differences of computational and mathematical thinking, two concepts that could potentially empower each other in school curricula. The three main ways to introduce how computational thinking has been integrated in the K-12 education was illustrated by the examples of three close countries: Finland, Estonia and Lithuania. While introducing computational thinking in K-12 education is seen as important and beneficial by many authors, making changes to the existing curriculum is never easy. Designing school curricula is a highly contextualized and politicized process, which is why every country has to find their own way for introducing computational thinking in schools. We have provided some arguments for adding computational thinking in everyday school-life as smaller pieces in the context of similar concepts like mathematics could be a solution for some countries, to avoid overwhelming the existing curricula.

References

1. Wing, J.M.: Computational thinking. Commun. ACM **49**(3), 33–35 (2006)
2. Grover, S., Pea, R.: Computational thinking in K–12: a review of the state of the field. Educ. Res. **42**(1), 38–43 (2013)
3. Papert, S.: "Mindstorms" Children. Computers and Powerful Ideas.Basic books, Inc., Publishers/New York (1980)
4. Tang, X., Yin, Y., Lin, Q., Hadad, R., Zhai, X.: Assessing computational thinking: a systematic review of empirical studies. Comput. Educ. **148**, 103798 (2020)
5. Brennan, K., Resnick, M.: New frameworks for studying and assessing the development of computational thinking. In: Proceedings of the 2012 Annual Meeting of the American Educational Research Association, Vancouver, Canada, pp. 1–25 (2012)
6. Weintrop, D., et al.: Defining computational thinking for mathematics and science classrooms. J. Sci. Educ. Technol. **25**(1), 127–147 (2016)
7. Denner, J., Werner, L., Ortiz, E.: Computer games created by middle school girls: can they be used to measure understanding of computer science concepts? Comput. Educ. **58**(1), 240–249 (2012)
8. Selby, C., Woollard, J.: Computational Thinking: the Developing Definition. University of Southampton (E-prints), UK (2013)
9. ISTE, CSTA. Operational Definition of Computational Thinking for K-12 Education (2011)
10. Yadav, A., Hong, H., Stephenson, C.: Computational thinking for all: pedagogical approaches to embedding 21st century problem solving in K-12 classrooms. TechTrends **60**(6), 565–568 (2016)
11. Gadanidis, G., Clements, E., Yiu, C.: Group theory, computational thinking, and young mathematicians. Math. Think. Learn. **20**(1), 32–53 (2018)
12. Kotsopoulos, D., et al.: A pedagogical framework for computational thinking. Dig. Experiences Math. Educ. **3**(2), 154–171 (2017)
13. Bocconi, S., Chioccariello, A., Earp, J.: The Nordic approach to introducing Computational Thinking and programming in compulsory education. Report prepared for the Nordic@ BETT2018 Steering Group, pp. 397–400. National Research Council of Italy, Institute for Educational Technology (CNR-ITD), Palermo, Italy (2018)
14. Burton, L.: Mathematical thinking: The struggle for meaning. J. Res. Math. Educ. **15**(1), 35–49 (1984)
15. Polya, G.: Mathematical Discovery: On Understanding, Learning and Teaching Problem Solving, 2 vol. combined, 1981st edn. John Wiley & Sons, New York (1965)
16. Harel, G., Sowder, L.: Advanced mathematical-thinking at any age: its nature and its development. Math. Think. Learn. **7**(1), 27–50 (2005)
17. Cuoco, A., Goldenberg, E.P., Mark, J.: Habits of mind: an organizing principle for mathematics curricula. J. Math. Behav. **15**(4), 375–402 (1996)
18. OECD: PISA 2015 Assessment and Analytical Framework: Science, Reading, Mathematic, Financial Literacy and Collaborative Problem Solving, revised edition. PISA, OECD Publishing, Paris (2017)

19. OECD: PISA 2018 Assessment and Analytical Framework. PISA, OECD Publishing, Paris (2019)
20. PISA, OECD: Mathematics Framework (Draft). Retrieved from PISA (2022). https://pisa2022-maths.oecd.org/files/PISA%202022%20Mathematics%20Framework%20Draft.pdf. Last accessed 22 May 2023
21. Halmos, P.R.: The heart of mathematics. Am. Math. Mon. **87**(7), 519–524 (1980)
22. Stanic, G., Kilpatrick, J.: Historical perspectives on problem solving in the mathematics curriculum. In: Charles, R., Silver, E. (eds.) The teaching and assessing of mathematical problem solving, pp. 1–22. National Council of Teachers of Mathematics, Reston, VA (1988)
23. Wing, J.M.: Computational thinking and thinking about computing. Phil. Trans. R. Soc. A: Math. Phys. Eng. Sci. **366**(1881), 3717–3725 (2008)
24. Sneider, C., Stephenson, C., Schafer, B., Flick, L.: Exploring the science framework and NGSS: computational thinking in the science classroom. Sci. Scope **38**(3), 10 (2014)
25. Bråting, K., Kilhamn, C.: Exploring the intersection of algebraic and computational thinking. Math. Think. Learn. **23**(2), 170–185 (2021)
26. Malara, N.A., Navarra, G.: New words and concepts for early algebra teaching: sharing with teachers epistemological issues in early algebra to develop students' early algebraic thinking. In: Kieran, C. (ed.) Teaching and Learning Algebraic Thinking with 5-to 12-Year-Olds, pp. 51–77. Springer, Cham (2018)
27. Pei, C., Weintrop, D., Wilensky, U.: Cultivating computational thinking practices and mathematical habits of mind in lattice land. Math. Think. Learn. **20**(1), 75–89 (2018)
28. Kallia, M., van Borkulo, S.P., Drijvers, P., Barendsen, E., Tolboom, J.: Characterising computational thinking in mathematics education: a literature-informed Delphi study. Res. Math. Educ. **23**(2), 159–187 (2021)
29. Stephens, M., Kadijevich, D.M.: Computational/algorithmic thinking. In: Lerman, S: (ed.) Encyclopedia of Mathematics Education, pp. 117–123. Springer, Cham (2020)
30. Dagiene, V., Stupuriene, G.: Bebras – a sustainable community building model for the concept based learning of informatics and computational thinking. Inform. Educ. **15**(1), 25–44 (2016)
31. Bocconi, S., Chioccariello, A., Dettori, G., Ferrari, A., Engelhardt, K.: Developing computational thinking in compulsory education-Implications for policy and practice (No. JRC104188). Joint Research Centre, Seville (2016)
32. Bocconi, S., et al.: Reviewing Computational Thinking in Compulsory Education, JRC128347. In: Inamorato Dos Santos, A., Cachia, R., Giannoutsou, N., Punie, Y. (eds.). Publications Office of the European Union, Luxembourg (2022)
33. Kupiainen, S., Hautamäki, J., Karjalainen, T.: The Finnish education system and PISA. opetus-ja kulttuuriministeriö (2009)
34. Maaranen, K., Stenberg, K.: Teacher effectiveness in finland: effectiveness in finnish schools. In: Grant, L.W., Stronge, J.H., Xu, X. (eds.) International Beliefs and Practices That Characterize Teacher Effectiveness, pp. 125–147. IGI Global, Hershey, PA (2021)
35. Eurydice: Finland: Compulsory education extended until the age of 18. https://eacea.ec.europa.eu/national-policies/eurydice/content/finland-compulsory-education-extended-until-age-18_en. Last accessed 26 Mar 2022
36. Estonian Education System: https://www.educationestonia.org/about-education-system/, Last accessed 26 Mar 2022
37. Preschool, basic and secondary education: https://www.hm.ee/en/activities/pre-school-basic-and-secondary-education. Last accessed 26 Mar 2022
38. Niemelä, P., Pears, A., Dagienė, V., Laanpere, M.: Computational thinking–forces shaping curriculum and policy in Finland, Sweden and the Baltic Countries. In: Passey, D., Leahy, D., Williams, L., Holvikivi, J., Ruohonen, M. (eds.) Digital Transformation of Education and Learning – Past, Present and Future. OCCE 2021. IFIP Advances in Information and

Communication Technology, vol. 642, pp. 131–143. Springer, Cham (2021). https://doi.org/10.1007/978-3-030-97986-7_11
39. Haaristo, H.-S., et al.: Elukestva õppe strateegia vahehindamine. Tallinn: Poliitikauuringute Keskus Praxis, Rakendusuuringute Keskus CentAR (2019)

What Students Can Learn About Artificial Intelligence – Recommendations for K-12 Computing Education

Tilman Michaeli[1(✉)], Ralf Romeike[2], and Stefan Seegerer[2]

[1] TUM School of Social Sciences and Technology, Computing Education Research Group, Technical University of Munich, Munich, Germany
tilman.michaeli@tum.de

[2] Computing Education Research Group, Freie Universität Berlin, Berlin, Germany
{ralf.romeike,stefan.seegerer}@fu-berlin.de

Abstract. Technological advances in the context of digital transformation are the basis for rapid developments in the field of artificial intelligence (AI). Although AI is not a new topic in computer science (CS), recent developments are having an immense impact on everyday life and society. In consequence, everyone needs competencies to be able to adequately and competently analyze, discuss and help shape the impact, opportunities, and limits of artificial intelligence on their personal lives and our society. As a result, an increasing number of CS curricula are being extended to include the topic of AI. However, in order to integrate AI into existing CS curricula, what students can and should learn in the context of AI needs to be clarified. This has proven to be particularly difficult, considering that so far CS education research on central concepts and principles of AI lacks sufficient elaboration. Therefore, in this paper, we present a curriculum of learning objectives that addresses digital literacy and the societal perspective in particular. The learning objectives can be used to comprehensively design curricula, but also allow for analyzing current curricula and teaching materials and provide insights into the central concepts and corresponding competencies of AI.

Keywords: Artificial Intelligence · Machine Learning · Computing Education · Curricula · Competencies

1 Introduction

Artificial Intelligence is a central topic of computer science and has been a driving force of research and developments from the very beginning. In CS education, AI topics have always been an attractive way to motivate students to engage in the field of computing. As such, the development of games to play against the computer, or robotics, are common practice in CS education all around the world [1]. However, recent developments pushed the importance of AI forward significantly, attracting the attention of the media and making politicians require stakeholders in education to put a stronger emphasis on AI

Published by Springer Nature Switzerland AG 2023
T. Keane et al. (Eds.): WCCE 2022, IFIP AICT 685, pp. 196–208, 2023.
https://doi.org/10.1007/978-3-031-43393-1_19

education. As a result, an increasing number of CS curricula are being extended to include the topic of AI. Furthermore, AI competencies are increasingly discussed as an important aspect of digital literacy for both teachers of all subjects (who need to understand the impact and application of AI technologies in their domain) and students (who experience a growing presence of AI technologies in their daily lives). A fundamental understanding of AI technology provides a key for two doors: the responsible use of such technology, and an informed discussion about the impact of AI on society.

Technological advances in the context of the digital transformation with increasingly powerful computing systems and a steadily growing volume of data are the basis for the rapid developments in the field of AI in the last years, especially in the field of machine learning. Consequently, whether computational thinking needs to be complemented by "AI thinking" [2] or as "CT2.0" [3] is a topic of discussion in CS education.

With longtime expertise in research on AI education and in developing teaching and learning materials for bringing the central concepts and ideas of AI to all levels of students, we frequently received requests by educational stakeholders for advice: What can and should be learned in the context of AI? Obviously, it is not sufficient to define content to be "taught"; it is necessary to define and discuss learning objectives that connect well to the established structures of educational systems and the understanding of teachers and students [4]. For AI, this remains a particular challenge since CS education research on central concepts and principles of AI is not yet sufficiently elaborated.

In order to address this challenge, in this paper, we present a curriculum of learning objectives suitable for mapping and understanding the field of AI education. In the following section, we discuss underlying goals and theories that such a curriculum needs to take into account with the goal of situating the topic and its challenges in the context of computing education. Section 3 highlights major developments in AI as well as related work on AI competencies in K-12 education. Section 4 presents the curriculum of learning objectives with a brief contextualization. The paper closes with a discussion of its applications and necessary future developments.

2 AI in the Context of CS Education

There is a consensus in computer science education research that teaching should focus on aspects fundamental to the subject and relevant in the long term. Short-lived technical developments, however, should play a lesser role. For this reason, various catalogs of principles, ideas, and concepts that characterize CS or one of its fields have been proposed over the past 30 years. These catalogs can be used, for example, in preparing new topics for teaching, as the foundation for curriculum development, and to provide insight into the field and its central aspects. According to [5], such characterizations also increase comprehensibility by shifting the focus from a technological perspective to underlying principles. They also enable achieving a "balance between concepts and practice" (ibid.) by highlighting the practices of the field and helping to provide a broader overview. Approaches such as the Fundamental Ideas of Computer Science according to Schwill [6], the Great Principles of Computing [7] or the Big Ideas of Computer Science according to Bell et al. [8] structure and characterize CS or its subfields by means of central terms, ideas, concepts, or underlying principles.

Since the field of AI is still undergoing rapid development with only little experiences and few studies on the integration of AI in education, we consider it important to start with the discussion of AI competencies and their contribution to general education. In order to be effective, such work needs to be put into perspective in a regional context and connect to the scientific and political discourse. In Germany, where this work originates from, a significant and helpful structure for understanding educational needs due to the digital transformation was achieved by the Dagstuhl Declaration [9]. Its stated objective is to enable students to use digital systems in a self-determined way. To this end, it is considered important to understand and explain digital systems, to evaluate them regarding their interaction with the individual and society, and to learn ways to use them creatively. Thus, for schools to fulfill their educational mission, phenomena, objects, or situations of the digital networked world should be viewed from three perspectives:

1. The technological perspective questions how digital systems work, explains their operating principles and teaches problem-solving strategies,
2. the socio-cultural perspective considers its interactions with individuals and society,
3. while the user-oriented perspective focuses on its effective and efficient use.

These equally important perspectives are referred to as the Dagstuhl triangle, which has also found its way into national education plans, e.g., in Switzerland. Considering these perspectives in the field of AI does not only connect well to the political discourse but may help assure that learning occurs based on a well-founded technological understanding, fostering applicability but also considering the significant impact AI has on society.

3 Developments in AI and Related Work

AI is the subfield of computer science that is concerned with replicating human cognitive abilities through computer systems and can be roughly divided into two major approaches: On the one hand, there are knowledge-based approaches to AI (sometimes also referred to as "classical" or "good old-fashioned" AI), which deal with the representation of knowledge and the drawing of conclusions through automated reasoning. Machine learning (ML) approaches, on the other hand, derive or identify rules, behaviors, or patterns themselves based on data – in other words, they "learn". This acquired knowledge is stored in a model and can subsequently be applied to new situations or new data.

AI problems are typically characterized either by a high degree of complexity or by the fact that they cannot be formalized conclusively, e.g. because of uncertainty. AI approaches build upon heuristics, probabilistics, statistics, planning, generalization, or reasoning that allow for dealing with these characteristics. However, typical AI systems are structured modularly and consist of multiple CS and/or AI tasks that work closely together. For example, speech recognition systems may involve aspects of hardware, software, pattern recognition, audio processing, and knowledge-based and ML approaches of AI.

Intending to develop guidelines for teaching AI to K-12, a working group identified five big ideas of AI [10]. These ideas comprise of the following:

1. Computers perceive the world using sensors.
2. Agents maintain models/representations of the world and use them for reasoning.
3. Computers can learn from data.
4. Making agents interact comfortably with humans is a substantial challenge for AI developers.
5. AI applications can impact society in both positive and negative ways.

So far, four of the ideas have been underpinned with concepts and learning objectives. However, the comprehensive list also includes learning objectives that are not specific to AI, such as how images or audio are represented digitally in a computer or illustrating how computer sensors work. Furthermore, discussions with stakeholders and teachers alike have revealed that they need a compact curriculum which serves their needs by connecting to both technical literature of the academic field (such as provided by [11]), as well as to established educational standards.

Another approach was chosen by Long and Magerko [12]. Based on an exploratory literature review of 150 documents such as books, conference articles, or university course outlines, the authors identified key concepts, which then formed the basis for their conceptualization of AI literacy – a set of competencies that everyone needs in the context of AI. They subdivide AI Literacy into five overarching themes in the form of questions: What is AI?; What can AI do? How does AI work?; How should AI be used?; How do people perceive AI? However, this approach is limited to a "historical" perspective, as it only reflects on existing material. This might be particularly problematic considering that CS education research on central concepts and principles of AI is not sufficiently elaborated yet. Furthermore, the competencies identified are on a rather general and abstract level.

In recent years, numerous methodological approaches have been developed for teaching AI in the classroom. They range from interactive experiments, unplugged-activities [13], configuring AI models/systems [14, 15], using models within programming projects [16–18] to implement AI algorithms [19, 20]. All these approaches are mostly limited to a small set of particular competencies, but impressively illustrate the breadth of learning approaches for teaching a topic sometimes considered "too hard to understand".

4 Approach

This work was triggered by requests for a curriculum of learning objectives for the field of AI, which connects well with the recent political discourse, can be understood by teachers and stakeholders and takes the comprehensive experiences in CS education into account. It was started within a working group of experts from computing education research and practice. Over the course of one year, a list of AI learning objectives derived empirically as well as stated normatively with respect to the political discourse was curated, contrasted with technical literature and learning resources on AI, and compiled into a preliminary catalog of learning objectives. This catalog was then discussed with experts from the field of AI and K-12 CS education. The learning objectives were refined with the expert group once more, after incorporating this individual feedback, in an iterative process.

The developed catalog aims at two objectives:

(1) The curriculum of learning objectives should support the integration of AI as a topic in existing CS curricula. Thus, learning objectives typically already addressed in existing curricula are not included. Furthermore, learning objectives that are relevant in the field of CS, but not inherent to AI or AI systems, such as sensors or actuators, are omitted.
(2) The curriculum of learning objectives should underpin the importance of computing education as a basis for digital literacy and preparation for living in the digital world. To this end, learning objectives should not only focus e.g., on pure technological or pure societal aspects.

For educators and stakeholders of non-computing domains, this catalog may provide insight into the central concepts and corresponding competencies of AI.

5 Learning Objectives for Artificial Intelligence in Secondary Education

5.1 Technological Perspective (T)

The technological perspective provides insight into how phenomena, artifacts, and systems function or how they are structured. This is particularly difficult for the field of AI, considering that both the term and what is or is not considered AI are under a constant process of change. This ambiguity is reflected within common definitions of the field, such as "AI is the study of how to make computers do things at which, at the moment, people are better" [21]. Therefore, it is even more important that students are able to recognize AI systems in their daily lives, face different definitions and their implications, and characterize AI problems – in contrast to other problems in CS – and typical application areas. As the recent advancements in the field are primarily driven by advances in machine learning, there is a significant amount of attention on this particular domain of AI. However, other relevant approaches to AI must not be ignored – from a CS, as well as a computing education perspective (Fig. 1).

Machine learning deals with algorithms that improve through experience over time [22]. Three different approaches to how machines can learn can be distinguished, which strongly depend on the overall goal and available data: supervised, unsupervised, and reinforcement learning. The corresponding competencies allow students to understand phenomena of their daily lives. For each of these approaches, there are various concrete methods that can make this idea of "learning" accessible within teaching. Crucial for machine learning and its success or failure is the available data which needs to be selected and preprocessed. As machine learning algorithms only learn from data (and therefore past experience), the difference between correlation (that those methods can identify) and actual causality is of utmost importance to assessing the capabilities and limits of such AI systems. The complexity of the models that are learned often provides a further challenge, as individual decisions of the system cannot be comprehended anymore. Therefore, understanding this loss of transparency and ways to tackle it (such as *explainable AI*) are crucial to enabling students to profoundly analyze the consequences of the usage of this technology.

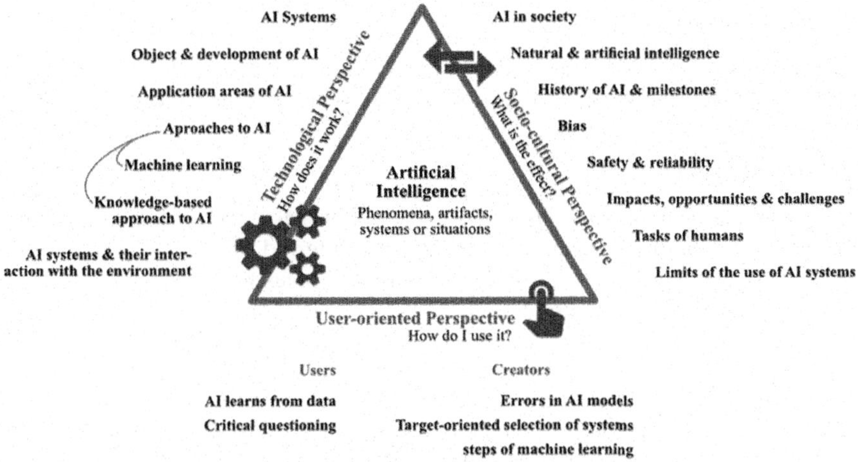

Fig. 1. Learning objectives for AI in secondary computing education according to the three perspectives provided by the Dagstuhl triangle

Knowledge-based approaches to AI, however, are characterized by representing human knowledge in such a way that the computer can then be used for automatic reasoning. Often, knowledge-based and machine learning approaches are used together, supplementing each other. Given the goal of mimicking human intelligence, perceiving (using sensors) and interacting (using actuators) with the environment is a central task in many AI systems. Knowing that such systems typically have a modular structure and, for example, in working with language or images, consist of multiple computer science and/or AI tasks, is a core competency for understanding AI systems.

Students should be able to…

T1 AI Systems

…identify technologies that use AI methods.
…give indicators for when they are interacting with an AI system (e.g. with reference to the Turing test).

T2 Object and Development of AI

…discuss different definitions of AI,
…distinguish between strong and weak AI and give an example for each of these categories.
…distinguish between "AI problems" and other problems in computer science (e.g. with respect to uncertainty, direct relation of input and output) and describe approaches to deal with them (e.g. heuristics, probabilistics, statistics, planning, generalization, predictive and logical reasoning).
…explain the role of artificial intelligence in the history of computer science as well as the developments in computer science that have led to advances in the field (e.g. computing power, Big Data, "AI winter" and "AI summer").

T3 Application Areas of AI

…characterize application areas of artificial intelligence given their specifics (e.g. robotics, language processing, image processing, cognitive systems, artificial life).

T4 Approaches to AI

…distinguish and explain knowledge-based (sometimes also referred to as symbolic or "classical") and machine learning (sometimes also referred to as subsymbolic or data-driven) approaches to AI, state the fundamental differences between these approaches, and give typical examples of applications.

T4.1 Machine Learning

…describe different approaches to machine learning (reinforcement learning, supervised learning, unsupervised learning), explain their differences, and give examples of application in each case.
…assign concrete methods to the different approaches of machine learning and explain their basic functionality (e.g. k-nearest neighbors, decision tree learning, neural networks, linear regression, KMeans, vector quantization, Q-table learning).
…select the appropriate method in light of given data and goals.
…configure the hyperparameters (such as the number of neighbors for k-nearest neighbors) in suitable tools (e.g. in Orange).
…implement a concrete method to solve a problem.
…specify criteria to evaluate a trained model.

T4.1a Data Selection and Preparation

…decide which kind of data is needed for a given problem and prepare the data appropriately.
…explain why different design choices lead to different models.
…justify the procedure of dividing a data set into training and test data.
…describe how the training examples provided in an initial data set can affect the results of an algorithm.

T4.1b Correlation and Causality

…explain the difference between correlation and causality, give an example of each, and explain where these concepts are relevant in the field of AI.

T4.1c Transparency and Explainability

…distinguish transparency and explainability of AI systems.
…explain why the transparency of AI systems is often difficult to establish.
…name principles of algorithmic transparency and accountability.

T 4.2 Knowledge-based Approach to AI

...explain the approach and methods of knowledge-based AI approaches with reference to knowledge representation and reasoning.
...model knowledge explicitly in a representation form (e.g. as facts and rules, or semantic network,...).
...explain different methods of reasoning (e.g. search, logical reasoning, probabilistic reasoning).

T 5 AI systems and Their Interaction With the Environment

...describe the modular structure of AI systems and divide an AI problem into different AI and computer science tasks.
...explain how AI systems collect data via sensors and interact with the world via actuators.
...illustrate that different sensors support different types of representation and thus give different insights about the world.

5.2 Socio-Cultural Perspective (S)

Within the socio-cultural perspective of the Dagstuhl triangle, the interactions of technology with individuals and society are addressed. Undoubtedly, AI severely affects society in many ways. The implications are vast but sometimes subtle. Therefore, it is all the more important that students are able to identify societal areas affected by AI. Furthermore, learning about AI also helps to strengthen understanding about humankind and natural intelligence in general and how the advancements of AI systems dovetail with the history of technology and society. As AI systems are increasingly incorporated into decision making, students have to be aware of the possibility of bias inherent in the data used for training and its influence on fairness and reliability of AI systems – once more reflecting other areas where e.g., problems resulting from representation issues are also common. As future shapers of society, students must be enabled to analyze the impact, opportunities, and challenges of AI. Furthermore, they have to know about ways to tackle potential problems of AI usage that help ensuring its responsible use. For this, it is crucial to clearly characterize the role humans are playing in creating AI systems. Only this way, an informed debate regarding the future of our society that takes opportunities as well as limits into account is possible.

Students should be able to...

S1 AI in Society

...identify and characterize areas of society affected by AI and find examples of AI from their daily life and classify them.

S2 Natural and Artificial Intelligence

...identify differences between artificially and naturally intelligent systems.

S3 History of AI and Milestones

…explain the history of AI and state milestones in its development and its importance to society (e.g. Deep Blue, Watson, AlphaGo, voice assistants).

S4 Bias

…explain why biases in data affect the results of machine learning and discuss implications for the use of AI systems.

S5 Safety and Reliability of AI Systems

…discuss the reliability of AI systems.
…name attack scenarios on AI systems (adversarial attacks) and classify them in terms of level (physical level, data level, protocol level).

S6 Impacts, Opportunities and Challenges

…analyze the implications, opportunities, and challenges of artificial intelligence for our society (e.g. the impact of automation on human workforce needs, idea of singularity, diversity, responsibility).
…explain ways to counter the problems (e.g. fake news in the context of deep fakes, analyzing and influencing human behavior) resulting from the use of AI (e.g. democratically determined fairness criteria, regulation of AI use, explainability).

S7 Human Tasks

…describe the tasks of humans when using AI systems (e.g. configuring, designing, critically assessing data).

S8 Limits of the Use of AI Systems

…explain the limits of the use of AI systems.
…explain misconceptions about the use of AI systems (e.g. Eliza effect, Tale-Spin effect and SimCity effect).

5.3 User-Oriented Perspective (U)

In the Dagstuhl triangle, the user-oriented perspective focuses on the purposeful selection of systems and their effective and efficient use. It includes questions about how and why tools are selected and used. For AI systems, we have to distinguish between two user scenarios within the user-oriented perspective:

(A) Consumers or end-users who use technology that passively incorporates AI (e.g. implicitly in apps, translation software, Alexa and co., self-driving cars) and.
(B) Users who use AI actively for creating their own artifacts or solving AI problems by processing their own data sets – meaning they create, configure and use AI models explicitly (i.e. in systems such as Orange, MS Azure AI, LightSide or calling APIs such as Huggingface).

(A) **Consumer or End-User (Non-Creative)**
For consumers or end-users who use applications that have AI systems embedded, (especially reflective) competencies described in the socio-cultural perspective are sufficient. There are no AI-specific "operating skills", as AI is geared towards the user. However, since AI systems do have an enormous impact on our personal lives, it is all the more important to (based upon the technological perspective) be able to interpret and use the results provided by an AI system:

Students should be able to…

UA-1 AI Learns from Data

…explain that AI systems can learn from available data, including personal data, and make informed decisions regarding the disclosure of data in the interaction with AI systems.
…distinguish AI systems that apply generic AI models and AI systems that adapt to the user.

UA-2 Critical Questioning

…critically question the results of the conscious and unconscious use of AI systems (e.g. suggestions and prices in online stores).

(B) **Users Who Use AI Actively for Creating Their Own Artifacts**
In contrast to mere end-users, users that employ AI in a "creative" manner by creating, configuring, and using AI models need to be familiar with AI methods and tools, but also be able to identify and correct possible underlying errors. In addition, respective tools must be chosen purposefully, and actual tool-specific "operating skills" are needed:

Students should be able to…

UB-1 Errors in AI Models

…explain why results of AI systems may contain errors, question obtained results, and identify and correct errors.

UB-2 Target-Oriented Selection of Systems

…name and justify selection criteria (e.g. with regard to data protection, bias, etc.) for deciding on an effective, efficient system in light of the data to be used and the goal.

UB-3 Steps of Machine Learning

…apply the steps of ML to solve a specific data-based problem (collect data, label as appropriate, select method, apply method, interpret results) in suitable tools.

6 Discussion and Outlook

Working with the catalog of learning objectives provided impressive insights into how much interested stakeholders and teachers can learn by simply reading it. Due to the recent omnipresence of machine learning, many are not aware of the breadth of the field of AI and the relevance of knowledge-based approaches. However, this part of AI has been very important in history, offers valuable learning experiences for understanding many AI approaches and may play a crucial role in hybrid approaches to AI which are getting increasingly important in AI research and development.

Furthermore, the socio-cultural perspective in particular is often overseen when new materials for AI topics are developed [23]. In line with the Dagstuhl triangle, we believe it is important that potentials and societal challenges are not discussed in isolation but based on a sound fundamental understanding of the technical fundamentals of AI.

An interesting question was to identify those learning objectives related to the use of AI systems: It is an inherent requirement of AI systems to be intuitive to use, removing the need for any special AI application skills. Similar to the proliferation of computer technology in the 1960s and 1970s, "demystification" is often seen as a primary educational goal, which can be achieved through the comprehension of basic methods [19]. Just as standard software that enables ordinary users to creatively implement their own problems and goals became increasingly important in the 1980s, we are also seeing more and more AI systems that enable ordinary users to evaluate their own data using AI methods to develop creative solutions. With the digital transformation and the digitization-related advancements of all disciplines, we believe that this aspect will become particularly important in schools in the future.

With the primary goal of answering the question of which distinct AI learning objectives might be important in secondary education, the question of an order and the relative importance of competencies, as well as that of the competency levels, was not considered in this work. Considering the currently very heterogeneous attempts to integrate the topic of AI into the curricula, this approach does not seem to be purposeful to us. Thus, the presented catalog can be used to comprehensively design half a year of CS lessons, but also to give students a brief insight into the topic. Furthermore, it allows for analyzing what competencies are addressed in current curricula and teaching materials and provides insight into the central concepts and corresponding competencies of AI – even for stakeholders of non-computing domains.

With the approach taken, it is obvious that the catalog does not include competencies on detailed levels, as i.e., AI4K12 [10] are slowly progressing to. However, the abstraction level chosen allows for quickly grasping possible focus areas of AI education and allows other disciplines to connect e.g., ICT/Media education to the application-oriented perspective or the humanities with the societal perspective.

Eventually, AI competencies must be merged into CS curricula. To this end, in a first step, what can and should be learned in the context of AI needs to be characterized. With this catalog of learning objectives, we present a recommendation to address this need, which has already proven to be helpful for several stakeholders in creating CS curricula.

References

1. Hubwieser, P., et al.: A global snapshot of computer science education in k-12 schools. In: Proceedings of the 2015 ITiCSE on working group reports, pp. 65–83 (2015)
2. Touretzky, D.S., Gardner-McCune, C.: Artificial intelligence thinking in K–12. In: Kong, S.-C., Abelson, H. (eds.) Computational Thinking Education in K–12: Artificial Intelligence Literacy and Physical Computing, pp. 153–180. The MIT Press (2022). https://doi.org/10.7551/mitpress/13375.003.0013
3. Tedre, M., Denning, P., Toivonen, T.: Ct 2.0. In: Proceedings of the 21st Koli Calling International Conference on Computing Education Research, pp. 1–8 (2021)
4. Brabrand, C., Dahl, B.: Constructive alignment and the solo taxonomy: a comparative study of university competences in computer science vs. mathematics. In: Conferences in Research and Practice in Information Technology, vol. 88, pp. 3–17. Australian Computer Society (2008)
5. Denning, P.J.: Great principles in computing curricula. In: Proceedings of the 35th SIGCSE Technical Symposium on Computer Science Education, pp. 336–341 (2004)
6. Schwill, A.: Fundamental ideas of computer science. Bull.-Eur. Assoc. Theor. Comput. Sci. **53**, 274 (1994)
7. Denning, P.J.: Great principles of computing. Commun. ACM **46**(11), 15–20 (2003)
8. Bell, T., Tymann, P., Yehudai, A.: The big ideas in computer science for k-12 curricula. Bull. EATCS **1**(124) (2018)
9. Brinda, T., Diethelm, I.: Education in the digital networked world. In: Tatnall, A., Webb, M. (eds.) WCCE 2017. IAICT, vol. 515, pp. 653–657. Springer, Cham (2017). https://doi.org/10.1007/978-3-319-74310-3_66
10. Touretzky, D., Gardner-McCune, C., Martin, F., Seehorn, D.: Envisioning ai for k-12: what should every child know about AI? Proc. AAAI Conf. Artif. Intell. **33**(01), 9795–9799 (2019). https://doi.org/10.1609/aaai.v33i01.33019795
11. Russel, S., Norvig, P: Artificial Intelligence: A Modern Approach, 4th edn. Pearson (2020)
12. Long, D., Magerko, B.: What is AI literacy? competencies and design considerations. In: Proceedings of the 2020 CHI conference on human factors in computing systems, pp. 1–16 (2020)
13. Lindner, A., Seegerer, S., Romeike, R.: Unplugged activities in the context of AI. In: Pozdniakov, S.N., Dagienė, V. (eds.) ISSEP 2019. LNCS, vol. 11913, pp. 123–135. Springer, Cham (2019). https://doi.org/10.1007/978-3-030-33759-9_10
14. Carney, M., et al.: Teachable machine: Approachable web-based tool for exploring machine learning classification. In: Extended Abstracts of the 2020 CHI Conference on Human Factors in Computing Systems, pp. 1–8 (2020)
15. Zimmermann-Niefield, A., Turner, M., Murphy, B., Kane, S.K., Shapiro, R.B.: Youth learning machine learning through building models of athletic moves. In: Proceedings of the 18th ACM International Conference on Interaction Design and Children, pp. 121–132 (2019)
16. Druga, S.: Growing up with AI: Cognimates: from coding to teaching machines. Ph.D. thesis, Massachusetts Institute of Technology (2018)
17. Kahn, K.M., Megasari, R., Piantari, E., Junaeti, E.: AI programming by children using snap! block programming in a developing country. In: EC-TELPractitioner Proceedings 2018:13th European Conference on Technology Enhanced Learning (2018)
18. Lane, D.: Explaining artificial intelligence. In: HelloWorld, 4, (2018)
19. Jatzlau, S., Michaeli, T., Seegerer, S., Romeike, R.: It's not magic after all–machine learning in snap! using reinforcement learning. In: 2019 IEEE Blocks and Beyond Workshop (B&B). pp. 37–41. IEEE (2019)

20. Michaeli, T., Seegerer, S., Jatzlau, S., Romeike, R.: Looking beyond supervised classification and image recognition–unsupervised learning with snap! CONSTRUCTIONISM 2020 395 (2020)
21. Rich, E.: Artificial Intelligence. McGraw-Hill, New York, NY USA (1983)
22. Mitchell, T.: Machine Learning, New York. McGraw-Hill, NY USA (1997)
23. Zhou, X., Van Brummelen, J., Lin, P.: Designing AI learning experiences for k-12: emerging works, future opportunities and a design framework. arXiv preprint arXiv:2009.10228 (2020)

Robotics in Primary Education: A Lexical Analysis of Teachers' Resources Across Robots

Christophe Reffay[1(✉)], Gabriel Parriaux[2], Béatrice Drot-Delange[3], and Mehdi Khaneboubi[4]

[1] University Bourgogne Franche-Comté, Besançon, France
christophe.reffay@univ-fcomte.fr
[2] University of Teacher Education, Lausanne, Switzerland
gabriel.parriaux@hepl.ch
[3] University of Clermont Auvergne, Clermont-Ferrand, France
beatrice.drot-delange@uca.fr
[4] CY Cergy Paris University, Paris, France
mehdi.khaneboubi@u-cergy.fr

Abstract. Through a lexical analysis, this study examines the relationship between the terms used in various educational resources about robots. These resources were authored by novice or expert teachers in primary schools. Our hypothesis is that the computer science concepts discussed in an activity are different depending on the type of robot. The first results confirm dependence between the type of robot and the lexicon used in the resources. The corpus is explored according to three thematic sets of terms: Computer Science (CS), Pedagogy and Move with special attention for CS terms to compare the vocabulary used for sequential and event-driven programming robots.

Keywords: educational robotics · event-driven programming · sequential programming · teacher education

1 Introduction

In the recent years, we have witnessed in several countries an important movement towards the introduction of Computational Thinking (CT) skills in the curricula for compulsory education. In 2022, a publication of the European Union indicates that 15 countries have CT skills integrated in primary education and 12 countries have CT skills as a compulsory element in both primary and secondary level. 15 countries have renewed their curriculum between 2016 and 2021 to include CT skills [1].

In this context, programming is being considered a central element in the development of these new CT skills [2]. Depending on the educational goals and the material available in class, teachers design learning activities and make use

Published by Springer Nature Switzerland AG 2023
T. Keane et al. (Eds.): WCCE 2022, IFIP AICT 685, pp. 209–220, 2023.
https://doi.org/10.1007/978-3-031-43393-1_20

of different Computer Programming Learning Environments. Many activities are based on the use of tangible artifacts such as robots.

In France and Switzerland, pre-assembled mobile robots (e.g. Beebot, Thymio) appear to be the most common used in class at primary level. They are also among the tools often presented to teachers in teacher education programs on CT skills. Robotics kits, including components that have to be built (e.g. LEGO®-Mindstorms™) also exist, but their use seems to be less widespread. In terms of competencies, pre-assembled robots let kids focus on the programming tasks, where robotics kits are more oriented towards the development of engineering/technology ones [3].

Pre-assembled mobile robots can be very diverse, from simple automata like Beebot or Bluebot that are being programmed with buttons and have no sensors to more advanced robots like Thymio that have sensors and can react to their external environment.

According to the classification of Computer Programming Learning Environments for primary education proposed by [4], Beebot and Bluebot robots fall in the "Logo family programming environments" category and more precisely in the "Roamers" (floor turtles) subcategory. In this category, a program is defined as a sequence of ordered instructions having a beginning and an end. Ozobot and Thymio robots are falling in another category named "Physical Computing Environments" and subcategory "Educational robotics environments." These last two robots may use a programming language leading on event-driven programming, associating events and actions to define their behavior, i.e.: a very different way to define a program.

In terms of programming, there is an important difference between those two categories, one being uniquely focused on sequential programming and the other being more oriented towards event-driven programming.

2 Educational Robotics and Programming Paradigms

Robots are now widely used in primary education in many countries and researchers like [5] estimate their use can have a potential impact on the way science and technology is taught at all levels. Positive results can be seen in the use of educational robotics to develop an understanding of concepts related to STEM [5,6] and also, in more specific contexts, to foster 21st century skills [7].

Even if the development of social competencies using educational robotics is welcome, we should keep in mind that one of the main goal of introducing robots in classrooms is to let pupils learn basic computer science and programming concepts [8]. We are interested in understanding what programming notions and skills are taught by teachers with the different categories of robots.

The two central concepts in event-driven programming are *events* (something that occurs) and *event handlers* (a piece of program that executes as a reaction to an event). The main difference with sequential programming (where a program gets executed from a beginning to an end) is that an event-driven program waits indefinitely for events to occur and reacts to any considered events happening.

With the classic procedural approach, there is an *inversion of control* because the execution order depends on external events.

Such a different approach of programming can be challenging for young pupils to handle. First, it might be difficult to grasp the logic of functionality when it is distributed across event handlers. Then, understanding event-driven programming might require the comprehension of more advanced notions that are not seen in introduction courses like *origins* and *routing of events*, *device drivers*, *parallelism* and *concurrency*, *states* or *model-view-controller*. Depending on the programming environment, some parts of an event-driven program might be completely hidden from the user, making it impossible to trace code from the beginning to the end [9]. The same authors observe that students who are introduced to programming using event-driven approaches do not develop some algorithmic skills that other students would generally acquire through imperative-procedural programming languages leading on a sequential execution model.

Unfortunately, we couldn't find a research paper about the set of concepts that students should learn to master event-driven programming, or about their misconceptions of those concepts.

In the field of Educational robotics, the question of programming paradigms for robots has received little attention in the scientific literature. Among the 105 papers analyzed in their systematic review on event programming, [10] note that only two of them concern robots (Social Robot Toolkit, Thymio). We couldn't find any research articles that addresses the best practices for teachers in such a context either [10].

Based on these observations, we propose to investigate the link between the type of robots in educational robotics activities and the lexicon used to describe those activities.

3 Research Questions

We propose to look at pedagogical resources produced by teachers for activities in educational robotics to see if we can find any significant difference between them according to different variables. Considering teacher education as a long term development process, we compare resources authored by novices (i.e.: pre-service teachers) in our schools of education vs resources produced and published on the Internet by experienced teachers or teams.

By using lexical analysis, we capture the vocabulary used by teachers in their pedagogical resources. Then, we formulate the hypothesis that the lexicon is significantly different according to the type of robots that they are using. More precisely, we investigate if some specific terms reveal different CS notions or programming paradigms depending on the type of robots used. Finally, we can formulate our research question as follows:

RQ1 *Validation: Is the lexicon used in pedagogical resources statistically dependent on the type of robots used in educational robotics?*

RQ2 *Exploration: Which are the specific terms used in pedagogical resources for the various types of robots?*

RQ3 *Do we have lexical differences between resources authored by pre-service teachers and experts?*

4 Methods: Data Collection and Analysis

4.1 Corpus: A Collection of 120 Pedagogical Resources

The corpus contains 120 texts authored by teachers in two French-speaking countries. They describe activities in the field of educational robotics for pupils in primary schools. 59 of these texts are documents preparing or presenting pedagogical activities produced by pre-service teachers in the context of their studies in three different teacher education institutions. These 59 texts were selected from a corpus of 135 productions analyzed in a previous study on pedagogical strategies used by pre-service teachers [11]. Other 61 texts were collected from the web following a standardized query protocol and are authored by experienced teachers (teams). The resulting corpus of 120 texts is also qualified by the following criteria: the robot used in the activity the age of target pupils and the country from which the educational system depends. Table 1 presents the composition of the corpus according to the author's expertise and robots' names grouped by types (sequence-based vs. event-based).

Table 1. Number of resources distributed in the corpus according to authors expertise and robot used

Author	Sequence based robots				Event based robots			All
	Beebot	Bluebot	Other_Seq	Sum Seq.	Ozobot	Thymio	Sum Event	Sum
Novice	17	20	7	44	2	13	15	59
Expert	16	12		28	17	16	33	61
All	33	32	7	72	19	29	48	120

Non formatted text has been automatically extracted from original documents: text contained in presentations in various formats (.pptx, .key), in text documents (.odt, .docx) or in PDF files, and audio speech from video (excluding visual text appearing on images or video files). Some cleaning was necessary to get a syntactically correct text content.

4.2 Lexical Analysis

Using a textometry software TXM, we built the lexicon (12,008 different words), lemmatised according to French rules (resulting in 7,881 distinct lemmas) from the entire corpus (252,960 words). The lemmas frequencies range is [1–17, 403]. Considering the list of lemmas in decreasing order of their frequency, we found that the lemma *robot* was the first meaningful term having the highest frequency (2,250).

In Table 1, the maximum number of resources in a subset is 20 (Novice - Bluebot). This implies that a term appearing only once in each resource of this subset and in no others would have 20 occurrences. Consequently, we decided to consider only lemmas having a frequency f (such as $20 \leq f \leq 2250$). This choice reduced the list of lemmas to be analysed from 7881 to 1104.

From these 1,104 lemmas, we manually selected the 373 ones that could be meaningfully associated to the three following themes: Pedagogy, Computer Science (CS) and Moves. Note that some lemmas (e.g. *séquence, programme*) may fall in more than one category (e.g. *séquence*: sequence of instructions or sequence of pedagogical activities; *programme*: computer code or national curriculum; these two words may refer either to CS or Pedagogy). In other words, our sets of lemmas are not mutually exclusive.

In the resulting extraction, we have 195 lemmas for Pedagogy (e.g. *activité, évaluer, collaborer, élève, enseignant...*; i.e.: activity, evaluate, collaborate, pupil, teacher...), 134 lemmas for CS (e.g. *algorithme, boucle, capteur, effecteur...*; i.e.: algorithm, loop, sensor, effector...) and 77 lemmas for Moves (e.g. *position, grille, tourner, gauche, droite, derrière, devant...*; i.e.: position, grid, turn, left, right, backward, forward...).

4.3 Statistical Analyses

We conducted statistics using R [12] on the lexicon following different organization of our data. To deal with categorical variables we constructed contingency tables to search for relations between robots and terms used in the resources. Chi-square test was performed. Correspondence analysis [13] plots let us represent in a two-dimension space our variables in order to interpret the kind of proximity or distance that we could find between our categories.

5 Results

5.1 Dependence Between Lexicon and Resources Classified by Robots—Words Grouped by Theme

In a first set of analyzes, we group words by theme (CS, Pedagogy and Move) and pedagogical resources by robot. Because of the very small numbers of texts for Cubetto (1), Mouse (4) and Robotdoc (2) we decided to group these 7 texts into a single category named: "Other_Seq" referring to "other sequence-based robots" (as presented in Table 1).

For each robot and corresponding resources, we counted the number of occurrences of each individual word from each theme and sum them. This gives us a contingency table with 5 categories of robots and 3 categories of words.

As a result, Pearson's chi-square test shows that we can reject the null hypothesis ($\chi2(8) = 1365.8, \mathrm{p} < 0.01$). There is a significant dependence between the frequency of the words grouped by theme and the type of robot. But they are only weakly associated (Cramer's V of 0.1105).

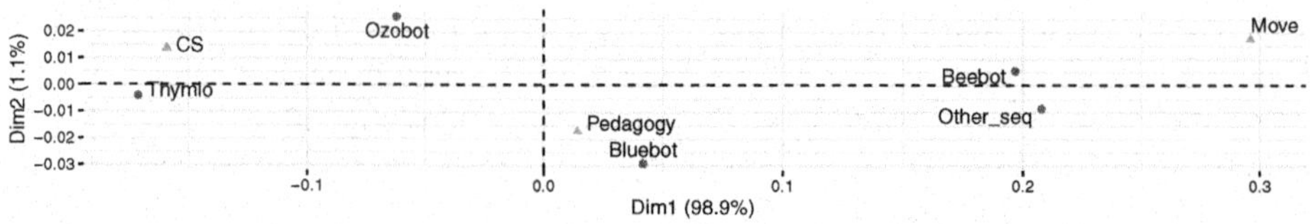

Fig. 1. Correspondence Analysis: Robots - Themes

Figure 1 spreads the different themes and robots on a factorial plan for correspondence analysis (CA).

On Fig. 1, the first axis (Dim 1) is strongly discriminant (almost 99%). This first factor of the CA seems to separate mostly between CS and Move categories of words. Pedagogy, being near the origin, doesn't discriminate according to this first factor. This first factor also serves to discriminate between event-based robots (Thymio and Ozobot Bit), which are closer to CS, and sequence-based robots. The latter (Beebot and Other_Seq) are closer to Move. Bluebot does not seem to discriminate according to this factor.

This first analysis shows us that there is a dependence—even weak—between words classified by theme and pedagogical resources classified by robots. An association exists between CS lexicon and resources produced on event-based robots on one side, and between Move lexicon and resources produced on sequence-based robots on the other side.

5.2 Dependence Between Lexicon and Resources Classified by Robots/Level of Expertise of Authors—Words Grouped by Theme

In order to observe how the level of expertise influences these positions, we conduct a second set of analyzes splitting each robot category from Fig. 1 to identify those authored by novices and those by experts in Fig. 2. We obtain a contingency table with 9 categories mixing robots and level of expertise and 3 categories of words.

Pearson's chi-square test shows that we can reject the null hypothesis ($\chi2(16) = 1761.8, \mathrm{p} < 0.01$). There is a significant dependence between the frequency of the words grouped by theme and the type of robot when we take into account the level of expertise. But they are only weakly associated (Cramer's V of 0.1255).

Again, on the CA presented in Fig. 2, the first axis is strongly discriminant (83%). As in our previous analysis, the first factor of the CA seems to separate mostly between CS and Move categories of words. If we look at the pedagogical resources grouped by robot and by level of expertise, we see the separation between resources produced by experts for event-based robots (Thymio and Ozobot)—associated to CS—and resources produced for sequence-based robots—associated to Move—without real distinction in the level of expertise.

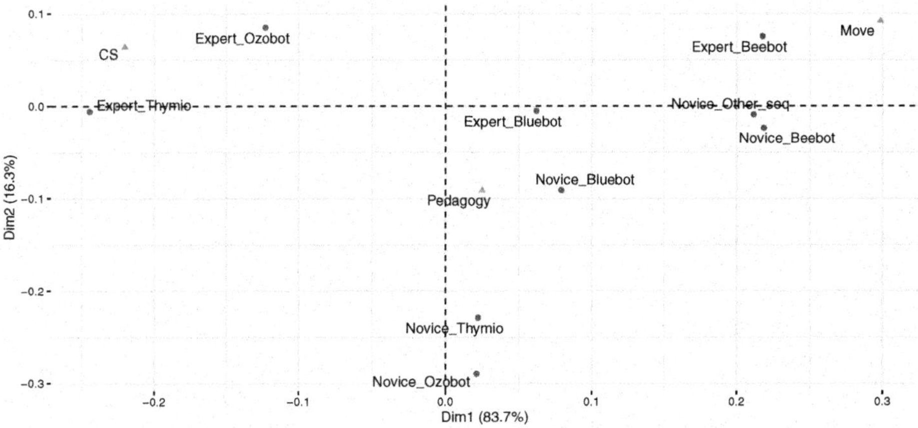

Fig. 2. Correspondence Analysis: Authors - Robots - Themes

This second analysis shows us that there is a dependence—even weak—between words classified by theme and pedagogical resources classified by robots and by level of expertise of their authors. An association exists between CS lexicon and resources produced by experts on event-based robots on one side, and between Move lexicon and resources produced on sequence-based robots on the other side.

5.3 Dependence Between CS Lexicon and Resources Classified by Robots—Words Taken Individually

Having considered until now our lexicon as an aggregation of words grouped by themes, we analyze now our data considering each word of the lexicon separately.

In this third set of analysis, we first extract from the lexicon all the words belonging to the CS theme, drop the others, and keep all pedagogical resources. Then we grouped resources by robot. For each robot and corresponding resources, we counted and summed the number of occurrences of each individual word from the CS theme. Other sequential robots (Cubetto, Robotdoc and Mouse) with few corresponding resources had to be abandoned as they had a lot of zero values. For the same reason, words appearing in too few resources were removed. This gives us a resulting contingency table with 94 words from the CS lexicon and four robots (Beebot, Bluebot, Thymio and Ozobot Bit).

In this case, Pearson's chi-square test shows that we can reject the null hypothesis ($\chi 2(279) = 5600.6, \mathrm{p} < 0.01$). There is a significant dependence between the frequency of the words of the vocabulary in the theme "CS" and the type of robot on which pedagogical resources are based. The strength of the association is moderate (Cramer's V of 0.3312).

Correspondence analysis offers a representation where the first two factors cover 80% of variance (49.38 and 30.99 respectively). To facilitate the interpretation, we display a bi-plot of the 30 most contributive variables in Fig. 3.

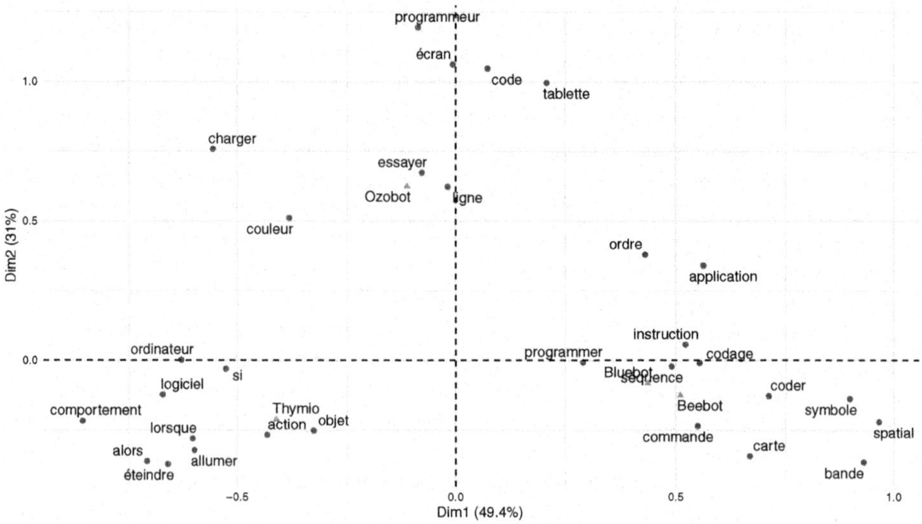

Fig. 3. Correspondence Analysis with CS lexicon: most contributive words

According to the first axis, there is an opposition between Thymio/Ozobot and the couple Beebot/Bluebot. On the second axis, we observe an opposition between Ozobot Bit (always used in following lines mode) and the three other robots.

We observe a so-called "Guttman effect" with points drawing a kind of parabolic shape. It means that there is a link between variables. We can interpret it by saying that the vocabulary is discriminant.

If we look at the vocabulary, the first axis separates words related to the machine and to the technical dimension (*comportement, allumer, éteindre, action, objet...*; behavior, switch on/off, action, object...)—associated with Thymio—from words related to programming (*instruction, symbol, order, séquence, coder...*)—associated with Beebot and Bluebot.

5.4 Dependence Between CS Lexicon and Novices' Resources Classified by Robots—Words Taken Individually

In a fourth set of analyses, we conduct the same analysis, now considering only resources authored by novices. Having only two resources on Ozobot authored by novices, this robot is not considered here. Taking into account only a sub part of the corpus, the set of CS terms also differs.

In the case of novices, we obtain a contingency table with 54 words from the CS lexicon and three robots (Beebot, Bluebot and Thymio). Pearson's chi-square test shows that we can reject the null hypothesis ($\chi 2(106) = 448.37, \mathrm{p} < 0.01$). For novices, there is a significant dependence between the frequency of the words of the vocabulary in the theme "CS" and the type of robot on which pedagogical resources are based. The strength of the association is still moderate (Cramer's

V of 0.2955), but less than in the previous analysis: when we did not separate resources by level of expertise.

Correspondence analysis offers a representation where the first two factors cover 100% of variance (57.70 and 42.29 respectively). To facilitate the interpretation, we display a biplot of the 30 most contributive variables in the case of novices in Fig. 4.

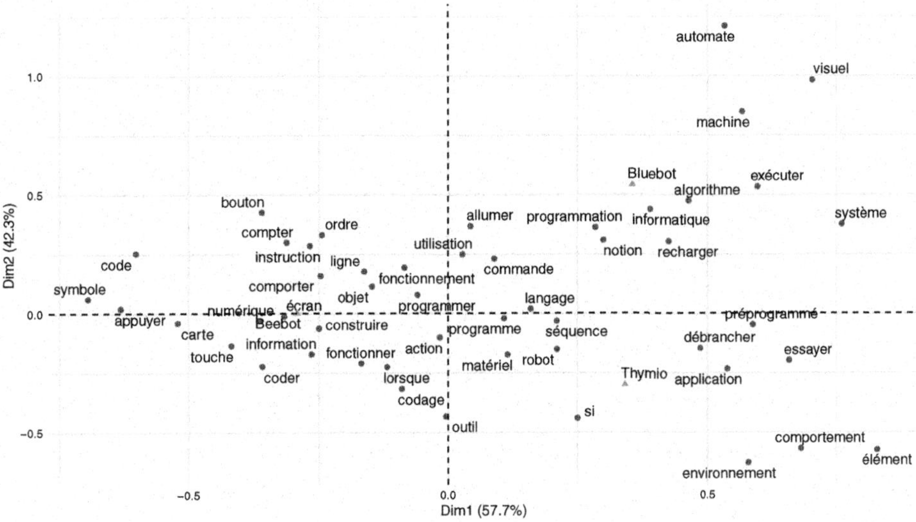

Fig. 4. Correspondence Analysis with CS lexicon (novices): most contributive words

For the first axis, the most discriminant words—those with the highest contribution to the orientation of the axis 1 (*contrib*) and those best represented by axis 1 (cos^2)—are *code, carte, appuyer* on the left-hand side (i.e.: code, card, push—*contrib=12.60, 11.62 and 8.61*; $cos^2 = 0.850, 0.994$ *and* 0.999 respectively) and *robot* (i.e.: robot—*contrib=7.75*, $cos^2 = 0.657$) on the right-hand side. On this dimension, we observe an opposition between the Beebot and the other two robots. For the second axis, the most discriminant words are *automate, programmation, bouton, machine* (automaton, programming, button, machine—*contrib=10.80, 7.18, 6.57 and 5.70*; $cos^2 = 0.837, 0.618, 0.584$ *and* 0.692 respectively) on the top and *si* (if—*contrib=9.66*, $cos^2 = 0.756$) on the bottom. This second dimension shows an opposition between Thymio and Bluebot. If we compare Fig. 3 with Fig. 4, we can see that the very similar robots Beebot and Bluebot are plotted near each other on Fig. 3 (all authors) but very far away on Fig. 4 (novices only).

If we look at the vocabulary, it's not so easy to interpret. But we can find:

- near Beebot (on the left-hand side): vocabulary typically used for the first manipulation of such a toy with young pupils: *appuyer, carte, touche, code, objet* (i.e.: push, card, button, code, object)

- near Bluebot (in the upper right quadrant): the terms rather used one step further in programming: *informatique, algorithme, programmation, exécuter, notion, automate* (i.e.: CS, algorithm, programming, to execute, notion, automaton)
- and finally near Thymio (in the lower right quadrant): the words describing the behavior of a reactive object in its environment: *matériel, robot, si, comportement, environnement* (i.e.: material, robot, if, behavior, environment).

However, these are the terms we were able to interpret and that we expected to find in the neighbourhood of each of these robots. But other words have positions that are difficult to explain. For example, the word *séquence* appears near Thymio and far away from Beebot and Bluebot. These two robots being considered as sequence-based ones we expected that this word would be placed near to them and not near to the event-based robot: Thymio. An in-depth read of the 47 occurrences of the word *séquence* in resources authored by novices reveals that 44 of them refer to a pedagogical sequence and only 3 concern a sequence of actions. Another word, *objet* (i.e.: object) is placed near Beebot on Fig. 4. When checking the 18 occurrences of *objet* in the novices' resources, we verified that all of them designate a physical object to be manipulated or detected by the robot. It never refers to object oriented programming.

5.5 Dependence Between CS Lexicon and Experts' Resources Classified by Robots—Words Taken Individually

In the case of experts, we obtain a contingency table with 83 words from the CS lexicon and 4 robots (Beebot, Bluebot, Thymio and Ozobot).

The first observation is that CS lexicon is narrower for novices (54 words) than for experts (83 words).

Pearson's chi-square test shows that we can reject the null hypothesis ($\chi2(246) = 4635.4, \mathrm{p} < 0.01$). For experts, there is a significant dependence between the frequency of the words of the vocabulary in the theme "CS" and the type of robot on which pedagogical resources are based. The strength of the association is moderate and a little bit greater than for novices or than in the case when we did not separate resources (Cramer's V of 0.3426).

The correspondence analysis for resources from experts draws the robots nearly in the same position as in the previous analysis which did not take into account the level of expertise and presented on Fig. 3.

6 Conclusion

Our exploratory research compared the lexicon of pedagogical resources authored by novices and experienced teachers. A focus has been made on Computer Science terms to analyse differences across the robots used in educational robotics: sequence-based versus event-based. The statistical analysis shows a significant dependence between vocabulary and type of robots used. This dependence is even greater for experts who tend to use more CS terms than novices. The discriminant terms oppose technical object description (machine aspects) for Thymio to more general programming concepts for Beebot and Bluebot.

Coming back to our research questions, we were asking whether the lexicon used in pedagogical resources was statistically dependent on the type of robots used in educational robotics (RQ1). All our analyzes have shown that there was a significant dependence between the lexicon used inside pedagogical resources and the type of robots it was focusing on. We could find in the pedagogical resources that we analyzed three lexical fields that were different for each group of robots. We can answer positively to our first question.

Then we were asking what were the specific terms used in pedagogical resources for the various types of robots (RQ2). We have seen that there were differences according to the level of expertise, with experts differentiating more clearly between a vocabulary around programming when using sequence-based robots and a vocabulary around machine when using event-based robots. Such a difference of vocabulary has not been observed so clearly with novices.

Finally, we wanted to know if there were lexical differences between resources authored by pre-service teachers and experts (RQ3). We have seen that CS vocabulary is less developed in resources produced by novices. We have also observed that the distribution of words according to the factors of the Correspondence analysis were not the same for novices than for experts, with a distinction between basic manipulation of a robot and more general programming vocabulary for novices where experts were opposing programming to machine. We can also answer positively to our third question.

We are aware of some limits for these results. In data collection, the words appearing on images or video files were not captured and then are not considered in the statistical analyses. The nature of the productions authored by novices and experts is different. Novices produced shorter preparation document to conduct an activity with their pupils. Experts documents were three times longer (as a mean) and more explicit because the goal was to share with peer teachers. This can partly explain the unbalanced use of CS terms.

Our conclusions can not easily be generalized, as our analyses might be specific to the context of the three institutions of teacher education where they were conducted. The cultural aspect can also play a role and other countries could have very different situations.

Based on this study, one can see that event-based robots are the one used in primary school to discover machine aspects of technical objects and sequence-based programming robots are rather used to initiate pupils to sequential programming. The authors of this article, involved in the field of teacher education on computational thinking, note that different types of robots are presented during teacher training sessions as equivalent alternatives. This might represent a difficulty for teachers who want to teach programming concepts to their pupils. This could be more explicitly explained to pre-service teachers in their teacher education sessions. Another possible road in teacher education could be to teach the distinction between the two notional models: sequential or event-driven, changing the locus of control from the programmer to the environment.

References

1. Bocconi, S., et al.: Reviewing Computational Thinking in Compulsory Education (2022). ISBN 9789276472087
2. Balanskat, A., Engelhardt, K.: Computing our future: computer programming and coding-priorities, school curricula and initiatives across Europe. European Schoolnet (2014)
3. Misirli, A., Komis, V.: Robotics and programming concepts in early childhood education: a conceptual framework for designing educational scenarios. In: Karagiannidis, C., Politis, P., Karasavvidis, I. (eds.) Research on e-Learning and ICT in Education, pp. 99–118. Springer, New York (2014). https://doi.org/10.1007/978-1-4614-6501-0_8
4. Fessakis, G., Komis, V., Dimitracopoulou, A., Prantsoudi, S.: Overview of the computer programming learning environments for primary education. Rev. Sci. Math. ICT Educ. **13**(1), 7–33 (2019)
5. Alimisis, D.: Educational robotics: open questions and new challenges. Themes Sci. Technol. Educ. **6**(1), 63–71 (2013)
6. Benitti, F.B.V.: Exploring the educational potential of robotics in schools: a systematic review. Comput. Educ. **58**(3), 978–988 (2012)
7. Theodoropoulou, I., Lavidas, K., Komis, V.: Results and prospects from the utilization of educational robotics in Greek schools. Technol. Knowl. Learn. **28**, 225–240 (2021). https://doi.org/10.1007/s10758-021-09555-w
8. Mussati, A., Giang, C., Piatti, A., Mondada, F.: A tangible programming language for the educational robot Thymio. In: 2019 10th International Conference on Information, Intelligence, Systems and Applications (IISA), pp. 1–4. IEEE (2019)
9. Halland, K., Malan, K.: Reflections by teachers learning to program. In: Proceedings of the 2003 Annual Research Conference of the South African Institute of Computer Scientists and Information Technologists on Enablement Through Technology, pp. 165–172 (2003)
10. Lukkarinen, A., Malmi, L., Haaranen, L.: Event-driven programming in programming education: a mapping review. ACM Trans. Comput. Educ. (TOCE) **21**(1), 1–31 (2021)
11. Drot-Delange, B., Parriaux, G., Reffay, C.: Futurs enseignants de l'école primaire: connaissances des stratégies d'enseignement, curriculaires et disciplinaires pour l'enseignement de la programmation. RDST. Recherches en didactique des sciences et des technologies (23), 55–76 (2021)
12. R Core Team: R: A Language and Environment for Statistical Computing. R Foundation for Statistical Computing, Vienna, Austria (2020). https://www.R-project.org/
13. Benzecri, J.P. (ed.): L'analyse des données. II: L'analyse des correspondances. 3e ed. comportant de nouveaux programmes. Avec collab, 2nde edn., vol. 2. Dunod, Paris (1980)

Introducing Artificial Intelligence Literacy in Schools: A Review of Competence Areas, Pedagogical Approaches, Contexts and Formats

Viktoriya Olari(✉), Kamilla Tenório, and Ralf Romeike

Freie Universität Berlin, Königin-Luise-Str. 24-26, 14195 Berlin, Germany
{viktoriya.olari,kamilla.tenorio,ralf.romeike}@fu-berlin.de

Abstract. Introducing artificial intelligence (AI) literacy to school students is challenging. As AI education is constantly growing, educators can struggle to decide *which* content is relevant and *how* it can be taught. Therefore, examining which practices and formats have already been evaluated with students and are used repeatedly and which are challenging or should be explored further is necessary to facilitate teaching AI and encourage the development of new activities. In this literature review, we address this need. Using a directed and conventional content analysis, we systematically analyzed 31 cases of introducing AI literacy in schools in terms of three categories: (a) competence areas, (b) pedagogical approaches, and (c) contexts and formats. When analyzing the results, we identified underrepresented competence areas and summarized common pedagogical practices and recurrent formats and contexts. Additionally, we investigated the approach to using data to make abstract AI knowledge accessible to novices.

Keywords: Artificial intelligence literacy · AI education · data literacy

1 Introduction

Integrating artificial intelligence (AI) literacy into schools has been on the educational research agenda for several years. As students interact with AI technologies every day, they should be empowered to critically evaluate these technologies [1, 2], use them as a tool for effective human–machine collaboration [3], and be aware of how insights are gained from data at an early age [4]. Consequently, initiatives to foster AI literacy are emerging worldwide, and the number of educational materials and tools is increasing.

Several studies have been published in recent years to provide educators with a solid foundation for AI education. Most of these secondary studies in the field have focused on conceptualizing AI literacy [2, 5, 6] or examined specific topics in AI education, such as machine learning [7–9]. However, in addition to answering the question of *which* content is essential in AI education, there is also a clear need to explore *how* AI should be introduced to students.

T. Keane et al. (Eds.): WCCE 2022, IFIP AICT 685, pp. 221–232, 2023.
https://doi.org/10.1007/978-3-031-43393-1_21

In this study, we address this need by conducting an exploratory review of 31 AI case studies that were empirically evaluated with students in schools. Each study is systematically analyzed in terms of three categories: (a) competence areas, (b) pedagogical approaches, and (c) contexts and formats. The main contributions of this paper are the following: (a) analysis of common pedagogical practices, particularly the use of data to make AI knowledge accessible to novices; (2) identification of underrepresented competence areas in AI education; and (3) investigation of recurrent formats and contexts in this field. From a historical perspective, these contributions provide an overview of the current AI education landscape in schools, which can be used for comparisons in the future.

The paper is organized as follows: In Sect. 2, we provide background on AI literacy in school education and discuss related works. In Sect. 3, we describe the methods used for this exploratory review. In Sect. 4, we outline the analysis results; the presentation of results is organized into the three categories that served as the basis for the analysis. We discuss the findings in Sect. 5 and, finally, offer suggestions for future research in Sect. 6.

2 Artificial Intelligence Literacy in School Education

According to Long and Magerko [2], *AI literacy* is a set of competencies that enable individuals to evaluate AI technologies critically; communicate and collaborate effectively with AI; and use AI as a tool online, at home, and in the workplace. Although some suggestions confine AI education to machine-learning education [7, 9], researchers also use the term "AI education" to describe approaches that focus on introducing AI to school students [10, 11].

Several guidelines have been published on AI literacy in schools. Long and Magerko [2] provided a conceptual framework, including a detailed set of AI literacy competencies for learners and design considerations of learner-centered AI for developers. Tedre et al. [4] proposed a concept of computational thinking 2.0, which extends basic computational thinking by adding the mental skills and practices students need for training machines. Touretzky et al. [1] suggested five major ideas of AI that should be introduced to every student in their education: perception, representation and reasoning, learning, natural interaction, and societal impact. Researchers have often referred to this framework when developing local guidelines for AI instruction in schools (e.g., [12]). Zhou et al. [5] provided guidelines for designing AI learning experiences for K–12 students based on prior research and presented a list of future opportunities to strengthen the effectiveness of AI curricula.

In addition to conducting intense conceptual work on AI literacy guidelines, researchers have empirically evaluated several approaches with school students. For example, Sintov et al. [13] and Williams et al. [14] investigated the use of robots and game-based learning to introduce AI to school students and found the approaches successful. Srikant and Aggarwal [15] suggested that collecting and analyzing students' data would enhance students' learning of AI.

Nevertheless, little emphasis has been put on systematically inspecting practices and pedagogical approaches for introducing students to AI at the school level. However, before new materials and tools are developed, researchers and educators should ideally know which approaches and formats have already been evaluated with students and are effectively and frequently used and which are challenging or should be investigated in more detail in the future. Moreover, knowing which competence areas educators are focusing on in practice and which areas are underrepresented in the current AI education would also be valuable to determine whether all pertinent dimensions are being covered or whether adjustments will need to be made in the future when new approaches are developed.

Consequently, in our exploratory literature review, we focused on the following two research questions:

- **RQ1:** Which competence areas are underrepresented in the current AI literacy approaches?
- **RQ2:** What are the common pedagogical practices, recurrent formats and contexts in AI education?

3 Method

To answer the research questions, we conducted an exploratory literature review using qualitative research methods. In this section, we describe the selection of studies for the review and analysis process in detail.

3.1 Selection Process

To find relevant literature, we used the snowballing and keyword search approaches. Snowballing refers to using the reference list of a paper or the citations to the paper to identify additional relevant papers [16]. While snowballing, we studied the bibliographies of the works cited on AI education provided by Long and Magerko [2], who analyzed 150 documents on AI literacy, and by Zhou et al. [5], who reviewed 49 more recent works on AI education. We included the studies whose titles indicated practical implementation of AI topics with students in the start set for further analysis. The search helped us find relevant keywords for the second stage of the search.

Afterward, to include more recent studies, we used the following search string on Association for Computing Machinery (ACM) Digital Library: [All: "ai education"] OR [All: "ai literacy"] OR [All: "machine learning education"] OR [All: "artificial intelligence literacy"] OR [All: "artificial intelligence education"] AND [Publication Date: (01/01/2020 TO 01/31/2022)]. We chose this database since ACM is the world's largest educational and scientific computing society [17] and because its digital library provides access to a vast number of contributions to the computer science field [18]. Additionally, we searched Google Scholar for the same terms and evaluated the first 50 search results.

We selected relevant papers based on the following inclusion and exclusion criteria: The selected study (a) is grounded in research, (b) the primary objective is the introduction of AI literacy in school education, (c) is evaluated with students, (d) is published in English, and (e) is accessible. Using these criteria, we first filtered out studies by reviewing their abstracts and keywords. Of the remaining studies, additional studies were excluded after reading the full texts, resulting in 31 studies published between 2010 and 2021. The complete list of all studies selected for the literature review can be provided upon request.

3.2 Analysis Process

For analyzing the selected studies, we used a combination of directed and conventional qualitative content analysis methods [19]. The directed analysis methods rely on existing theories or prior research that can be used for coding the text passages and include the definition of codes prior to the analysis. If no code is suitable, a new code can be created during the analysis. Conventional content analysis is an inductive method and does not require prior theory. The codes are defined as part of the analysis. Section 4 explains in detail how we determined the codes.

In the first step, one researcher (data extractor [20]) defined the codes, read the studies, and coded the relevant passages using predefined codes. The relevant text segments were then extracted into a table. In the second step, another researcher (data checker) reviewed the coding for six random papers to validate the first researcher's coding. The data checker either confirmed that the coding was correct or discussed the issues with the data extractor to reach an agreement. Initially, the data checker agreed on 89.17% of the coded text passages. After discussion, the data extractor and data checker reached 97.5% agreement. In the end, for the codes defined for the directed analysis method, we calculated the frequency of their occurrence with respect to the totality of studies. The complete results of coding can be provided upon request.

4 Results

We conducted an exploratory literature analysis according to the three categories: (1) competence areas, (2) pedagogical approaches, and (3) contexts and formats. In the following three subsections, we present the results. Each subsection is similarly organized. First, we explain how we coded and analyzed the text passages. We have chosen to explain the definition of the codes in this section rather than in Sect. 3 for ease of reading. Second, we summarize the results of the analysis for each category.

4.1 Category 1: Competence Areas

To analyze the underrepresented competence areas and answer RQ1, we used the Dagstuhl triangle, a framework for describing the phenomenon of digitization that should be included in education [21]. This approach involved examining each study from three perspectives: (a) technological ("Does the study foster technological competencies? Did the students learn how AI works?"), (b) socio-cultural ("Does the study promote socio-cultural competencies? Did students learn what the impact of technology is?"), and (c) user-oriented ("Does the study promote a user-oriented perspective? Did the student learn how to use AI?").

From the technological perspective, most of the analyzed approaches aimed to enable students to understand the technical background of AI. This trend can be observed in all age groups. For instance, Vartiainen et al. [24] argued that young children (< = 6 years) should be able to explain how a computer learns to classify emotions and illustrate how this goal might be achieved. For middle school students, DiPaola et al. [22] claimed that the students should be able to articulate how recommendation systems function. For high school students, the requirements are more specific and extensive. Vachovsky et al. [23] developed a summer school concept that provides participants with an overview of the technical methods used in humanitarian applications.

The socio-cultural perspective was addressed by just over half of literature. Approaches ranged across the spectrum, from assessing the societal impact of AI technologies [22] to examining algorithmic bias [25] and from describing the limitations of AI in real-world settings [26] to considering issues of data privacy [27].

The third perspective, user-oriented, was also considered in most approaches. The analysis indicates that students are expected to use technology to accomplish the assigned task, such as training the device to recognize gestures [28] and deploying machine learning models using given software [12, 29]. Only a few works reported that the students learn how to meaningfully use AI in their everyday lives and solve problems relevant to their everyday lives [28, 30].

In short, we found that the analyzed literature covers all three perspectives of the Dagstuhl triangle to varying degrees. However, a small number of the studies covered all three perspectives simultaneously. The technological and user-oriented perspectives were evidently dominant, meaning that most studies concerned students' ability to know how AI systems work and how to use them but not what their effects are.

4.2 Category 2: Pedagogical Approaches

We based the analysis of the pedagogical approaches on Sheard and Falkner's [31] classification of the key pedagogical practices used in computing education for answering the first part of the RQ2. Each approach we identified was allocated to one or multiple practices from the following list: (a) active learning (a range of practices in which students are involved in actively doing and reflecting on their learning), (b) collaborative learning (a range of practices wherein students collaborate in the learning process), (c) contributing student pedagogy (a range of collaborative practices in which students produce valued artifacts to contribute to other students' learning), (d) blended learning (a range of active instructional practices that blend modes of learning, typically online and face to face), and (e) massive open online course or MOOC (pedagogic approaches built on top of the MOOC format). If the analyzed approach did not fit into any of our criteria or explicitly built upon other approaches, we included it in the category "Other approaches."

Furthermore, from a pedagogical perspective, research suggests that using concrete data instead of abstract concepts may be beneficial for educating school students on AI [5]. Srikant and Aggarwal [15] proposed that being involved in collecting and entering data could provide students with greater ownership of the exercise and enhance the activity element. Register and Ko [32] showed that one way to develop self-advocacy skills in the domain of machine learning is to teach the learner with their personal data. Consequently, we decided to explore how data is used in current pedagogical approaches to introducing AI in schools. For the analysis, we used the data lifecycle provided by

Grillenberger and Romeike [33] as a structuring framework because the data lifecycle is widely used to describe content and competencies relevant in the context of data and data literacy [34]. For every stage of the data lifecycle (acquisition, cleansing, modeling, implementation, optimization, processing/analysis, visualization, evaluation, sharing, erasing, archiving), we answered the question: "Is this stage covered by the respective approach, and if so, how is it embedded?".

The analysis of pedagogical approaches indicates that active learning was a key factor in learning AI in all the studies considered. For instance, students taught conversational agents and evaluated how well the agents learned [35], or they redesigned YouTube to understand how it uses stakeholders' needs and users' data to deliver content [22]. Collaboration was also evident in the analyzed studies, although to a lesser extent than active learning. Several researchers have described students working in pairs or groups [23]. However, some researchers found it challenging to implement collaborative learning due to COVID-19 [11]. Overall, we found that pedagogical approaches were characterized as "low floor" [28], "hands-on" [36], "playful" [37], and "project-based" [28]. No use of blended learning or MOOCs was reported.

After analyzing the literature for how the data was used in each of the studies, we found that most works involved using data for introducing machine learning concepts. Two studies reported the use of data in the context of knowledge-based systems [14, 36]. The most common stages of the data lifecycle to which the activities referred are the analysis and evaluation stages. Occasionally, the acquisition, modeling, and implementation stages were addressed. Students were reported to collect the data using scientific tools and methods and build machine learning models by experimenting with different features and adjusting model parameters to predict a better outcome [29]. Even young children were reported to be able to use subjectively meaningful data, such as their bodily expressions, to train the machine learning models and to reason about when the model breaks and why [24]. However, information about the specific content is sometimes lacking, e.g., what techniques the students used for "basic data processing" [38] while preparing the data. Although cleansing, optimization, and especially visualization are common practices in AI when conducting explorative data analysis or evaluating model performance [39], studies rarely address them.

In summary, we found that active learning and collaborative learning were common approaches, whereas blended learning and MOOCs were not reported to be used. Most studies involved one or more phases of the data lifecycle, suggesting that educators often used data literacy in AI educational contexts.

4.3 Category 3: Contexts and Formats

To investigate the pedagogical context and answer the second part of RQ2, we used the structure proposed by Charlton and Poslad [40]. For coding, we also used the method of conventional content analysis method. Each study was investigated for (a) student context and purpose setting (for each study, the following questions were answered: "How is the study embedded in students' everyday lives? Can young people get creative with AI and solve problems they care about?") and (b) the formal context in which the reported intervention took place ("Did the reported intervention occur during computer science school lessons, in context of other subjects, or outside the regular school lessons?). While evaluating formats and contexts, we also collected statistics on the duration, target group, sample size, participants' background knowledge, and teacher involvement.

The findings indicate that the activities described in the studies were aligned with the students' context though they had an artificially created purpose. While the studies referenced contexts from students' everyday life (such as games [30], friends [15], animals [12], food [41]), students performed artificially created tasks (e.g., using particular software to train a classification model with a dataset that is prepared by the educator [42]) and did not transfer their knowledge into other domains. Students applying knowledge to new contexts and working on projects they cared about were rarely reported (e.g., [43]).

The formats used in the analyzed studies ranged from short activities and one-day workshops to summer schools lasting several weeks. Most activities reported were not part of the regular computer science curriculum and occurred in the context of other subjects (e.g., social sciences [38]) or outside regular school classes. The activities were based on the assumption that students had no prior knowledge of AI and were conducted by researchers, though the studies did not specify whether school teachers were also involved in the education process. Only Heinze et al. [44], Burgsteiner et al. [36], Williams and Breazeal [45], Kaspersen et al. [38] reported involving teachers and preparing them to be multipliers and test AI materials.

In summary, we found that the topic of AI was embedded in various subjects but rarely in computer science classes. Students were more reported to learn about AI in restrictive, artificially created contexts than in projects that interested them and in which they could transfer their knowledge to other domains.

5 Discussion

We conducted an exploratory review of 31 studies that focused on introducing AI literacy in schools. We analyzed each study in terms of the three categories and presented our results in Sect. 4. In this section, we discuss the key findings.

1. Most studies were concerned with developing students' ability to know how AI systems work and how to operate them but not what their effects are.

   While analyzing the competence areas, we observed that the socio-cultural perspective was clearly underrepresented, a concerning finding in light of the need to develop responsible practitioners and critical users of AI, as is stressed by organizations such as United Nations Educational, Scientific and Cultural Organization (UNESCO) [3]. This result is consistent with the findings of Zhou et al. [5], who noted that ethics are underrepresented in existing approaches to AI education. In contrast, the technological perspective was addressed in most studies. Interestingly, however, most of the studies were not anchored in the context of computer science education.
2. Students were actively engaged in the learning process. However, they were frequently reported to learn about AI in restrictive contexts. Moreover, they did not apply their knowledge to new domains.

   Analysis of the pedagogical practices showed that active learning was among the most common approaches, as well as collaborative practices. However, while investigating the context and purpose settings, we found that activities for introducing

AI mostly addressed artificially created, pre-structured tasks and that students were not expected to develop their knowledge and apply it to new contexts and domains. Such an approach is characterized by Bers [46] as a playpen environment in contrast to the playground, where the students have more room to move, explore, experiment, collaborate, and apply the knowledge to new contexts. Since the goal of modern education is to empower students to think creatively, playpen environments should be a stepping stone, not the destination [47].

3. AI education is still a marginal topic in schools. However, if the goal is to spread AI literacy widely, it should be integrated into regular school lessons. More formats should be available for advanced students, and teachers should be more involved.

   In terms of formats, the studies typically targeted students outside regular school hours, indicating that AI is still a marginal topic in school education. Approaches for more advanced students were rarely reported, which is expected and in line with the finding of [7], who emphasized that most instructional units address beginners. Moreover, there was little reported involvement of teachers. Consequently, at first glance, it appears that most studies were conducted by researchers. This trend is consistent with the statements of Marques [7, 48], who noted that there is little work involving K–12 teachers. One reason, as stated by Vazhayil et al. [49], could be that teachers have little belief in the potential of AI education. However, to sustain AI education in schools, teachers need to be involved and trained.

4. AI education appears to be inextricably linked to data literacy. However, a solid theoretical foundation that explores the relationship between AI and data literacy is lacking.

   In exploring the approach of using data in AI education, we found that data is used in the context of introducing machine learning and knowledge-based systems. Each study involved one or more phases of the data lifecycle, though there was a lack of details about the specific contents, e.g., which techniques the students used to optimize the model. This tendency indicates an inextricable link between AI education and data literacy—the ability to collect, manage, evaluate, and apply data critically [34], as already suggested by Long and Magerko [2], Zhou et al. [5], Tedre et al. [4]. However, a solid theoretical foundation that explores the relationship between AI literacy and data literacy (including related concepts such as critical big data literacy [50], and statistical literacy [51]) is lacking. Future research should explore the theoretical underpinnings of these concepts to clarify how AI education can be enhanced through data literacy.

6 Conclusions

This paper analyzed existing approaches reported in the literature to teach AI literacy to school students. After identifying underrepresented competence areas, we examined common tendencies regarding pedagogical practices and the formats and contexts in AI education. Subsequently, we investigated the approach of using data in AI education.

The findings indicate that the socio-cultural perspective is underrepresented in current practical studies. This finding is concerning if the goal is to achieve responsible practitioners and mature, critical users of AI who are aware of the general conditions surrounding AI. Consequently, future research could suggest ways to integrate more approaches from the field of ethics into AI education. Another tendency that we discovered is that students are often supposed to learn about AI in restrictive, predefined contexts rather than in subjectively meaningful projects they care about. However, since the goal of modern education is to empower students to think creatively, future research should investigate how educators can transfer from pre-defined, step-by-step instructions to more open-ended projects. Lastly, the analysis indicates that educators use data in various contexts of AI education, suggesting that AI literacy is inextricably linked to data literacy. Therefore, future research may investigate whether personally meaningful data may be used as a tool to promote AI playgrounds in the school context.

Although this exploratory study provides comprehensive insights into the research field and trends in AI education, it is not exhaustive as AI education is a dynamic field that is consistently evolving. Therefore, we recommend that future researchers conduct a systematic literature review to obtain a holistic picture of the research field. We also encourage to them to explore the relationship between AI and data literacy to support future practical concepts for AI education through the solid theoretical foundation.

References

1. Touretzky, D., Gardner-McCune, C., Martin, F., Seehorn, D.: Envisioning AI for K-12: What Should Every Child Know about AI? In: Proceedings of the AAAI Conference on Artificial Intelligence, pp. 9795–9799 (2019)
2. Long, D., Magerko, B.: What is AI Literacy? Competencies and Design Considerations. In: Proceedings of the 2020 CHI Conference on Human Factors in Computing Systems, pp. 1–16. Association for Computing Machinery, New York, NY, USA (2020)
3. UNESCO: Beijing Consensus on Artificial Intelligence and Education (2019)
4. Tedre, M., Denning, P., Toivonen, T.: CT 2.0. In: Proceedings of the 21st Koli Calling International Conference on Computing Education Research, pp. 1–8. Association for Computing Machinery, New York, NY, USA (2021)
5. Zhou, X., Van Brummelen, J., Lin, P.: Designing AI Learning Experiences for K-12: Emerging Works, Future Opportunities and a Design Framework (2020)
6. Ng, D.T.K., Leung, J.K.L., Chu, S.K.W., Qiao, M.S.: Conceptualizing AI literacy: An exploratory review. Comp. Edu. Artif. Intelli. **2**, 100041 (2021)
7. Marques, L.S., Gresse Von Wangenheim, C., Hauck, J.C.R.: Teaching Machine Learning in School: A Systematic Mapping of the State of the Art. Informatics in Education **19**, 283–321 (2020)
8. Gresse von Wangenheim, C., Hauck, J.C.R., Pacheco, F.S., Bertonceli Bueno, M.F.: Visual tools for teaching machine learning in K-12: A ten-year systematic mapping. Edu. Info. Technol. **26**, 5733–5778 (2021)
9. Tedre, M., et al.: Teaching Machine Learning in K–12 Classroom: Pedagogical and Technological Trajectories for Artificial Intelligence Education. IEEE Access **9**, 110558–110572 (2021)
10. Williams, R., Park, H.W., Breazeal, C.: A is for artificial intelligence: the impact of artificial intelligence activities on young children's perceptions of robots. In: Proceedings of the 2019 CHI Conference on Human Factors in Computing Systems, pp. 1–11. Association for Computing Machinery, New York, NY, USA (2019)
11. Olari, V., Cvejoski, K., Eide, Ø.: Introduction to machine learning with robots and playful learning. In: Proceedings of the AAAI Conference on Artificial Intelligence, pp. 15630–15639 (2021)

12. Ali, S., Williams, R., Payne, B.H., Park, H.W., Breazeal, C.: Constructionism, Ethics, and Creativity: Developing Primary and Middle School Artificial Intelligence Education. In: 28th International Joint Conference on Artificial Intelligence. Palo Alto, CA, USA (2019)
13. Sintov, N., et al.: From the lab to the classroom and beyond: extending a game-based research platform for teaching ai to diverse audiences. In: Sixth Symposium on Educational Advances in Artificial Intelligence (EAAI-16) (2016)
14. Williams, R., Park, H.W., Oh, L., Breazeal, C.: PopBots: Designing an Artificial Intelligence Curriculum for Early Childhood Education. In: Proceedings of the AAAI Conference on Artificial Intelligence, pp. 9729–9736 (2019)
15. Srikant, S., Aggarwal, V.: Introducing data science to school kids. In: Proceedings of the 2017 ACM SIGCSE Technical Symposium on Computer Science Education, pp. 561–566. Association for Computing Machinery, New York, NY, USA (2017)
16. Wohlin, C.: Guidelines for snowballing in systematic literature studies and a replication in software engineering. In: Proceedings of the 18th International Conference on Evaluation and Assessment in Software Engineering, pp. 1–10. Association for Computing Machinery, New York, NY, USA (2014). https://doi.org/10.1145/2601248.2601268
17. ACM: About the ACM Organization, https://www.acm.org/about-acm/about-the-acm-organization, last accessed 31 January 2023
18. Chen, L., Babar, M.A., Zhang, H.: Towards an evidence-based understanding of electronic data sources. In: 14th International Conference on Evaluation and Assessment in Software Engineering (EASE), pp. 135–138. Keele University, UK (2010)
19. Hsieh, H.-F., Shannon, S.E.: Three approaches to qualitative content analysis. Qual Health Res. **15**, 1277–1288 (2005)
20. Kitchenham, B., Charters, S.: Guidelines for performing Systematic Literature Reviews in Software Engineering. Keele University (2007)
21. Brinda, T., Diethelm, I.: Education in the digital networked world. In: Tatnall, A., Webb, M. (eds.) Tomorrow's Learning: Involving Everyone. Learning with and about Technologies and Computing, pp. 653–657. Springer International Publishing, Cham (2017)
22. DiPaola, D., Payne, B.H., Breazeal, C.: Decoding design agendas: an ethical design activity for middle school students. In: Proceedings of the Interaction Design and Children Conference, pp. 1–10. Association for Computing Machinery, New York, NY, USA (2020)
23. Vachovsky, M.E., Wu, G., Chaturapruek, S., Russakovsky, O., Sommer, R., Fei-Fei, L.: Toward More Gender Diversity in CS through an Artificial Intelligence Summer Program for High School Girls. In: Proceedings of the 47th ACM Technical Symposium on Computing Science Education, pp. 303–308. ACM, New York, NY, USA (2016)
24. Vartiainen, H., Tedre, M., Valtonen, T.: Learning machine learning with very young children: Who is teaching whom? Int. J. Child-Comp. Intera. **25**, 100182 (2020)
25. Schaper, M.-M., Malinverni, L.: Valero, cristina: Robot Presidents: Who should rule the world? Teaching Critical Thinking in AI through Reflections upon Food Traditions. In: Proceedings of the 11th Nordic Conference on Human-Computer Interaction: Shaping Experiences, Shaping Society, pp. 1–4. ACM, New York, NY, USA (2020)
26. Ali, S., DiPaola, D., Lee, I., Hong, J., Breazeal, C.: Exploring generative models with middle school students. In: Proceedings of the 2021 CHI Conference on Human Factors in Computing Systems, pp. 1–13. ACM, New York, NY, USA (2021)
27. Forsyth, S., Dalton, B., Foster, E.H., Walsh, B., Smilack, J., Yeh, T.: Imagine a More Ethical AI: Using Stories to Develop Teens' Awareness and Understanding of Artificial Intelligence and its Societal Impacts. In: 2021 Conference on Research in Equitable and Sustained Participation in Engineering, Computing, and Technology (RESPECT), pp. 1–2 (2021)
28. Hitron, T., Orlev, Y., Wald, I., Shamir, A., Erel, H., Zuckerman, O.: Can children understand machine learning concepts? The effect of uncovering black boxes. In: Proceedings of the

2019 CHI Conference on Human Factors in Computing Systems, pp. 1–11. Association for Computing Machinery, New York, NY, USA (2019)

29. Sakulkueakulsuk, B., et al.: Kids making AI: Integrating Machine Learning, Gamification, and Social Context in STEM Education. In: 2018 IEEE International Conference on Teaching, Assessment, and Learning for Engineering, pp. 1005–1010 (2018)
30. Voulgari, I., Zammit, M., Stouraitis, E., Liapis, A., Yannakakis, G.: Learn to machine learn: designing a game based approach for teaching machine learning to primary and secondary education students. In: Interaction Design and Children, pp. 593–598. Association for Computing Machinery, New York, NY, USA (2021)
31. Falkner, K., Sheard, J.: Pedagogic approaches. In: The Cambridge Handbook of Computing Education Research, pp. 445–480. Cambridge University Press, Cambridge (2019)
32. Register, Y., Ko, A.J.: Learning machine learning with personal data helps stakeholders ground advocacy arguments in model mechanics. In: Proceedings of the 2020 ACM Conference on International Computing Education Research, pp. 67–78. Association for Computing Machinery, New York, NY, USA (2020)
33. Grillenberger, A., Romeike, R.: About classes and trees: introducing secondary school students to aspects of data mining. In: Pozdniakov, S.N., Dagien\.e, V. (eds.) Informatics in Schools. New Ideas in School Informatics, pp. 147–158. Springer International Publishing, Cham (2019)
34. Ridsdale, C., et al.: Strategies and Best Practices for Data Literacy Education Knowledge Synthesis Report (2015)
35. Lin, P., Van Brummelen, J., Lukin, G., Williams, R., Breazeal, C.: Zhorai: designing a conversational agent for children to explore machine learning concepts. In: Proceedings of the AAAI Conference on Artificial Intelligence, pp. 13381–13388 (2020)
36. Burgsteiner, H., Kandlhofer, M., Steinbauer, G.: IRobot: teaching the basics of artificial intelligence in high schools. In: Proceedings of the Thirtieth AAAI Conference on Artificial Intelligence, pp. 4126–4127. AAAI Press (2016)
37. Kandlhofer, M., Steinbauer, G., Hirschmugl-Gaisch, S., Huber, P.: Artificial intelligence and computer science in education: From kindergarten to university. In: 2016 IEEE Frontiers in Education Conference (FIE), pp. 1–9 (2016)
38. Kaspersen, M.H., Bilstrup, K.-E.K., Van Mechelen, M., Hjorth, A., Bouvin, N.O., Petersen, M.G.: VotestratesML: A High School Learning Tool for Exploring Machine Learning and Its Societal Implications. In: FabLearn Europe / MakeEd 2021 - An International Conference on Computing, Design and Making in Education. ACM, New York, NY, USA (2021)
39. Perer, A., Shneiderman, B.: Integrating statistics and visualization: case studies of gaining clarity during exploratory data analysis. In: Proceedings of the SIGCHI Conference on Human Factors in Computing Systems, pp. 265–274. ACM, New York, NY, USA (2008)
40. Charlton, P., Poslad, S.: Engaging with computer science when solving tangible problems. In: Proceedings of the 3rd Conference on Computing Education Practice. Association for Computing Machinery, New York, NY, USA (2019)
41. Evangelista, I., Blesio, G., Benatti, E.: Why are we not teaching machine learning at high school? A proposal. In: 2018 World Engineering Education Forum - Global Engineering Deans Council (WEEF-GEDC), pp. 1–6 (2018)
42. Long, D., Padiyath, A., Teachey, A., Magerko, B.: The Role of Collaboration, Creativity, and Embodiment in AI Learning Experiences. In: Creativity and Cognition. Association for Computing Machinery, New York, NY, USA (2021)
43. Tedre, M., Vartiainen, H., Kahila, J., Toivonen, T., Jormanainen, I., Valtonen, T.: Machine Learning Introduces New Perspectives to Data Agency in K—12 Computing Education. In: 2020 IEEE Frontiers in Education Conference (FIE), pp. 1–8 (2020)

44. Heinze, C., Haase, J., Higgins, H.: An action research report from a multi-year approach to teaching artificial intelligence at the K-6 level. In: Proceedings of the AAAI Conference on Artificial Intelligence, pp. 1890–1895 (2010)
45. Williams, R.: How to train your robot: project-based AI and ethics education for middle school classrooms. In: Proceedings of the 52nd ACM Technical Symposium on Computer Science Education, p. 1382. Association for Computing Machinery, NY, USA (2021)
46. Bers, M.U.: Designing Digital Experiences for Positive Youth Development: From Playpen to Playground. Oxford University Press, USA (2012)
47. Resnick, M., Robinson, K.: Lifelong Kindergarten: Cultivating Creativity Through Projects. Peers, and Play. MIT Press, Passion (2017)
48. Williams, R., Kaputsos, S.P., Breazeal, C.: Teacher perspectives on how to train your robot: a middle school ai and ethics curriculum. Proceedings of the AAAI Conference on Artificial Intelligence. **35**, 15678–15686 (2021)
49. Vazhayil, A., Shetty, R., Bhavani, R.R., Akshay, N.: Focusing on teacher education to introduce AI in schools: perspectives and illustrative findings. In: 2019 IEEE Tenth International Conference on Technology for Education (T4E), pp. 71–77 (2019)
50. Sander, I.: What is critical big data literacy and how can it be implemented? Internet Policy Review **9**(2), (2020)
51. Kadijević, Đ.: Data science for novice students: a didactic approach to data mining using neural networks. Teaching of Mathematics **23**(2), 90–101 (2020)

What Type of Leaf is It? – AI in Primary Social and Science Education

Stephan Napierala[1(✉)], Jan Grey[2], Torsten Brinda[1], and Inga Gryl[2]

[1] Computing Education Research Group, University of Duisburg-Essen, Essen, Germany
{stephan.napierala,torsten.brinda}@uni-due.de

[2] Institut for Primary Social and Science Education, University of Duisburg-Essen, Essen, Germany
{jan.grey,inga.gryl}@uni-due.de

Abstract. Digitization is a crucial process that is transforming our modern lives. As such, it is essential for students to be able to act maturely in a digital world and to participate in society responsibly, based on their education [1]. This is where digital literacy comes in as a key competence for both: social participation and self-determination in a digital world. To gain a deeper understanding of the digital technologies that surround us, computing education is a valuable way to go. It can help to explain the underlying principles and phenomena of the digital world. Many countries have begun incorporating it into their primary school curriculum. In Germany, and in particular in its federal state North Rhine-Westphalia, computing education is embedded in the Primary Social and Science Education (PSE, in German Sachunterricht). However, there is currently a lack of comprehensive training and education concepts for (future) teachers and corresponding teaching materials to include computing education in this subject, aside from research projects. To support the integration of computing education into PSE, we have developed teaching materials on Artificial Intelligence (AI) using identification apps. These materials provide students with insights into how AI systems perform classification tasks, such as determining different types of leaves, and cover basic concepts of Machine Learning (ML). The materials have been tested in one primary school class and validated by student teachers during their teaching internship semester. This paper describes the action-oriented materials and first classroom experiences.

Keywords: artificial intelligence · machine learning · primary education

1 Introduction

The increasing digitization is changing the lives of children and young people [2], and it poses new challenges for socialisation and school education in our society. In particular in primary schools, the requirements of the digital world must be

T. Keane et al. (Eds.): WCCE 2022, IFIP AICT 685, pp. 233–243, 2023.
https://doi.org/10.1007/978-3-031-43393-1_22

addressed as early as in the school entry phase, so that students are empowered to act responsibly within their environment [3].

In Germany, the subject of Primary Social and Science Education (PSE) is focused on the students' experience realm, addressing phenomena from the living environment and using multi-perspective approaches. With regard to the digitized world, teaching *with* digital technologies as well as teaching *about* principles of digital technologies is subject of primary social and science education [4,5]. Principles that already play a major role in our and students' daily lives are Artificial Intelligence (AI) and Machine Learning (ML). They are used to make life more comfortable and appear, e.g., in voice assistants (such as Siri or Alexa), search engines on the internet, navigation systems, facial recognition software for unlocking smartphones or recommendations for streaming services. Students naturally interact with such systems without perceiving their presence or knowing anything about their functional principles. Taking up such objects and phenomena is part of a comprehensive digital education that should be delivered as early as possible, as outlined by the CECE: "All students must have access to ongoing education in computer science in the school system. Computing education should preferably begin in primary school, at the latest at the beginning of secondary school" [6].

To address this need, the project "Computing Education as a Perspective of Primary Social and Science Education in Teaching Internships during Teaching Degree Study Programs" aims to answer the question: How can prospective teachers be enabled to provide computing education in primary schools during their practical phase of their studies? At the Institute for Primary Social and Science Education at the University of Duisburg-Essen, university teacher training was redesigned to allow students to acquire scientific and educational concepts in computing and test teaching materials about AI and ML in practice, both before and during their teaching internships at school [7]. Developing appropriate teaching materials is crucial for all kinds of schools, but particularly for primary schools, where computing education is typically provided by generalist teachers who may not have specific training in computer science. Therefore, a broader support is required for both prospective and active teachers to acquire the necessary experiences, skills, interest, and self-confidence [8] to incorporate computing education into their teaching.

In our project, we pursue a two-part, future-oriented approach: On the one hand, we have embedded computing education into the PSE course at the university for students who will become primary school teachers. On the other hand, we have developed material for primary school teaching, in order to make low-threshold offers to active teachers in schools. This approach allows us to reach both future and active teachers, and to raise awareness about computing education in PSE. We have chosen this approach, because adequate training of both pre-service and in-service teachers is essential for successfully embedding computing education [9].

In this paper, we focus on supporting active teachers by presenting our developed material on AI and ML. Therefore, we first take a look at the curricular integration of computing education into primary education in Germany and especially AI and ML in Primary Education (Sect. 2). Afterwards we describe the development of the material in Sect. 3, practical experiences are presented in Sect. 4.

2 Related Work

2.1 Objectives and Curricular Embedding of Computing Education in Primary Social and Science Education in Germany

As previously mentioned, in Germany, computing education is not a standalone subject in primary school. Instead, it is integrated into the subject of Primary Social and Science Education (PSE), with the goal of promoting students' ability to act and empower them to participate in a digitally-shaped world and society [10]. This "digital" education, which is a central goal of school education in general [11], includes both using teaching and learning *with* and *about* digital media and technologies. The multi-perspective approach of PSE provides the opportunity to examine topics from both: a social science and natural science perspective. In relation to the digitally-shaped world, computing principles represent a perspective for PSE to engage with digital media. As a result, digital education and especially computing education are integrated into the PSE curriculum. The current curriculum for the state of North Rhine-Westphalia covers the principles of data processing (input-process-output principle), algorithmics, and programming [12]. The *German Informatics Society (GI)* provides an important framework, with recommendations for computing education in lower [13], upper secondary education [14] and primary education [15].

Incorporating computing education into PSE can help to address digitization-related (mis-)conceptions and to reflect on digital technologies. Since the curricular establishment is still comparatively new, it is not possible to assume a broad implementation in practice, yet. Reasons for this include inadequate concepts and materials, lack of knowledge and experience of teachers regarding teaching about digital media [9,16] and subjective competence assessment of teachers [17]. To address these challenges, the project presented here integrates computing education into university teacher training at three universities in North Rhine-Westphalia and develops, among other things, material in the fields of AI and ML. Although AI and ML are not explicitly stated in the primary school curriculum, they are an opportunity to understand how a variety of commonly used computing systems work. They can also be used to reflect on underlying value systems and to sensitize students to the possibilities, limitations, and risks of different computing systems. As AI and ML are increasingly present in students' everyday lives and are becoming increasingly important, they are relevant topics for school education [18,19]. Teachers should be able to educate students about the principles and phenomena of computing systems. By incorporating computing education into teacher education, we offer students the opportunity to develop basic computing education skills, which will enable them to create and carry out lessons about computing principles such as AI and ML [20].

2.2 AI and ML Material

Internationally, there are already several successful materials and approaches for teaching primary school students basic computing principles in the fields of AI and ML. The PopBots project [21] developed an AI curriculum that uses LEGO robots, which can be programmed in a block-based way to explore AI with young children. "Learn to Machine Learn" (LearnML) is another project in which an AI education framework and game-based material were developed for younger and older students which has already been used in teacher education [22]. The Teachable Machine[1] by Google is another project, which has already been successfully used with primary school students to teach them basic principles of ML [23].

However, all of these projects have a fundamental structural problem: they are only available in English and are not ready for use in other countries, as primary school students usually do not have a comprehensive knowledge of English. The material must therefore be translated into their native language first, which is not always possible, as some projects use specific software or websites. Therefore, several material can not be used in German-speaking primary schools. This lack of suitable material (in the national language) is a major obstacle to the successful implementation of computing education in primary schools.

While there is some material available in German for primary education in the field of AI and ML, it is mainly designed for older students and therefore not suitable for primary school. For example, the *AI + Ethics Curriculum for Middle School* project[2] has translations into German, Portuguese and Korean on the subject of AI, but it targets older students from grade 6 to 8 (aged 12–14). Similarly, the *AI Unplugged* material [18,24] is primarily intended for students in lower and upper secondary education (aged 12–18). Lindner et al. [18], however, point out that some activities could be used for younger students, for which they would probably need to be adapted. The material by Janssen [25] on AI, ML and facial recognition does not require any programming knowledge, which makes it initially appear more interesting for use in primary school. In addition to technical aspects, the material addresses the social, political, and ethical effects of AI systems. However, these materials are designed for older students (about 15 and 16 years), and are therefore not suitable for use in primary school. Due to the limited availability of German material on AI and ML for use in primary schools, the aim of our project is to develop and test further material. In the following, the specific conditions under which the project is carried out and first practical classroom experiences are described.

[1] https://teachablemachine.withgoogle.com/.

[2] https://www.media.mit.edu/projects/ai-ethics-for-middle-school.

3 Concept Development

3.1 Overall Conceptual Consideration

Combining Ideas from Biology and Computer Science. Our material was developed as part of a funded project. To combine ideas from Biology and Computer Science, we selected plant identification apps to introduce basic concepts of AI and ML. We chose this field to create unplugged teaching material because the identification of plants is part of the Primary Social and Science Education curriculum (content area "Animals, Plants, Habitats" [12]), and not the *Good-Monkey-Bad-Monkey Game* material by [18], which could lead to misconceptions about monkey behavior. The teaching material first focuses on the identification of plants without digital tools, but later also extends this process to a digital identification app for plants. During the unplugged activity, students take on the role of an AI system and complete a learning process in which they identify features of leaves and learn basic concepts of ML. The next section provides more detailed insights into the material and its usage.

Teaching Material and Approach. Our manual for teachers is divided into three parts: The first part discusses the curricular integration of computing education in primary social and science education. It explains how the inclusion of informatic phenomena aligns with the digitalization strategy outlined in [3] and the core curriculum for PSE in North Rhine-Westphalia [12] as well as the recommendations for primary schools provided by the German Computer Science association [15]. It also outlines the objectives and desired competencies of the module. The second part of the manual provides theoretical background information on computer science and biology that are essential for the module. This includes introducing the terms AI, ML, and decision trees in the computer science section and the structure and features of leaves in the biology section.

The third and final part of the manual presents detailed descriptions of several lessons and the associated lesson materials. The series of lessons follows a four-step approach to teach basic concepts of ML (supervised learning): 1. training data, 2. development of rules, 3. testing the model, 4. reflection.

1. The students are introduced to a set of training data, similar to an AI system. The data set consisting of 24 images of 12 different types of leaves. They are shown in pairs of photographs and schematic representations (see Fig. 1). With the self-developed memory game, the students try to find the pairs of leaves and discuss the relationships between the images and leaves. The memory game provides an interactive approach to the topic in which the students explore and practice biological technical terms for leaf components and discovering distinctive features of leaves (such as leaf shape, edge, tip). The naming of the leaf types is supported by the teacher, afterwards.
2. In the second step, rules are develop to distinguish the leaf types by creating decision trees using the distinctive features of the leaves from the memory game. This is done in a playful way by having the students try to guess a leaf

Fig. 1. Excerpt from the working material for the memory game.

that the teacher has chosen, asking questions about the leaf's features (e.g., *What does the edge of the leaf look like?*). Building on the questions asked, an incomplete decision tree is created. After that, the tree is completed by the students so that all the leaves from the memory game can be clearly identified. An incomplete decision tree is created, then completed by the students so that all the leaves from the memory game can be clearly identified. A possible resulting decision tree is shown in Fig. 2. The tree can be quite extensive, but could be reduced by decreasing the number of leaf types (memory cards). We did not use a binary decision tree here, which tends to be easier to understand, because the number of leaf features would have leaded to a more complex tree than the one shown in Fig. 2.

3. In the third step, the students test their own decision trees using unknown leaves (test data). Among them, there are also types of leaves which were not included in the memory game before. The students then discuss the limitations of the developed decision trees and add new elements to the tree, so that the unknown leaves can be identified. The opportunity to change the tree if new leaves appear gives students first insights into the limitations of AI systems (e.g., underfitting and overfitting).
4. In the final step, the students test the leaf identification app *Seek*[3], make assumptions about how it works, and discuss the limitations of identification apps by means of blurred images.

The material focuses on action-oriented learning and design-based research [26] in primary schools. Action-oriented learning is designed to integrate practical tasks into the classroom [27]. Therefore, [28] introduce the concept of "learning through action", which is opposed to that of "learning to act". In this

[3] https://www.inaturalist.org/pages/seek_app.

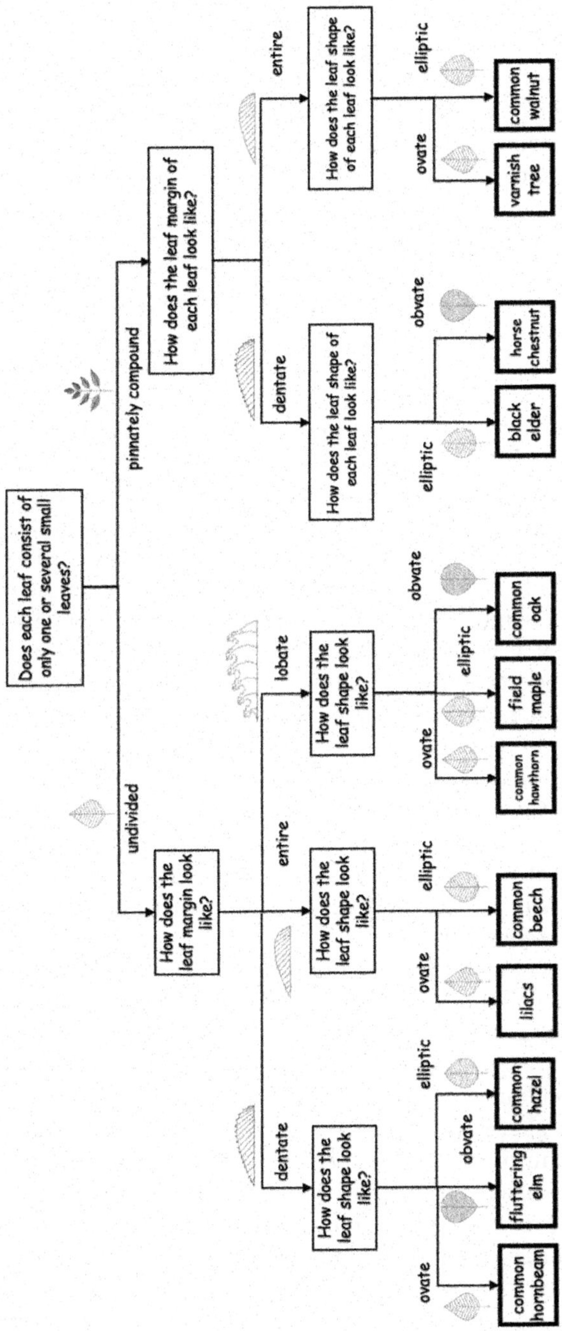

Fig. 2. Possible decision tree for the twelve different leaf types.

sense, action-oriented tasks attempt to convey subjects and material contents to students through their actions. Due to the structure of action orientation through raising an issue, planning of a solution, practical implementation and reflecting about the procedure [29], action-oriented instruction is suitable for the implementation of computing education in primary schools. Therefore, university teacher education must enable students to integrate computing education into (action-oriented) primary social and science education.

4 Implementation and Evaluation

The material was tested in a third-grade primary school class from March to April 2022 with 16 female students. It was used in a primary social and science education class and the teacher provided feedback on its applicability afterwards. Based on this feedback, the material was subsequently adapted.

Overall, the material could be used in class as anticipated and was found to be effective. Through the use of a memory game, students were able to identify essential features of leaves (shape, tip, and edge) and use these features to create a decision tree. However, extra guidance and moderation by the teacher was necessary during the creation of the decision tree. The extensive structure of the decision tree initially required basic knowledge on the purpose of decision trees. At the beginning, some students had difficulties in obtaining information from a decision tree. They wanted to "jump" within the tree and did not move along the edges. With additional material and explanations, this step was reasonably supported. Following these experiences, we added profiles of the corresponding leaves to the handout to enable teachers and students to failproof their worksheets. With the profiles, the developed features of the individual leaves are recorded, so that they can be accessed during the creation of the decision trees. Because the lessons do not always have to take place in the same classroom, it is difficult to collect intermediate results on posters in the classroom. Therefore, working sheets with profiles and material for cutting out are required, which were included subsequently.

Furthermore, the material was found to provide opportunities for students to communicate and collaborate on the problem-solving task of the memory game. For example the memory game requires discussions to find the "correct" solution, and to identify features of leaves, such as, the tip of the leaf. A positive effect was found in an enhanced practice of biological technical terms.

The students successfully applied their knowledge of self-created decision trees to make assumptions about the functioning principles of the identification app *Seek*. The transfer and application of knowledge appears smoothly. They were also able to provide explanations for why the app could not identify certain leaves, such as blurred images or multiple leaves in the camera image. Through guidance from their teacher, the students were able to transfer the principle of automatic recognition and its limitations to other everyday areas, such as face detection for unlocking smartphones and its limitations when wearing a mask.

However, some issues were identified and revisions to the material were needed. It turned out that the identification app *Seek* was unable to identify all leaves when photos of them were printed on paper. This was found to depend on the quality of the photographic material and print quality. Additionally, the variability within species caused discussions, as the photos of certain leaves (e.g. hazelnut) were ambiguous and displayed different characteristics in different photos (e.g. the tip on one photo looked rather round and more or less pointed on another).

4.1 Feedback by the Teacher

The supervising teacher acknowledged many positive aspects of the material. She highlighted the benefits of the material in terms of promoting communication about the subject, reinforcing biological terms and encouraging diverse, independent, and interactive work among the students. The teacher considered the material to have high potential for teaching primary social and science education, as it has many connections to biological topics covered in PSE curriculum. Furthermore, the decision trees can also be used to make connections to mathematics, as they share similarities with tree diagrams used in combinatorics. However, the teacher suggested that the material would be more appropriate for use in a fourth-grade class, due to its complexity and level of abstraction. Additionally, the teacher felt that additional concrete visualisations, such as maps, illustrations, craft forms and templates in the handbook would have been beneficial in some places to make it easier to prepare lessons. These have now been added in the revised handbook.

5 Conclusion and Outlook

In the future, the teaching material will be used by students during their teacher internship semester in primary social and science education studies, and will be tested to provide prospective teachers with an easy entry into AI and ML. The material will also be made available to active teachers in schools, allowing them to work independently with the material and expand their knowledge.

From a long-term perspective, incorporating the project and material into teacher education enables students to gain access to computer science during their studies and opens the possibility for them to approach digital technologies from a computer science and technical perspective. This can also help students to develop a positive computer science-related self-concept, interest in computing and, above all, skills in this area, which they can test and apply in practical contexts in school and university. This will equip prospective teachers with the skills and attitudes needed to lead digital education in schools.

References

1. European Commission. Joint Research Centre.: DigComp 2.2, The Digital Competence Framework for Citizens: With New Examples of Knowledge, Skills and Attitudes. Publications Office, Luxembourg (2022)

2. Kammerl, R., Kramer, M.: The changing media environment and its impact on socialization processes in families. Stud. Commun. Sci. **16**(1), 21–27 (2016)
3. KMK: Bildung in der digitalen Welt - Strategie der Kultusministerkonferenz. Beschluss der Kultusministerkonferenz vom 08.12.2016 in der Fassung vom 07.12.2017, Kultusministerkonferenz (2016)
4. Brinda, T., et al.: Frankfurt-Dreieck zur Bildung in der digital vernetzten Welt. In: Pasternak, A. (ed.) Informatik für alle, pp. 25–33. Gesellschaft für Informatik, Dortmund (2019)
5. K-12 Computer Science Framework Steering Committee: K-12 Computer Science Framework. Technical Report, Association for Computing Machinery, Code.org, Computer Science Teachers Association, Cyber Innovation Center, and National Math and Science Initiative, New York (2016)
6. CECE: Informatics Education in Europe: Are We All In The Same Boat? Technical report, The Committee on European Computing Education, New York, NY, USA (2017)
7. Kuckuck, M., et al.: Informatische Bildung in Praxisphasen des Sachunterrichts in NRW. In: Humbert, L. (ed.) Informatik - Bildung von Lehrkräften in allen Phasen, pp. 241–250. No. P-313 in Lecture Notes in Informatics (LNI), Gesellschaft für Informatik e. V. (GI), Bonn (2021)
8. Benton, L., Hoyles, C., Kalas, I., Noss, R.: Bridging primary programming and mathematics: some findings of design research in England. Digit. Experiences Math. Educ. **3**(2), 115–138 (2017)
9. Hubwieser, P., Armoni, M., Giannakos, M.N., Mittermeir, R.T.: Perspectives and visions of computer science education in primary and secondary (K-12) schools. ACM Trans. Comput. Educ. **14**(2), 1–9 (2014)
10. GDSU: Sachunterricht und Digitalisierung. Positionspapier erarbeitet von der AG Medien & Digitalisierung der Gesellschaft für Didaktik des Sachunterrichts (GDSU), Gesellschaft für Didaktik des Sachunterrichts, Online-Publikation (2021)
11. European Council: Recommendation of the European Parliament and of the Council of 18 December 2006 on key competences for lifelong learning. Technical Report 2006/ 962/ EC, Council of the European Union, Brussels (2006)
12. MSB NRW: Lehrplan für die Primarstufe in Nordrhein-Westfalen: Fach Sachunterricht. Auszug aus Heft 2012 der Schriftenreihe, Schule in NRW", Sammelband: Lehrpläne Primarstufe, Ministerium für Schule und Bildung des Landes Nordrhein-Westfalen, Düsseldorf (2021)
13. GI: Grundsätze und Standards für die Informatik in der Schule: Bildungsstandards Informatik für die Sekundarstufe I. Beilage zu LOG IN 28 (150/151), Empfehlungen der Gesellschaft für Informatik e.V. (2008)
14. Brinda, T., Puhlmann, H., Schulte, C.: Bridging ICT and CS: educational standards for computer science in lower secondary education. In: Proceedings of the 14th Annual ACM SIGCSE Conference on Innovation and Technology in Computer Science Education - ITiCSE 2009, Paris, France, p. 288. ACM Press (2009)
15. GI: Kompetenzen für informatische Bildung im Primarbereich. Beilage zu LOG IN 39 (191/192), Empfehlungen der Gesellschaft für Informatik e.V. (2019)
16. Dagienė, V., Jevsikova, T., Stupurienė, G., Juškevičienė, A.: Teaching computational thinking in primary schools: worldwide trends and teachers' attitudes. Comput. Sci. Inf. Syst. **19**(1), 1–24 (2022)
17. McGarr, O., Mcdonagh, A.: Digital Competence in Teacher Education. Output 1 of the Erasmus+ Funded Developing Student Teachers' Digital Competence (DICTE) Project., DICTE (2019)

18. Lindner, A., Seegerer, S., Romeike, R.: Unplugged activities in the context of AI. In: Pozdniakov, S.N., Dagienė, V. (eds.) ISSEP 2019. LNCS, vol. 11913, pp. 123–135. Springer, Cham (2019). https://doi.org/10.1007/978-3-030-33759-9_10
19. Shamir, G., Levin, I.: Teaching machine learning in elementary school. Int. J. Child-Comput. Interact. **31**, 100415 (2022)
20. Kim, S., Lee, M., Kim, H., Kim, S.: Review on artificial intelligence education for k-12 students and teachers. J. Korean Assoc. Comput. Educ. **23**(4), 1–11 (2020)
21. Williams, R., Park, H.W., Oh, L., Breazeal, C.: PopBots: designing an artificial intelligence curriculum for early childhood education. In: Proceedings of the AAAI Conference on Artificial Intelligence, vol. 33, pp. 9729–9736 (2019)
22. Voulgari, I., Zammit, M., Stouraitis, E., Liapis, A., Yannakakis, G.: Learn to machine learn: designing a game based approach for teaching machine learning to primary and secondary education students. In: Interaction Design and Children, Athens Greece, pp. 593–598. ACM (2021)
23. Toivonen, T., Jormanainen, I., Kahila, J., Tedre, M., Valtonen, T., Vartiainen, H.: Co-designing machine learning apps in K–12 with primary school children. In: 2020 IEEE 20th International Conference on Advanced Learning Technologies (ICALT), Tartu, Estonia, pp. 308–310. IEEE (2020)
24. Ossovski, E., Brinkmeier, M.: Machine learning unplugged - development and evaluation of a workshop about machine learning. In: Pozdniakov, S.N., Dagienė, V. (eds.) ISSEP 2019. LNCS, vol. 11913, pp. 136–146. Springer, Cham (2019). https://doi.org/10.1007/978-3-030-33759-9_11
25. Janssen, D.: Machine Learning in der Schule: Eine praxisorientierte Einführung in künstliche neuronale Netze, Gesichtserkennung und Co., 2nd edn. Science on Stage Deutschland e.V., Berlin (2020)
26. Van den Akker, J., Gravemeijer, K., McKenney, S., Nieveen, N. (eds.): Educational Design Research, Zeroth edn. Routledge (2006)
27. Jank, W., Meyer, H.: Didaktische Modelle. Cornelsen, Berlin, 14. auflage edn. (2021)
28. Möller, K.: Handlungsorientierung im Sachunterricht. In: Kahlert, J., Fölling-Albers, M., Götz, M., Hartinger, A., Miller, S., Wittkowske, S. (eds.) Handbuch Didaktik des Sachunterrichts, 2nd edn., pp. 403–407. Schulpädagogik, Klinkhardt, Bad Heilbrunn (2015)
29. McConnell, J.J.: Active learning and its use in computer science. In: Proceedings of the 1st Conference on Integrating Technology into Computer Science Education, Barcelona, Spain, pp. 52–54. ACM Press (1996)

Levels of Control in Primary Robotics

Ivan Kalas(✉) and Andrea Hrusecka

Comenius University, Bratislava, Slovakia
{ivan.kalas,andrea.hrusecka}@fmph.uniba.sk

Abstract. For several years, we have been developing educational content for informatics for lower primary education (years ranging from one to four and age ranging from six to ten). The resulting intervention is built of three complementary strands, with robotics as the most recently completed one. Here, pupils work with Blue-Bot programmable robots, equipped with blue wireless external control panels. Each team pairs the robot with the panel and controls it using small plastic command tiles. We also use the introduction of new content as a set of research instruments and aim to deepen our understanding of how pupils construct and extend their comprehension of basic computing concepts and related operations. We focus on determining which of these concepts are considered as more challenging to pupils. The current project is established on our previous research on *different levels of control* in programming and related *program representations*. Here, we focused on exploring whether, even when programming a physical robot using an external control panel, the transition from *direct control* to *programming* is a challenging cognitive transformation for young learners.

Keywords: Educational Robotics · Informatics · Lower Primary · Levels of Control · Representation of Program

1 Introduction

The implementation of informatics[1] in primary school has become a real trend. Issues, such as curriculum design, teacher professional development (PD), the development of computational thinking (CT), and related educational research activities, are the focus of researchers, educators and stakeholders. In Slovakia, informatics as a subject has been extended from secondary education as being compulsory in years 3 and 4 already (eight to ten years old pupils), see for example the recent EC JRC study [1]. However, the real challenge for educators and content designers is to fulfil the intention of the subject and to promote it in the sense of *computing for all* [2], sustainably and systematically, with suitably designed progression, respecting developmental appropriateness and knowledge of the pupils and continuously supporting primary teachers.

Our study involves informatics education in all mentioned aspects. Whenever we complete an iterative, evidence-based development (always focused on elementary programming at kindergarten, primary or secondary stages), we start using new intervention

[1] In various countries alternatively named informatics, computer science, computing or the like.

Published by Springer Nature Switzerland AG 2023
T. Keane et al. (Eds.): WCCE 2022, IFIP AICT 685, pp. 244–257, 2023.
https://doi.org/10.1007/978-3-031-43393-1_23

as an instrument for further research. This is based on our conviction that establishing informatics education and continuously supporting its development is not possible without in-depth knowledge of how pupils build their understanding of basic concepts and related operations, exploring which concepts and operations are more demanding for them than others. This is what we had in mind in the Robotics for Primary project which is a part of our long-term *design research*[2] project Informatics with Emil. Thanks to a robotics intervention, which we recently completed and started to disseminate in Slovak and Czech schools, we obtained an important complementary research instrument. In this paper, we present how we used it to additionally validate our observation from the development period: With appropriately chosen robotic equipment and suitable pedagogy, the cognitive demand of transitioning between control levels is surprisingly different from programming a virtual character on the screen.

The detailed findings presented here were reported in the symposium *Informatics in Primary*[3]*Education: Approaches, Current Issues and Lessons Learnt*, organised by the working group WG3.1 of The International Federation for Information Processing (IFIP) in August 2022 in Hiroshima, as a part of WCCE 2022.

2 Programming at Primary Stage

If we intend to build sustainable programming, starting as early as in primary, we should be clear about how we perceive programming, its difficulty and its role in pupils' education and lives. Especially, when we also strive to thoroughly consider the developmental specificities of these age groups. Here, we draw on Blackwell who believes that pupils start programming when they are not directly manipulating observable things, but specify "behaviour to occur at some future time" [5, p.5]. Blackwell [ibid] continues by pointing out that programming is hard because of (a) the loss of the benefits of direct manipulation and (b) introduction of notational elements to represent abstraction. Having this in mind, designers should always pay close attention to pupils' cognitive transitions between different concepts and related operations, levels of control and various forms of the control representations [6–8].

2.1 Educational Robotics

Educational robotics is an important context in which control and representation can be explored. Fortunately, content designers, educators and researchers agree that educational robotics provides great opportunities to develop computational thinking at every level of education, including primary (or even earlier, in kindergarten).

[2] Modern research design, see [3], suitable for interwoven development and research.

[3] For the purposes of the symposium and this paper, primary education is understood in the sense of the UNESCO ISCED [4] classification as a level of formal school education: (1) with the entrance age usually between 5 to 7, typically lasting until age 10 to 12, (2) focus on providing pupils with fundamental skills and establishing their solid foundation for learning, (3) often with one generalist teacher responsible for a group of pupils, facilitating most of the learning process (sometimes with other teachers for certain subjects).

According to Batko [9], educational robotics is an umbrella term for the rich field linked to pedagogy and using robots as a means to achieve educational goals. In our narrower perspective, it is also considered an important part of informatics education. Its history dates back to early 1970s when Papert and his team created a turtle [10], the world's first educational robot. After several pioneering projects in the 1980s, a new phase of educational robotics was launched in late 1990s with the ground-breaking Lego Mindstorms kit. However, it wasn't until the 2010s that a plethora of different educational robots emerged, and that's also when interest in educational robotics in schools boomed significantly.

Educators and researchers focus on the integration of robots into education for various purposes and in different forms. More importantly, from its very beginning, robots and various devices have also served as a means for exploring the learning process of children and pupils in elementary programming. In 1974, Perlman, then supervised by Papert, tried to explore the concept of procedure in a tangible programming interface for preschool children in her Tortis Slot Machine [11, 12]. Thus, she started studying the cognitive difficulties of some aspects of programming with pre-schoolers.

More recently, Sullivan and Heffernan [13] provide a systematic review of the research literature related to the use of robotics construction kits in K-12 learning in the STEM disciplines and refer to them as computational manipulatives for learning. El-Hamamsy et al. [14] present the informatics and robotics integration model for primary school, which identifies elementary informatics concepts suitable for primary school teachers to develop their understanding as part of the professional development (PD) programme without computers, through Robotics Unplugged activities that employ physical robots. Mikova and Krcho [15] analyse several cognitive taxonomies applied in the context of educational robotics and present their own taxonomy as a result of their research. Developmentally appropriate robotics kits and computational concepts that can be supported at primary level are also studied by Chalmers [16], focusing on sequencing and emerging awareness of loops and patterns.

Finally, we want to draw attention to an interesting systematic review of research trends in robotics education for young children and pupils. Jung and Won [17] report that most of the existing studies used constructivist and constructionist frameworks but suggest research agendas should be diversified and the diversity of research participants should be broadened. They also encourage researchers to study which skills are developed by young learners in the robotics context in connection to informatics education.

2.2 Exploring Control and Representation in Primary Programming

The above mentioned suggestion to focus on how young learners develop computational thinking and skills in the context of robotics is in line with our research's goals. In each of our recent design research projects, from ScratchMaths [7, 18] to date [8, 19], we have focused on gaining better understanding of the learners' cognitive processes in informatics, specifically in programming. In each of these research projects, we have exploited our framework [6]. In developing it, we have been thinking about how to explore and characterise the increasing difficulty of tasks in various educational contents for programming. For that purpose, we created a two-dimensional structure in which the first dimension represents four levels of control of a sprite (a character, a turtle, a robot, an object etc.) from:

- the simplest level of direct manipulation, when learners control (a) a physical robot by hand, for example on a floor mat, or (b) a virtual character by dragging it in the stage or 'manually' switching its costume in the Costumes tab of Scratch etc.
- to the most complex computational control when learners build a program, one or several scripts, for a robot or a sprite as a representation of a future behaviour.

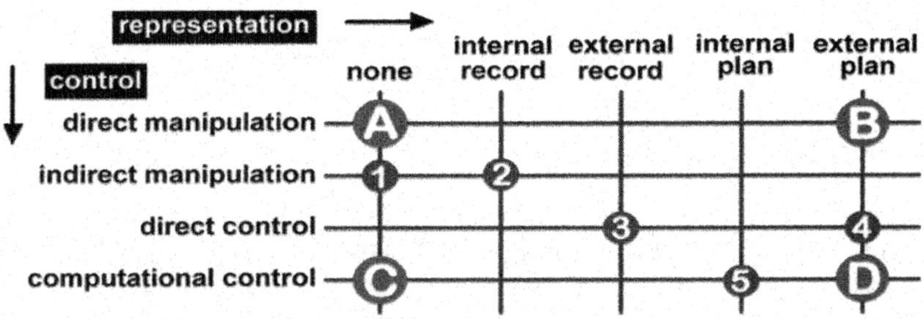

Fig. 1. Two dimensions of the framework for studying increasing cognitive demands of the programming tasks based on [6].

The second dimension allows studying the cognitive demand of the concepts and related operations from the perspective of the way in which the behaviour (the process) is represented. We identified three major types: having no representation at all, keeping a record of the steps, and building a program in advance, using certain notation. However, we found out that the second and third types should be divided into subtypes, thus revealing five types of representations altogether, see Fig. 1. Surprisingly, all of the grid points of the framework have meaningful interpretations in primary programming, including 'extremes' like Ⓑ and Ⓒ. In [6], we concluded that any programming content by its progression of activities usually tends to advance from a certain starting point of the grid towards point Ⓓ (in a Manhattan-style moves, i.e., from left to right and/or from top to bottom). In the first world (part) of Emil for Year 3, for example, the resulting progression is ❶❷❺ (i.e., progressing from ❶ to ❷ to ❺), and in its second world, it is ❸Ⓓ.

We will deal with further validation of the framework in other research, with the aim of applying it to assess the cognitive demands of the tasks in Emil for Year 4. We expect this may result in the framework's modifications and extension. However, in our current project, we use the above mentioned framework specifically to analyse the cognitive demands of learners' activities in educational robotics, as recommended by Jung and Won [17]. Specifically, we investigate whether the use of a blue control panel (see next section) affects the difficulty of transitioning from direct control with one externally represented command to computational control with an external plan, i.e., a sequence of commands.

2.3 Informatics with Emil

In this long-term data-based design research, we heavily draw on the intensive and formative study of Papert. Here, we mention the two following points in this context, as far as they frame our robotics development as well:

- Educational programming in its broad interpretation provides excellent opportunities to explore powerful ideas. Papert referred to his dream Mathland [10]. We can help pupils explore powerful computational ideas in informatics.
- We strive to help pupils to gradually transfer their focus from solving a problem to thinking about an explicit representation of the solution, often a program. In modern informatics education, it is our program that represents our idea, and the program becomes an object to think with and think about.

2.4 Robotics for Primary Project

We assume that robotics must form part of any informatics teaching content. Although this opinion is widely accepted by designers and educators, the available content only partially exploits opportunities to fully encounter powerful ideas of informatics. In our design, we focus on this prospect while maintaining possibilities to integrate technologies into other subjects also. We chose to devote five lessons to robotics in each year of primary, using TTS Blue-Bots equipped with the TacTile readers and control panels wirelessly connected to the robots, see Fig. 2. We decided to use the panels from the first lesson with the youngest pupils.

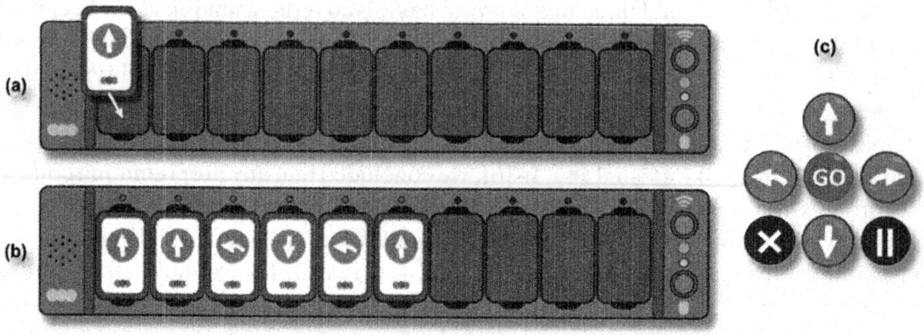

Fig. 2. (a) Pupils first pair the panel with the robot using the blue button on the right, then use the panel with a card as a remote control – they send the command to execute by using the green button. (b) However, they can also plan an entire program on the panel in advance. (c) The control buttons on the robot are locked after pairing with the panel.

In our robotics, we stick to the same pedagogical and design principles:

- We strive to respect and exploit all benefits of the 'primary style teaching'.
- Teachers do no explain but support their pupils to explore and discover.

- Pupils never work alone. In Emil, they work in pairs with one tablet, and in robotics, they work in teams of three or four pupils. They collaborate all the time, arguing within and between teams, communicate and discuss to learn together.
- Through the whole content, we work with multiple representations of the programs, positions, headings, paths and everything.
- We encourage pupils to 'think with their programs', to build, share, explain and modify them, come across various constraints and accept them and learn from each 'mistake'.

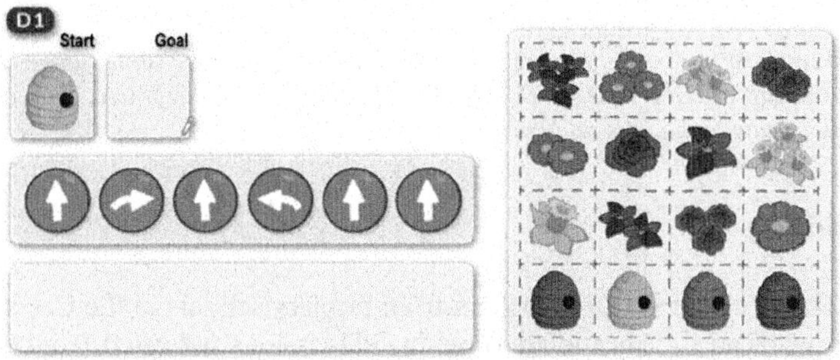

Fig. 3. An example from the First steps: *How will the robot go? Program it and find out. Draw the path and its goal. Use the blue panel and* ***return with the robot along the same path.***

In this research, within the robotics thread of the Emil project, we exploited our two-dimensional control/representation structure presented earlier. Namely, we explored the cognitive demands of the different levels of control applied in the primary robotics in the context of pupils using the external panel to control the robot.

In the numerous iterations of the design research [3] development, we closely collaborated with our university's partner design primary schools. Eventually, we settled on the structure of the content with four parts (or 'steps') of the activities. In the **First steps**, the external panel is used to control Ema (the robot) and the main goal is the progression from using one command to planning a program. Figure 3 illustrates an activity from this part. In the **Second steps**, pupils control Ema by using its own buttons, see Fig. 2(c) – with the program hidden inside the robot. In our framework, this is called an internal plan representation, see Fig. 3. In the **Third steps**, pupils use Ema's buttons also but represent their program in parallel, using paper cut-out cards with pictures of corresponding command. In the **Fourth steps**, a free choice to select working with any of these control/representation strategies stays with each team. Figure 4 illustrates an activity from the fourth part.

In this research, we focused on further verification of learners' acceptance of a blue panel to control Ema from the beginning. We formulated our objectives into the following research questions:

(RQ1) *How do pupils accept the use of the blue panels?*

(RQ2) *How do pupils progress from direct control to multiple commands planning?*

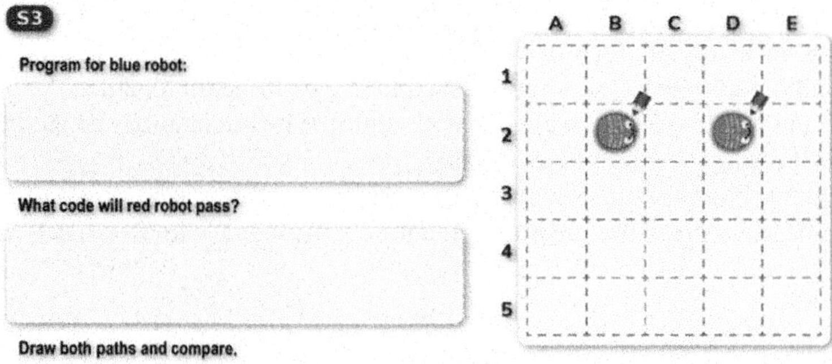

Fig. 4. An example from the Fourth steps: *Both robots will dance* ***the same dance****. Let the blue robot follow* ***the path coded D2 E2 E3 D3 D2 D1 C1****. Program the blue robot. What code will the red robot pass? Draw both paths and compare.*

3 Method

In early 2022, we contacted 176 teachers from primary schools in the Czech Republic and Slovakia who had already attended one-day PD sessions dedicated to our educational content Robotics for primary. The critical component of this PD session is devoted to the pedagogy that we exploit with our Blue-Bot Ema (and Emil[4]).

In the first stage of the research, we asked the teachers about their consent to participate in our research as well as some basic open-ended questions in the form of an electronic questionnaire about when they had participated in the training, whether they were already working with the new educational content with their pupils, in which years and how they had already progressed with the activities. Thus, we obtained valuable information about the levels of control and forms of representation that they were already applying with their pupils in robotics. Based on the replies, we identified a narrower sample for the second stage of the research, i.e., teachers who have already experienced their pupils working with blue control panels.

We obtained 36 consents and responses to our initial questions, whose descriptive overview is provided in Fig. 5. All respondents participated in a PD in robotics sometime between August 2021 and May 2022. Of the 20 teachers who have not yet begun working with Ema with their pupils (as of the date of that stage of the research, the 2021/22 school year), ten plan to begin in September 2022, some in the 2023 or 2024[5] school year or have not yet decided.

Our research focused on how learners adopted control panels and their role while transitioning from direct control to computational control, i.e., programming. As seen in Fig. 5 (b), all 16 teachers already working with our content have begun in each year of the primary stage. According to (c), in each year, they have started the First Steps part of the content. Hence, all pupils of the 16 teachers, in each year, have already started

[4] We have already briefly presented these pedagogical principles earlier in the paper.

[5] Czech primary schools are currently in the process of implementing informatics as a mandatory subject at primary level, and schools are encouraged to start teaching it not later than in September 2023 or September 2024.

controlling robot with a single command and have experienced the transition to planning several steps in advance with the program explicitly represented on the panel.

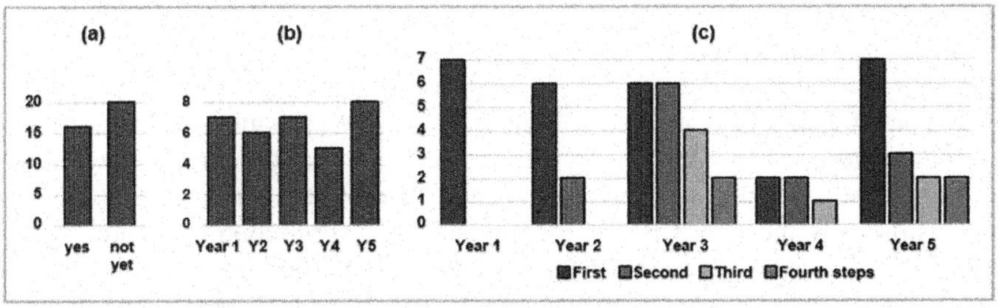

Fig. 5. Breakdown of n = 36 sample according to the number of teachers (a) already working with our content with their pupils, (b) working with pupils, by years, (c) who already started with First steps, Second steps etc., by Years of school.

In the second stage of the research, we addressed only those 16 teachers, thus forming our narrow purposeful sample with a set of questions focused on our current research questions. We also asked them to scan some of the already solved pages from the pupils' workbooks. The analysis of these, however, goes beyond the scope of this paper, and we will report the corresponding results separately.

At this stage of our research, we received responses from seven teachers who represent the situation in six Czech and Slovak primary schools and have experience of using our content in 21 classrooms with a total of 386 pupils. Part (a) of Fig. 6 shows that these were classes in all years of primary school: Three teachers started with Ema in Year 1, three in Year 2, and so on. Similar to n = 36, those n = 7 teachers (a subset of n = 36) most frequently started working with First steps in Year 3.

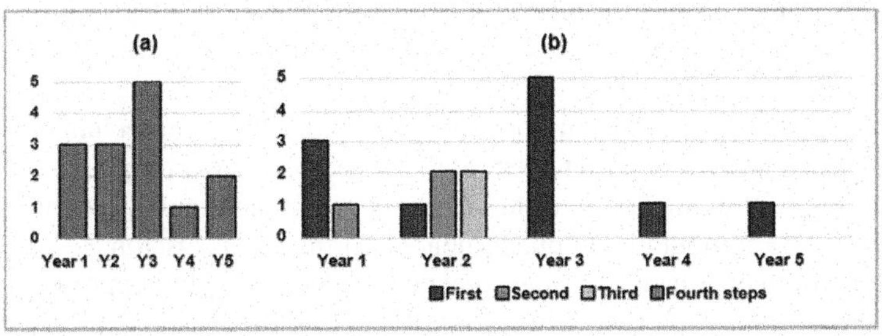

Fig. 6. Breakdown of n = 7 sample according to (a) teachers already doing our content with pupils, by Years, (b) teachers who already started with First steps, Second steps etc., by years.

To process and analyse the data obtained from the online questionnaire, we used a qualitative data analysis app QualCoder 3.1 [20] and applied standard method of coding and collapsing the codes into themes [21]. In the initial coding process, we applied over 30 codes, like order of the commands, debugging, collaboration, interrupting running program, pairing Ema and control panel and so on, which we subsequently collapsed into seven themes, presented and commented in the following section.

4 Results

By analysing the collected responses, we pursued our main objective. Specifically, we wanted to better understand how controlling a robot using a programmable panel similar to a remote control affects learners as they move from direct control (giving a single command to the robot) to planning and executing a program. An important feature of the panels used by the pupils is that a command or several commands are explicitly represented and visible. In presenting and interpreting the findings, we follow the five resulting themes that emerged from the data analysis. In our narrative, we first focus on the technical and organisational aspects, then on some affective aspects and the classroom atmosphere, and finally on the cognitive findings dealing with the different levels of mastery in compulsory informatics education in primary school.

5 Discussion

Among the results obtained, we would like to emphasize the following:

- Teachers in our sample know the importance of collaboration and the need to gradually develop it with our pupils. The educational content presented here and its pedagogy create numerous situations where teams in the classroom seek for and develop different collaborative practices (Figs. 3 and 4). When asked how they proceeded and collaborated in solving a particular problem, pupils also explain to each other, for example, the different strategies for dividing the tasks in the team. For example, it is faster and safer if the program is not being constructed on the panel by only one team member, but someone dictates or reads it and another looks up the tiles and hands them to the mate who puts the cards on the panel. Different strategies and forms of cooperation lead to different success in problem-solving and are worth discussing and sharing.
- Teachers also mention various minor problems (Table 1). Other technical problems – although rare – can also be used to benefit the development of computational thinking. For example, the simultaneous pairing of robots with panels and the connections cross by the teams is a computational phenomenon worthy of discussion.
- Teachers also consider it an advantage that pupils have an explicit representation of the program being built and executed in front of them on the panel. They can repeatedly execute the same program – unchanged – for Ema on different starting positions and with different initial headings. They can work with the program as an object of thought and can easily notice their program's properties. They can also easily spot a bug in the program and fix it by replacing one tile with another, which we consider a true affordance of the blue TacTile panels.
- Finally, the most significant result of this research is the following: Teachers in our sample confirmed that in most of the 21 participating classes, the use of the panels from the beginning of pupils' work with Ema – in every primary year – reduces

Table 1. Presentation and interpretation of the identified themes (In the left column are our findings from the analysis of the collected data; teachers' quotes are in italics; the right column contains our interpretations and comments).

Organisation and course of the lesson. Pupils work on the floor, divided in teams of three or four. Each team has their own mat and robot Ema Pupils either stand and walk around the mat with the blue panel in their hands while solving the problems or sit around the mat and rotate it on the floor or they just imagine Ema's current direction while programming and can plan a path containing **left** and **right** commands in this way also. Teachers believe that this is mainly how older and more mature pupils work	Papert [10] refers to this behaviour as *body syntonic learning*. Thanks to this identification with a robot that they control, learners can plan, execute and debug the program as early as in year one or even earlier
Technical issues. Pupils are sometimes confused about whether to start the program with the **Send** button on the panel or with the **GO** button on Ema Pupils do not know how to interrupt the program currently running from the panel Sometimes, the tiles did not work. Other times, the Bluetooth pairing between Ema and the panel did not work. Pupils had to learn how to turn the two devices off and on again and pair them afresh *... sometimes the panel remembered commands from the previous program...*	We believe this may happen if they had worked with Bee-Bots or Blue-Bots before, using a different pedagogy and not starting with the blue control panel immediately We have the same experience and do not know how to interrupt the running program either We have never experienced this; it is hard to know what exactly happened
Collaboration. It often depends on how well those in the team work together. First, they solve problems by taking turns. Gradually, however, they learn to work more efficiently and collectively. Teams happily solve tasks together and like to discuss *If there are good partners in the team, they thrive, and I am there to ask follow-up questions and inspire them to think further. If that's not the case, often I'm solving problems like 'I was next, but Don beat me to it...'*	The development of collaboration and communication is one of the key goals of our educational content in informatics and its pedagogy. We will get back to this in the concluding section

(*continued*)

Table 1. (*continued*)

Organisation and course of the lesson. Pupils work on the floor, divided in teams of three or four. Each team has their own mat and robot Ema Pupils either stand and walk around the mat with the blue panel in their hands while solving the problems or sit around the mat and rotate it on the floor or they just imagine Ema's current direction while programming and can plan a path containing **left** and **right** commands in this way also. Teachers believe that this is mainly how older and more mature pupils work	Papert [10] refers to this behaviour as *body syntonic learning*. Thanks to this identification with a robot that they control, learners can plan, execute and debug the program as early as in year one or even earlier
Pupils' attitudes and atmosphere in class. Pupils like what we do, the atmosphere in the class is great, busy, friendly, working and relaxed ... *sometimes even a pupil who did not do very well in informatics or other subjects will perform well!*	
Controlling robot by the panel. Most of the pupils of all years accepted using the panel without any problems. First, they had to get used to holding it correctly (e.g. not upside down), choosing the right tile and holding it correctly as well (so that, for example, they don't confuse the **back** command with the **forward**, if holding the tile wrongly). Also, some teachers report that some pupils, for a while, had problems with the correct order of the tiles One teacher pointed out that... *When Ema has to* ***go to the right****, we have to give two commands, in fact – turn* **right***and step* **forward**...	We consider order (in various forms and at various levels) to be one of the key phenomena of informatics. Therefore, it needs to be given corresponding attention in discussions with pupils This surprising remark enabled us to realise that in the PD session, we have to emphasise Ema does not know the command *go right*. We only have **left** and **right** turns and step **forward** or **backward**

(*continued*)

Table 1. *(continued)*

Organisation and course of the lesson. Pupils work on the floor, divided in teams of three or four. Each team has their own mat and robot Ema Pupils either stand and walk around the mat with the blue panel in their hands while solving the problems or sit around the mat and rotate it on the floor or they just imagine Ema's current direction while programming and can plan a path containing **left** and **right** commands in this way also. Teachers believe that this is mainly how older and more mature pupils work	Papert [10] refers to this behaviour as *body syntonic learning*. Thanks to this identification with a robot that they control, learners can plan, execute and debug the program as early as in year one or even earlier
Advantages and disadvantages. When working with the panel, pupils see the program in front of them. As they execute the program, the small LED lights above the commands light up one by one. Pupils can also easily see properties such as the number of commands in the program Working with the panel develops imagination and logical thinking. It helps pupils to quickly find an error in the program and easily correct it *… I was astonished how, out of eight tiles of a program, pupils* (of years 1 and 2) *easily identified the one that was incorrect…* One teacher noted that pupils prefer to work without panels: *Working with the panels requires more time; the panel has a limited number of commands*	This observation underscores the importance of the explicitly represented program and the opportunity to see the program as an object of our thinking about the problem, Papert [10]. We will get back to this in the Discussion Unfortunately, we do not have more details. It does, however, support our belief that this research must continue by observing pupils at work with blue panels and interviewing them
From one command to several. Pupils controlled Ema using the panel with one tile for just a few seconds and immediately moved on to programming more steps on their own. They understood the principle right away, it was quite natural for them In one case, teachers began the lesson by explaining, then the pupils immediately started using panel with multi commands A small group of pupils kept controlling the robot with one tile but soon they discovered another possibility or saw how others were doing it *… sometimes they moved from a single tile to the whole program even faster than I wanted …*	This approach, however, contradicts the pedagogy of Emil and Ema. Through various activities and tasks, we create situations where pupils identify the need for something new: a tool, a concept, an option or a procedure among others. Soon, they will discover and explore it early on in collaboration with other classmates, scaffolded by their teacher

the transition from direct control to programming from a cognitive point of view to a practically trivial one. This conclusion distinguishes educational robotics, i.e., controlling a physical object on a floor mat from controlling a virtual character on a screen. The panel contributes to this by its design, i.e., by motivating pupils to move immediately from single-command to multi-command control.

As some of the teachers' responses are not entirely consistent with this conclusion, we plan to extend our research by visiting schools, observing lessons in person and interviewing pupils involved in the process.

Acknowledgments. This work has been funded in part by VEGA Slovak Agency under project Productive gradation of computational concepts in programming in primary school 1/0602/20 and APVV under the Contract no. APVV-20-0353.

References

1. Bocconi, S., et al.: Reviewing Computational Thinking in Compulsory Education. Publications Office of the European Union, Luxembourg (online), Joint Research Centre (2022)
2. Sentence, S.: Moving to mainstream: Developing computing for all. In: Proc. of WiPSCE'19, pp. 1–2. ACM, New York (2019)
3. Plomp, T., Nieveen, N. (eds.) Educational design research. Part A: An Introduction. SLO, Netherland (2013)
4. UNESCO UIS Homepage, https://isced.uis.unesco.org/, last accessed 02 October 2022
5. Blackwell, A.F.: What is Programming? In: 14th Workshop of the Psychology of Programming Interest Group, pp. 204–218 (2002)
6. Kalas, I., Blaho, A., Moravcik, M.: Exploring control in early computing education. In: Pozdniakov, S., Dagienė, V. (eds.) Informatics in Schools. Fundamentals of CS and Software Engineering. ISSEP 2018. LNCS, vol. 11169, pp. 3–16. Springer, Cham (2018)
7. Kalas, I., Benton, L.: Defining Procedures in Early Computing Education. In: Tatnall, A., Webb, M. (eds.) Tomorrow's Learning: Involving Everyone. Learning with and about Technologies and Computing. Proc of WCCE 2017, pp. 567–578. Springer, Cham (2017)
8. Kalas, I., Horvathova, K.: Programming Concepts in Lower Primary Years and Their Cognitive Demands. In: Passey, D., Leahy, D., Williams, L., Holvikivi, J., Ruohonen, M. (eds.) DTEL OCCE 2021. IFIP Advances in Information and Communication Technology, vol. 642, pp. 28–40. Springer, Cham (2021)
9. Batko, J.: Educational robotics in the education at primary schools in the Czech Republic. (in Czech). J of Technol. Info. Edu. **10**(1), 5–16 (2018)
10. Papert, S.: Mindstorms: Children, computers, and powerful ideas. Basic Books, New York (1980)
11. Perlman, R.: Using Computer Technology to Provide a Creative Learning Environment for Preschool Children. AI Memo 360, MIT (1976)
12. Morgado, L., Cruz, M., Kahn, K.: Radia Perlman – A pioneer of young children computer programming. Current Developments in Technology-Assisted Education, pp. 1903–1908. Formatex (2006)
13. Sullivan, F.R., Heffernan, J.: Robotic construction kits as computational manipulatives for learning in the STEM disciplines. J. Res. Technol. Educ. **48**(2), 1–24 (2016)

14. El-Hamamsy, L., Chessel-Lazzarotto, F., Bruno, B., et al.: A computer science and robotics integration model for primary school: Evaluation of a large-scale in-service K-4 teacher-training program. Educ. Inf. Technol. **26**(1), 2445–2475 (2021)
15. Mikova, K., Krcho, J.: Cognitive taxonomy and task gradation in educational robotics. Preliminary results. In: Tardioli, D., Matellán, V., Heredia, G., Silva, M.F., Marques, L. (eds.) ROBOT2022: Fifth Iberian Robotics Conference. ROBOT 2022. LNNS, vol 589. Springer, Cham (2022)
16. Chalmers, C.: Robotics and computational thinking in primary school. Int. J. Child-Comp. Intera. **17**(1), 93–100 (2018)
17. Jung, S.E., Won, E.: Systematic review of research trends in robotics education for young children. Sustainability **10**(4), 905 (2018)
18. Benton, L., Hoyles, C., Kalas, I., Noss, R.: Bridging primary programming and mathematics: Some Findings of Design Research in England. Digital Experiences in Mathematics Education **3**(2), 115–138 (2017)
19. Kalas, I., Blaho, A., Moravcik, M.: Programming in Year 4: An Analysis of the Design Research Process. In: Proc of CSEDU, vol 2, pp. 425–433. SCITEPress, Vienna, Austria (2022)
20. QualCoder, https://qualcoder.wordpress.com/, last accessed 02 October 2022
21. Creswell, J.W.: Educational Research. Pearson, London (2012)

Digital Education in Higher Education

How ICT Tools Support a Course Centered on International Collaboration Classes

Shigenori Wakabayashi[1(✉)], Jun Iio[2], Kumaraguru Ramayah[3], Rie Komoto[4], and Junji Sakurai[4]

[1] Department of English Studies, Chuo University, Tokyo 197-0393, Japan
swkbys37@tamacc.chuo-u.ac.jp
[2] iTL, Chuo University, Tokyo 162-8478, Japan
iiojun@tamacc.chuo-u.ac.jp
[3] Language Academy, Universiti Teknologi Malaysia, Johor, 81310 Bahar, Malaysia
kumar@utm.my
[4] Workshop Initiative for Language Learning, Chiba 277-0841, Japan
riekomoto.will@gmail.com, sakurai@sekisaibo.co.jp

Abstract. Here we describe a course centered on three international online collaboration classes. The participants were students at Japanese and Malaysian universities and the course used Information and Communication Technology (ICT) tools to contribute to university students' language ability, willingness to study, and knowledge about their own cultures and those of their interlocutors. Various communication tools were used to support and monitor the project. The use of these ICT tools, including a newly developed application program (Dialogbook), will be presented. We describe how Dialogbook was used to set up small-group discussions, exchange comments, provide feedback between the instructor and students, and enable students' reviewing of their performance via rubric questions. The availability of such a one-stop support tool for students in the collaboration classes reduced the burden on teachers. The data collected with this application is closely examined both quantitatively and qualitatively, and the results show that the course successfully facilitated students' engagement in the project, with high motivation levels.

Keywords: Application · Collaboration · Communication · English · Group Activities · ICT

1 The Purpose and the Structure of This Article

This article reports on a university-level course as part of an Information and Communication Technology (ICT) based global education project [the SMILE project (Students Meet Internationally through Language Education)], centered on a series of international collaboration classes (November and December in 2021) based on ICT tools, where a commercial conference system (Webex), Social Networking Service (SNS) (WhatsApp), and an original, newly developed Learning Management System (LMS) for collaboration (Dialogbook) were used.

Published by Springer Nature Switzerland AG 2023
T. Keane et al. (Eds.): WCCE 2022, IFIP AICT 685, pp. 261–274, 2023.
https://doi.org/10.1007/978-3-031-43393-1_24

The SMILE project has three major characteristics as an educational program: Participants enjoy opportunities for communicating with peers of their own generation using English as a lingua franca; Goals, activities and achievements are clearly presented and recorded through the project and reviewed systematically during and after each activity; and the project can apply to any subject or content matter, including applied linguistics and information technology, and can be adjusted to the pedagogical needs of participants and courses.

This paper focuses on the description of one course carried out at a tertiary level of education, describing the ICT tools used in the course and the data collected with one of the tools, Dialogbook. The data collected as answers to rubric descriptors showed that participants' expectations and confidence in the SMILE project were both very high, and analysis of their language production showed that participants used rich varieties of vocabulary.

This paper is structured as follows: In the rest of Sect. 1, the background of the SMILE project will be given: This project was not initiated as a solution to obstacles caused by COVID-19, but rather had its roots in the authors' long-held sense of mission as educators at this global era. In Sect. 2, the constructs of the project will be given: The whole program will be described, focusing on a specific course implemented in 2021. In Sect. 3, we focus on the ICT tools for the project, including an original application newly developed by the second author (Dialogbook), which was employed to carry out many tasks. In Sect. 4, part of the records kept with Dialogbook will be presented and discussed. These data show that the project raised learner awareness of similarities and differences between their own and their peers' cultures and their proficiency in English. Most importantly, data show that the experience gained through the course helped participants to raise their motivation for further studies. In Sect. 5, a summary and a further direction of the project will be given.

2 The Background of the SMILE Project

Throughout the last half of the 20th century and onward, innovations in transportation provided humankind with incredible global mobility. This, along with other factors, resulted in increased numbers of second-language speakers using lingua franca, which is primarily English in East and Southeast Asia. Studies in second language acquisition and global education have developed much during these several decades, and have revealed various phenomena, but no theory of language acquisition proposes that language can be acquired without it being used or that language experience is unimportant [1]. Some crucial aspects of interactional competence can be improved only through interaction [2].

Concerning language education, it is desirable to supply opportunities to meet fellow non-native speakers of the target second language: Communicating in English among learners who share their first language is not 'natural' as a form of genuine communication, although it is a classroom activity observed at schools in countries around the world, including Japan. Yet most learners have little experience using English genuinely with those who do not share their first language, except perhaps (near) native-speaker teachers in their classes. With regards to cultural awareness, it is important for learners to meet people who do not share their backgrounds to become aware of cultures and values different from their own, which also deepens their understanding of their own culture and values.

Given the internet and ICT tools currently available, it may appear easy to set up opportunities where learners use English as a genuine means of communication. However, the reality is different: Instructors and institutions have little 'practical' connection with other instructors or institutions outside their own community. Besides, they generally appear to lack knowledge relevant to utilizing ICT to set up such collaboration. The first two authors of this paper were involved in international collaboration projects at Chuo University, Tokyo, from 2011 to 2015, when the university received a substantial grant from the Ministry of Education, Culture, Sports, Science, and Technology of Japan to promote global education. With our colleagues, we set up several credit-awarding classes, in which Japanese students visited institutes abroad, worked with non-Japanese students, and interacted with foreign students in collaboration classes via a teleconference system. These global project-based courses established human resource networks, making it possible to carry out the SMILE project.

The principle aim of the SMILE project is simple and clear: To provide students with opportunities to meet and communicate with speakers who do not share their first languages via the internet (and physically in person if conditions allow). From the viewpoint of second language acquisition, students should have plentiful opportunities to use the target language to become proficient interactors in the language. Experiencing genuine use of the target language should help learners obtain the integrative and internal motivation to keep them studying. It should be mentioned here that, in addition to the course described in this paper, three other collaborations (Japan-Taiwan high school collaboration; Japan-Indonesia high school collaboration; and Japan-Thailand university collaboration) were carried out around the same time, but for reasons of space, we do not elaborate on these collaborations here. Interested readers are referred to the website of the Workshop Initiative for Language Learning [3].

3 Overview

3.1 Participants

Participants in the collaboration classes consisted of two groups of students: One included 12 Japanese university students (nine third-year and two fourth-year undergraduate students, plus one first-year Master's student), all of whom were majoring in English linguistics. They belonged to the Department of English Studies, and their proficiency in English was evaluated as A2-B1 in Common European Framework of Reference for Languages (CEFR); the other group included ten second-year university students in Malaysia, who studied in a teacher-training (TESL) course and studied the Japanese language as well. They were recruited from a Japanese class, and participation was voluntary. Their proficiency in English was B1 or higher. The 22 students were divided into six groups, three to four members each (two from Japan and one or two from Malaysia). The professors from Japan and Malaysia and a coordinator attended the collaboration classes. No support technician attended the class. Because of COVID-19, all students from Malaysia participated in the class from home, while most students from Japan gathered in a classroom. All participants understood the purpose of the project and the data collection and signed an informed consent form before the course started.

3.2 Preparation, Main Events, Wrap-up, and Review

Preparations for this specific course started with the first author's invitation to the third author. The two professors have known each other for more than 10 years and their established relationship helped to set up the project. In early September 2021, they finalized the dates of three collaboration classes. A coordinator, who might be regarded as a teaching assistant in the regular term, ensured that everything went as planned. During the collaboration, nothing occurred to seriously disturb ICT communication or classroom activities, but a large typhoon hit Malaysia, and we had to make sure that students from Malaysia would be able to attend the collaboration class (see Sect. 3). In this situation, the coordinator played a critical role as an anchorperson between the two institutes.

The classroom activities on the Japan side in the Japan-Malaysia joint program are summarized in Table 1: The course on the Japan side was taught once per week, and each class lasted for 100 min. Japanese students prepared three dimensions in advance for the collaboration classes during the first three classes of their course: English skills, contents, and manipulation of ICT. These classes included exchanging information, and students did their own research and preparation outside of the classroom. The main event of the course was the three collaboration classes where Japanese students met their Malaysian peers in small groups online. A discussion session lasted for 25–30 min, and they participated in two sessions during each class, resulting in a total of six sessions. The participants in the first and second sessions were the same throughout these classes. One student on the Japan side missed two classes, but the rest attended all classes. One interim review and preparatory class was placed between the first and second collaboration classes on the Japan side because that day was a national holiday in Malaysia. After the three collaboration classes, two classes on the Japan side were used for wrap-up and review of the collaboration classes.

4 ICT Tools

This section describes the ICT tools used during the collaboration classes. It should be mentioned that the collaboration classes and the rest of the course could not have been carried out without them, even if a human resource network were available. The most important tool was the newly developed application, Dialogbook, which was used throughout the course for multiple purposes.

4.1 Tools for the Communication Among the Instructors and the Coordinator

The ICT tools used for this course included email, Webex, and WhatsApp, and they were used to exchange information among the instructors and a coordinator. Setting up a communication bypass during the sessions proved to be quite important. WhatsApp was used just before the third session when a typhoon hit Malaysia; otherwise, the Malaysian students might not have been able to attend the collaboration classes (Fig. 1).

Table 1. The summary of the course (Japan side).

No	Dates	Activities	Contents
1	20 Oct	Preparation	Overall description of the course. Practice using ICT
2	17 Nov	Preparation	Lecture on Malaysian culture and education system
3	24 Nov	Preparation	Mock collaboration, with practice using ICT
4	1 Dec	Collaboration	Topic: Self-introduction
5	8 Dec	Preparation	Discussions to decide the topic of the third collaboration
6	15 Dec	Collaboration	Topic: Japanese and Malaysian culture
7	22 Dec	Collaboration	Topic: Varies among groups
8	12 Jan	Wrap-up	Discussion on what they found in the collaboration classes
9	19 Jan	Data analysis	Discussion on how to analyze the video-recorded data

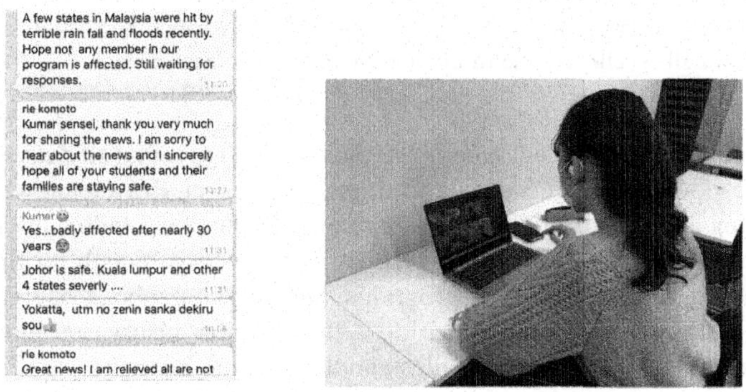

(a) (b)

Fig. 1. (a): Communication via WhatsApp. The second last message is in Japanese, saying, "Relieved to hear that all from Malaysia can join." (b): An image from one of the collaboration classes. This student is communicating in a group of four students using Webex.

4.2 Tools for Preparing and Reviewing the Classroom and Out-of-Class Activities

Dialogbook ver.2 is a software application developed by the second author and was used here as a one-stop platform. The main page of each student site (Fig. 2a) has a space for interaction between the instructor and student (left), sharing URLs for Webex meeting rooms (center), and for answering the rubric question (right). The questions appear when the blue button "update your evaluation" on the main page, as in Fig. 2b.

The teacher page is similar to the student one but differs in that responding to student comments and uploading the rubric descriptions and self-scoring results are available. All operations are recorded and can be read afterward by downloading from the teacher account in the form of a Microsoft Excel file for rubric questions and JSON files for the student-instructor correspondence.

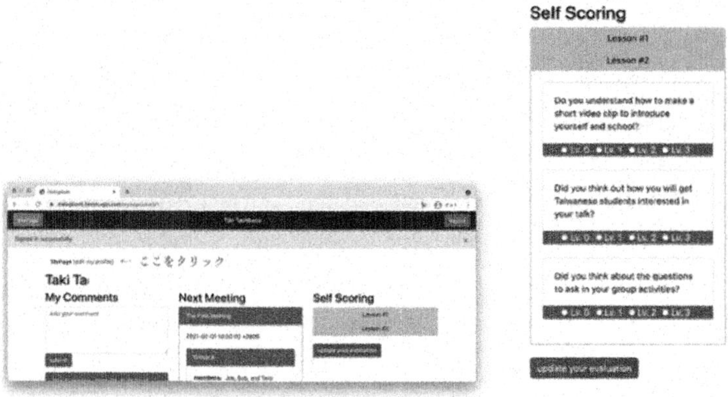

(a) (b)

Fig. 2. (a): The main student page of Dialogbook ver.2: The left column is to write comments/reviews of the class to be shared with the teacher; the middle column is to share the URL of the meeting room with peers; and the right column is to answer rubric questions. (b): When one of the yellow cells is clicked, the rubric questions for the class appear.

The advantages of using Dialogbook are three-fold. One is that all data, except video recording, are stored in and retrievable from the application. Reviewing what a student has done during and after the course is important to evaluate individual learners and the whole course (see Sect. 4), so keeping records must be easy enough for those without intensive training with ICT tools or programs. Second, Dialogbook operates independently of other LMS, SNS, and file-sharing systems so that instructors and students do not get lost in the massive number of files and tools on the internet.

Dialogbook is also user-friendly on other points. For example, the URLs for Webex meetings on the screen are automatically replaced by the next one 2 h after the preceding session, and consequently, the list of URLs on the site are always relevant for the next class. This simple and user-friendly appearance helped the first author immensely because he tends to get lost, especially during the last couple of years when dealing with several courses online became a necessity. As shown in Sect. 4, the students who participated in the course from the Japan side were not very well accustomed to using a new ICT tool; a streamlined system like this one is also necessary and quite helpful to them.

The last and most important feature is the ease of sharing information between two institutions. Sharing information may cause no problems among non-educational companies, but when it comes to educational institutions in Japan, protecting students' privacy is at the top of the list for security. Sharing information is generally dealt with among instructors. Of course, students and instructors should be careful when sharing any information with others but meeting other people with different cultural and linguistic backgrounds is highly valuable and cannot be replaced by any other means, hence establishing this kind of simple and safe one-stop service for sharing information between institutions is extremely valuable. (An earlier version of Dialogbook did not have this function [4]).

When the first author carried out a collaborative project similar to the current one from 2015 to 2018 between his institute and a university in Australia, sharing the URLs for Zoom sessions was carried out through a platform provided by the Australian university (and by email), but to log into the platform, the instructors at that university had to make special arrangements so that students and the instructor from the Japanese institute could receive login credentials as visitors. Thanks to Dialogbook, the students and instructors did not have to tackle such obstacles in this project.

4.3 Tools for Carrying Out, Recording, and Analyzing Collaboration Classes

Webex was used for collaboration classes. Japanese students hosted all group activities and recorded the meetings on their devices. The recorded videos were transcribed with the automatic subtitle generation tool available on YouTube, and then the Japanese student who hosted the session checked it. The transcription did not follow a strict format used in linguistic research, but the process of checking the texts allowed them to notice characteristics of their own and their peers' use of English while watching the videos.

5 The Outcome of the Project

In this Section, data collected with Dialogbook will be presented, including students' answers to rubric questions, message exchanges between students and instructors on the Japan side, and some comments sent to Malaysian instructors from his students.

5.1 Scores of Rubric Questions

As shown in Tables 2 and 3, no more than six questions with a scale of four levels (0–3) were set for each class so that students could evaluate themselves without much effort. These questions were aimed at revealing how much progress participants made towards the objectives of each class, including the contents of the class and homework, skills for using ICT tools, and attitudes. Since the questions covered such diverse aspects of the course, the instructor (the first author) set up the questions without referring to any specific descriptors such as CEFR. Tables 2 and 3 present the self-evaluation scores (mean and standard deviation) by eight students who answered all items, though one student failed to answer three items. Here we treat the scores from an ordinary scale as from an interval scale, similar to a Likert Scale. The data from the other four students are omitted because they skipped more than five questions. The numbers in the first column correspond to the class numbers in Table 1.

Some questions were asked repeatedly with the same or different wording, and student responses changed. One example is the question concerning the use of ICT tools: Answers to Question Items 1, 9, and 23 are concerned with setting up Webex rooms, and the means for these questions are 1.88, 3.00, and 3.00, respectively. This is naturally explained by the fact that Question Item 1 was given after the first trial of the setting of Webex room when some students did not do well. Later, all students became proficient at setting up Webex rooms. The same goes with the Questions concerning the

Table 2. Rubric questions and students' scores (To be continued).

Cl	Item	Rubric Questions	M	SD
1	1	Did you succeed in setting up a Webex room and recording what you discussed in that room?	1.88	1.25
1	2	Did you succeed in using YouTube to transcribe your video recording?	1.14	1.21
1	3	Did you edit the text the YouTube transcriber had created?	1.38	1.19
1	4	Do you think you are good at transcribing spoken data?	1.25	1.16
2	5	Do you understand what we will do during the rest of the seminar classes?	2.86	0.38
2	6	Do you think that the collaboration classes will give you good chances to improve your English?	3.00	0.00
2	7	Do you understand how general education in Malaysia is different from that in Japan?	3.00	0.00
2	8	Do you find any reasons for the differences in primary and middle educations between Japanese schools and Malaysian ones?	2.88	0.35
2	9	Did you succeed in setting up a Webex meeting, having a conversation with your partner, recording the conversation and viewing what you have recorded?	3.00	0.00
2	10	Did you understand the purpose of the collaboration classes?	2.88	0.35
3	11	Did you enjoy talking with your partner in the first session?	2.50	1.07
3	12	Did you enjoy talking with your partner in the second session?	2.88	0.35
3	13	Did you check the video recording after the class?	2.75	0.71
3	14	Was your and your partner's voice clear enough to transcribe?	2.86	0.38
3	15	Did you understand how to transcribe your video using YouTube?	2.71	0.76

(continued)

Table 2. (*continued*)

Cl	Item	Rubric Questions	M	SD
3	16	Are you looking forward to talking with XXX students?	2.86	0.38
4	17	Do you think your talk was interesting to the members of your group?	2.25	0.71
4	18	Did you prepare the materials for your talk?	2.75	0.46
4	19	Did you ask any good questions in the group activities?	2.13	0.83
4	20	Did you understand the members of your group well?	2.38	0.74
4	21	Did you enjoy the group activities?	2.88	0.35
4	22	Did you learn anything new in the group activities?	2.63	0.52
5	23	Did you set up a meeting room for the next collaboration class?	3.00	0.00
5	24	Do you understand how to get the transcription of the recorded data using YouTube?	2.13	0.99
6	25	Did you understand what Malaysian students talked about their culture?	2.63	0.52
6	26	Did you set up the topics of the next and last collaboration class?	2.63	0.52
6	27	Did you prepare well for presenting Japanese culture in this collaboration class?	2.38	0.74
6	28	Did you enjoy talking during the first and second sessions?	2.88	0.35
6	29	Did you find out anything that you had not been aware of in Malaysian culture?	2.75	0.46
6	30	Did you find out anything that you had not been aware of in Japanese culture?	2.38	0.74
7	31	Did you prepare well for presenting Japanese culture in this collaboration class?	2.63	0.74
7	32	Did you enjoy talking during the first and second sessions?	2.88	0.35

use of YouTube and its subtitle generator (items 2, 3, 4, 15, and 24). The mean scores for the first three are below 1.4, but those for the last two are above 2.1.

Table 3. Rubric questions and students' scores (Continued).

Cl	Item	Rubric Questions	M	SD
7	33	Did you understand what Malaysian students talked about?	2.38	0.74
7	34	Did you contribute to your discussion?	2.63	0.74
8	35	How do you evaluate yourself through the three collaboration classes?	2.13	0.83
8	36	How do you evaluate Chuo University students, including yourself, through the three collaboration classes?	2.63	0.52
8	37	How do you evaluate your group in the first session through the three collaboration classes?	2.38	0.52
8	38	How do you evaluate your group in the second session through the three collaboration classes?	2.63	0.52
8	39	Did you find the collaboration classes interesting?	2.88	0.35

In other questions, obvious changes were not observed. Question Items 27 and 31 are identical, asking whether they were prepared for presenting Japanese culture, but two participants answered differently, which resulted in a small increase of the mean score from 2.38 to 2.64. Question Items 25 and 33 are almost identical, asking whether they understood Malaysian students, and two participants answered differently, which resulted in a small decrease in the mean score from 2.64 to 2.38.

Lastly, the scores on some questions are very high. Japanese learners looked forward to the collaboration classes at the early stage of collaboration: Answers to Question Items 6 and 16 are 3.00 and 2.86 (one answered 2 and one failed to answer), respectively. They enjoyed the collaboration classes: Answers to Question Items 11, 12, 21, 28, 32, and 39 were 2.50 or 2.88: One student answered 2, but the rest answered 3 (and one failed to answer Question 11). This is consistent with Japanese and Malaysian students' comments, some examples of which we will describe in the next subsection.

5.2 Student Comments

Student comments collected on the Japan side with Dialogbook are analyzed at a linguistic level, and the results are given in Table 4 and Fig. 3 below. Although a previous study of collaboration classes between Japanese and Taiwanese high schools reported an increase of words and lemmas across three collaboration classes [5], such development was not observed in this project; probably because students had well-developed writing skills and high motivation even before starting the collaboration classes, and their attitudes toward the activities remained positive throughout the course.

The quantitative descriptions of words with Wordclouds are given in Fig. 3. The font sizes reflect the frequency of words in the messages. Those large words are closely related to the topics in each session, i.e., self-introduction, culture, education, and others, respectively. Therefore, quantitatively no change seemed to occur in the performance. However, qualitative differences are reflected in the answers.

Table 4. The summary of lexical use in message exchanges.

Classes	Numbers of words	Numbers of lemmas	Numbers of sentences	Words per sentences	Lemmas per sentences
Before the collaboration classes	2476	1802	172	14.40	10.48
After 1st collaboration class	669	522	52	12.87	10.04
After 2nd collaboration class	936	672	78	12.00	8.62
After 3rd collaboration class	939	615	69	13.61	8.91
Total	5020	3611	371	13.53	9.73

Fig. 3. From left to right: After the 1st, 2nd, and 3rd collaboration classes.

Now let us examine the student comments qualitatively. Some examples are given in Table 5, where spelling errors were corrected, but grammatical errors were left in the original. The comments in the bottom line were sent to the Malaysian instructor from his students. Before the first collaboration, all the participants said that they were looking forward to the collaboration class. A few students were also worried about their English skills (s4, s11). After the first collaboration class, they said they had enjoyed themselves (s2). Some commented about their English skills (s5). Other comments revealed that learners were motivated to study more because of this experience (s10). Student comments after the second collaboration class, whose topic was ‘cultures,’ referred to the contents more often than those after the first one, where the students introduced themselves. Through the three collaboration classes, the number of mentions regarding the contents in their interaction increased. After the third and final session, they expressed their enjoyment of the class as well as their interest in the contents they had dealt with. They also referred to their proficiency in English. Some mentioned networking among students and all Japanese students appeared interested in keeping contact with Malaysian friends. After the three collaboration classes, Malaysian students commented to the Malaysian instructor. The examples are given in the last row of Table 5. They show that the Malaysian students also appreciated the course.

Table 5. Comments from Japanese students. The numbers in ( ) are the student IDs.

	Examples
Before 1st Collaboration class	"I'm looking forward to my first class with UTM next week. (s3)" "I can't wait to talk with the students of UTM. (s9)" "I'm looking forward to learning about the culture of Malaysia, but I'm worried about my English. (s4)" "I am worried about my English skill, but I will do my best in the next lesson. (s11)"
After the 1st collaboration class	"I enjoyed talking with UTM students. It was a lot of fun.... Anyway, it was a good opportunity to speak in English. (s2)" "I enjoyed talking Malaysian, but I felt a lack of my English power. (s5)" "It was lots of fun! I have realized what I forgot; you can communicate and be friends with people without advanced English command. I found Malaysian friends tended to talk about their hometown, probably because they were proud of their hometown. I should emulate them and know about my own hometown. If only we had had more time! (s10)"
After the 2nd collaboration class	"We had second times collaborations with UTM students. I introduced them to Japanese Wagashi. It seems that they were enjoying my presentation, and they asked me some questions. It was happy for me to answer the question. (s2)" "I introduced the Japanese language to Malaysian students. They were especially interested in kanji. This experience helped me to rediscover my own culture. (s8)" "On 15 December, we could enjoy talking with UTM students. We talked about Japanese culture and Malaysian culture. Also, we talked about how to spend in winter. In Malaysia, they spend 31 December hanging out and going night market. We talked about many things, and it was very wonderful. (s9)"

(continued)

Table 5. (*continued*)

	Examples
After the 3rd collaboration class	"Today, we talked about the education system and school events. It was interesting to know the difference between these schools, but I realized there is a lot of the same things. Especially, I was surprised at the school uniform. Some students who belong to a school representative or librarian wear different uniforms. This was fresh information for me. Through this session, I could talk with Malaysian students. This experience is rare and interesting. In one day, I want to talk about them face to face. (s2)" "At first, I was worried about if I could talk with Malaysian students in English. So, I got ready for UTM. Then, I enjoyed talking with them, and we exchanged cultures of each other's countries. This project became a good experience for me. (s8)" "22 Dec: I enjoyed the sessions again, and I miss the students who I talked to in this class. We exchanged our Instagram accounts with each other. I hope we can meet someday. In the three collaboration classes, I understood my level of speaking English. I need to keep studying English in the future. (s11)"
Message from Malaysian students after the 3rd collaboration class	"Tq so much, sensei, for giving us this golden opportunity to join the program." "Thank you, sensei, for the amazing opportunity. I would be so glad to participate in this program again in the future (hopefully physically)."

All students enjoyed the collaboration classes. Japanese students probably spent more time preparing for this project than they did in other classes, but no complaints was found in their comments. All in all, the project achieved considerable success.

6 Conclusion

This paper describes an international collaboration course between Japanese and Malaysian universities. The international relations among the individuals involved and the ICT tools used made it possible to carry out this course, where students were given occasions to use English as a genuine means of communication. The answers to rubric questions and student comments collected through the course showed that they became aware of the skills needed for communication, increased their motivation to study the language, and became more curious about the world and themselves.

Further studies should be carried out in at least two directions. First, participants' real interaction during the collaboration classes should be analyzed to reveal what takes place in group works. Second, how this type of international project-based study could be implemented with different course subjects (e.g., science) and schools (e.g., primary schools) should be examined. Although, in practice, some other practical issues (e.g., finding a class to pair with) need to be resolved to carry out a SMILE, we believe that any teacher with enthusiasm will be able overcome them with support from WILL [3].

Acknowledgments. This project was supported by Grant for Establishing Interdisciplinary Research Cluster (PI Jun Iio), Chuo University. We would like to thank John Matthews for his comments on the English and Loh Khai Xian for his support in administrating the participation of Malaysian students in the project. This study is supported by KAKENHI 22K00689.

References

1. Mitchell, R., Myles, F., Marsden, E.: Second Language Learning Theories, 4th edn. Routledge, New York (2019)
2. Doehler, S.P.: On the nature of development of L2 interactional competence. In: Salaberry, M.R., Kuniz, S. (eds.) Teaching and Testing L2 Interactional Competence, pp. 25–59. Routledge, New York (2019)
3. WILL Homepage: https://kotoba-kobo.jp/e. Last accessed 24 Jan 2022
4. Iio, J., Wakabayashi, S.: Dialogbook: a proposal for simple e-portfolio system for international communication learning. Int. J. Web Inf. Syst. **16**(5), 611–622 (2020)
5. Iio, J., Wakabayashi, S., Sakurai, J., Ishikawa, S., Kijima, Y.: Providing a platform for intercultural communication education and its practices. Trans. Digit. Pract. **2**(3), 58–67 (2021)

Multiple Platform Problems in Online Teaching of Informatics in General Education, Faced by Part-Time Faculty Members

Hajime Kita[1(✉)], Naoko Takahashi[2], and Naohiro Chubachi[3]

[1] Kyoto University, Yoshida, Sakyo, Kyoto 606-8501, Japan
kita.hajime.7a@kyoto-u.ac.jp
[2] Kokugakuin University, Higashim-Shibuya, Tokyo 150-8440, Japan
n.takahashi@kokugakuin.ac.jp
[3] Takasaki University of Commerce, Negoya 741, Takasaki 370-1214, Japan
n-chubachi@uv.tuc.ac.jp

Abstract. The curriculum for an undergraduate program in Japanese universities usually comprises a general education and special/major education programs, and in general education programs, informatics is widely taught. It is one of the characteristics of the informatics education in Japan. A nationwide survey on the informatics education in Japanese universities conducted in 2016 revealed that the teaching of informatics in general education depends largely on part-time faculty members as well as full-time ones. During the COVID-19 pandemic, most Japanese universities were forced to conduct their classes online for 2020 and 2021 academic years. Online teaching was carried out in several modes, using various learning management systems and video conferencing services and student access terminals that differed across universities. Furthermore, the permission to access information systems depends on the employment contract renewal. In such situations, part-time faculty members faced various problems while using multiple platforms that were rarely recognized by full-time members. In this study, the authors point out these multiple platform problems faced by part-time faculty members and propose a common platform for informatics teaching in general education to resolve the issue and improve the teaching quality.

Keywords: Informatics in general education · Multiple platforms · Online teaching · Part-time faculty member · Identity management · Educational service provision

1 Introduction

The curriculum for undergraduate programs in Japanese universities usually consists of general education and special/major education programs, and in general education programs, informatics is taught widely, and a large number of students

Published by Springer Nature Switzerland AG 2023
T. Keane et al. (Eds.): WCCE 2022, IFIP AICT 685, pp. 275–285, 2023.
https://doi.org/10.1007/978-3-031-43393-1_25

take these courses. Informatics in general education will be subsequently referred to as IGE in our study. It is one of the characteristics of the informatics education in Japan.

For general education courses commonly taken by many students, such as informatics and languages, securing teaching staff is an important consideration for universities. A nationwide survey on the informatics education in Japanese universities was conducted in 2016 [1]. It showed that teaching informatics in general education depends largely both on part-time faculty (PTF) and full-time faculty (FTF) members.

The outbreak of cornavirus (COVID-19) in 2019 escalated into a worldwide pandemic. During the pandemic, most Japanese universities were forced to have their teach online for the 2020 and 2021 academic years. The online mode of teaching taken up by several universities became an "emergent evacuation of teaching." Hence, different styles of teaching, the use of learning management systems (LMSs), and information terminals used by students varied one university to another. In such a situation, PTFs faced the problem of using several teaching methods and various information environments. Furthermore, there was also the administrative issue of the renewal of employment contracts and access permissions to educational information systems linked to them. This was recognized as a serious problem in online classes taught by PTFs.

This study highlights the problems faced by IGE PTFs. As shown below, it addresses problems faced by PTFs even before the pandemic. However, the problems exacerbated during the pandemic and were recognized by the IGE teaching community. Recognizing these problems, the authors conducted a domestic symposium focusing on the issues that arise in online teaching in 2021 [2]. While we have not surveyed this problem yet in a wider PFT community, in this study, the authors addressed the problems by sharing the insights that gained from the discussion at the symposium.

Furthermore, the authors propose a common IGE platform to solve the problems. With this common platform, we can also expect an improvement in the teaching quality of IGE.

This paper is organized as follows. In the next section, Sect. 2 provides an outlook on IGE in Japan. Section 3 discusses the role of PTFs in IGE and highlights multiple platform problems faced by PTFs. In Sect. 4, we share the experiences of the authors on this issue. In Sect. 5, a common teaching platform for IGE to solve the problems is proposed. Section 6 concludes the paper.

2 General Education of Informatics in Japanese Universities

As mentioned before, the curriculum for an undergraduate program in Japanese universities usually consists of general education and special/major education programs. Prior to World War II (WWII), general education was provided in high schools, and universities provided only special/major education. In the reform for the Japanese educational system after WWII, new universities were organized by combining old high schools and universities, and hence new universities included both types of education in their mission.

Along with the introduction of computers in universities, classes on treating computers were introduced to the curriculum of universities. Currently, several universities have courses on informatics in their general education programs, and taken by many students. It is one of the characteristics of informatics education in Japanese universities.

As for the academic community, the Information Processing Society of Japan (IPSJ) covers the computer science field, and pays attention to field education as well as academic research. It established the Information Processing Education Committee [3]. This committee proposes periodically curriculum standards for special/major subjects of the field. Furthermore, under this committee, a committee for general education (GE) was also established. GE proposes the Body of Knowledge for IGE (GEBOK), and textbooks alongside the GEBOK have been published by some members of the GE committee [4].

Concerning informatics education in Japanese universities, a nationwide survey was conducted in 2016 [1]. It included IGE, as well as special/major field education.

The survey results showed that IGE was conducted in many universities and a large number of students took such courses. While a wide range of topics were treated in these courses, computer literacy, information ethics, and security were taught in many of them. Furthermore, relating conceptual knowledge on information networks, digitization of information, and elements and structure of computers were also selected often.

The teaching staff of IGE largely comprised PTFs as well as FTFs. The percentage of PTFs in the teaching staff is about 30%. They usually have the background of research fields such as computer science while among the FTFs who teach IGE, those with a research background are few.

3 Multi-platform Problems in Online Teaching

Online teaching is carried out by combining various technologies and administrative matters as discussed subsequently (See Fig. 1). The selection of technologies is done by each university. Furthermore, administrative options are also decided by each university. In such a situation, PTFs who teach at several universities may find it challenging to cope with multiple technologies and administrative options sets.

3.1 Technological Options in Online Education

During the COVID-19 pandemic, many universities in Japan were forced to continue their educational activities online. From a technological point of view, online education is carried out with various layered technologies listed as follows:

Authentication System: User accounts and their authentication are the basis of information systems. Usually, accounts are issued separately by universities. Furthermore, some universities issue different accounts for different information systems, while some introduce unified accounts with centralized authentication systems. Some accounts were issued by major IT service providers. Additionally, some universities introduced multi-factor authentication to enhance information security, while others used conventional ID/PW authentication.

Learning Management Systems and Related Information Services: Learning Management Systems (LMS) is a key component of online education. In Japan, various LMS are independently selected by universities. Some universities introduce campus-wide LMS, while others may use different LMSs by departments. Some may use LMSs of a cloud service type, and others run their selected LMSs on-premise.

Additionally, student information systems (SIS) for course registration by students and grade registration by instructors, portal services serving as an entrance for several web-based services are also introduced independently by universities. Furthermore, inter-system coordination among SIS and LMS such as the feeding of course rosters from SIS to LMS depends on universities as well.

Support of Online Communication and Collaboration: E-mail is a conventionally yet commonly used communication service in universities. Usually, e-mail accounts are issued by universities to faculty members, non-teaching staff, and students. Services for online storage and web-based teleconferencing are becoming increasingly common these days. In particular, web-based teleconferencing services have been newly introduced as key components of online teaching during the pandemic. Furthermore, on-demand video delivery solutions are also used in some universities.

PC Terminals: Online education requires network connection and PC terminals at the student side. For IGE classes, various application software such as office tools and programming environments are also required.

Before the pandemic, classes were held using campus computer laboratories with PC terminals maintained by universities, or on students' laptops whose specifications were approved by universities. However, in rapidly taken online education during the pandemic, universities and teachers had to consider a wide variety of students' environments, and not only personal computers but also tablet terminals and smartphones.

Furthermore, under the initiative of 'GIGA school' [5], senior high schools started to introduce access terminals for all students. In Japan, most public senior high schools are run by prefectures, the second-level local governments consisting of several first-level ones such as cities and towns. Some prefectures are asking students to buy their laptops/tablets. While universities mostly introduce PC-type terminals with Windows or macOS, high schools introduce tablet-type terminals with iPadOS, ChromeOS, or Windows. In 2025, students who experienced GIGA school environments will start to enroll in universities, and the variety of information terminals held by students may increase.

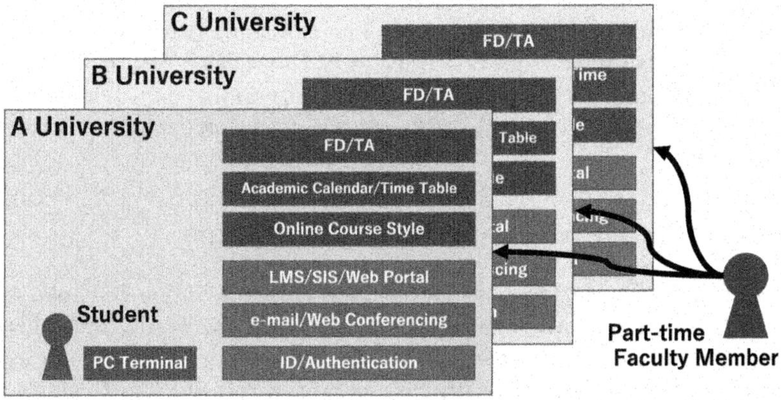

Fig. 1. Technical elements and administrative options for online teaching.

3.2 Administrative Issues

Administrative issues related to online teaching were also decided by each university.

Online Teaching Style: There are several online teaching styles.
- Synchronous type using teleconferencing systems.
- Asynchronous type where course materials are distributed via an LMS and/or video delivery services, and obtain responses as assignments, etc. using LMS

In the case of having in-person classes, hybrid/hyflex type operation of classes had to be considered for students who are unable to attend due to various reasons. Furthermore, the assessment in classes was also an important issue during the pandemic in which we experienced difficulty conducting an in-person examination. Policies of course assessment were also decided by universities independently.

Contract Renewal of PTF: Renewal of the contracts for PTFs is typically done annually, and new contracts usually start at the beginning of the semester. However, preparation of online teaching takes time, and PTFs may want to start it during the previous academic year. In the case of newly contracted PTFs, it gets difficult because new accounts and access permission to relating information systems such as LMS are not prepared within the academic year before commencement of classes.

FD and TA: PTFs usually do not participate in the decision-making process, and their access to informal/tentative information is limited. It may also be difficult for PTFs to attend university activities for faculty development (FD) because of time constraints. Access to teaching assistants and communication with them may be difficult for PTFs who stay outside the universities.

Academic Calendar and Timetable: The academic calendar and timetable of the course also vary from one university to another. While online education may save commuting time, adjustment of various class schedules due to national holidays is also a problem for part-time faculty members even before the pandemic.

4 Experience of Multi-platform Problems

Problems of multiple platforms for PTFs who conduct online IGE classes were recognized through teaching during the COVID-19 pandemic, and this study points out and addresses the issue. However, we do not have enough evidence (e.g. survey results) on the issue. In this section, we would like to share author experiences.

4.1 Background of Identity Management of PTFs

Kita, the first author of this paper, had served as director-general of the Institute for Information Management and Communication (IIMC), the central ICT organization of Kyoto University for more than four years until the end of 2020.

In Kyoto University, SIS uses its original accounts while LMS and other information systems use unified campus accounts. For students and FTFs, these two accounts are well linked via the portal sites, and information on SIS such as course rosters are automatically fed to LMS; hence usability of these systems was good. However, in the renewal of employment, PTFs' employer numbers are alter every year, thus from the SIS, PTFs cannot create course sites on the LMS for the classes they teach themselves. Furthermore, the SIS accounts were issued to all PTFs for registration of syllabus and grades, but the unified campus accounts were issued upon their request, a limited number of PTFs used the LMS before the pandemic.

Under such conditions, the IIMC faced a very heavy workload in issuing new accounts to PTFs, setting up course sites on LMS taught by them manually, giving instruction of usage of LMS and other linked services in in-person or online seminars to PTF, and answering many questions on LMS and web-conferencing services from PTF at the help desk. This problem was reported by Kita [6] from a viewpoint of system administration. Kinoshita [7] who taught language classes as a PTF reported the issue from PFT's point of view.

4.2 Notes on Work as a PTF for IGE

Takahashi, the second author of this paper, has taught IGE at several universities as a PTF as well as at Kokugakuin University as an FTF. She experienced difficulties as a PTF in applications for the LMS account, the LMS authentication processes, and campus networks differing across universities.

The followings are notes on the points to work as a PTF:

- Usually, prior to the start of the PTF contract, the university issues an account to enter the syllabus of the course held in the next academic year. However, with such an account, only the syllabus system may be accessible, and an access to LMS may be unavailable. Hence he/she has to obtain a permission to access LMS. Even in the case of contract being extended, an access to LMS may be restricted temporally at the end of the academic year, and he/she must confirm it.
- For communication from the university, he/she has to register his/her mail address or has to use a mail address with the domain name of the university issued by the institution. In the latter case, he/she also has to confirm the mail system of the account, availability of Web-mail, and set forwarding to the address for daily use. During the pandemic, there was a case that a new mail account was issued to introduce new online services in a university.
- At the beginning of a new semester, a PTF has to confirm the availability of his/her account at the LMS, check the course roster, the way of sending announcements to course students, communicate with particular students, prepare course contents, and uploading of them to LMS. In the case of renewal of contract, he/she has to check availability of course contents used during the previous year. If cleared, the same procedure was to be followed for the first year. In LMS operation, available functions and resources for PTFs may differ from those of FTFs. If students can use the same functions and resources as the FTFs, they cannot be explained by the PTFs in their classes.
- IGE classes are held in campus computer laboratories with PC terminals. PTFs have to confirm the way of logging into the terminals. A login account may be different from the LMS account. Depending on universities, other than the use of the same ID with the LMS, there are various login ways such as the use of e-mail address for a login account, use of special account for computer laboratories, log in with electronic ID cards read by a card reader of the terminal etc.

If a PTF is employed by another university as an FTF and has experience working as a PFT as well, he/she can ask or check the environment and necessary procedures in advance. However, if he/she works only as PTFs of several universities, preparation of classes may lead to anxiety.

As an actual case, Takahashi experienced the following in a university: This university introduced a portal web site that had the function of LMS. The e-mail address is used for logging into it, while the faculty ID number was used before. The login procedure of the PC terminal for the instructor is different from that of the PC terminal for student use. Different mail systems are used for faculty members (Microsoft) and students (Google). The cloud storage used by FTFs is not available for PTSs, and hence the PTFs cannot explain such services to students as same as the FTFs.

4.3 Organizational Aspect of Computer Laboratories

Chubachi, the third author of this paper, was an FTF in four universities and a PTF in two, and served as an instructor for IGE classes that use university computer laboratories. He points out the importance of recognizing organizational structure that manages computer laboratories as a PTF or an FTF newly joined to a university. A new staff had to check the relationship of the department of educational affairs and that for information systems. In the teaching of IGE classes, we have to use computer laboratories and have to confirm the specification of PC terminals, e-mail addresses of the universities, authentication systems, university portal sites, and LMSs. To learn these things, faculty members have to know the departments managing these systems and their operational information.

In many Japanese universities, the departments of educational affairs do not pay much attention to activities held in classes, and hence they may not offer an adequate environment for each class. Even IGE classes, computer laboratory may not be assigned unless the instructor requires. If such courses are also held in the previous year, usually the same room is assigned, but for newly open courses, the instructor has to pay attention to room assignment. Depending on universities, different departments manage computer laboratories. If computer laboratories are managed by the department for information systems, the instructor has to submit an application for using a room, while other procedures are taken at other departments. If communication between two departments is poor, this can lead to problems.

For example, Chubachi encountered various issues in computer laboratories. There was a case when the available software on PC terminals was different in each room, and classes were assigned to the room that did not have the necessary software. Another case was that an update of software versions or replacement of PC terminals were held without notification, and hence course materials had to be revised after the classes commencement. When a teacher starts working in universities as an FTF or PTF for the first time, the start of courses becomes difficult without obtaining relating information in advance, knowing the relationship of departments in charge of the matter. Thus, for the success of IGE courses, knowing the relationship of the organization and services necessary for the class is a key issue.

5 Proposal of a Common IGE Platform

This section proposes the construction of a common platform for IGE to solve the multi-platform problems discussed above. It is expected that this common platform can improve the quality of IGE teaching as well as solve the aforesaid problems.

The common platform consists of two key components: an identity management system and a learning management system. See Fig. 2.

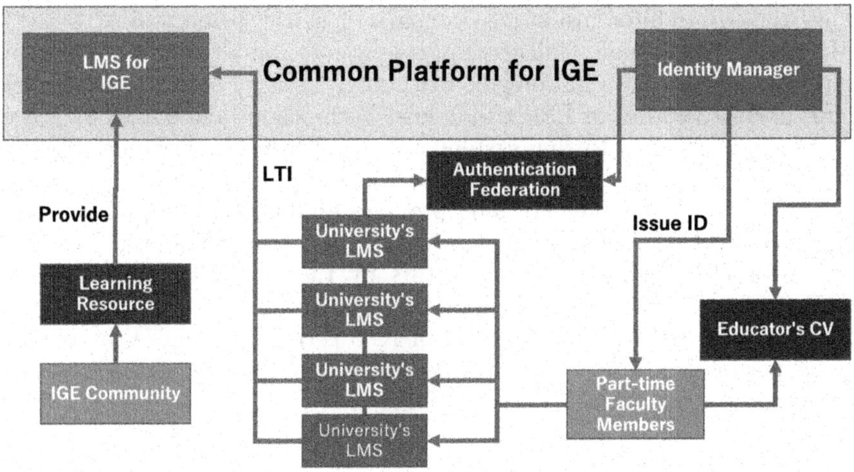

Fig. 2. Proposal of a Common Platform for IGE

5.1 Identity Management of Part-Time Faculty Members

As for the authentication among Japanese universities, the Academic Access Management Federation in Japan (GakuNin) formed in 2009 connects identity (IdP) and service providers (SP), and many universities and companies join this activity as IdP or SP [8]. With GakuNin, various services of SP can be used with the ID provided by IdP.

By introducing an identity management system that works as an identity provider of an authentication federation, and if LMS's of universities having classes join the federation as service providers, instructors can log in to various LMSs of universities where they teach using the same accounts.

This identity management system will also work as a platform for instructors of IGE to join original platform activities such as training opportunities, sharing good practices, and collaboration projects for development of curriculum and IGE learning material.

5.2 LMS for IGE

The other key component is LMS as a unified teaching environment of IGE across universities. In the concept of the Next Generation Digital Learning Environment by EDUCAUSE [9], the LMS works as a hub that connects various educational services. It can be implemented using LTI [10], a standard proposed by IMS Global for connecting an LMS to various services. With this, instructors can teach their courses in a unified environment that can be accessed via the LMS of each university they teach. Connecting various services from LMSs via LTI has already been widely experienced by universities, and administrative workload at the university side is quite light.

This kind of architecture is also considered in the project of MEXCBT of the Ministry of Education, Culture, Sports, Science, and Technology, Japan [5]. It is trying to construct a nationwide learning system for school education with learning portals (a kind of LMS) that host each school and MEXCBT, a centralized computer-based testing system connected from the learning portals via LTI.

The unified LMS for IGE not only provides a unified environment for teaching but also works for efficient dissemination of learning materials, tests, and questions for CBT, support of instructors by the community such as GE in IPSJ. For example, there is a learning material developed by a community of IGE instructors, and it is widely used in IGE [11]. Furthermore, by obtaining adequate permission on learning records stored in this LMS, it can be used for the evidence-based improvement of teaching.

5.3 Qualification of Instructors

Furthermore, the unified environment for IGE will provide the instructors with training opportunities and qualifications as well. Activity records such as qualification as well as taught courses can be exported to electronic CV such as ORCID [12], a global ID system for researchers.

5.4 Management Issues on the Common Platform

So as to achieve the proposed concept, we also think about the management of the platform as well as technological issues, that is, an institution that runs the platform, and ways to cover its cost.

A similar situation is also observed in several subjects taught in general education in universities. Classes are taken by many students, but universities face difficulties to have a sufficient number of FTFs to teach such classes. Hence, many PTFs are required to teach such classes. Foreign language classes are a typical example. The proposed common platform may also encourage the education of such classes.

6 Conclusion

In this study, the authors discussed problems of multiple-platform in the online teaching of informatics in general education (IGE) in Japanese universities. The nation-wide survey shows IGE depends largely on part-time faculty members (PTFs), and during the pandemic, they seemed to face problems of multiple platforms used by universities both in technological and administrative aspects. While there is still no statistical evidence, the authors pointed out the problems by sharing their experiences. Furthermore, they also propose a concept of a common platform for IGE considering recent trends of technologies for teaching. This common platform is designed to improve the issues experienced and the quality of teaching. To confirm the feasibility of this proposal will be the subject of future study.

Acknowledgements. Discussion of the problems of multiple-platform was based on the discussion in the Symposium "Future Informatics Education for University Students" 2021. The authors sincerely express their gratitude to the GE committee of the Information Processing Society of Japan, SIG-ITE of the Academic eXchange for Information Environment and Strategy (AXIES), the cosponsored organizations of the symposium, and its participants.

References

1. Kakeshita, T., Takahashi, N., Mika Ohtsuki, M.: Survey and analysis of computing education at Japanese universities: informatics in general education. Olympiads Inform. **13**, 81–98 (2019)
2. Kita, H.: "Petagogy" for future: education of informatics in multiplatform era—a report of symposium "future informatics education for university students" 2021. Mag. Inf. Process. Soc. Jpn. **63**(10), 568–571 (2022). (in Japanese)
3. Jyoho-Shori-Kyouiku-Iinkai (Education Committee), Information Processing Society of Japan. https://www.ipsj.or.jp/annai/committee/education/index.html. Accessed 17 Jan 2022. (in Japanese)
4. Jyoho-shori-gakkai Ippan-jyoho-kyouiku-Iinkai (GE Committee of IPSJ) ed.: Ippan-Jyoho-Kyoiku. Ohmsha, Tokyo (2020). (in Japanese)
5. Ministry of Education, Culture, Sports, Science and Technology: GIGA School KOUSOU NO JITSUGEN. https://www.mext.go.jp/a_menu/other/index_00001.htm. Accessed 20 Jan 2022. (in Japanese)
6. Kita, H.: Jyugyou no online-ka to hijyoukin-koushi - Kyoto Daigaku no jireikara. https://edx.nii.ac.jp/lecture/20200731-07. Accessed 21 Jan 2022. (in Japanese)
7. Kinoshita, Y.: Zenki no enkaku-jyugou no genba to sono kadai—Hijyoukin-koushi no baai. https://edx.nii.ac.jp/lecture/20200821-05. Accessed 21 Jan 2022. (in Japanese)
8. About GakuNin. https://www.gakunin.jp/en. Accessed 20 Feb 2022
9. Brown, M.: The NGDLE: We Are the Architects (2017). https://er.educause.edu/articles/2017/7/the-ngdle-we-are-the-architects
10. IMS Global: Learning Tools Interoperability. https://www.imsglobal.org/activity/learning-tools-interoperability. Accessed 20 Jan 2022
11. JYOHO-RINRI Digital Video. https://axies.jp/report/video/. Accessed 20 Jan 2022. (in Japanese)
12. ORCID. https://orcid.org/. Accessed 20 Jan 2022

Design and Effectiveness of Video Interview in a MOOC

Halvdan Haugsbakken(✉)

Østfold University College, B R A Veien 4, 1757 Halden, Norway
Halvdan.Haugsbakken@hiof.no

Abstract. Video is just one of several modalities used in online courses to create digital learning experiences for learners. On the other hand, the development, design, and use of videos in Massive Open Online Courses (MOOCs) are poorly understood, a matter that is reflected in current research. For example, research on the use of videos is primarily approached from a learning analytic perspective which means mapping of user patterns and video performance. In fact, we find few studies that outline the design work and the use of different video genres in MOOCs. That said, the goal of this paper, is therefore to explore the learning design process and the effectiveness of a particular video genre that is seldom studied in online courses, video interview. To examine this matter, the paper explores the learning design process of using video interview and how it performed in a MOOC by analyzing click stream data. The study found that video interview can have a high view completion rate among learners.

Keywords: MOOC · video · interview · learning design

1 Introduction

We can define *genre* as a type of communication of socially-agreed-upon conventions [1]. In Massive Open Online Courses (MOOCs), which can be defined as an open-access online course (i.e., without specific participation restrictions) that allows for unlimited (massive) participation [2], a common video genre is *talking head* videos. They are characterized by that an educator talks directly into the camera, representing a lecture-centric pedagogy where information is transferred through explanation.

In contrast, video-based learning is an unexplored terrain and represents many possibilities which we have yet to explore in full detail. Maybe, one of these can be found in the affordances of the structured conversation, *the interview*. An interview can loosely be defined as a structured conversation between two or several persons where one participant, the interviewer, asks questions, while the other participant, the interviewee, provides answers. Also, an interview is usually associated with knowledge transfer. On the other end, the interview has other affordances; it can be used for reflection and spark learning which in turn can generate knowledge [3]. For example, two or more persons can engage into an unstructured conversation and exchange opinions and learn from

Published by Springer Nature Switzerland AG 2023
T. Keane et al. (Eds.): WCCE 2022, IFIP AICT 685, pp. 286–297, 2023.
https://doi.org/10.1007/978-3-031-43393-1_26

each other. Thus, the interview can be embedded into the pedagogy of an online learning design and facilitate for learning.

That said, the goal of this paper is therefore to conceptualize how the interview can be used as part of a learning design in a MOOC. To capture its affordance, the paper conceives a particular video genre, *video interview*, and analyzes how it was designed and used by learners in a MOOC that ran on the course platform FutureLearn. In the MOOC, the learners engaged with a story arch about a female teacher who used digital technologies in her classroom practice. To engage the learners, non-interactive video interviews with the teacher were made and embedded into the course structure as a means to establish a connection between the course material and the learner. In the video interviews, the teacher explained and reflected upon the challenges in changing to a technology-rich classroom practice.

To construct an analysis, the paper breaks down the above matter and asks the following research questions (RQs):

- RQ1: How can video interviews be conceptualized in a learning design?
- RQ2: What is the performance of video interviews in a MOOC?

To answer the RQs, the paper provides an analysis over three parts. The first part outlines relevant research. The second part accounts for the data analysis. This section describes how video interview can be conceptualized and employed in the overall course design in a MOOC. In addition, by analyzing clickstream data from two course runs, the effectiveness of this particular video genre is considered. The third part discusses and concludes the analysis.

2 Relevant Research on Use of Videos in MOOCs

In general, researchers approach use of videos in MOOCs from at least two research perspectives. First, a research stream measures video performance and *map user patterns* and *learner engagement*. Guo et al. [4] found that various videos styles provide different outcome on perceived use. Based on a data sample of 6.9 million video sessions, it was established that short videos and videos with instructor involvement were more accepted than traditional formats used in video lecturing. Mamgain et al. [5] did a survey where they asked about various video features embedded in Coursera and edX. The study showed that learners preferred short videos over in-built video-quiz features. Other studies also establish that learners watch videos at fast speed as scholars now possess exact data on where learners stop watching, a topic examined in a study by Kim et al. [6]. Click-level interaction (playing, pausing, and quitting patterns) were analyzed and uncovered that long videos are not preferred among learners. Briton and colleagues [7, 8] applied clickstream data from video-watching to build algorithms that can predict learner behavior in use of videos which can lay the foundation for customizing assignments and assessment in new ways.

Later studies have found that learners engage with videos in more complex ways. For example, Li et al. [9] collected data on learners watching video lectures and established that learners create new video user patterns which are matched to personal learning strategies and perceived difficulty of the learning contents. Bonafini et al. [10] completed a study where they calculated that video watching and participation in discussion forums increase the probability of course completion. That said, we see the tendency that videos become more interactive and are embedded with quizzes, a matter studied by Kovacs [11]. Kovacs showed that learners engage more deeply with in-video quizzes, as he demonstrated that users who start watching a video will engage in a following in-video quiz. Researchers have also turned to eye-tracking technologies. Sharma and colleagues [12, 13] used this technology to show that gaze patterns influence the attention of the student having implication on engagement. They found that learners who watch videos and at the same time engage with other learners, have better learning outcome than students who only engage with video material.

Second, a research stream analyzes *video styles* used in MOOCs [14]. Still, we can by and large say that talking head video is a common video style in MOOCs, but researchers have started to refine our current understanding of the recorded lecture. Early on, studies indicated that the simple recorded lecture video was not the most dominant video style. Instead, it could be divided into smaller parts. Guo et al. [4] classified six types of instructional videos used in MOOCs: (1) classroom lecture with instructor on the blackboard; (2) talking head of instructor at desk; (3) digital drawing board (Khan-style); (4) slide presentation; (5) studio without audience; and (6) computer coding session. Later, we can observe more variety in the lecture-centric video styles. Rahim and Shamsudin [15] completed a study on video lectures and found more than fifteen ways they can be designed and made. In this regard, researchers have recently started outlining new ways to conceptualize videos. For example, studies argue that it is more meaningful to view videos as either speaker-centric (a visible person speaks about the contents) and board-centric (a large rectangular surface displays the contents) which are also preferred video styles among learners [16, 17]. Furthermore, researchers begin to develop new video styles from categories to *taxonomies over video* and are instead interested in establishing their dimensional value which are determined by human presence and the type of instructional media [18]. Missing from this research stream, nonetheless, are case studies that try to conceptualize the educational value of the structured conversation, such as an interview video, and what role it can play in learning and online courses.

3 Methods

In order to conceptualize the video interview genre, a research design was devised. The study applied a mixed method approach which meant use of qualitative and quantitative methods [19]. These were used to perform different types of analysis.

First, a qualitative research approach as described by Brinkmann and Kvale, the hermeneutical approach [3], was used to conceptualize the use of the video interview genre. It focuses on interpretation and meaning condensation as a mean to process and analyze qualitative data. But it is also an inductive, iterative and creative approach that can be applied to reflect on teaching practice and for knowledge creation. This latter aspect was employed in this study, as it was applied to conceptualize the role of the interview video genre and to make it fit to an overall MOOC course design. That said, the qualitative research design consisted of two approaches. On the one hand, the researcher decided to make a MOOC of a doctoral study, as an approach to thinking differently about research dissemination. To design the MOOC, the researcher used the course template provided by the MOOC provider where the online course was operated. The course template was used to prepare the learning material and the learning and assessment activities. On the other hand, after completing the course development process, the researcher applied a thematic analysis approach [20]. This approach was employed to identify patterns of meaning and to better conceptualize the video interview genre. This involved analyzing the course template, production notes, storyboards, video treatments, and evaluating the role videos played in the overall course design. The production period lasted from August 2017 to May 2019.

Second, after the course development period concluded, in October 2019 the MOOC was launched on FutureLearn. The MOOC has had several runs, but for the purpose of this paper, we focus on two runs that lasted three weeks each. The first run lasted from October to November 2019, and the second one from April to May 2020, which coincided with the first wave of the Covid-19 pandemic. The first run had roughly 500 learners and a course completion rate of about 15%, while the second one had about 2.150 learners with a course completion rate of about 21%. In order to examine the performance of the interview video, predefined datasets provided by FutureLearn were analyzed. FutureLearn provides course creators with a limited number of datasets which contain anonymized data and predefined variables. A separate dataset for videos was also provided and was data cleaned and analyzed.

4 Data Analysis

In this part, the data analysis is performed by answering the paper's RQs. The following analysis will answer them by first outlining the design approach for making video interviews, while the second part describes their effectiveness.

4.1 The Design Approach for Making Video Interview

The Topic of the MOOC

The MOOC 'Digital Transformation in the Classroom' (DTC) is an online course that runs on the online course platform FutureLearn. DTC was created to use the MOOC concept as an alternative way to disseminate research. The online course is based on a sociological study of a teacher working in a Norwegian high school. The study used qualitative research strategies to investigate how the teacher used digital technologies to organize foreign language training. In 2016, the study was published as part of a doctoral dissertation covering about 400 pages [21]. A separate chapter in the thesis describes the teacher's teaching practice and contains 80 pages. The study is a hard read for practitioners. For example, a practice lens on technology implementation was used as theoretical framework, not pedagogical theory [22]. The study relied on contextualization, applying a thick description approach [23]. The study describes the teacher's classroom practice from a process perspective which includes planning and implementation of lessons. Later, it would become unfeasible to adapt the study into a journal article. Instead, a MOOC was made. In this format, the research could reach a larger target group, teachers. Therefore, a three-week online course was made.

The Role of a Predefined MOOC Platform Pedagogy

In order to develop the video interviews, the course designer had to make adaptions and adjust the subject matter to a predefined online pedagogy. FutureLearn has formulated a MOOC pedagogy which uses storytelling, which can be better described as a *conversational pedagogy*. The pedagogy ensures that the learner engages with an overall story arch and at the same time learns from social interaction with other learners. It supports three principles of pedagogy: (1) telling stories; (2) provoking conversations; (3) and celebrating progress [24]. The pedagogy assumes that when engaging with stories, learners will learn, remember, and structure knowledge. In practice, Future Learn uses discussion forums to operationalize the conversational pedagogy.

That said, the predefined MOOC pedagogy sets constraints but also gives possibilities on course design work. When creating a MOOC, course designers can approach the conversational pedagogy in two ways. First, the conversational pedagogy is embedded into the setup of the MOOC platform. The platform is an "interactive book" following an xMOOC educational model, being a lecture-instructed centric pedagogy. To learn from the conversation, the learner follows a predefined learning path arranged with learning goals, learning material, assignments, and assessment forms. In online courses which use Learning Management Systems (LMS), it is not uncommon to use a file structure or a module setup. Here, FutureLearn's course structure differs. Instead, the interactive book is based on an instructional design where the learner starts on an introductory web page and works him or herself from web page to web page which contains the learning contents. On each web page, a discussion forum feature is default. Also, instead of using traditional LMS framing, a different terminology stands out. For example, FutureLearn calls a module a "Week", while a subsection within a Week is called an "Activity". Each Activity contains one or more "Steps". A step is a web page and can be structured by the limited features in the platform. A step can be made as an article, a video, a discussion thread, poll, or quiz. Second, FutureLearn provides a course design template which is an Excel sheet that gives an overview of Weeks, Activities, and Steps, and is intended to help course designers to plan and visualize an online course. The course design template is a complex tool that challenges the educator to think thoroughly through what their course will look like. As FutureLearn recommends that a Week should contain no more than 20 Steps, the course design template is justified. The course design template could be described as a learning goal maze and is full of learning goals which need to be formulated by the educator.

In contrast, the template does not provide recommendations on where and when to use videos, moreover, it does not explain what suitable video genres can be employed. In fact, that is for the course creator to decide. Then, to have an effective use of video, course designers are challenged to outline their own video course design plan. Therefore, videos need to be carefully considered, so they support the conversational pedagogy and are not for "pedagogical decoration" serving no learning purpose.

Designing a Story Arc About the Teacher Inger

When it was clear that the learning experience needed to be structured against a superimposed pedagogy, a story needed to be devised which the learner could engage with. Therefore, the course designer scaffolded a learning path that operationalizes the challenging concept of *digitalization* which enables the learner to see it from an everyday perspective. In so doing, the learner engages with a story arch that tells the story about preparing teachers for how to plan and enact classroom practice by following the experiences of a high school teacher who used digital technologies in foreign language training. In the story, the learner meets the "main character", Inger, the same person who was the participant in the doctoral study. Over three weeks, the learner engages with the story and learns about different ways to conceive digitalization. In the first week, the main goal is to address 'digitalization' and structure a learning path for the learner, so that they can express it from their own point of view. Digitalization is connected to sociological perspectives on social networks and how new technologies are implemented in organizations. In the second and third week, the learner learns about Inger's teaching practice, as a way to be more specific about how digitalization affects classroom practice. The learner engages with the approaches Inger used to plan her lessons using digital technologies, but also explores what happened when she implemented her lesson plans.

On the other hand, to address the learning contents making up the story arch, we can look at particular excerpts. The overall theme for the second week, is the planning phase for using digital technologies in a classroom setting and is displayed in Table 1. The second week addresses the meaning of modeling digital classroom practice as an approach to prepare teachers to use digital technologies in teaching. The learner is presented four strategies which Inger used when she planned her classes. First, the learner is introduced to ways to stay updated on new technologies. Second, the learner is presented with node-mapping, a strategy for charting students' user pattern of digital technologies. Third, the learner is introduced to a theme approach, which is a different way to operationalize learning goals. Fourth, the learner is presented with examples of how to design and organize learning activities using digital technologies.

The General Use of Videos

As noted, FutureLearn does not provide a course template nor pedagogical recommendations on how to design and use videos to support the conversational pedagogy. For example, there are no set guidelines for video length. In this regard, a separate video course plan had to be designed which determined the pedagogical role and the planning, production, and post-production video process. That said, one of the first matters that needed a solution was deciding the number of videos, those that could be reused and those required to be made. This is essential as video production consumes vast resources in MOOC making. Also, the course designer had to consider the imperative design question; does a video really need to be made? In fact, this is a critical design choice. Therefore, a distinction between *self-produced* and *embedded videos* was made. A self-produced video refers to videos made particularly for DTC while embedded video are reused YouTube videos. All in all, DTC contains 40 videos, 28 self-produced and

Table 1. Week 2, "Planning for digital transformation".

Week 2	Activity title	Step	Step name
Planning for digital transformation	Designing a digital classroom practice	2.1	What to learn in week 2
		2.2	Modelling the classroom
		2.3	Decouple and reconnect
		2.4	What have you learned?
	Choosing the digtech kit	2.5	Selecting and creating article
		2.6	Inger's digtech kit video
	Mapping social networks	2.7	Node-mapping
		2.8	What learning goes on
		2.9	Share your experience
	Forming knowledge	2.10	Create knowledge
		2.11	Themes over chapters
		2.12	Working with themes
	Meaningful learning activities	2.13	Acts for engagement
		2.14	The news round
		2.15	Share your experience
		2.16	Blog and YouTube
		2.17	Recap week 2

12 embedded ones. DTC's videos can be classified as short and are between 3 to 5 min long, except some embedded YouTube videos.

DTC used six video genres which were adapted to FutureLearn's pedagogy and include: (1) talking head; (2) introduction; (3) interview; (4) illustration; (5) lecture; and (6) short documentary. Addressing each video genre, talking head videos are distinguished by that the course leader reads from a script and talks into the camera while it is overlayed with pictures, illustrations, interviews, etc. Talking head videos serve different instructional purposes. For example, they are used for explaining learning goals while others outline theoretical concepts. Introduction is mainly used for marketing purposes. Interview is a video genre we will describe in the next section. Illustration is used for demonstration of concepts and are embedded YouTube videos. Lecture is also a video genre that serves the purpose of explaining concepts and understand their consequences. In DTC, lecture are videos of group conversations between experts or recorded conference keynotes and are also embedded YouTube videos. Short documentary is a video genre consisting of interviews and videos that report on factual events on a given topic. Also here, YouTube videos were used.

The Learning Design of Video Interview

Video interview as a genre can be defined as an instructional style where persons converse, express, and reflect upon a particular topic. Interviews are most used in the context of asking questions to an expert who responds with an opinion of some sorts, meaning knowledge transfer. In this case, we can assume that information is a type of objective knowledge or true representation of reality that is stored in the minds of people which can be collected and presented. In a way, by using the interview, deductive representation can be displayed. At the other end of the spectrum, the interview can serve other purposes and affordances, foremost being a means for inductive thinking. It can be used for exploration and people can exchange opinions in order to raise greater awareness of a particular topic. In other words, an interview can be used for reflection or retrospection to foster sense-making and knowledge creation, not simply for information transfer. It is within this latter meaning that the video interviews were designed and used in DTC, implying that they have different instructional purposes.

Table 2. Overview of self-made video interviews.

No	Step	Name step	Degree of full interview use	Duration
1	1.2	Who is Inger?	Complete interview	2:43
2	2.6	Inger's digitech kit	Interview excerpt	4:03
3	2.8	What learning goes on?	Interview excerpt	3:27
4	2.12	Working with themes	Complete interview	2:43
5	2.15	Share your experience	Complete interview	3:03
6	2.16	Blog and YouTube	Interview excerpt	4:41
7	3.6	Share your experience	Complete interview	4:13
8	3.7	Reflect on your actions	Complete interview	1:33
9	3.9	Reflect by debriefing	Complete interview	3:05
10	3.12	Enacting the newsround	Complete interview	2:40
11	3.14	Share your experience	Complete interview	3:56

First, the use of interview video is designed to challenge the learner to engage with the overall conversational pedagogy. Moreover, the objective is to enable a better relationship between learning material and learner experience by focusing on real-life scenarios from a classroom. To achieve that, *requires careful deliberation on what role a video interview plays in the general arch story line* in the MOOC. The video interviews are therefore intentionally situated in exact Steps and Weeks in the overall course structure and are grouped according to which themes and learning goals a Week addresses. For example, DTC contains eight video interviews with the main character, Inger, where she reflects upon her teaching experience. She explains and reflects upon a rich selection of topics which are relevant for planning and implementation of a technology-rich classroom practice. Such challenges include explaining why she chooses to use digital technologies; what role digital technologies have in the planning of learning activities; reflections on where she succeeds and flops with learning activities; what role digital technologies play in the training of the students' digital literacies; and strategies to assess the students' learning, etc. Therefore, the interview videos must be situated in a course structure where these topics are specifically addressed. A used learning design strategy in DTC, for example, is to apply interview videos as a means to provoke conversation. In the overall course structure, there are many Steps called "share your experience", and they contain a video interview with Inger. There, the learner is going to watch an interview video and thereafter answers questions and contributes to a thread in the discussion forum.

Second, the other approach in use of the interview video, is their design and production. All the videos containing elements of the interview format are displayed in Table 2. The table indicates that some videos are "complete interview" while others are labeled "interview excerpt". The difference between them, is that the first video interview type is a comprehensive and edited interview with Inger while the latter is a talking head video containing an interview excerpt. As noted earlier, DTC contains eight complete video interviews with the teacher which are based on an in-depth interview. The complete video interviews are edited according to a three-point tell, meaning that each one explains three essential experiences related to the topic that the video addresses. The three-point tell is an approach that condenses relevant citations from a long interview and makes them more coherent for the learner. For example, in an interview video, Inger explains a learning activity she designed, the news round; the video covers three topics related to this learning activity.

4.2 Effectiveness of Interview Videos

Table 3. Performance of interview videos in 1st run. View completion in percent.

	Views	5%	10%	25%	50%	75%	90%	100%	Dur.
Who is Inger?	194	86.6	86.1	80.4	73.7	70.6	65.4	63.9	2:43
Inger's digitech kit	67	80.6	80.6	79.1	74.6	73.1	65.6	64.1	4:03
What learning goes on?	53	83.0	84.9	79.2	73.5	71.7	69.8	66.0	3:27
Working with themes	44	75.0	72.7	68.2	65.9	61.3	61.3	52.2	2:43
Share your experience	42	73.8	76.2	64.3	64.2	61.9	61.9	59.5	3:03
Blog and YouTube	42	73.8	71.4	71.43	64.2	59.5	57.1	52.3	4:41
Share your experience	39	64.1	64.1	61.5	58.9	56.41	56.4	51.2	4:13
Reflect on your actions	33	72.7	66.6	66.6	63.6	60.6	57.5	57.5	1:33
Reflect by debriefing	34	67.6	61.7	55.9	44.1	41.1	35.2	29.4	3:05
Enacting the newsround	32	71.8	71.8	65.6	68.7	56.2	53.1	43.7	2:40
Share your experience	30	66.6	63.3	66.6	56.6	46.6	46.6	30.0	3:56

To move to part two of the analysis, nonetheless, we have the possibility to address the performance and effectiveness of the video interviews from two course runs. Clickstream data showing view completion rates are displayed in Tables 3 and 4. In this regard, we can extrapolate and make certain general remarks about learner viewer patterns which we stress are limited. We can observe two general viewer patterns in both datasets. First, the data shows that all video interviews have a general decline in view completion in terms of percentage. Both datasets find that from the 1st and 2nd run that most video interviews drop from 15 to almost 20%. Second, the dataset from the two runs suggest that we observe a general decline in 10%, when we consider 50% view completion rate. In other words, when the learners view half the interview videos, the view completion rate suggests being low. Although we do not possess exact data, an interpretation, however, is that the interview videos suggest not having high degree of quitter pattern, something which would have been indicated in a steep decline in view completion. When we look at some of the runs, only a couple of video interviews appear to have high degree of quitter patterns. This quitter pattern is among others indicated in interview videos from the 1st run as displayed in Table 3.

Table 4. Performance of interview videos in 2nd run. View completion in percent.

	Views	5%	10%	25%	50%	75%	90%	100%	Dur.
Who is Inger?	890	92.2	90.5	85.1	79.2	76.4	73.4	70.1	2:43
Inger's digitech kit	294	82.6	79.2	76.8	73.1	68.7	66.6	64.2	4:03
What learning goes on?	252	84.1	82.5	78.9	73.8	69.4	65.0	59.5	3:27
Working with themes	230	83.9	82.6	80	76.5	70.4	67.8	61.3	2:43
Share your experience	203	81.2	79.3	74.3	71.4	65.0	62.5	60.5	3:03
Blog and YouTube	201	79.1	75.1	71.6	68.1	66.6	64.1	61.1	4:41
Share your experience	175	79.4	77.7	74.2	66.8	62.2	58.2	58.2	4:13
Reflect on your actions	146	79.4	78.0	74.6	72.6	69.1	67.8	65.7	1:33
Reflect by debriefing	165	81.2	77.5	72.7	69.7	62.4	58.7	57.5	3:05
Enacting the newsround	159	80.5	76.7	73.5	70.4	69.8	64.7	56.6	2:40
Share your experience	142	77.4	73.2	69.0	64.0	61.2	58.4	56.3	3:56

5 Discussion and Conclusion

Broadly speaking, the research review outlined in the start of the paper established that research on the use of videos in MOOCs, either measures their effectiveness [4] or categorizes them into different pedagogical styles [18] where variants of talking head videos are very dominant. As a video genre, talking head videos suggest mirroring a behavioristic pedagogical principal, meaning transfer of information from educator to learner. We can argue that the video genre reflects an extension of the traditional lecture into the digital format. In contrast, videos can be designed and produced in many ways to support learning. This can among other be achieved with the posed interview video genre. On the one end, video interviews can be based on the premise of informing. This can be rendered by staging an activity where an expert transfers his or her knowledge about a particular topic. On the other hand, interview videos can be designed using the pedagogical principle of retrospection, meaning that one or several persons use personal reflection of events, situations, practices, activities, and experiences with the goal of to further gain knowledge and new understandings. This latter approach has been used and explored in this paper, meaning a novel contribution to research on use of videos in MOOCs.

That being said, it becomes important to outline what implications interview videos can have on educational practice. We mention a few. First, interview videos can be employed to create conditions for more *diverse online learning experiences* for learners which is suggested to be an important instructional design principle [25]. In contrast, we often see that this is not always persistent with how MOOCs are generally made. Educators who make their first online course often turn to established ways of teaching, meaning the lecture format. The outcome of the practice are often talking head videos. But by using interview videos, the video genre can complement talking head videos, implying more varied ways to online learning for learners. Second, research on use of MOOC suggests that learners engage more deeply with videos when they are embedded with quizzes [11] which can be enabled with H5P technologies. H5P is an interactive video format that provides the learner with the ability to click within the video for an action to occur. Within a video, different learning contents and activities can be embedded such as quizzes and short presentations. Video interviews can also embed such contents, implying facilitation for active learning opportunities. Third, to have effective use of video interviews in MOOCs, will require large effort in other places, foremost in planning, design, and production, meaning that the craft of online learning design becomes ever-more important for educators to master in practice. It goes without saying, however, that video-based learning demands resources and time. To make high quality interview videos, educators need to consider many factors like the learning intention behind an interview video, how interview videos align with learning goals, and what role they play in conjunction with other modalities in a digital learning environment. In other words, to design and make interview videos, will most likely require learning design thinking and consideration of an important question – when is there really a need for making videos?

References

1. Devitt, A.J.: Genre. In: Heilker, P., Vandenberg, P. (eds.) Keywords in Writing Studies, pp. 82–87. State University Press, Utah (2015)
2. Kaplan, A.M., Haenlein, M.: Higher education and the digital revolution: about MOOCs, SPOCs, social media, and the cookie monster. Bus. Horiz. **59**(4), 441–450 (2016)
3. Brinkmann, S., Kvale, S.: InterViews: learning the craft of qualitative research interviewing, 3rd edn. Sage Publications, Thousand Oaks, California (2015)
4. Guo, P.J., Kim, J., Rubin, R.: How video production affects student engagement: an empirical study of MOOC videos. In: L@S 2014 - Proceedings of the 1st ACM Conference on Learning at Scale, pp. 41–50. ACM, New York (2014)
5. Mamgain, N., Sharma, A., Goyal, P.: Learner's perspective on video-viewing features offered by MOOC providers: coursera and edX. In: Proceedings of the 2014 IEEE International

Conference on MOOCs, Innovation and Technology in Education, pp. 331–336. IEEE MITE (2014)
6. Kim, J., Guo, P.J., Seaton, D.T., Mitros, P., Gajos, K.Z., Miller, R.C.: Understanding in-video dropouts and interaction peaks in online lecture videos. In: L@S 2014 - Proceedings of the 1st ACM Conference on Learning at Scale, pp. 31–40. ACM, New York (2014)
7. Brinton, C.G., Buccapatnam, S., Chiang, M., Poor, H.V.: Mining MOOC clickstreams: video-watching behavior vs. in-video quiz performance. In: IEEE Transactions on Signal Processing, pp. 3677–3692. IEEE (2016)
8. Brinton, C.G., Chiang, M.: MOOC performance prediction via clickstream data and social learning networks. In: Proceedings - IEEE INFOCOM, pp. 2299–2307. IEEE (2015)
9. Li, N., Kidziński, Ł., Jermann, P., Dillenbourg, P.: MOOC video interaction patterns: what do they tell us? In: Conole, G., Klobučar, T., Rensing, C., Konert, J., Lavoué, É. (eds.) EC-TEL 2015. LNCS, vol. 9307, pp. 197–210. Springer, Cham (2015). https://doi.org/10.1007/978-3-319-24258-3_15
10. Bonafini, F.C., Chae, C., Park, E., Jablokow, K.W.: How much does student engagement with videos and forums in a MOOC affect their achievement? Online Learn. J. **21**(4), 223–240 (2017)
11. Kovacs, G.: Effects of in-video quizzes on MOOC lecture viewing. In: L@S 2016 - Proceedings of the 3rd 2016 ACM Conference on Learning at Scale, pp. 31–40. ACM, New York (2016)
12. Sharma, K., et al.: Looking AT versus looking through: a dual eye-tracking study in MOOC context. In: Computer-Supported Collaborative Learning Conference, CSCL (2015)
13. Sharma, K., Jermann, P., Dillenbourg, P.: "with-Me-Ness": a gaze-measure for students' attention in MOOCs. In: Proceedings of International Conference of the Learning Sciences, pp. 1017–1021. ICLS (2014)
14. Aryal, S., Porawagama, A.S., Hasith, M.G.S., Thoradeniya, S.C., Kodagoda, N., Suriyawansa, K.: Using pre-trained models as feature extractor to classify video styles used in MOOC videos. In: 2018 IEEE 9th International Conference on Information and Automation for Sustainability, pp. 1–5. IEEE (2018)
15. Rahim, M.I., Shamsudin, S.: Categorisation of video lecture designs in MOOC for technical and vocational education and training educators. J. Tech. Educ. Training **11**(4), 11–17 (2019)
16. Santos-Espino, J.M., Afonso-Suárez, M.D., Guerra-Artal, C.: Speakers and boards: a survey of instructional video styles in MOOCs. Tech. Commun. **63**(2), 101–115 (2016)
17. Lai, Y.C., Young, S.S.C., Huang, N.F.: A preliminary study of producing multimedia online videos for ubiquitous learning on MOOCs. In: 2015 8th International Conference on Ubi-Media Computing, UMEDIA 2015 - Conference Proceedings, pp. 295–297. IEEE (2015)
18. Chorianopoulos, K.: A taxonomy of asynchronous instructional video styles. Int. Rev. Res. Open Dist. Learn. **19**(1), 294–311 (2018)
19. Creswell, J.W.: Research design: qualitative, quantitative, and mixed methods approaches. 5th ed. Research design. SAGE, Los Angeles, California (2018)
20. Braun, V., Clarke, V.: Using thematic analysis in psychology. Qual. Res. Psychol. **3**(2), 77–101 (2006)
21. Haugsbakken, H.: Using social media the inside out: a qualitative study of four different local models for organizing social media in organizations. NTNU, Trondheim (2016)
22. Orlikowski, W.J.: Using technology and constituting structures: a practice lens for studying technology in organizations. Organ. Sci. **11**(4), 404–428 (2000)
23. Geertz, C.: The Interpretation of Cultures: Selected Essays. Basic Books, New York (1973)
24. FutureLearn: The Pedagogy of FutureLearn How our learners learn. London (2018)
25. Nilson, L.B., Goodson, L.A.: Online Teaching at Its Best: Merging Instructional Design with Teaching and Learning Research. Jossey-Bass Inc., Publishers, San Francisco (2017)

Tracking Epistemic Interactions from Online Game-Based Learning

Eric Sanchez[1(✉)] and Nadine Mandran[2]

[1] TECFA, Geneva University, Geneva, Switzerland
eric.sanchez@unige.ch
[2] LIG, Grenoble Alpes University, Grenoble, France
Nadine.Mandran@univ-grenoble-alpes.fr

Abstract. This paper draws on an empirical work dedicated to assessing the relevance of an online training course for pre-service teachers. The course is dedicated to the legal rules governing the use of digital educational resources. It consists of a game-based learning session with *Tamagocours*, an online Multiplayer Tamagotchi. The players take care of a character by feeding it with "digital educational resources". If the choice of resources does not respect copyright legislation, the character withers and eventually dies. Based on the digital traces collected from 242 players, we conducted a factor analysis to classify the players according to the interactions that took place during the game session. Our analysis shows that the game is played in very different ways depending on the teams. It also provides evidence that the interactions that take place are not always epistemic interactions and that some players use avoidance strategies that work against learning. Our contribution therefore focuses on a method for understanding how a game is played and the potential effects of playing on learning. In addition, these results may offer new perspectives for the design of learning games. Indeed, the result of the study emphasize the need to focus on the player's learning experience in terms of epistemic interactions.

Keywords: Game-based Learning · Epistemic Interactions · Collaborative Learning · Playing Analytics

1 Introduction

This paper deals with an empirical study into a game called *Tamagocours* [1] and dedicated to pre-service teacher training about copyright legislation. A previous paper based on the same data [2] and published in 2017 drew on the strategies performed by players. For this paper, we built new indicators and we focus on epistemic interactions that take place during the game session. Indeed, epistemic interactions are considered to provide important insight about the learning process and, therefore, the efficiency of the game.

In the next section, we describe the context of the study, the game, and the expected learning outcomes. The third section of the paper summarizes the background of the study. We discuss how interactions can take place during a game session and to what

Published by Springer Nature Switzerland AG 2023
T. Keane et al. (Eds.): WCCE 2022, IFIP AICT 685, pp. 298–308, 2023.
https://doi.org/10.1007/978-3-031-43393-1_27

extent these interactions are epistemic, i.e. foster the learning process. We describe the method of data production and data analysis of the study in the fourth section. We elaborate on the data collected, the indicators that we built and how we processed the data with a Principal Component Analysis [3] followed by a Hierarchical Ascendant Classification [4]. The last section is dedicated to the discussion of the results and the implication of the finding for game designers.

2 Tamagocours: An Online Multiplayer Tamagotchi

The *Tamagocours* game (Fig. 1) was designed and developed by a multidisciplinary team of researchers, computer scientists and students according to a collaborative and user-centered design approach [5]. It aims to offer pre-service teachers, a synchronous and online training about the legal rules governing the use of digital resources in an educational context. The game is also adapted to the training of numerous students (up to 250–300 each year for our context), not available at the same time and, for most of them, not really interested in the subject.

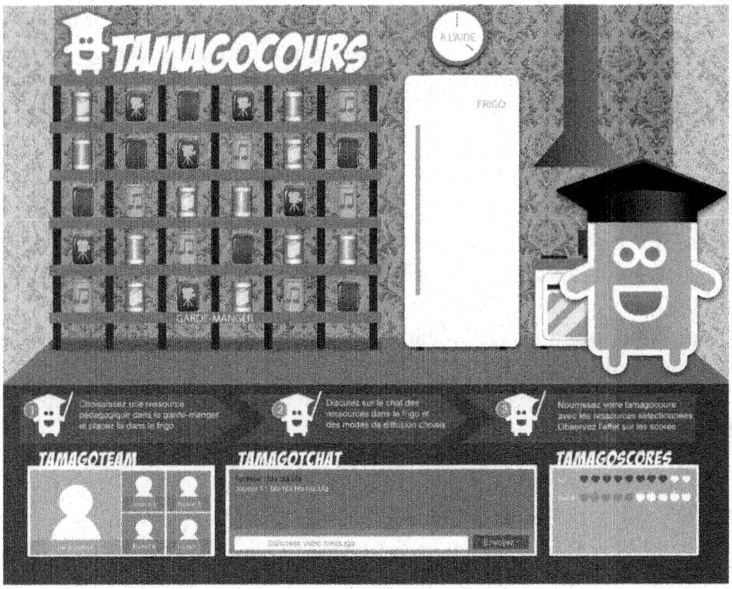

Fig. 1. Print screen from the Tamagocours game

The *Tamagocours* game is a Tamagotchi. It consists of taking care of a character by feeding it with "digital educational resources". If the choice of resources does not respect copyright legislation, the character withers and eventually dies (which means that the game level is lost and that the team must try again). Otherwise, the player earns points and can complete the 5 levels of the game. The students play the game online, in teams of 3 to 4 players. Players choose resources from shelves, drag and drop the selected resources in a refrigerator before feeding the character. This way, each player can see the resources selected by his teammates. Players can also send and read messages via a chat room. A game session lasts about 2 h at a maximum, but this duration varies greatly from team to team.

The game aims at offering the students a learning by doing experience. Indeed, they are expected to learn, from trial and error, which characteristics of a digital educational resource should be considered to comply with copyright legislation. The game also aims at offering the students a collaborative learning experience. Learning by doing and collaborative learning result from epistemic interactions described below.

3 Epistemic Interactions and Game-Based Learning

3.1 Game-Based Learning as Experiential Learning

Game-based learning is often seen as experiential learning [6, 7]. From this point of view, game-based learning is rooted in Dewey's philosophy [8]. An individual's experience is constituted through his interactions with his environment. This experience is at the service of learning when the interactions take a particular form that aims to produce effects on this environment. Thus, Dewey develops a theory of learning based on the idea of *knowing experience* [9]. Kolb describes experiential learning as a cyclic pattern [10]. Action (active experimentation) leads to feedback (concrete experience). Then, reflective observation on this experience allows for abstract conceptualization which frames new action.

Thus, the importance of the game for the learning process results in the quality of feedback it produces in response to the player's actions. Depending on the consequences of these actions, the player will learn if they are relevant or not and will be led to confirm or revise his way of thinking and acting. The expression "reflection in-action" [11] describes this form of learning.

According to this point of view, learning results from the setting up of interactions resulting from an "artificial conflict" [12] between a player and a game. Since they allow the player to learn from reflection on his successes and failures, these interactions can therefore be qualified as epistemic interactions.

3.2 Game-Based Learning as Collaborative Learning

Game-based learning is also seen as collaborative learning [13]. Indeed, playing in a team fosters interactions between players. During the game, knowledge is made explicit, shared, discussed, and assessed. The positive effect of these interactions on learning depends on the epistemic quality of dialogs [14]. Good dialogs are epistemic interactions [15], i.e. different interactive processes such as explanation, production of an articulated discourse, elaboration of meaning or clarification of views [16].

The Theory of Didactical Situation [17] distinguishes 2 different categories of situations depending on the epistemic interactions that take place. A *formulation situation* means that the player makes previous implicit knowledge explicit. Knowledge is put into words to be communicated. This communication allows the sharing of this knowledge within the team. From a learning point of view, a formulation situation is therefore useful to the one who formulates the knowledge and to the one who receives it. Interactions between players are then seen as a form of cooperation, i.e. a sharing of knowledge.

The Theory of Didactic Situations also distinguishes *validation situations*. These are interactions between players that aim to establish the validity of a statement. Arguments are produced to validate or invalidate the ideas expressed. Thus, these interactions result in an argumentative process that also contributes to learning. Indeed, the learner brings arguments to convince of the ideas he puts forward.

3.3 Research Questions

Based on what has been written above, a game can foster 2 categories of epistemic interactions: interaction with the game (an artificial conflict to be addressed) and interactions with teammates (formulation and validation situation when players collaborate). As a result, we hypothesize that the quality of a game dedicated to learning can be evaluated by revealing its capacity to allow epistemic interactions to take place.

Thus, we wish to answer the following research questions:

Q1: What kinds of interactions take place during the game session with *Tamagocours*?

Q2: To what extent can these interactions be considered epistemic interactions?

We hypotheses that the players differ in terms of interactions they have with the game and their teammates. We also hypotheses that these differences might have consequences on the learning process. These research questions are addressed by a playing analytics method described below.

4 Method: Playing Analytics

The study is a playing analytics method [2] *i.e.* a form of learning analytics [18] adapted to game-based learning. The method encompasses the collection, the coding, the visualization, and the analysis of digital traces of the interactions automatically collected.

We collected the digital traces from 242 pre-service teachers (Traces from 10 players were not considered due to technical issues). The raw data were processed to build indicators of the students' behaviors. The messages collected were coded depending on their meaning. Table 1 describes the main selected indicators.

Patterns AF and *SAF* are indicators of two different strategies. The players review (*pattern_SAF*) or does not review (*pattern_AF*) the resources before feeding the Tamagochi. *Patterns AF* are not indicators of epistemic interactions since such interactions mean that the player does not anticipate the result of his choice and thus, do not allow the players to identify the relationship between their actions and their consequences.

In addition, messages *Chat_F* (number of messages explaining a rule) and *Chat_V* (number of messages about the discussion of a rule) provide evidence that the players are involved in formulation and validation situations and thus, in epistemic interactions and collaborative learning. The reviews, by a player, of the resources selected by teammates (*ShowItemFridgeOthers*, number of readings of the characteristics of a resource selected by a teammate) is also an indicator of collaboration while *Chat_OJ* and *Chat_NC* (number of messages that do not rely to the use of educational resources and copyright legislation) show that players are not engaged into the expected tasks.

Other indicators such as *feedTamagoGood*, *P_feedgood* or *feedTamagoBad* show off the success or failure of the player and *HelpLink* provide insight about the use of the documentation about copyright legislation.

Table 1. Selected indicators

ID	Indicators
totalAction	Nb of performed actions
feedTamago	Nb of feedings
feedTamagoGood	Nb of successes
P_feedgood	% of successes
feedTamagoBad	Nb of failures
showItemCupboard	Nb of readings of the characteristics of a resource
ShowItemFridgeOthers	Nb of reading of the characteristics of a resource selected by a teammate
HelpLink	Nb of clicks on the help button
Chat_V	Nb of messages about the discussion of a rule (*validation*)
Chat_F	Nb of messages explaining a rule (*formulation*)
Chat_OJ	Nb of messages about the game itself
Chat_NC	Nb of other messages
Pattern_AF	Pattern of successive actions ShowItemCuboard – AddToFridge - FeedTamago
Pattern_SAF	Pattern of successive actions ShowItemCuboard – AddToFridge - FeedTamago

In short, the data analysis encompasses the following steps:

(1) Data are automatically collected when the students play. The different actions performed are recorded along with a time stamp.
(2) Raw data are cleaned and stored in a csv format file. They are also anonymized.
(3) Messages are coded according to the indicators of epistemic interactions described in Table 1 (Chat_V, Chat_F, Chat_OJ or Chat_NC).
(4) Aggregate data are produced from raw data.
(5) We perform a Principal Component Analysis (PCA) [3] based on the indicators described in Table 1. The PCA is followed by a Hierarchical Ascendant Classification [4] to classify the player according to the selected indicators (interactions with the game and their teammates).

We expect to find different categories of players depending on how they interact with the game.

5 Results

5.1 Different Categories of Players' Behaviors

The Principal Component Analysis provides 4 axes with eigenvalues greater than 1. The percentage of inertia (total variance) considered is 69.3%. The first factorial plan (axes 1 and 2) explains 48.4% of the inertia. Figure 2 shows the independence between the different types of patterns and actions and the number and type of messages.

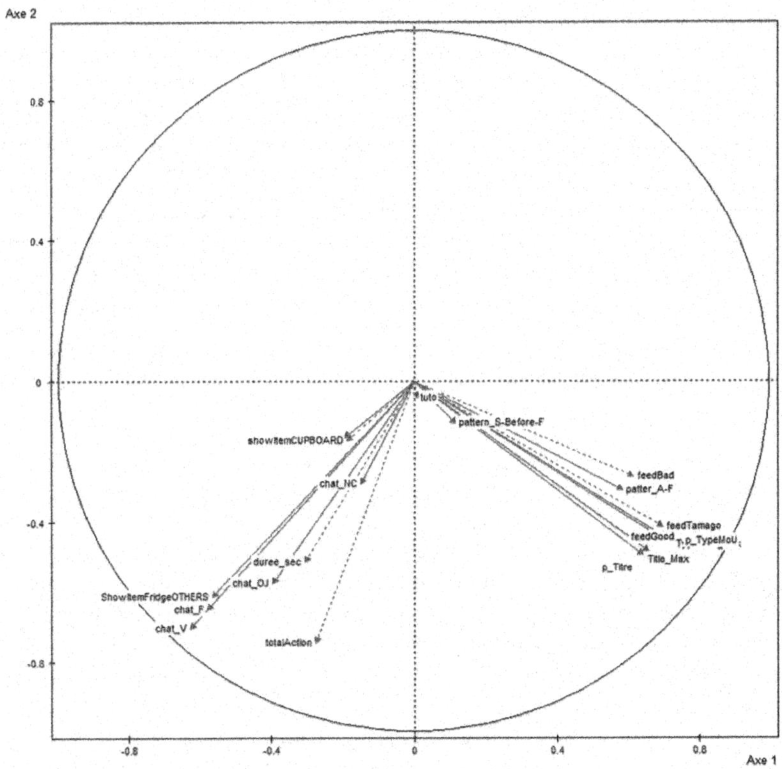

Fig. 2. Result of the Principal Component Analysis

We classify the players according to the coordinates of individual on the 4 factorial axes. The Hierarchical Ascendant Classification allows us to highlight 6 classes of players. The interpretation of the classes is based on the variables for which the class average is higher (positive) or lower (negative) than the general average.

- Class 1 (n = 43, 18%): These players feed the tamagotchi with resources whose characteristics they have not checked (*pattern_A-F* positive, *showItemCupboard* negative). Furthermore, they rarely refer to the assistance provided by the game (*helpLink* negative).
- Class 2 (n = 33, 14%): The behavior of these players is the opposite of players from class 1. They check the characteristics of the resources (*pattern_A-F* negative, *showItemCupboard* positive). They consult the help provided by the game (*helpLink* negative).
- Class 3 (n = 26, 11%): Players from this class send messages to their teammates and these messages are about the quality of the game or other subject (*chat_NC* and *chat_OJ* positive). They also rarely succeed (*p_feedgood negative*).
- Class 4 (n = 51, 20%): For this class of players all the variables are negative. It means that they perform very limited actions.
- Class 5 (n = 82, 34%): Players from class 5 are efficient (*p_feedgood* positive,*feedbad* negative) and this success rate seems linked with a strategy based on the checking of the selected resources (*showItemCupboard* positive). However they do not often succeed (*p_feedgood* negative) and they do not often interact about the game with their teammates (*chat_OJ* and *chat_NC* negative) and they perform a limited number of actions (*totalAction* negative).
- Class 6 (n = 7, 3%): Different indicators show that the players from this class collaborate with their teammates. The collaboration takes the form of messages about the copyright legislation (*chat_V* and chat_F positive) and attention paid to the resources selected by their teammates (*ShowItemFridgeOthers* positive)

Based on these results, we can state that the way the game is played varies greatly among players. In the following, we examine the consequences of the strategies in terms of epistemic interactions and learning process.

5.2 Tamagotchi Force-Feeders vs. Trial-and-Error Testers

Players from class 4 are inactive players in terms of actions performed. Different reasons might explain their inactivity: misunderstanding of the game, refusal to play a game considered childish, and fear of failure. These reasons are confirmed by the messages collected. Indeed, the messages sent by the players show that some of them consider this mode of learning to be unsuitable and that others did not understand what to do. They are disengaged or, at best, spectators.

Players from class 3 are different since they send messages to their teammates. However, these messages do not relate to the subject to be learned. We call Tamagotchi force-feeders the player from class 1. Indeed, they try to feed the Tamagotchi but, since they rarely review the characteristics of the resources that they select, they are unlikely to find the relationship between the characteristics of an educational resource and its licit or illegal nature. Thus, for these 3 classes of players (49%) we consider that the game failed to foster epistemic interactions and that there is significant doubt that the players have learned something.

Players from classes 2 and 5 (48%) are engaged in an individual strategy based on the testing of selected resources. This testing opens the room for the setting up of epistemic interactions since the feedback provided by the game to the action performed by the players can be interpreted in light to the characteristics of the selected resource. The observed success of players from classes 2 and 5 supports the hypothesis that they managed to identify the characteristics of the resources that play a role in terms of legacy to use.

5.3 Collaboration, Cooperation, and Mutual Support

Players from class 6 are different from other classes. The duration of the game and the number of performed action is higher than the mean. The main feature of these players is that they send many messages to their teammates. Some messages are about opinions about the game itself or messages non-related to the game (*Chat_OJ* or *Chat_NC*), but they also write to their teammates the rules to follow (*Chat_F*) and provide arguments (*Chat_V*). Table 2 is an excerpt from an exchange between players 143 and 31 from team 48. It illustrates how a player tries to convince his teammates.

Table 2. Excerpt from a chat between 2 players

Player ID	Quote
48_143	La Vie est belle, I have some doubts
48_31	Why, for la vie est belle ?
48_31	**Normally, you can broadcast 6 min max**
48_143	Frank Capra hasn't been dead very long
48_143	ah right

The resource, "*La Vie est belle*" is a movie from Frank Capra. Since Frank Capra died in 1991, his work is not yet in the public domain and teachers are not allowed to show more than 6 min of the film in a lesson. The rule is formulated by players 31 (in bold characters) and agreed by his teammates. Thus, player 31 emphasizes the maximum broadcasting time and player 143 underlines the need to take the date into consideration. "Normally, you can broadcast 6 min max" is coded as *Chat_F* while "Frank Capra hasn't been dead very long" is coded as *Chat_V*.

6 Discussion

Based on the empirical work carried out with the game *Tamagocours*, we can state that players adopt different gameplays. This result confirms previous works that underline the subjective nature of playing [19]. In addition, as predicted by our model, we found 2 categories of epistemic interactions:

- Approximately half of the players interact with the game; they take decisions and select resources to feed the Tamagotchi. The epistemic nature of these interactions lies in the fact that they give the player the opportunity to test misconceptions and hypotheses about the criteria that should be considered for selecting educational resources. However some players use avoidance strategies that work against learning. The fact that players do not check the characteristics of the resources show that they are not selected based on explicit criteria and that the player does not try to anticipate the consequences of his actions. It means that these players cannot interpret the feedback of the game and cannot give meaning to successes and failures. In other words, though there is evidence that approximatively 80% of the players participated in the game, a minority of them play according to the expectations of the game designers and, therefore, have some chance to achieve the expected learning outcomes.

- Teammates use the chat to share messages. However, only 3% of the players are deeply involved in epistemic interactions and collaborative learning. Most written messages relate to discussions about the quality of the game or other issues. It means that the game does not fully meet our expectations regarding this issue. Thus, even though almost all teams managed to complete the 5 levels of the game, some doubts remain about the quality of learning. Indeed, a deep understandind of the copyright laws applicable for the use of digital educational resources result from the capacity to formulate the rules that should be followed. The data does not provide evidence of such capacity for most students.

Based on the results of this study, we consider that the tracking of epistemic interactions is a good way to assess the quality of learning outcomes for game-based learning. Indeed, the method allows for identifying the learners who manage to succeed with avoidance strategies that work against learning (for our study, the players who do not review the resources before feeding the Tamagotchi). The method also enables to identify the players who are deeply involved into in-depth discussion about the knowledge to be learned (for our study, the players involved in formulation and validation situations with teammates).

However, the method suffers from limitations since game-based learning is not limited to the use of the game. Learning also result from the debriefing conducted under the supervision of the trainer. We also know that debriefing is important for the transfer of knowledge [20, 21], and being able to formulate the legal rules for the use of digital educational resources does not guaranty that these rules will be applied in a relevant way.

Besides, the players who do not perform any action are not necessarily inactive from a cognitive perspective. We can hypotheses that some of them are attentive to the actions performed by their teammates and that they learn from what they observe. From a methodological perspective, the epistemic model of a player is inferred from its behavioral model built with the digital traces collected. In absence of such record, we know nothing about what the students managed to learn.

In addition, it is worth to notice that the picture drawn with the analysis of the digital traces does not consider that players might have changed their strategy during the game session. Indeed, the work carried out in a previous study [2] demonstrated that there is a majority of inactive players at the beginning of the game session and that they become more active later on. Thus, the factor analysis conducted on the data set only gives an overall idea of how a player plays and the epistemic interactions that take place vary over time.

7 Conclusion

We carried out an empirical study dedicated to assessing the relevance of an online and game-based training course for pre-service teachers. This assessment was based on a theoretical model which distinguishes 2 categories of epistemic interactions. We found that players adopt different ways of playing that are not always in favor of learning. Most players choose to be inactive or to develop strategies that do not allow epistemic interactions. However, we also found players who play according to the expectations of the game designers and who are involved in epistemic interactions with the game itself or with other players.

We consider that the contribution of this study is two folds. First, it consists of the development of a method adapted to track epistemic interactions and to assess the quality of learning. Indeed, this study allowed us to build a method to analyze epistemic interactions. On the one hand, we have highlighted the data to be collected to study these behaviors (i.e. relevant interactions in terms of activity and messages) and the appropriate data analysis methods. Thus, we propose an analysis model based on two categories of epistemic interactions. Second, these results may offer new perspectives for the design of learning games. Indeed, the result of the study emphasize the need to focus on the player's learning experience in terms of epistemic interactions. A learning game should offer the player both to interact with the game and with teammates. In addition, we consider that leaderboards should offer the trainers involved in the monitoring of the game the opportunity to track epistemic interactions and to identify the players who use avoidance strategies that work against learning.

References

1. Sanchez, E., Emin Martinez, V., Mandran, N.: Jeu-game, jeu-play vers une modélisation du jeu Une étude empirique à partir des traces numériques d'interaction du jeu Tamagocours. STICEF **22**(1), 9–44 (2015)
2. Sanchez, E., Mandran, N.: Exploring competition and collaboration behaviors in game-based learning with playing analytics. In: Lavoué, É., Drachsler, H., Verbert, K., Broisin, J., Pérez-Sanagustín, M. (eds.) EC-TEL 2017. LNCS, vol. 10474, pp. 467–472. Springer, Cham (2017). https://doi.org/10.1007/978-3-319-66610-5_44
3. Bro, R., Smilde, A.: Principal component analysis. Anal. Methods **6**(9), 2812–2831 (2014)
4. Lebart, L., Salem, A., Berry, L.: Exploring Textual Data. Kluwer Academic Publishers, Dordrecht (1998)
5. Lallemand, C., Gronier, G.: Méthodes de design UX: 30 méthodes fondamentales pour concevoir et évaluer les systèmes inter-actifs. Editions Eyrolles, Paris (2015)
6. Sanchez, E.: Game-Based Learning, in Encyclopedia of Education and Information Technologies, Tatnall, A. (ed.) pp. 1–9. Springer International Publishing, Cham (2019)
7. Wu, W.H., Hsiao, H.C., Wu, P.L., Lin, C.H., Huang, S.H.: Investigating the learning-theory foundations of game-based learning: a meta-analysis. J. Comput. Assist. Learn. **28**(3), 265–279 (2012)
8. Dewey, J.: Experience and Education. Collier Books, New York (1938)
9. Dewey, J.: The Influence of Darwin on Philosophy and Other Essays in Contemporary Thought. SIU Press (2007)

10. Kolb, D.A.: Experiential Learning: Experience as the Source of Learning and Development. FT press (2014)
11. Schön, D.: The Reflective Practitioner. Temple Smith, London (1983)
12. Salen, K., Zimmerman, E.: Rules of Play, Game Design Fundamentals. MIT Press, Cambridge, MA (2004)
13. Sanchez, E.: Competition and collaboration for game-based learning: a case study, in instructional techniques to facilitate learning and motivation of serious games. Wouters, P., van Oostendorp, H. (eds.) Springer, Heidelberg. pp. 161–184 (2017)
14. Van der Meij, H., Albers, E., Leemkuil, H.: Learning from games: does collaboration help? Br. J. Educ. Technol. **42**, 655–664 (2011)
15. Ohlsson, S.: Learning to do and learning to understand: a lesson and a challenge for cognitive modeling. In: Reiman P., Spade, H. (eds.) Learning in Humans and Machines: Towards an Interdisciplinary Learning Science, Elsevier Science, Oxford, UK. pp. 37–62 (1995)
16. Baker, M.J.: Argumentation and constructive interaction. In: Coirier, P., Andriessen, J. (vol eds.) Foundations of Argumentative Text Processing, pp. 179–202. University of Amsterdam Press, Amsterdam, NL (1999)
17. Balacheff, N., Cooper, M., Sutherland, R.: Theory of didactical situations in mathematics: didactique des mathématiques (Didactique des Mathématiques, 1970–1990). Kluwer Academic Publishers, Dordrecht, The Netherland (1997)
18. Siemens, G., Baker, R.: Learning analytics and educational data mining: towards communication and collaboration. In: Proceedings of the 2nd International Conference on Learning Analytics and Knowledge, pp. 252–254 (2012)
19. Henriot, J.: Le jeu. Presses Universitaires de France, Paris (1969)
20. Sanchez, E., Plumettaz-Sieber, M.: Teaching and learning with escape games from debriefing to institutionalization of knowledge. In: Gentile, M., Allegra, M., Söbke, H. (eds.) GALA 2018. LNCS, vol. 11385, pp. 242–253. Springer, Cham (2019). https://doi.org/10.1007/978-3-030-11548-7_23
21. Lederman, L.: Debriefing: toward a systematic assessment of theory and practice. Simul. Gaming **23**(2), 145–160 (1992)

Distance Learning in Sports: Collaborative Learning in Ice Hockey Acquisition Processes

Masayuki Yamada[1(✉)], Yuta Ogai[2], and Sayaka Tohyama[3]

[1] Kyushu Institute of Technology, 680-4 Kawazu, Iizuka, Fukuoka, Japan
yamada@lai.kyutech.ac.jp

[2] Tokyo Polytechnic University, 1583 Iiyama, Atsugi, Kanagawa, Japan
ogai@t-kougei.ac.jp

[3] Shizuoka University, 3-5-1 Johoku, Naka-ku, Hamamatsu, Shizuoka, Japan
tohyama@inf.shizuoka.ac.jp

Abstract. Is it possible to induce collaborative learning in non-face-to-face learning? The objective of this research is to collaboratively support the sports skill acquisition process in non-face-to-face learning, which is currently growing and becoming widespread, and to study the characteristics of the cognitive aspects therein. An experiment concerning the ice hockey "stickhandling" skill was implemented in a non-face-to-face fashion, with two university students as the participants. In the experiment, a descriptive questionnaire was used concerning cognitive aspects in the acquisition process. The experiment was conducted over the course of eight months. The results of analyzing the descriptive questionnaire revealed a number of descriptions where the participant viewed the other person's movements, aiming to improve their own movement. However, descriptions concerning a participant attempting to improve the other subject's movement could not be observed. In contrast, in a previous study targeting online meetings, collaborative speech was observed. The findings suggested that in a non-face-to-face sports skill acquisition process, with merely an environment that allows for comparative study of the other person's movement and thinking, it would be difficult for collaborative settings regarding the other person's movement to occur. However, the possibility was mentioned for collaborative learning occurring with the addition of online meetings.

Keywords: Sports Skill · Non-Face-to-Face Collaborative Learning · Visualization System

1 Introduction

Is it possible to induce collaborative learning in non-face-to-face learning?

In recent years, research on collaborative learning to develop a knowledge-based society has been widely conducted (e.g. [1, 2]). Traditional research known as "Intercultural Learning Network" project suggested that students from different countries

Published by Springer Nature Switzerland AG 2023
T. Keane et al. (Eds.): WCCE 2022, IFIP AICT 685, pp. 309–319, 2023.
https://doi.org/10.1007/978-3-031-43393-1_28

exchanged their experimental or observational results and discover ideas through discussions about differences between the results [3]. Asynchronous collaborative learning examples aimed for "knowledge building" are widely known [4] in the Computer Supported Collaborative Learning (CSCL) field. CSCL learning environments have been provided in both face-to-face and distance learning situations to support communities of learners [5].

In sports skill learning situations, there are many collaborative settings where people train together as teammates. It is thought that the conversations in these settings implicitly turn into learning support. For example, in the scenario of two people playing catch, one person remarks on the other's form, while the other player then corrects this form in accordance with the received comment, which can be seen in everyday life. Since these collaborative learning settings are too routine and unremarkable, they have not been made into the subject of research. In recent years, such research on implicit physical learning have been widely conducted [e.g., 6, 7].

However, today our lives in the COVID-19 situation include a big part of non-face-to-face learning: many schools are implementing a significant number of non-face-to-face classes. Sports learning is no exception. The conventional act of practicing together with a friend in a field has now become difficult. Clarification regarding where non-face-to-face implementation is possible is required to support learning going forward.

In sports learning, is it possible to perceive and grasp the process of acquisition, and is non-face-to-face collaborative learning possible in sports skill acquisition processes?

In the present study, asynchronous-type training is defined as non-face-to-face learning. Here, we have compared such training with synchronous-type training including online meetings.

This study was conducted on non-face-to-face collaborative sports skill acquisition processes, targeting stickhandling in ice hockey. This research is about "acquisition," the process of being able to display matured performance in a particular field, such as a sport. Much research in this domain has come to utilize techniques by comparing professionals and amateurs [8]. In today's world, where there is a need for non-face-to-face training, implicit collaborative processes like the ones described above have not been established. Due to this, the current situation is one that has not been examined previously. Online tools are thought to be effective for supporting non-face-to-face collaborative training, but it would be challenging to describe them as fully sufficient (the reason for this being that the shift to non-face-to-face was not foreseen). Due to this, there is a need to focus on non-face-to-face collaborative sports skill acquisition processes, and determine what kind of learning processes will arise in completely non-face-to-face learning. Moreover, there is a need for consideration regarding collaborative learning that can be induced with the introduction of remote online meetings.

There is a need to focus on cognitive aspects that apply to human thinking for research concerning collaborative learning. For example, in research on programming learning [9], analysis has been performed on the cognitive aspects of constructive interactions in the learning process [10]. In sports, we can observe one's performance like programming. The analysis of cognitive aspects using discourse and the learning process is needed based on the observed performance data. Further, some research revealed characteristics in a long-term learning process by cutting-edged technology. For example, Roy [11] recorded all the speech of his son from his birth to age three at home and revealed a case of the process of language acquisition. Long-term data will also be necessary to examine the process of sports skill acquisition.

In research on cognitive aspects in the acquisition process [12], with ice hockey acquisition processes as the subject, cognitive aspect descriptions were indicated via a network diagram, and consideration was made concerning the circumstances of the changes therein. In research on activities conducted as an entire team, game and cognitive analyses were carried out [13], as was analysis of the athletes' respective cognitive aspects. However, since investigations on collaboration between athletes were not implemented, there is a need for such research going forward. In prior studies that developed a system for visualizing collaborative sports skill acquisition processes [14], there was a need for extended application in the implementation of the system, as well as for consideration of collaborative learning processes. Each of these research examples included an everyday, in-person practice environment and was built upon natural forms of learning; given this, there is a need to explore how collaborative learning between athletes takes place online.

2 Objective

This study was conducted on how non-face-to-face sports skill acquisition processes—which are currently growing more common—should be collaboratively supported, and considerations were made regarding the characteristics of the cognitive aspects therein.

3 Non-Face-To-Face Collaborative Training Experiment

3.1 Experimental Participants & Targeted Skills

In this research, an experiment was conducted in a non-face-to-face collaborative training environment. The participants were two university students. The present study took the approach of examining this process through long-term observation. Thus, rather than taking numerous participants as subjects, the study considered only the process of one pair. Collaborative learning settings as a team were assumed, and having explained this background, the experiment was executed for the two participants, who had no prior ice hockey experience. In the experiment, the participants were asked to act as teammates and facilitate improvements in each other's movements by reviewing those movements using the system. One of the participants was a male who played soccer. The other participant was a female who did not play sports. Both had different experiences with sports. However, in Japan, ice hockey is not at all a well-known sport. Most people have never encountered it. Thus, it was believed that the participants' experiences with sports would have little impact upon the results. Beginners were selected because it was believed that this would enable observation of the skill acquisition process. In studies of skill acquisition, experiments often take beginners as subjects.

The targeted skill in the study was "stickhandling." In ice hockey, stickhandling is the skill of using one's stick to move the puck (ball) as one desires. A person can carry out training for this skill on their own, but doing so with another person instead might result in applicable feedback for both individuals. The experiment used a university laboratory (meaning that dryland training took place), and adjustments were made so that experimentation for each participant was conducted on different dates and times. After implementing the experiment for a set period of time with the condition of it taking place in a completely non-face-to-face manner (hereinafter "first half"), similar experimentation continued, and was carried out with the condition of one online meeting per month being set (hereinafter "second half"). The experimentation for both the first and second halves lasted around four months. However, the first half was halted at approximately two months due to the COVID-19 pandemic that emerged immediately after experimentation began.

3.2 The Number of Experimental Implementations

As mentioned earlier, the experimentation schedule was adjusted (by the first author); the general standard was once per week, and the number of instances differed between the participants. The experiment was conducted eight times in the first half and 14 times in the second half for Participant A, as well as six times in the first half and 13 times in the second half for Participant B. A video conferencing system was used in the second half of the experiment, and remote online meetings were held four times. In these meetings, the system described below was utilized, and goals for the coming month were established, which were to be realized while continuing to access each other's movements with regards to the matter of "what should be done to improve each other's movement."

3.3 Training and Test Content

The training and performance tests in the experiments utilized the company HOCKEY REVOLUTION's "My Puzzle Systems" [15] (see Fig. 1). This system took place via tablet app, and has plates with colors and numbers arranged in six locations, designed in a way so that instructions concerning where one should move pucks appear.

Fig. 1. The Experimental Environment

The experimental procedure was as follows: (1) The system (described below) was used, and a reflection was conducted (time: freely chosen); (2) Next, training was implemented for a 10-min period, and its contents were set by the participant; (3) After training, a skill test was conducted; (4) Finally, a descriptive questionnaire (described below) was filled in (time: freely chosen) (see Fig. 2). The duration of the skill test was 30 s. In the test, one of the following instructions was given every 1.5 s: color, number, or pass to right or left. In accordance with these instructions, participants either handled the task on that tile or passed to the right or left. The number of participants' successful responses to each instruction was calculated by reviewing the video on site. Subsequently, the researchers determined whether the number was correct. In this research, the focus was on the cognitive aspects. Due to this, test results were not subjected to analysis. We hope to introduce details concerning performance at another opportunity in the future.

Fig. 2. The Experimental Procedure Was as Follows

The system used a speech and movement visualization system for collaborative sports skill acquisition processes, assumed to be in person (HDMi system [14]). With this system, speech and descriptions indicating cognitive aspects in sports competencies were visualized via a network diagram (see Fig. 3) to help users making relations between their physical performances and their meta-cognitive awareness. In the network diagram, words appeared as nodes, and words that co-occur in the same sentence were connected by edges. Further, physical movements were analyzed through OpenPose [16]; the movement for each body part was rendered in graph form (see Fig. 4). To analyze the participant's reports, we used KBDeX [17]. We separately analyzed the participant's responses and plotted a network of the collocations in each sentence. We then analyzed this network focusing on collocations between collocating words associated with "stickhandling" specifically, words describing maneuvers, and words describing body-part positions. In Fig. 4, in the first letter of each item is "R," which indicates the right side of the body parts; if it is "L," it indicates the left side. If the last letter of each item is "X," it represents the horizontal value, and if it is "Y," it represents the vertical value. The remaining letters indicate the location of the part. RShoulderY is the right shoulder, RWristY is the right wrist, and RHipY is the right side of the hip.

A characteristic trait of the system is that, as collaborative skill acquisition settings are assumed, a comparative study of the participant and the other person's current and past movement and descriptive questionnaire data become possible (see Fig. 5). In Fig. 5, along with videos of different participants, the viewer may observe performance assessments, self-assessments, the results of descriptive questionnaire network analysis (the network diagram in the upper-middle part of the figure), as well as body-part coordinates on an x and y-axis in the videos (the two graphs in the lower-middle part of the figure). The descriptive questionnaire was administered upon the pre-training reflection, as well as upon post-test data entry. In the first half of the experiment, the entry items were: "Seeing and thinking about the system, where did you focus during implementation? Why did you think about focusing there?" and "After the training and test ended, where did you think about focusing the next time? Why did you think that?" In the second half,

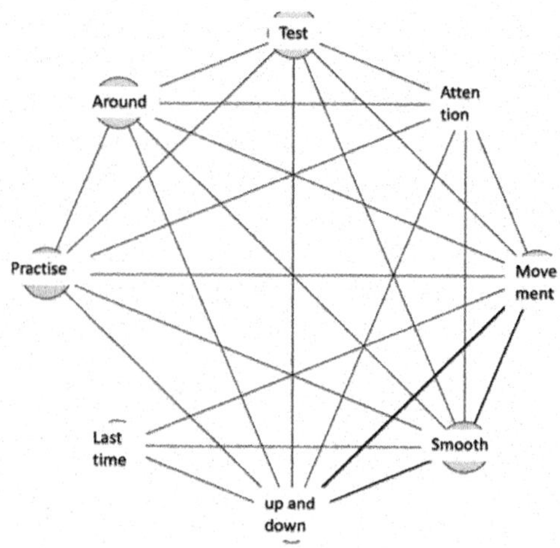

Fig. 3. Network Diagram of Descriptive Questionnaire Data

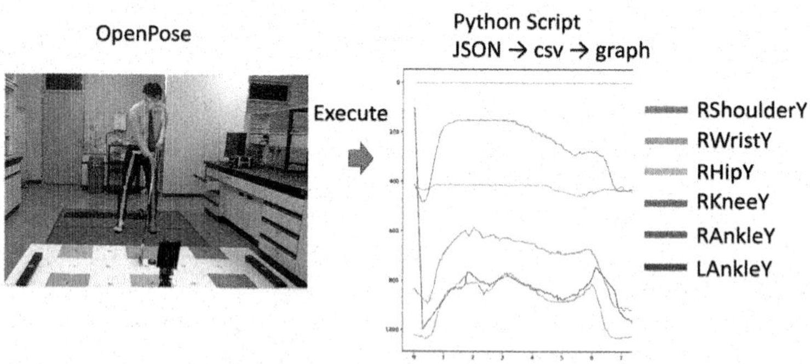

Fig. 4. System Development

even if the activities were non-face-to-face, the aim was to utilize data and for collaborative learning to emerge, and the following item was added: "Viewing the movement of the other person and thinking that you want to improve your own movement, what would you do for your goals, including those with the other person?".

4 Analysis

For protocol analysis, a tool was used to examine cognitive aspects—such as thinking [18] techniques for coding speech—following which such aspects were counted. In this research, "coding-and-counting analysis" [19] was employed. This method categorizes and counts data for speech and descriptions that indicate cognitive aspects of an objective established in advance. The objective of this research was to focus on cognitive aspects of collaborative acquisition processes in a non-face-to-face sports skill training environment, and to determine the characteristics therein. In an example of prior research

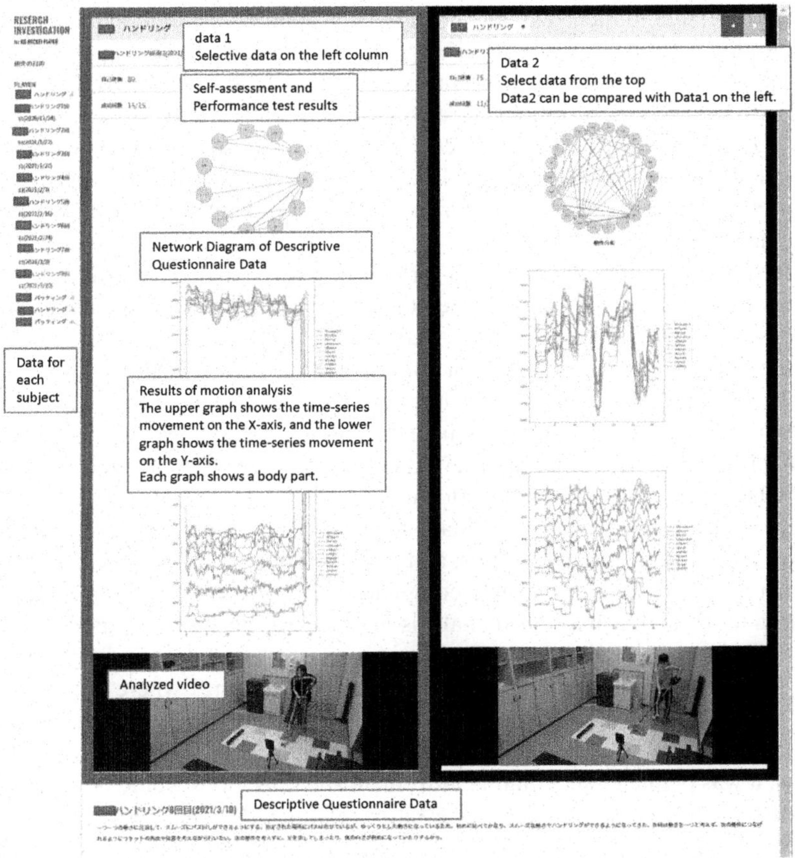

Fig. 5. Visualization System.

that utilized the same system and studied collaborative acquisition processes [20], it was shown that in the process of two children acquiring horizontal bar skills as they conversed, speech relating to their respective thoughts and movements was observed. In this research, consideration was made concerning to what degree collaborative descriptions about the other person were observed in an environment that allowed for mutual observation of each other's movements and cognitive aspects in a non-face-to-face collaborative sports acquisition setting.

In this research, the following two categories were established, and the number of descriptive questionnaires included in each was counted. The unit used was a written description provided by the participant, and a study was conducted regarding how many instances of these appeared.

In the first category, written text was extracted where the participant inspected the other person's data present in the system, and subsequently used it as a reference with their own movement. With in-person skill acquisition processes, situations can be observed in everyday life where a person views another's movement data and then makes improvement to their own movements. This component, functioning as collaborative learning, often takes place implicitly. This experiment was non-face-to-face, and as with in-person cases, there are instances of being described as a part that is implicitly processed. Further, descriptions were utilized, and consideration was made regarding whether collaborative learning took place. Concretely, subject-written text was extracted that included descriptions where it could be determined that they were explicitly viewing and inspecting the other person's movement, such as "Looking at Person B's movement, I thought to do XX."

As for the other category, a subject-written text was extracted where the objective was to view the system and improve the other person's movement. In team sports, it is highly possible that in settings where a person trains with another, encouragement for improving the other person's movement will arise. This occurs because goals are shared as a team, and teammates build each other up. Concretely, a subject-written text was extracted that included descriptions where it could be determined that the participant was explicitly trying to correct the movements of the other person, such as "I think it would be better if Person B crouched down more."

In this research, extractions were made from descriptive questionnaires, with regard to the two above mentioned categories, and the matter regarding what degree of collaborative learning was taking place in a completely non-face-to-face setting was studied. In addition to the above mentioned analysis, a study was performed regarding whether collaborative speech (such as that seen in prior research examples) arose during online meetings. This consideration targeted speech in four meetings where the system was used, actions were mutually reflected upon, and shared objectives were set. In the online meetings, the two participants reflected and prepared their next objectives. With online meetings, it was predicted that mutual movement and sensations would be shared due to the establishment of goals, and that conversation relating to "mutual movement improvements" would naturally take place. Due to this, the analysis considered whether "mutual movement improvements" related to speech were included in meetings or not.

5 Results and Considerations

In this analysis, the two categories of "descriptions concerning corrections in one's own movements, having viewed the other person's movements and data" and "descriptions concerning corrections in the other person's movements" were established. Further, the descriptive questionnaires entered into the system were analyzed. Moreover, a study was conducted regarding whether analysis of speech in online meetings included the presence of "speech relating to mutual movement improvement."

The results extracted from both participants' descriptive questionnaires showed that there were two instances of "descriptions concerning improvement of one's own movements, having viewed the other person's movements and data" in the first half, and three in the second half for Participant A. There were no instances in either period for Participant B (see Table 1). There were no instances of "descriptions concerning corrections in the other person's movements" for either participant. Given the fact that in the eight months spanning the experiment for each, the experiment was implemented 22 times for Participant A and 19 for Participant B, with the appearance of merely five instances can be considered a value that may be extremely low. In prior research that utilized the same system with in-person practice, speech (such as that described above) could be seen taking place in natural conversation [20]. However, in this non-face-to-face-type experiment, almost no such descriptions of utilizing collaborative advantageous points were observed.

Table 1. The Results Extracted from Both Participants' Descriptive Questionnaires

	Number of practices	Descriptions concerning corrections in one's own movements, having viewed the other person's movements and data	Descriptions concerning corrections in the other person's movements
Participant A First half	8	2	0
Participant B First half	6	0	0
Participant A Second half	14	2	0
Participant B Second half	13	0	0

Speech relating to "mutual movement improvement" occurred in every online meeting. That is to say, if a system is utilized where even remotely both individuals can discuss and view learning processes online, then it is highly probable that collaborative learning will take place. It was not the case in this research that training was implemented for two people together online. Nonetheless, utilizing a visualization system may allow for a comparative study of each person's respective training images, movement analysis, and descriptive questionnaires, which will make it possible to induce collaborative learning with online viewing and discussions. Such speech may be related to coaching. Further, such collaborative interactions may be thought of as circumstances similar to a setting wherein people train in real time.

6 Outlook

The objective of this research was to collaboratively support non-face-to-face learning in sports skill acquisition settings, focusing on cognitive aspects and studying their characteristics. It was implied that with training that enables, via a system, the viewing of a variety of data concerning the movement and thinking of the other person, it would be difficult for collaborative settings to occur with regard to each other's performance. It suggests that sharing a video in a gymnastics class for sports education will not encourage students to comment on each other. Moreover, it may be difficult for collaborative learning to take place in completely non-face-to-face, text-only interactions (for example, forums or message boards), which is not strictly limited to sports. In the background here, with text-only interactions, it is difficult for detailed nuances to be conveyed. However, in online meetings, training where past learning processes were viewed and inspected, it was implied that it is possible for collaborative learning to occur. In educational settings such as at schools, the construction of training that allows for mutual viewing of completely in-person individual learning processes, and the introduction of discussion actions through online meetings, can make it possible for collaborative learning to occur.

This research contains the implications of an experiment with a single pair of participants. There is a need for such studies, which focus on remote collaborative learning on a larger scale. Specifically, it is necessary to increase the number of participants as well as the amount of data. However, in a previous study by Roy [11], there was a significant impact upon the one participant in the study. In regard to these results as well, our plan is to follow up with continued long-term observation and to also consider the generalization of results.

Additionally, implementing detailed analysis, such as what kind of visualization system for information was utilized, may lead to the development of systems with greater learning effectiveness. In a previous study [7], postures were converted into numbers, and a cluster analysis of the relevant changes was displayed in the form of color bars. The system used here shows movements in the various video coordinates. We expect that it will be difficult to understand such coordinate data itself and to carry out investigations using it. For this reason, it is necessary to devise visualization methods that support learning by beginners. It is also necessary to consider whether these experimental results were brought about by the later addition of online meetings and whether there was any problem with the visualization of movements.

A study on performance in sports learning is also essential. For example, lowering one's waist is suggested in the ice hockey shooting skill acquisition process [21]. In terms of what kind of information may be visualized in support systems in various skill learning situations to lead to better support, the matter is one of domain specificity; thus, there is a need to examine systems that are based on the respective learning matters and interests of the participants. In this study, the analysis does not focus on individual reflections. However, we would introduce a statement as follows: "I'm getting better at passing the ball smoothly, but I need to pay attention to seeing the ball and giving it straight to where I want it to go." It suggests that the system helped her look back: thinking about other tasks after completing one task. In the future, we would like to continue studying when the subjects hope to cooperate with their partner and how the cooperation impacts their performances due to the provided technology.

Acknowledgements. This work was supported by JSPS KAKENHI Grant Numbers 22K12315.

References

1. Zhang, J., Scardamalia, M., Reeve, R., Messina, R.: Designs for collective cognitive responsibility in knowledge building communities. J. Learn. Sci. **18**(1), 7–44 (2009)

2. Bransford, J., Brown, A., Cocking, R. (eds.).: How People Learn. National Academy Pres, Washington (1999)
3. Levin, J.A., Riel, M., Miyake, N., Cohen, M.: Education on the electronic frontier: teleapprentices in globally distributed educational contexts. Contemp. Educ. Psychol. **12**(3), 254–260 (1987)
4. Scardamalia, M., Bereiter, C.: Higher levels of agency for children in knowledge building: a challenge for the design of new knowledge media. J. Learn. Sci. **1**, 37–68 (1991)
5. Koschmann, T., Hall, R., Miyake, N.: CSCL 2: Carrying forward the Conversation. Lawrence Erlbaum Associates, NJ (2002)
6. Suwa, M.: Re-representation underlies acquisition of embodied expertise: a case study of snowboarding. In: Proceedings of 27th Annual Meeting of the Cognitive Science Society, Stresa, Italy, p. 2557 (2005)
7. Nishiyama, T., Suwa, M.: Visualization of posture changes for encouraging metacognitive exploration of sports skill. Int. J. Comput. Sci. Sport **9**(3), 42–52 (2010)
8. Ericsson, A., Charness, N., Felotovich, P., Hoffman, R.: Expertise and Expert Performance. Cambridge University Press, Cambridge (2006)
9. Tohyama, S., Matsuzawa, Y., Yokoyama, S., Koguchi, T., Takeuchi, Y.: Constructive interaction on collaborative programming: case study for grade 6 students group. In: Tatnall, A., Webb, M. (eds.) WCCE 2017. IAICT, vol. 515, pp. 589–598. Springer, Cham (2017). https://doi.org/10.1007/978-3-319-74310-3_59
10. Miyake, N.: Constructive interaction and the iterative process of understanding. Cogn. Sci. **10**(2), 151–177 (1986)
11. Roy, D.: New Horizons in the study of child language acquisition. In: Proceedings of Interspeech 2009 (2009)
12. Yamada, M., Suwa, M.: How does cognition change in acquiring embodied skills? –a case study of an ice hockey player. In: International Symposium on Skill Science 2007, Japan (2007)
13. Yamada, M., Suwa, M.: Practicing 'off ice' collaborative learning in a university ice hockey team. In: 34th annual meeting of the Cognitive Science Society, Japan (2012)
14. Ogai, Y., Rin, S., Tohyama, S., Yamada, M.: Development of a web application for sports skill acquisition process visualization system. In: 7th International Symposium on Educational Technology, pp.235–237, Japan (2021)
15. MY PUZZLE SYSTEMS - Dryland Training Flooring Kit For Stickhandling, https://hockeyrevolution.eu/products/my_puzzle_systems. Accessed 5 Feb 2022
16. Zhe, C., Gines, H., Tomas, S., Shin-en, W., Yaser, S.: Openpose: realtime multi-person 2D pose estimation using part affinity fields. Eprint ArXiv:1812.08008 (2019)
17. Matsuzawa, Y., Oshima, J., Oshima, R., Niihara, Y., Sakai, S., KBDeX: a platform for exploring discourse in collaborative learning. In: Procedia - Social and Behavioral Sciences, vol. 26, pp.198–207 (2011)
18. Ericsson, A., Simon, H.: Protocol Analysis. The MIT Press, Cambridge (1996)
19. Vogel, F., Weinberger, A.: Quantifying qualities of collaborative learning processes. In: Fischer, F., Hmelo-Silver, C.E., Goldman, S.R., Reimann, P. (eds.) International Handbook of the Learning Sciences, pp. 500–510. Routledge, New York, NY (2018)
20. Tohyama, S., Yamada, M., Ogai, Y.: A case study of collaborative discussion about expertise in horizontal bar practices. JSiSE Research Report **35**(7), 119–125. Japan (2021). (in Japanese)
21. Yamada, M., Kodama. K., Shimizu. D., Ogai, Y., Suzuki. S.: Visualization of cognition and action in the shooting skill acquisition process in ice hockey. In: Proceedings of Fifth International Workshop on Skill Science (SKL 2018), JSAI International Symposia on AI 2018, pp.34–52, Japan (2018)

Instructional Methodologies for Lifelong Learning Applied to a Sage Pastel First-Year Module

Tania Prinsloo(✉), Pariksha Singh, and Komla Pillay

University of Pretoria, Pretoria 0002, South Africa
{tania.prinsloo,pariksha.singh,komla.pillay}@up.ac.za

Abstract. Lifelong learning is a useful and beneficial skill to learn. In this paper, students from a university in South Africa are taught Sage Pastel in their first-year of study using the Instructional Methodologies Framework for Lifelong Learning. This framework includes problem-based learning, e-learning, reciprocal teaching, professional portfolios, reflections, and knowledge maps. The students were asked how they experienced the module and their responses were mapped to the framework to demonstrate their journey. It is concluded that the majority of the students found the approach useful as a lifelong learning skill, with an 85% positivity indicator. The teaching environment used for this paper is unique, as the data was gathered in 2021 when the university was teaching only online because of Covid-19 restrictions, but the benefits of following a lifelong learning approach are evident. Future research will include comparing this module to other first-year modules that follow a similar approach to determine if students do become life-long learners.

Keywords: Lifelong Learning · Sage Pastel · Instructional Methodologies · Learning Management System · Sustainable Development Goals

1 Introduction

"Wisdom is not a product of schooling, but the lifelong attempt to acquire it." – Einstein.

Lifelong learning is a skill that is widely recognized as beneficial and useful [1–3]. Lifelong learning can be translated to learning that can occur at all phases of life [4], irrespective of age. More recent interpretations are that lifelong learning should be entrenched in all perspectives, from learning center to employment, family, and society [5], ensuring that lifelong learning is never neglected. It is for this reason that the Sustainable Development Goals (SDGs) focus specifically on lifelong learning in SDG 4, which states that it needs to "ensure inclusive and equitable quality education and promote lifelong learning opportunities for all" [6, p.1] which directly implies literacy and numeracy skills for all [7]. The learning culture is thus the idea of a society in which every person, regardless of age or location, has access to learning opportunities [8].

Published by Springer Nature Switzerland AG 2023
T. Keane et al. (Eds.): WCCE 2022, IFIP AICT 685, pp. 320–331, 2023.
https://doi.org/10.1007/978-3-031-43393-1_29

In this paper, the focus is on a first-year module – Sage Pastel – that is incorporated into an accounting module. It combines essential competency skills such as learning how to learn, and the knowledge of how to acquire new information, as detailed by Kaplan [2]. The aim of this paper is to determine if using Instructional Methodologies can enhance or promote lifelong learning for first-year students.

2 Background and Literature Review

At a higher education institution in South Africa, a cohort of approximately 2200 students typically enroll for a first-year Sage Pastel module. Sage Pastel is a cloud-based accounting application used worldwide. The main objective for the students is to apply accounting strategies and processes in the Sage Pastel application. The accounting principles and methods are acquired in an accounting course, and these transferable skills are practiced and enhanced in the Sage Pastel module. Our university works very closely with other modules in the program to increase the effectiveness and understanding of the Sage Pastel module. The Sage Pastel curriculum evolved in 2020 to be an integral part of the accounting programs offered at our university. The enhanced curriculum changed from an examination module to a continuous assessment module which enhances lifelong learning. The module carries three credits that equate to thirty notional hours of learning. The students are required to write two semester tests, but the rest of the module is based on assignments. Some of the principles of lifelong learning that were further integrated are to teach for understanding by using an interactive eBook and videos, applying their knowledge in the corresponding accounting module, and applying the accounting concepts rather than the facts. Students frequently interact with their lecturers via the online discussion boards and the Learning Management system (LMS) (BlackBoard) sessions.

Throughout the semester, active student-centered learning is implemented. The Sage Pastel Blackboard module incorporate online resources, including videos and written exercises. These Blackboard resources can be used to prepare for lessons, or as post-class tasks to reinforce content. Facilitators can also be contacted online during their designated consultation hours. Students can use the designed yearly schedule and assessment calendar to help them prepare for learning sessions and submitting assignments on time. This also allows students to manage their own timetable, thus entrenching lifelong learning skills. This method of online learning is referred to as hybrid learning.

Transformation of the online module to adapt it to lifelong learning was undertaken as follows:

- The print textbook was traded for an eBook that was easily accessible through the LMS.
- The traditional tests and assignments tested surface knowledge. This method was re-designed to higher-order questions with scenario-based real-world examples. The approach used was "Learning to Be Productive and Employable" [22, p. 170].
- Navigating of the LMS was adapted to simplify finding the right resources in a minimal amount of time
- The recording of all live online presentations was made available for reference and reinforcement of content knowledge.

Instructional practices adapted from Mahajan et al. [9] promote lifelong learning practices by engaging learners in self-directed, self-assessed, problem-oriented learning as depicted in Fig. 1 below.

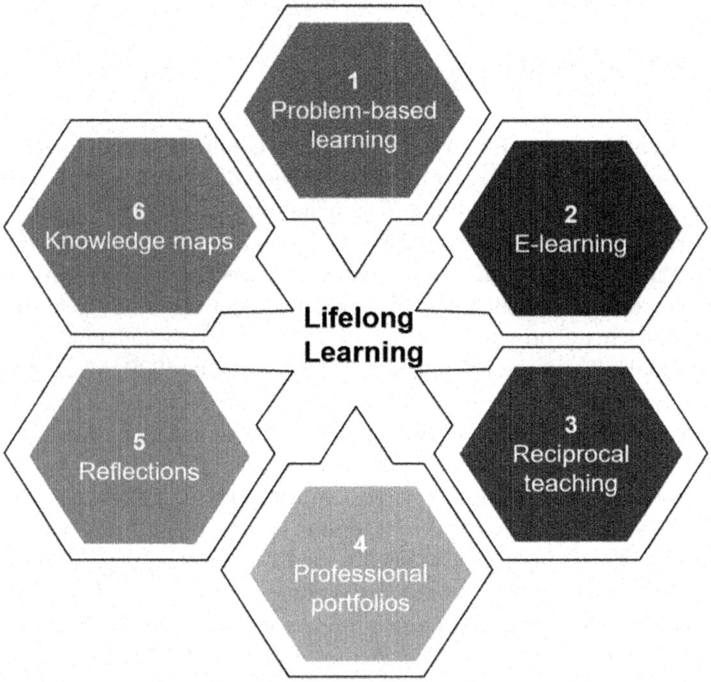

Fig. 1. Instructional methodologies for cultivating and promoting life-long learning skills adapted from Mahajan et al. [9].

2.1 Problem-Based Learning

Problem-based learning focuses on a well-designed practical challenge, methodologies of instruction for establishing and promoting lifetime learning abilities [10]. Problem-based learning is developing lifelong learning abilities through an educational cycle in which students assess their learning needs, conduct research, and connect theory and practice, shown in Fig. 2. It is a four-phase educational cycle that helps students acquire lifetime learning abilities through active involvement.

In Sage Pastel, the problem-based learning approach is used to promote lifelong learning. Students are assigned problems in their major accounting module that they solve using Sage Patel software. Students in a group first determine what they need to know, distribute the workload according to their strengths, and then return to the group with the skills they need and share these skills with the group. This approach promotes lifelong learning, and students learn how to solve and apply knowledge to real-world problems.

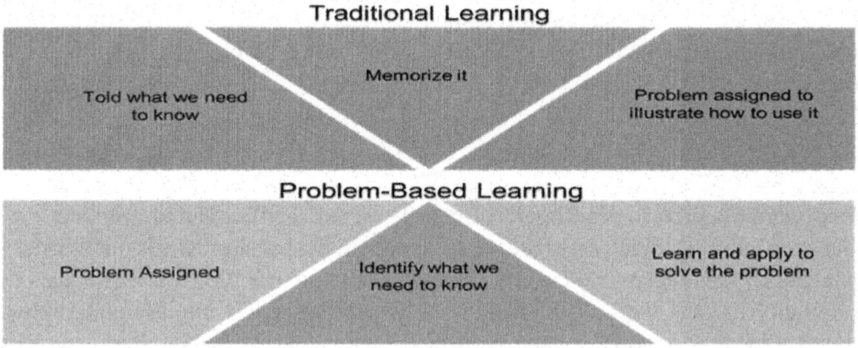

Fig. 2. Traditional Learning versus Problem-Based Learning adapted from Ali [10].

2.2 E-learning

E-learning encompasses all teaching and learning activities carried out by individuals or groups using computers and other electronic devices, whether online or offline, synchronous or asynchronous [9, 11]. Web-based learning, online learning, internet-based learning, computer-based learning and mobile learning are all terms used to describe e-learning. It is more adaptable, and learners are to some extent responsible for setting their own pace of learning [9]. These characteristics of e-learning, combined with e-assessment, make it possible to promote self-motivated learning, provide opportunities for self-assessment, reflection and gap analysis, and support lifelong learning. E-learning is a teaching and learning tool that is increasingly used for lifelong learning outside the traditional learning centre [11]. E-Learning in Pastel Accounting is conducted via the LMS that is zero-rated. Zero-rating means that internet users do not have to pay any fees to access and use specific internet sites. This is an agreement between the service provider and the university. The LMS houses resources and content available for the course, and these resources are available to use at any time by the students. Due to connectivity and load shedding issues, the readily accessible resources make it easier for the students to engage with the module's content. Recorded sessions, videos and notes are accessible for download. A discussion board for all queries are answered du-ring office hours. Online live sessions are presented every day for the students who require more engagement. All assessments are also easily accessible online via the LMS and offer students the flexibility to complete them.

2.3 Reciprocal Teaching

Reciprocal teaching is a classroom activity where students take on the role of the presenter in small groups. Lecturers help model this activity for students and help them to lead group discussions using four strategies: Summarizing, Asking Questions, Clarifying and Predicting. This is applicable in the Sage Pastel course, as after a session students are asked to summarize the content covered for that day and how it is relevant to other subjects. Students ask questions in the session on the chatbox and in the discussion boards to eliminate any confusion or query; other peers or facilitators can answer these questions. Students form small groups using the breakaway sessions in the LMS tool and discuss content, thereby clarifying any misconceptions. Reciprocal teaching promotes lifelong learning [12, 13].

2.4 Portfolios

Students were required to develop portfolios. These are a collection of a student's work that has been carefully selected to create a story about the learner. This is not a collection of a student's tasks done over the course of a semester or a year. Portfolios contain a carefully chosen subset of their work. Traditionally, creating a portfolio assignment begins with a form of goal or story for the portfolio. As a result, portfolios are characterized by the specific purpose fulfilled, the number and type of items included, the activity of pinning down the included items, how and whether a student responds effectively to the selected activities, and all preceding portfolio decisions [14–16]. The Sage Pastel module used four subsets of tasks to help create this portfolio with specific objectives in the module. These objectives were portrayed in real-life examples needed to be captured using the Sage Pastel system.

2.5 Reflections

Reflection is a process of paying intentional, structured, and intellectual attention to one's own ideas, behaviours, and thoughts concerning specific observations to promote perceptions of reactions to present and future experiences [9]. Regardless of the definition, reflection is critical thinking that occurs during or after the learning process and involves connecting new learning experiences and ideas to previous experiences to generate more complex concepts and promote higher-order thinking. Reflection encourages students to take improved ownership of their learning, which can lead to more 'reflective practice' in the workplace later on and the development of lifelong learning abilities [10, 17]. Reflection in the Sage Pastel module was promoted after each assessment. Students connected via an online tool – either with Discussion Boards or Collaborate Sessions - to discuss and demonstrate understanding of the parts of the assessment that needed clarification. Reflection also helped students transfer knowledge from one module to another by using the information gained in the Sage Pastel course and completing assessments in their main accounting modules. Reflections on the feedback from students at the end of the course also helped better develop the LMS and content components.

2.6 Knowledge Maps

A knowledge map is a method of surveying and connecting objects of knowledge and information, usually visibly, in such a manner that the mapping actually generates deeper knowledge, such as understanding where skills and expertise are located, and how they move through the system [18]. Mind maps and concept maps are examples of knowledge maps. The knowledge maps can be handwritten or created digitally. The use of concept maps for learning activities involving group discussion and interaction can generate assessment criteria identified by the students. All peer assessments contribute to instilling a lifelong learning mindset by strengthening self-monitoring abilities [20]. The creation of knowledge maps necessitates a great deal of subjective levels of understanding of subject-related topics; students employ analytical abilities to solve problems, communication is enhanced, and teamwork skills are instilled, all of which develop lifelong learning skills [20]. The process of generating maps involve the following seven steps: 1. Start with the most important concepts, ideas and words. 2. Then add other concepts. 3. Connect all the concepts with arrows or lines. 4. Give the linking lines meaningful labels. 5. Organize and order your maps by concepts. 6. Be creative and use multiple colors in your maps, in this way you will differentiate between concepts. 7. Customize your map by adding additional items, for example links or files [21]. The Sage Pastel course, together with the fundamental accounting modules, enforced the ideas of concept maps and mind maps to complete integrated assessments. Students are grouped in teams of four to five members where cross-module activities need to be performed. This enhances lifelong learning skills. Students complete Knowledge maps and mind Maps are used to complete projects with real-world examples across first-year subjects.

3 Research Chapter and Methodology

The main research question addressed in this paper is: Was the introduction of Instructional Methodologies used in the Sage Pastel module successful in promoting and enhancing lifelong learning for students during the Covid-19 pandemic?

This research design is a cross-sectional, randomised survey where the data are collected at one point in time from a sample selected to represent a larger population. The survey was administered online via the student LMS. All the required ethical consent was obtained before the survey was administered. In order to obtain ethical clearance, an application was submitted to the ethics committee, and the committee gave feedback and requested minor adjustments. The survey was distributed once final approval was obtained. The target population was the students required to complete the Sage Pastel module. The sample selection was simple randomised sampling where every student in the target population had an equal chance to complete the voluntary survey. Descriptive statistics were used as a qualitative method to discuss the findings.

A survey comprising of thirteen questions was administered to the 2021 cohort of students in the Sage Pastel module; the survey was voluntary and aimed at sustainable Development Goal 4: Quality Education and Lifelong Learning in Higher Education focusing on Lifelong learning. The survey was completed by 363 students and a statistician used SPSS version 13 to analyse the data collected. Table 1 below shows how each question in the survey maps to the Instructional Methodologies.

Table 1. The mapping of the administered questions to the Instructional Methodologies.

Question	Mapping to Instructional Methodologies
1. Do you feel that you had the necessary skill set to work through the content of the module?	• 2. E-learning • 5. Reflections
2. Do you feel that the teaching material matches your interest?	• 3. Reciprocal teaching • 6. Knowledge maps
3. Do you find the assessments useful?	• 4. Professional portfolio
4. Did you know what this module was about before you started?	• 5. Reflections
5. Do you believe this module will help you in your personal development?	• 1. Problem-based learning • 2. E-learning • 3. Reciprocal teaching • 6. Knowledge maps
6. Do you believe the subject will help in your professional development?	• 1. Problem-based learning • 2. E-learning • 3. Reciprocal teaching • 6. Knowledge maps
7. Which module resources contributed the most to your understanding of the content? Rank the resources from the most useful to the least:	• 2. E-learning and • 6. Knowledge maps
8. Do you only engage with the module when necessary i.e. when you have a test or assignment due?	• 1. Problem-based learning
9. Do you engage with the module on a weekly basis, as prescribed?	• 1. Problem-based learning
10. Do you make use of external resources that is not provided by the module? For example, YouTube videos?	• 2. E-learning and • 6. Knowledge maps
11. Do you prefer doing assignments in groups or as an individual?	• 1. Problem-based learning • 2. E-learning • 3. Reciprocal teaching • 6. Reflections
12. Do you share or impart knowledge with other students, like peer-to-peer learning?	• 3. Reciprocal teaching
13. Do you want to extend your knowledge of the module?	• All methodologies used

4 Findings

The responses of the students were analyzed for each question:

Question 1: Do you feel that you had the necessary skill set to work through the content of the module?

The finding indicates that 66.5% of the students had some skills before the module began due to the module being run from April to September. The students learned digital literacy skills and fundamental accounting concepts in the first three months at university. Learning progresses primarily due to prior knowledge and only secondarily from the resources presented to students. The students acquired the skill for this module in the first quarter of the year when they had to attend their main accounting modules. One of the instructional methodologies for lifelong learning is reflection; students use the skills from core modules to navigate the content in Sage Pastel. Another key instruction methodology that is relevant is based on e-learning. Students attain this module's digital literacy skills in a compulsory course that all university students register for.

Question 2: Do you find the teaching material matches your interest?

Approximately fifty eight percent (57.8%) of the students agreed that the course material matched their interests, whereas 21.1% were unsure. In comparison, 21.1% of the students believe the teaching material does not match their interest = appears to be a duplication. The coordinators integrated Sage Pastel with other first-year courses, which showed students the relevance of Sage Pastel in the corporate world. The instruction methodology followed for this was getting the students to create knowledge maps on integrated assessments and enhancing their portfolios with integrated knowledge. Students also learnt from one another using reciprocal teaching methods.

Question 3: Do you find the assessment useful?

Sixty nine percent (69%) of the students agreed that the assessments were useful. Students were actively involved in the learning process when they were assessed as learners. The assessments emphasized critical thinking abilities, problem-solving techniques and encouraged students to set realistic objectives for themselves and track their progress objectively. This leads to lifelong learning [22]. The instructional methodology used to enhance lifelong learning was the development of a professional portfolio. Students created portfolios to showcase the work-integrated across first-year modules.

Question 4: Do you know what this module was before you started?

The findings indicate that 21.9% of the students agreed that they understood the module's objectives before the start date of the second quarter of the academic year; however, 78.1% of the students did not fully understand what was required of them at the start of the module. The instructional methodology used for this was a reflection on the work covered in the accounting module, and the digital literacy module. These modules should equip students to start the Sage Pastel module with a degree of confidence.

Question 5: Do you believe this module will help you in your personal development? And Question 6: Do you believe this module will help you in your professional development?

The finding indicates that 70.7% of the students that completed the survey agreed or very strongly agreed that the Sage Pastel module enhanced their personal development. Approximately eighty-five percent (84.7%) of the students agreed that their professional development will be enhanced. Lifelong learning entails seeking out or creating learning opportunities for both personal and professional objectives. This style of learning is applicable to everything students learn throughout their lives, not only in the classroom. Students can make better, more educated decisions if they keep learning. It improves their social skills, understanding of the world around us, and ability to grow and develop. Students can also use lifelong learning to help them advance their careers [23]. The integration of three first-year modules allows students to interact socially, integrate knowledge, and are exposed to real-world examples. This lifelong instructional methodology used for personal and professional development was problem-based learning, where students solved real-world problems using Sage Pastel. E-Learning also helped students to gain technology skills to complete the module. Reciprocal learning was used in the online sessions to enhance their facilitation skills, while knowledge maps enhanced development. This all leads to improving lifelong learning skills. Learning progresses primarily incorporate prior knowledge and only secondarily the resources presented to students. Constructivism suggests that past information is used to create new knowledge. It is based on the educational notion that facilitators must draw connections between what is new and what students have learned already. Knowledge must be contextualised and connected to students' existing knowledge and experiences. Importantly, information should be tailored to regional and cultural contexts, considering the value of knowledge to students [24].

Question 7: Which module resources contributed the most to your understanding of the content? Rank the resources from the most useful to the least:

Two hundred and eighty three students ranked videos as their first or second preference. Two hundred and seventeen students ranked the Blackboard Collaborate sessions as their first or second preference. Two hundred and thirteen students ranked eBooks as their first or second preference. Lastly, only 9 students ranked the discussion board as their first or second preference. The order of preference is videos, Blackboard Collaborate sessions, eBooks and then the discussion board. Good e-learning design means ensuring that there are various modes of learning available to the student. It is also easy for students to switch between learning modes, thereby promoting self-motivated learning.

Question 8: Do you only engage with the module when necessary, that is when a test or assignment is due?

The results showed that 53.7% of students only engaged with the module when an assessment was due. The module assessments are all very practical in nature. All assessments adopt the problem-based learning approach of "Problem Assigned", "Identify what we need to know", and "Learn and apply to solve the problem". Students are presented with in assessment scenarios which is the problem assigned; students sift through all the content to determine how to apply the relevant content to the correct scenario.

Question 9: Do you engage with the module on a weekly basis, as prescribed?

Out of the sample, 62.6% of respondents engage with the module weekly. Consistent engagement with the module results in the students practicing and improving their ability to apply gained knowledge to solve problems. Students are consistently presented with scenario learning in order to upskill themselves at their own pace.

Question 10: Do you make use of external resources that is not provided by the module? For example, YouTube videos?

The results indicate that 84.2% of respondents did not use resources that were not provided by the module. The module provides various formats of learning material – students were happy with the available formats of the material and therefore did not need to spend time looking for external resources.

Question 11: Do you prefer doing assignments in groups or as an individual?

Of the 361 students who answered this question, thirteen students preferred both, working in groups or alone, whichever suited their schedule better. The balance was split between working in groups – 109 – and working individually – 239. A large portion of first-year students in 2021 stayed at home, as all classes were presented online, leading to no interaction with fellow students as would normally be the case. In terms of lifelong learning, group work is ideal to instill important concepts [8] and the skewed picture should change in future. For group work, reciprocal teaching is applicable, while problem-based learning fits better with individual work. Students had to reflect on their experiences to be able to answer this question and in both instances, students used an e-learning platform.

Question 12: Do you share or impart knowledge with other students, like peer-to-peer learning?

It became evident that the students did not interact with one another often. Of the 361 students, only 93 indicated that they shared their knowledge with fellow students. Those that did share their knowledge, did so by making use of reciprocal teaching.

Question 13: Do you want to extend your knowledge of the module?

Out of the 362 students that answered this question, 243 indicated that they do not feel the need to extend their knowledge beyond the module. However, the remaining 119 uses all the aspects of the instructional methodologies proposed to extend their knowledge of the module.

5 Discussion of Findings

Based on the findings in the previous section, it is evident that Questions 1 to 3, 5 to 11, and 13 confirmed that instructional methodologies introduced within the Sage Pastel course can influence lifelong learning. The response to Question 4 can be attributed to students not understanding the integration of different first-year modules or the required knowledge needed to start the Sage Pastel module. Question 12's response can be attributed to the Covid-19 pandemic, where students did not have the luxury of attending university and seeing other students face-to-face, therefore they did not feel comfortable with reciprocal teaching. During the Covid-19 pandemic, as was the case when this paper's data was collected, it created a unique environment for students having to study only online. It enabled the researchers to apply instructional methodologies to promote lifelong learning. The researchers were able to instill lifelong learning principles uniquely in 2021. It is up to lecturers to design the LMS in such a manner that it continues to foster these principles. This can be achieved with an adapted instructional design going forward.

6 Conclusion and Future Research

Of the 13 questions, 11 indicated the conformance to lifelong learning principles, with an 85% positivity indicator. Students can be inspired to pursue lifelong learning for self-development and advancement when applying instructional methodologies. Based on their requirements and ambitions, learners can continue pursuing lifelong learning for personal and professional improvement. Lifelong learning is about much more than obtaining a qualification. Educators and facilitators can encourage lifelong learning by creating inclusive learning centers to foster the characteristics of a lifelong learner. Future research will include to compare this module's success to other modules that follow a similar lifelong learning approach and to compare students' perceptions. Also, the students can be asked to reflect on the module now that some teaching will again be presented face-to-face once Covid-19 restrictions have been lifted.

References

1. Illeris, K.: A comprehensive understanding of human learning. In: Contemporary Theories of Learning, pp. 1–14, Routledge (2018)
2. Kaplan, A.: Lifelong learning: conclusions from a literature review. Int. Online J.Primary Educ. (IOJPE), 5(2) (2017). ISSN: 1300–915X, 5(2)
3. Mezirow, J.: An overview on transformative learning. In Lifelong learning, 40–54 (2008)
4. Palumbo, M., Proietti, E.: Adult lifelong learning and counselling in life transitions: Challenges for universities. In: Paper presented at the Eucen Studies eJournal of University Lifelong Learning. Eucen Conference and Autumn Seminar, vol. 2, no. 1, pp. 21–26 (2018)
5. Charungkaittikul, S.: Building a learning society: perspective from Thailand. New Dir. Adult Continuing Educ. **2019**(162), 25–36 (2019)
6. United Nations.: Sustainable Development Goal 4: Targets and indicators [dedicated webpage]. https://sdgs.un.org/goals/goal4. Accessed 15 Dec 2021
7. Hanemann, U.: Examining the application of the lifelong learning principle to the literacy target in the fourth sustainable development goal (SDG 4). Int. Rev. Educ. **65**(2), 251–275 (2019). https://doi.org/10.1007/s11159-019-09771-8
8. Green, A.: The many faces of lifelong learning: recent education policy trends in Europe. J. Educ. Policy **17**(6), 611–626 (2002). https://doi.org/10.1080/0268093022000032274
9. Mahajan, R., Badyal, D.K., Gupta, P., Singh, T.: Cultivating lifelong learning skills during graduate medical training. Indian Pediatr. **53**(2016), 797–804 (2016)
10. Ali, S.S.: Problem based learning: a student-centered approach. Engl. Lang. Teach. **12**(5), 73–78 (2019)
11. Mouzakitis, G.S., Tuncay, N.: E-learning and lifelong learning. Turk. Online J. Distance Educ. **12**(1), 166–173 (2011)
12. Ahmadi, M.R., Gilakjani, A.P.: Reciprocal teaching strategies and their impacts on English reading comprehension. Theory Pract. Lang. Stud. **2**(10), 2053–2060 (2012)
13. Mccombs, B.L.: Motivation and lifelong learning. Educ. Psychol. **26**(2), 117–127 (1991)
14. Nkhoma, C., Nkhoma, M., Tu, L.K.: Authentic assessment design in accounting courses: a literature review. Issues in Informing Sci. Inf. Technol. **15**, 157–190 (2018)
15. Kim, Y., Hinchey, P.H.: Educating English Language Learners in an Inclusive Environment. United States of America, Peter Lang Verlag, New York (2018)
16. Tiwari, A., Tang, C.: From process to outcome: the effect of portfolio assessment on student learning. Nurse Educ. Today **23**(4), 269–277 (2003)

17. Al-Sheri, A.: Learning by reflection in general practice: a study report. Educ Gen Prac **7**(1995), 237–248 (1995)
18. Ebneyamini, S., Sadeghi Moghadam, M.R.: Toward developing a framework for conducting case study research. Int. J. Qual. Methods **17**(1), 1–11 (2018)
19. Stäuble, B.: Using concept maps to develop lifelong learning skills: a case study. The reflective practitioner. In: Proceedings of the 14th Annual Teaching Learning Forum, Perth, Murdoch University. (2005)
20. Hanewald, R.: Cultivating life-long learning skills in undergraduate students through the collaborative creation of digital knowledge maps. Procedia Soc. Behav. Sci. **69**(2012), 847–853 (2012)
21. Ria, H., Dirk, I.: Digital knowledge mapping in educational contexts. In: Ifenthaler, D., Hanewald, R. (eds.) Digital Knowledge Maps in Education, pp. 3–15. Springer, New York (2014). https://doi.org/10.1007/978-1-4614-3178-7_1
22. Biesta, G.: What's the point of lifelong learning if lifelong learning has no point? On the Democratic deficit of policies for lifelong learning. Eur. Educ. Res. J. **5**(3–4), 169–180 (2006)
23. UNESCO Institute for Lifelong Learning (UIL).: Embracing a culture of lifelong learning: contribution to the Futures of Education initiative. UNESCO Institute for Lifelong Learning, Hamburg, Germany (2020)
24. Laal, M.: Benefits of lifelong learning. Procedia. Soc. Behav. Sci. **46**(2012), 4268–4272 (2012)

Enhanced Online Academic Success and Self-Regulation Through Learning Analytics Dashboards

Yassine Safsouf[1,2,3](✉), Khalifa Mansouri[2], and Franck Poirier[3]

[1] LIMIE Laboratory, ISGA Group, Centre Marrakech, Marrakech, Morocco
yassine.safsouf@isga.ma

[2] Laboratory MSSII, ENSET of Mohammedia, University Hassan II of Casablanca, Casablanca, Morocco
khalifa.mansouri@enset-media.ac.ma

[3] Lab-STICC, University Bretagne Sud, Rennes, France
franck.poirier@univ-ubs.fr

Abstract. In the wake of the COVID-19 health crisis, governments around the world made educational continuity during school and university closure a priority. Many countries adopted online education as an alternative to face-to-face courses. This situation has led to an awareness of the importance of analyzing learning traces and data left by students to measure, evaluate and improve the learning process. This paper presents an interoperable online learning analytics dashboard that allows teachers to easily track the progress of their learners as well as to predict and remedy dropouts. For learners, the dashboard offers the possibility to visualize their learning process, analyze it and develop better self-regulation skills. The results of the study conducted on a blended learning course, showed that the dashboard led learners to spend more time on their online training, to perform the proposed activities much better and to respect the deadlines better, and finally to improve their academic success.

Keywords: Learning Experience · Learning Analytics · Self-Regulated Learning · Learning Analytics Dashboards · Learner Success

1 Introduction

In many countries, the COVID-19 pandemic has dramatically accelerated the shift, partially or fully, to online learning in higher education. It is a significant change in the way the student learns and, for the teacher, in the way the educational activities are organized and the student's work is monitored and evaluated. Current learning management systems (LMS) have little or no ability to motivate students and facilitate their work, nor to effectively monitor their work by the teacher. It is therefore necessary to design tools and integrate them into LMS to enable both students and teachers to be effective in online learning, in a general perspective to ensure a good learning experience (LX).

Published by Springer Nature Switzerland AG 2023
T. Keane et al. (Eds.): WCCE 2022, IFIP AICT 685, pp. 332–342, 2023.
https://doi.org/10.1007/978-3-031-43393-1_30

For students, one of the most important factors for success in an online learning environment is the ability to self-regulate their activities. Zimmerman who developed the theory of self-regulated learning defines self-regulation as "processes whereby students activate and sustain cognitions, affects, and behaviors that are systematically oriented toward the attainment of personal goals" [1].

In theory, learning analytics (LA) and teaching analytics (TA) helps measure and support students' self-regulated learning (SRL) in online learning environments by harnessing the hidden potential of interaction data generated by the use of learning management systems (LMS) [2]. According to Sclater [3], the goal of learning analytics is to analyze the digital traces left by learners in order to better understand them and optimize learning.

However, in a review paper analyzing 54 articles on self-regulated learning and learning analytics, Viberg et al. [4] show that there is little evidence of contribution of LA for SRL in these articles. LA performs mainly to measure rather than to support SRL among learners in online environments. Hence, there is a critical need to design tools such as learning analytics dashboard that leverage learner interaction traces to help learner self-regulation.

So, the research challenge is to collect learner interaction traces to analyze them in order to propose an effective visualization of the analysis results to the different users (students and teachers) [5].

In this paper, we propose a learning analytics dashboard which is a visual communication tool, designed as a dashboard for teachers and learners that provides an analysis of learning data to facilitate the monitoring and control of the learning process, with the aim of improving the engagement, enjoyment of learning and success rate of online learners.

This paper begins with a literature review on the influence of self-regulated learning theory and learning analytics on online learners' success. Then, we share the reports of our tool created in the form of learning trace analysis dashboards. The next section is dedicated to the methodology our experiment, and finally the discussions of the results. Finally, we present a conclusion with some perspectives.

2 Related Work

2.1 Self-Regulated Learning Theory

Self-regulated learning theory (SRL) defines learning as a dynamic process in which the learner plans, monitors and evaluates his or her learning, applying appropriate strategies to achieve the goals [6]. It is a set of activities that individuals do by themselves in a proactive way [7].

Panadero [8] published an article that presents a review of the six most popular self-regulated learning models, the article concludes that, most of these models are composed of three essential phases, namely, (1) the preparation phase, (2) the performance phase, and (3) the reflection phase. As presented in the model of phases and subprocesses of self-regulation by Zimmerman and Campillo [9], the preparation phase includes task analysis, planning, goal detection, and goal achievement; the performance phase involves the performance of the actual task completed while monitoring and controlling progress; and the final reflection phase, where the learner self-assesses, reacts, and adapts for future performance.

Winne and Hadwin [10] proposed another model of self-regulation composed of four linked phases that are open and recursive and controlled by a feedback loop: (1) task definition (understanding of the task), (2) goal setting and planning (goals and plan to achieve the task), (3) enacting tactics and strategies for learning (actions needed to reach those goals), and (4) adaptations (metacognitive processes for long-term modification of motivations, beliefs and strategies). Each task can be modeled by five facets called COPES model: Conditions, Operations, Products, Evaluations and Standards. The learner's performance depends in part on evaluation (Evaluations facet), i.e. internal and external feedback.

Many studies agree on the relevance of self-regulated learning as a predictor of academic success in online learning systems. Liaw and Huang [11] investigated learner self-regulation to better understand learners' attitudes toward online learning. The results show that the factors perceived satisfaction, perceived usefulness, and interactive learning environments were identified as predictors of perceived self-regulation in the online learning context. In a study on formal and informal learning using social media [12], the authors showed that the use of social media as pedagogical means, to encourage students to control their autonomies.

2.2 Learning Analytics Dashboards

One of the most common applications of learning analytics is the production of dashboards to provide stakeholders (primarily teachers and learners) with visual interpretations of the overall learning process [13]. Schwendimann [14] defined these tools as a set of single displays that aggregate many indicators about the learning process and/or context into one or more visualizations. In general, these dashboards are steering tools that summarize the company's activities and results by process; thus, allowing to supervise the achievement of any set objective [15].

Jivet [16] proposed a literature review to better understand and describe the theoretical underpinnings behind the use of dashboards in educational settings. The study revealed that the most common foundation for the design of analytic dashboards is SRL. This theory is primarily used in the awareness and triggering of reflection, providing some support for the performance and self-reflection phases of the SRL cycle. Research conducted by Nicholas and colleagues to see how dashboards would be able to predict student outcomes at different points in a course shows that learner outcomes can be predicted with a supervised machine learning algorithm. These predictions were integrated into an instructor dashboard that facilitates decision making for learners classified as needing assistance [17].

In a review paper analyzing 29 learning analytics dashboards (LAD), Matcha et al. [18] find that the information presented in the dashboards is difficult to interpret. They criticize the lack of theoretical grounding of the dashboards (SRL theories is not explicitly considered in the design of LADs), they also note the weaknesses of dashboard evaluations in the experiences described and ultimately their relatively low impact on learner behavior. The critical analysis of the 29 LADs leads to the proposal of the Model of User-centered Learning Analytics Systems (MULAS) which identifies four dimensions that should be considered by dashboard designers: theory, design, feedback and evaluation.

From this state of the art, we identify two research objectives. First, it is to draw on critical analyses and proposed models in the literature to design a learning analytics dashboard that provides quality and effective feedback to learners and teachers on their learning activity. Second, to conduct an experiment in order to evaluate the contribution of the dashboard to learners' self-regulation and success.

In the following, we present our dashboard called TaBAT for Tableau de Bord d'Analyse des Traces d'apprentissage in French.

3 Design of the Learning Analytics Dashboard TaBAT

LMS platforms provide a variety of integrated reports based on journal data but they are primarily descriptive. They tell participants what happened but not why and they do not predict outcomes or advise students on how to improve their academic performance. These tools are mostly programmed to work with a single platform.

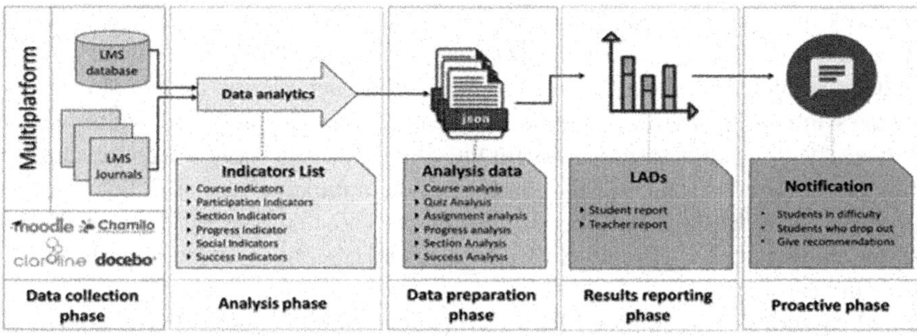

Fig. 1. The phases of the operating process.

Created to work with different online platforms, TaBAT is designed as a dashboard accessible online via the following link https://safsouf.net/tabat. It allows to see what happened during the online course (descriptive aspect), to see which students will or will not succeed in the online course (predictive aspect), to know why students were declared as dropouts (diagnostic aspect) and finally to get information on the actions to be taken to improve students' progress and success in the online course (proactive aspect).

As shown in Fig. 1, the operating process of TaBAT consists of extracting learner data from data sources (student learning tracks), selecting and calculating assessment indicators, presents reports in various diagrams (based on the learning traces generated from the LMS platform in JSON files to ensure interoperability). Two independent views are presented: the student report and the teacher report.

3.1 Data Collection Phase

The first phase is to determine the source of the data, choose the LMS, prepare and retrieve the data we use for our reports. The data can be located either in a database in logstore tables (in Moodle for example), log files or both.

3.2 Analysis Phase

In this second phase we create analysis algorithms based on the data collected from the previous phase. The goal of these algorithms is to specify and create indicators as well as to analyze student activity traces. The indicators we use are classified into six different categories:

- **Course category**: Gives general information about the course. The three chosen indicators are: the number of students enrolled in the course, the number of sections planned and the number of activities/resources created.
- **Participation category**: This category is more focused on the actions that can be done which consider students active. We distinguish two types of possible actions: consultation actions and contribution actions.
- **Section category**: Here, the two chosen indicators are: the activities/resources consulted by the student within each section (Lessons, Quizzes, Assignments, etc.) and the number of activities/resources contained in each section. These two indicators are used to calculate the student's level of progress in each section of the course.
- **Progression category**: A student's progress represents his or her status within a course. The three chosen indicators for the calculation of progress are: the number of activities the student has already completed, the number of activities not completed in respect of a deadline and the number of activities defined by the teacher at the beginning of the year. The level of progress will also be calculated on the basis of these indicators.
- **Social category**: This category focuses on the social interactions that can take place during the course which considers the students socially active on the LMS.
- **Success Category**: This category is specific to our approach. It is based on our previous research work that models a learner's success in an online course. This category is intended to provide an estimate of a learner's success. In our previous research, we proposed and statistically validated a causal model for evaluating online learner success (e-LSAM) [19]. This model allowed to identify the success factors associated with e-learning and to examine which factors explain a learner's success in an LMS. The result of our study shows that success is explained, with a prediction rate of 80.7%, by 24.1% of self-regulation (represented in our case by the level of progression with success) and by 75.7% of continuity in using the system. The latter is explained by 38.5% of the level of social interaction and 61.5% of the level of course participation.

The indicators presented above give us a numerical value representing the data corresponding to a specific student. We have decided to represent the significance of the numerical data in the form of color indicators.

3.3 Data Preparation Phase

The third phase plays a main role in the process of our tool, it is the relay between the analysis phase and the results presentation phase. It is also an essential phase to ensure the interoperability of our tool. The goal is to allow, as well as to gather transform and prepare the essential data for our tool in order to generate data in JSON files with a standardized structure. Thus hiding their main source (we are talking here about platforms or data sources) and on the other hand to give the possibility to other developers to extend the use of our tool to other LMS platforms, by using any programming language which allows the generation of these same files (for example: PHP or Python).

3.4 Results Reporting Phase

In this phase, the reports in form of LADs are presented. These reports communicate directly with JSON files to get the necessary data back. Two aspects are presented independently: the report for the student and for the teacher.

Report for the Teacher

The report for the teacher (showed in Fig. 2) presents statistical data during the online course. The first page (1) includes the number of students enrolled, the number of sections, activities and resources in the course, the number of students who actively participate in the course, statistics on monthly connections for the current year, as well as statistics on the number of times students consult the activities and resources.

The quiz analysis page (2) provides a table that shows, for each student, the list of quizzes taken or not taken, the number of questions answered, the total number of questions, the final score obtained as a percentage, and the time recorded for taking the test.

The assignment analysis page (3) provides a summary of the assignments that may (on time or late) or may not be returned by students.

The dropout page (4) presents a table that displays the list of students with an estimation of the overall time spent on the course, an indicator representing the level of success (based on the results of our theoretical model called e-LSAM (for e-learner Success Assessment Model) [19, 20]) and finally a prediction status. This status indicates the result of the prediction either: risk of dropping out, minimal risk or success. A color coding allows to visually differentiate if the assignment is submitted or not, if the quizzes are done or not and the risk of dropping out or not.

Report for the Student

The report for the student gives an overall view of each student's progress in the course. The three available interfaces are shown in Fig. 3.

The first interface (1) gives a positioning of the student's progression level for each section of the course with two other levels: the level of progression of the best student and the level of the average student in the class. It also displays a ranking table of all learners in the class. This interface aims to motivate and support students' metacognition and self-regulation processes.

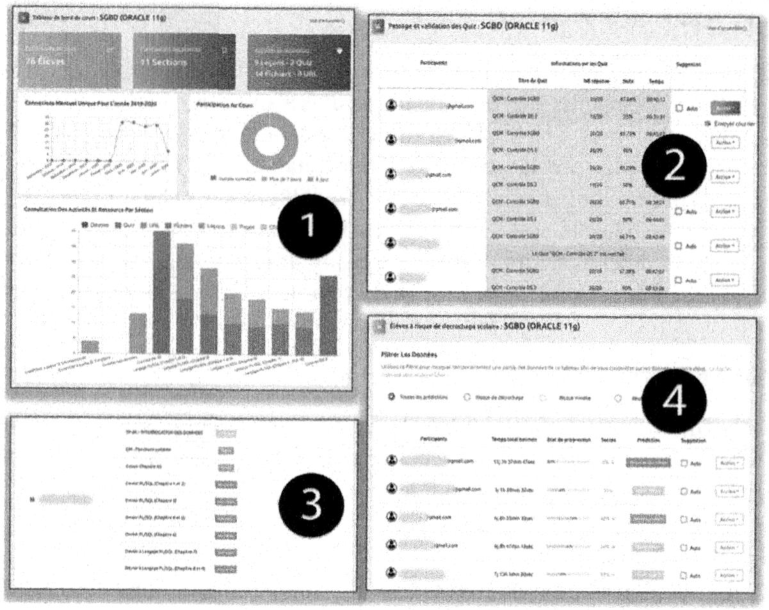

Fig. 2. General view of report of the teacher dashboards.

For the second interface (2), the student can see the details of his/her progress in the course. A chart presented in the form of a vertical progress bar summarizes the student's progress for each section of the course. This interface displays the details of the student's progress in each section.

The last interface (3) is the notification interface. Here the student can view the list of notifications (marked as unread) sent automatically by the system. Notifications are displayed by type, with a message indicating the actions to be taken. A script is scheduled to send notifications automatically twice a day; at 08:00 in the morning and again at 08:00 in the evening. If the same notification has already been sent and has not been read yet, the sending is not done.

3.5 Proactive Phase

This last phase allows the teacher to contact the students manually or to schedule automatic notifications. The goal is to have alerts on the student's side about a variety of available actions. The last three pages of the report for the teacher (2, 3 and 4), gives him the opportunity to select the learner(s) who will receive automatically suggestions (or notifications) regarding their achievements, assignments to submit or quizzes to do, resources to consult or even lessons to view. Each page also includes a contact button to send the student an email.

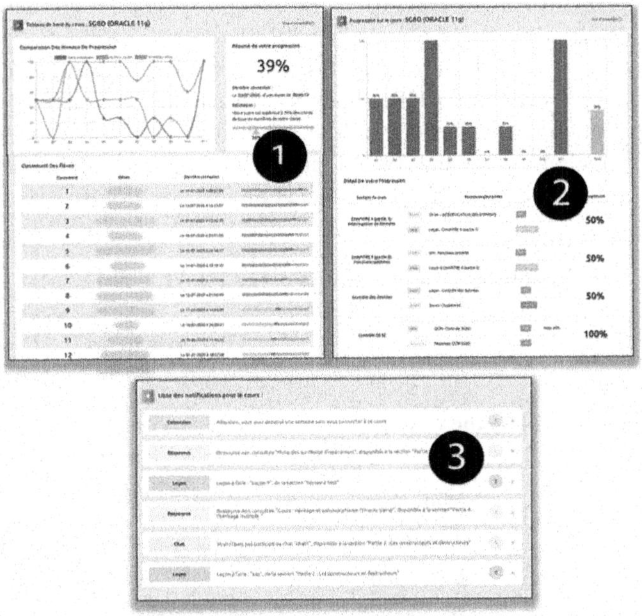

Fig. 3. General view of report of the student dashboards.

4 Methodology and Date Analysis

4.1 Context of the Study and Participants

This study aims to see the impact of the TaBAT dashboard, on the self-regulation and prediction of success of students in a higher institute in Morocco (ISGA of Marrakech).

The target population is composed of 46 students who have participated in a course organized in a mixed modality. The class is divided into two groups of 23 students each (15 female and 31 male), aged between 18 and 35 years (39 between 18 and 25 years and 7 between 26 and 35 years). In terms of time of use of the Internet and computer devices per day, 5 students reported their time of use to be between two and five hours, 31 between five and ten hours, and another 10 more than ten hours per day.

4.2 Study Methodology

The course was available in a blended learning format, which combines face-to-face and online training. Students in both groups, all took a face-to-face course entitled "Object Oriented Programming", with some chapters online on the Moodle 3.8 platform, over an eight-week period, finalized by a supervised face-to-face exam.

To evaluate the impact of using the tool on self-regulation and prediction of student success online, one of the two groups was given the experiment to use the TaBAT tool (exposed group), while the second group did not have access to the dashboard (control group).

4.3 Study Results

The part of the online course followed by all students consists of 7 sections (parts), with 7 lessons, 3 files to download, 7 URL links to visit, and 2 assignments due on dates planned at the beginning of the course. The analysis of the individual student traces in each group was done using the TaBAT dashboards via the teacher report. Table 1 describes the result of the experiment conducted on the two groups.

Table 1. Usage statistics of the TaBAT tool.

		Exposed group	Control group
Number of active users		23/23	21/23
Cumulative time to complete the course		129 h 15 min	78 h 37 min
Percentage progress score	**Max**	100%	100%
	Min	52%	16%
	Average	73.21%	56.93%
Percentage of assignments	**Returned on time**	81.22%	58.73%
	Returned late	11.62%	14.93%
	Not returned	7.16%	26.34%
Prediction of success (online success)		23/23	16/23
Effective success (validation of the face-to-face exam)		20/23	18/23

4.4 Discussion

We note at first that the 23 students in the exposure group all logged into the online course, while for the control group, 2 students did not take the online part of the course. This is because the only way to communicate with the teacher was face-to-face. Whereas for the exposed group, the teacher had the possibility through the TaBAT dashboard to contact each student via e-mail, which allowed for individual monitoring.

The second observation concerns the total time spent doing the online course activities. This time is represented in Table 1, cumulated for each group. Students in the exposure group spent significantly more time (65% more) than those in the control group following and completing the online course activities and resources. The learners enjoy their own time online, at their ease, to meet the objectives of the online course. This reflects independent functioning and resistance to distractions, making work at home a particular form of self-regulated learning.

The third remark concerns the performance of each group, this performance is represented in Table 1 by three score values, the maximum, minimum and average score of progression in the online course. The progress of each student represents the number of activities or resources consulted or accomplished over the number of activities or resources defined by the teacher at the beginning of the course. We notice a significant improvement in the performance of the exposed group mainly by an increase in the minimum value (3.25 times more) and the average progress (28% more) of the participants. This progression is mainly explained by the proactive actions made manually by the teacher or sent automatically by the TaBAT tool (proactive phase), in order to remind the students (with the help of notifications) if they have not yet accessed certain resources (file to download or URL to visit) or unaccomplished activities (lesson, homework, quiz to do, etc.). Not to mention the important role of the student report that allows each learner to self-assess and use their own online time at their convenience to achieve the objectives.

The fourth remark concerns the analysis of the return of homework. Indeed, the exposed group had a rate of 92.84% of assignments (planned at the beginning of the course) returned on time (assignments returned on time with those returned late), while for the control group, the same rate was 73.66%. This significant improvement is particularly due to the notifications received if there is an assignment due or not handed in on time (late). The notification includes the date and the number of days to hand in the assignment.

The final point concerns student success. In this study, the level of success calculated by the TaBAT tool based on our online learner success assessment model (e-LSAM) is compared to that obtained after the final exam. Table 1 shows that the TaBAT tool was able to demonstrate a high ability to predict the success of students for both groups in our experiment.

5 Conclusion

The development, implementation and experimentation of the learning analytics dashboard TaBAT represents the completion of our modeling work, which was design to identify factors that reduce the dropout rate of learners, and at the same time improve their success in online courses.

We proposed in this paper a study to test the effectiveness of the learning analytics dashboard TaBAT in the analysis of learning traces in an online course planned by an engineering school in Morocco. The results of this study confirmed that the use of TaBAT increased the learners' performance, improved their autonomy, and finally improved their academic success.

In our future work we would like to extend the use of TaBAT to other online courses (of different natures and specialties), in order to generalize our experience and to see the impact of the tool on the performance and the real success of learners.

References

1. Zimmerman, B., Schunk, D.: Handbook of Self-Regulation of Learning and Performance. Routledge, New York (2001)
2. Ferguson, R.: Learning analytics: drivers, developments and challenges. Int. J. Technol. Enhanced Learn. **4**(5–6), 304–317 (2012)
3. Sclater, N.: Learning Analytics Explained (2017). ISBN-13: 978–1138931732

4. Viberg, O., Khalil, M., Baars, M.: Self-regulated learning and learning analytics in online learning environments: a review of empirical research. In: ACM LAK 2020, pp 524–533 (2020)
5. Labarthe, H., Luengo, V.: L'analytique des apprentissages numériques. Rapp. Rech. LIP6 - Lab. d'Informatique Paris 6, (2018)
6. Zimmerman, B.J., Moylan, A.R.: Self-Regulation, Where Metacognition and Motivation Intersect. Handb. Metacognition Educ., pp. 299–315 (2009)
7. Zimmerman, B.J.: From cognitive modeling to self-regulation: a social cognitive career path. Educ. Psychol. **48**(3), 135–147 (2013)
8. Panadero, E.: A Review of self-regulated learning: six models and four directions for research. Front. Psychol. **8**, 422 (2017)
9. Zimmerman, B.J., Campillo, M.: Motivating Self-Regulated Problem Solvers, pp. 233–262 (2003)
10. Winne, P. H., Hadwin, A. F.: Studying as self-regulated engagement in learning. In: Hacker, D., Dunlosky, J., Graesser, A. (eds.) Metacognition in Educational Theory and Practice, pp. 277–304 (1998)
11. Liaw, S., Huang, H.: Perceived satisfaction, perceived usefulness and interactive learning environments as predictors to self-regulation in e-learning environments. Computational Education, vol. 60, no. 1, pp. 14–24 (2013)
12. Matzat, U., Vrieling, E.M.: Self-regulated learning and social media – a 'natural alliance'? Evidence on students' self-regulation of learning, social media use, and student–teacher relationship. Learn. Media Technol. **41**(1), 73–99 (2016)
13. Verbert, K., Duval, E., Klerkx, J., Govaerts, S., Santos, J.L.: Learning analytics dashboard applications. Am. Behav. Sci. **57**(10), 1500–1509 (2013)
14. Schwendimann, B.A., et al.: Understanding learning at a glance: an overview of learning dashboard studies. In: ACM International Conference on Proceeding Series, vol. 25–29-Apri, pp. 532–533 (2016)
15. Fernandez, A.: Les tableaux de bord du manager innovant: Une démarche en 7 étapes pour faciliter la prise de décision en équipe (Management). Eyrolles. 12 april (2018)
16. Jivet, I.: Adaptive learning analytics dashboard for self-regulated learning. https://research.ou.nl/ws/portalfiles/portal/9497006/2018_08_Chile_Research_Visit.pdf. Accessed 20 Feb 2022
17. Nicholas, D., Grover, S., Eagle, M., Bienkowski, M., Stamper, J., Basu, S.: An instructor dashboard for real-time analytics in interactive programming assignments. In: ACM International Conference Proceeding Series, pp. 272–279 (2017)
18. Matcha, W., Ahmad Uzir, N., Gasevic, D., Pardo, A.: A systematic review of empirical studies on learning analytics dashboards: a self-regulated learning perspective. IEEE Trans. Learn. Technol. **13**(2), 226–245 (2019)
19. Safsouf, Y., Mansouri, K., Poirier, F.: An analysis to understand the online learners' success in public higher education in Morocco. J. Inf. Technol. Educ. Res. **19**(2020), 87–112 (2020)
20. Safsouf, Y., Mansouri, K., Poirier, F.: A new model of learner experience in online learning environments. In: Rocha, Á., Serrhini, M. (eds.) EMENA-ISTL 2018. SIST, vol. 111, pp. 29–38. Springer, Cham (2019). https://doi.org/10.1007/978-3-030-03577-8_4

Analysis of Facial Expressions for the Estimation of Concentration on Online Lectures

Renjun Miao(✉), Haruka Kato, Yasuhiro Hatori, Yoshiyuki Sato, and Satoshi Shioiri

Tohoku University, RIEC Main Building, 2-chōme-1-1 Katahira, Aoba Ward, Sendai, Miyagi, Japan
{miao.renjun.s1,haruka.kato.p8,yhatori,yoshiyuki.sato.e4, satoshi.shioiri.b5}@dc.tohoku.ac.jp

Abstract. The present study aimed to develop a method to estimate the state of attention from facial expressions while students are in online lectures. We conducted an experiment to measure the level of attention based on reaction time to detect an auditory target, which was the disappearance of noise sound, while watching lecture videos, assuming that reaction time for the detection of contents-irrelevant noise is longer when learners are focusing attention more to the contents of the videos. We sought facial features that are useful for predicting the reaction time and found that reaction time can be estimated in some amount from facial features. This result indicates that facial expressions are useful for predicting attention state, or concentration level while attending lectures.

Keywords: Attention · Facial Features · Online Lecture

1 Introduction

In order to improve education quality, it is critical to estimate the level of learners' concentration on studies. For online learning, a web camera can be used easily for recording learners' faces and the facial expressions can be used for estimation of concentration levels. There are several attempts to evaluate mental states with facial expressions. For example, there are reports that attempted to estimate image preference from facial expressions [1–3], which suggest that facial expressions are useful features for estimating subjective judgments of image preference. Similarly, Thomas and Jayagopi recorded images of students' faces in a classroom while they were studying with video material on a screen and estimated the level of engagement from students' facial expressions [4]. Their engagement prediction showed a certain level of accuracy suggesting that facial expressions are useful for estimating the level of engagement or concentration as well. However, previous studies, including Thomas and Jayagopi, were based on subjective judgments. It is crucial to develop a method to estimate the level of concentration objectively. In this study, we focused on estimating attention states using a typical psychophysical measurement, that is, reaction time to detect a target. We designed an

Published by Springer Nature Switzerland AG 2023
T. Keane et al. (Eds.): WCCE 2022, IFIP AICT 685, pp. 343–348, 2023.
https://doi.org/10.1007/978-3-031-43393-1_31

experiment, in which participants were asked to detect an auditory target while watching a lecture video. Understanding the lecture was the primary task and participants answered quizzes after watching the video. Detection of the target was the secondary task and reaction time was used as an objective measure of attention levels when watching the lecture videos, assuming that reaction time to a target that is not related to the primary task is longer when participants are focusing on the videos. Images of participants' faces were recorded while they were watching the videos and facial expressions were analyzed after the experiment. The purpose of the study is to estimate the reaction time from the facial expressions to develop the method to estimate concentration level from images of learners' faces.

2 Experiment

The aim of the experiment was to obtain reaction times to an auditory target as a measure of attention level. Simple reaction time to the appearance of light or sound is used to estimate how much attention is paid to the target (shorter reaction time if more attention is paid to a target). Although this assumption could be too much simplified and the other factors should also be considered (see Discussion), we started with this for the first attempt. We used the disappearance of a continuous noise sound as the target. The reason we used disappearance instead of presentation was to avoid the influence of bottom-up attention, which could reduce the effect of attention on the lectures because salient stimulus attract attention independently of other factors such as concentration on the lectures.

Nine participants took part in the experiment and their average age was 22.8. They had normal or corrected-to-normal vision and normal audition. The task of the experiment was to detect changes in white noise (whose frequency spectrum is uniform) sound while watching online learning material. The target was the disappearance of the white noise. The learning materials were the introductory PHP (PHP is a computer language) course with nine lectures on YouTube [5], and we describe watching one lecture as one session. Participants watched videos on a computer display (MacBook Pro retina 15inch late 2013) with headphone (Sony dynamic stereo headphones MDR-7506) in an experimental booth, with no light source except for the display. Average loudness of lecturer's voice was 70 db and that of white noise was 0.66 db.

Participants were instructed to watch each video lecture to learn PHP and respond to quizzes after watching each lecture. They were also instructed to press a key when they noticed the auditory target, the sudden disappearance of the white noise. This was a secondary task to estimate the attention state at the time of target presentation. The participants were informed that understanding the lecture was the main task of the experiment. The white noise disappeared after the period randomly selected between 25 and 35 s. The white noise started again right after the key press for the detection and started after a pause of 10 s when there was no key press. There were nine sessions of watching one lecture, and one lecture time was between 10 and 20 min. At the end of each lecture, a set of quizzes were provided to evaluate the learning effect (Fig. 1).

There were two control sessions, where the participants were not asked to watch the video displayed, but to focus on white noise. The control session was to evaluate the

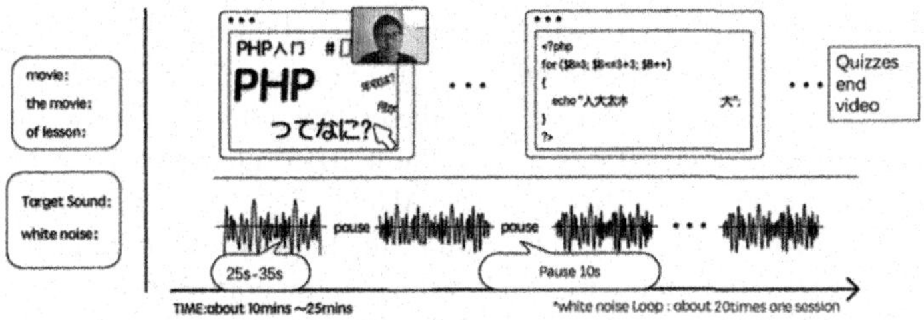

Fig. 1. Experimental design.

detection task per se in the condition without paying attention to the lecture. In the control session, the same video lectures were used so that the participants knew the content and had little or no reason to be attracted to the content. Each participant participated in nine lecture sessions and two control sessions, and the total time of watching videos was about 134 min. The experiment was conducted in two days. The first control session was conducted at the 6th session with the video of the first lecture repeated and the second control session was conducted at the 11th session with the video of 6th lecture. Five lecture sessions and the first control session were performed on the first day and the remaining four lecture sessions and the second control session were performed on the second day.

3 Facial Feature Analysis

Videos were recorded of participants' faces during the lectures and facial features were analyzed after the experiment. We analyzed video data frame by frame, using OpenFace [6] to analyze the facial feature as action units (AU). AUs of participants' faces from 3 s to 0 s before the target presentation (disappearance of white noise) were analyzed to search for facial expressions that predict reaction times, with which, we assume, the level of attention can be estimated at around the time of target presentation.

The Facial Action Coding System (FACS) [7] is a system that displays a series of facial muscle movements corresponding to the displayed emotion. An Action Unit (AU) code is assigned to each facial movement. For example, AU1 indicates the raising of the eyebrows; AU4 indicates the lowering of the eyebrows.

To predict reaction time from facial expression, we used a machine learning method, Light GBM [8], to model the relationship between AUs and reaction time.

Light GBM is a gradient boosting model, which is considered to be fast with relatively accurate performance. This choice of Light GBM followed a previous study which used several other methods and found similar results [1–3]. For the model evaluation, we used a five-fold cross-validation method. All the data were divided into 5 groups and 4 of them were used for training and the remaining one was used for the test. In the procedure, each group was tested once and used for training four times. The average of the five test scores was used as the final score. The prediction performance was evaluated by root mean square error (RMSE) from the prediction and the coefficient of correlation between data and prediction.

The features of the facial expressions were extracted throughout each session from the recorded video, using an open-source facial expression analysis tool, OpenFace, which automatically recognizes faces and analyzes facial landmarks, head orientation, and gazes. Two types of AU outputs are available: 0–5 intensity of 17 different AUs (AUr) and a binary value of 18 different AUs (AUc).

We used AU data between 3 s and 0 s before the target presentation (disappearance of white noise) for statistical indexes of AU values of the period, which were the mean, minimum, maximum, standard deviation, 25%, 50% (median) and 75% for AUr and means and standard deviation for AUc. The total number of indexes were 155 (17 AUr × 7 and 18 AUc × 2) (Fig. 2).

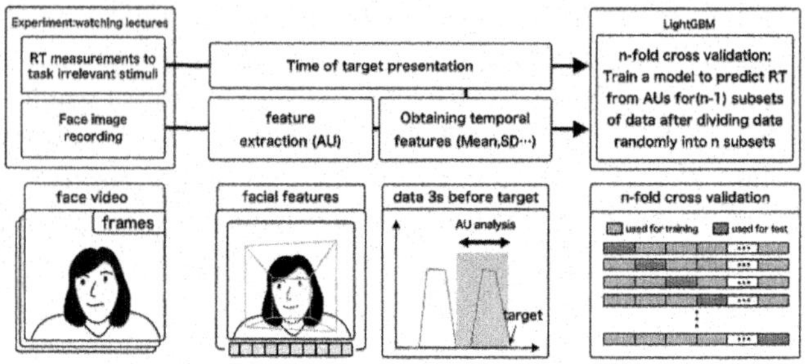

Fig. 2. Analysis of facial expressions.

4 Results

The average reaction time of all participants was 1.63 s on all lecture sessions and the standard deviation was 2.186. Since the reaction time varied among participants, we normalized the reaction time data as Z-scores after taking logarithm, which was to reduce the asymmetry in the distribution. Using the normalized values of AUs, we applied Light GBM for modeling the relationship between reaction time and facial expressions, and tested the model by the five-fold cross-validation method. Data without response within 10 s were excluded. Such target presentations were 1.03 on average.

The left side of Fig. 3 shows the relationship between the reaction time results (horizontal axis) and the prediction from Light GBM (vertical axis). Each point represents each target presentation from all sessions of all participants and different colors indicate different training-test combinations (five colors in the figure). The RMSE of data deviation from the predictions is 0.7, which is smaller than RMSE from the average, that was 1 after normalization. The correlation between data and predictions was statistically significant ($p < 0.001$, $t = 38.2$, $r = 0.716$). These results suggest that facial expressions can be used to predict the participant's reaction time to the target that was irrelevant to the contents of the lectures. We assume that reaction time to the target varies depending on attention states so that we claim that facial expressions contain useful information to estimate the level of attention while learning in lectures. That is, the prediction of reaction time, in turn, predicts the attention state during learning.

A further analysis revealed the contribution level of each AU to the prediction, that is, how much each AU is important for the prediction: Sharpley additive explanations (SHAP). Figure 3b shows the results of SHAP. AU45 (Blink), AU15 (Lip Corner Depressor) and AU7 (Lid Tightener) are the three largest contributors among all AUs. The Discussion provides consideration of why these three indexes are important.

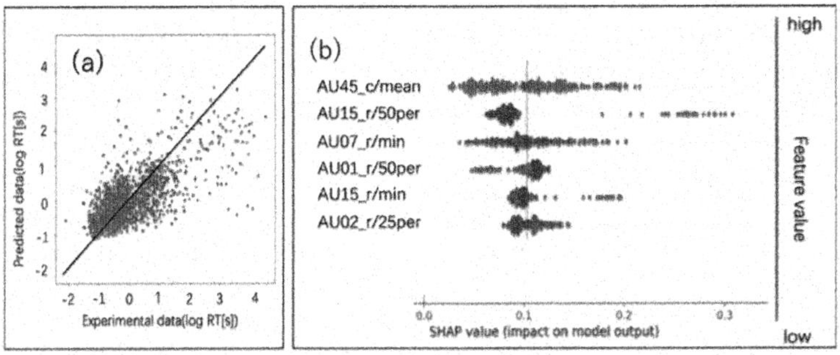

Fig. 3. (a) Correlation between measured reaction time and prediction of the model. (b) Indexes are arranged according to the level of contribution to the prediction obtained using a method (SHAP). The color, red/blue, indicates positive/negative contribution. (Color figure online)

5 Discussion

In this study, we used a machine learning technique to predict the reaction time for detecting an auditory target using facial images of participants who were watching video lectures. From the reaction time, we can infer how attentive a person is: a slower response suggests that the person is highly attentive to the lecture, paying less attention to the target. We identified facial features that contribute the most to the prediction, which are the action units of AU45 (Blink), AU15 (Lip Corner Depressor), and AU7 (Lid Tightener). We speculate the reasons why they are important features to predict reaction time. Blinks are known to be related to task given [9], and our results suggest that attention states could be estimated from blink. AU15 (Lip Corner Depressor) may be related to the condition where a person feels difficulty or confusion to understand the lecture and tries to attend more to the lecture. AU7 (Lid Tightener) may be related to sleepiness because the brow corners are tense when people are sleepy. These speculations may be valid, but further investigation is required with a larger number of participants to clarify the issue, since there are significant individual differences for the AUs of largest contribution. We should be cautious about generalizing the present results.

The assumption of reaction time and attention to the lecture could be too simplified. Longer reaction time to the target can be due to lowering the general arousal level, for example, instead of stronger attention to the lecture. In our control condition, participants were asked to detect the target without paying attention to the video lecture. This reaction time can be considered as reaction time with full attention to the target detection. The average reaction time across all participants was 0.68 s for the two control sessions.

The time is much shorter than 1.63 s, which is average reaction time of lecture sessions. Although this does not deny the possible influence of change in arousal level on the reaction time for lecture sessions, reaction time to the target can be a good measure to estimate attention level to the lectures. We also analyzed the results removing data of sessions where participants appeared to be sleepy. By watching the face videos of all sessions of all participants, the first author judged whether each session might have been influenced by sleepiness or not. The similar prediction performance was obtained for the data to the original results, suggesting that sleepiness or arousal level is not major factors of reaction time variation. Since this was an unofficial attempt, we do not conclude that the arousal level did not influence the present results. Only further investigation can make the issue clearer. Indeed, an analysis of the reaction time change with the progress of the lecture during a session showed a trend of increase in reaction time as the lecture progressed. This may indicate attention changes following the progress of a lecture toward the direction of reducing attention, which may be interpreted by change of arousal level or effect of sleepiness.

In conclusion, we have developed a method to evaluate attention state using facial expressions of learners. This method can be used to improve education quality when learners' face images are available, such as during online lectures.

References

1. Shioiri, S., Sato, Y., Horaguchi, Y., Muraoka, H., Nihei, M.: Quali-informatics in the society with yotta scale data. In: 2021 IEEE International Symposium on Circuits and Systems (ISCAS), pp. 1–4 (2021)
2. Sato, Y., Horaguchi, Y., Vanel, L., Shioiri, S.: Prediction of image preferences from spontaneous facial expressions. Interdiscip. Inf. Sci. **28**(1), 45–53 (2022)
3. Horaguchi, Y., Sato, Y., Shioiri, S.: Estimation of preferences to images by facial expression analysis. IEICE Tech. Rep. **120**(306), HIP2020-67, 71–76 (2020)
4. Thomas, C., Jayagopi, D.B.: Predicting student engagement in classrooms using facial behavioral cues. In: Proceedings of 1st ACM SIGCHI International Workshop on Multimodal Interaction for Education, pp. 33–40. ACM, New York (2017)
5. https://www.youtube.com/watch?v=uVaOzQLxXt0. Accessed 02 Oct 2022
6. Baltrušaitis, T., Robinson, P., Morency, L.P.: OpenFace: an open source facial behavior analysis toolkit. In: 2016 IEEE Winter Conference on Applications of Computer Vision (WACV), pp. 1–10. IEEE, New York (2016)
7. Ekman, P., Friesen, V.W.: The Facial Action Coding System: A Technique for The Measurement of Facial Movement. Consulting Psychologists Press, San Francisco (1978)
8. https://lightgbm.readthedocs.io/. Accessed 02 Oct 2022
9. Doughty, M.J.: Consideration of three types of spontaneous eyeblink activity in normal humans: during reading and video display terminal use, in primary gaze, and while in conversation. Optom. Vis. Sci. **78**(10), 712–725 (2001)

Development of Education Curriculum in the Data Science Area for a Liberal Arts University

Zhihua Zhang(✉), Toshiyuki Yamamoto, and Koji Nakajima

Kansai University of International Studies, Kobe, Hyogo 650-0006, Japan
{z-zhang,to-yamamoto,kj-nakajima}@kuins.ac.jp

Abstract. Data Science has emerged as a field that will revolutionize science and industry. The development of human resources for Data Science has become an urgent issue in every aspect of the digitizing society. However, a curriculum to meet the needs in such a digitizing society is not available to higher education in Japan, especially in the realm of liberal arts. In response to the situation required of the approved program for Mathematics, Data Science, and AI Smart Higher education (MDASH), we proposed a conceptual curriculum model for the Data Science education program, which systematically incorporates the knowledge module of Data Science while remedying the weakness in the basic math skills and barriers to be considered in the process of learning Data Science concepts. This paper aims to propose an integrated curriculum based on the conceptual model for the faculty members in a small-sized private liberal arts university, where students lack basic math skills, IT skills, and the basic knowledge of Data Science. Issues consisting of curriculum on knowledge areas and subjects, implementation approach of Data Science education courses, and fusion of Data Science with expertise education are discussed. A sample course will be showcased at the end.

Keywords: Conceptual Curriculum Model · Curriculum Development · Data Science Education · Liberal Arts University · Stage-wised Refinement Model

1 Introduction

With the advancement of advanced information technology, work across nearly all domains is becoming more data-driven in society, where various kinds of data are generated and relatively easy to obtain. It is required to utilize these data to create new value. Digital transformation is also being promoted speedily in all industries so that new digital technologies can be used to develop new business models. In various fields of social, industrial, and business situations, problem-solving based on the existence of big data is emphasized. Therefore, there is an urgent need to develop human resources who own mathematical thinking ability and data analysis/utilization ability and who can create value and solve problems based on this, in addition to specialized education, in each field of humanities or science. Today, as more data and ways of analyzing them

Published by Springer Nature Switzerland AG 2023
T. Keane et al. (Eds.): WCCE 2022, IFIP AICT 685, pp. 349–360, 2023.
https://doi.org/10.1007/978-3-031-43393-1_32

become available, more aspects of the economy, society, and daily life will become further dependent on data. Educators, administrators, and students must start now to consider how to best prepare for and keep pace with this data-driven era of tomorrow [1].

In response to the situation required of MDASH, which is an approved program for Mathematics, Data Science, and AI Smart Higher education, an accredited education program promoted by the Japanese Ministry of Education, Culture, Sports, Science and Technology, universities nationwide are actively developing their own mathematical, Data Science, and AI education curriculums [2]. On the other hand, a literacy level and applied level model curriculum formulated by the Inter-University Consortium for Mathematics and Data Science Education is limited to about four credits each. Here, to secure the opportunity for all university students to take courses, it has no choice but to enroll in common basic education, even when considering securing teachers in charge of classes due to academic arrangement [3].

In general, data scientists need to acquire knowledge of mathematics and statistics, IT, especially programming skills, and domain expertise, and the range are wide. In addition, there are systematic patterns due to the remarkable difference in difficulty, but the ones that are suitable for liberal arts college students are not organized. Whether it is possible to realize a systematic curriculum model that comprehensively considers "knowledge module", "implementation approach" and "barriers to be considered" in the lesson design of Data Science Education at a private university of liberal arts.

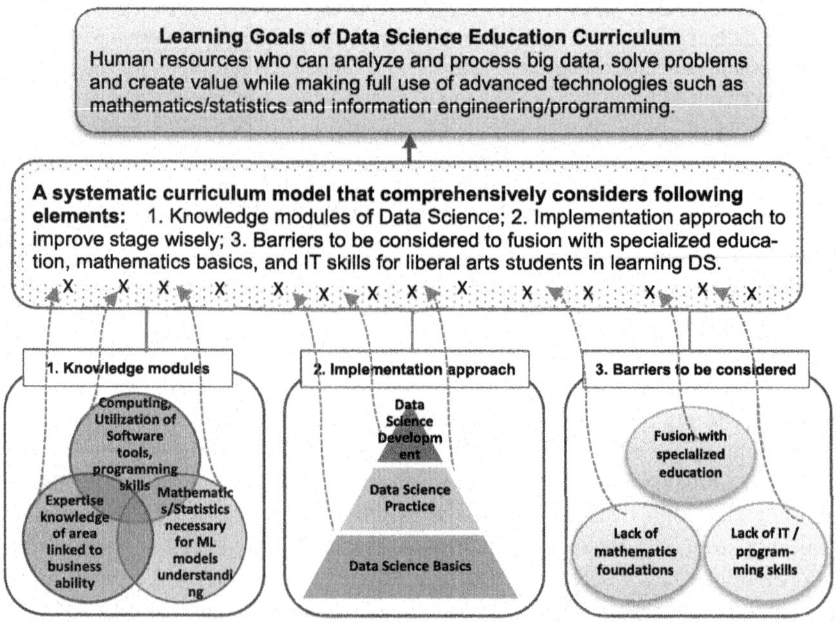

Fig. 1. Academic questions about the systematic curriculum model.

Here, we proposed a conceptual diagram (model) of curriculum design for our university's Data Science education program (see Fig. 1).

In this conceptual model, firstly, we define the learning contents of Data Science as the relevant "knowledge modules"; secondly, we define the educational "implementation approach" as the learning stage that is step-wised refinement from simple to complex; finally, the "barriers to be considered" for liberal arts students, such as the characteristics of weak mathematical knowledge, insufficient basic information skills and programming skills, and how to integrate Data Science education into the education of their major field knowledge in teaching and other considerations, to achieve a systematic Data Science teaching plan for liberal arts college students. These are the academical questions about the systematics curriculum model we defined.

2 Knowledge Area and Subjects of Data Science Education Curriculum

2.1 Knowledge Area of Data Science Education

Data Science is a growing field of study that combines discipline expertise, computer programming skills, and knowledge of mathematics and statistics to derive meaningful insights from the data. Moreover, Data Science experts should apply machine learning algorithms to numbers, texts, images, videos, audio, and more to build artificial intelligence (AI) systems that can perform tasks that require human intelligence. Because it has become possible to handle big data efficiently, Data Science is creating a lot of new opportunities, not only in business but in other contexts. In Data Science, we can easily get valuable insights into business models and consumer behavior in e-commerce through data analysis. However, when it comes to visualizing and combining data, it can be challenging to interpret the results in a way that is useful for the business. Therefore, it's important for students to learn how to practically apply their Data Science knowledge to tackle these challenges effectively.

However, despite being used as a general term covering multiple disciplines, Data Science is difficult to define. The definition from Drew Conway's Venn diagram (2013) [4], consists of the knowledge of substantive expertise, mathematics and statistics, and computer and programming technology. The Japan Data Scientist Association talks about the qualities of the Data Science skillset required as a data scientist with the following three powers. 1) Business problem solving: Ability to organize and solve business problems after understanding the background of the problem; 2) Data Science: Information science for instance information processing, artificial intelligence, and statistics. And the ability to understand and implement and operate Data Science in a meaningful way; 3) Data engineering: Ability to use, implement, and operate Data Science in a meaningful way.

On the other hand, the ACM's Computing Competencies for Undergraduate Data Science Curricula [5] is intended to materialize the knowledge and skills required for the purpose of majoring in Data Science, including engineering courses. In the report of the National Academies of US for the undergraduate education in Data Science [1], the following points were made: The new majors and minors will begin by integrating components from established courses, specifically in the areas of computer science, statistics, business analytics, information technology, optimization, applied mathematics, and numerical computing. But this research is intended for Data Science literacy education purposes in common basic subjects. The two have some things in common, but they are not necessarily the same. Our emphasis is on targeting lower-grade liberal arts colleges who are weak in mathematics and ICT skills.

The knowledge modules designed in this research include basics of statistics, use of software tools, basics of data analysis, as well as students' acquisition of critical thinking and presentation skills. It becomes possible to select and combine these knowledge modules while combining them with specialized knowledge that leads to business practice, making the construction of the syllabus more flexible.

2.2 Subjects Related to the Knowledge Area

Based on the knowledge area classification of the above Data Science education courses, we have designed the corresponding related subjects, which are detailed below.

Area I, Basic Statistics and Its Utilization: Area I consists of the three subjects shown in Table 1. It is mainly about the foundations of mathematics/statistics skills.

Table 1. "Data Science Education Curriculum" the Area I Subjects

Subject name	Contents	Credit
Basic Statistics A	A subject related to basic knowledge for reading official statistics, simple research reports, and fieldwork dissertations. Educational content includes how to read descriptive statistical data such as simple tabulation, frequency distribution, representative value, dispersal degree, cross-tabulation, and correlation coefficient; how to read graphs, and how to calculate and create them	2
Basic Statistics B	A subject on the basic knowledge of inference statistics necessary for compiling and analyzing statistical data. Educational content includes basics of probability and probability distribution, population and sample, basic statistics and its properties, test/estimation theory and its application, and basics of regression analysis	2
Introduction to Research	A subject about acquiring basic knowledge and skills on qualitative and quantitative research, tabulation, and analysis. Specific survey methods, observation surveys, interview surveys, and questionnaire surveys will be taken up, and the basics of the survey will be acquired in an exercise format	1

Area II, ICT and Programming Skills: Area II consists of the three subjects shown in Table 2. It is mainly about Area II is about ICT and Data Science basics on utilization of software tools and programming skills.

Table 2. "Data Science Education Curriculum" the Area II Subjects

Subject name	Contents	Credit
ICT Literacy	The purpose is to familiarize yourself with how to use data analysis using Excel or R using BYOD and to give lectures and exercises on the basics of data analysis and basic techniques of data visualization	2
Utilization of ICT A	The purpose is to familiarize yourself with how to use Python and R language and programming technology using a personal computer and to give lectures and exercises on the basics of analysis using actual data and basic techniques of data visualization	2
Data Science	Learn about changes occurring in society, technologies for data and AI utilization, social impact, and the latest trends of it. In part of data literacy, students will learn the basic techniques of DS, such as reading data, explaining data, and handling data. In addition, the introduction on ELSI, GDPR, AI ethics and threats, and utilization of data and AI as points to consider when dealing with data and AI	2

Area III, Basics of Big Data and AI Evolving Subjects on Problem-Solving: Area III consists of the three subjects shown in Table 3. Area III is for the programming practice techniques and the basics of IoT, big data, and AI evolving subjects in the basics of problem-solving content.

3 Implementation Approach of the Data Science Education Courses

Using Data Science and artificial intelligence technology to solve practical problems in the business field is an extremely complicated process. It concerns variously skilled Data Science professionals with diverse technical and business backgrounds. Also, it is multiple tasks across the Data Science life cycle. According to the data analysis model (CRISP-DM), a standard cross-industry data analysis process includes six items:

1) Understanding of business: This is to understand the situation and issues of on-site business and set project goals. It is essential to have the ability to accurately grasp the business situation numerically from the marketer's point of view and select themes.
2) Understanding of data: This is to examine whether the data is available. For instance, to investigate data items, quantities, quality, etc. Often, it includes outliers and missing values. Ability to make data available is required.
3) Data preparation: As a pre-processing for mining, the usable data is shaped into data suitable for analysis. It includes tasks such as missing value processing, data type maintenance, normalization, sampling, etc.

Table 3. "Data Science Education Curriculum" the Area III Subjects

Subject name	Contents	Credit
Data Science Theory	For beginners in programming, the R language is easier to understand. For this reason, R is useful in statistical processing that aims to analyze data and explain something based on the results. In this course, students will acquire practical DS skills through R language programming techniques, involvement with Data Science, data analysis, and visualization of actual problems	2
Data Science Practice Exercise	Python is a simple, readable, and versatile programming language. Python has abundant libraries in all fields such as statistical analysis of data, AI application/machine learning, and IoT data utilization, and is used in a wide range of application fields. This subject is to learn the basic knowledge of Python, deepen the understanding of algorithms through Python programming, and learn how to utilize typical APIs and services	2
Basics of Artificial Intelligence	Learn basic technologies of information system engineering such as algorithm/data structure, information security, information communication network, and artificial intelligence related to the characteristics of big data and the utilization of AI. Introductory level engineering knowledge subjects. Content created by external organizations (MOOC, etc.) may be used	2

4) Modeling: The ability of model creation or method selection is required. It includes correlation analysis, regression analysis, market basket analysis, cluster analysis, genetic algorithm (GA), decision tree, etc.
5) Evaluation: Evaluate from a business perspective whether the model is sufficient to achieve well-defined business goals.
6) Implementation: Make concrete plans to apply the results of data mining to a specific business field and take concrete actions to achieve the set goals.

Many companies have had considerable difficulty in developing human resources with these abilities. Most of the time, the first introduction to Data Science was successful, but it could not have a holistic view of where to start in subsequent practice and advanced problem-solving. For students to have such abilities, it is essential to have a PBL-type lesson using actual data after understanding the basics of statistics and mathematics, an introduction to Data Science, basic program languages and programming techniques, etc.

To carry out Data Science education smoothly, and let the Data Science talent training course succeed, we proposed a Stage-wised Refinement Model in the Data Science education program according to the defined educational implementation approach in the conceptual model [6].

As shown in Fig. 2, it consists of four stages from bottom to top as pillars that support the educational curriculum of Data Science at our university. The difference from the conceptual model is the addition of "Stage 0: Invitation to Data Science". This is a result of consideration given to the lack of basic mathematics and ICT skills at liberal arts universities.

The other three stages are: Stage 1- Data Science basics; Stage 2- Data Science practice; and Stage 3-Data Science development, respectively, which will be described below in detail.

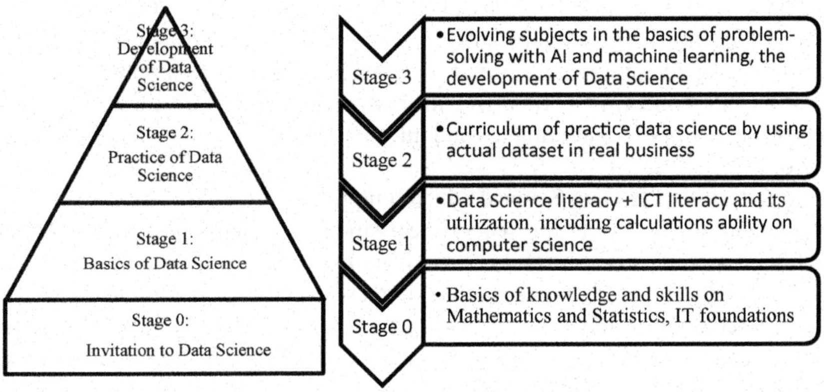

Fig. 2. Concept of Stage-wised Refinement Model in Data Science education program.

Stage 1: Basics of Data Science, the contents include the Data Science literacy corresponding to the points of introduction in the consortium model curriculum, in addition, to ICT literacy skills including the ability of calculation in computer science.
Stage 2: Practice of Data Science, the contents include the practice of Data Science by using actual datasets in real business or simulation with a specific domain application. Learn how to handle data and databases for liberal arts students and analyze data using statistical analysis software R or entry of programming language Python.
Stage 3: Development of Data Science, the contents include evolving subjects in the basics of problem-solving with AI and machine learning. Learn how to perform machine learning using actual data by using Python or R programming language, AI tools, etc. If it is possible, take it to PBL education that practices problem-solving and value creation.
Stage 0: Invitation to Data Science, the contents include the basics of knowledge and skills in Mathematics and Statistics which is purposed to clear the hurdles for liberal arts students in Data Science study.

For liberal arts students, the foundations of mathematics (including statistics) are indispensable for Data Science to study Data Science literacy level in the future, to take future developmental curriculum, and to acquire problem-solving ability beyond literacy level. It is necessary to have a minimum of strength in the foundations of mathematics, as well as IT (including programming) skills.

The ultimate purpose of Data Science is to provide an academic basis for making rational decisions in the business field, etc., based on the analyzed data. Thus, Data Science is closely related to the basics of mathematics and IT skills an inseparable field. That is why we add "Stage 0: Invitation to Data Science" to the Stage-wised Refinement Model shown in Fig. 2.

4 Barriers to be Considered on the Implementation Approach

4.1 Problems of Lack of Mathematics Basics and Information Technology Skills

In the framework developed by Conway [4], the Data Science education curriculum consists of the knowledge of substantive expertise, mathematics/statistics, computer, and programming technology, etc. First, one starting point is to assume a curriculum organization that conforms to this. But in this process, it is hard to say that the student's learning history of mathematics and information subjects in high school was fully considered.

The university-wide Data Science education program presented in this paper is primarily intended for first year and second-year students at liberal arts universities. At a private liberal arts university such as our university, where most of the students are not good at mathematics and IT basics, even if literacy level mathematics and Data Science education are conducted, the basic ability of students' mathematics and information will be a big challenge. In some cases, you may also need remedial education in mathematics and IT foundations in junior high school and high school.

To solve this problem, we are newly constructing basic mathematics content for Data Science education for college students in the liberal arts, which will be developed by on-demand learning. In other words, we decided to develop learning content that utilizes Python programming and corresponds to the middle and high school math knowledge modules that are indispensable for Data Science learning.

As an effect of this effort, it is expected to be foundational research of the Data Science education curriculum model, which is a field under development in the practice of Data Science education. Remedial education of mathematics basics and IT basics necessary for implementing the Data Science education curriculum at the university can be smoothly realized, and it is expected to contribute to the implementation of educational content suitable for the actual situation of students and the guarantee of Data Science education quality. From the perspectives of teachers and students, the following advantages are noted:

Teacher

- On-campus resources in Data Science education and programming education for liberal arts students will be available.
- Teachers in the field of education can provide learning opportunities with the teaching materials of this project for the problems of students' foundations of mathematics and ICT literacy.

Student

- Overcome the consciousness that students are not good at mathematics before taking Data Science. It will be an opportunity to improve the IT literacy and programming skills of students and they will be able to keep up with the learning of Data Science.
- Become able to understand the basic mathematics and the basics of IT literacy that was lacking in high school.
- The mindset of Data Science will be the cornerstone of lifelong learning.

4.2 Problem of the Fusion of Data Science Education with Substantive Expertise Education

Another problem with the practice of Data Science education is how to deal with the relationship between Data Science education and expertise education in each major. Discussions held above are under the policy of promoting the concreteness of curriculum as a pillar in the framework of Conway. It turns out that at least "expertise" is lacking in the latter. However, considering that Data Science education is positioned as a university-wide education that goes beyond that framework, apart from expertise education, it is natural to think that "expertise knowledge" is educated in the specialized field of each faculty to which it belongs.

But can we become data scientists in a specialized field without expertise and fusion with Data Science? The answer to this question is no, and it can be said that education on thinking and processes that lead to value creation by comprehensively utilizing the knowledge and background cultivated in each field is indispensable.

Almost common at many faculties, there is a need for human resources who can analyze data scientifically with a deep understanding of their expertise field data. For that purpose, education is aimed at acquiring the ability to utilize data based on the "expertise knowledge". Therefore, regarding the introductory education in the proposed systematic curriculum model, first, Data Science is centered on the utilization of big data to understand the image of Data Science that utilizes the three elements of mathematics/statistics, information technology, and specialized knowledge. However, we have prepared "Data Science" and "Utilization of ICT A" as the entry subjects to provide the lecture on what is the brought about in solving social problems, including case studies if necessary.

We think that the most significant background to acquire in practicing Data Science is not just the skill to master the software tools and the data processing method. But the imagination and creativity to envision value creation on site. Generally, data acquisition is costly, so it is important to emphasize what can be done by using data and clearly show the usefulness of acquiring and accumulating data.

Therefore, we designed neatly what kind of data is likely to be obtained in what form in the area targeted for problem-solving, and what kind of value can be created by utilizing it. Subjects at the stage of "Data Science development" in the Stage-wised Refinement Model, need to be done in connection with specialized knowledge education. The essence of Data Science education is to develop the ability to systematically explain, but the key is how to deepen the experience. And it is considered effective to incorporate PBL (Project Based Learning), which deals with practical issues in collaboration with the real site, into the curriculum, although it is commonplace.

In addition, subjects such as computer science, business analysis, information technology, applied mathematics, and mathematical calculation are also essential in the common curriculum. Further discussion is necessary on these issues in the future.

5 Course Structure and Qualification Certification

From this academic year, we started the university-wide Data Science Education Program at the Kansai University of International Studies (KUISs). As a case study, the course structure of the education program is designed based on the proposed systematic curriculum model that is necessary to comprehensively develop the subjects on computer and information system knowledge, statistics-related skills, domain knowledge of specific fields. At the same time, we focus on developing students' problem-solving, critical thinking, communication and presentation skills.

The practice work performed mainly considers two aspects. First one is to systematize the relationships between the subjects while standardizing the contents of the subjects that are currently being implemented. Second one is going to award a "Data Science Education Curriculum Certificate" by acquiring the prescribed credits from the group subjects (see Fig. 3), for the purpose of encouraging students to actively participate in Data Science education programs.

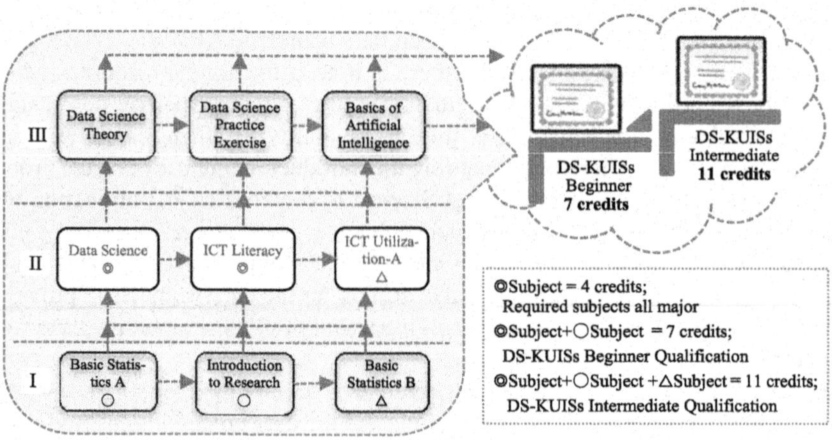

Fig. 3. Course structure and qualification certification at KUISs.

Each subject in the subject group I, II, and III as shown in Fig. 3 corresponds to the three category-level subjects described in the knowledge area of Sect. 2. This is the Course Structure and Qualification Certification of the Data Science Education Program at KUISs. Here, the symbol of double circle ◎ means the compulsory subjects, the circle ○ means the elective subjects, and the triangle △ means the recommended subjects. In this program, students acquire the target certification program by taking a combination of three category-level courses. If they got a certain number of credits, they should be qualified for Data Science.

Curriculum subjects including Area I and Area II are called DS-KUISs beginner, while Area III is reached are called DS-KUISs Intermediate. If a student has completed the prescribed four subjects from it with 7 credits, he/she will be reached the "Data Science Education Curriculum Beginner's level". If for DS-KUISs Intermediate, he/she should complete the prescribed six subjects with 11 credits and will be recognized as the "Data Science Education Curriculum Intermediate level".

6 Conclusion

As an umbrella term, Data Science includes a broad range of theories, algorithms, methodologies, and software tools that help us to use datasets to understand and solve problems in the real world. The knowledge area of Data Science also widely includes mathematics/statistics, programming skills, data management techniques, and in some cases, machine learning models and algorithms generally used in the sciences, engineering, humanities, education, medicine, and business. In addition, due to the rapid development of digital transformation in society, there is an urgent need to develop human resources who have mathematical thinking ability and data analysis/utilization ability and who can create value and solve problems based on this, in addition to specialized education in each field, regardless of whether it is humanities or science.

We have proposed a conceptual curriculum model for Data Science education program, which systematically considered the knowledge module related to Data Science learning and the implementation approach as an educational method. The discussions take place within the framework of promoting curriculum specificity and implement ability. As a case study, this paper discussed the development of a curriculum for Data Science education at a liberal arts university. However, this is a result of the fact that Data Science education is positioned as university-wide education that transcends that framework, apart from specialized education.

To ensure that the educational program runs smoothly, it is expected to contribute to the implementation of educational content suitable for the actual situation of students of liberal arts for the guarantee of Data Science education quality. That is the discussion on clear the barriers of liberal arts students and the problem of the fusion of Data Science education with substantive expertise education. The essence of Data Science education is to develop the ability to systematically explain, but the key is how to deepen the experience. It is considered effective to incorporate PBL-based learning, which deals with practical issues in collaboration with real business site problems.

Finally, we describe the Data Science education program starting from this year as a case study, the course structure, and the qualification certification of the Data Science education program at KUISs. As a future research topic, we plan to conduct a questionnaire survey of students regarding the actual implementation status and evaluate the courses that have been implemented. We will set up a class questionnaire and conduct the evaluation, including items such as course completion status, achievement of learning goals, attitudes toward Data Science before and after learning, and satisfaction with educational methods including active learning and on-demand learning. Then we will improve the proposed model, and let it be able to withstand the construction of a curriculum for minors in combination with existing undergraduate courses.

Acknowledgment. This work was supported by MEXT/JSPS KAKENHI Grant Numbers JP (22K02930).

References

1. NASEM: National Academies of Sciences, Engineering, and Medicine 2018. Data Science for Undergraduates: Opportunities and Options. The National Academies Press, Washington, DC (2018)
2. MEXT: "Mathematical/Data Science/AI Education Program (Literacy Level) Requirements. Open call for participants briefing materials (2021). https://warp.ndl.go.jp/info:ndljp/pid/12099644/www.mext.go.jp/content/20210305_mext_senmon01-000012801_1.pdf. Accessed 20 Apr 2021
3. JIUC. The Japan Inter-University Consortium for Mathematics and Data Science Education, Mathematics/Data Science/AI (literacy level) Model curriculum. http://www.mi.u-tokyo.ac.jp/consortium/model_literacy.html. Accessed 20 Mar 2020
4. Conway, D.: The data science Venn diagram (2013). http://drewconway.com/zia/2013/3/26/the-data-science-venn-diagram. Accessed 01 Mar 2020
5. ACM Data Science Task Force: Computing competencies for undergraduate data science curricula (2021). https://dl.acm.org/doi/book/10.1145/3453538
6. Zhang, Z.: A study of digital transformation human resources development and data science education programs at a private liberal arts university. Bull. Kansai Univ. Int. Stud. Res. Ser. **15**, 163–175 (2022)
7. Zhang, Z.: The development of new information technology and necessity of data science education. Bull. Sanyo Women's Coll. **41**, 1–20 (2020)
8. Cabinet Office Japan: AI Strategy 2019 -AI for all people, industry, regions, and governments-, Integrated Innovation Strategy Promotion Council Decision (2019). https://warp.ndl.go.jp/info:ndljp/pid/12251721/www.kantei.go.jp/jp/singi/ai_senryaku/pdf/aistratagy2019.pdf. Accessed 11 Dec 2021
9. Krensky, P., et al.: Magic Quadrant for Data Science and Machine Learning Platforms (2021). https://www.gartner.com/en/documents/3998753. Accessed 24 Feb 2022
10. Ross, J.: The Digital Challenge: How to Transform Your Business in the Midst of Crisis, MIT Industrial Liaison Program Webinar Series. https://ilp.mit.edu/watch/2020-digital-transformation-jeanne-ross. Accessed 27 Apr 2020
11. The recommendations of the Science Council of Japan, Training of Human Resources for the Big Data Era (2014). https://www.scj.go.jp/ja/info/kohyo/pdf/kohyo-22-t198-2.pdf
12. Matsuo, T., Tamada, K.: Issues in data science education at liberal arts and private universities. Bull. Edogawa Univ. **31**, 249–255 (2021)
13. ASA. Curriculum Guidelines for Undergraduate Programs in Statistical Science (2014). https://www.amstat.org/asa/files/pdfs/EDU-guidelines2014-11-15.pdf
14. UCI Data Science Initiative. http://datascience.uci.edu/about/. Accessed 25 Nov 2020

Educational Data Mining in Prediction of Students' Learning Performance: A Scoping Review

Chunping Li[1(✉)], Mingxi Li[1], Chuan-Liang Huang[2], Yi-Tong Tseng[1], Soo-Hyung Kim[3], and Soonja Yeom[1]

[1] University of Tasmania, Hobart, Australia
{Chunping.Li,Mingxil,Tsengyt,Soonja.Yeom}@utas.edu.au
[2] National Chung Hsing University, Taichung City, Taiwan
Lin210346@gmail.com
[3] Chonnam National University, Gwangju, South Korea
Shkim@chonman.ac.kr

Abstract. Students' academic achievement is always a target of concern for educational institutions. Nowadays, the rapid development of digital transformation has resulted in huge amounts of data being generated by Learning Management Systems. The deployment of Educational Data Mining (EDM) is becoming increasingly significant in discovering ways to improve student learning outcomes. Those approaches effectively facilitate dealing with students' massive amounts of data. The purpose of this review is to evaluate and discuss the state-of-art EDM for predicting students' learning performance among higher education institutions. A scoping review was conducted on twelve peer-reviewed publications that were indexed in ACM, IEEE Xplore, Science Direct and Scopus between 2012 and 2021. This study comprehensively reviewed the final inclusion literature on EDM in terms of tools, techniques, machine learning algorithms and application schemes. We have found that WEKA (tool) and classification (technique) were chosen in most of the selected studies carried out in their EDM settings. This review suggested that Tree Structured algorithms as supervised learning approaches can better predict students' learning performance, as it has been validated in several comparative analyses of other algorithms. In the present study, we demonstrate a future trend toward improving the generalizability of prediction models that can deal with a diverse population and the predictive results can be easily interpreted and explained by educators in the general market.

Keywords: Student Learning Performance · Data Mining · EDM · Machine Learning · Algorithms

T. Keane et al. (Eds.): WCCE 2022, IFIP AICT 685, pp. 361–372, 2023.
https://doi.org/10.1007/978-3-031-43393-1_33

1 Introduction

In the era of Big Data, scientists and engineers have developed data mining techniques and algorithms to transform the data into understandable information [1]. Data mining improves efficiency, predicts future trends, and makes more informed operational decisions. This method can be used in many fields, especially universities because students' success is crucial for higher education. Moreover, higher educational institutions collect large amounts of data from their students, staff, and organisational system. Then, the data is transferred to information by the application of Educational Data Mining (EDM), which higher institutions can use to improve instructional and intervention strategies. EDM can be applied to various fields; it can be used to predict academic performance, assist instructors, recognise struggling students, improve online learning systems, etc.

This paper focuses on predicting students' academic performance through different methods of algorithms and techniques because it can figure out the possible challenges of students and guide students' career possibilities. Student academic performance is always a target of concern among educational institutions. EDM has been proven to be one of the useful methods to analyse educational data and then evaluate the performance of students [2, 3]. Fortunately, most scholars from different fields have been studying and developing techniques to improve students' learning performance, and this review provides one part of a solution to improve student learning outcomes by discussing the authors' points of view in detail and eventually identifying some effective analytical techniques.

EDM is becoming increasingly significant in discovering ways to improve student learning performance. Many scholars have undertaken their research and analysis on identifying the effective methods of students using such methods [4]. However, the employment, as well as the application, of educational data mining methods are still not getting enough attention. Most of higher educational institutions commonly increase their interest in further improving their academic quality [5]. Educational data, such as the student learning activities, objectives, preferences, participation, learning marks, and achievement, is found to impact students' performance and outcome [6, 7].

Therefore, the purpose of this review is to provide insights into the implementation of EDM in higher education by analysing currently published research outcomes to analyse and discover how EDM can be used to predict students' performance with higher predictive accuracy. Higher educational institutions can deploy this recommended EDM method to predict students' learning in the future.

2 Background

Academic achievement is a huge concern for institutions of higher learning around the world. Massive amounts of learning and teaching data are generated through the use of learning management systems [4]. Institutions can deploy data mining methods to improve students' learning performance by making better decisions, planning better directions for students, predicting future trends and individual behaviour, and maximising resources.

The benefit of applying EDM in the higher education domain has been well documented in recent research [2, 8–10]. Data mining methods were used to assist academic performance in two primary categories: prediction and detection of undesirable learning outcomes. Most of the studies in this review focused on predicting students' grades, achievement or performance based on historical data (personal, educational, behavioural, and extra-curricular features); while Dabhade et al. [11] indicate that the involvement of behavioural data would increase the accuracy for the prediction of results. This statement could be the cause of the behavioural features consisting of traits related to students' learning process [12]. Some studies developed models based on data mining techniques on learning behaviour analytics to discover students' undesirable learning patterns or poor learning habits. The importance of the pattern of studying activity and learning habits is highlighted in EDM, which provides instructors with useful information related to students' acceptance of the current curriculum and learning behaviour. With the assistance of EDM, adaptive learning materials can promptly be developed for students, helping to correct study habits, improving academic performance, and facilitating students' learning [6]. The possible reason for the lack of research in this aspect is the differentiation in chosen parameters for data mining algorithms. In addition, there is a steep cost involved in implementing data mining tools and techniques because they deal with vast amounts of data [13].

This scoping paper is an attempt to gain insight into more learning challenges that prior studies have not been able to address as well as the effective methods to improve students' learning from the ICT perspective. Data mining techniques and algorithms are used primarily for two schemes: prediction analytics (dropout, grade, and achievement) and learning behaviour analytics (learning pattern and behaviour). In most selected studies, predictive functions were utilised to suggest ways to enhance students' performance and learn better in academic achievement.

3 Methodology

This review aims to explore the implementation and performance of educational data mining methods in predicting students' learning performance. Hence, this scoping review was conducted in order to provide answers to the following two research questions:

Research Question 1: *What are the typical tools involved in EDM settings for predicting student performance?*
Research Question 2: *In student performance prediction studies, which data mining approaches and algorithms are mostly employed with high accuracy?*

3.1 Search Protocol

The scoping review was conducted to answer research questions based on PRISMA-ScR guidelines [14]. Based on the research question, search terms were selected to reflect the broad scope of the review. The same search strategy was used in both databases: ((educational data mining) OR (data mining)) AND ((student performance) OR (student outcome)) AND ((higher education) OR (university)). At the initial search stage, filters were used to limit articles written in English and published between 2012 to 2021.

Four international databases of authoritative academic resources were used to search for relevant studies, which are the Association for Computing Machinery (ACM) Digital Library, ScienceDirect, Institute of Electrical and Electronics Engineers (IEEE) Xplore and Scopus. The article selection process was detailed in Fig. 1. Two hundred and sixty-seven (267) articles were acquired after removing duplicates. Followed by screening of title and abstracts and full-text articles based on selection criteria, a total of twelve (12) articles were included in this scoping review.

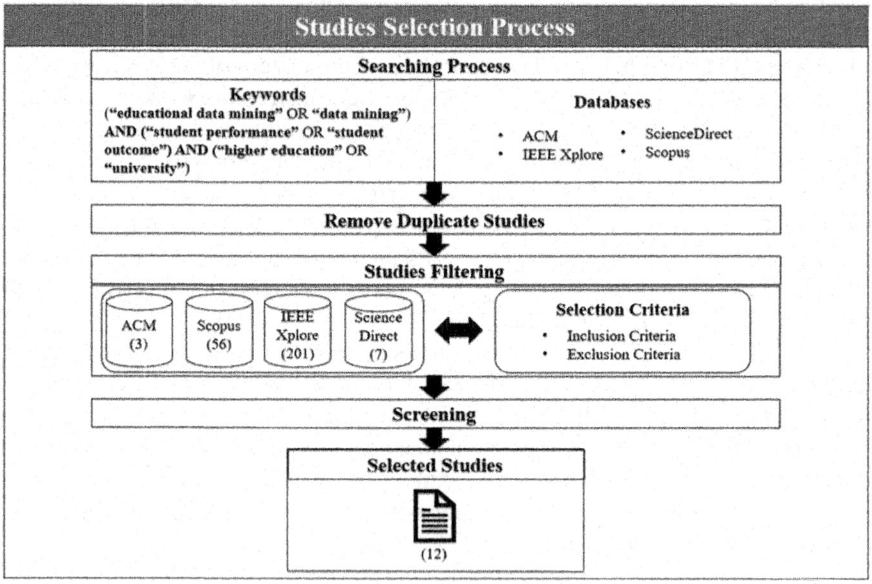

Fig. 1. Flow of article selection process following PRISMA-ScR guidelines.

3.2 Selection Criteria

Inclusion Criteria. After the pre-screening process, the consideration of the advanced filters of paper selection was applied based on the employ of EDM methods, which are the clarity of the finding and the accuracy of the result. The inclusion of criteria to determine the relevant literature are listed below:

- Studies that were published from 2012 to 2021.
- Studies that were written in English.
- Studies that were peer-reviewed publications in journal or conference.
- Studies related to the usage of data mining techniques in students' learning performance prediction.
- Studies that clearly described the setting of EDM.
- Algorithms were applied in predicting learning performance along with empirical research evidence.

- Comparable prediction evaluation indicators were provided based on more than one applied algorithm.

Exclusion Criteria. Furthermore, the following criteria were used to exclude literature that is considered unsuitable for this review:

- Studies were published before 2012.
- Studies were written in language other than English.
- Studies were not providing a clear description of the use of methods/algorithms/techniques of education data mining.
- Studies did not provide relevant evidence to contribute to the research questions.

4 Results

This scoping review aims to explore the techniques and algorithms to obtain an accurate performance in the prediction of students' academic learning outcomes. Twelve eligible articles were considered directly related to the research questions and were comprehensively reviewed in terms of tools, prediction approaches, algorithms and evaluation methods used in the EDM setting. A summary of the included studies is presented in Table 1.

4.1 Data Mining Framework and Tools

There are three articles that followed the framework Cross Industry Standard Process for Data Mining (CRISP-DM) [3, 18, 20]. CRISP-DM is the data mining model that deals with DM from different perspectives with the aim of increasing knowledge of the data [24].

The tools mentioned in selected studies are listed in Fig. 2, two out of twelve articles have not mentioned the tools. The most common tool used to prepare data and implement the predictive model was Waikato Environment for Knowledge Analysis (WEKA) for machine learning approaches [3, 4, 15, 18–23]. Other machine learning tools included Jupyter Notebook [11] and Orange Data Mining [20]. Data storage and pre-processing tools were MATLAB, Minitab, Microsoft SQL Server and Excel.

4.2 EDM Approaches and Algorithms

From Table 1, it is observed that supervised machine learning approaches were employed in all twelve selected studies, then followed by deep learning approaches (5 studies). There are 20 different algorithms in use in all reviewed literature, which are mainly divided into classification, regression and deep learning techniques (Fig. 3).

Classification techniques are the most frequently used, specifically, tree structured algorithms which contain normal Decision Trees [16, 17, 22], Random Forest [3, 16, 17, 22, 23], J48 [3, 15, 19–21, 23], ID3 [4, 19, 20] and CART [18, 19]. Other applied classification techniques are Naïve Bayes (NB) [3, 4, 15, 18, 21, 23] and Bayesian

Table 1. Summary table of twelve included studies.

Reference	Dataset Size	Tools	Approaches	Algorithms	Evaluation
[15]	225	WEKA	Classification, Deep Learning	NB, Bayesian Network*, ID3, J48, NN	Precision, Recall, F-Measure, Accuracy
[4]	N/A	WEKA	Classification, Deep Learning	NB, ID3*, NN, SVM	Precision, Recall, F-Measure, Accuracy
[3]	441	WEKA, SQL	Classification	Random Tree*, J48, NB, OneR, Stacking	Precision, Kappa index, Absolute Error
[16]	480	N/A	Classification, Regression	Logistic Regression*, SVR, Decision Tree, Log-LR, Random Forest, PLS-R	Mean Absolute Error, Root Mean Squared Error, R-Squared
[17]	500	N/A	Classification, Regression	LR, Decision Tree, SVM, Random Forest*	R-Squared, Mean Square Error, Root Mean Square Error
[11]	85	MS-Excel, Jupyter	Classification, Regression	MLR, SVM*	Mean Absolute Error, Mean Squared Error, Root Mean Squared Error, R-Squared
[18]	385	WEKA	Classification	NB, CART, IBK*	False positive rate, True positive rate, Accuracy
[19]	234	WEKA	Classification	ID3, J48*, CART*	Accuracy, Specificity, Precision, Recall, F-measure

(*continued*)

Table 1. (*continued*)

Reference	Dataset Size	Tools	Approaches	Algorithms	Evaluation
[20]	1374	WEKA, Orange, Minitab, MATLAB	Classification, Deep Learning	J48*, ANN	Accuracy, Root Mean Squared Error
[21]	120	WEKA	Classification, Deep Learning	NB*, J48, ML, Nearest Neighbours, SVM	Accuracy, F-measure
[22]	300	WEKA	Classification	Decision Tree*, Random Forest	Accuracy, Precision, Recall, F-measure
[23]	395	WEKA	Classification, Deep Learning	NB, MLP, J48*, Random Forest	Rescission Recall F-measure

*Denotes algorithms proven to have the best performance based on their evaluation criteria.

Fig. 2. Tools used in selected EDM studies and the number of studies.

Network [15], Support Vector Machine (SVM) [4, 11, 16, 17, 21], OneR classifier [3], Stacking [3], IBK [18] and Nearest Neighbours [21].

Regression techniques include Logistic Regression [16], Linear Regression (LR) [17], Log-Linear Regression (Log-LR) [16], Partial Least Squares Regression (PLS-R) [16], Multiple Linear Regression (MLR) [11].

Deep Learning contains Neural Network (NN) [4, 15], Artificial Neural Network (ANN) [20] and Multi-Layer Perceptron (MLP) [21, 23].

4.3 EDM Performance and Evaluation

Making a machine learning model effective depends largely on evaluating it. Different metrics were adopted in the use of model performance evaluation, which refers to the ability of the model to correctly predict student performance with the applied dataset. Table 1 illustrated the applied measures for each selected study. The algorithms' performance can be evaluated by the predictive classification accuracy (such as true positive rate, false positive rate, precision, recall, f-measure, accuracy), the error measurement (such as mean square error, relative absolute error and root relative squared error) and

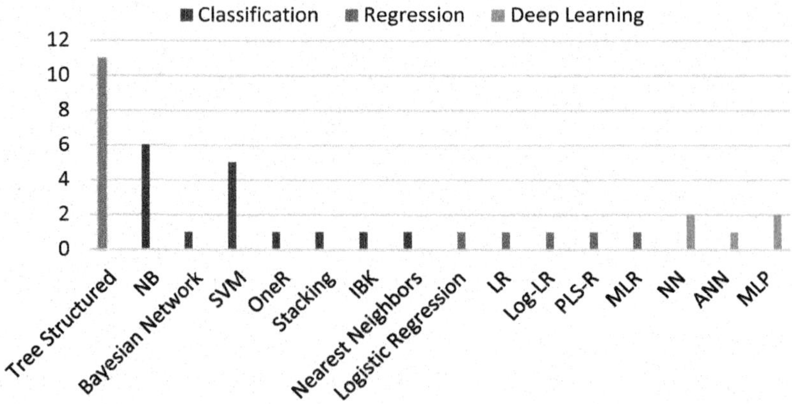

Fig. 3. Frequency of applied machine learning algorithms in EDM.

regression quality judgement (such as R-squared). Overall, performance indicators, accuracy [4, 15, 18–22], precision [3, 23] and R-squared [11, 16, 17] scores are the common measures in the comparative analysis to assess various algorithms' performance.

The paper has reviewed clearly explain how EDM is used in predicting student performance. To identify the best algorithms in data mining based on educational data, the highest value of the evaluation method was exacted for analysis. Figure 4 summarised algorithms identified with more accurate performance and better quality of the predictive model in the reviewed studies. Seven of the 12 articles identified that tree structured algorithms outperformed other algorithms. Among the tree structured method, ID3 achieved 75.47% accuracy, which is greater than 52.83% in NB, 57.47% in NN and 66.04 in SVM [4]; Random Forest had better precision (96%) [3] and R-squared (88.59%) [17]; the best accuracy was attained by J48 with 98.30% compared with ID3 [19] and 98.10% compared with ANN [20], and the most precision of 92.40% in comparison of NB, MLP and random forest (below 90%) [23]. It is worth noting that Bayesian Network has only appeared in one article, and it reached an accuracy rate of 92%, superior to other algorithms, including J48, ID3, NB and NN [15].

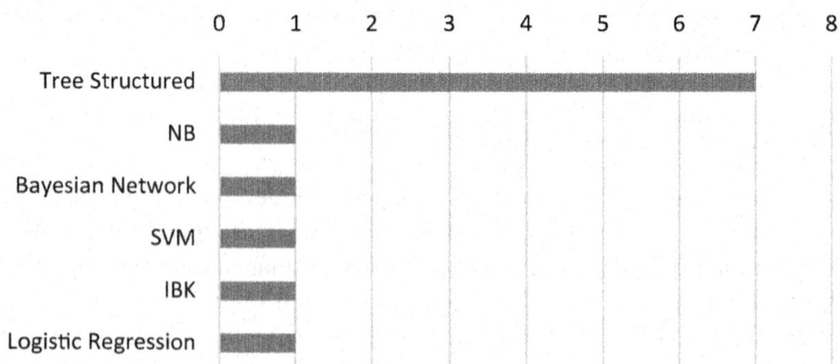

Fig. 4. The frequency of accurate algorithms identified.

5 Discussion

This paper aims to analyse and organise the methods of general techniques and algorithms usage in educational data mining and focuses on a higher accuracy rate in predicting students' learning performance. EDM methods can predict students' learning performance and refine academic decision-making for educational institutions.

Research Question 1: *What are the typical tools involved in EDM settings for predicting student performance?*

In the surveyed articles, the WEKA is found to be the most common tool used for machine learning approaches. WEKA is a Java software tool of the machine learning algorithm for data mining collection to analyse different datasets. It is an open source tool source tool includes a set of visualisation tools, which makes a smooth graphical user interface (GUI), together with a collection of machine learning algorithms [25]. Its easy accessibility makes it widely used with data miners working in the educational field [26].

Research Question 2: *In student performance prediction studies, which data mining approaches and algorithms are mostly employed with high accuracy?*

The purpose of using EDM algorithms is to acquire a higher accuracy rate in the dataset calculation. The prediction of students' academic performance is the main target to explore using the EDM algorithm in this review paper. It is apparent from this scoping review that classification approaches are employed extensively in EDM, in particular in Tree Structured algorithms with relative higher accuracy of predictive model.

A majority of studies have attempted to predict student performance using supervised machine learning. Nevertheless, research on other data mining techniques (such as unsupervised, semi-supervised and hybrid machine learning) are still understudied in identifying the best algorithms among them. It is possible to reap endless advantages from supervised and deep learning techniques. The generalisability and ease of interpretation of the results may be the possible reason for researchers' adoption [27]. The performance accuracy of supervised learning algorithms can benefit from the size of the training dataset and labelled data [28]. In general, supervised machine learning tend to be more accurate than unsupervised learning with a large training dataset. While the use of other techniques to understand student behaviour is generally lacking, such as clustering. Considering the overfitting risks in supervised learning approaches, other data mining approaches can be explored. Other researchers can take advantage of this finding in the future to fill a valuable research gap.

It is observed that tree structured (Decision Tree and Random Forest), Naïve Bayes and SVM are dominant in the selected studies for predicting student academic performance (Fig. 3). The possible reason may be due to the interpretability of these algorithms. The tree structured algorithms outperformed other applied algorithms in 7 out of 12 articles. Decision Tree is popular because it is one of the five top algorithms used, and the most popular supervised learning algorithm. It has often been discussed and compared with others algorithms [1, 3, 4, 15–17, 19, 21–23]. The articles mentioned the advantages of the Decision Trees, which are easy to understand, interpret, and handle noisy data and do not require normalisation of data [22]. In addition, J48 has the potential for data result illustration in visual classification [29]. Among the selected studies, J48 Decision Tree has been found to achieve the highest accuracy rate (98.10%) [20]. It is worth noting that the predictive model was fitted with 1374 student records, which is the largest dataset compared to other selected studies with an 85–500 sample size (see Table 1). Predictive models need a lot of data to be trained accurately by machine learning. The model accuracy largely depends on the dataset range, the larger dataset has more precise results, therefore classifying more clear patterns for student learning behaviour and outcome [27, 28]. The limited sample size (below 1000 instances) could be one of the limitations identified in this review; it requires explored with sufficient students' data to improve the training model and draw accurate conclusions in future research.

The results in this scoping review indicate that the use of data mining techniques could contribute a great deal of insight into students' learning outcomes and reveal valuable patterns. Factors of academic performance analysis can be examined and analysed through EDM to decrease students' academic performance failure or dropout [10]. Machine learning algorithms employed in Dabhade et al. [11], the evidence indicated that the most important factor when predicting future performance is recent past performance. EDM was also utilised to analyse learning behaviours to assist students in correcting study habits to enhance learning performance [6] and to identify at-risk students of academic failure in online learning environment [30, 31]. EDM supports decision-making in learning by providing insights into strategies that will help students to enhance overall learning outcomes [32]. The implementation of EDM has implications in improving students' performance during the learning process, we emphasise the need to develop predictive models that have higher generalizability that can work with a diverse population, greater explainability which can be interpreted by stakeholders easily and an early prediction purpose instead of prediction made after the student has completed current courses.

6 Conclusion

This scoping review has analysed the current literature on Educational Data Mining (EDM) in student performance prediction to provide insight into how EDM was implemented in the research field. EDM provides insight into students' performance and academic failure risk based on the evaluation of students' personal data, historical and current academic performance and learning behavioural features. The study reveals that WEKA is among the most applied tools in implementing different EDM approaches. The findings imply that supervised learning, particularly classification techniques (Tree Structured algorithms), is commonly adopted in developing the predictive model with higher accuracy compared to other algorithms.

The application of EDM in a learning context allows one to uncover hidden patterns of student learning behaviour and knowledge relates to learning process in large amounts of data; thus, the prediction-making of outcomes or behaviours is crucial [4]. The findings of this paper can be used as guidance for EDM implementation aiming to develop predictive model with higher accuracy. These reviewed tools, approaches and algorithms can serve as a map to foster research in facilitating student academic performance.

This scoping review is limited by the scope of reviewing comparative analysis of machine learning algorithms in the EDM field. It is possible that valuable publications have been omitted because employed due to the lack of evidence for the comparative analysis form different algorithms. Additionally, as this is a scoping review, more theoretical contributions should be explored than methodological implications in order to reach a more in-depth conclusion. Therefore, these limitations can be addressed by expanding this review by examining the sample dataset used to develop prediction models and evaluating the factors and attributes that impact student performance in the EDM.

Acknowledgement. This research was supported by the Institute of Information & Communications Technology Planning & Evaluation (IITP). Grant funded by the Korean government (MSIT) (No. 2021-0-02068, Artificial Intelligence Innovation Hub).

References

1. Chalaris, M., Gritzalis, S., Maragoudakis, M., Sgouropoulou, C., Tsolakidis, A.: Improving quality of educational processes providing new knowledge using data mining techniques. In: 3rd International Conference on Integrated Information (IC-ININFO), vol. 147, pp. 390–397 (2014)
2. Khanna, L., Singh, S.N., Alam, M.: Educational data mining and its role in determining factors affecting students academic performance: a systematic review. In: Proceedings of the 2016 1st India International Conference on Information Processing (IICIP), Delhi, India. IEEE (2016)
3. Moscoso-Zea, O., Saa, P., Luján-Mora, S.: Evaluation of algorithms to predict graduation rate in higher education institutions by applying educational data mining. Australas. J. Eng. Educ. **24**(1), 4–13 (2019)
4. Francis, B.K., Babu, S.S.: Predicting academic performance of students using a hybrid data mining approach. J. Med. Syst. **43**(6), 162 (2019)
5. Alzafari, K., Kratzer, J.: Challenges of implementing quality in European higher education: an expert perspective. Qual. High. Educ. **25**(3), 261–288 (2019)
6. Tsai, Y.R., Ouyang, C.S., Chang, Y.K.: Identifying engineering students' English sentence reading comprehension errors: applying a data mining technique. J. Educ. Comput. Res. **54**(1), 62–84 (2016)
7. Li, C., Herbert, N., Yeom, S., Montgomery, J.: Retention factors in STEM education identified using learning analytics: a systematic review. Educ. Sci. **12**(11), 781 (2022)
8. Gupta, S.B., Yadav, R.K., Shivani: Analysis of popular techniques used in educational data mining. Int. J. Next-Gener. Comput. **11**(2), 137–162 (2020)
9. Jin, Y., Yang, X., Yu, C., Yang, L.: Educational data mining: discovering principal factors for better academic performance. In: Proceedings of the 2021 the 3rd International Conference on Big Data Engineering and Technology (BDET), Singapore, Singapore (2021)
10. Pradeep, A., Das, S., Kizhekkethottam, J.J.: Students dropout factor prediction using EDM techniques. In: Proceedings of the 2015 International Conference on Soft-Computing and Networks Security (ICSNS), Coimbatore, India. IEEE (2015)
11. Dabhade, P., Agarwal, R., Alameen, K.P., Fathima, A.T., Sridharan, R., Gopakumar, G.: Educational data mining for predicting students' academic performance using machine learning algorithms. Mater. Today-Proc. **47**, 5260–5267 (2021)
12. Amrieh, E.A., Hamtini, T., Aljarah, I.: Mining educational data to predict student's academic performance using ensemble methods. Int. J. Database Theory Appl. **9**(8), 119–136 (2016)
13. Zoric, A.B.: Benefits of educational data mining. In: Proceedings of the 44th International Scientific Conference on Economic and Social Development, Split, Croatia (2019)

14. Tricco, A.C., et al.: PRISMA extension for scoping reviews (PRISMA-ScR): checklist and explanation. Ann. Int. Med. **169**(7), 467–473 (2018)
15. Almarabeh, H.: Analysis of students' performance by using different data mining classifiers. Int. J. Mod. Educ. Comput. Sci. **9**(8), 9–15 (2017)
16. El Guabassi, I., Bousalem, Z., Marah, R., Qazdar, A.: Comparative analysis of supervised machine learning algorithms to build a predictive model for evaluating students' performance. Int. J. Online Biomed. Eng. (iJOE). **17**(2), 90–105 (2021)
17. El Guabassi, I., Bousalem, Z., Marah, R., Qazdar, A.: A recommender system for predicting students' admission to a graduate program using machine learning algorithms. Int. J. Online Biomed. Eng. (iJOE) **17**, 135–147 (2021)
18. Ayinde, A., Omidiora, E., Adetunji, A.: Comparative analysis of selected classifiers in mining students' educational data. Commun. Appl. Electron. (CAE) **1**(5), 5–8 (2015)
19. Saheed, Y., Oladele, T., Akanni, A., Ibrahim, W.: Student performance prediction based on data mining classification techniques. Niger. J. Technol. **37**(4), 1087–1091 (2018)
20. Blasi, A.H., Alsuwaiket, M.: Analysis of students' misconducts in higher education using decision tree and ANN algorithms. Eng. Technol. Appl. Sci. Res. **10**(6), 6510–6514 (2020)
21. Salal, Y., Abdullaev, S.: Optimization of classifiers ensemble construction: case study of educational data mining. Comput. Technol. Autom. Control Radio Electron. **19**(4), 139–143 (2019)
22. Kaunang, F.J., Rotikan, R.: Students' academic performance prediction using data mining. In: Proceedings of the 2018 Third International Conference on Informatics and Computing (ICIC), Palembang, Indonesia. IEEE (2018)
23. Kiu, C.-C.: Data mining analysis on student's academic performance through exploration of student's background and social activities. In: Proceedings of the 2018 Fourth International Conference on Advances in Computing, Communication & Automation (ICACCA), Subang Jaya, Malaysia. IEEE (2018)
24. Chapman, P., et al.: CRISP-DM 1.0: step-by-step data mining guide. SPSS inc. **78**, 1–78 (2000)
25. Adekitan, A.I., Salau, O.: The impact of engineering students' performance in the first three years on their graduation result using educational data mining. Heliyon **5**(2), e01250 (2019)
26. Kabakchieva, D.: Predicting student performance by using data mining methods for classification. Cybern. Inf. Technol. **13**(1), 61–72 (2013)
27. Shafiq, D.A., Marjani, M., Habeeb, R.A.A., Asirvatham, D.: Student retention using educational data mining and predictive analytics: a systematic literature review. IEEE Access **10**, 72480–72503 (2022)
28. Chaovalit, P., Zhou, L.: Movie review mining: a comparison between supervised and unsupervised classification approaches. In: Proceedings of the 38th Annual Hawaii International Conference on System Sciences, Big Island, HI, USA. IEEE (2005)
29. Toivonen, T., Jormanainen, I.: Evolution of decision tree classifiers in open ended educational data mining. In: Proceedings of the Seventh International Conference on Technological Ecosystems for Enhancing Multiculturality, Le6n, Spain (2019)
30. Rodrigues, M.W., Isotani, S., Zarate, L.E.: Educational data mining: a review of evaluation process in the e-learning. Telematics Inform. **35**(6), 1701–1717 (2018)
31. Baradwaj, B.K., Pal, S.: Mining educational data to analyze students' performance. Int. J. Adv. Comput. Sci. Appl. **2**(6), 63–66 (2012)
32. Parmar, K., Vaghela, D., Sharma, P.: Performance prediction of students using distributed data mining. In: Proceedings of the 2015 International Conference on Innovations in Information, Embedded and Communication Systems (ICIIECS), Coimbatore, India. IEEE (2015)

Using a Cloud-Based Video Platform for Pre-service Teachers' Reflection

Tomohito Wada(✉), Chikako Kakoi, Koji Hamada, and Chikashi Unoki

National Institute of Fitness and Sports in Kanoya, Kagoshima 891-2393, Japan
{wada,chichicaco,hako,unoki}@nifs-k.ac.jp

Abstract. A cloud-based video platform was deployed into the pre-service PE teacher training course. One hundred and five students were enrolled in the course, and all demonstration (demo) lessons performed by students were video recorded and shared with the system. After each demo lesson, students were required to conduct two types of assessments by marking up the video with tags. As a result, the tags marked into each video clip were widely spread, and this suggests that it prevented a decrease in a student's concentration to observe them. The number of tags became relatively large in some teams, and this suggests that mark-up may be influenced by tags that were marked in advance by their peers. Except for a few cases, students conducted the assessments correctly through the system. According to the survey completed by students, most of the comments were positive. This trial gave a direct and visual feedback of the demo lessons, and it provided a good opportunity for students for their reflection.

Keywords: Cloud-based video platform · Microteaching · Reflection · Teacher training

1 Introduction

In pre-service teacher training courses at higher education institutions, demonstration (demo) lessons are generally implemented to develop students' teaching skills. In these demo lessons, students are divided into two groups, one as the teacher and the other as students, and are required to conduct lessons which simulate real lectures. Demo lessons in a planned series of five to ten-minute encounters with a small group of real students, often with an opportunity to observe the results on video tape, are called microteaching [1]. Video viewing in teacher education and professional development is a unique and potentially powerful tool [2], and there appears to be a general consensus on the benefit of using video to develop reflection among teachers [3].

In our pre-service teacher training courses, the microteaching method was adopted and video recordings have been used for reflection [5]. Since 2013, the video has been shared using a Learning Management System (LMS), a web-based application installed at university, so that students can replay video regardless

Published by Springer Nature Switzerland AG 2023
T. Keane et al. (Eds.): WCCE 2022, IFIP AICT 685, pp. 373–378, 2023.
https://doi.org/10.1007/978-3-031-43393-1_34

of time or place. However, LMS has only a simple playback function so the video was used just for a means of observation. Thus, more sophisticated functions that utilize video recording were expected.

To make a qualitative assessment of physical education lectures, Takahashi proposed a method called "duration recording of teaching episodes" [6] which classify a lecture into four category, i.e. instruction, management, cognitive activity and physical activity. This is one well-known method to assess PE lectures which contain comparatively long physical activities. A dedicated application for duration recording of PE lessons has been developed and is available in Japan [4].

Video recordings of a demo lesson and the duration recording of teaching episode are effective methods to develop teaching ability of pre-service teachers. However, it is not easy to employ them especially into a class with a lot of students. To share video with the LMS it takes a lot of work e.g. preparing camera, shooting, copying into a computer, trimming, encoding and then uploading. The dedicated application can simplify these processes, however due to cost it is often difficult to implement the application into university classes.

Recently a cloud-based video platform service called Vosaic was released [7]. Vosaic provides fundamental functions for video sharing with user management, and a mark-up function into the video. The mark-up function is often called 'tagging'. Users can access all of these functions with a web browser, so it is easy to deploy the system into our courses.

Therefore, through the use of the cloud-based video platform, this study will examine where this service can be effectively used in a course for pre-service teacher development.

2 Methods

This study was carried out at a college which provides courses for pre-service physical education teacher. The Vosaic system was introduced into "Methods of Teaching Health and Physical Education IV". This course was for the 3rd grade students, and 105 students were enrolled in 2021.

The students were divided into 18 teams of 5 to 6 students. Six teams of students formed a group, and each group conducted a demo lesson in parallel. Four members from a team took turns as a teacher, the remaining team member recorded a video with an iPad which the lecturer provided. The remaining members in the group (around 30 students) played the role of students for the demo lesson. The lesson themes were Softball, Judo, Physical Fitness, Gymnastics, Creative Dance, Rhythm Dance and Health. Lessons were held in the gymnasium or the dance studio except Health. The duration of demo lesson was around 30 min.

The Vosaic system [7] was hired as a video platform. The system administration including user management was carried out by a IT staff in the college. Lecturers of the course were registered as "Educators" and students were registered as "Users" on Vosaic. After the class, the video recorded during demo lessons were uploaded by a lecturer of the course.

After the demo lesson, students of the team who took charge of teachers used Vosaic to conduct two types of assessments of the lesson. The first one was named "Good/Bad (GB) assessment". Students marked good acts as "Good" and moments that need improvement as "Bad" by observing the video. The second one was "Duration recording of teaching episode" proposed by Takahashi [6]. Every moment of the demo lessen was marked into four episodes: "Instruction", "Management", "Cognitive activity" and "Physical activity". All team members individually completed the GB assessment, while a team representative performed the duration recording because it might have less individual difference. Timelines marked by teammates were shared and every team member could see the results of other team members' assessments.

With Vosaic, results of assessments can be marked as tags with buttons displayed on a web browser. Figure 1 shows an example of a display with Vosaic. Users can tag the scene with the green and red buttons at the right side while playing the video. These tags are then displayed on the timeline at the bottom of video. In Fig. 1, Good/Bad assessments tagged by team members are shown in five separate timelines.

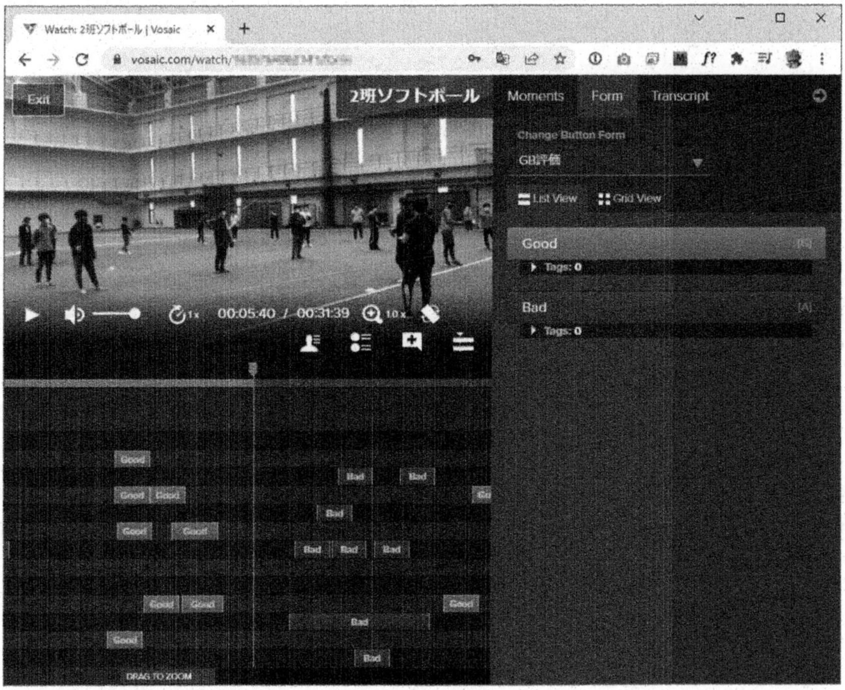

Fig. 1. An example of Good/Bad assessment with Vosaic.

3 Results

As a result of conducting the course, two demo lessons' video clips for each team, 36 clips in total, were uploaded to the Vosaic. The total time of the video clips was 20 h 30 min (1230 min). At the beginning of the semester it was planned that each team would have 3 demo lessons, however it was decreased due to the coronavirus pandemic. The total number of tags marked into the video was 3,553 for the GB assessment, 1,439 for the duration recording method.

Time variation of the number of GB tags per minute marked by students into video clips is shown in Fig. 2. This shows that tags were widely spread on video clips. In general, people tend to get tired of watching the long video clips. However, by requiring to mark moments as an assessment, it might prevent a decrease in a student's concentration to observe these video.

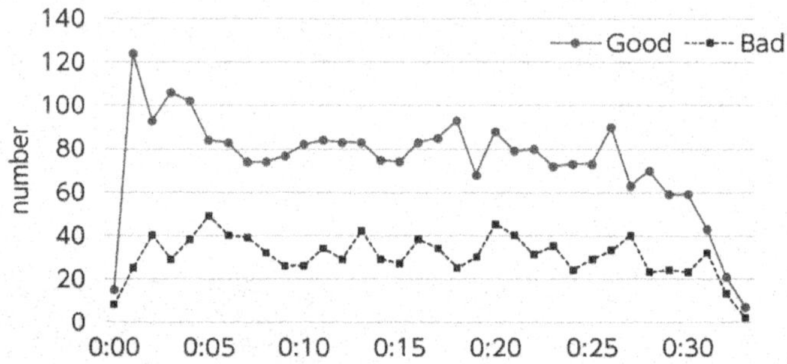

Fig. 2. Time variation in the number of GB tags per minute.

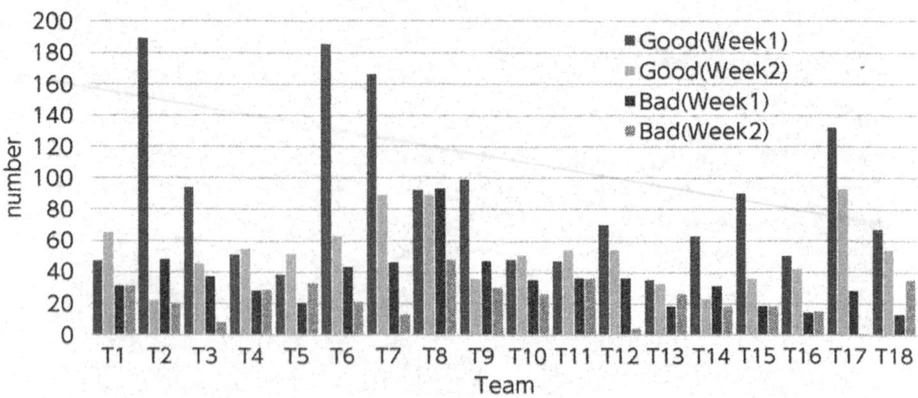

Fig. 3. The total number of GB tags for each team.

The total number of attached GB tags for each team is shown in Fig. 3. The average number of Good tags were 86.8±49.9 and 53.1±21.0 for the first and the second demo lesson, Bad tags were 34.6 ± 18.3 and 22.9 ± 12.1. In some teams, a larger number of "Good" tags were identified in the first demo lesson as if clicking a lot of "like" buttons in SNS. In this Vosaic setup, all marked tags were shared with teammates, and it can be considered that some students may have been influenced by tags marked in advance by their teammate. Therefore, before the second demo lessons, lecturers told students that a tag should be attached to one teaching action, and too many tags may obscure the salient features of the demo lesson. This should be one of the reasons in the decrease of tags in the second demo lesson.

Results from duration recording tabulated by lesson theme are shown in Table 1. In most of clips, teaching episodes was assessed correctly through the system. However, in four demo lessons in three teams, the duration recording assessment was not carried out properly, even though GB assessment was carried out in these lessons. On the Vosaic system, the buttons for the duration recording assessment were set as "Toggle button". The toggle button allows users to control the length of the moment by pressing it once to mark the beginning, and press it again to mark the end of the moment. This difference in operation between two assessment forms might confuse some students.

Table 1. The ratio of activities of demo lesson by duration recording.

Theme	Instruction	Physical Activity	Cognitive Activity	Management
Health	57%	1%	33%	8%
Judo	52%	39%	2%	7%
Creative Dance	48%	31%	9%	12%
Gymnastics	37%	39%	7%	17%
Softball	35%	33%	10%	21%
Physical Fitness	32%	22%	25%	21%
Rhythm Dance	31%	37%	19%	13%
Total	43%	25%	18%	14%

4 Conclusion

A cloud-based video platform enabled students to share and assess videos of demo lessons in a simple operation even in a class with over 100 students. There was little guidance for the system, but most of students were able to use it without trouble. According to the survey taken at the end of the course, most of the comments regarding the use of the system were positive. This trial gave direct and visual feedback of the demo lessons, and it brought a good opportunity for pre-service teachers reflection. In the GB assessment, many students pointed out that criteria for assessments were similar to those of other students. The duration recording and its timeline display also made students reconsider their time management.

In this research, we propose a method with binary tags called GB assessment. The previous study [8] which utilized video for pre-service teachers indicated that students were able to discern particular aspects of teaching that were both strengths and weaknesses. The GB assessment can enable students to focus on their distinctive features, and had the effect of promoting this type of reflection.

In this trial, some students tended to mark too many GB tags into the video. The video-enhanced reflection facilitates teacher reflection and increase the quantity of things teachers notice about their teaching [9]. Vosaic provides a brief and intuitive method and it might boost the number of GB tags for some students. The appropriate number of tags is still unclear, and it should be clarified in future studies.

Some students also pointed out that they could not understand the reasons for tagging by peers in some cases. Adding a comment to a GB tag or increasing the type of tag could be a solution for that. These also will be the subjects of future studies.

At last, it is worth mentioning that even during the coronavirus pandemic, we were able to continue and enhance our course activities by utilizing the cloud-based video platform.

References

1. Allen, D.W. (ed.): Micro-teaching: A Description. Stanford Teacher Education Program, Palo Alto (1967)
2. Gaudin, C., Chalies, S.: Video viewing in teacher education and professional development: a literature review. Educ. Res. Rev. **16**, 41–67 (2015)
3. Hamel, C., Viau-Guay, A.: Using video to support teachers' reflective practice: a literature review. Cogent Educ. **6**(1), 1673689 (2019)
4. Lesson Study Analyst for Physical Education. https://pes-analyst.jp/. Accessed 27 Feb 2022
5. Sato, Y., Kakoi, C.: Case study reports and reflection of Health and Physical Education Teacher Education IV (2014) in NIFS – For construction of practical leadership development system in active learning type tuition for Experiential Learning Model. Ann. Fitness Sports Sci. **52**, 35–67 (2016). (in Japanese)
6. Takahashi, T.: Observation and Evaluation of Physical Education Class - Authentic assessment for improvement. Meiwa Publishing, Tokyo (2003). (in Japanese)
7. Vosaic: Video Coaching, Video Feedback, Video Analysis. https://vosaic.com/. Accessed 27 Feb 2022
8. Coffey, A.M.: Using video to develop skills in reflection in teacher education students. Aust. J. Teach. Educ. **39**(9), 86–97 (2014)
9. Wright, G.A.: Improving teacher performance using an enhanced digital video reflection technique. In: Spector, J., Ifenthaler, D., Isaias, P., Kinshuk, Sampson, D. (eds.) Learning and Instruction in the Digital Age, pp. 175–190. Springer, Boston (2010). https://doi.org/10.1007/978-1-4419-1551-1_11

Awareness Support with Mutual Stimulation Among People to Enrich Group Discussion in AIR-VAS

Mamoru Yoshizoe(✉) and Hiromitsu Hattori

Ritsumeikan University, 1-1-1 Noji-higashi, Kusatsu, Shiga, Japan
{yoshizoe,hatto}@fc.ritsumei.ac.jp

Abstract. While the Internet has made it possible for people all over the world to be connected, they continue to face the barrier of value diversity. Although we often have to consider or respect other people's values, it is not easy to sense them due to the limitations of our knowledge, experience, and imagination. We tackle this issue by developing AIR-VAS, a discussion support system that supports the mutual consideration of unfamiliar values and thus encourage synergistic communication. AIR-VAS is a group discussion system that supports awareness of other people's values. AIR-VAS can recognize characteristic opinions raised in a session and share them among all discussion participants. Through the sharing of opinions, people can obtain different viewpoints on the issues currently being discussed so AIR-VAS can stimulate people to generate/evaluate/analyze ideas. AIR-VAS has the function of visualizing statements presented during a discussion in the form of a word co-occurrence network. We realized opinion sharing as the process of network re-construction, including the use of sub-networks to represent the opinions of other groups. Experiments show that the system successfully enhances the diversity of ideas.

Keywords: Discussion support · Idea generation support · Awareness · Word co-occurrence network · Summarization

1 Introduction

Society is becoming more globalized and complex with the development of information technology, and people's values are becoming more diverse. As a result, it has become necessary for society to be aware of diverse and changing values, and to have a broad perspective on all issues.

A wide variety of information is now being exchanged on the Internet, and anyone can easily refer to and post such information. However, this has led to the frequent occurrence of "flaming" [1] on social networking services (SNS), such as Twitter, where people post their thoughts and feelings based on certain values only to find that they are criticized and pilloried by many viewers. In addition, with the development of the Web and social networking services, Internet users

Published by Springer Nature Switzerland AG 2023
T. Keane et al. (Eds.): WCCE 2022, IFIP AICT 685, pp. 379–388, 2023.
https://doi.org/10.1007/978-3-031-43393-1_35

are exposed only to information that matches their interests and the communities to which they belong or have close relationships, which isolates them from information that differs from their point of view and makes them isolated in a homogeneous cultural and ideological bubble. This problem, known as the "filter bubble" [2], continues to become stronger.

These problems suggest that we may lose the opportunity to be exposed to a variety of information and that we may not be able to perceive things from a broad perspective. To prevent such a situation, it is necessary to recognize ideas that differ from our own ideas. To achieve this goal, we believe that technologies and mechanisms are necessary to gain awareness of diverse viewpoints in various situations. In addition, we think that awareness of new perspectives helps to support the generation of new ideas and encourage new ways of perceiving others.

Our research group (AIR: Acceptable Intelligence with Responsibility) has been discussing processes and approaches to make people aware of various viewpoints and has been trying to implement and verify a prototype system that incorporates such mechanisms.

To advance this research, we designed and implemented a system that promotes ideas by presenting new perspectives in the discussions. Specifically, we assume a frequent situation in workshops where participants are divided into several groups and discuss the same topic in parallel. By making it possible to refer to information from parallel discussions that cannot normally be accessed easily, we aim to bring the perspectives of many other participants into each group's discussion, thereby stimulating and improving the overall quality of the discussion. In this paper, we detail the design of the system and evaluate its effectiveness in an experiment.

2 Related Work

Various methods for supporting idea generation have been developed, such as brainstorming [3] and brainwriting [4], and various extent systems incorporate these methods [5–7]. These systems visualize the content of the discussion as labels and catch phrases on the screen, and share them with group members to help organize the keywords and main points.

Research on visual-based idea support systems has led to many studies focused on "Awareness" [8–10]. Dourish [8, p. 107] defines awareness as "awareness is an understanding of the activities of others, which provides a context for your own activity". For example, displaying other people's information on a screen or working on a virtual shared screen [11–13] are attempts to support "awareness" based on Dourish's definition. Awareness is a major theme in idea generation support systems, and it has been shown that better awareness of team activities and events that may affect the team can lead to increased team productivity [14]. Robert investigated how awareness of others affects the search task and showed that being aware of the behavior of other users can lead to improved performance and reduced effort in the search task. Wikum+ [15] is a collaborative document writing tool that allows groups working together to discuss and summarize the issues in a single space. In Wikum+ experiments, the system yielded a reduction in user effort, and the integration of new ideas.

However, these discussion support systems visualize the status of discussions in a group and assume support for discussions within just that group. These systems do not support awareness beyond the group, a key function of the proposal made in our research. The proposed system allows interaction among groups in real-time and improves the quality of the overall workshop discussion through interaction differs from the usual group-discussion style workshop in which people share characteristic viewpoints and opinions of each group when the group discussion is over. The originality of this system is that it improves the quality of discussion in the workshop as a whole through real-time interaction between groups.

3 AIR-VAS System

3.1 System Design

We present the AIR-VAS system that supports idea generation and awareness of diverse values via intuitive presentation of other people's information. We targeted a framework that could provide a new perspective by sharing discussion information among groups beyond the borders of discussion groups. By receiving idiosyncratic information from other groups in real-time, we can expect the people to recognize diverse viewpoints and ideas, so that the discussion broadens and deepens by taking account of various values and factors surrounding the discussion theme.

In a group-work style discussion where participants are divided into several groups and discuss the same topic in parallel, the system visualizes the status of the discussion in each group and use the information of other groups to stimulate the entire discussion. AIR-VAS aims to exchange the perspectives of the groups and so improve the final quality and efficacy of the discussion. Sharing information raised in different groups and communities, the participants are challenged to expand their perspectives. In addition, by incorporating the perspectives of other groups, we can expect development of new unexpected visions, which may lead to more efficient workshops. The system will also contribute to the creation of learning opportunities in school education and corporate employee training, where people will learn to recognize other people's viewpoints, respect them, and learn the skills to incorporate them into their activities.

The system architecture is shown in Fig. 1, while Fig. 2 shows a UI screen. Each group has a PC and microphone. The system visualizes information extracted from each group's discussion speech text, forms group-specific summaries, and displays them on the appropriate screen. For visualizing the information, we adopt the co-occurrence network method [16]. Word co-occurrence networks are a method of expressing co-occurrence relationships between words in terms of network connections, and they offer effective discernment of the structure and features of text data [17]. Brief explanations of each modules in Fig. 1 are given here.

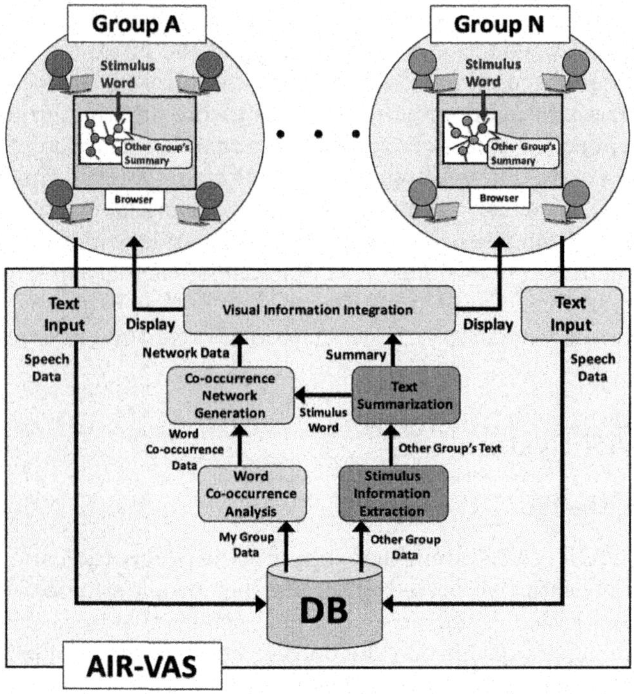

Fig. 1. The AIR-VAS system architecture.

Text Input Module
The module that enters the discussion text into the database. Web Speech API[1] is used for speech recognition.

Word Co-occurrence Analysis Module
The module that analyzes the co-occurrence relationship of the words in the database.

Co-occurrence Network Generation Module
The module that generates the co-occurrence network diagram from the word co-occurrence data of top 50 frequent words and stimulus word data.

Stimulus Information Extraction Module
The module that extracts the other group's discussion text data from the database.

Text Summarization Module
The module that summarizes the other group's discussion text by using a Transformers-based summarization model.

Visual Information Integration Module
The module that integrates the visual information to create the browser display.

[1] https://developer.mozilla.org/ja/docs/Web/API/Web_Speech_API.

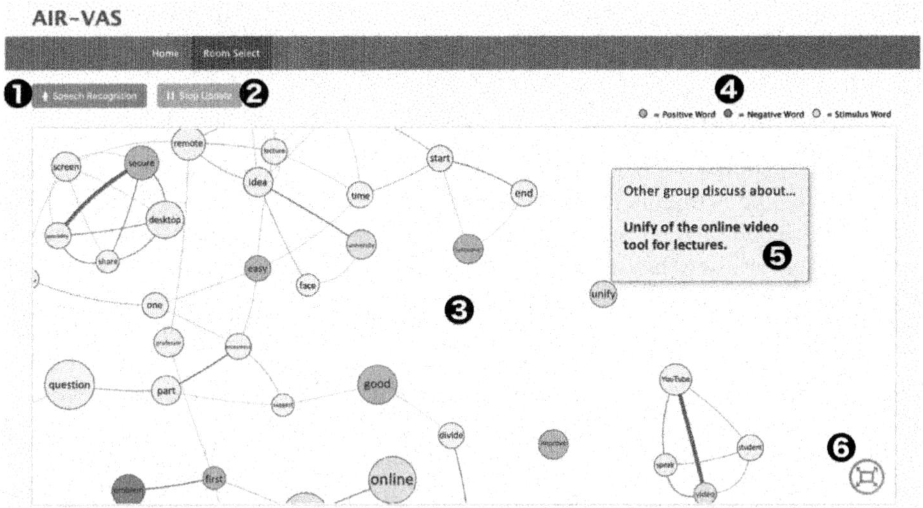

Fig. 2. The AIR-VAS system UI. (1) Speech recognition button. (2) Network update stop button. (3) Co-occurrence network view. Users can scroll and zoom. (4) Node color definitions; green shows positive, red shows negative, yellow shows stimulus words. (5) The selected node shows speech text in which the word is used; The stimulus word represents other group's summary. (6) Network stabilize button. (Color figure online)

3.2 Word Co-occurrence Network

The *Word Co-occurrence Analysis Module* calculates the co-occurrence of words. We use the *Jaccard* index [18] for this calculation. The Jaccard index of two words w_1, w_2 is calculated as shown by formula (1).

$$Jaccard(w_1, w_2) = \frac{|V_1 \cap V_2|}{|V_1 \cup V_2|} \tag{1}$$

V_1, V_2 includes co-occurrence words of w_1, w_2.

The *Word Co-occurrence Analysis Module* inputs word co-occurrence data to the *Co-occurrence Network Generation Module*, and then, the co-occurrence network diagram is made from frequent word data and stimulus word data (Fig. 2 (3)). The co-occurrence network diagram is displayed by javascript package vis.js[2] on the browser. Figure 2 (1) is the button for speech recognition and Fig. 2 (2) (6) are network function buttons. Users can check the network using zoom-in-out and stop physical network simulation. We set three node colors so the network diagram can offer intuitive recognition of the discussion (Fig. 2 (4)). The green node shows positive feelings, the red node shows negative feelings, the yellow node shows stimulus words, while other nodes are default white. We

[2] https://visjs.org/.

defined the emotional polarity of positive or negative by applying the Polar Phrase Dictionary [19] and the opinion lexicon[3] of Hu and Liu [20].

3.3 Stimulus Information

The system displays the other group's word and discussion summary as stimulus information. The *Stimulus Information Extraction Module* picks up other group's discussion text from the database and defines the target text to be summarized. In this system, we set the discussion text of the last 5 min as the target part (left of Fig. 3). The discussion text of the target part is input to the *Text Summarization Module* which then outputs a summary of the other group's discussion (Fig. 2 (5)). This extraction of stimulus information is iterated at 5 min intervals. Therefore, if the discussion takes 20 min, stimulus information is created at 5, 10, and 15 min.

For text summarization, we use the abstractive summarization model of T5 [21]. T5 is a pre-trained model for language generation, translation, and comprehension. It has high performance on many generation tasks, including summarization and abstractive question answering. We adopt the generative model T5[4], and fine-tune it for the short text summarization task [22]. We use this fine-tuned model for summarization in the *Text Summarization Module.* The model outputs a summary of the discussion text, and a word is selected as the stimulus word; this word is not been added to the co-occurrence network (right of Fig. 3).

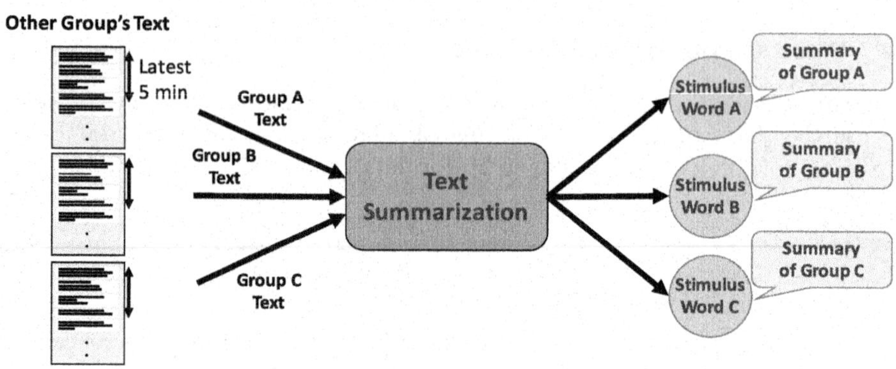

Fig. 3. Text Summarization Module overview

4 Evaluation

We conducted a discussion experiment with the system to examine how stimulus information affects the diversity of the discussion and the awareness of diverse

[3] http://www.cs.uic.edu/~liub/FBS/opinion-lexicon-English.rar.
[4] https://huggingface.co/google/mt5-base.

values and perspectives. The discussion was undertaken as a Zoom online meeting. We recruited 16 college students for the experiment, and formed four groups of four people. Two groups (G1, G2) could refer to stimulus information, while the other two groups (G3, G4) could not. The experiment had two rounds for 20 min, one for each condition. The discussion members were shuffled at the beginning of round 2, so all members have experienced two conditions. In the first round, each group discussed how to improve campus dining options and mobile food stands. In the second round, each group discussed how they would like their lectures to operate if classes continued to be online in the next semester due to COVID-19. In both rounds, we asked each group to write ideas and proposals about the theme posed and answer a questionnaires at the end of the experiment. We compared discussion status and user experiences in both conditions on the point of whether the system's display of information from the other group helped them become aware of diverse values and perspectives.

4.1 Activation by Stimulus Information

The users answered a questionnaire on the discussions at the end of the experiment. From the quantitative results in Fig. 4, users felt that stimulus information helped in discovering diverse ideas (Round1: $t(11)= 3.000$, $p = 0.012$; Round2: $t(10)= 2.494$, $p = 0.032$) and in satisfaction with the discussion (Round1: $t(10)= 2.236$, $p = 0.049$; Round2: $t(12)= 2.393$, $p = 0.034$). The results of the number of ideas that each group wrote in the discussion also reflected the efficacy of the information provided. The groups that could refer to stimulus information had more ideas and proposals than the groups that could not (Table 1).

In the questionnaire responses, many users commented that the stimulus information helped to find new ideas. One user explained "*I was able to get ideas from the stimulus information. I think it had an impact on the discussion that followed.*" Another user said "*I was able to find a new starting point for the conversation from the stimulus words. In particular, the stimulus words seemed to advance the discussion more.*" In addition, some users felt that stimulus information helped when the discussion stalled. One user explained "*I felt the discussion less often because the stimulus words allowed us to look at them and talk about them even after everyone had expressed their opinions*". Another user said "*I had the impression that the discussion was less likely to get stuck when there was stimulus information.*" On the other hand, one user commented, "*It was difficult to understand how the node word impacted the flow of the discussion*", and pointed out that it is necessary to present not only the word by itself but also the context of the word.

In Fig. 4, the stimulus information and summary were positively evaluated (high scores) by users. One user said, "The summary of the other group was natural sentences, and it was useful". Another user said "As for the stimulus information, it was short and coherent and helped to develop the discussion".

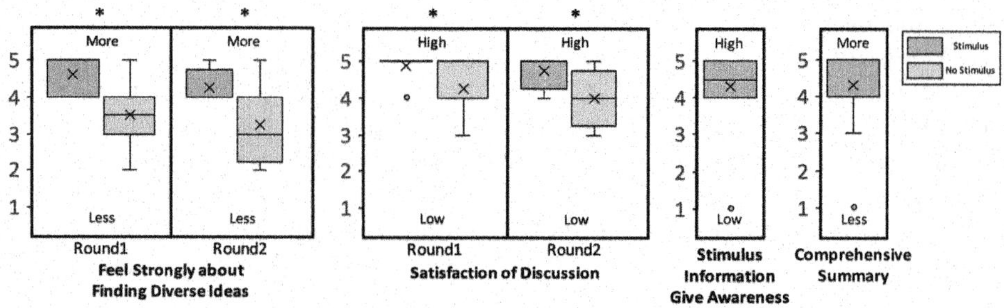

Fig. 4. Box plots showing quantitative values (out of 5). Scores that resulted in different means from t-tests are starred ($p < 0.05*$).

Table 1. The number of ideas

Group	Condition	Number of ideas (Round1)	Number of ideas (Round2)
G1	Stimulus	11	6
G2	Stimulus	11	9
G3	No Stimulus	8	4
G4	No Stimulus	7	5

4.2 Impact on Discussion Direction

Based on the speech-to-text logs, we investigated how the stimulus information impacted the direction of the discussion.

Round1. In round 1, each group discussed how to improve campus dining options and mobile food stands. We found that G3 discussed "*the cafeteria gets crowded during lunchtime...*", and G2 explained "*it would be convenient to be able to see the menu of the cafeteria and pay via our smartphone.*" The system summarized these discussion texts, "The problem of crowded cafeterias during lunchtime" and "Useful ways to use the smartphone", and sent the summaries to G1 as stimulus information. G1 received this stimulus information, and they developed a discussion about a smartphone application for checking the crowding of the cafeteria in real-time (left of Fig. 5). In the questionnaires, one user of G1 said "*The stimulus information about "smartphone" gave the discussion a distinctly different orientation from the previous discussions*".

Round2. In round 2, each group discussed how to improve campus education in the environment of COVID-19 restrictions. We found that G3 discussed the video recording of lectures, and the resulting stimulus information increased the discussion scope of G1 and G2. One user of G1 said "*The discussion had been going in the direction of making online classes better, but negative comments from other groups led to a renewed discussion of the advantages and disadvantages of both online and face-to-face classes.*" and another user of G2 explained "*From the stimulus information about recording the lectures, we discussed the effects of recording and measures to counter skipping classes.*" (right of Fig. 5).

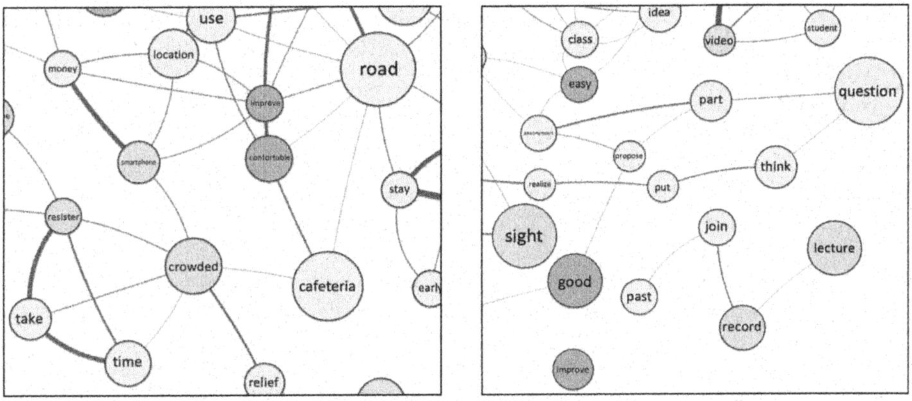

Round1 – G1 **Round2 – G2**

Fig. 5. The co-occurrence network diagram of round1-G1 (left) and round2-G2 (right).

5 Conclusion

In this paper, we presented the AIR-VAS system; it supports idea generation and awareness of diverse values by exchanging summaries of other people's discussions. The system allows users to recognize the ideas and perspectives of other discussion groups in real-time through stimulus information. Using an abstractive summarization model, AIR-VAS allows users to intuitively perceive the contents of another group's discussion. The results of an experiment on an implemented AIR-VAS system showed that stimulus information activated the discussion and gave awareness of different perspectives of the discussion theme. A limitation of this study is that it considers only a single fixed pattern of timing and frequency with which the system presents stimulus information. In future work, we will intend to investigate more variation in the information display parameters and focus on differences in the semantic distance of the contents of the discussion.

References

1. Jane, E.A.: Flaming? What flaming? The pitfalls and potentials of researching online hostility. Ethics Inf. Technol. **17**(1), 65–87 (2015)
2. Pariser E.: The Filter Bubble: What the Internet is Hiding from You. Penguin Press (2011)
3. Osborn, A.F.: Applied Imagination. Scribner's, New York (1953)
4. VanGundy, A.B.: Brain writing for new product ideas: an alternative to brainstorming. J. Consum. Mark. **1**(2), 67–74 (1984)
5. Stefik, M., Foster, G., Bobrow, D.G., Kahn, K., Lanning, S., Suchman, L.: Beyond the chalkboard: computer support for collaboration and problem solving in meetings. Commun. ACM **30**(1), 32–47 (1987)

6. Foster, G., Stefik, M.: Cognoter: theory and practice of a colaborative tool. In: Proceedings of the 1986 ACM Conference on Computer-Supported Cooperative Work, pp. 7–15 (1986)
7. Watabe, K., Sakata, S., Maeno, K., Fukuoka, H., Ohmori, T.: Distributed multiparty desktop conferencing system: MERMAID. In: Proceedings of the 1990 ACM Conference on Computer-Supported Cooperative Work, pp. 27–38 (1990)
8. Dourish, P., Bellotti, V.: Awareness and coordination in shared work spaces. In: Proceedings of the 1992 ACM Conference on Computer-Supported Cooperative Work, vol. 92, pp. 107–114 (1992)
9. Gutwin, C., Greenberg, S.: A descriptive framework of workspace awareness for real-time groupware. Comput. Supported Coop. Work (CSCW) **11**(3–4), 411–446 (2002)
10. Schmidt, K.: The problem with awareness: introductory remarks on awareness in CSCW. Comput. Supported Coop. Work (CSCW) **11**(3–4), 285–298 (2002)
11. Cadiz, J.J., Venolia, G., Jancke, G., Gupta, A.: Designing and deploying an information awareness interface. In: Proceedings of the 2002 ACM Conference on Computer Supported Cooperative Work, pp. 314–323 (2002)
12. Gross, T.: Supporting effortless coordination: 25 years of awareness research. Comput. Supported Coop. Work (CSCW) **22**(4–6), 425–474 (2013)
13. Tee, K., Greenberg, S., Gutwin, C.: Providing artifact awareness to a distributed group through screen sharing. In: Proceedings of the 2006 20th Anniversary Conference on Computer Supported Cooperative Work, pp. 99–108 (2006)
14. Villa, R., Gildea, N., Jose, J.M.: A study of awareness in multimedia search. In: Proceedings of the 8th ACM/IEEE-CS Joint Conference on Digital Libraries, pp. 221–230 (2008)
15. Tian, S., Zhang, A.X., Karger, D.: A system for interleaving discussion and summarization in online collaboration. In: Proceedings of the ACM on Human-Computer Interaction, CSCW3, Article 241, vol. 4, pp. 1–27 (2020)
16. Fruchterman, T.M.J., Reingold, E.M.: Graph drawing by force-directed placement. Softw. - Pract. Exp. **21**(11), 1129–1164 (1991)
17. Liu, Y., Goncalves, J., Ferreira, D., Xiao, B., Hosio, S., Kostakos, V: CHI 1994–2013: mapping two decades of intellectual progress through co-word analysis. In: Proceedings of the SIGCHI Conference on Human Factors in Computing Systems, pp. 3553–3562 (2014)
18. Jaccard, P.: Etude comparative de la distribution florale dans une portion des Alpes et des Jura. Bull. Soc. Vaudoise Sci. Naturelles **37**, 547–579 (1901)
19. Kaji, N., Kitsuregawa, M.: Automatic construction of polarity-tagged corpus from HTML documents. In: Proceedings of the COLING/ACL on Main conference poster sessions (COLING-ACL 2006). Association for Computational Linguistics, pp. 452–459 (2006)
20. Hu, M., Liu, B.: Mining and summarizing customer reviews. In: Proceedings of the tenth ACM SIGKDD International Conference on Knowledge Discovery and Data Mining, pp. 168–177 (2004)
21. Raffel, C., et al.: Exploring the limits of transfer learning with a unified text-to-text transformer. J. Mach. Learn. Res. **21**(140), 1–67 (2020)
22. Kodaira, T., Komachi, M.: The rule of three: abstractive text summarization in three bullet points. In: Proceedings of the 32nd Pacific Asia Conference on Language, Information and Computation. Association for Computational Linguistics (2018)

Foundations of Computer Science in General Teacher Education – Findings and Experiences from a Blended-Learning Course

Stefan Seegerer[1(✉)], Tilman Michaeli[2], and Ralf Romeike[1]

[1] Computing Education Research Group, Freie Universität Berlin, Berlin, Germany
{stefan.seegerer,ralf.romeike}@fu-berlin.de

[2] TUM School of Social Sciences and Technology, Computing Education Research Group, Technical University of Munich, Munich, Germany
tilman.michaeli@tum.de

Abstract. With regards to the digital transformation, the consensus that computer science education plays a central role in shaping "digital education" is now emerging: Beyond the efficient and reflective use of information systems, new topics and methods arise for all school subjects that require computer science competencies and must be anchored in general teacher education. However, in light of students' heterogeneity, the question of how motivation, subject-specific demands, and applicability in subject teaching can be harmonized presents a particular challenge. This paper presents key findings and experiences from the research-led development and subsequent evaluation of a blended learning course offering. This course offering provides student teachers of all subjects and school types with basic computer science competencies for teaching in the digital world. On this foundation, success factors and good practices in the design of the course are identified. It is shown that the design of such courses can be successful if illustrative examples are used, communication and collaboration are promoted and, in particular, references and application perspectives for the respective subjects are taken into account.

Keywords: computing education · digital education · general teacher education · blended learning

1 Introduction

With the digital transformation, the way we communicate, use technologies, work, or gather information is changing in all areas of life. School subjects are also affected by this transformation process – and increasingly it is acknowledged that computer science competencies are not only relevant for the efficient and reflective use of digital media or information technology systems [1]. For example,

Published by Springer Nature Switzerland AG 2023
T. Keane et al. (Eds.): WCCE 2022, IFIP AICT 685, pp. 389–399, 2023.
https://doi.org/10.1007/978-3-031-43393-1_36

in science classes, simulations and data analysis – also referred to as the third and fourth pillars of science – are used to gain insights. Additionally, sensors may be used to collect digital measurements. In economics classes, digital business models and their impact on the labor market are addressed; and in religion classes, ethics are discussed in the context of algorithms and artificial intelligence. These changes, which affect not only content such as artificial intelligence but also methods such as data analysis or simulations, represent an important aspect of "digital education".

Teachers of all subjects and school types need the corresponding competencies to be able to address these changes appropriately in their teaching. Computing Education plays a central role in this context: Only with competencies in handling and evaluating data, or by having a basic understanding of algorithms, are teachers able to address corresponding phenomena in the classroom in a well-founded way. Accordingly, the training and continuing education of teachers is a central task in the context of digital education, in which computer science must assume a leading role. In light of the students' heterogeneity, the question arises as to how motivation, content and applicability in the classroom can be harmonized. Therefore, this paper presents key findings and experiences from the research-led development and subsequent evaluation of a blended learning course. This course provides student teachers of all subjects and school types with basic computer science competencies for teaching in the digital world. The course has been running successfully now for 4 years with almost 1000 students participating at 3 universities.

2 Related Work

Digital education means new topics and methods for all school subjects [1], which go beyond the efficient and reflective use of computer science systems. This means they have to be anchored particularly in the education of teachers of all subjects and school types. There is now a consensus – not limited to the perspective of computing education – that computer science education plays a central role in the design of this kind of digital education and that teachers of all school subjects need corresponding computer science competencies. Various parties are calling for the necessary foundations of computer science to be anchored in teacher training. Following the strategy "Education in the Digital World" of the German Standing Conference of the Ministers of Education and Cultural Affairs, the *Research Group Digital Campus Bavaria* has formulated 19 competencies for teaching in the digital world [2]. There, so-called media-related computer science skills are explicitly required, which include "conceptual knowledge of databases and algorithms". An expert commission convened by the German Ministry for Education and Research also calls for "[a]ll institutions of teacher education [...] to [promote] computer science competence (in the sense of algorithmic thinking, data literacy, computational thinking, and data security)" [3]. Also, on an international level, several initiatives emphasize the importance of computer science for digital literacy, such as the "informatics for all" strategy [4].

However, few approaches anchoring the foundations of computer science in general teacher education exist. One such approach is the lecture series "Computer Science in Everyday Life" at the University of Wuppertal [5]. The course focuses on everyday phenomena which are analyzed and evaluated from the perspective of computer science, in order to provide future teachers with "expert access to the science of computer science". Furthermore, Yadav et al. [6] integrated a one-week module (2 × 50 min lecture) on computational thinking (CT) into a psychology course for student teachers. This short module focuses specifically on the related concepts of abstraction, reasoning, algorithms, and debugging, and explaining their importance in the classroom in more detail. Other scholars developed courses specifically designed for prospective elementary school teachers [7,8]. The focus of these courses was on teaching computer science content for teaching at a primary level. Therefore, in addition to subject-specific content, computer science education topics, e. g. the use of unplugged activities, were addressed as well.

To summarize, existing offers either choose a subject-oriented approach, are comparatively short, or primarily aim at enabling the teaching of computer science competencies. In contrast to this, the applicability in the respective subject, which is necessary due to the change of all subjects by the digital transformation, has not been the focus research so far. According to previous experience, with an approach focusing primarily on computer science content knowledge, this can be established "only to a limited extent" [5]. There is a lack of research on how the teaching of the foundations of computer science can be designed for student teachers of all subjects and school types in order to contribute to applicability in the subject. However, this would enable future teachers to address the new contents and methods, that are a result of the digital transformation, in their teaching.

3 Approach

In the following section, we present the central findings and experiences of the research-led development, testing, and evaluation of a study program, which provides student teachers of all subjects and types of schools with fundamental computer science competencies for teaching in the digital world. In the first step, conditions and challenges for the design of such a study program will be identified. Based on this step, the implementation is presented in the form of organizational decisions and theoretically-derived design principles. These have been refined in the course of the accompanying research in order to address the corresponding conditions and challenges. The evaluation accompanying the module is used to examine how certain design decisions were perceived. Finally, the entire study program is evaluated in a pre-post design. This allows for the drawing of conclusions regarding the suitability of the design principles and organizational decisions.

4 Design Parameters, Implementation and Outcomes

4.1 Conditions and Challenges

Motivation. Computer science education is increasingly seen as an important part of general teacher education. However, it can be assumed that due to long-term established stereotypes, a lack of prior knowledge [8] and insufficient conceptions of computer science and its role in the digital transformation, only few students exhibit an intrinsic interest on topics of computer science. Furthermore, computer science is perceived as complex [5] and often reduced to working with computers [6]. Many students do not see the need to change their role from "outsider" to "insider" [9]. Also, the discourse on digital education is often dominated by the use of digital media in the classroom. In our view, the most important challenge thus arises from the motivation: *How can we attract students to want to deal with computer science topics and how can we continuously maintain motivation while contributing to a positively-shaped image of computer science?*

Organizational Conditions. The organizational conditions still pose a particular challenge for such a course, as at most institutions, digital education is not a (mandatory) part of teacher education curricula. Furthermore, there is a lack of corresponding qualified staff and resources: *How can the numerous student teachers per institution be provided with a well-founded computer science education offer in a timely, financially-feasible, and scalable manner that meets the demands of good education as elaborated in computing education over the last 30 years (for example, contextualized, modeling-based, idea-based)*?

Content-Wise Challenges. Many years of experience in computer science education at all age levels show that the design of computing education programs poses special challenges. Computer science is often abstract and thus difficult to grasp, requires problem-solving skills, has a wide range of topics, and technical skills are needed to implement computer science models, which are regularly perceived as demotivating in particular in the context of learning to program [10]. Furthermore, a great heterogeneity of students is to be expected, both in terms of their prior computer science experience and in terms of the types of schools and subjects studied. *Given the students' expected heterogeneity, how can computer science competencies be developed in a way that offers concrete application possibilities for subject teaching in various subjects?*

4.2 Design of the Course

Organizationally, the course was designed and advertised as an optional blended learning course (5 ECTS) for "competencies for teaching in the digital world", addressing the aforementioned challenges as follows: By embedding it in the larger context of digital education, the prospect of being able to apply the acquired competencies to subject teaching, and the close cooperation and joint implementation with colleagues from media education, the computer science core was intended to remain in the background. Five of the twelve modules of the course deal with the acquisition of computer science competencies, whereby exemplary topics from the broad spectrum in computer science were interwoven with the requirements in the context of digital education (cf. Table 1)[1]. The comprehensive and appealing presentation of the modules as online learning units should, on the one hand, take into account the expected heterogeneity of the students, so that they can work as far as possible independently and at their own pace, as well as pursue personal interests. On the other hand, the few permanently-available staff and material resources should be used in such a way that as many students as possible can benefit from the offer. Within the ongoing scaling and the Covid19 pandemic, the synchronous part was reduced to the implementation and presentation of the final project phase. The loss of the opportunity to engage in collaborative learning experiences in face-to-face encounters was handled with appropriate alternatives considered in the design principles.

Table 1. Modules of the course, modules with focus on computer science in **bold**.

Modules 0–5	Modules 6–11
0: Digital literacy in the subject classroom	6: Research, store, and evaluate digitally
1: **Fundamentals of digitalization**	7: Communication, interaction, and collaboration
2: Media Culture History, Theory, and Ethics	8: **From data to professional knowledge**
3: **Computers and the Internet**	9: **Simulations in the professional context**
4: Creativity in digitalization	10: Social networks
5: **Solving subject-specific problems with algorithms**	11: Outlook: Digital opportunities and boundaries

The **content and methodological design** is guided by design principles initially grounded in theory and later sharpened during the accompanying research, which, in addition to meeting the challenges outlined, aim to illustrate the relevance, applicability, and creative possibilities of computer science:

Through *scaffolding*, the learning process is supported by guiding assistance and the degrees of freedom in performing a task are initially limited [11]. This (optional) temporary support is intended to help with the understanding of new concepts so that learners can later work on similar tasks independently. In the context of the course, the use-modify-create approach [12] was used for this purpose, explanatory videos were created, and practical tasks were initially guided in small steps, which was intended to take into account the students' limited prior experience. The free-text responses to the module-accompanying

[1] A publicly accessible version of the modules can be found at blindedforreview.

evaluations showed that the exercises on programming were challenging, but the explanatory videos were rated as particularly helpful, so that such assistance for programming tasks was consistently expanded.

To achieve *contextualization* in different subjects, examples of application or relationships to the subjects were shown and social implications taken into account [13]. The examples were transferred by the students to their own subjects in reflection tasks to ensure applicability in their teaching. The feedback from the students showed that the contextualization was important for recognizing the contents' significance for their own subject and teaching. Furthermore, the evaluations showed that the relevance of programming, in particular, must be made clear through appropriate contexts and illustrative examples.

The consistent *application of the "pedagogical double-decker"*, which refers to the idea of training teachers with methods and examples they themselves can use for their later teaching, is intended to underline the practical relevance of what has been learned and to make the learning processes more sustainable by making the contents also tangible at the action level [14], but the activities can also be applied directly or transferred into teaching. In the evaluations, students continuously emphasized this as particularly useful for their own teaching.

The continuous *promotion of communication and cooperation* turned out to be one of the most important design principles regarding the implementation as a blended learning course, both for motivational factors and the professional exchange. For this purpose, discussion forums, digital bulletin boards or tasks that required explicit collaboration were used. On the one hand, this stimulated exchange between the subjects, thus highlighting the interdisciplinary importance of the digital transformation with regards to changing subjects and schools, and on the other hand, it addressed the great amount of heterogeneity. The students found the tasks for the mutual exchange of ideas to be enriching, precisely because they contributed to the relevance of the content.

In order to lower motivational and technical hurdles for the students, *low-threshold access* through active learning and playful tinkering was applied as a consistent design principle [15]. Animations, applets, games, and the programming environment Snap*!* were used for this purpose, among others. The latter is not only very accessible but also allows for easy creation, investigation, and further development of simulations or data analysis, which additionally directly provides applicability in subject teaching. These elements were often mentioned positively by the students in the free-text comments and described as motivating.

4.3 Overall Evaluation

Since the piloting of the first modules in winter term 2018/19, the course has been offered every semester at three universities due to increasing interest. Overall, out of the 709 students thus far, an exceptionally high proportion of female students (75%) for computer science courses stands out. This is notably due to the fact that a large proportion of the participants could be recruited from the elementary school teacher training program. Given the growing importance of computer science education in elementary school [16], this is particularly gratifying.

Looking at interest in computer science, before the course began, 62% of the 424 participants in the evaluation already agreed with the statement "computer science is interesting"; 17% of the respondents initially saw computer science as rather boring. In the pre-post comparison of interest, the Wilcoxon signed-rank test[2] yields a significant increase with medium effect size according to [17] at a significance level of $\alpha = 0.05$ with a median of 5 in the pretest and a median of 6 in the posttest ($n = 231$, $p < 0.001$, $r = 0.36$) – 79% of the respondents now see computer science as at least rather interesting, only 8% as rather boring. It is likely that demonstrating the width of computer science and the corresponding creative and collaborative opportunities have contributed to the increase in interest.

A central goal of the course is to promote computer science competencies, particularly ensuring their applicability in the subject classroom. The students' self-assessment of computer science competencies (for example, on the components of a computer, the coding of data, or the subject-specific effects of algorithms), we found only little prior knowledge – in line with our expectations (cf. Fig. 1). Comparing the results of those who attended computer science within their K-12 education (46%), the only significant difference was for the question "I can explain how computers store data in 0 and 1" (Mann-Whitney U tests at a significance level of $\alpha = 0.05$).

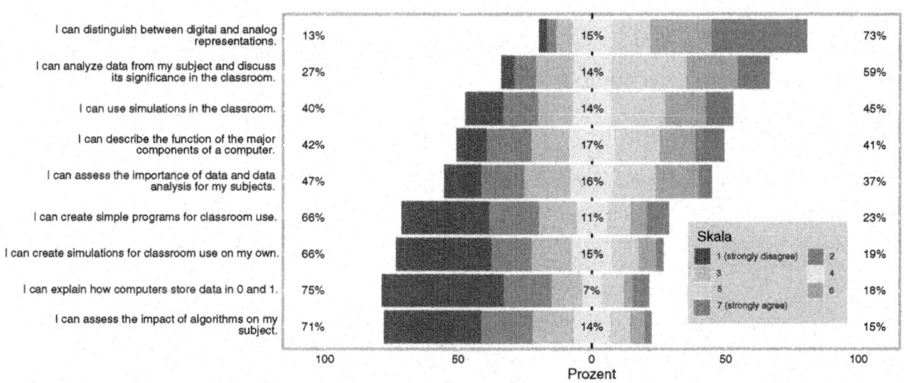

Fig. 1. self-assessment of students in pretest (n = 424)

In the posttest, matching was established for 231 participants based on the individual participant code. According to the Mann-Whitney U test, the answers of the participants for whom this matching was possible did not differ significantly at a significance level of $\alpha = 0.05$ in both the pretest and the posttest (in all questions except the one about the importance of data and data analyses for own subjects) from those for whom no matching was available. Therefore, it

[2] Due to the absence of a normal distribution, non-parametric test procedures were used consistently.

can be assumed that the results are sufficiently representative. In Table 2, the respective medians, the p-value of the Wilcoxon signed-rank test (H_0: No or negative trial effect)[3] and the correlation coefficient r[4] are used as a measure of effect size.

Table 2. Self-assessment of competencies (n = 231, Likert scale from 1 (does not apply) to 7 (applies completely)).

Statement	med pre	med post	Wilcoxon-Test	r
I can explain how computers store data in 0 and 1	2	6	$p < 0,001^*$	0, 67
I can assess the impact of algorithms on my subject	2	5	$p < 0,001^*$	0, 66
I can assess the importance of data and data analysis for my subjects	4	6	$p < 0,001^*$	0, 62
I can use simulations in the classroom	4	6	$p < 0,001^*$	0, 59
I can create simulations for classroom use on my own	3	5	$p < 0,001^*$	0, 61
I can analyze data from my subject and discuss its significance in the classroom	5	6	$p < 0,001^*$	0, 52
I can describe the function of the major components of a computer	4	6	$p < 0,001^*$	0, 54
I can create simple programs for classroom use	3	6	$p < 0,001^*$	0, 63
I can distinguish between digital and analog representations	6	7	$p < 0,001^*$	0, 38
Total	3.66	5.78	$p < 0,001^*$	0, 69

The results in the pre-post comparison show a significant increase for the self-assessment of competencies – in all sub-questions as well as overall. The effect sizes are strong in almost all cases.

[3] Significant test results to a significance level of $\alpha = 0.05$ are indicated by a $*$.

[4] The correlation coefficient r is defined as $r = \frac{z}{\sqrt{n}}$, where z indicates the standardized test statistic of the Wilcoxon signed-rank test and n indicates the sample size. According to [17], $r = 0.10$ and above is considered a weak effect, $r = 0.30$ and above is considered a medium effect, and $r = 0.50$ and above is considered a strong effect.

5 Discussion and Conclusion

Anchoring computer science foundations in general teacher education is a central task in the context of digital education. Our results confirm the assumption that high heterogeneity and low prior experience of students in particular have to be taken into account for the design of appropriate course offerings. Furthermore, we found no significant influence of prior K-12 computer science education.

A notable observation of the implementation was that the *digital transformation* in the students' view was initially almost exclusively related to media *use*. Within the course, the consequences of the digital transformation for everyday life and the subjects and scientific disciplines were emphasized. As can be seen from the feedback, the students were thus able to better understand phenomena or topics that are gaining relevance in their subjects in the course of the digital transformation after the course. Therefore, the modules create the necessary basis for discussing the effects of digital change in their subjects. We see the consistent transfer of interdisciplinary computer science education to a contextualized view in relation to the subject studied as a central criterion for success. However, programming remains a particular but rewarding challenge for students. Here, we have learned that – especially in online environments – intense scaffolding is necessary. Furthermore, appropriate contextualization is central to clarify relevance and thus contribute to motivation, so that most students could say of themselves, not without pride: "I have programmed for the first time".

The students' interest in computer science also increased slightly during the course of the study program. Such an increase cannot be taken for granted. For example, [6] finds that prospective teachers' interest in computer science did not change as a result of their corresponding course offerings, and [18] concludes that interest in computer science actually declined slightly in an after-school learning lab regardless of the module, with older visitors' interest actually declining slightly more in comparison.

In summary, it can be seen that not only can foundations of computer science be prepared in an appropriately accessible way for students of all subjects and school types, but that students were also able to recognize the meaningfulness or necessity of these computer science concepts and that their confidence in their competencies for teaching in the digital world could be strengthened. A strong contextualization in the respective subjects, intensive scaffolding, the promotion of communication and collaboration, playful approaches, and the use of the "pedagogical double-decker" proved to be particularly successful in the design. The results thus provide promising guidelines for the development of computer science courses for general teacher education that prepare future teachers for teaching in the digital world.

References

1. GFD: Fachliche Bildung in der digitalen Welt – Positionspapier der Gesellschaft für Fachdidaktik [professional education in the digital world – position paper of the society for subject matter teaching and learning] (2018). https://www.fachdidaktik.org/wp-content/uploads/2018/07/GFD-Positionspapier-Fachliche-Bildung-in-der-digitalen-Welt-2018-FINAL-HP-Version.pdf. Accessed 01 Aug 2022
2. Forschungsgruppe Lehrerbildung Digitaler Campus Bayern: Kernkompetenzen von Lehrkräften für das Unterrichten in einer digitalisierten Welt [core competences of teachers for teaching in a digital world]. Merz **4**, 65–74 (2017)
3. van Ackeren, I., et al.: Digitalisierung in der lehrerbildung: herausforderungen, entwicklungsfelder und förderung von gesamtkonzepten [Digital transformation in teacher education: challenges, areas of development and advancement of concepts]. Die Deutsche Schule **111**(1), 103–119 (2019)
4. Caspersen, M.E., Gal-Ezer, J., McGettrick, A., Nardelli, E.: Informatics for all the strategy. ACM (2018)
5. Losch, D., Humbert, L.: Informatische Bildung für alle lehramtsstudierenden [Computer science education for all pre-service teachers]. In: Pasternak, A. (ed.) Informatik für alle, pp. 119–128. GI, Bonn (2019)
6. Yadav, A., et al.: Computational thinking in elementary and secondary teacher education. ACM TOCE **14**(1), 1–16 (2014)
7. Casali, A., Monjelat, N., San Martín, P., Zanarini, D.: Primary level teachers training in computer science: experience in the argentine context. In: Pesado, P., Arroyo, M. (eds.) CACIC 2019. CCIS, vol. 1184, pp. 389–404. Springer, Cham (2020). https://doi.org/10.1007/978-3-030-48325-8_25
8. Döbeli Honegger, B., Hielscher, M.: Vom Lehrplan zur LehrerInnenbildung - Erste Erfahrungen mit obligatorischer Informatikdidaktik für angehende Schweizer PrimarlehrerInnen [From curriculum to teacher training - first experiences with compulsory computer science education for pre-service swiss primary teachers]. In: INFOS 2017, pp. 97–107. GI (2017)
9. Schulte, C., Knobelsdorf, M.: Attitudes towards computer science-computing experiences as a starting point and barrier to computer science. In: Proceedings of the Third International Workshop on Computing Education Research, ICER 2007, pp. 27–38. Association for Computing Machinery, New York (2007). https://doi.org/10.1145/1288580.1288585
10. Kinnunen, P., Simon, B.: Experiencing programming assignments in CS1: the emotional toll. In: Proceedings of ICER 2010, pp. 77–86. ACM, New York (2010)
11. Lin, T.C., et al.: A review of empirical evidence on scaffolding for science education. Int. J. Sci. Math. Educ. **10**(2), 437–455 (2012)
12. Lee, I., et al.: Computational thinking for youth in practice. ACM Inroads **2**(1), 32–37 (2011)
13. Guzdial, M.: Does contextualized computing education help? ACM Inroads **1**(4), 4–6 (2010)
14. Arnet-Clark, I., Smeets-Cowan, R., Kühnis, J.: Competences in teacher education at Schwyz University of teacher education (PHSZ), and the swiss education policy. e-Pedagogium (2), 88–99 (2015)
15. Petre, M., Richards, M.: Playful pedagogy: empowering students to do, design, and build. In: Leicht-Scholten, C., Schroeder, U. (eds.) Informatikkultur neu denken - Konzepte für Studium und Lehre, pp. 41–54. Springer, Wiesbaden (2014). https://doi.org/10.1007/978-3-658-06022-0_3

16. European Union and Audiovisual and Culture Executive Agency Education: Digital education at school in Europe. Publications Office of the European Union, Brussels (2019)
17. Cohen, J.: A power primer. Psychol. Bull. **112**(1), 155–159 (1992)
18. Bergner, N.: Konzeption eines Informatik-Schülerlabors und Erforschung dessen Effekte auf das Bild der Informatik bei Kindern und Jugendlichen [Conceptualisation of a computer science student laboratory and research of its effects on the view of children and adolescents on computer science]. Ph.D thesis, RWTH, Aachen (2016)

Digital Innovation in Assessment During Lockdown: Perspectives of Higher Education Teachers in Portugal

Ana Amélia Carvalho[1(✉)], Daniela Guimarães[1], Célio Gonçalo Marques[2], Inês Araújo[1], and Sónia Cruz[1]

[1] University of Coimbra, LabTE, CEIS20, 3000 Coimbra, Portugal
{anaameliac,inesaraujo}@fpce.uc.pt, Danidesg@gmail.com, Soniacatarinacruz@gmail.com

[2] Polytechnic Institute of Tomar, LIED, TECHN&ART, 2300 Tomar, Portugal
Celiomarques@ipt.pt

Abstract. During the COVID-19 pandemic, lockdown policies forced higher education teachers to adopt remote teaching. This disruptive situation challenged teachers to continue delivering classes and carrying out assessment online. In order to investigate higher education teachers' perceptions about the online assessment, a survey was conducted in Portugal. The study focuses on digital tools and methodologies used in online assessment, first-time digital tools used, and the tools and methodologies that teachers intend to maintain in face-to-face assessment, as well as confidence in students' results. Data was collected online from May to July 2021. Participants (n = 868) were from all fields of science and technology. Most of them (80%) reported the use of new assessment tools and methodologies during this period. The majority (72%) has confidence in the results obtained by the students. However, some of them (36%) reported academic fraud situations. Digital tools related to summative assessment are the most prevalent, but methodologies related to formative assessment were also used. Some teachers (49%) intend to use methodologies and tools in face-to-face classes used for the first-time during the lockdown.

Keywords: Digital Assessment · Innovation · Higher Education

1 Introduction

This paper focuses on the consequences of COVID-19 pandemic on education, particularly on assessment during educational lockdown. The move from face-to-face education to online technologies forced teachers and students to adapt to a new teaching and learning context. Video conferencing and collaborative platforms became widely used and infrastructure for internet access had to be reinforced.

Online learning challenged teachers and students and brought up serious issues to those with limited internet access. Even in countries with good internet infrastructure,

Published by Springer Nature Switzerland AG 2023
T. Keane et al. (Eds.): WCCE 2022, IFIP AICT 685, pp. 400–411, 2023.
https://doi.org/10.1007/978-3-031-43393-1_37

there are questions about the ability of teachers and students to interact effectively through video conferencing. Although some teachers had already online teaching competencies, others were not prepared at all. In a very short period, higher education institutions provided training to teachers. They had to cope with increased preparatory work, difficulty gauging students' understanding, and encouraging students' class participation [1, 2]. Due to all this effort to adapt to remote emergency teaching, several questions emerged related to assessment online. Did teachers carry out assessment during lockdown? What kind of digital tools did they use? After emergency remote teaching will they continue to use those digital tools? Did the pandemic contribute to accelerating the appropriation of technology? These are some of the questions that we intend to answer with an online survey that addressed higher education teachers in Portugal.

This paper presents a descriptive study aiming to understand the online assessment, the new tools and methodologies used and the ones that teachers intend to keep in their classes, and the confidence on students results.

2 Emergency Remote Teaching

Emergency remote teaching was a solution to the COVID-19 pandemic crisis. Such practice is quite different from distance education or well-planned online learning experiences [3].

2.1 Digital Education in Higher Education

Some higher education institutions (HEI) had educational support to prepare instructors to teach, and to update their training particularly with the pedagogical integration of new educational technologies, apps, or videoconferencing systems. During the last decade, several Portuguese institutions started to offer training to their teachers.

Portuguese legislation for distance learning programs (Decree Law 133/2019) and the Portuguese Agency for Higher Education Evaluation and Accreditation, responsible for the Evaluation and Accreditation of programs on higher education, demand pedagogical training. Due to this demand several institutions are developing courses to promote pedagogical training. However, several teachers are always resistant to change and avoid training.

During COVID-19 lockdowns, HEI moved to courses taught online. This was a new situation. It had been necessary to train teaching staff and to improvise quick solutions [3]. There was a general lack of preparation of HEI, teachers, and students [4].

In Portugal, even before the general lockdown decreed by the government on the 16th March 2020, most HEI were already on remote online classes. Training was needed. Each institution made an effort to solve this problem. Two important stages to train teachers for remote teaching emerged: synchronous tools and then online assessment.

First of all, the training focused on using videoconferencing systems. It was a possible solution for keeping classes going on. To complement the teachers training during lockdown, several webinars and workshops were organized to help teachers. As noted by Suswanto et al. [5], learning through online media, such as Google Classroom, Zoom, and Microsoft Teams, has been successfully implemented during pandemic.

Along with the lockdown, another problem arose: assessment online. This was the second stage in training for remote teaching. Tools for questionnaires and quizzes online were the most demanded. Training also addressed the use of LMS to do tests and the use of proctoring systems, for example, Exame.net, to avoid academic fraud. Most institutions sent guidelines for online assessment to help teachers and to minimize academic fraud.

2.2 Digital Innovation and Assessment

The integration of digital technologies in educational innovation "can result in a range of fundamentally different ways of learners and teachers' access, engage with, and build knowledge" [6, p. 2310]. Innovation in education, according to UNICEF, means solving a real problem in a new, simple way to promote equitable learning. Innovation demandes creativity, and creative people demonstrate the trait of openness to experience.

Using digital tools in teaching practices is not always synonymous of digital innovation. Genlott et al. [7] consider the existence of a "first-order change", related with an adjustment to the practice, by doing the same things done before, but using new ways to do it, and a "second-order change" that implies a redefinition of the nature of activities. The authors also emphasize the existence of intrinsic barriers to the "second-order change", mostly related to traditional classroom practices. "People may adopt the mechanical parts of an innovation without adopting its purposes, theories and evaluation measures. In that case the innovation is lost" [7, p. 3025].

The way students learn is shaped by the structure of assessment. Teachers need to be aware of this when selecting assessment methods and in thinking about the relationship between formative and summative assessment. Formative assessment is more focused on the process of learning itself, referred to as assessment for learning [8, 9]. It enables students to develop their learning through assess and feedback. It gives student opportunities to experiment, make mistakes and take risks. It helps students to identify their own gaps. Also, it promotes teacher reflections about the contents that need to be reinforced. By contrast, summative assessment is assessment of learning, is punctual, and it quantifies students' learning with a mark. What teachers do with assessment information determines whether the event is formative or summative. Formative and summative assessments in conjunction with appropriate feedback systems are used to support learning in higher education [4].

Although some doubts can arise in teachers' confidence about online assessment [4, 10–12], there is evidence of no differences between the academic performance when students went online [11, 13].

2.3 Cheating

Cheating is the antithesis of mastery forms of motivation and student engagement [14]. Mastery approach goals are counterintuitive to cheating behavior [15]. Cheating is also dependent on how performance is evaluated [16–18]. The authors determined that students were more likely to commit fraud when the focus was on results-based evaluation, instead of process-based evaluation.

Most university courses tend to use result-based evaluation, in typical learning conditions [19]. However, some institutions changed this focus when instruction and assessment moved into remote delivery.

Students report being almost four times more likely to be dishonest in online courses (42%) than in-person courses (10%) [20]. King and Case [21] identified that the percentage of students who admitted to academic cheating activity increased over a five-year period, but almost three in four students felt it was either very easy or somewhat easy to cheat on an online exam.

Academic fraud is a problem that HEI cannot ignore. It is important to clarify students what academic fraud is and its ethical and legal implications, something that many institutions already do. A possible solution is to rethink the type of assessment.

3 Method

We used a single-administration survey [22] to collect higher education teachers' perspectives about online assessment.

The questionnaire has demographic questions and four dimensions, namely: i) online assessment, ii) use of some digital tools for first-time, iii) confidence in students' results, and iv) intention to keep the same kind of assessment used during lockdown in face-to-face classes.

In order to describe the sample, the demographic questions were about gender, age, service years as a teacher in HE, and the field of science and technology (FOS), classification in the Frascati Manual.

3.1 Procedures

In May 2021, we posted a link to the questionnaire on social media platforms including Facebook and LinkedIn, and we also contacted higher education institutions to send the link to their teaching staff. However, some HEI declined to undertake the questionnaire, due to being overwhelmed with requests to answer questionnaires.

The questionnaire is in line with the Ethical Charter published by the Portuguese Society of Education Sciences [23]. The questionnaire was approved by the Ethics Committee and the Data Protection Committee.

After clicking the link, participants accessed an informational letter outlining the details of the study, the estimated time - approximately 4 min - to fill in the questionnaire, and the consent to collect data.

The questionnaire was anonymous, and the respondents' participation was voluntary. The questionnaire was available on LimeSurvey, from May to July 2021.

3.2 Participants

A convenience sample of 868 higher education Portuguese teachers answered the questionnaire, 53.5% were female and 46.5% male. Their age ranged from 24 to 70 years old. Their average age is 51.6, the mode is 53 years, and the median is 53 years old. They were from all fields of science and technology (FOS), in the following order of respondents: Social Sciences (28.3%), Engineering and Technologies (23.9%), Exact and Natural Sciences (19.8%), Medical and Health Sciences (14.2%), Humanities (12.6%), and Agricultural Sciences (1.2%).

Most of the sample were highly experience in teaching in higher education (Table 1). More than 60% of respondents had 21 to 40 years of teaching experience, followed by 11 to 20 years (15.8%). Lastly, teachers with less and with more teaching experience, namely up to 5 years (13.4%) and over 41 years (3.9%).

Table 1. Service years as a teacher in higher education.

Length of service	f	%
up to 5 years	116	13.4
6 to 10 years	59	6.8
11 to 20 years	137	15.8
21 to 30 years	305	35.1
31 to 40 years	217	25.0
Over 41 years	34	3.9

Most of the teachers (81%) carried out online assessment during HEI' lockdown.

4 Results and Discussion

From a sample of 868 teachers of HEI with classes online due to confinement, 701 did online assessment. Several reasons were pointed out by 19% of respondents for the non-appliance of assessment: 10% did not need to do it and 5% did not feel confident with the results. Other reasons with less expression (until 1%) were also mentioned, such as: the use of other assessment methods, assessment was carried out in face-to-face due to institution decision, the assessment took place after the lockdown period, they did not know how to carry it out, and because they had a previous bad experience.

4.1 Institutional Guidelines for Assessment Online

For most of the HEI, assessment online was something new. According to respondents, most of them (78.9%) reported that their institutions created guidelines for conducting the online assessment.

To keep the camera always on was the most common guideline provided by the HEI according to 66.9% of respondents. Record the session during the assessment (14.7%), use two cameras (one pointing to the hands and the other pointing to the face) during the test (14.7%), and sign a declaration of non-copying honor (13.3%) were also guidelines to teachers. Other guidelines were also mentioned, but with lower percentage, such as: students should have the microphone on, to include the non-copying declaration of honor in the heading of the test, to confirm the students' identification when conducting assessment, and to use tools specially designed for online assessment. However, some recommendations were abandoned since they were not aligned with the General Data Protection Regulation, especially the ones that invaded the privacy of learners like the obligation of having the camera always on or the recording of the online assessment session.

4.2 Online Assessment

Online assessment carried out by teachers during lockdown is presented in Table 2.

Table 2. Assessment online.

Assessment	f	%
Tests (e.g., MSWord, Moodle, MSTeams…)	565	80,6
Group work	386	55,1
Individual work	354	50.5
Multimedia presentations by students	260	37.1
Oral tests	213	30.4
Handwritten activities (photographed)	164	23.4
Online Quizzes	135	19.3
Students participation in forums	95	13.6
Videos made by students	90	12.8
Peer review	88	12.6
Portfolios	71	10.1
Students participation in chats	44	6.3
Concept maps	36	5.1
Mental maps	22	3.1

Most of the teachers evaluated students through tests, whether using MS Word, Moodle, or MS Teams (80.6%), online quizzes (19.3%), oral tests (30.4%) or even through handwritten activities (23.4%) that were photographed or digitally scanned and sent by email, social networks, or learning management system. Teachers also used group work (55.1%), individual work (50.5%) and students' presentations, both multimedia (37.1%) and videos (12.8%).

With lower percentage, students' participation in forums (13.6%) and in chats (6.3%), assessment based on peer review (12.6%), and portfolios (10.1%). Finally, concept maps (5.1%) and mental maps (3.1%), as knowledge representation assessment.

4.3 Digital Tools Used for the First Time in Assessment

Teachers were asked if, during lockdown, they started using digital tools for assessment that, usually, they did not use. Most teachers (80.3%) answered positively.

Inquired about which digital tools they used for the first time in assessment, the most used are tests (71%), questionnaires (28.8%), and online quizzes (14.2%).

With lower percentage, they used Padlet or similar (8%), Drive (5.5%), and portfolios (5%). Finally, with minimum representation, concept maps (2.8%), mental maps (1.8%), wikis (1.4%), and blogs (1.1%).

4.4 Confidence in Students' Results

Three aspects were considered related to results achieved: teachers' confidence in the results achieved by students, if the results were better or worst than those achieved usually in face-to-face, and finally if they identified cheating.

Results Achieved

Teachers were invited to compare results achieved in assessment during lockdown with results usually achieved in their courses (see Fig. 1).

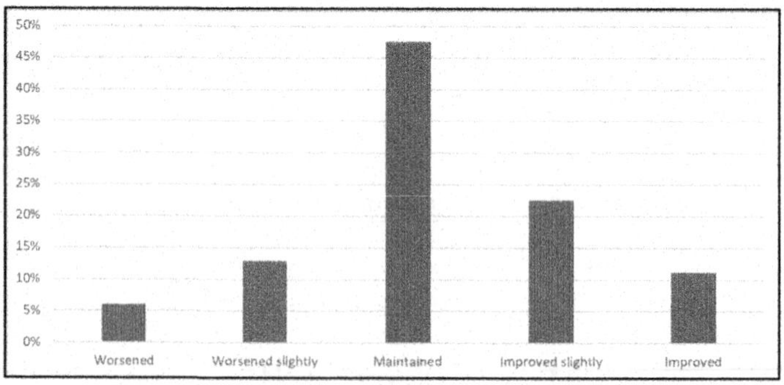

Fig. 1. Students' results worsen or improved during lockdown.

For almost half of the teachers the results remained the same (47.5%), for some the results improved (33.6%), and for a few they worsened (18.8%). Teachers' perceptions are in line with other studies [11, 13].

Confidence in Online Results

Teachers were questioned about their confidence in online assessment during faculty closure, through a five points scale, from 1 (not at all confident) to 5 (very confident) (see Table 3).

Most of the teachers were confident with the results achieved (72.2%), and some were not confident (27.8%). The mean of the data is 3.18, the mode 4 and the median is 3.

Table 3. Teachers confidence in results achieved online during lockdown.

Confidence in students results	f	%
Not at all confident	72	10.3
Slightly confident	123	17.5
Confident	188	26.8
Quite confident	246	35.1
Very confident	72	10.3

4.5 Cheating During Online Assessment

Respondents were asked if they had identified some kind of cheating. Some identified some cheating (36.2%), all others did not (63.8%). Different strategies of cheating were reported, namely: students cooperated with each other to answer the test (24.5%), students consulted not allowed information or tools during the test (18.8%), students sent the answers to other colleagues (18.4%), the test was answered by someone else (5.3%), students got illegitimate (qualified) help during the test (4.4%), and students gained access to the test, before it was carried out, with the help of someone (0.1%).

Teachers were asked to compare online summative assessment with face-to-face summative assessment, and to point in which one do teachers consider it is easier for students to commit fraud (see Table 4). The majority considered it easier to commit fraud in online assessment (79.2%), than in face-to-face (1.0%) assessment. For some (13.6%) there are no differences and others (6.3%) do not know. These results about being easier to cheat online are similar to those obtained by other studies [17, 20, 21].

Table 4. Easier for students to commit fraud: online or face-to-face.

Easier to commit fraud	f	%
Online assessment	555	79.2
Face-to-face assessment	7	1.0
There are no differences	95	13.6
I do not know	44	6.3

We also collected data from students (n = 3,754). They considered that it is easier to cheat during online assessment (57.9%) than during face-to-face assessment (4.9%), others considered that there are no differences (16.2%), and some do not know (21.1%). These results coincide with the opinions of Portuguese teachers on academic fraud and with other studies [17, 20, 21].

Although students recognized that it is easier to cheat online, they would prefer to be assessed face-to-face (65.7%) than online (34.3%).

4.6 Assessment Used that Teachers Intend to Keep

After this upgraded effort to assess students online, we asked teachers if they intend to keep some of the tools or methods used during lockdown in their face-to-face classes. Surprisingly, half of them do not (51.2%), and others are divided into maybe (32.7%) and yes (16.1%).

Those that intend to keep the assessment used during lockdown in face-to-face classes and those that answered maybe (n = 342), selected the options presented in Table 5. The most selected are: group work, individual work, and tests. A second set follows, comprising multimedia presentations by students, online quizzes, students' participation in forums, peer review, and videos made by students. A third set includes students' participation in chats, concept maps, portfolios, and mental maps.

Table 5. Keeping in face-to-face assessment used during lockdown

Assessment	f	%
Group work	198	57.9
Individual work	180	52.6
Tests (e.g., MSWord, Moodle, MSTeams, Classroom)	175	51.2
Multimedia presentations by students	144	42.1
Online quizzes	106	31.0
Students participation in forums	77	22.5
Peer review	68	19.9
Videos made by students	67	19.6
Students participation in chats	31	9.1
Concept maps	30	8.8
Portfolios	23	6.7
Mental maps	17	5.0

According to the selection presented on Table 5, teachers gave priority to student's reflection, creativity and collaborative work.

There is a moderate Pearson correlation between the assessment done online and the assessment teachers intend to keep, related to mental maps ($r = 0.71$), concept maps ($r = 0.68$), peer review (0.61), videos made by students ($r = 0.60$), students' participation in chats ($r = 0.57$), group work ($r = 0.54$), and online quizzes ($r = 0.53$).

4.7 Limitations and Future Directions

Although our findings provide important insights into online assessment during emergency remote learning, there are some limitations. First, participants represent a convenience sample of higher education teachers who used social media platforms or accepted the invitation sent by email by their institutions to participate in the study. As such, these findings cannot be generalized to all teachers. Nonetheless, the number of respondents is quite high.

Second, the questionnaire was short to stimulate respondents, and some topics were not deeply investigated. In future research we intend to interview teachers to better understand their challenges and difficulties, as well as the impact of this experience in their teaching and assessment practices. Particularly, the appropriation of digital tools used for online assessment, and if they returned to the most commonly used assessment of learning, instead of an assessment for learning.

As a recommendation, we advise teachers to design courses with diversity of assessment to minimize cheating. They need training about assessment practices [24, 25], and preventing cheating techniques [24], taking advantage of the innovation for conducting assessments during the confinement due to COVID-19.

Higher education teachers need to step forward in what concerns assessment and take advantage of the digital tools and alternative assessment methods that can further engage students even in face-to-face assessment, rather than limit assessment to the most traditional methods usually used in HEI.

5 Conclusion

From one moment to the next, HEI had to adapt to remote teaching due to the pandemic. This situation exposed major discrepancies both in terms of ownership of the technology and in terms of skills to use it. Not all teachers and students had convenient access to the Internet, adequate equipment and appropriate spaces, and few had pedagogical training in the use of technology.

From a sample of 868 teachers of higher education with online classes due to lockdown, 701 (81%) did online assessment. As online teaching was something new for many teachers, most of them reported that their institutions created guidelines for conducting online assessments, as occurred worldwide [3, 4].

Most teachers evaluated students through tests, whether using MSWord, Moodle or MS Teams. They also used group work, individual work, students' multimedia presentations, oral tests or even handwritten activities that were photographed or digitally scanned and sent by email, social networks, or learning management systems, trying to avoid cheating.

Tests, questionnaires, and online quizzes were the digital tools most used for the first time in assessment. Some teachers used Padlet or similar, Drive, and portfolios. A few teachers used concept maps, mental maps, wikis, and blogs.

Although most teachers recognized the higher likelihood of fraudulent attempts in online assessment, than in face-to-face, they were confident on the results achieved by students. These findings are in line with other studies [11, 13, 17].

Using summative and formative assessment may be a more efficient way of reducing possible fraud situations, focusing on process-based assessment, and reducing result-based assessment [4, 16, 17]. Moreover, formative assessment, as reported, is more effective on academic motivation and self-regulation skill [26].

Despite teachers' effort to assess students online during the lockdown, half of the teachers do not intend to add some of the tools or methods used when returning to face-to-face classes. It seems that some teachers could not perceive usefulness or ease of use, as identified in other studies [27].

The pandemic contributed to accelerating the appropriation of technology and the digital innovation in assessment, but there is still a long way to go. Teachers and institutions should take advantage of the lessons learned during the pandemic to promote the improvement of teaching and learning practices [24–27], including assessment practices.

References

1. Azizan, S., et al.: Online learning and COVID-19 in higher education: the value of IT models in assessing students' satisfaction. Int. J. Emerg. Technol. Learn. (iJET) **17**(3), 245–278 (2022)
2. Rose, S.: Medical student education in the time of COVID-19. JAMA **323**(21), 2131–2132 (2020)
3. Hodges, C., Moore, S., Lockee, B., Trust, T., Bond, A.: The difference between emergency remote teaching and online learning. EDUCAUSE Review (2020). https://er.educause.edu/articles/2020/3/the-difference-between-emergency-remote-teaching-and-online-learning
4. Guangul, F., Suhail, A., Khalit, M., Khidhir, B.: Challenges of remote assessment in higher education in the context of COVID-19: a case study of Middle East College. Educ. Assess. Eval. Account. **32**(4), 519–535 (2020)
5. Suswanto, B., Sulaiman, A., Sugito, T., Weningsih, S., Sabiq, A., Kuncoro, B.: Designing online learning evaluation in times of Covid-19 pandemic. Int. Educ. Res. **4**(1), p18–p18 (2021)
6. Howard, S., Schrum, L., Voogt, J., Sligte, H.: Designing research to inform sustainability and scalability of digital technology innovations. Educ. Tech. Res. Dev. **69**(4), 2309–2329 (2021)
7. Genlott, A., Grönlund, Å., Viberg, O.: Disseminating digital innovation in school–leading second-order educational change. Educ. Inf. Technol. **24**(5), 3021–3039 (2019)
8. Oldfield, A., Broadfoot, P., Sutherland, R., Timmis, S.: Assessment in a digital age: a research review. Bristol: University of Bristol (2013). http://www.bristol.ac.uk/media-library/sites/education/migrated/documents/researchreview.pdf
9. Stiggins, R., Chappuis, J.: An Introduction to Student-Involved Assessment for Learning, 6th edn. Pearson, New York (2012)
10. Pauli, M., Ferrell, G.: The future of assessment: five principles, five targets for 2025. JISC, Bristol (2020). https://www.jisc.ac.uk/reports/the-future-of-assessment
11. Hope, D., Davids, V., Bollington, L., Maxwell, S.: Candidates undertaking (invigilated) assessment online show no differences in performance compared to those undertaking assessment offline. Med. Teach. **43**(6), 646–650 (2021)
12. Stack, A., et al.: Investigating online tests practices of university staff using data from a learning management system. Australas. J. Educ. Technol. **36**(4), 72–81 (2020)
13. Jaap, A., Dewar, A., Duncan, C., Fairhurst, K., Hope, D., Kluth, D.: Effect of remote online exam delivery on student experience and performance in applied knowledge tests. BMC Med. Educ. **21**(1), 1–7 (2021)
14. Daniels, L., Goegan, L., Parker, P.: The impact of COVID-19 triggered changes to instruction and assessment on university students' self-reported motivation, engagement and perceptions. Soc. Psychol. Educ. **24**(1), 299–318 (2021)
15. Pulfrey, C., Vansteenkiste, M., Michou, A.: Under pressure to achieve? The impact of type and style of task instructions on student cheating. Front. Psychol. **10**, 1624 (2019)

16. Daumiller, M., Janke, S.: The impact of performance goals on cheating depends on how performance is evaluated. AERA Open **5**(4) (2019)
17. Tuah, N., Naing, L.: Is online assessment in higher education institutions during COVID-19 pandemic reliable? Siriraj Med. J. **73**(1), 61–68 (2021)
18. Şenel, S., Şenel, H.C.: Remote assessment in higher education during COVID-19 pandemic. Int. J. Assess. Tools Educ. 181–199 (2021)
19. Yüksel, H., Gündüz, N.: Formative and summative assessment in higher education: opinions and practices of instructors. Eur. J. Educ. Stud. **3**(8), 336–356 (2017)
20. Watson, G., Sottile, J.: Cheating in the digital age: do students cheat more in online courses? Online J. Dist. Learn. Adm. **13**(1) (2010). https://mds.marshall.edu/cgi/viewcontent.cgi?article=1000&context=eft_faculty
21. King, D., Case, C.: E-cheating: incidence and trends among college students. Issues Inf. Syst. **15**(1) (2014)
22. Fowler Jr, F.: Survey Research Methods. Sage Publications (2013)
23. SPCE – Sociedade Portuguesa de Ciências da Educação (2020). Carta Ética. SPCE. https://bit.ly/3IcCahg. Accessed 15 Dec 2021
24. Yazici, S., Yildiz Durak, H., Aksu Dünya, B., Şentürk, B.: Online versus face-to-face cheating: the prevalence of cheating behaviours during the pandemic compared to the pre-pandemic among Turkish University students. J. Comput. Assist. Learn. **39**(1), 231–254 (2023)
25. Latif, M.M.M.A., Alhamad, M.M.: Emergency remote teaching of foreign languages at Saudi universities: teachers' reported challenges, coping strategies and training needs. Educ. Inf. Technol. (2023)
26. Ismail, S.M., Rahul, D.R., Patra, I., Rezvani, E.: Formative vs. summative assessment on academic motivation, attitude toward learning, test anxiety, and self-regulation skill. Lang. Test. Asia **12**, 40 (2022)
27. Saleem, I., Shamsi, M.A., Magd, H.: Impact assessment of ease and usefulness of online teaching in higher education in post Covid era. Int. J. Inf. Educ. Technol. **13**(1), 102–113 (2023)

The Role of Technology in Communities of Learning Collaboration and Support

Maina WaGioko[1](✉) and Janet Manza[2](✉)

[1] Aga Khan Schools, Aga Khan Academy, Mombasa, Kenya
gioko@agakhanacademies.org
[2] Presbyterian Primary School, Mombasa, Kenya
janetpetermanza@gmail.com

Abstract. Continuous Professional Learning is gaining currency in Kenya due to several factors, including the Teachers' Service Commission's policy (appraisal and development). This has facilitated practicum session inclusion. This explorative interpretive study undertook artifact analysis to establish the role of social media in practicum. The study reviewed 560 schools from 38 counties after a three-day face-to-face session during the school term practicum. Six platforms, Edmodo, WhatsApp, Slack, Kaizala, Twitter, and Facebook were reviewed. Activity logs (posts and contents) were analyzed over 12 months of practicum (communities of learning) sessions. The document analysis focused on enrolment, traffic, content, type of activities, quality of engagement, and opportunities for support and learning. The findings revealed that currency, relevance, importance, camaraderie, and learning as factors that guided the engagement. The use of social media extended the learning experiences, continued cohort engagement, increased numbers reached, and facilitated the transfer of principles into practice.

Keywords: Practicum · Professional Learning · Technology infusion

1 Introduction

Globally, education has been an important aspect of human resource development, due to the knowledge, skills, attitude, values, and competencies gained from it. Education improves integrity and relationships among individuals. A Community of Learning (CoL) is a group of teachers with a shared commitment to reflect on their teaching practice and to learn, both individually and in teams, about the pedagogies that are most effective for improving learners' learning. The CoL members also reflect on challenges and successes, material development, differentiated instruction, and learning activities through social network technologies, among many other approaches. Social networks can be infused into the CoL, as they allow educators to share ideas irrespective of time and geography. Sharing and comparing classroom teaching content, teaching techniques, and learning methods can help teachers enhance the learning experiences in their classrooms. Social networking allows teachers to connect within and across schools. These

Published by Springer Nature Switzerland AG 2023
T. Keane et al. (Eds.): WCCE 2022, IFIP AICT 685, pp. 412–422, 2023.
https://doi.org/10.1007/978-3-031-43393-1_38

networks are useful, as they keep the teachers abreast of innovative and contextual curriculum deployment, changes in the curriculum, and content across schools, counties, and, perhaps, beyond, in other countries. The connectivity enables teachers to access authentic experiential information, leading to professional growth as they build a network of references from peers and experts. While this is often not talked about, contacts are key to professional learning. The world today revolves around whom you know. Establishing relationships with others in different schools can help teachers to enhance their careers. Social networking for teachers can be used to build contacts with teachers from other schools and help keep their options open. In CoL, Edmodo, WhatsApp, Slack, Kaizala, and Facebook were used in the post-training phase during the practicum for the transfer of principles into practice. This paper aims to explore how social platforms were used in a community of learning to leverage collaboration and support.

2 Nature of the Platforms

This section describes the platforms that were used in the community of learning practicum.

2.1 Edmodo

Edmodo is an educational website that takes the ideas of a social network and refines them and makes them appropriate for a classroom. Using Edmodo, students and teachers can reach out to one another and connect by sharing ideas, problems, and learning resources. This powerful app enables the users to become part of a safe network that provides full privacy. It guarantees full confidentiality so that one can easily store their unique ideas and class projects without worrying. With Edmodo, there is endless collaboration. It means that you can, instantly, connect and get the required information from other students and teachers. It allows interaction in a virtual professional learning community of practice [1].

2.2 WhatsApp

WhatsApp is a free messenger application that works across multiple platforms and is being widely used among students and teachers to send multimedia messages. It enables one-on-one communication, as well as communication in closed, members-only groups. It facilitates interactive, multimedia discourse with quick exchanges of text, images, audio, and video on people's mobile phones. WhatsApp's popularity has been attributed to the fact that it imitates face-to-face communication best and to the sense of immediacy it affords, as messages synchronously flow between group members [2]. WhatsApp groups function as "micro-communities" [3] and establish a sense of community space, where informal communication takes place between the members of the closed group.

2.3 Slack

Slack allows communities, groups, or teams to join through a specific invitation sent by a team admin or owner [4]. Although Slack was meant for organizational communication, it has been slowly turning into a community platform, a function for which users had previously used message boards. According to Peraita and Robey [4], many of these communities are categorized by topics that a group of people may be interested in discussing.

2.4 Facebook

Facebook is a social networking site created in 2004 by Jack Zuckerberg, which has since obtained over a billion users, and it has the potential to facilitate learning in the classroom. With the widespread use of Facebook in society, it simply makes sense to investigate ways it might be used in higher education. Several studies have been done by scholars in different disciplines regarding the use of Facebook (in general and in academia). Students come to school wired and are willing and eager to use technology, but higher education has a well-established trend toward non-adoption of new technologies. Studies on the use of Facebook [5, 6], indicate that there are a wide number of potential benefits to using Facebook as an educational tool.

2.5 Kaizala

Kaizala is like WhatsApp, but a superior one that makes professional engagements more fulfilling [7]. Through Kaizala, you can schedule meetings, undertake surveys, and share files, among others. It is a private platform, where data is safe, and engagement is protected [8].

2.6 Twitter

Twitter is an online news and social networking site, where people communicate in short messages called tweets [9]. Tweeting is posting short messages to anyone who follows you on Twitter, with the hope that your messages are useful and interesting to someone in your audience [10]. Another description of Twitter and tweeting might be micro-blogging. Some people use Twitter to discover interesting people and companies online, opting to follow their tweets [11]. Twitter has been used in education for various purposes [12–17].

The six social network platforms were used to offer a choice from the alumni preference in a diverse differentiated approach.

3 Literature Review

A teacher in the 21st century is expected to be competent in a range of technologies that have proliferated in today's digital world [18]. This is congruent with preparing learners to cope with the demands of the 21st-century job market through the development of digital and information literacies [19]. The "ability to effectively and thoughtfully evaluate, navigate and construct information using a range of digital technologies" [20: p. 128] are key elements that facilitate a teacher's facility to function effectively in a digital world.

Tobin [21] coined the term "Personal Learning Network," to describe a network of people and resources that support ongoing learning. While the terms Professional Learning Network and Communities of Learning are often used interchangeably, in this study CoL is used because this study focused on teachers' learning after a course related to their professional work. According to Tobin, employees can learn by observing and talking with their network of colleagues and with individuals who have relevant expertise. He asserted that "learning doesn't take place just in training programs but should be part of every employee's everyday activity. You learn every time you read a book or article, every time you observe how someone else is doing work like your own, every time you ask a question" [21, para 1]. Tobin, thus, defined CoL as an ongoing and multifaceted process.

CoL can be understood as learning systems built upon an architecture of participation that can come to exist with or without specific objectives. In such systems "learning is understood in terms of on-going, recursively elaborate adaptations through which systems maintain their coherences within dynamic circumstances" [22, p. 151]. Individual agents engage in these systems through various forms of participation such as from committed engagement to more peripheral lurking that is generally transactional in nature. As people interact in a system there is a dual change happening to them as well as to the systems. The responsive nature of CoLs might offer teachers access to interactions and resources necessary to grow professionally.

Many researchers and educators have attempted to define and envision the purpose of CoL for teachers [e.g. 23–26], but there is no agreed-upon definition. CoL has been described as a "reciprocal learning system[s]" [25, p. 8], "vibrant, ever-changing group[s] of connections," [27, para. 4], "network[s] of fellow educators and resources" [Catapano, n. d. in 28], "the sum of all social capital and connections" [23], and "online communities that allow the sharing of lesson plans, teaching strategies, and student work, as well as collaboration across grade levels and departments" [24]. Various scholars, authors, and educators conceive of CoL in unique, and somewhat disparate ways. Understanding how educators conceive of and utilize CoL may help bring more clarity to the construct.

CoL offers new spaces in which teachers may learn and grow as professionals with support from a diverse network of people and resources. With recent advances in technology and widespread access to the Internet, teachers can expand their web of connections beyond their face-to-face networks, seek help and emotional support, and aggregate vast quantities of professional knowledge at any time and from anywhere [14, 26, 29]. CoL can also be from online communities, networks of practice [30], and social media sites. Online communities are groups of people who connect for a shared purpose, while a network refers to a "set of nodes and links with affordances for learning" [31, p. 9]. Social media sites are digital tools that people can use to connect and communicate with others. Each of these terms refers to a single medium for connecting with others. CoL is a broader, multifaceted system, that often incorporates multiple communities, networks of practice, and sites that support both on- and offline learning. Researchers have yet to explore CoL as complex systems of people, resources, and digital tools.

Even though educators seem to be giving CoL more attention, there is a dearth of research about CoL and its effects. Most studies about online teacher learning focus on the learning experiences of the teachers in a single community, a network of practice, or a site, such as Twitter [13–17, 32]. Similar to CoL, teachers participate in these online spaces to find, share, and create professional knowledge [16, 32, 33], and to collaborate with and feel supported by a community of education professionals [12, 14, 17, 32]. Some researchers have also explored how participation in online spaces shapes teachers' identities [34, 35].

While some teachers have explored the immediate, potential, and applied value of certain online communities and networks [31], there is still a significant gap in the literature regarding the value of CoL, and how they shape teaching and learning. Given the limited nature of research about CoL, in this study, we sought to further understand teachers' experiences with social media within the CoL.

Social networks allow teachers to share ideas. Comparing notes on classroom teaching techniques and learning styles can help teachers enhance the learning experience in their classroom. Teachers can also share lesson plans and visual aid ideas. Social networking allows teachers to connect with teachers in other schools. These partnerships are useful as the teachers keep abreast of innovations and contextual curriculum deployment, changes in curriculum and content in other counties and, maybe, even other countries. Teachers can also use social networking to connect with teachers and experts from other countries. This can help them get accurate information on other countries and not just use content from the Internet that is often outdated. For example, the teachers can plan a virtual field trip, with ease and accuracy. The virtual connection can also offer live interactions with engagement. The study aimed to investigate how teachers use social networks to support their learning post-face-to-face sessions.

3.1 The Issue and the Problem of the Study

Educators' professional learning sessions are usually done face-to-face after which the educators receive a certificate. This has led to educators earning certificates without transferring what they learned into practice. Similarly, after the training, the educators return to their stations where some of them attempt to implement the new ideas and give up on a slight challenge. Reflection on the approach has led many service providers to introduce a practicum session, where the community of learning approaches is implemented. In the community of learning, the educators collaboratively implement the new ideas, where the collaboration is mediated by social media. More so, the educator also enriches their learning further by connecting to others who were not on the course within and outside the County. Social Media has been used in social interaction and the focus on professional work has been interrupted by the social aspect. The study aimed at exploring how these interruptions can be curtailed and how the focus on professional learning is enhanced in social media as well as how connectivity through social media facilitated collaboration and support in communities of learning.

4 Methodology

The study was explorative interpretive in approach. Artifact analysis was done by tracking the educators who were invited, had joined, and participated actively from the cohort of teachers and school leaders in Kenya who had attended a face-to-face session. A cohort of educators was selected based on their use of social media in their CoL as well as representation across the courses and the regions where the course was implemented. The design of the program the educators were attending has a face-to-face and an 8-week practicum session hence a favourable design to explore the use of social media. The CoL activities included posting artifacts (videos, pictures, documents, publications, sound), discussions, reflections, and information. The activities were tracked to identify the frequency, type, level of discussion and nature of responses. The tracking of engagement was done to identify the evolvement of what was going on. The interactions were tracked across cohorts, and across platforms, where the findings were analyzed. The analysis developed emerging thematic areas for insights into the role of social media in CoL. The aim was to analyze the post-face-to-face activities and establish how social media was scaffolding the transfer of principles into practice in a collaborative peer-supported environment.

4.1 Limitations

Educators who are not technically advanced faced challenges, especially accessing shared information, due to the type of phones they had, electricity issues, and connectivity. Although 99% of the population owned smartphones, not all smartphones supported sending information, especially video clips, certain photos, and recorded clips. These were limitations that lead to a further selection of only those who were able to engage actively in the CoL.

5 Findings and Discussion

Out of the six, Twitter was the least used forum (Table 1). Twitter has analytics that can present the Twitter handle traffic, tweets, retweets (with or without comments), likes, and comments. Twitter continues to be used by the facilitators after the study and it became a platform connecting to the government semi-autonomous agencies such as the Ministry of Education, Kenya Institute of Curriculum Development (KICD), Centre for Mathematics, Science and Technology Education in Africa (CEMASTEA), as well as other partners such as Universities and other agencies such as I choose life Africa, and British Council, among others. Twitter was later utilized by the facilitators as a page for creating awareness of what is happening and got more connections with outsiders than the alumni. One of the limitations was the word limit and the lack of usage. It might be useful to introduce tweeting during the educator's preparation so that they see the importance of it in sharing learning.

Edmodo, Slack, and Kaizala were introduced during the face-to-face sessions. The use of platforms for task submission of deliverables, and undertaking surveys, quizzes, and tests proved to be useful for understanding navigation and utility. Attempts to use

Table 1. Platforms Utility Post Face-to-Face Sessio

Platform	Edmodo	Slack	WhatsApp	Twitter	Kaizala	Facebook
Educators Invited	330	150	600	150	224	160
Educators Joined	260	130	550	30	156	140
Educators Active	164	87	480	22	122	130

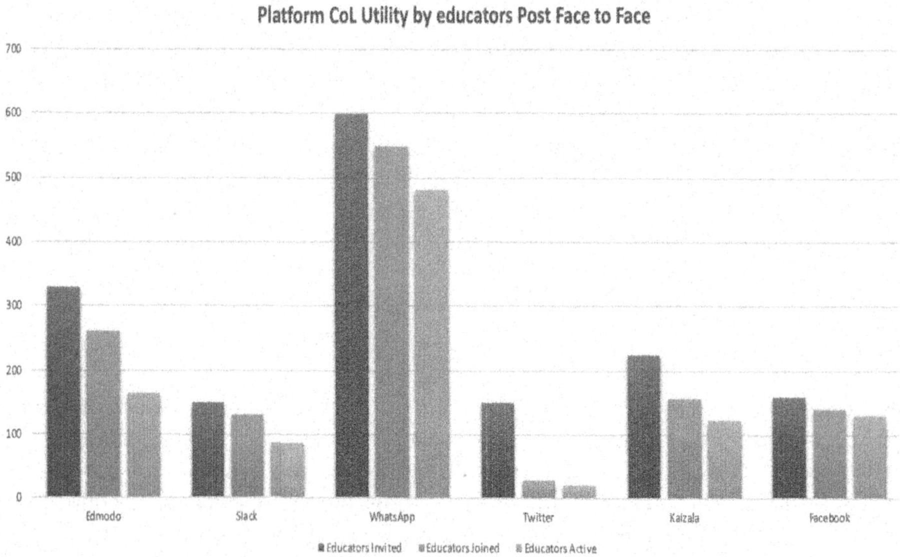

Fig. 1. The distribution of Participants Across Platforms

them after graduation was not sustainable as the traffic dwindled fast over time (Table 1). They were key during the face-to-face session and the demand for deliverables, reflection, and quizzes increased their currency, thereafter, they dropped in value after graduation. These apps have mobile functionality, so mobility was not the reason for the decline. It may be attributed to the participant's comfort and what they like using mostly. These apps have become preferable due to the variety of functions, hence, they invite officialdom. The social media mentality is of casual approach and engagement. It will take more exposure and comfort levels for this cohort to embrace the superior apps which are not frequently used social media tools.

Facebook and WhatsApp (Fig. 1) stood the test of time with over 80% of the participants engaging in post-face-to-face sessions. There was a group on WhatsApp and a Facebook page that was private and invite only. On both platforms, there was traffic ranging from sharing activities, papers, information (videos, pictures, documents), and discussions (posing and responding to questions, modeling pedagogical activities). Some of the alumni took a natural leadership role by action and they shared their areas of implementation ranging from leadership, literacy, numeracy, and professional learning.

The analysis of social media engagement brought out the five critical aspects of support that is currency, relevancy, importance, camaraderie, and educators as learners.

5.1 Currency

Most of the posts were about current issues or what was happening during the moment of posting. This included announcements on educational events and news about educational incidents or happenings. The platforms became like a live bulletin, where updates and information and or discussion of current issues were shared. The currency of the participation was aligned to the mainstream media newspaper, radio, and television on education matters. The currency could have been a level driving the level of engagement.

5.2 Relevancy

Most of the posts were about learning, classroom work, or the teaching profession. These were designed directly by the teachers or downloaded from a website or forwarded from a post on another platform or group/page within the same platform. Relevance was a multiplier, it provided information (Knowledge, Skills, Values, Attitudes, Competency) to the educators. It was a learning center.

5.3 Importance

The information posted may not have been important to everyone in the group, but it spoke to specific members of the group, depending on what was posted. For example, a post on lesson planning resonated with those who were planning lessons or had an issue with lesson planning. The variety of members in the groups and the convergence of having taken the same course meant that the posts reflecting the transfer of principles into practice were important to certain groups within the cohort. The idea of posting inquiry questions made the responses posted important as they responded to an inquiry. The platform became a go-to platform as the educator wanted to learn from the frequently asked questions. The questions brought out the needs of educators and, hence, the facilitators were able to offer comprehensive responses with additional guidance based on the trends.

5.4 Camaraderie

Within the group, different friendships evolved, based on what was being posted. For example, some educators forwarded education matters/ideas/innovations and the responses would come from a certain group who liked such posts. A sense of identity based on interest was established and people coalesced around what they perceived as valuable additions in their professional work. For example, a post on technology infusion in literacy would attract those who are interested in that area, and they would engage more and establish a micro-CoL within the CoL. This would lead to the appreciation and identification of such a team who, later, became resource providers for engaging in that topic and deepening their learning hence identifying their areas of interest as educators.

The educators appreciated the aspect of learning and, hence, the social media CoL activities became a medium for learning. The educators gained knowledge, skills, competencies, values, and attitudes that enabled them to gain insight into issues of time management, teaching/learning approaches, ethics, and digital literacy, all of which inform teaching practices. The social media platform became a source of information, ideas, exemplars, questions, and answers. The more it is offered, the more the teachers and school leaders can become learners.

6 Conclusion

Social media has been observed to support continuous professional learning opportunities. The following areas were seen as the areas of support that can extend professional learning, facilitate continued engagement of the cohorts, enable the transfer of learning into practice, and increase reach:

Extend Professional Learning. This was enabled as the learning continued through sharing resources, sparking questions, and collaborating in activities, among others. The participant continues referring to the course materials. There was a co-creation and co-generation of learning among educators as they shared.

Continued Engagement of the Cohorts. The engagement on the virtual platforms keeps the cohort in touch, hence, the professional bond they developed in the session was extended and might be beneficial to their professional learning. This removed the geographical limitation, and the engagement was across schools and beyond.

Enabling the Transfer of Learning into Practice. As the participants implement what they were taught, they were transferring the principles into practice. By sharing their experiences, they reinforced the transfer, as well as shared challenges and learned from each other. The reinforcement was enhanced by the contextualization nature, and this triggered ownership and authorship which was critical in the take-up.

Increasing the Reach. New members are added to the list and might not have been part of the cohort, but they learn from the cohort. As much as the platform was created for a particular cohort, opening it up facilitated the reach of information to other educators who had not attended the face-to-face sessions.

7 Recommendations

The benefits of social media in communities of learning are immense. To further enhance the benefits there are need to address the learning element, diversity, and modeling.

Learning Element. In all sessions, the virtual engagement should be started within the session, so that it becomes part of the learning approach before the cohort completes the course.

Diverse Social Network. Exploring the networking sharing resources available in diverse social media and giving feedback enhance the spirit of collaboration as a driving force. Presenting a variety will provide opportunities for choice and voice by the educators.

Model. The practice should be modeled during the face-to-face session. This will create ease and acceptance as support is available. The assimilation could improve the take-up.

References

1. Ayling, D., Owen, H., Flagg, E.: Thinking, researching, and living in a virtual professional development community of practice. ASCILITE (2012). http://ascilite.org.au/conferences/wellington12/2012/images/custom/ayling,_diana__thinking.pdf
2. Ariel, Y., Avidar, R.: Information, interactivity, and social media. Atl. J. Commun. **23**(1), 19–30 (2015)
3. Karapanos, E., Teixeira, P., Gouveia, R.: Need fulfillment and experiences on social media: a case on Facebook and WhatsApp. Comput. Hum. Behav. **55**(Part B), 888–897 (2016)
4. Peraita, K.K., Robey, S.: 4 Reasons Slack Will Change How You Teach (2018). https://www.insidehighered.com/digital-learning/views/2018/09/19/four-reasons-slack-will-change-how-you-teach-opinion. Accessed 3 Oct 2020
5. Aydin, S.: A review of research on Facebook as an educational environment. Educ. Tech. Res. Dev. **60**(6), 1093–1106 (2012)
6. Bissessar, C.S.: Facebook as an informal teacher professional development tool. Aust. J. Teach. Educ. **39**(2), 9 (2014)
7. Foley, M.J.: Microsoft is ramping out the rollout of its Kaizala group communications app (2018). https://www.zdnet.com/article/microsoft-is-ramping-out-itsrollout-of-its-kaizala-group-communications-app/. Accessed 2 Oct 2020
8. Roy, P.: Learn better with Kaizala. https://kaizala007.blog/2020/04/21/kaizala-for-education/. Accessed 2 Oct 2020
9. PBIS, Using Twitter as Your Personal Learning Network (PLN). https://www.pbisrewards.com/blog/twitter-personal-learning-network-pln/. Accessed 2 Oct 2020
10. Cox, J.: How Can Twitter Be Used in the Classroom? (2020). https://www.teachhub.com/technology-in-the-classroom/2020/02/how-can-twitter-beused-in-the-classroom/. Accessed 2 Oct 2020
11. Gil, P.: What Is Twitter & How Does It Work? (2021). https://www.lifewire.com/what-exactly-is-twitter-2483331. Accessed 8 Mar 2021
12. Carpenter, J., Krutka, D.: How and why educators use Twitter: a survey of the field. J. Res. Technol. Educ. **46**(4), 414–434 (2014)
13. Gesthuizen, R.: Why build your PLN? In: ACEC2012: Australian Computers in Education Conference, Perth, Australia (2012)
14. Hur, J., Brush, T.: Teacher participation in online communities: why do teachers want to participate in self-generated online communities of K-12 teachers? J. Res. Technol. Educ. **41**(3), 279–303 (2009)
15. Kelly, A., Antonio, A.: Teacher peer support in social network sites. Teach. Teach. Educ. **56**, 138–149 (2016)
16. Trust, T.: Deconstructing an online community of practice: teachers' actions in the Edmodo math subject community. J. Digit. Learn. Teach. Educ. **31**(2), 73–81 (2015)
17. Visser, R., Evering, L., Barrett, D.: #TwitterforTeachers: the implications of Twitter as a self-directed professional development tool for K–12 teachers. J. Res. Technol. Educ. **46**(4), 396–413 (2014)
18. McKnight, K., O'Malley, K., Ruzic, R., Horsley, M.K., Franey, J., Bassett, K.: Teaching in a digital age: how educators use technology to improve student learning. J. Res. Technol. Educ. **48**(3), 323–333 (2016)

19. Silva, E.: Measuring skills for 21st-century learning. Phi Delta Kappan **90**(9), 630634 (2009)
20. Kereluik, K., Mishra, P., Fahnoe, C., Terry, L.: What Knowledge is of most worth. J. Digit. Learn. Teach. Educ. **29**(42014), 127–140 (2013)
21. Tobin, D.R.: Building your learning network, Corporate learning strategies (1998). http://www.tobincls.com/learningnetwork.htm. Accessed 15 June 2021
22. Davis, B.: Inventions of Teaching: A Genealogy. Routledge, London (2004)
23. Couros, A.: Developing personal learning networks for open and social learning. In: Veletsianos, G. (ed.) Emerging Technologies in Distance Education, pp. 109–128. Athabasca University Press, Edmonton, Canada (2010)
24. Flanigan, R.: Professional learning networks are taking off. Education Week (2011). http://www.edweek.org/ew/articles/2011/10/26/09edtech-network.h31.html?tkn=NXCFrTi53Q/RNUP7oI3Dyieu/9gskTJyoOc/
25. Powerful Learning Practice: Connected educator month starter kit (2012). https://dl.dropboxusercontent.com/u/8413898/CE14/connected-educator-month-starter-kit-2014.pdf
26. Trust, T.: Professional learning networks are designed for teacher learning. J. Digit. Learn. Teach. Educ. **28**(4), 133–138 (2012)
27. Crowley, B.: 3 steps for building a professional learning network. Education Week (2014). http://www.edweek.org/tm/articles/2014/12/31/3-steps-for-building-aprofessional-learning.html
28. Trust, T., Krutka, D., Carpenter, J.P.: "Together we are better": professional learning networks for teachers. Comput. Educ. 15–34 (2016)
29. Trust, T.: Beyond school walls: teachers' use of professional learning networks to seek help on a global scale. Int. J. Soc. Media Interact. Learn. Environ. **1**(3), 270–286 (2013)
30. Brown, J., Duguid, P.: The Social Life of Information. Harvard Business Press, Cambridge (2000)
31. Wenger, E., Trayner, B., de Laat, M.: Promoting and assessing value creation in communities and networks: a conceptual framework. Ruud de Moor Centrum, The Netherlands (2011)
32. Carpenter, J., Krutka, D.: Engagement through microblogging: educator professional development via Twitter. Prof. Dev. Educ. **41**(4), 707–728 (2015)
33. Duncan-Howell, J.: Teachers making connections: online communities as a source of professional learning. Br. J. Educ. Technol. **41**(2), 324–340 (2010)
34. Barab, S., Kling, R., Gray, J.H.: Designing for Virtual Communities in the Service of Learning. Cambridge University Press, Cambridge (2004)
35. Luehmann, A., Tinelli, L.: Teacher professional identity development with social networking technologies: learning reform through blogging. Educ. Media Int. **45**(4), 323–333 (2008)

Trends of Checklist Survey of Computer Operational Skills for First-Year Students: Over the Past Four Years

Daisuke Kaneko[1(✉)], Yukiya Ishida[2], Masaki Omata[3], Masanobu Yoshikawa[3], and Takaaki Koga[4]

[1] Hokusei Gakuen University, Sapporo, Hokkaido, Japan
kaneko@hokusei.ac.jp
[2] Chitose Institute of Science and Technology, Chitose, Hokkaido, Japan
y-kawani@photon.chitose.ac.jp
[3] University of Yamanashi, Yamanashi, Japan
omata@hci.media.yamanashi.ac.jp, yoshi@yamanashi.ac.jp
[4] Saga University, Saga, Japan
d4062@cc.saga-u.ac.jp

Abstract. Information literacy has become extremely important not only in elementary and secondary education but in higher education as well. Thus, the quality of first-year information literacy education must be improved. To do this, it is necessary to visualize students' information literacy and improve the curriculum accordingly. For this study, the authors surveyed basic information and communication technology (ICT) knowledge and developed a self-assessment checklist to assess computer operational skills. The checklist (designed as placement and achievement tests) contained a total of 40 items across four categories: (a) computer operations, (b) internet/e-mail, (c) Word, and (d) Excel/PowerPoint. Students selected an item if they could perform the operation described in that item. The authors conducted the study over four years with participation from 17,086 students at six universities in Japan. The results indicate that the placement test score in 2018 was lower than in other years, and the achievement test scores were markedly higher than the placement test scores in all years. By category, (d) Excel/PowerPoint had lower placement test scores than the other categories. However, even in category (d), achievement test scores were higher than the placement test scores. The results suggest that the first-year information literacy education programs were effective in these universities.

Keywords: Information Literacy · Computer Operational Skills · First-Year Students · Self-Assessment Checklist

1 Introduction

The new courses of study (the fundamental standards for curriculums by the Ministry of Education) were announced in Japan in 2017 (2018 for high schools). These courses aimed to develop language skills, information literacy (including information morals),

Published by Springer Nature Switzerland AG 2023
T. Keane et al. (Eds.): WCCE 2022, IFIP AICT 685, pp. 423–428, 2023.
https://doi.org/10.1007/978-3-031-43393-1_39

and problem-solving skills as the qualifications and abilities that form the foundation of learning. It is interesting to note that information literacy was stated for the first time as part of the new courses of study. Over time, the importance of information literacy has been established across primary, secondary, and higher education stages.

Subsequently, improving students' ability to use information and the corresponding development of information literacy education has been a major discussion in higher education and across universities. In particular, information literacy education for first-year students has been considered very important.

To improve the quality of information literacy education for first-year students, it is necessary to measure students' information literacy abilities. Previous literature provides insight into studies that focused on assessing these abilities. For example, Nishino et al. [1] attempted to provide standardized placement test questions for knowledge of information, and Fukada et al. [2] developed survey items on information ethics that can be used at multiple universities.

However, these measurements have to be conducted as needed. The current study proposes that by visualizing their abilities continuously, students can learn what they need to learn. Additionally, the quality of the educational program can be improved by analyzing the results.

We distinguished between measuring students' basic information and communication technology (ICT) knowledge and their level of operational skills. We focused on measuring students' level of acquisition of basic ICT knowledge through a survey consisting of 40 multiple-choice questions covering 14 learning areas [3].

We continued to investigate techniques to measure computer operational skills required in information literacy education for first-year students. For example, it would be possible to survey students' computer operational skills using certificate examinations such as Microsoft Office Specialist (MOS). However, having all students take such exams consistently is extremely difficult. Considering the examination fee and the number of available computers, the feasibility is low. Additionally, each university has different requirements for operational skills that students should learn. Therefore, we developed a self-assessment checklist for assessing computer operational skills [4].

We conducted this survey for four years at several universities. Specifically, we examined the results of skill checks conducted on incoming first-year students from 2018 to 2021.

2 Computer Operational Skills Checklist

The self-assessment checklist (developed by the authors) allows students to evaluate whether they can perform the operations described in the list. The checklist contains 40 items divided into the following four categories: (a) computer operations, (b) internet/e-mail, (c) Word, and (d) Excel/PowerPoint.

Computer operations (a) consist of 10 items related to the operation of the computer itself, such as mouse operations and file operations. Internet/e-mail (b) consists of six items related to Internet browsing; for instance, using a browser, such as entering URLs, and e-mail operations, such as sending attached files. Word (c) consists of 14 items related to Microsoft Office Word operations, such as changing the font and table insertion. Excel/PowerPoint (d) consists of 10 items related to Microsoft Office Excel and PowerPoint operations, such as entering rudimentary functions and creating graphs. The students were also required to checkmark all items they could perform. Further, another option stating "I can do nothing" was set for each category. The purpose is to have students check this if they cannot check any other items in the category. It is possible to distinguish whether a student is not checking because of a lack of applicable items or because of a mistake.

Apart from these, we also included an item asking students about the types of computers and mobile devices they use.

3 Results from a Four-Year Survey

3.1 Participant Data

The results of checklist surveys from 2018 to 2021 were analyzed in this study. A placement test was administered to new students at the time of their enrollment, and the same survey was administered six months or one year later as an achievement test. The survey was administered to 17,086 students across six universities (national and private universities) in Japan.

Table 1 illustrates the number of students and universities for each year. Students who have taken the tests more than once are counted separately. The number of students for the achievement test in 2021 is lower than in other years since it reflects the data accumulated before writing the research paper.

Table 1. Number of students and universities for each year

	2018	2019	2020	2021	Total
Placement Test (PT)	1,322 (3)	3,070 (5)	3,325 (5)	2,387 (5)	10,104
Achievement Test (AT)	2,284 (5)	1,870 (3)	2,078 (4)	750 (2)	6,982

Note: Number of students (universities)

3.2 Total Score

Table 2 illustrates the mean and standard deviation for each test conducted from 2018–2021. Firstly, we consider the trend of the total number of checked items (total score). Figure 1 illustrates a box-and-whisker plot of total scores. Scores on the placement test were low in 2018 and have since increased, with a slight drop in 2021. Scores on achievement tests show slight differences every year.

The results indicate that compared to the placement test, the achievement test scores have increased in all years. Furthermore, 77.9% of the students scored 36 points or higher on the achievement test. High achievement test scores must indicate that all participating universities had introduced information literacy education for first-year students as part of their regular curriculum.

Table 2. Mean and standard deviation for the test conducted each year

	18PT	18AT	19PT	19AT	20PT	20AT	21PT	21AT
N	1,322	2,284	3,070	1,870	3,325	2,078	2,387	750
Total	23.14	36.28	27.24	36.97	28.38	36.98	26.69	37.78
PS = 40	10.04	6.05	9.58	4.97	9.12	5.09	9.43	4.09
(a) Computer	7.52	9.55	8.35	9.75	8.62	9.61	8.25	9.69
PS = 10	2.90	1.38	2.42	1.01	2.17	1.16	2.37	0.90
(b) Internet	4.28	5.54	4.64	5.56	4.76	5.63	4.46	5.64
PS = 6	1.69	1.03	1.47	0.90	1.39	0.82	1.45	0.75
(c) Word	7.99	12.90	9.61	13.09	10.02	13.11	9.43	13.27
PS = 14	4.28	2.28	4.06	1.93	3.86	1.95	4.04	1.62
(d) Excel/Ppt	3.35	8.29	4.63	8.58	4.99	8.63	4.55	9.19
PS = 10	2.99	2.46	3.30	2.13	3.24	2.11	3.25	1.55

Note: Above: mean, below: standard deviation, PS: perfect score

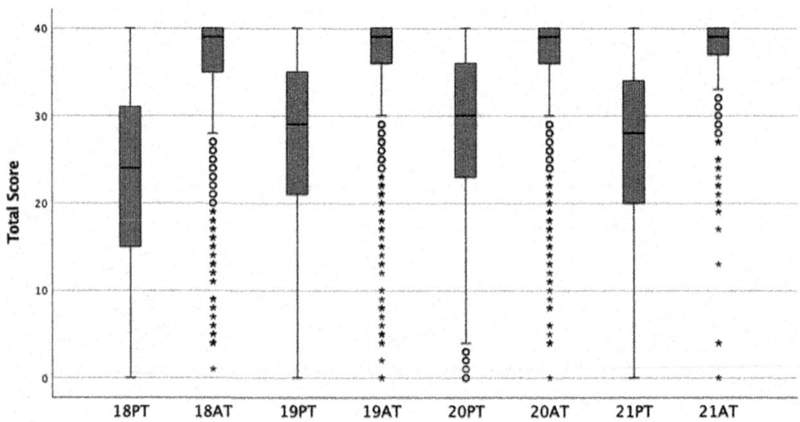

Fig. 1. A box-and-whisker plot of total scores

3.3 Scores by Category

Table 2 indicates the mean and standard deviations for each category of the self-assessment checklist. Figure 2 illustrates a box-and-whisker plot of the scores for each category. Similar to the trend observed in the total scores, placement test scores in 2018 in each category were also lower than in the following years. In addition, achievement test scores were higher than placement test scores in all categories.

In categories (a) and (b), many students achieved high scores on the placement test. In category (a), 66.5% of the students scored 9 or 10 points, and in category (b), 60.0% of the students scored 5 or 6 points. The percentage of students scoring high on the achievement test increased by 93.7% in category (a) and 91.5% in category (b). These

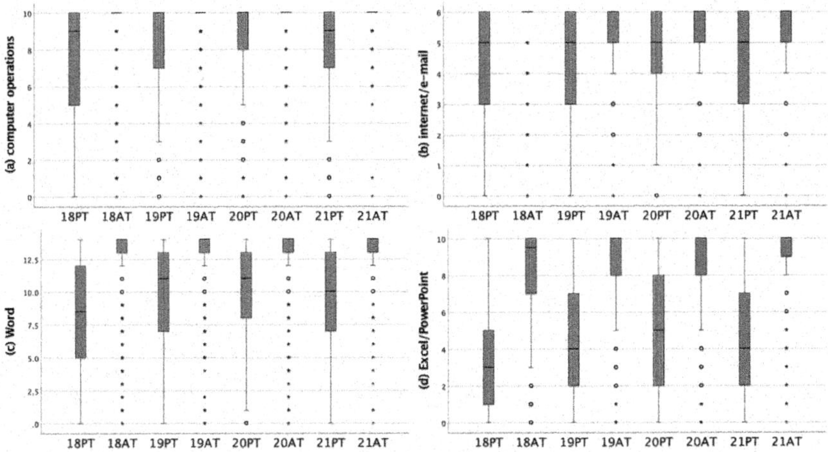

Fig. 2. A box-and-whisker plot of the scores for each category

results suggest that most students had already used a computer in some form or another by the time they entered university and were familiar with computer operations and internet/e-mail.

Scores on the placement test slightly varied in category (c). However, 88.3% of students scored 12 or higher on the achievement test. In category (d), placement test scores are considerably lower than in the other categories. The achievement test scores are also lower than the other categories (except 2021) but demonstrate a large increase in performance compared to the placement test.

Table 3 illustrates the items in category (d) for which the percentage of students who checked the item was particularly low. The percentages in the table are calculated by summing the responses over the four years. All items are related to the operations of Excel. However, even for these low percentages, the percentages of these items in the achievement test were very high.

Table 3. Items in category (d) with particularly low percentages in the placement test

Item	PT	AT
I can copy formulas using absolute cell reference so that the cell address does not move relatively when using AutoFill	21%	70%
I can change the number of decimal places to the specified number of digits (round off to the second decimal point, and so on)	29%	80%
I can paste a graph created in Excel onto a Word document	33%	87%

4 Conclusions

To improve the quality of information literacy education for first-year students, it is necessary to visualize their information literacy abilities and capture the changes after imparting the necessary education. Subsequently, we developed a basic ICT knowledge survey and a self-assessment checklist to receive quantitative feedback. The checklist measured the level of computer operation skills of students. A survey using the developed checklist was administered to approximately 17,000 students from six universities as a placement and achievement test.

The total scores on the placement test and the achievement test, as well as the scores for each category, were compared over four years. The results demonstrate that the placement test scores in 2018 were lower than in other years. The reason the results of the placement test after 2019 are better than those of 2018 is not clear. However, computer literacy education in high schools has improved against the background of the revision of the courses of study. In particular, considering the large increase in (c) Word and (d) Excel/PowerPoint scores after 2019, it is possible that more exploratory classes using this software took place in upper secondary schools.

In addition, the achievement test scores were markedly higher than the placement test in all years. By category, (d) Excel/PowerPoint had lower placement test scores than the other categories since some items had a response rate of between 20%–30%. However, even in category (d), scores on the achievement test were considerably higher. It can be said that students had already been familiar with computer operations by the time they entered university, and the first-year information literacy education programs were effective at the universities where the survey was conducted.

As mentioned in the introduction, we are simultaneously surveying basic ICT knowledge in addition to the survey using the computer operational skills checklist. In the future, it is necessary to analyze the data in conjunction with the basic ICT knowledge survey and the skills checklist survey. In addition, it is also necessary to refine the survey items to better reflect students' information literacy skills.

References

1. Nishino, K., Kayama, M., Fuse, I., Takahashi, S.: Investigations and considerations of university freshmen's knowledge of the subject "information". In: IEICE Technical Report, ET2006-41, vol. 106, no. 249, pp. 29–34. IEICE, Tokyo (2006)
2. Fukada, S., Nakamura, A., Okabe, S., et al.: Analysis on judgmental and behavioral aspects of information ethics among university students. Jpn. J. Educ. Technol. **37**(2), 97–105 (2013)
3. Kaneko, D.: Improving the fundamental ICT knowledge survey for first-year university students and the results of five years in a Japanese University. In: Proceedings of E-Learn, pp. 1117–1122. AACE, San Diego (2017)
4. Kaneko, D., Ishida, Y., Omata, M., Yoshikawa, M., Koga, T.: Development of a self-evaluation checklist of computer operational skills for first-year university students. In: Proceedings of E-Learn, pp. 530–534. AACE, San Diego (2018)

Universities of the Future and Industrial Revolution 4.0: The Academy Transformation

Maria Teresa Pereira[1,2](✉), Manuel S. Araújo[3], António Castro[4], and Maria J. Teixeira[5]

[1] Associate Laboratory for Energy, Transports and Aerospace (LAETA-INEGI), Porto, Portugal
[2] Porto School of Engineering, Polytechnic of Porto, Porto, Portugal
mtp@isep.ipp.pt
[3] Porto Accounting and Business School, (CEOS), Polytechnic of Porto, Mamede Infesta, Portugal
manuelsalvador@iscap.ipp.pt
[4] Escola Secundária Fontes Pereira de Melo (ESFPM), Porto, Portugal
[5] Monteiro Ribas Indústrias, SA, Porto, Portugal
jt@mri.pt

Abstract. This article aims to reflect on the changes that are taking place today, considering them from different perspectives, as well as to describe the impact that results from these changes in social, economic, ethical, and academic terms, and the role of creative learning in this transformational process. A description is made of the main characteristics of this moment, mainly in what is considered the industrial 4.0 revolution, as well as the main global trends that are associated with it in this third decade of the millennium. Presenting the Universities of the Future (UoF) project, an assessment of its main results is made, as well as essential questions that must be asked so that several levels of decision-makers can consider as valid in building a different and better future for the planet we inhabit. Part of the answers found seem to suggest that the different social institutions must converge in a collaborative paradigm, in which the free sharing of knowledge, the distribution of resources, and the focus on common problems with different approaches and by different players, bring more creative, efficient, and sustainable solutions and knowledge.

Keywords: Industry 4.0 · I4.0 · Universities of Future · Creative Learning

1 Introduction - One Accelerated Transformational World

The world is undergoing such a rapid process of transformation, and there seems to be no other phenomenon of equal magnitude in the history of civilization [1–5]. The turn of the millennium brought the acceleration of digitalization triggered by technological advances in what would be called the fourth industrial revolution (I4.0), commonly understood to mean a range of manufacturing technologies that fuse the physical and digital worlds due to increasing interconnectivity and smart automation. But what are

Published by Springer Nature Switzerland AG 2023
T. Keane et al. (Eds.): WCCE 2022, IFIP AICT 685, pp. 429–440, 2023.
https://doi.org/10.1007/978-3-031-43393-1_40

we talking about when we talk about the I4.0 revolution? The social representation of this expression I4.0 is not the same in different social and professional groups. For the common citizen it is vaguer and more diffuse, and for professionals who deal with it more specifically, the construct is clearer and more objective. We will now address some of the main features that seem to characterize the I4.0.

Industrial Revolution 4.0. There does not seem to be a clear consensus on this expression, but it appears recurrently associated with automation technologies, data exchange, and using the concepts cyber-physical systems, internet of things and cloud computing, with the focus being the efficiency/effectiveness of the processes. I4.0 is a new paradigm of production systems highly focused on creating intelligent products and processes, using intelligent machines and the transformation of conventional production systems into intelligent factories [6, 7]. All these changes involve not only increasing the efficiency of resources and time, but more highly, changing the way people work. This new industrial paradigm encompasses a set of industrial developments, having emerged in 2010 in Germany, through a project focused on technological solutions and which consisted of the fusion of traditional production methods with the latest technological developments in the areas of information and communication. It represents an evolution of production systems that creates benefits for organizations: cost and energy reduction, increased safety and quality, improved process efficiency, etc. It is the revolution of massive digitization, the *Internet of Things*, *Machine Learning,* and *Robotization*, but also *Nanotechnology* and new materials, *Biotechnology* – technologies that merge the physical, digital, and biological worlds, applied to production processes [8, 9]. The concepts of *Digitalization* (transforming analog formats into digital formats), *Intelligence* (solving problems, normally attributed to humans but increasingly acquired by machines that autonomously communicate with each other and make decisions based on the data received), and *Smart Factory* (factories that could manage complexity, are less prone to disruption and produce products more efficiently) [10], have been associated with discussions about I4.0. Regarding *Smart Factories*, Burke et al. [11], from Deloitte, highlighted 5 main features: 1) connectivity; 2) optimization; 3) transparency; 4) proactivity; and 5) flexibility. These characteristics reduce the need for manual tasks, allow real-time access to the production process, control and monitoring, better human-machine interface, and better use of new technologies such as robotics. Nine pillars of technological advancement are considered and comprise the following technologies: *Big Data* [12]; *Autonomous Robots* [13]; *Internet of things (IoT)*[14]; *Simulation* [15]; *Integrated systems*[16]; *Cyber Security* [17]; *Cloud computing* [13]; *Additive Manufacturing* [18] and, *Augmented Reality* [19, 20]. See Fig. 1.

Social and Natural Changes. If it is true that technological changes have brought about significant changes, it is no less true that the social and natural changes of this *Anthropocene* period are also increasingly present. Although there is still no great consensus on the date of its beginning, the *Anthropocene* has been pointed out by some as having started with the first industrial revolution in the 18th century, and some scholars even refer to the beginning of agriculture, as it begins to change greatly, the ecosystem. While considerable social and natural changes are taking place, we have chosen to present the *Demographic Pressure, Political Changes, Climate Change* and *Pandemic* outbreaks as major concerns in their relationship to the future of industry, academia, and humanity.

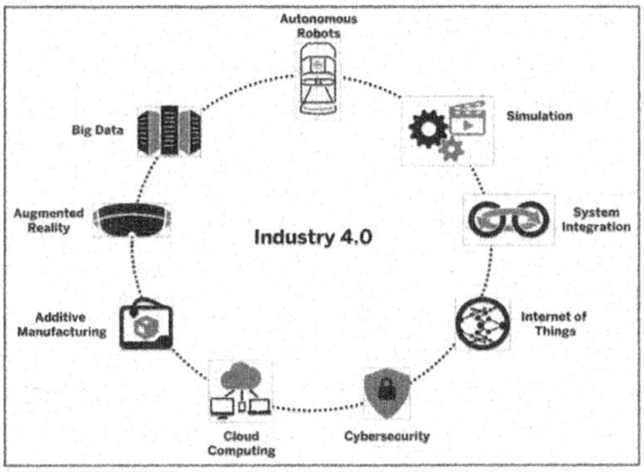

Fig. 1. Main components of I4.0.

Demographic Pressure. In 2022 we have a global population of almost 8 billion people, values that are estimated to increase dramatically in the coming decades, a reality that creates considerable pressure in terms of the distribution of resources at a planetary level. With a planet with limited resources and an increasing population density and with more consumption demands, it creates an extreme situation with consequences at different levels [10, 21]. On the other hand, the population pyramid is increasingly ageing, requiring this population to create solutions that also involve their inclusion in the productive and social process and not be assumed as a negative liability. If it is true that excess population creates challenges for humanity, it is no less true that population imbalances in different parts of the globe create migration problems, as well as considerable educational needs on the part of educational institutions, as upskilling and upskilling for dealing with this new industrial revolution.

Politics Changes. The geostrategic interests of different governments and large companies must be variables to be included in this equation of Politics Changes [22]. The recent crisis in Europe, in which Russia's recognition of the independence of the provinces of Donetsk and Lugansk, followed by military invasion, creating a terrible world tension with damages in human and economic terms at a global level, with a tenuous reaction of international institutions, which does not favor the realization of the 2030 agenda, and therefore the goals most associated with the I4.0 and the transformation of higher education institutions. More aggressive political leadership is not conducive to the social climate of collaboration that we aspire to. On the stage of the different powers, worrying instability processes are unleashed, as they are almost always based on economic paradigms in which short-term economic profit prevails, without much regard for higher values, such as human rights. The need for peace, strong institutions, solid partnerships, respect for human life and the sustainability of the planet is therefore unequivocal, and without political leaders aligned with these democratic values, the challenge of a different and better future through the I4.0 it gets harder to reach.

Climate Change. There is immense evidence of climate change on the planet we inhabit, and human activity is the main explanation for this change. It is irrefutable that human activities are responsible by climate change (warming the atmosphere, ocean, and land)

[23]. Scientists from different areas and in different parts of the globe are unanimous in the conclusion that these changes are unequivocal and have great potential to negatively affect life on Earth. By way of illustration, scientific evidence reveals that current warming is occurring roughly ten times faster than the average rate of ice-age-recovery warming. Carbon dioxide from human activity is increasing more than 250 times faster than it did from natural sources after the last Ice Age. Global Temperature Rise, Warming Ocean, Shrinking Ice Sheets, Glacial Retreat, Decreased Snow Cover, Sea Level Rise, Declining Arctic Sea Ice, Extreme Events, and Ocean Acidification continue in this negative spiral, which as you can imagine are not good signs. Given the evidence of these changes, once again science must support the solutions leading not only to their mitigation, but also to our better adaptation to these changes. Intervention for greater sustainability of resources and greater solidarity with future generations and biodiversity involves: increasing energy efficiency; increasing the use of renewable energy; reducing direct and indirect greenhouse gas emissions; conserving and protecting water resources through efficiency, reuse, and stormwater management; eliminating waste; preventing pollution; increasing recycling; designing, constructing, maintaining, and operating high-performance sustainable buildings; supporting economic growth and livability of the communities, and other different ways to protect the planet.

Pandemic. At the end of 2019, in a city in the People's Republic of China, a new virus was identified with an infection capacity with Pandemic characteristics. Quickly, the epicenter of this event was no longer limited to a part of the globe and became a serious problem for all human beings. Faced with the unknown and the gravity of the phenomenon (deadly or highly debilitating), individuals, organizations, communities, cities, countries, regions, in short - society, put immense efforts into dealing with this global threat. It was interesting to witness a phenomenon of international collaboration that has not been seen for some time in the history of humanity. Scientists, laboratories, public and private research centers, universities, associations, governments, federations, international organizations, and even the simplest person, left their usual selfish goals, to focus on this common problem of fighting the so-called Pandemic of COVID-19. The Mantra of that time was sharing, collaboration, transparency, solidarity, alignment of government measures, effort and sacrifice, mobilization, isolation, and multiple restrictions in terms of freedom and even economic functioning, with unequivocal consequences in terms of business survival and families. It was exciting to watch the sharing, for example, of the knowledge that pharmaceutical companies had (and which they normally hide from their competitors for commercial reasons), to make advances in terms of creating a vaccine to fight the new virus. It is true that "the time window" in which this occurred was short, having quickly turned to "closing the so open sharing of knowledge", then generated by these different actors. However, this interregnum in the more competitive attitude of people, corporations and states resulted in an exponential acceleration of the creation of a new vaccine. What would normally take 5 to 10 years was significantly reduced in terms of the average time to obtain a solution. Different solutions emerged with an interesting degree of effectiveness, empirically validated by the reduction of cases, as well as the reduction of their severity. In addition to this vaccine phenomenon, society also adapted to a new reality, or even a "new normal" after successive pandemic waves passed, with a significant transformation of behavioral patterns, consumption, socialization, work, among many other changes that were taken for granted before the Pandemic. The vulnerability that this global experience brought, as well as the role that technology played in dealing with it, has refocused the purpose of many decision-makers and many individuals without these greater responsibilities.

The industrial revolution 4.0 and the different changes that are taking place at the planetary and human levels, force us to make fundamental decisions to survive the times ahead. New Eras bring new threats and new challenges, which is why the role that creative learning can play in the co-construction of a better and different future seems fundamental to us. Concerns about sustainability and humanity set the tone for the foundations of the so-called Industrial I5.0 Revolution - Digital transformation to a Sustainable, human-centric industry.

2 Universities of Future Project

Industry 4.0 is assuming its rhythm in today's business environment and strategies. Companies are changing their working processes dramatically and this poses major challenges requiring proactive adaptation by businesses/industries, governments, and Higher Education Institutions (HEIs). The industry 4.0 main components are presented (Fig. 1). The major focus of the companies' investment will be on digital technologies (DT) [24]. DT itself is not a leverage issue for the business results, a strategic plan should be done for a sustainable investment. In addition, companies are also investing in training employees and driving organizational change. One main concern relies on occupations' transformation towards a digital culture, where some occupations are threatened by redundancy, others are growing rapidly, and a third set of new occupations will emerge. The Universities of the Future project (UoF) addresses the existing gaps in higher education offers by developing new, innovative, and multidisciplinary approaches to teaching and learning, stimulating entrepreneurship and entrepreneurial skills of higher education teaching staff and company staff, and facilitating the exchange, flow and co-creation of knowledge through a true community of practice and using design thinking methodology.

The UoF project is to form – and sustain - a community of HEIs, Companies, Government entities, Students, and alumni to address: a) the qualification of teachers and students in the Industry 4.0 age; b) the reskilling and up-skilling of industry staff for the digital transformation towards Industry 4.0; c) the instruments and resources with which HEIs, educators/trainers, businesses and government decision-making bodies should be equipped with to ensure a smooth sailing on this journey.

The objectives set for this project resulted in the following outcomes:

1) A common body of knowledge on industry 4.0's readiness/maturation by regions/business and its subsequent impact on skills' shifting, up/re-skilling. *A Blueprint and a Best Practice report* were developed and publicly available on the UoF website and on the UoF platform.
2) *A Community of practice and co-creation units for university-business cooperation*: 33 small-scale events were organised to engage the four elements of the quadruple helix into providing input for the success of the outputs or outcomes of the project.

3) *Educational resources for teacher training, for re- and up-skilling*:

   Creating innovative lessons on core topics/main components of Industry 4.0, targeting bachelor/master students - 12 autonomous lessons of circa 30 min: Artificial Intelligence, Soft skills, Smart Teams and Transformation Leadership, 5G and I4.0, Internet of Things, Intellectual Property, Introduction to I4.0, System thinking, Sensors for Cyber-physical systems, Wireless communication for IoT devices, Tips to Improve Communication, Personal Branding, Basics of Prototyping, Basics of Additive Manufacturing, made publicly available at the UoF platform (requiring a simple registration), directed to the target groups and in the four working languages.

   Continuous training programmes/short courses on core topics/main components of Industry 4.0, for employees interested in re/upskilling - 10 short courses, with two European Credit Transfer and Accumulation System (ECTS), 24 contact hours, on the topics: Machine Learning and Data Analytics to Predictive Maintenance; Building Internet of Things Solutions; Vanguard Leadership Program for Industry 4.0; Additive Technology - 3D Modelling and Printing; Circular Economy in Industry 4.0 - a practical approach; Systemic Design for Sustainability; Business Processes Modelling; User-Centred Product Development; Ethical Product Development; Sustainable Product Development – made publicly available at the UoF to target groups – e.g. SMEs – platform in the four working languages.

   An international joint post-graduation (PG) program designed using creative strategies applied to industry 4.0, and targeting workers interested in applying pilot projects to accelerate their companies' digital transformation - PG in I4.0 – Digital Transformation - supported by the Virtual Platform. The PG was initially designed to be developed in a mixed format – online and face-to-face, depending on students' mobilities, with a common timetable (8 h 30 a.m.-10 h 30 a.m.) (Fig. 2).

   Classes were recorded and uploaded to the virtual platform, offering to the students the possibility to attend offline. To abide by Portuguese legislation on Higher Education programmes, the joint PG comprised 30 ECTS, 210 Contact Hours (CH), and six modules: Module 1 - Project: with six challenges briefed by the companies to be developed in co-creation (mentoring and coaching), using design thinking methodology (52 CH) throughout the duration of the post-graduation, included three bootcamps with a week; Module 2 - Transferable and Soft Skills (52 CH) running simultaneously with Module 1. Modules 3 to 6 were small hands-on projects and cooperative work on team challenges (24 CH). Module 3 - IT driven 4.0: Introduction to I4.0, IoT, Cyberphysical Systems, Cybersecurity; Module 4 - New Business and Digital Transformation: Development of New Business in the I4.0 and Digital Transformation scope; Data Analytics and Machine Learning; Co-creation in innovation and, Entrepreneurship; Module 5 - Information Systems and Decision Support Systems (IS&DSS): Training in IS/IT to Support de Digital Transformation, Systems Interoperability, Business Process Management and Notation - BPMN – and Power BI. Module 6 - Sustainable Enablers – Logistics and Supply Chain Management 4.0, Augmented and Virtual Reality and Sustainability. Due to COVID-19 the PG programme was delivered online using the same strategy/methodology.

4) *Guiding and supporting resources* directed to HEIs, business and government decision-making bodies, as well as to educators/trainers - Two Tool Kits for Teachers:

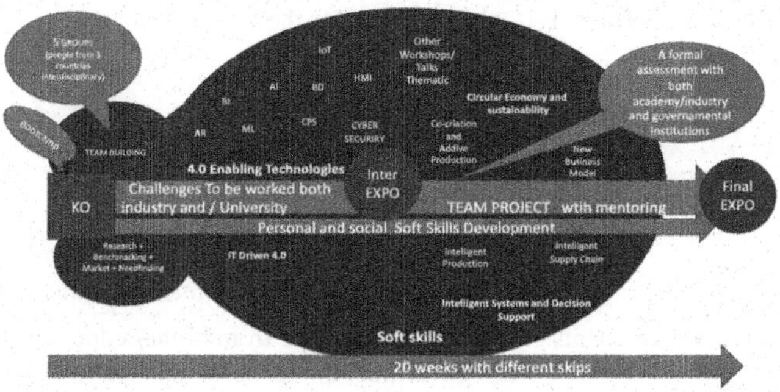

Fig. 2. Joint Post-graduation in Industry 4.0 Framework

i) Tools & Methods - with the tools and methods that can be used to support learning and teaching; ii) Technologies - with the most advanced and used technologies available to support the teaching and learning activities; one Tool Kit for HEIs, where Industry 4.0 is briefly presented and its potential benefits and threats for HEIs are highlighted, and one Tool Kit for Industry, where Industry 4.0 is briefly presented and its potential benefits are highlighted, and models for assessing maturity in I4.0 are also presented. Furthermore, it promotes fruitful cooperation between Industry and HEIs. The toolkits translated into four languages are public on the UoF website and the UoF Platform.

5) *A robust virtual teaching and learning factory for industry 4.0* providing ample tools and resources enabling the direct contact of the target-groups with the main components of Industry and Education 4.0. A UoF Platform providing i) an area for companies to present briefings and challenges for collaboration – to be used as classroom case studies, or to be developed by international multidisciplinary groups as real-life projects with tangible outcomes; ii) Open educational resources (OER) autonomous lessons; iii) short courses available to be reproduced and adapted to the target groups; iv) post-graduation in Industry 4.0 Innovation and Digital Transformation.

2.1 The UoF Project Results

The Blueprint for the universities of the future report [25], was one of the first outputs in the project UoF, supported by the methodologies/tools: expert interviews, focus group and a survey, see Table 1. Investigation also included research into weak signals and megatrends. This information was used to create a start scenario to chart us a direction of where we would like to go and define the educative assets and tool kits that support the leverage for the future scenario.

Concerning challenges in society the main issues identified were the lack of a skilled workforce. Students have often expressed a worry that they don't know what skills they should be learning, and that by the time they graduate, these skills will not be useful anymore. Furthermore, the lack of mobility between countries and regions can exacerbate the shortage problem. Additionally, the lack of a skilled workforce is increased by the gender imbalance and unequal access to opportunities; New ways of working – flexibility in working life, that is not tied to a place, time, or single employer; An ageing

Table 1. Collected data for the blueprint

Method	Data
Literature review	137 journal articles of Industry 4.0 competencies
Interview	86 experts of Education 4.0
Review	205 educational solutions for Industry 4.0
Benchmarking	35 international forerunners of Education 4.0
Workshops and co-creation events	143 participants from higher education, industry, governmental agencies, and students

population - concern over who will care for the elderly; Achieving carbon neutrality by 2050 – sustainable solutions are critical; Lack of common vision on technology – many companies that have expressed that there is no common vision on how to use the available technology, or how to start developing it; Legislation is not updated to address all these challenges. Based on that the UoF recommendations for HEIs for the three coming decades can be seen in [25].

The UoF workshops often approached the question, "What is the role for higher education institutions?" and "Are they sufficiently adapting to the new educational needs of society?" The latter question mainly referenced responders' perceptions of the slow creation of new curriculum, and bureaucratic requirements that made the process even slower.

The educative assets developed under the UoF alliance showed that clusters of collaboration can be used to also develop online learning technology and content, which in turn also increases scalability. When it comes to online learning, student mobility definition should be included, as online learning is a tool that increases educational accessibility and promotes inclusion. Unequal access to education diminishes the efforts for reskilling and upskilling, and online learning can be both accessible and a tool to increase accessibility to create more opportunities for high quality education online. Interdisciplinary education programmes and real projects developed in co-creation with companies have proven a valuable tool to provide a more rounded education to students. Not only by providing experiences which more closely resemble real working life, but also by providing the students the opportunity to learn to work with, and learn from people from different fields, and by becoming a topic expert within their own group. The development of these types of programmes is not easy though and requires more effort in terms of time or resources, than more traditional teaching.

Educational clusters, therefore, can aid in the co-development of these programmes by the mutual pooling of resources, and by creating a larger audience to take part in these programmes. Interdisciplinary programmes are meant to bring students from different backgrounds together to teach them skills related to solving problems, so they can see how they can use their skills in real life, as well as to better understand what people from other disciplinary backgrounds can do. It can increase their understanding and the type of communication skills that are required in working life. It can also create the type of personal connections that can later lead to entrepreneurial activity.

2.2 Universities of the Future, I4.0 and Creative Learning

The industrial revolution 4.0, as well as all the previous revolutions that preceded it, challenged society to a set of changes necessary to accompany them on the path of civilizational progress. Companies and academia have been adjusting their methods and content to better align with the new technological requirements. Due to the characteristics of this last industrial revolution, the transformations that need to be carried out in society are of a gigantic order of magnitude, since the mindset that is required is considerably different [26, 27]. As we had the opportunity to present before, the universities of the future will have to reinvent themselves, leaving once and for all the "distance" from the real world that surrounds them, increasingly incorporating in their DNA the valences of the industry, as well as the leadership of technological innovation, or intervention in social problems. The new generations that arrive at universities are not only made up of young people, but also older audiences who return to meet the demands of digital literacy so necessary to this new paradigm. The terms upskilling and reskilling have been increasingly repeated by the most diverse protagonists, and it seems to have been familiar with the idea that basic training is not enough to keep up to date, and for that very reason, make a master, a post-graduation, an MBA, a doctorate, a specialization, or different other shorter training courses, are the "new normal", which people are already used to fulfilling. If it is true that the academy continues to be the stage where the population normally goes to fulfill this training need, it is no less true that companies have created their own training offers, some of them with a degree of sophistication and innovations that are worthy of admiration. On the other hand, the worker himself invested and created training options for himself in a self-taught way, using his own technology to inform himself and develop professional skills. Part of the success of the UoF project came from the ability of higher education institutions, companies, and government entities to join forces to align objectives, provide knowledge, but most of all, collaborate so that everyone's needs could be met, in true teamwork, in which the collaborative spirit spoke louder. In a way, it was as if "each of these three entities decided to leave their homes and meet in the city's central square to talk about their experiences and discover that they could be useful in a unique synergy".

Jeffrey [28] states that people are themselves the builders of the meanings that matter when they are involved in the learning process, in the continuity of the developmental-constructivist school since Piaget. Chappell and Craft [29, p. 382] advocate that "creative learning conversations are a way of contributing to change, which moves us towards an education future fit for the twenty-first century". These same authors, consider that traditional forms of teaching and learning suffer from a certain lethargy, in the sense that the degree of participation and commitment of the multiple interested parties of the community interact in a coalescence of talents and synergistic (individual, interpersonal and group processes). A comparative study with successful students in South Korea and the United States sought to identify perceptions about the most creative learning skills and receptive learning skills. The results describe an assessment of lower competence in critical thinking compared to receptive learning competencies in both countries. However, as the school years progress, American students seem to develop a perception of improvement in their creative and critical thinking skills. The authors explain that there may be some influence here from culture, and epistemological beliefs on critical and creative learning [30]. To have a society of high innovative capacity, it is essential to verify and guarantee the quality of the education system, which is only possible with an ecosystem in which learning creativity is fostered [31]. This learning creativity is based on six fundamental pillars [32, 33]: infrastructures, intellectual capital, integrity, incentives, institutions, and interaction. It seems obvious to us to conclude that if our commitment is not linked to investment in these areas, we will see our economic and human development unequivocally conditioned. To what extent are we promoting these creativity skills in our institutions? Do we, education professionals, have the skills to develop these skills in our students, or do we remain in a classic paradigm of teaching content and in a very receptive and passive methodology for acquiring knowledge? In the European community, the Bologna process aimed to place the student at the centre of the learning process, an intention that goes against this idea of promoting in the person who learns a great responsibility to build their learning, but how could one not fail to be, it also needs a new profile of educators, new methodologies, new resources, new institutions. To what extent are we truly heading in that direction? What does the future of creative learning hold for us? Smitsman and Smitsman [34] presented a very interesting proposal to build the design of learning tasks for the thrivability of creativity: a) need to include activities on how to bring forth future states and emerging worlds from within their present states of reality; b) need to enable the game of diversity through a creative exploratory process that can show wholeness and unity, as skills grow; c) need to provide meaningful feedback and feed-forward interactions that promote future creating behaviors; d) need to make it possible to combine existing capabilities into new patterns by shifting stances; e) need to evoke development of empathy, joy, compassion, care, and trust; f) need to include a supportive environment for exploration; g) need to bring the future into the here and now of a person. The same authors consider that these needs can be met with strategies such as role-play or group dialogues, exercises to visualize a different and better future self, opportunities for communication and storytelling, projects and opportunities for collaboration, training, and education in making their creative future viable, training in systems dynamics (in order to make complexity more visible), training in mindfulness and internal harmony, among others.

3 Conclusions

Otto Scharmer and Senge [5] explore a set of reflections related to our capacity for transformation, whether in individual, team, organizational or even social as Humanity. We certainly still have a long way to go to make our society more eco and less ego, but it seems to be evident that part of the solution requires our ability to learn to be more creative and this is impossible to achieve without others. Our brains are fabulous at creating new solutions for new and old problems, but this requires a set of conditions that do not limit this power, on the contrary, it forces the different decision-makers to provide the context, the tools and the culture of freedom and collaboration that creating the future requires.

Projects such as universities of the future seek to bring together different entities, define strategies, and promote methodologies that favour this "organic soup" that promotes creative learning. Like this project, many others are going in this direction, but not as many as could be needed to accelerate the process of changing the educational paradigm. Therefore, it is imperative that the great world and national institutions commit themselves to this purpose of "freeing the natural creative capacity of individuals" so that they can give back to society much more than what they received from it.

References

1. Kotter, J.P.: Accelerate: Building Strategic Agility for a Faster-Moving World. Harvard Business Review Press, Boston (2014)
2. Kotter, J.P., Rathgeber, H.: That's Not How We Do It Here!: A Story about How Organisations Rise and Fall–and Can Rise Again. Portfolio/Penguin, New York (2016)
3. Kotter, J.P., Akhtar, V., Gupta, G.: CHANGE: How Organisations Achieve Hard-to-Imagine Results Despite Uncertain and Volatile Times. Wiley, Hoboken (2021)
4. Scharmer, O., Käufer, K.: Leading from the Emerging Future: From Ego-System to Eco-System Economies, 1st edn. Berrett-Koehler, San Franciso (2013)
5. Scharmer, O., Senge, P.: Theory U: Leading from the Emerging Future. A BK Business Book, 2nd edn. Berrett-Koehler, San Francisco (2016)
6. Kagermann, H., Helbig, J., Hellinger, A., Wahlster, W.: Recommendations for implementing the strategic initiative INDUSTRIE 4.0: securing the future of the German manufacturing industry; final report of the Industrie 4.0 Working Group. Forschungsunion/acatech, Munich, Germany (2013)
7. Nakayama, R.S., Spínola, M.M, Silva, J.R.: Towards I4.0: a comprehensive analysis of evolution from I3.0. Comput. Ind. Eng. **144**, 1–15 (2020)
8. Schwab, K.: A quarta revolução industrial. Tradução de Daniel Moreira Miranda. Edipro, São Paulo, Brazil (2016)
9. Schwab, K., Davis, N.: Aplicando a quarta revolução industrial. Tradução de Daniel Moreira Miranda. Edipro, São Paulo, Brazil (2018)
10. World Economic Forum: The Future of Jobs. World Economic Forum, Geneva, Switzerland (2016). http://www.weforum.org/docs/WEF_Future_of_Jobs.pdf. Accessed 22 Feb 2022
11. Burke, R., Mussomeli, A., Laaper, A., Hartingan, M., Sniderman, B.: The Smart Factory: Responsive, Adaptive, Connected Manufacturing. Deloitte University Press, New York (2017)
12. Luo, J., Wu, M., Gopukumar, D., Zhao, Y.: Big data application in biomedical research and health care: a literature review. Biomed. Inform. Insights **8**, 1–10 (2016)
13. Dang, L.M., Piran, M.J., Han, D., Min, K., Moon, H.: A survey on internet of things and cloud computing for healthcare. Electronics **8**(7), 768 (2019)
14. Cordes, F., Stacey, N.: Is UK Industry Ready for the Fourth Industrial Revolution? The Boston Consulting Group, Boston (2017)
15. Ferreira, W., Armellini, F., Santa-Eulalia, A.: Simulation in industry 4.0: a state-of-the-art review. Comput. Ind. Eng. **149**, 106868 (2020)
16. Pérez-Lara, M., Saucedo-Martínez, J.A., Marmolejo-Saucedo, J.A., Salais-Fierro, T.E., Vasant, P.: Vertical and horizontal integration systems in Industry 4.0. Wirel. Netw. **26**(2), 4767–4775 (2018)
17. Carvalho, J.M.C:. Integração de Edge Computing e IoT em equipamento CNC de 5 Eixos (2021). http://media.daimler.com/marsMediaSite/en/instance/ko.xhtml?oid=9905147. Accessed 18 Feb 2022
18. Tofail, S.A.M., Koumoulos, E.P., Bandyopadhyay, A., Bose, S., O'Donoghue, L., Charitidis, C.: Additive manufacturing: scientific and technological challenges, market uptake and opportunities. Mater. Today **21**(1), 22–37 (2018)

19. Arena, F., Collotta, M., Pau, G., Termine, F.: An overview of augmented reality. Computers **11**, 28 (2022)
20. Ma, M., Jain, L.C., Anderson, P.: Future trends of virtual, augmented reality, and games for health. In: Ma, M., Jain, L.C., Anderson, P. (eds.) Virtual, Augmented Reality and Serious Games for Healthcare 1, pp. 1–6. Springer, Heidelberg (2014)
21. World Economic Forum: The Global Risks Report 2022 World Economic Forum, Geneva, Switzerland (2022)
22. Weiss, T.G., Forsythe, D.P., Coate, R.A., Pease, K.-K.: The United Nations and Changing World Politics, 8th edn. Routledge, Abingdon-on-Thames (2017)
23. NASA How do we know climate change is real? https://climate.nasa.gov/evidence. Accessed 27 Feb 2022
24. PwC: Global Industry 4.0 Survey – Industry 4.0: Building the digital enterprise. PwC, London (2016)
25. Universities of the Future project. universistiesofthefuture.eu. Accessed 23 Apr 2023
26. Dweck, C.S.: Mindset: The New Psychology of Success. Random House, New York (2006)
27. Dweck, C.S.: Mindset: How You Can Fulfil Your Potential. Constable & Robinson Limited, London (2012)
28. Jeffrey, B.: Creative learning identities. Education 3-13 **36**(3), 253–263 (2008)
29. Chappell, K., Craft, A.: Creative learning conversations: producing living dialogic spaces. Educ. Res. **53**(3), 363–385 (2011)
30. Yeh, H.-Y., Yang, S.-H., Fu, J., Shih, Y.-C.: Developing college students' critical thinking through reflective writing. High. Educ. Res. Dev. **42**(1), 244–259 (2023)
31. Crosling, G., Nair, M., Vaithilingam, S.: A creative learning ecosystem, quality of education and innovative capacity: a perspective from higher education. Stud. High. Educ. **40**(7), 1147–1163 (2015)
32. Nair, M.: The DNA of the new economy. Econ. Bull. **8**(December), 27–59 (2007)
33. Nair, M.: Inclusive innovation and sustainable development: leapfrogging to a high-income economy. In: Ramasamy, R. (ed.) ICT Strategic Review 2011/12: Transcending into High Value, pp. 226–256 (2011)
34. Smitsman, A., Smitsman, A.: The future-creative human: exploring evolutionary learning. World Futures **77**(2), 81–115 (2021)

A Conceptual Framework for Automatic Generation of Examinations Using Machine Learning Algorithms in Learning Management Systems

Emma Cheserem[1(✉)], Elizaphan Maina[1], John Kihoro[2], and Jonathan Mwaura[3]

[1] Kenyatta University, Nairobi, Kenya
{cheserem.emma,maina.elizaphan}@ku.ac.ke
[2] The Cooperative University of Kenya, Nairobi, Kenya
[3] Northeastern University, Boston, MA, USA
j.mwaura@northeastern.edu

Abstract. The transition of education from face-to-face to electronic learning (e-learning) has been accompanied by the application of artificial intelligence and machine learning techniques to improve teaching, learning and assessment processes. Learning Management Systems (LMS) are used to conduct electronic learning (e-learning), and to facilitate student assessment through automatic generation of examinations from a question bank. However, the perceived low quality of these examinations has led them to be used for formative assessments and not for summative assessments. One way to ensure that high quality exams are generated by LMS systems would be to ensure that the questions cover different levels of difficulty as specified by an educational taxonomy. One commonly used taxonomy is Bloom's Taxonomy, later updated to the Revised Bloom's Taxonomy (RBT). In this research, we review studies on automatic generation of examinations from question banks. From this review, we define the parameters necessary for a quality exam based on RBT. Finally, we propose a conceptual framework that applies machine learning algorithms to automatically generate a quality exam from an LMS question bank. We intend to do further research by developing a prototype based on the conceptual framework.

Keywords: Automatic Generation of Exams · Machine Learning · Bloom's Taxonomy

1 Introduction

In recent decades there has been an accelerating shift from face-to-face learning to distance learning to electronic learning (e-learning), a change accelerated by the COVID-19 pandemic [1]. E-learning is made possible through Learning Management Systems (LMS) such as Moodle, Blackboard Learn and Canvas, tools that permit instructors

Published by Springer Nature Switzerland AG 2023
T. Keane et al. (Eds.): WCCE 2022, IFIP AICT 685, pp. 441–450, 2023.
https://doi.org/10.1007/978-3-031-43393-1_41

and learners to interact synchronously or asynchronously. As the shift to e-learning has occurred, machine learning (ML) techniques are being used to enhance the LMS systems in order to get better outcomes for instructors and learners [2, 3]. Studies show that applications of ML can improve learner engagement by providing individualised feedback to the student, provide rapid assessment and feedback to the student, enable intelligent agents to advise students, enhance administration and assessment in education, among many other applications [2, 4–6].

A normal teaching cycle requires an instructor to prepare several assessments, possibly including two continuous assessment tests (CATs), one regular examination and one supplementary examination, for each unit that s/he is teaching. This is a time-consuming and effortful process. One of the challenges faced, particularly in the setting of examinations, is ensuring that questions cover different levels of difficulty, to enable the instructor to determine the comprehension of students regarding the subject matter in a specific unit.

In LMS systems, examinations are generated by random selection of questions from a question bank, with no particular selection criteria [7–9]. Studies show that because it is expensive to generate a quality exam that tests different cognitive levels, online tests generated within LMS systems are primarily used for formative assessment, and not summative assessment [5]. However, research reveals that a quality examination should include questions that test both higher and lower order thinking skills. This can be done by ensuring that the questions in an examination cover all levels of an educational taxonomy such as Revised Bloom's Taxonomy (RBT) [10]. RBT assists the lecturer in preparing intended learning outcomes (ILOs) and assessments [11]. While research has been done into coverage of RBT by examinations, most research does retrospective labelling of examination questions, not classification of questions prior to including them in examinations. However, using ML techniques to classify questions, it is possible to label questions in a question bank and thus enable generation of good quality examinations within an LMS.

The aim of this paper is to explore how machine learning algorithms can improve the quality of automatically generated exams in LMS systems. This study was guided by the following research questions:

1. What methods are used to automatically generate examinations from question banks in LMS systems?
2. What machine learning algorithms have been used to classify examination questions into different cognitive levels?

In this paper, we develop a conceptual framework to integrate ML techniques in the automatic generation of quality exams in LMS systems.

2 Methodology

For this review paper the Khan et al. [12] method was selected. It involves five steps: (i) framing research questions for a review, (ii) identifying relevant work, (iii) assessing the quality of studies, (iv) summarising the evidence, and (v) interpreting the findings. The review questions have been stated above. Subsequently, we identified primary studies and systematic reviews using appropriate search keywords [13]. The following keywords were used:

- Automatic Examination Generation
- Online Test Generation
- Intelligent Test Paper Generation
- Automated Question Paper Generator System

The databases used for the search were Google Scholar and *IEEE Xplore*. The search period covered was 2011 - 2021. Out of this search, over 50 articles were selected, but scanning the abstracts allowed us to reduce the number to 10 papers relevant for this research, published between 2011 and 2021.

2.1 Examinations

The need to evaluate the learning attained by students is significant in Higher Education Institutions (HEIs). This is done through assessment tools such as quizzes, tests and final examinations. However, due to the significant time and effort required to set these assessments, some examinations are poorly designed, and fail to properly assess the achievement of the intended learning outcomes (ILO) of a specific course [14]. A good final examination should cover all the ILOs and have questions that can distinguish good from poor learners. RBT can be used to ensure questions of different difficulty level are included in the examination.

2.2 Question Bank

In an LMS system, a question bank is created when large numbers of individual questions of different types are drafted and placed in a repository. When an examination is required, questions are selected from the bank [14]. These questions may have undergone review and revision before they are added to the bank, or after being included in a test [15]. A good examination should contain questions from different levels of Revised Bloom's Taxonomy (RBT). We propose to use RBT to classify questions, prior to their inclusion in an examination generated from the test bank of an LMS.

An Automatic Examination Generator (AEG) is a tool that selects questions from a question bank and generates an examination. The AEG will use a pre-determined template to guide coverage of ILOs, randomize questions in order to avoid repetition and distribute marks fairly over the various questions in the exam [14].

Due to unfamiliarity with the process, or distrust of the quality of examinations produced, lecturers using LMS systems in HEIs use a hybrid of online and offline tools to conduct assessment [16–18]. To enhance the confidence of HEI examiners in automatically generated examinations, an AEG should produce a quality examination from the question bank, which tests different cognitive levels and covers the selected ILOs [19].

2.3 Bloom's Taxonomy

Educational taxonomies help the instructor to set learning objectives which then guide the learning activities and assessments [20]. One of the best known educational taxonomies is Bloom's taxonomy. It was developed in 1948 by a group of university lecturers attending the American Psychological Association Convention in Boston. Led by Benjamin Bloom, these educators collaboratively created a framework to classify learning outcomes [21]. They believed that this framework, named Bloom's Taxonomy, could promote standardisation in assessment and teaching [22]. Bloom's taxonomy had three components, the cognitive, the affective and the psychomotor domains. The cognitive component was widely adopted in education.

In 2001 the taxonomy was revised by a group of cognitive psychologists and assessment specialists including David Krathwohl, Lorin Anderson and other educational experts. They expanded Bloom's taxonomy from a single dimension to a two-dimensional taxonomy, updating the verbs and introducing a knowledge dimension [22]. In the Revised Bloom's Taxonomy (RBT), the categories in the cognitive dimension were renamed Remember, Understand, Apply, Analyse, Evaluate and Create as shown in Fig. 1 below [23].

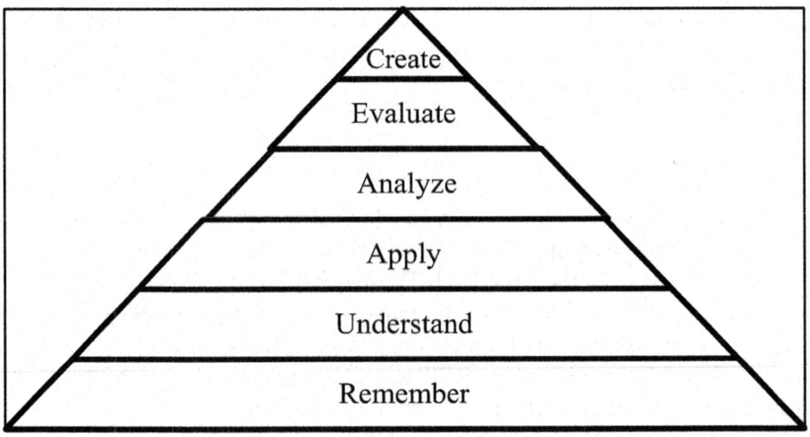

Fig. 1. Revised Blooms Taxonomy

2.4 Use of ML Techniques to Classify Examination Questions

ML techniques are used widely to classify examination questions. A review of the literature showed several popular ML techniques, including Support Vector Machines (SVM), K-Nearest Neighbour (kNN), Convolutional Neural Networks (CNN), Long Short-Term Memory (LSTM), Naïve Bayes, Logistic Regression, Decision Trees and Random Forest used to classify questions into a level of RBT. Of these ML techniques, SVM was one of the most popular, attaining 86% correct classification as seen in the analysis of results below.

3 Results

In this section we critique studies on the automatic generation of examinations with an emphasis on how questions are selected for inclusion in an examination. A good examination covers the ILOs of a course, and contains questions that range over the different levels of RBT. This means that the questions test both higher and lower order thinking skills, enabling the examiner to use the examination as a tool to discriminate between students who have a shallow understanding and those who have a deep understanding of the subject. Such an examination should also align with the question paper format desired by the examiner [24].

Kale and Kiwelekar [24] designed a AEG that enables the examiner to choose the examination questions according to learning outcome, the cognitive skill level of RBT to be covered, the difficulty level, and the desired marks per question. The algorithm then selects questions from the question bank as long as they meet the desired criteria. This question paper generator depends on the examiner to correctly specify the RBT level of the question, and it does not include any ML techniques.

Amria et al. [14] present a framework that allows educators to map questions to ILOs based on RBT. In their system, the educator is responsible for defining a question and mapping it to a predefined ILO. Questions that are mapped to a lower level of RBT such as remembering, understanding, and applying are placed in the first part of the exam while those at a higher RBT level are placed in the latter part of the exam. Their tool allows tutors to enter different question types such as True/False, essay questions and others. Output formats include XML (for electronic exams), PDF, or Document. This tool uses a random algorithm to select questions to be included in the exam, while categorization based on RBT is done by the examiner when adding questions to the question bank.

Several of the papers we found showed the steps taken to classify examinations according to RBT. In a 2016 study, Jayakodi et al. [25] used Natural Language Processing (NLP) techniques to identify the RBT category for exam questions from the Computer Science domain. Using NLP to develop a set of rules for classification, their system was able to correctly categorise 82% of 147 questions that had been previously labelled by a domain expert. The study could be extended to cover a broader range of questions from different educational domains.

A similar study by [26] used a rule-based approach and NLP to identify the keywords in a question, and subsequently categorized a set of 100 questions into the different RBT levels. The study emphasised that a certain keyword in a question does not automatically determine the RBT category. Their research calculated the question category based on weights calculated by subject matter experts (SMEs).

Other studies in our review classified the questions in examinations into RBT using ML techniques. Laddha et al. [27] investigate the use of CNN and LSTM to classify 844 exam questions into RBT levels. Using a dataset labelled with both cognitive and knowledge dimensions, they trained the CNN and LSTM models on a 70% training set and tested on the remaining 30%. The limitation of this study was the low accuracy levels of 66.67% for CNN, and 44% for LSTM.

An empirical research by [11] used a Python script to match the action word in the examination question to a RBT keyword list. Using a dataset of 1,000 examination questions, they then used an open source tool named orange and the machine learning algorithms SVM and kNN to classify the questions into the 6 different RBT levels. The accuracy for SVM was 69% and for kNN was 60.5%.

Mohammed & Omar [10] use term frequency–inverse document frequency (TF-IDF) and word2vec to improve the performance of exam question classification according to Bloom's Taxonomy. In their research, they evaluate the performance of SVM, Logistic Regression (LR), and kNN. Their findings were that SVM had superior performance over LR and kNN, achieving an average of 89.7%, 89.4%, and 85.44% weighted F1-measure respectively. Their research classified questions from two datasets containing a total of 741 questions. They found ML techniques useful in classifying examination questions from different domains.

The research done by Rahim et al. [7] takes a database of 500 examination questions and uses the Genetic Algorithm to select the questions to be included according to coverage of RBT levels. This research describes a good examination as that which covers 3 to 6 levels of RBT. Although this research was restricted by the quantity of questions they had available for their research, they were able to generate examinations that had on average 70% coverage of RBT.

Sangodiah et al. [28] investigated the performance of the SVM algorithm in classifying questions using different taxonomy-based features. The questions in the study were classified into RBT levels by domain experts. The questions were pre-processed using WordNet, while Stanford Parser was used to tag parts-of-speech. The output was then passed through a feature extraction process and the extracted features used to train the SVM classifier. The findings were that bag-of-words combined with general and specific taxonomy terms were the most useful features in question classification. The classifier was able to achieve 72.9% accuracy. A summary of the ML techniques used in examination question classification is shown in Table 1 below.

3.1 Proposed Conceptual Framework for the Automatic Generation of Exams

In this section we propose a machine learning enabled conceptual framework for the automatic generation of examinations from a question bank in an LMS. The variables in this framework include coverage of ILOs, coverage of RBT, marks distribution, and random selection of question [7, 14]. The questions used in the automatic generation of exams will originate from a question bank populated by different types of questions in a specific subject domain. The question bank can be created by manual input of questions by the instructors; alternatively questions may be generated using artificial intelligence techniques including NLP [10, 29].

From the studies reviewed, it is evident that a number of researchers are using NLP techniques and ML algorithms to classify examination questions into the different RBT levels. Concurrently, several researchers have developed AEGs that produce examinations; however these use random selection of questions that fit predetermined criteria.

Based on the above reviews, we propose to improve AEGs by using ML techniques to label the questions with the correct RBT levels prior to their selection for inclusion in an examination. The performance of the ML model would improve over time as questions are added to the question bank. We opine that the use of ML techniques would result

Table 1. Summary of ML Techniques used in classifying examination questions

	Authors	ML Algorithm (Accuracy)	Question datasets used
1	Laddha et al. [27]	• CNN (80%) • LSTM (71%)	A dataset of 844 questions
2	Patil & Shreyas [11]	• Used SVM and kNN to classify the questions into 6 different levels • SVM (69%) • kNN (60.5%)	The data set consisted of 1,000 questions collected from various external sources related to operating system course
3	Mohammed & Omar [10]	• Support Vector Machine (SVM) (89.7%) • Logistic Regression (LR) (89.4%) • K-Nearest Neighbour (kNN) (85.4%)	Dataset 1 – 141 questions Dataset 2 – 600 questions
4	Rahim [7]	• Genetic Algorithm • Exams generated had 70% coverage of RBT	A dataset of 500 questions
5	Sangodiah et al. [28]	• Domain experts • SVM (72.9% accuracy)	A dataset of 415 questions

in good quality examinations that can be used for generating summative exams from LMS systems. The diagram below illustrates how the proposed ML-enabled AEG would work.

The conceptual framework below envisions examination questions entered into the question bank, then using a trained ML model, the questions are then classified into different RBT levels. Subsequently, an examination can be automatically generated that adheres to a defined question paper format, comprising questions covering the ILOs as prescribed by the examiner and covering all the RBT levels (Fig. 2).

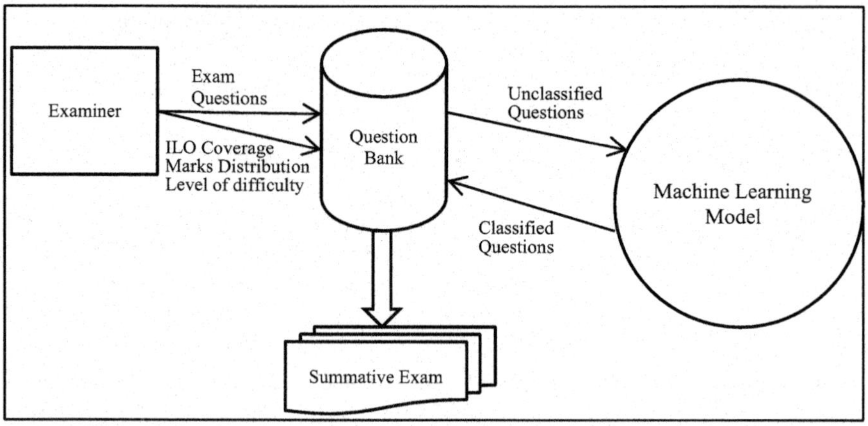

Fig. 2. Proposed Conceptual Framework

4 Conclusion

This study reviewed a number of studies on the automatic generation of examinations using machine learning techniques. From the review, we have defined a number of parameters necessary for the automatic generation of examinations using machine learning algorithms to label the questions in a question bank. Having noted the need to generate good examinations, we propose a conceptual framework that will utilise a trained machine learning model to label the questions prior to their inclusion in a quality exam. We propose to validate this framework by developing a prototype based on the conceptual framework. Using this prototype, examinations will be produced for a specific subject domain in an LMS system.

Acknowledgement. This research was supported by the National Research Fund 2016/2017 grant award under the multidisciplinary-multi-institutional category involving Kenyatta University, University of Nairobi, and The Cooperative University of Kenya. The research is investigating how artificial intelligence can be used to enhance e-learning in HEIs.

References

1. Schiff, D.: Out of the laboratory and into the classroom: the future of artificial intelligence in education. AI Soc. **36**(1), 331–348 (2020). https://doi.org/10.1007/s00146-020-01033-8
2. Popenici, S.A.D., Kerr, S.: Exploring the impact of artificial intelligence on teaching and learning in higher education. Res. Pract. Technol. Enhanc. Learn. **12** (2017)
3. Zawacki-Richter, O., Marin, V.I., Bond, M., Gouverneur, F.: Systematic review of research on artificial intelligence applications in higher education – where are the educators? Int. J. Educ. Technol. High. Educ. **16** (2019)
4. Araka, E., Maina, E., Gitonga, R., Oboko, R.: Research trends in measurement and intervention tools for self-regulated learning for e-learning environments-systematic review (2008–2018). Res. Pract. Technol. Enhanc. Learn. **15** (2020)

5. Boitshwarelo, B., Reedy, A.K., Billany, T.: Envisioning the use of online tests in assessing twenty-first century learning: a literature review. Res. Pract. Technol. Enhanc. Learn. **12** (2017)
6. Luckin, R.: Towards artificial intelligence-based assessment systems. Nat. Hum. Behav. **1** (2017)
7. Rahim, T.N.T.A., Aziz, Z.A., Rauf, R.H.A., Shamsudin, N.: Automated exam question generator using genetic algorithm. In: 2017 IEEE Conference on e-Learning, e-Management and e-Services, IC3e 2017, pp. 12–17. IEEE (2017)
8. Kalaluka, K.M.: Exam paper generating system: automated exam system. Int. J. Multi-Discip. Res. 1–4 (2017)
9. Noor, N.M., Napi, N.M., Amin, I.F.I.: The development of autonomous examination paper application: a case study in UiTM Perlis branch. J. Comput. Res. Innov. (JCRINN) **4**, 21–30 (2019)
10. Mohammed, M., Omar, N.: Question classification based on Bloom's taxonomy cognitive domain using modified TF-IDF and word2vec. PLoS ONE **15**, 1–21 (2020)
11. Patil, S.K., Shreyas, M.M.: A comparative study of question bank classification based on revised bloom's taxonomy using SVM and K-NN. In: 2nd International Conference on Emerging Computation and Information Technologies (ICECIT), pp. 1–7. IEEE (2017)
12. Khan, K.S., Kunz, R., Kleijnen, J., Antes, G.: Five steps to conducting a systematic review. J. Roy. Soc. Med. **96** (2003)
13. Kitchenham, B.: Guidelines for performing Systematic Literature Reviews in Software Engineering Version 2.3 EBSE Technical Report EBSE-2007-01 (2007)
14. Amria, A., Ewais, A., Hodrob, R.: A framework for automatic exam generation based on intended learning outcomes. In: Proceedings of the 10th International Conference on Computer Supported Education (CSEDU 2018), pp. 474–480 (2018)
15. Crisp, V., Shaw, S., Bramley, T.: Should we be banking on it? Exploring potential issues in the use of "item" banking with structured examination questions. Asses. Educ.: Princ. Policy Pract. **27**, 655–669 (2020)
16. Mimirinis, M.: Qualitative differences in academics' conceptions of e-assessment. Assess. Eval. High. Educ. **44**, 233–248 (2019)
17. Rolim, C., Isaias, P.: Examining the use of e-assessment in higher education: teachers and students' viewpoints. Br. J. Educ. Technol. **50**, 1785–1800 (2018)
18. Ivanova, M., Bhattacharjee, S., Marcel, S., Rozeva, A.: Enhancing Trust in eAssessment - The TeSLA System Solution. Technical University of Sofia (2019)
19. Tetali, D.R., Rani, P.K.: Automated course outcomes assessment for multiple choice questions (auto_assess). Int. J. Adv. Res. Comput. Sci. **8**, 189–192 (2017)
20. Van Niekerk, J., von Solms, R.: Using Bloom's taxonomy for information security education. In: Dodge, R.C., Futcher, L. (eds.) WISE 2009/2011/2013. IAICT, vol. 406, pp. 280–287. Springer, Heidelberg (2013). https://doi.org/10.1007/978-3-642-39377-8_33
21. Bloom, B.S., Engelhart, M.D., Furst, E.J., Hill, W.H., Krathwohl, D.R.: Taxonomy of Educational Objectives: The Classification of Educational Goals. Taxonomy of Educational Objectives, p. 207 (1956)
22. Anderson, L.W., et al.: A Taxonomy for Learning, Teaching, and Assessing: A Revision of Bloom's Taxonomy of Educational Objectives (2001)
23. Krathwohl, D.R.: A revision of Bloom's taxonomy: an overview. Theory Pract. **41**, 212–218 (2002)
24. Kale, V.M., Kiwelekar, A.W.: An algorithm for question paper template generation in question paper generation system. In: The International Conference on Technological Advances in Electrical, Electronics and Computer Engineering (TAEECE), pp. 256–261. IEEE (2013)

25. Jayakodi, K., Bandara, M., Perera, I.: An automatic classifier for exam questions in engineering: a process for Bloom's taxonomy. In: Proceedings of 2015 IEEE International Conference on Teaching, Assessment and Learning for Engineering, TALE 2015, pp. 195–202 (2016)
26. Omar, N., et al.: Automated analysis of exam questions according to Bloom's taxonomy. Proc. - Soc. Behav. Sci. **59**, 297–303 (2012). 8
27. Laddha, M.D., Lokare, V.T., Kiwelekar, A.W., Netak, L.D.: Classifications of the summative assessment for revised Bloom's taxonomy by using deep learning. Int. J. Eng. Trends Technol. **69**, 211–218 (2021)
28. Sangodiah, A., Ahmad, R., Ahmad, W.F.W.: Taxonomy based features in question classification using support vector machine. J. Theor. Appl. Inf. Technol. **95**, 2814–2823 (2017)
29. Kumar, V., Ramakrishnan, G., Li, Y.-F.: A framework for question generation from text. In: 2019 IJCAI Workshop SCAI: The 4th International Workshop on Search-Oriented Conversational AI (2019)

Developing Informatics Modules for Teachers of All Subjects Based on Professional Activities

Torsten Brinda[1], Ludger Humbert[2], Matthias Kramer[1(✉)], and Denise Schmitz[2]

[1] University of Duisburg-Essen, Schützenbahn 70, 45127 Essen, Germany
{torsten.brinda,matthias.kramer}@uni-due.de
[2] University of Wuppertal, Gaußstraße 20, 42119 Wuppertal, Germany
{humbert,dschmitz}@uni-wuppertal.de

Abstract. In recent years it has become clear that teachers need digital competency to master their everyday work. However, this digital competency is based on informatics concepts and phenomena that cannot be addressed in an appropriate way without informatics education. This article describes an approach to basic informatics education for all teachers, regardless of their subjects or stage of their professional life. The results of a funded project in the federal country of North Rhine-Westphalia in Germany are presented in which, among other things, a community of practice (CoP) with members from all three phases of teacher education (pre-service, induction and in-service) developed and tested a modular concept of basic interactive informatics teaching units.

Keywords: Informatics competency · Digitalization-related competency · Teacher education

1 Introduction

What became evident by the results of international studies in recent years, see e.g. the evaluation of the PISA results 2018 [1], was even more reinforced in times of a global pandemic: publishing learning material for students on internet platforms, using end-to-end-encrypted messengers for communicating with students and their parents as well as selecting and using platforms for distance learning were only a few of the tasks, which posed problems to teachers in schools during the last years. In this context, educators are expected to be competent both in using digital technologies as professional educators [2] as well as in educating students on this topic [3]. At the same time, such competency has been required for decades [4], but has not been systematically anchored in teacher education until recently. Teachers need such competency for the competent handling of computing systems (e.g. mobile devices and apps) that they want to or should use for professional activities. The PISA results show that teachers' competencies are key: even if they want to implement digital alternatives to traditional

Published by Springer Nature Switzerland AG 2023
T. Keane et al. (Eds.): WCCE 2022, IFIP AICT 685, pp. 451–462, 2023.
https://doi.org/10.1007/978-3-031-43393-1_42

teaching, they often lack the skills and abilities to do so efficiently and competently. Training on selected products might be a short-term solution. Yet, the acquired skills become obsolete as soon as tools, programs and platforms that are considered popular today are replaced in a few years . All these products are the result of a modeling and implementing process and as such are based on informatics concepts and principles. So that all teachers can act competently – when teaching with current and future digital technologies (e.g. with a virtual laboratory), during other profession-related activities (e.g. for communication via messenger), or when creating subject-specific references to digital technologies in class (e.g. discussion about artificial intelligence) – they will therefore also have to acquire, to a certain extent, facets of informatics competency (see Subsect. 2.1), as explained in [5]. This could enable them to select and to use digital resources according to scientific criteria, to react competently to occurring phenomena when using such resources and – finally – to become self-determined citizens in a world shaped by digitalization, which has also been emphasized already in other works (e.g. [6,7]).

This article describes processes and results of a large funded project in North Rhine-Westphalia in Germany, in which stakeholders from twelve universities, centers for practical school teacher training (in German *Zentren für schulpraktische Lehrerausbildung*) and from schools as well as ministries work together to address competencies related to digitalization in teacher education. Within the project, communities of practice (CoP) on different aspects of digitalization-related competency of teachers are the main way of cooperation. The authors of this paper are the members of the management team of a CoP that deals with the development of basic informatics competency in all teachers.

The rest of the paper is structured as follows: Sect. 2 first presents the background of the work. Section 3 gives an overview of the development of a modular interactive informatics teaching concept oriented along teachers' professional activities, presents one learning unit in detail as well as first experiences in pilot courses. The paper ends with summary and conclusions in Sect. 4.

2 Theoretical Background and Related Work

The aim of the paper is to present a concept of how informatics can be integrated into general teacher education by developing modular teaching units that can be used at all stages of teacher education. First, an overview of educational recommendations and existing models is given. Then, the German teacher education system is briefly described. The section ends with a brief description and discussion of related projects.

2.1 Digital Competency and Informatics Competency

During the last years, an often heard demand in all educational fields from primary to higher education has been the call for *digitalization* accompanied by the development of *digital skills*, *digital literacy* as well as *digital competency*, although the terms have been and still are used inconsistently. The definitions of these terms comprise a multitude of skills, knowledge and attitudes such as awareness for safety issues or the ability to develop a computing system by oneself [8, pp. 50–52] as well as a combination of generic digital competency, subject/didactic digital competency and profession-oriented competency [9, p. 217]. In general, any usage of computing systems to perform a certain task can be found using the terms *digitalization* or *digital media*. And even though different authors refer to different concepts, wider or narrower, there is usually not much debate about the importance of skills and competency related to digitalization, as these are "at the top of the European Policy Agenda" [3, p. 2].

On a European level, detailed competency frameworks addressing the competencies students at school as well as their teachers are expected to acquire have been published (e.g. DigComp [3], DigCompEdu [2]). The DigComp framework focuses on using digital media in all subjects and beyond school-life and DigCompEdu assumes that teachers have developed exactly these competencies, before they include such technologies in their classrooms as well as in other facets of their professional life. Informatics competency has almost not at all – at least not explicitly – been included in these models. However, other competency frameworks addressing informatics competency also exist (such as the K12CS recommendations, cf. k12cs.org, and the educational standards for computer science [10]). As argued before, teachers also need to deal with informatics phenomena occurring when using computing systems in the classroom and they need to address certain informatics aspects which occur in the digital transformation of the underlying disciplines of the subjects they teach. This general idea has already been anchored in the famous TPACK model [11], which describes the knowledge and skills teachers need to have when teaching a subject in a technology-rich environment and in which the description of the underlying "technological knowledge" combines digital skills as well as informatics competency [4]. To better connect all these different models and frameworks, an interdisciplinary working group developed an approach to integrate the aforementioned models and more in a new integrated model [5, p. 8] of digitalization-related competency of teachers. The key idea of this model is a broad and integrative understanding of digitalization-related competency, which covers using and understanding digital technologies, their informatics background as well as impacts, such technologies have on society. This broad understanding then determines the competency facets in the main pillars of teacher development in this context, namely learning and teaching with and about digital technologies and using digital technologies in other profession-related activities. This broad understanding of digitalization-related competency of teachers, which explicitly integrates informatics competency, will be used for the rest of this paper.

2.2 The German Teacher Education System

As this work refers to specifics of the German teacher education system, a brief overview is given. Teacher education in Germany is separated into three distinct phases or stages: The first stage covers academic education with a duration of at least five years (finishing with a *Master of Education*). Usually, prospective teachers study at least two subjects they will later teach in schools plus a selection of topics on education, e.g. foundations of psychology, educational theories, school development etc. In the process, prospective teachers specify one type of school (e.g. primary, secondary or vocational school) and learn specific requirements for this selected type of school. If informatics education should be integrated in this stage of teacher education, it should be provided in the typical form for this stage, i.e. a seminar or a lecture.

A Master's degree is required to enter the second stage, so called assistant teacher stage (in German *Vorbereitungsdienst*). For at least 18 months, assistant teachers work the majority of the time in schools, teaching their two (or more) subjects to students. In the beginning of this phase, the assistant teachers work with experienced teachers who support them in the development and teaching of their first series of lessons. A smaller amount of time (usually once a week) is spent in close-by seminars, located in centers for practical school teacher training, with other assistant teachers to foster their knowledge on educational theories, both general and subject-specific. They finish the second stage with an exam, thus receiving their official teaching degree which allows them to teach in a selection of public schools in Germany. If informatics education should be integrated in this stage of teacher education, this should be accomplished by integrating aspects in learning units which take place at the centers for practical school teacher training.

Having passed the second stage, teachers enter the third and final stage where they receive in-service training about selected topics. If informatics education should be integrated in this stage of teacher education, it should be accomplished by integrating learning units in in-service teacher training offers at their schools.

It is worth noting that the three stages of teacher education are organized by completely different institutions and that is why the supervisors of these institutions often do not cooperate with each other in a systematically organized way. The described project also had the aim to establish new and better ways of cooperation between educators in the different phases of teacher education.

2.3 Related Projects

Provided that all teachers should develop informatics competency, the next question to be answered is, how such informatics education can be implemented in teacher education. Just as mathematics is taught as an independent subject but is needed in other subjects, such as physics or social sciences, concepts and methods of informatics are applicable in a wide contextual range.

One possible way to educate teachers in informatics is to present core informatics concepts to them and to let them transfer these principles into their subjects. This approach was used in several projects. For example, Seegerer and Romeike [7] investigated where informatics-related topics can be found in other school-relevant disciplines and described, how a course can be structured that deals with informatics foundations which are then applied within different subject domains [12]. The benefit of this approach is obviously that teachers can immediately apply their knowledge in their respective subjects and hence can use it directly in their classes. However, all scientific fields need different approaches and transfers, e.g. the principles applicable in STEM subjects might differ from the ones applicable in liberal arts, sports, music etc.

Another facet of teachers' activities is their professional engagement ([2,5]). Hence, another approach would be to start from their everyday profession-related activities. For example, teachers have to ensure that the data they store about their students (and possibly their parents) such as addresses, grades, medical issues etc. are accessible solely by those who are permitted to access them. They also have to communicate with parents and colleagues. If they choose to use a messenger, then they have to ensure that neither the service provider nor anyone in the routing path can access any private information. As explained in Subsect. 2.1, to make a competent decision for or against an existing program, teachers need to understand at least on a basic level how these programs work, i.e. how they process input data, which features they do and do not incorporate and which consequences would follow from using a specific tool, e.g. for the privacy of their students' data. This approach is described by Braun et al. [13] and the work presented in this paper is also based on this approach. The obvious advantage is that the contents are independent of a specific subject group, i.e. they are relevant for all teachers of all subjects. This, however, is also a disadvantage, especially for in-service trainings in later stages: Teachers tend to prefer in-service trainings with accompanying material which they can include directly into their lessons.

2.4 Interim Conclusion

Demands for *digital competency* are high and become increasingly frequent. They comprise a multitude of skills and all of them include the competent usage of computing systems. As informatics is the science that enables and drives all digital transformation, demands for *digital competency* imply demands for *informatics competency*. Teachers are the key actors in the education system. Not only do they need to understand how the subjects they teach and the teaching methods they use are influenced by computing systems, i.e. by informatics concepts, many further professional activities in school are also increasingly shaped by the usage of computing systems. As informatics has not yet been implemented as a mandatory school subject in Germany, all prospective and current teachers need to develop informatics competency in any of the stages of teacher education, so any approach should take this broad need into account. To be motivating and convincing especially for practicing teachers, any approach should be oriented towards teachers' profession-related activities, so that they can directly understand, how this new competency help them for their job as a teacher and beyond. Subject-independent activities have the advantage that they are relevant for all teachers of all subjects. That is why this approach was chosen for the project described here. Based on such a foundation, connections to informatics concepts within other (groups of) school subjects can then be developed in a following step.

3 Digitalization-Related Competency for All Teachers

The ComeIn[1] project (communities of practice in North Rhine-Westphalia for innovative teacher education, funded by the German Ministry of Education and Research, 2020–2023) has two main objectives: (1) to further develop digitalization-related competency of teachers, (2) to use communities of practice as a cooperation method to better network the three phases of teacher education. In the project, more than 200 stakeholders from all three phases of teacher education collaborate in five subject-specific (e.g. STEM, humanities) and three interdisciplinary CoPs (e.g. basic informatics education, inclusion).

3.1 Key Steps in the Development Process in the CoP "Basic Informatics Education"

In order to anchor basic informatics concepts in teacher education, the CoP[2] decided at the start of the project to develop a course whose accompanying material can be used completely or partly in all phases of teacher education.

Longer discussions followed on the question of which informatics concepts or competency facets should be taught or developed in such a course. First, the idea of choosing school-relevant informatics concepts, such as "algorithms" or "languages and automata" [10, p. 289] as a starting point was discussed, since these are known and established both nationally and internationally. CoP members from the second and third phase of teacher education criticized this approach, because it did not seem practical enough for practicing teachers. Instead, explicit or implicit references to informatics concepts in other subjects or groups of subjects as well as in subject-independent, profession-related activities with a connection to informatics were discussed as an alternative starting point, from which underlying informatics competency facets should then be developed. Since this alternative approach also connects university teacher education with school practice, in accordance with the explanations in Subsect. 2.3, this approach was chosen as the starting point of the course development.

As explained in Subsect. 2.2, the possibilities to integrate new educational elements are quite different for each stage of teacher education. For example, while a lecture seems appropriate for student teachers in university, visiting a weekly lecture seems completely unmanageable for teachers who work full-time in schools. Hence, the CoP agreed on developing a collection of interrelated but essentially independent teaching units (referred to as *modules* in the following) for several reasons: (1) There are neither national nor federal guidelines regarding the extent to which digitalization-related competency should be anchored in university teacher education. As a result, the curricular space available for such competency development varies greatly between universities. A modular concept offers the advantage of being able to integrate only selected modules into courses with a broader thematic focus, as well as being able to offer specific courses with a

[1] https://comein.nrw/.

[2] https://comein.nrw/portal/cop-igb/.

focus on informatics competency development. (2) In the second and third phase of teacher education, key competencies such as digitalization-related competency are usually addressed in (a series of) half-day or full-day workshops. A modular concept also offers the necessary flexibility here.

Based on the decision to orientate the module development along subject-independent teacher activities, the CoP collected a set of prototypical activities derived from several digitalization-related competency frameworks (see Subsect. 2.1). For example, such a digitalization-related activity is chosing an appropriate program to communicate with colleagues, students, parents, institutions etc. To make an appropriate choice, e.g. for communicating via messenger, mail or any communication via internet, this choice must be based on certain criteria that distinguish the communication methods from each other. As one concern in professional communication of teachers is the data privacy of students or parents, teachers must be aware of communication methods that keep these data secure. This also means that they are aware of possible points of data privacy breach. And this means, they have to know in general how the internet works. Only then can an informed choice about forms of communication be made, i.e. which forms of communication should be chosen and which should be rejected. Similarly, other activities of teachers have been selected, e.g. protecting student data from unauthorized access, using collaboration platforms when collaborating with colleagues or searching and remixing existing resources to generate new learning material.

3.2 Developed Modules

Following the process described above, by September 2022, members of the CoP had developed nine modules related to teachers' professional activities, see Table 1.

Each module is the result of a intensive brainstorming and discussion process among the CoP members, reflecting their individual expertise on competency frameworks as well as professional requirements and general conditions in school. The starting point was the analysis of school-relevant competency frameworks related to digitalization in order to ensure that these competencies are also being addressed in the module. The German implementation of DigComp [3] is the strategy "Education in the digital world" developed by the Standing Conference of the German Ministers of Education and Cultural Affairs (KMK) [14]. Even though this strategy is mostly directed towards competencies of students, for all profession-related actions of teachers it is assumed that they have also at least developed these competencies. Currently, there isn't a comparable national strategy document for digitalization-related competency development of teachers, however, on a federal level such documents exist, such as the "Orientation framework: teachers in a digitalized world" [15]. As these are compulsory standards for teacher education, at first competency specifications from these frameworks were analyzed and grouped regarding typical profession-related activities of teachers, such as communication with others via internet. For every activity represented by a group of competency descriptions a module

Table 1. Overview of the developed modules, the underlying informatics concepts, and the relevance for teachers

Module title	Informatics concepts and competency facets	Important for teachers, because ...
M1: Informatics - from science to practice	Definition of terms, objects and methods of informatics, subject areas of informatics	... arguing with informatics first needs an insight into what informatics is and what not
M2: Information search and text design	Search engines, word processing systems and text design, bibliographical objects	... they use search engines to find teaching material and to combine the results into new material
M3: The "secure" chat with colleagues	Internet as interconnected networks, communication in networks, client-server architecture, encryption	... they must select appropriate ways for communicating with colleagues, parents, students etc.
M4: Artificial intelligence	History, machine learning, recommendation systems, neural networks, new learning and teaching situations with AI	... the term "artificial intelligence" is ubiquitous and it is especially relevant in schools (automatic language translators, automated assessment)
M5: From paperstacks to databases	Change of data management, possible uses of databases, querying data from the database, e.g. with SQL commands	... especially on management level they need to manage data of students, most probably from more than one class for several years
M6: Create, recall, protect data	File management on computing systems, encryption and decryption, backups, file management of apps	... they need to manage data of their students (contact data, grades, health remarks etc.)
M7: Shaping school life together	File properties, client-server model, persistence of data, versioning	... they need to cooperate with each other via shared platforms or documents
M8: Digital self defense	Password security, data tracking on websites, data transfer on the internet, malware	... they use the internet frequently, for lesson preparation or enhancement
M9: Creating legally compliant teaching material	Licenses as attributes of every digital artefact, structure of documents	... they frequently use and remix material they find on the internet

was specified. Each such module was then analyzed for informatics-related competency which should be addressed in the module. This process was continued with the remaining competency descriptions, until the majority of competency specifications in all documents were addressed, which resulted in the presented nine modules. Subsequently, responsibilities for modules within the CoP were defined and their concept was developed and refined by those responsible. Then the teaching material for the modules was developed and mutual feedback was given in internal peer reviews.

The resulting modules consist each of presentation slides, accompanying notes for educators with further examples as well as necessary files to illustrate examples in the module. In each of these modules, first a scenario from everyday lives of teachers is presented. This scenario is based on one or more of the collected professional activities. Based on this scenario, the related informatics concepts are explained. Every module also includes practical exercises for the (prospective) teachers to develop specific informatics competency facets. At the end, the introductory scenario is presented again and reviewed with regard to the concepts presented in the module.

To give a more detailed example, we use the third module *The "secure" chat with colleagues*. Professional communication, not only with colleagues but also with students, parents, institutions that students visit etc., is part and parcel of the teacher job and it definitely is an important part in every major framework that deals with digital skills, cf. [3, p. 15], [2, p. 19], [4, p. 39]. For example, in DigCompEdu, educators on levels B1 and B2 are expected to "use different digital communication channels and tools, depending on the communication purpose and context" as well as "select the most appropriate channel, format and style for a given communication purpose and context" [2, p. 35]. To make an informed decision about which tool or channel to use implies that educators can distinguish between different programs and channels based on certain (non-trivial) features. This means, they know how their communication data is processed in which way and can therefore choose or reject a certain program. The module starts with a scenario, where the students are faced with the situation that a messenger for communication with colleagues in the near future should be selected. Afterwards, the participants learn about different parts of the internet (client, server, router, internet provider, DNS), their respective functions and what this has to do with the messengers they are using. Next, they have to explore a simulation of a "small" internet, where one client asks for a website from a browser and two other clients exchange mails. Subsequently, they are presented with the logs from the servers to experience which parts of their requests and data can be seen by a server. Based on this, the participants learn that encryption can be a valid tool to keep data protected, their own as well as those of their students. Based on what has been experienced until then, a list of properties for messengers is derived with the participants and exemplary messengers are rated regarding these properties. Finally, the scenario is picked up and students have to reflect their own messenger use, both private and professional. The presented content as well as the embedded exercises present a possibility for participants to develop informatics competency facets, such as distinguishing between clients, routers and servers, explaining communication in the internet or using encryption to protect data privacy. Furthermore, these informatics competency facets are necessary to develop the demanded "digital" competency descriptions, such as selecting "the most appropriate channel, format and style for a given communication purpose and context" [2, p. 35].

In a similar way, all of the presented modules are designed. The competency specifications from national and international frameworks build the foundation. Afterwards, a scenario from the professional school life is constructed so that participants can relate the following contents to their job. Then, informatics concepts and their relation to the scenario are presented to clarify, why a competent execution of the given task requires informatics competency.

The modules are designed in such a way that they can be presented independently of each other as well as combined to form a larger sequence of modules. Since the modules do not focus on isolated informatics concepts but on school context, certain topics naturally occur in several modules, e.g. backups: In the module M6, different backup strategies are shown through which participants should develop their own strategies for their everyday lives. This is reflected in module M8 with a focus on specific ransomware where the backup acts as a protective mechanism. Among other things, this engagement with data is used to achieve the required competencies from DigCompEdu [2, p. 49].

3.3 First Experiences

The modules were first tested in the year 2022 on several occasions. In the summer term (15 weeks from April to July), an optional lecture was organized for student teachers at the university of Duisburg-Essen. It was a virtual lecture with integrated practical exercises that was held every week for 90 min. As module M9 was still in production, the modules M1 to M8 were presented in the order M1 - M6 - M2 - M3 - M8 - M7 - M5 - M4, as this sequence – according to the CoP – best reflects and supports the development of the underlying informatics competency. The number of participants was very small, even for an optional course. While 17 students subscribed to the course, only seven showed up regularly and participated in the final survey. Overall, the course was rated by the remaining students as profitable and useful for their future work as a teacher, although this might as well be interpreted as *survivorship bias*. It would have been also very interesting to hear about the drop out reasons of the other students, but there was no possibility to reach out to them, after they had removed themselves from the course. One of these students commented before that she had difficulties to understand even very basic informatics terms such as "sourcecode" or "compiler" and that the amount of technical terms overstrained her. Therefore, technical terms are reduced where they occur in masses and a glossary will accompany future material. Other students pointed out that some parts of the lecture contained too much presentation and gave not enough time to actually perform the tasks. To address this point, several modules are currently being enhanced with more interactive exercises, which is also beneficial for in-service training in the third stage.

In addition, at least four modules were integrated in existing lectures and seminars in universities of other CoP members. At least three times selected modules were tested in the third stage of teacher education, where about 15 to 20 teachers received an in-service training. In particular, the feedback from the latter situations was extremely valuable as these teachers could provide immediate feedback about the usefulness, strengths and weaknesses of the material. In addition to the positive feedback, almost all of participants agreed that all teachers should get educated in informatics, especially since lots of them associated informatics with "just programming" before. Whenever the material became too theoretical, participants gave us the advice to constantly clarify the necessity of certain concepts for teachers' work.

The feedback has then been and will further be used to revise and to update the material. It will also be published as Open Educational Resource (OER) at https://www.orca.nrw. Overall, it can be stated that the development of loosely connected informatics modules, each of which is oriented towards profession-related activities of teachers, has proven to work in general teacher education.

4 Summary and Conclusions

In order to implement the digital transformation of the school education system and to develop and to foster digital competency at all students, all teachers also need digital competency both for their own professionalization and for teaching with and about digital technologies as well as for other profession-related activities. Such professional activities require – among other things – informatics competency. As long as informatics has not been adequately anchored as a compulsory subject for all students in school education, such competency needs to be developed by the teacher education system for prospective and practicing teachers. In the paper at hand, a concept for modular informatics teaching units based on professional activities of teachers was motivated and described, which has already proven to be promising in initial teaching interventions. In the remaining project time until September 2023, the concept and the specific modules will be further tested and refined. Accompanying material with didactic comments for each module will be created so that the modules can be used by any educator in the three phases of the German teacher education system and not only by the developers of the modules. Further trials will take place in the second and third phases of teacher education. Based on the experiences, the modules will be further enhanced. In doing so, the COP members are in constant contact and consultation with members from the national and international community.

References

1. OECD: PISA 2018 Results (Volume V): Effective Policies, Successful Schools. OECD Publishing, Paris (2020). https://doi.org/10.1787/ca768d40-en
2. Redecker, C., Punie, Y.: European framework for the digital competence of educators: DigCompEdu. Scientific analysis or review, Policy assessment, Technical guidance KJ-NA-28775-EN-C (print), KJ-NA-28775-EN-N (online), Luxembourg (Luxembourg) (2017). https://publications.jrc.ec.europa.eu/repository/handle/JRC107466
3. Vuorikari, R., Kluzer, S., Punie, Y.: DigComp 2.2: the digital competence framework for citizens - with new examples of knowledge, skills and attitudes. Scientific analysis or review KJ-NA-31006-EN-N (online), KJ-NA-31006-EN-C (print), Luxembourg (Luxembourg) (2022). https://publications.jrc.ec.europa.eu/repository/handle/JRC128415
4. National Research Council: Being Fluent with Information Technology. The National Academies Press, Washington (1999)
5. Borukhovich-Weis, S.: An integrated model of digitalisation-related competencies in teacher education. In: Passey, D., Leahy, D., Williams, L., Holvikivi, J., Ruohonen, M. (eds.) OCCE 2021. IFIP Advances in Information and Communication Technology, vol. 642, pp. 3–14. Springer, Cham (2022). https://doi.org/10.1007/978-3-030-97986-7_1
6. Diethelm, I.: Informatische Bildung für alle Lehrkräfte - Position des GI-Arbeitskreises Lehrkräftebildung. In: Humbert, L. (ed.) INFOS 2021–19. GI-Fachtagung Informatik und Schule, pp. 311–311. Gesellschaft für Informatik, Bonn (2021)

7. Seegerer, S., Romeike, R.: Computer science as a fundamental competence for teachers in other disciplines. In: Proceedings of the 13th Workshop in Primary and Secondary Computing Education. WiPSCE 2018, Association for Computing Machinery, New York, NY, USA (2018). https://doi.org/10.1145/3265757.3265787
8. Ala-Mutka, K.: Mapping digital competence: towards a conceptual understanding. Technical note, Luxembourg (Luxembourg) (2011)
9. Gudmundsdottir, G.B., Hatlevik, O.E.: Newly qualified teachers' professional digital competence: implications for teacher education. Eur. J. Teach. Educ. **41**(2), 214–231 (2018). https://doi.org/10.1080/02619768.2017.1416085
10. Brinda, T., Puhlmann, H., Schulte, C.: Bridging ICT and CS: educational standards for computer science in lower secondary education. In: Proceedings of the 14th Annual ACM SIGCSE Conference on Innovation and Technology in Computer Science Education, pp. 288–292. ITiCSE 2009, Association for Computing Machinery, New York, NY, USA (2009). https://doi.org/10.1145/1562877.1562965
11. Koehler, M., Mishra, P.: What is technological pedagogical content knowledge (TPACK)?. Contemp. Issues Technol. Teach. Educ. **9**(1), 60–70 (2009). https://www.learntechlib.org/p/29544
12. Seegerer, S., Romeike, R.: Employing computational thinking in general teacher education. In: Proceedings of International Conference on Computational Thinking Education 2019, pp. 86–91. CoolThink@JC, The Education University of Hong Kong, Tai Po, New Territories, Hong Kong (2019)
13. Braun, D., Pampel, B., Seiss, M.: Informatik-Grundlagen für Lehramtsstudierende. In: Humbert, L. (ed.) INFOS 2021–19. GI-Fachtagung Informatik und Schule, pp. 193–202. Gesellschaft für Informatik, Bonn (2021)
14. The Standing Conference of the Ministers of Education and Cultural Affairs (KMK): The Standing Conference's "Education in the Digital World" strategy - Summary (2016). https://t1p.de/afap2. Accessed 22 Aug 2023
15. Eickelmann, B.: Lehrkräfte in der digitalisierten Welt - Orientierungsrahmen für die Lehrerausbildung und Lehrerfortbildung in NRW (2020), Medienberatung NRW, Düsseldorf. https://t1p.de/y7y3x

Informatics for Teachers of All Subjects: A Balancing Act Between Conceptual Knowledge and Applications

Daniel Braun, Melanie Seiss(✉), and Barbara Pampel

University of Konstanz, Konstanz, Germany
{d.braun,melanie.seiss,barbara.pampel}@uni-konstanz.de

Abstract. In this paper we argue for the need to incorporate basic informatics training for teachers of all subjects. We suggest that topics need to be carefully motivated by application scenarios all teachers can connect to. We present our ideas on which content should be taught in a course for teacher education students at a university, citing motivating examples. We then give insights into how the participants of our course judged the content to be relevant for them and to which extend they considered it to be part of general knowledge.

Keywords: Digital education · Teacher education · Computer Science · Informatics

1 Introduction

In recent years it has become more and more clear that children need to be equipped early on for the challenges of the digitalised world. In many approaches, the competencies needed also include basic knowledge of informatics.[1] In Germany, the Standing Conference of the Ministers of Education and Cultural Affairs published a strategy ("KMK strategy" [1]) that lists which digital competencies school children should acquire. One component of this strategy defines the competencies to recognise and understand algorithms in digital tools and to plan and use structured algorithmic sequences to solve problems. Similar perspectives exist in many countries and the discussion about basic informatics knowledge of school children has moved from the question whether such knowledge is actually needed (e.g. [2,3]), to more detailed questions on how such content can be incorporated into the curriculum (e.g. [4,5]). Further, the International Computer and Information Literacy Study (ICILS) 2018 [6,7] not only

[1] There are many slightly different interpretations of the term *informatics*. In this paper we use it synonymous with the term *computer science*, i.e. referring to the scientific discipline concerned with the study of computation, automation and information. In this sense, we consider teaching computational thinking as a subpart of informatics education.

Published by Springer Nature Switzerland AG 2023
T. Keane et al. (Eds.): WCCE 2022, IFIP AICT 685, pp. 463–474, 2023.
https://doi.org/10.1007/978-3-031-43393-1_43

evaluated the students' skills in using a computer, gathering information, producing information and digital communication, but also included a sub-study on the students' competencies in computational thinking [2], which shows that they consider computational thinking to be relevant.

The discussion whether teachers of all subjects should have such basic knowledge of informatics is, at least to our knowledge, not very advanced yet in the international context. The framework DigCompEdu [8], for example, lists many skills teachers need for teaching in a digitalised world, but it does not explicitly incorporate informatics knowledge or knowledge about computational thinking, while Yadav et al. [9] report about incorporating concepts of computational thinking in a required educational psychology class for future K-12 teachers.

In Germany, the KMK strategy [1] and its additional recommendations [10] propose that imparting digital competencies should be incorporated into various subjects. This fact, together with the aim that school children should acquire basic informatics competencies, lead to extensive claims that teachers of all subjects should acquire some basic competencies in informatics [11–14] as well as first proposals of what courses for teacher education students should look like [15–17]. This call for the incorporation of informatics competencies has now also been taken up in recent official political recommendations, explicitly by the Scientific Commission of the Standing Conference of the Ministers of Education and Cultural Affairs [18]. In their recommendations, they acknowledge the need for a comprehensive education of teachers (as well as school children) in the field of digitalisation and basic informatics competencies.

Thus, while it is relatively clear that informatics should be included in teacher education programmes, it is not established yet what content should be taught and how this should be taught. Findings [19,20] suggest that teacher education students are less digitally inclined and proficient than students of other study programmes. This probably implies that, on average, they are also less interested in and open for informatics knowledge. They may think that informatics does not play a role in their subjects or in their daily work because the underlying concepts of informatics are not obvious at first glance. However, this misconception can quickly reveal limits when technical aids or informatics applications do not work or must be (re)adapted.

This means that a course designed for such students needs to demonstrate how informatics knowledge can support their professional goals. Such a course should therefore carefully select the topics that are relevant for teachers of all subjects and link the content to practically relevant problems. It should provide students with a sufficient breadth of informatics topics that go beyond a pure user perspective, to avoid the mere acquisition of non-transferable product or user knowledge. On the other hand, it should still show the relevance of the treated topics with selected application examples from the everyday life of teachers as well as highlight the socio-cultural perspective. Such an offering then makes it possible to acquire informatics knowledge even for those students who have particular reservations and uncertainties with regard to their own prerequisites and abilities. This, in turn, can enable them to recognise the effects of informatics systems and principles with respect to digitalisation in their own subjects and to take an active role in these areas.

We discuss which topics and motivating application examples should be included in an informatics course for teacher education students from all subjects from our perspective. As an example, we present our experience with designing and teaching such a course at the University of Konstanz for students studying to become secondary school teachers. In a study with the participants of the course, we evaluated their perspectives about the relevance of the selected informatics topics for their future profession as a teacher as well as their general importance in a digitalised world. In the remainder of this paper, we present the course as well as the evaluation results. We also address new ideas of how to enhance the motivation for those topics that were still rated as less relevant.

2 Background Information

Our course has been offered at the University of Konstanz each term since the winter term 2020/21. The University of Konstanz is a university in Southern Germany with approximately 11,000 students (of which approximately 1500 are teacher education students) and belongs to the "Universities of Excellence" in Germany. The course was designed as part of the project "Edu 4.0: Digitalisation in Teacher Education" [21], which is funded by the Federal Ministry of Education and Research in the framework of the joint "Qualitätsoffensive Lehrerbildung" of the federal and state governments, a quality enhancement campaign in teacher education.

Besides our course, the project offers other courses for students in education programmes on topics like how to incorporate digital media in teaching. This means that in our course we can concentrate on informatics aspects and motivate them by application examples, but we do not need to teach a comprehensive introduction of how digital media can be used for teaching.

The project also includes training for university lecturers and tries to incorporate digital education into the curriculum of teacher education programmes. In this way, the project itself has a wide scope and tries to change the orientation of the university's teacher education programmes towards including digital and informatics aspects more generally.

In addition, a cross-disciplinary programme called "Advanced Data and Information Literacy Track (ADILT)"[2] aims to teach informatics competencies to students of all study programmes, i.e. it is also open for teacher education students [22]. The ADILT is part of the government's Excellence Strategy and allows students to obtain an additional certificate in Data Computing. Our course and also the other courses offered by the Edu 4.0 project can be credited towards this certificate, which means that our course can function as a stepping stone for further engagement with digital and informatics topics.

[2] https://www.uni-konstanz.de/en/adilt/.

3 Description of the Course

As already mentioned in the introduction, our course is offered to teacher education students of all subjects. Therefore, the course is offered in the area of educational sciences as an elective course with 3 ECTS credits and 2 weekly teaching hours. Every week a new topic is introduced for which we rely on a purely digital learning environment including learning videos or digital units created with the help of an authoring tool. Further, students need to hand in compulsory exercises, some of which are corrected automatically and others assessed by tutors. In addition, we offer live video conferences on selected topics (e.g. algorithmics). Here, questions can be clarified directly with the lecturers and tutors and, if necessary, it is also possible for students to work together on assignments in break-out rooms.

This setup enables us to prepare and integrate important informatics content digitally in an appropriate way for prospective teachers. We maximize the relevance of this course for teachers by considering concrete examples of how to use this content from the outset of the course. The content of the units was deliberately compiled to ensure maximum transferability as we target our course at teacher education students who are not scientifically oriented towards informatics. This means that as many examples as possible are integrated that could play a role in their future professional life. The knowledge and skills should be as universally applicable as possible to concrete situations since the primary aim is to impart conceptual rather than product knowledge. In case of doubt, we can adjust the technical level of the course because the students can attend other introductory courses in informatics as an alternative or a supplement.

Despite the focus on motivating application examples and the adaption of the technical level, the course aims at imparting conceptual knowledge rather than pure troubleshooting for problems teachers could encounter in their teaching. Relevant informatics content and concepts are usually difficult to recognise for those not familiar with the subject. This is because one aspect of the widespread digitalisation (in the teaching profession) is that these competencies often only play a role in the background, as software or services are usually designed to be as user-friendly as possible. But making tools easy and straightforward to use often leads to their usage being rather restricted, leading to the lack of user's conceptual knowledge becoming problematic when difficulties or application errors arise and need to be solved independently. This is where the following questions come in: What conceptual knowledge is important from our perspective? Which application examples can we use to effectively demonstrate the added value?

As no official recommendations for informatics basics for prospective teachers exist so far, as has been laid out in the introduction, we chose the topics for the course based on those considerations and adapted the motivating examples as well as the deeper informatics content according to the feedback provided in the course. The first session covers the organisational matter as well as a general introduction what informatics is. In this session, we also provide the students with insights about the current educational political developments, i.e. of how informatics is incorporated in the school curriculum. After this first session, we cover the following topics in our seminar plan: *computer systems*, *encoding and storing data*, *data protection and security*, *computer networks*, and *algorithmics and programming*. In Table 1, each topic is briefly presented with key points on content and relevance or practical examples to provide an overview of the applications on which emphasis has been placed. Following this, the individual topics are described with further details to provide a more concrete insight.

Table 1. Topics and contents of the course

Topic	Contents	Application (relevance)
Computer systems	Components of a computer, Von-Neumann-Architecture	Purchase of appropriately equipped computers
Encoding and storing data	Number systems, encoding of numbers, characters, colours, images, file formats for tables and texts	Creating texts and graphics; Collaboration (cross-system)
Data protection and security	Basic aspects of data protection regulation, encryption	Messenger-services, Meta's data policy, encrypting emails and documents
Computer networks	Addressing (IPv4, IPv6), DNS, client-server model, encryption and certificates	Tracking, censorship, security aspects, VPN
Algorithmics and programming	Variables, loops, iteration, recursion, machine learning, artificial intelligence	Data processing, technical systems, image recognition

3.1 Computer Systems

The unit on *computer systems* is the first unit after a general introduction to the course and the definition of informatics. It covers the main components of a computer, e.g. the mainboard, CPU, hard disk, working memory etc. For these components, we also address existing standards. This is especially important when learners are used to the packed design of mobile devices that cannot be opened. In the unit, the students gain an insight into these components and can for example make an informed decision when buying a new computer.

The unit also covers the Von-Neumann-Architecture and the basic concepts of encoding and storing data with a focus on logic and gates. It also includes the distinction between kilobytes and kibibytes to draw the attention to potential differences between the specifications of a product and the storage size the computer shows.

3.2 Encoding and Storing Data

Following the unit on *computer systems*, we introduce the basics of encoding data in more detail, including the binary system and the conversion between different systems. Information on encoding standards for numbers and characters (here ASCII, Unicode and UTF-8) is then motivated by problems that occur with different encodings across different systems when working together on a document, for example. We then move on to discuss the encoding of images. This knowledge will for example help teachers learn the difference between pixel graphics and vector graphics. Based on the advantages and disadvantages of each encoding, they can then make an informed decision about which format should be used. If high scalability is needed, vector graphics might be more appropriate, but in contrast, pixel graphics are often better supported by older projectors or printers, for example.

3.3 Data Protection and Security

Teachers need to be able to store and share personal data confidentially and securely due to privacy and data security requirements. Thus, two units of the course deal with data protection and security. In the first unit, we concentrate on data protection guidelines and give them a brief introduction to the EU's General Data Protection Regulation (GDPR), its applications in German schools and the conflicts that arise when using US tools that do not adhere to these strict data regulations. The aim of this unit is to provide the students with a basic understanding of the regulations so that they can follow ongoing discussions about data protection in general and in the school context. The assignments thus not only deal with the basic rules of the GDPR but also involve dealing with recent discussions in this context, i.e. with the question of whether WhatsApp or Youtube can be used in schools.

While this unit makes clear that teachers need to take care when dealing with student data, the second unit discusses how data can be protected. To understand the basic underlying mechanisms, we introduce some historic encryption methods such as Caesar and Vigenère cipher and point out the basic principles of modern encryption methods such as symmetric and asymmetric keys. For those interested, we also offer additional material explaining the public key encryption methods RSA and Diffie-Hellman in more detail. This should then enable the students to understand how end-to-end encryption basically works. For practical applications, they are asked to encrypt a file with a well known encryption tool and set up email encryption.

3.4 Computer Networks

Many devices and apps in class nowadays need a permanent connection to servers in the school network or the internet. In many application scenarios, the app then no longer works, although the device is actually fully operational. The consequence can be that the lesson content has to be postponed. This is why the topic of computer networks is of fundamental importance for teachers because with basic background knowledge they can solve typical challenges arising from simple network problems themselves. Furthermore, when using web-based services, teachers need to pay additional attention to aspects of data privacy and data security, which are covered in previous units.

In the first of two units the client-server model, IP addressing in subnets and MAC addresses as well as DNS are covered. With this knowledge we can already show the added value. For example, knowledge about addressing in IP networks can help when devices such as network printers cannot be reached or internet access is blocked. Furthermore, understanding DNS queries is essential, for example, to deal with censorship in class or to evaluate the effectiveness of web blocking.

The second learning unit focuses even more on practical application examples, as it deals with questions about traces on the internet and safe surfing. This is also in line with the KMK strategy and the education plan, which stipulates that aspects of consumer education are addressed in all subjects. In a digitalised consumer society, safe surfing is particularly relevant. In detail, the unit clarifies how users may be extensively spied on online through geo-IP tracking, metadata in text messages or in emails as well as tracking cookies. As an extension to the *data protection and security* unit, the cryptographic goals of confidentiality and authenticity are addressed. The application reference is the secure handling of certificates and the use of VPN or proxy servers.

3.5 Algorithmics and Programming

In these units we first introduce the idea of *computational thinking* [2] and try to give the students examples of how this affects far more areas than those where the connection to informatics is clearly visible. The students then receive an introduction to programming with the help of a visual language (SNAP!) and implement the contents in a continuous project, here a rudimentary text editor. We start with the core of imperative programming with I/O-commands, expressions and assignment, control structures (loops, decisions), procedures and functions. We then introduce the concepts of iteration and recursion, all using little examples that contribute to the text editor project. Although the coding examples make the units very practical, those concepts are usually hidden behind a user interface in a real text editor and there is no need (or even the possibility) to have an influence on the code. Hence, for these units, the actual application relevance remains more abstract than in the other subject areas.

In the last session, we give students a general idea of how artificial intelligence works. Although the previous units include an introduction to basic algorithmics and programming concepts, the gap in the technical details of classical machine learning or even deep learning is huge. Therefore we cover the topic by showing practical examples, discussing current technical and ethical limitations, and applying a hands-on session using "Teachable Machines"[3] and "Machine Learning for Scratch"[4], in which students can train and test their own machine learning models.

[3] https://teachablemachine.withgoogle.com/.

[4] https://scratch.machinelearningforkids.co.uk/.

3.6 Further Topics

In most of the units described above, we offered additional material for those students interested in more details of the topics. For example, we also present material on audio and video formats in the unit about encoding and students especially interested in programming can work on more challenging exercises in the units about algorithmics. In response to a request of the students, we also designed an optional unit on information retrieval with a focus on how search engines work.

By offering this optional content, we try to meet the students' different prior knowledge and interests. Nevertheless, we continue to focus on including topics for which a practical application can be found. For this reason, we did not include some topics that can generally be found in a curriculum of an introductory informatics course. From the field of theoretical computer science, formal languages and grammars, automata theory as well as computational complexity are not included because their relevance for all subjects is difficult to demonstrate. Similarly, we do not address database systems other than mentioning certain aspects which are relevant for other topics.

4 Evaluation and Discussion

We have offered the course each term since the winter 2020. The list of participants shows that we have successfully reached students from all subjects, including all natural sciences but also languages, history, economics and physical education. We also have a remarkably high percentage (66%) of female students.

As described in the previous sections, our course focuses on knowledge which is necessary for professional activities of teachers, motivated by concrete examples. To see whether this approach was successful, we need to know how important the participants of the course consider these topics to be, for their professional future on the one hand and the general importance in a digitalised world (general knowledge) on the other hand.

In an evaluation at the end of each course we asked the participants to rate the different topics we covered on a scale from 1 to 5 (see Fig. 1). The evaluation was conducted at the end of every course because to our experience many participants do not really have a correct idea about the content of these topics earlier in the course. Many students in Germany still start university without ever having learned basic informatics concepts. The following analysis is done on the data from four terms between the winter 2020 and summer 2022 and contains answers from 66 students.

For the question whether the covered topics are considered relevant for the work of a teacher, all but one topic were rated above 3, which stood for "undecided". Only the units on *algorithmics and programming* were rated slightly below. All topics have an average rating above 3 for the question whether they are considered important as general knowledge in a digitalised world. For all topics the ratings of their importance for general knowledge were higher than for their importance for teachers.

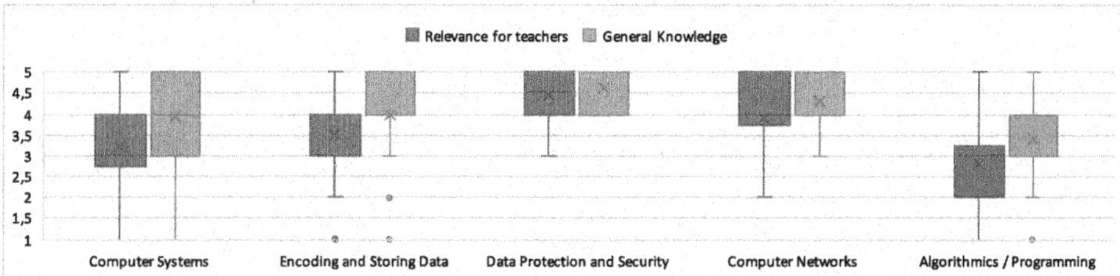

Fig. 1. Feedback on "The content of these course units is relevant for my professional future" and "I consider the content of the course units to be important general knowledge in a digitalised world." on a scale 1 (I strongly disagree) to 5 (I strongly agree).

The units on *data protection and data security* were rated as particularly relevant for teachers, which is no surprise because this is a topic many are very aware of since the introduction of the European General Data Protection Regulation. Many people, not just teachers, are still very unsure about what is allowed under these regulations. The participants rated knowledge about *computer networks* as almost equally important. Here the students were especially interested in aspects of safe surfing, hacking, tracking and what traces we leave online. The units about *computer systems* and *encoding and storing data* were considered of average importance.

The only units rated as less relevant were those on *algorithmics and programming*, although we always tried to emphasise how important the idea of computational thinking is for other subjects, especially the STEM subjects. It might be true that computational thinking and algorithmic content have significantly fewer practical application examples for teachers of other subjects, both for their own professional activities as well as for the concrete subject contents. However, it is difficult, for example, to explain the idea of machine learning and artificial intelligence without any background knowledge in algorithmics and some experience with computational thinking. According to the KMK strategy and the curricula of many subjects, these topics will become more and more relevant. This gap between theoretical and technical necessity on the one hand and the visibility of relevance for our target group on the other hand shows us the need to further develop and adapt our course at this point. Teacher education students need to recognise the relevance of computational thinking for their work at this stage of their education and lay foundations so that these issues can be addressed and adapted during the course of their subsequent education. We will address this problem by putting even more emphasis on the aspect of computational thinking in these units and by including the unit on information retrieval as a mandatory unit. At the same time, we will only include the most necessary concepts. For example, we will make the algorithmic concept of recursion optional as it is difficult for the students with little experience to understand how a computer executes recursive algorithms although the very first definition seems quite simple. Further, the complexity of the mandatory practical programming tasks will be reduced.

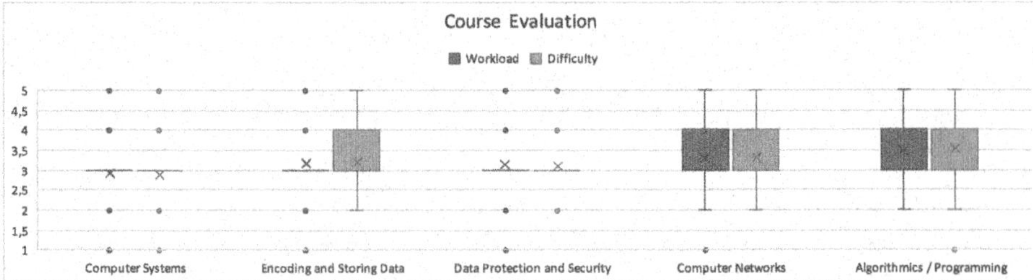

Fig. 2. Feedback on "The workload relative to the ECTS credits for the course was" and "The theoretical/technical requirements were" on a scale 1 (much too low) and 5 (much too high).

We also asked the participants about the workload relative to the 3 ECTS credits for the course and their perception of the difficulty for all covered topics (see Fig. 2). Overall we found a good balance between the credits earned for completing the course and the workload as well as the difficulty. Unfortunately the ratings for *algorithmics and programming* were highest. The participants rated both workload and difficulty a little to high, which is especially problematic, since here the ratings for the relevance were lowest.

5 Conclusion

This paper presented our insights from developing a basic informatics course for teacher education students of all subjects in which we balanced the introduction of basic informatics knowledge with applications of teaching with digital media. Overall we can say that we implemented the course very successfully. The relevance of most topics is apparent to the participants through the application perspective and concrete scenarios we used. Despite the difficulties with the units on *algorithmics and programming*, the course has a very high satisfaction rate (4.4 on a scale from 1–5) and is always fully enrolled.

Our idea of using concrete application examples from scenarios that arise when teaching with digital media distinguishes our course from others for (prospective) teachers which concentrate on the question of how teachers can incorporate informatics knowledge in their teaching of a specific subject directly (e.g. [15,23,24]). We think that both approaches are important and valuable and we plan to reach out to the lecturers of other didactics courses to develop ideas on how informatics can contribute to the different subject specific didactics. In this way we might reach even more students and motivate them to take our course or even other courses in informatics and digital media education, which are offered widely at our university.

References

1. Kultusministerkonferenz: Bildung in der digitalen Welt: Strategie der Kultusministerkonferenz (2016). https://www.kmk.org/fileadmin/pdf/PresseUndAktuelles/2018/Digitalstrategie_2017_mit_Weiterbildung.pdf
2. Wing, J.M.: Computational thinking. Commun. ACM **49**(3), 33–35 (2006)
3. Passey, D.: Computer science (CS) in the compulsory education curriculum: implications for future research. Educ. Inf. Technol. **22**, 421–443 (2017)
4. Barendsen, E., Chytas, C. (eds.): Informatics in Schools. Rethinking Computing Education. Proceedings of the 14th International Conference on Informatics in Schools: Situation, Evolution, and Perspectives, ISSEP 2021, Virtual Event, November 3–5, 2021. Springer, Heidelberg (2021). https://doi.org/10.1007/978-3-030-90228-5
5. Dagienė, V., Hromkovič, J., Lacher, R.: Designing informatics curriculum for K-12 education: from concepts to implementations. Inform. Educ. **20**(3), 333–360 (2021)
6. Eickelmann, B., et al. (eds.): ICILS 2018 #Deutschland. Computer- und informationsbezogene Kompetenzen von Schülerinnen und Schülern im zweiten internationalen Vergleich und Kompetenzen im Bereich Computational Thinking. Waxmann (2019)
7. Fraillon, J., Ainley, J., Schulz, W., Friedman, T., Duckworth, D.: Preparing for Life in a Digital World: IEA International Computer and Information Literacy Study 2018 International Report. Springer, Heidelberg (2020). https://doi.org/10.1007/978-3-030-38781-5
8. Redecker, C., Punie, Y.: European framework for the digital competence of educators (DigCompEdu) (2017). https://op.europa.eu/en/publication-detail/-/publication/fcc33b68-d581-11e7-a5b9-01aa75ed71a1
9. Yadav, A., Mayfield, C., Zhou, N., Hambrusch, S., Korb, J.T.: Computational thinking in elementary and secondary teacher education. ACM Trans. Comput. Educ. **14**(1), 1–16 (2014)
10. Kultusministerkonferenz: Lehren und Lernen in der digitalen Welt: Die ergänzenden Empfehlungen zur Strategie "Bildung in der digitalen Welt" (2021). https://www.kmk.org/fileadmin/veroeffentlichungen_beschluesse/2021/2021_12_09-Lehren-und-Lernen-Digi.pdf
11. Brinda, T.: Stellungnahme zum KMK-Strategiepapier "Bildung in der digitalen Welt" (2016). https://fb-iad.gi.de/fileadmin/FB/IAD/Dokumente/gi-fbiad-stellungnahme-kmk-strategie-digitale-bildung.pdf
12. Barkmin, M., Bergner, N., Bröll, L., Huwer, J., Menne, A., Seeger, S.: Informatik für alle?! - Informatische Bildung als Baustein in der Lehrkräftebildung. In: Beißwenger, M., Bulizek, B., Gryl, I., Schacht, F. (eds.) Digitale Innovationen und Kompetenzen in der Lehramtsausbildung, pp. 99–120. Universitätverlag Rhein-Ruhr, Duisburg (2020)
13. Van Ackeren, I., et al.: Digitalisierung in der Lehrerbildung: Herausforderungen, Entwicklungsfelder und Förderung von Gesamtkonzepten. Die Deutsche Schule: Zeitschrift Erziehungswissenschaft Bildungspolitik pädagogische Praxis **111**(1), 103–119 (2019)
14. Gesellschaft für Informatik e.V.: Offensive Digitale Schultransformation (2020). https://offensive-digitale-schultransformation.de/
15. Nenner, C., Damnik, G., Bergner, N.: Integration informatischer Bildung ins Grundschullehramtsstudium. In: Humbert, L. (ed.) INFOS 2021–19. GI-Fachtagung Informatik und Schule, pp. 103–112. Gesellschaft für Informatik, Bonn (2021)

16. Braun, D., Pampel, B., Seiss, M.: Informatik-Grundlagen für Lehramtsstudierende: ein Spagat zwischen Grundlagen- und Anwenderwissen. In: Humbert, L. (ed.) INFOS 2021 – 19. GI-Fachtagung Informatik und Schule, pp. 193–202. Gesellschaft für Informatik, Bonn (2021)
17. Seegerer, S., Michaeli, T., Romeike, R.: Informatische Grundlagen in der allgemeinen Lehrkräftebildung. In: Humbert, L. (ed.) INFOS 2021 – 19. GI-Fachtagung Informatik und Schule, pp. 153–162. Gesellschaft für Informatik, Bonn (2021)
18. Köller, O., et al.: Digitalisierung im Bildungssystem: Handlungsempfehlungen von der Kita bis zur Hochschule: Gutachten der Ständigen Wissenschaftlichen Kommission der Kultusministerkonferenz (SWK) (2022)
19. Schmid, U., Goertz, L., Radomski, S., Thom, S., Behrens, J.: Monitor Digitale Bildung: Die Hochschulen im digitalen Zeitalter. BertelsmannStiftung (2017)
20. Senkbeil, M., Ihme, J.M., Schöber, C.: Empirische Arbeit: Schulische Medienkompetenzförderung in einer digitalen Welt: Über welche digitalen Kompetenzen verfügen angehende Lehrkräfte? Psychol. Erzieh. Unterr. **68**(1), 4–22 (2020)
21. Bonnes, C., Schumann, S.: Didaktisierung des Digitalen: Zur Entwicklung berufs- und wirtschaftspädagogischer Studiengänge. bwp@ Berufs- und Wirtschaftspädagogik - online **40**, 1–17 (2021). https://www.bwpat.de/ausgabe40/bonnes_schumann_bwpat40.pdf
22. Hutter-Sumowski, C.V., Möhrke, P., Pöhnl, V., Schmidt-Mende, L., Zumbusch, A.: Lehre in Zeiten digitalen Wandels: Das ADILT Programm der Universität Konstanz. Bunsen-Mag. **24**(5), 182–184 (2022)
23. Gumpert, A., Zaugg, P.: Fit für den Lehrplan 21 - Wie Klassenlehrpersonen auf den Informatikunterricht vorbereitet werden (können). In: Pasternak, A. (ed.) Informatik für alle, pp. 201–210. Gesellschaft für Informatik, Bonn (2019)
24. Waterman, K.P., Goldsmith, L., Pasquale, M.: Integrating computational thinking into elementary science curriculum: an examination of activities that support students' computational thinking in the service of disciplinary learning. J. Sci. Educ. Technol. **29**, 53–64 (2020)

A System to Realize Time- and Location-Independent Teaching and Learning Among Learners Through Sharing Learning-Articles

Seiyu Okai[1(✉)], Tsubasa Minematsu[1], Fumiya Okubo[1], Yuta Taniguchi[1], Hideaki Uchiyama[2], and Atsushi Shimada[1]

[1] Kyushu University, Fukuoka, Japan
{okai,minematsu,fokubo,yuta.taniguchi,atsushi}@limu.ait.kyushu-u.ac.jp
[2] Nara Institute of Science and Technology, Ikoma, Japan

Abstract. Teaching and learning from one another is one of the most effective ways for learners to acquire proactive learning attitudes. In this study, we propose a new learning support system that encourages mutual teaching and learning by introducing a mechanism that guarantees sustainability. Learners submit articles called "learning-articles" that summarize their own learning and knowledge. The proposed system not only accumulates and publishes these articles but also has a mechanism to encourage the submission of necessary topics. The proposed system has been in operation since the academic year 2020, and it has collected learning-articles across our university's nine academic disciplines from more than 300 learners. To investigate the effects of sharing learning-articles on education from the learners' perspectives, a questionnaire was distributed among 25 students.

Keywords: learner-centered design · learning-article · educational support system

1 Introduction

Teaching and learning from one another have been considered important for a long time [1]. In recent years, some educational methods, such as cooperative learning [2,3] and flipped learning [4–6], have attracted particular attention. The increased interest in these educational methods is due to a shift away from traditional educational methods toward new ones that emphasize learner independence. In the case of conventional educational methods, learners may assume that they cannot acquire the ability to learn independently, and thus, will be taught by the teacher [7]. This ability is, however, necessary to respond to the accelerating pace of social change resulting from the expansion of globalization

Published by Springer Nature Switzerland AG 2023
T. Keane et al. (Eds.): WCCE 2022, IFIP AICT 685, pp. 475–487, 2023.
https://doi.org/10.1007/978-3-031-43393-1_44

and the development of information technology. Therefore, educational methods that integrate teaching and learning from one another [2–6] are expected to enable students to acquire a proactive attitude toward learning and also learn more effectively.

Computer based education has two main types of systems, "synchronous" and "asynchronous," to assist learners in teaching and learning from one another [8–11]. "Synchronous" learning support includes chat tools [8] and videoconferencing systems [9]. This type of system enables learners to quickly discuss the results among themselves in real time. However, its disadvantage is that the learners' knowledge is shared within a small group of learners who belong to the same class and knowledge sharing across generations is not possible.

"Asynchronous" learning support involves learners compiling their learning knowledge into articles (including texts and diagrams) and storing them in a database for other learners to read. A typical example is a "wiki," which allows learners to collaboratively edit articles on various topics from a textbook [10,11]. Though the development of "asynchronous" learning support entails the advantage of passing on learners' knowledge to the next generation, the challenge is how to ensure sustainability. For example, if learners were free to submit articles, many of them could be concentrated on simple or major topics that appear in textbooks. However, there might be fewer articles dealing with more advanced or novel topics that do not appear in textbooks. If this situation continues, it could soon become difficult for learners to submit articles that are useful to other learners. Therefore, it is not enough to simply accept and publish articles; a system that monitors the balance of topics in the articles submitted to the system and encourages learners to submit articles on topics that are currently in demand is needed.

Based on the above discussion, this paper proposes a learning support system that encourages teaching and learning from one another and is assisted by a mechanism to enhance sustainability. In the proposed system, learners can teach and learn from one another by sharing "learning-articles" that summarize their own learning in the form of articles. The proposed system consists of two subsystems. The first is a front-end subsystem, which accepts article submissions, browses through articles, and calls for submissions. The second is a back-end system, which includes a database for storing submitted articles and an analytics module for extracting topics that need to be submitted. Section 2 provides an overview of the proposed system and a detailed description of each subsystem. In Sect. 3, we report the results of a demonstrative experiment conducted in a class at our university, and show the usefulness of the learning-articles and the effectiveness of the calls for submission.

2 Proposed System

This section provides an outline of the proposed system (Fig. 1), which consists of two subsystems. The first is the learning-article publication system (LAPS), which accepts the submissions of learning-articles and presents the search results for them. In addition, LAPS solicits submissions based on rankings to ensure that the submitted learning-articles are not skewed toward a particular topic. The second is the learning-article management system (LAMS), which consists of a database and an analytics module in which information on learning-articles and the operation logs of learners are stored. The aim of the proposed system is to enable learners to acquire an attitude of actively sharing their knowledge with others and trying to learn from others. In the following sections, we explain LAPS and LAMS in more detail.

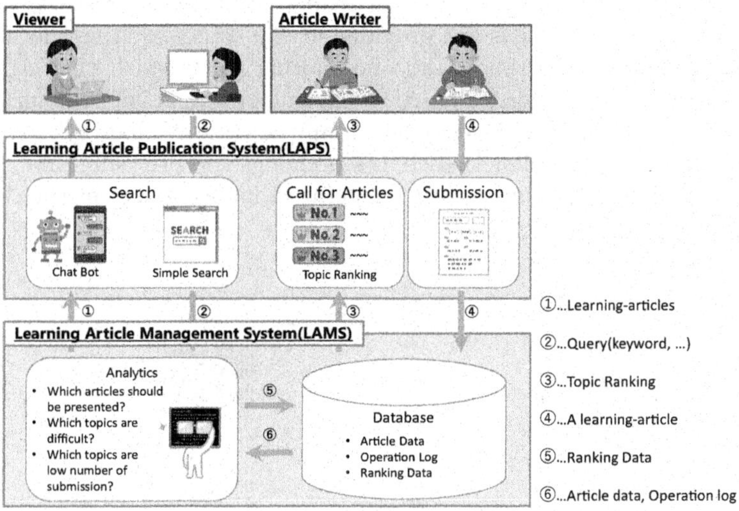

Fig. 1. Diagram of the proposed system

2.1 Learning-Article Publication System (LAPS)

In this section, we explain each module of LAPS, which is typically three in number. The first is the "Submission module," which is used when learners submit their articles. The second is the "Call for learning-articles module," which encourages learners to submit articles on specific topics. The third is the "Search module," which learners use to search for articles to read. By using the modules provided by the LAPS, learners can submit and read learning-articles regardless of time and location.

Submission Module. The submission module is used by learners to submit learning-articles with the intent of sharing their knowledge with other learners. Figure 2 shows the screen used for submitting a learning-article. In LAPS, students can insert images, diagrams, and hashtags in the article. After entering the title and body of the article, the learner must click on the "Submit" button at the bottom left of the screen to submit the article. The data on the learning-articles submitted are stored in the learning-article data table of the database. To guarantee the quality of the published articles, the LAPS has instituted an approval process overseen by teaching assistants (TA) and teachers (approvers). If an article submitted by a learner contains incorrect information or the content is incomprehensible, the approver will ask the learner (writer) to correct it. An example of a submitted article is shown in Fig. 3. This article was posted for the course "Digital Signal Processing," and explains the difference between "Periodic Signal" and "Aperiodic Signal." In this learning article, a hashtag was added at the top of the text. To prevent readers from identifying the author of each article, only their initials are provided at the top of each article. By using the search module, learners can read one another's articles. If they agree with the article, they can also give feedback by clicking on the "Like" button. Though learners do not explicitly give feedback in any other way than by pressing the "Like" button, implicit feedback, such as search logs and browsing time, is stored in the system. These logs are used to generate topic rankings in the Analytics module.

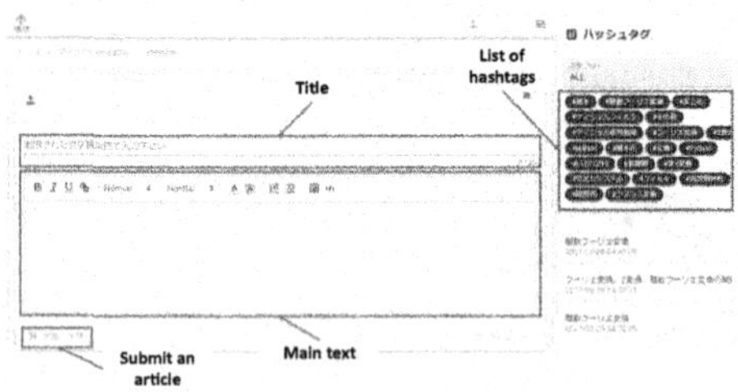

Fig. 2. The screen when submitting a learning-article

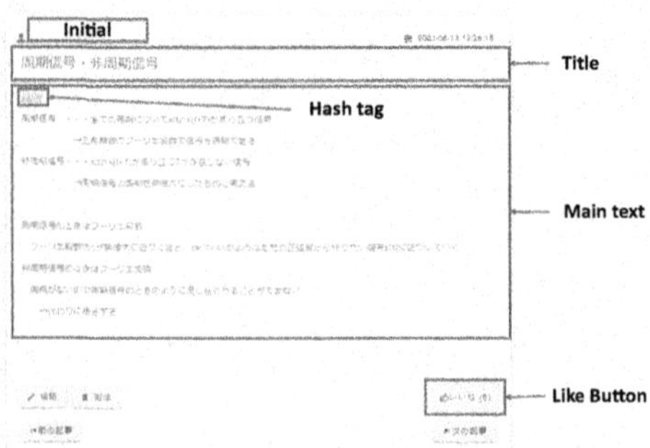

Fig. 3. Example of a posted learning-article.

Call for Learning-Articles Module. The call for the learning-articles module obtains data related to two learning-topic rankings (learning-topic ranking table in Sect. 2.2) from the database and presents the ranking before learners to encourage them to submit learning-articles. In the proposed method, a learning topic comprises a combination of keywords and article types. Article types are of the following four kinds: "basic," "development," "summary," and "other." The following two learning-topic rankings were displayed to the learners:

1. The ranking of topics for which many learners have searched but have not found the desired article. (This is called the "Ranking of difficult topics")
2. Topics with a limited number of submissions are ranked according to the number of submissions. (This is called "Ranking of few topics".)

The ranking screen presented to the learners is shown in Fig. 4. Learners can view the corresponding rankings by selecting a course from the buttons on the upper left of the screen. The left side of the screen shows the "Ranking of difficult topics," whereas the right gives the "Ranking of a few topics" from 1 to 10. The rules of ranking are explained in Sect. 2.2. If a learner finds a topic that they want to write about among the topics presented in the rankings, they can follow the following steps: first, click on the corresponding topic; next, click on the Submit button in the upper-right corner of the screen, which will take you to the page shown in Fig. 2; the hashtag related to the selected topic will be automatically added to the learning-article that you have posted. If a learner cannot find the topic they want to write about in the rankings, they can submit articles on new topics or topics outside the rankings.

The call for the learning-article module plays a major role in ensuring that a balance of topics of the submitted learning-articles is maintained by presenting the rankings to the learners and encouraging them to contribute.

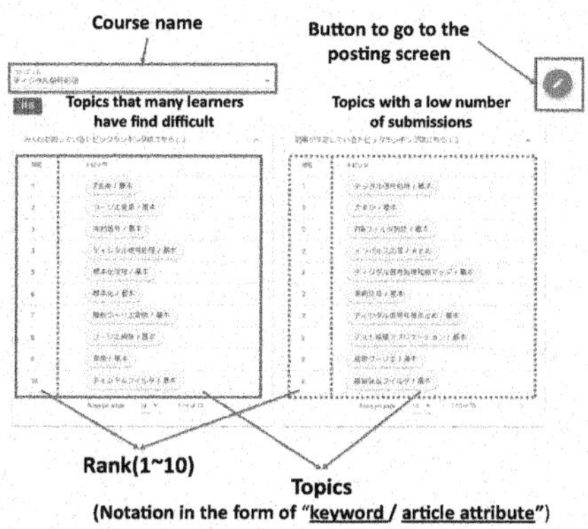

Fig. 4. The screen when displaying the ranking of learning topics

Search Module. The search module is used by learners to search for the desired articles. Either a personal computer or a smartphone can be used for this purpose; on a smartphone, articles can be searched for with the help of a chatbot. Regardless of the method used, all operations performed by the learner are stored in the operation log table of the database (Sect. 2.2).

Figure 5 shows a screenshot of the system when used from a personal computer. At the top of the screen there are options to set various parameters for the search. Articles can be narrowed down mainly using the following parameters.

- Keywords of the learning-article
- Hashtags
- Year of posting
- Course of study
- Sorting by date, time, title, or number of likes (learners can click the "Like" button for learning-articles they like)

When using a smartphone to conduct the search, the chatbot provides repeated prompts in order to narrow down the articles. The learner is asked for the following information: keywords, the type of learning-article, and the course of study. Based on the information obtained, the chatbot extracts three learning-articles and presents them to the learner.

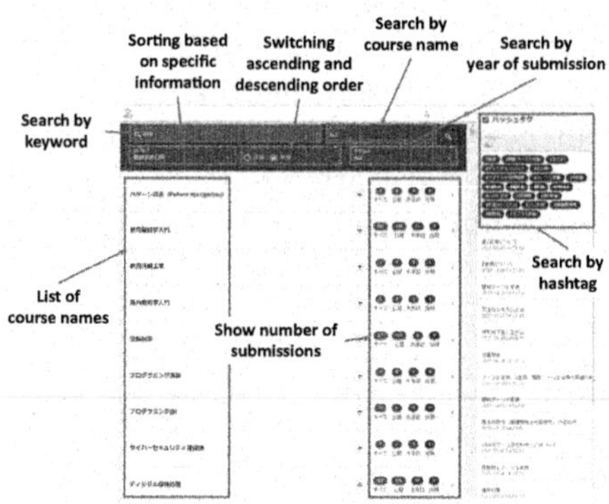

Fig. 5. The screen when searching for learning-articles

2.2 Learning-Article Management System (LAMS)

Unlike LAPS, LAMS does not directly interact with learners, but plays an important role in facilitating the sharing of learning-articles. The database accumulates the information necessary for the operation of the proposed system. The analytics module analyzes the data accumulated in the database and extracts the articles to be presented to learners as search results and learning topic rankings.

Database. This section describes the three important tables in the database. The first is the articles' data table, which mainly stores the following data sent from the submission module (Sect. 2.1) for each article:

- Id
- Article title
- Text of the body of the article
- Last modified time (e.g., "2021/01/01 13:20")
- Author name
- Year of submission (e.g., 2019)
- Article topic (e.g., "Fourier transform/basic," "Fourier transform/development")
- Subject name (e.g., "linear algebra,", "digital signal processing,", "pattern recognition")
- Number of "Likes"

The second is the operation log table, which stores the following data sent by the main search module (Sect. 2.1).

- The ID of the learning-article
- Operation name (e.g., "browse," "click 'Like' button," "feedback on smartphone," "submit a learning-article")
- Time of the operation
- Name of the learner who performed the operation

The third is the learning-topic ranking table, which is used to store the ranking information presented to learners when they use the call for learning-articles module (Sect. 2.1). It stores the following data:

- The name of the learning topic
- Type of ranking ("Ranking of difficult topics" or "Ranking of few topics")
- Course name
- Number of places
- Date and time when the rank was generated

Analytics Module. The LAMS analytics module has two main functions. The first is to determine which articles are to be presented to the learner as search results. As shown in Fig. 5, when a learner initiates a search using a personal computer or smartphone, the module extracts the learning-articles that contain the specified keywords, subject name, and year specified by the learner. If the learner requests for the search results to be sorted, then they are returned after sorting. The data necessary for extracting the learning-articles are stored in the article data table.

The second function is to decide which topics to present in the learning topic ranking list based on the data from the article data table and the operation log table. The module stores the data in the ranking data table based on the analytics results. The ranking of difficult topics is generated by collecting the number of times learners failed to find the desired article for each learning topic and sorting them in order of increasing frequency. More specifically, the weighted sum of the number of times the learner viewed and pressed the "Like" button for each topic is calculated. The ranking of a few topics is generated by aggregating the number of posts of learning-articles for each topic from the article data table and sorting them according to topics with the least numbers of posts. The relation between topics and articles is determined based on the keywords and hashtags included in the title.

3 Experiment

The proposed system has been in operation at our university since the academic year 2020, and as of April 2022, it has collected learning-articles across nine academic disciplines (e.g., digital signal processing) from 314 undergraduate learners. In this section, we report on the effects the learning-articles have on learning (Sect. 3.1) and the impact of the call for learning-article module on learners (Sect. 3.2), both of which we investigated during the aforementioned period. If ranking can be proven to have an effect on encouraging submissions, the prospects for the sustainability of the proposed system are high.

3.1 Evaluation of the Usefulness of Learning-Articles

A questionnaire was prepared to investigate the effects of sharing learning-articles on education from the learners' perspectives. The questionnaire was distributed among 25 students who had undergone training in digital signal processing in 2020 when the proposed system was put into operation. As homework after the final lecture, the learners posted articles based on their own learning and read the articles of others. The learners were informed by their teachers that their submission and reading of learning-articles would be used to evaluate their engagement in determining their grades. Thereafter, they responded to the questionnaire.

The results of the experiment are presented in Table 1. Four questions on the questionnaire required responses on a 5-point scale. Questions 1 (Q1) and 2 (Q2) asked the respondents to assess the process of contributing learning-articles. About half of the learners returned positive scores of 4 or 5, indicating that writing learning-articles helped them understand the main points of the lessons and the course content that was previously unclear. Questions 3 (Q3) and 4 (Q4) asked the respondents to assess the effect of the learning-articles on their learning. About half of the learners returned positive scores to each of these questions, indicating that for some learners, reading articles written by other learners helped them understand the course content and resolve points that they did not originally understand.

Table 1. Results of the questionnaire for learners about the learning-articles. 5-point scale, 1: don't agree at all, 2: don't agree, 3: can't say, 4: agree, 5: fully agree. The units are n.

Question	1	2	3	4	5	Average
Q1. Writing learning-articles helped you to better understand the main points of the course	1	2	8	10	4	3.6
Q2. Writing learning-articles helped you to determine what you didn't understand	1	1	7	12	4	3.7
Q3. By browsing articles by other learners, you were able to understand the course content	1	2	7	10	5	3.6
Q4. By browsing learning-articles by other learners, you were able to identify the points you did not understand	0	2	10	8	5	3.6

3.2 The Result of the Call for Learning-Articles Module

In 2021, the second year of implementing the system, we launched the call for learning-articles module for the course "Digital Signal Processing.", which is structured over a span of fifteen weeks. The class had 116 undergraduates in their third year. Similar to the experiment in Sect. 3.1, the learners were told by their teachers that their posting and reading of learning-articles would be used to evaluate their engagement in determining their grades.

Some of the topics that were presented to the learners in the ranking category of difficult topics and few topics are shown in Table 2. The total number of topics of the learning-articles on "Digital Signal Processing" posted by the end of the experiment period was 449. The total number of difficult topics presented to the learners during the experiment was 11, which constitutes 2.4% of the total number of topics. There was almost no change in the ranking of difficult topics throughout the experiment. The total number of few topics presented to the learners during the experiment was 124, which constitutes 27.6% of the total number of topics. As for the ranking of few topics, the number of topics with only one post was very high, which suggests that numerous topics were presented to the learners in the ranking.

Table 2. Correspondence table between each group and the ranking to be viewed

Ranking name	Topic		
Ranking of difficult topics	Sampling theorem/Basic	Discrete-time systems/Basic	Signals/Basic
Ranking of few topics	Python/Basic	Noise reduction/Basic	Block matrix/Basic

3.3 An Effect of Call for Learning-Articles Module

This was conducted as an experiment in the class (same as Sect. 3.2). Students were divided into four groups to examine the effects of the two lists when presented together and separately. Table 3 shows the correspondence between each group and the ranking. A "✓" indicates that the students had browsed the corresponding list; "×" means that the students had not browsed the corresponding list. Students in Groups A to C could use the call for learning-articles module, but the ranking list presented to each group was different. The students in Group D were used as the reference group and were not allowed to use the call for learning-articles module; they submitted learning-articles from the LAMS without browsing the rankings.

Table 3. Correspondence table between each group and the ranking to be viewed

Ranking name	Group A	Group B	Group C	Group D
Ranking of difficult topics	✓	×	✓	×
Ranking of few topics	×	✓	✓	×

To examine how the call for the learning-articles module changes the topics posted, the number of posts on the topics presented in the ranking for each group and the percentage of posts in the group were tabulated (see Table 4). In row 2 of Table 4, a comparison between the totals for each group shows that Group A had the highest number of submissions (30) and Group C the second highest (23). Both of these groups were shown the ranking of difficult topics, and the number of posts was greater for these groups than that for Groups B and D, which were not shown the ranking of difficult topics. In addition, more than half of the topics posted by Groups A and C were related to the topics presented in the list of difficult topics. In row 2 of Table 4, Group B was the most common, followed by Group D. Group B was shown the list of topics with the fewest submissions. In addition, more than one-third of the topics posted by Groups B and D were related to the topics presented in the list of a few topics.

We found that the number of posts related to the presented topic increased when the ranking of difficult topics was presented. In addition, in the ranking of few topics, the total value of Group C was lower than that of Group D. This means that it is difficult to expect an increase in the number of submissions related to the ranking of few topics when two rankings are shown simultaneously.

The students in Groups A to C completed a questionnaire about the usefulness of the call for learning-articles module, the results of which are presented in Table 5. In Question 1, there was a slight difference between Groups A to C, ranging from 3.7 to 3.9, but the difference was not statistically significant. When the results of Groups A to C were combined, it was found that 28 of the 41 students selected a positive rating of 4 or 5 for Question 1. These results indicate that the presentation of the ranking was helpful for more than 60% of the

Table 4. A comparison of the number of posts on the topics that appeared in the ranking during the experiment and their percentage of the total number of posts (the value in brackets indicates that they account for n% of the total number of posts in the group).

Ranking name	Group A	Group B	Group C	Group D
Ranking of difficult topics	30 (68%)	13 (25%)	23 (59%)	12 (33%)
Ranking of few topics	2 (5%)	19 (37%)	5 (13%)	11 (31%)

Table 5. Questionnaire results for the evaluation of the call for learning-articles module. Question 1 is 5-point scale, 1: don't agree at all, 2: don't agree, 3: can't say, 4: agree, 5: fully agree. Question 2 is also 5-point scale, 1: very few, 2: few, 3: about right, 4: many, 5: very many. The units are n.

Questionnaire	Group	Evaluation					
		1	2	3	4	5	Ave
Question. 1 The call for learning-articles module was helpful in deciding the topic of the learning-article to be posted	A	1	0	2	9	3	3.9
	B	0	0	4	5	3	3.9
	C	0	2	4	4	4	3.7
Question. 2 The number of rankings displayed in the call for learning-article module was sufficient	A	1	4	8	1	1	2.8
	B	1	4	5	2	0	2.7
	C	0	4	7	2	1	2.9

students in deciding the topic when submitting a learning-article. In Question 2, there was no significant difference in the distribution between Groups A and C. About 20% of the students felt that the number of rankings was too high, and about 40% felt that the number was too few. This suggests that the appropriate number of rankings varies greatly among learners. As a countermeasure, we are planning to increase the flexibility of the number of rankings that the module can offer.

3.4 Discussion

From Table 4, it can be concluded that the call for learning-articles module is expected to increase the number of submissions on topics where the number of submissions is low and many learners cannot find the desired articles. The results in Table 5 suggest that the information provided by the call for learning-articles module is what learners can demand. In addition, although we do not explain it in detail in this paper, when we compared the number of "Likes" on articles posted under the influence of the call for learning-articles module and those without the module, we found no significant difference. Based on these results, it can be said that the introduction of the call for learning-articles module in the proposed system can encourage learners to submit articles while adjusting the balance of topics of learning-articles stored in the database. In common with previous studies, reading each other's writing has been proven to have a certain effect on learning. As no previous study has evaluated learner-centered systems from the perspective of sustainability, the contribution of this study is significant [10,11].

Our study has some room for improvement. First of all, the effectiveness of the proposed method can be demonstrated in a more general perspective by combining it with Adaptive Comparative Judgement and the Delphi Technique. During this experiment, 119 articles were submitted, and it took about five hours for one TA to approve them. Considering that the system will be deployed in large-scale lectures, it is important to improve the efficiency of the approval process for learning-articles and to secure more approvers. In addition, the learners submitted the articles after receiving instructions from the faculty that they would be added to the engagement evaluation in the lecture. Therefore, it is unclear to what extent learning-articles would be used if faculties encouraged the writing and viewing of learning-articles in a manner that was not used for their grades. Also, it is unclear whether there are cases where articles are approved by teachers even if they are difficult to read from the learners' point of view.

4 Conclusion

In this study, we propose a new framework that enables learners to teach and learn from each other through learning-articles posted online. The results indicate that the learners could indeed understand the course contents and solve their problems by utilizing the articles. In addition, the call for learning-articles module could play an important role in gathering articles needed by learners based on the analytics. We believe that the proposed system is designed so as to become a self-sustaining operation. In the future, we will obtain learning progress data from quizzes, and so on, and clarify what kind of progress is generated from reading learning-articles. In addition, we will conduct detailed user evaluations of the submission and search modules as these were not done in the current study. In the long-term, we will conduct cross-analyses among learning activities from other systems, such as digital textbooks, the learning management system, and test scores. We would like to identify particular linkages, such as the types of activities that have high correlations or contribute to the posting of relevant articles in order to provide individualized support for posting learning-articles.

Acknowledgements. This work was supported by JST AIP Grant Number JPMJCR19U1, JSPS KAKENHI Grant Number JP18H04125, and JP22H00551, Japan.

References

1. King, A.: Transactive peer tutoring: distributing cognition and metacognition. Educ. Psychol. Rev. **10**(1), 57–74 (1998). https://doi.org/10.1023/A:1022858115001

2. Lazakidou, G., Retalis, S.: Using computer supported collaborative learning strategies for helping students acquire self-regulated problem-solving skills in mathematics. Comput. Educ. **54**(1), 3–13 (2010)
3. Jeong, H., Hmelo-Silver, C.E.: Seven affordances of computer-supported collaborative learning: How to support collaborative learning? How can technologies help? Educ. Psychol. **51**(2), 247–265 (2016)
4. Fidalgo-Blanco, A., Martinez-Nuñez, M., Borrás-Gene, O., Sanchez-Medina, J.J.: Micro flip teaching-an innovative model to promote the active involvement of students. Comput. Hum. Behav. **72**, 713–723 (2017)
5. LaFee, S.: Flipped learning. Educ. Digest **79**(3), 13 (2013)
6. Hao, Y.: Exploring undergraduates' perspectives and flipped learning readiness in their flipped classrooms. Comput. Hum. Behav. **59**, 82–92 (2016)
7. Vermunt, J.D.: Metacognitive, cognitive and affective aspects of learning styles and strategies: a phenomenographic analysis. High. Educ. **31**(1), 25–50 (1996). https://doi.org/10.1007/BF00129106
8. Rodríguez-Bonces, M., Ortiz, K.: Using the cognitive apprenticeship model with a chat tool to enhance online collaborative learning. GIST Educ. Learn. Res. J. **13**, 166–185 (2016)
9. Nancy Flanagan Knapp: Increasing interaction in a flipped online classroom through video conferencing. TechTrends **62**(6), 618–624 (2018). https://doi.org/10.1007/s11528-018-0336-z
10. Medero, G.S., Albaladejo, G.P., et al.: The use of a wiki to boost open and collaborative learning in a Spanish university. Knowl. Manag. E-Learn. Int. J. **12**(1), 1–17 (2020)
11. Sula, G., Sulstarova, A.: Using wikis as a teaching tool for novice teachers-pedagogical implications. J. Learn. Dev. **9**(2), 163–175 (2022)

Computing in Higher Education

Evaluation of a System for Generating Programming Problems Using Form Services

Takumi Daimon[1] and Kensuke Onishi[2](✉)

[1] Graduate School of Science, Tokai University, 4-1-1, Kitakanme, Hiratsuka, Kanagawa 259-1292, Japan
daimon@fuji.tokai-u.jp

[2] Tokai University, 4-1-1, Kitakanme, Hiratsuka, Kanagawa 259-1292, Japan
onishi@tokai-u.jp

Abstract. Programming must be evaluated as a subject when taught in high schools. As a result, increasing the efficiency of question generation and grading has become a pressing concern. Waquema is a system for automatically generating and grading programming problems that we created. Waquema is available in the following two versions: web (generates web pages) and cloud (generates Google Forms). At our university, we used the questions generated by Waquema's cloud version for exercises and exams in lectures. The system was then evaluated using a student questionnaire survey. We also conducted a questionnaire survey of the teachers who used the system and evaluated the time required for the exercises and examinations. The results showed that the difficulty level of the generated problems was appropriate for the students, and that the system could reduce the time required to prepare for the exercises.

Keywords: Programming education · problem generation · automatic grading

1 Introduction

In Japan, with the revision of the Courses of Study, the previous information will be reorganized, and "Information I" and "Information II" will be taught as high school subjects beginning in 2022. Students will learn programming in the "Computers and Programming" unit of "Information I," a required subject. Programming must be evaluated before when it can be taught as a subject. Therefore, programming exercises and examinations are required to assess students' understanding.

Teachers can conduct written exams or use learning management systems when developing exercises and exams. Exams that can be administered on a computer can be created with a learning management system. Written exams have the advantage of being administered without the use of a computer; however, they necessitate teachers spending time for not only preparing the questions

Published by Springer Nature Switzerland AG 2023
T. Keane et al. (Eds.): WCCE 2022, IFIP AICT 685, pp. 491–503, 2023.
https://doi.org/10.1007/978-3-031-43393-1_45

to be asked but also grading them. Improving the efficiency of question preparation and grading is an urgent issue to promote the reform of teachers' working styles.

The online judging system has the advantage of making it simple to judge the correctness of a question by submitting a program. Conversely, majority of the questions in the online judging system necessitate the implementation of a program whose output matches the example answers. It is preferable for beginners and novices who are trying to improve their understanding to have a variety of randomly generated problems based on the topic being studied. Several systems, primarily in the Java language, automatically generate and grade programming problems. Systems created by university students and teachers [1] are mostly used in universities, but there are no systems that generate randomized problems based on the unit being studied.

Waquema [2] is a system that automatically generates and grades programming problems in Python, JavaScript, and C++, which are educational programming languages for high school Information I and II. Waquema is available in the following two versions: web (generates web pages) and cloud (generates Google Forms). The development and evaluation of the cloud version are described in this paper. The following is the structure of this paper: Sect. 2 introduces related research in this field, Sect. 3 provides an overview of the system, Sect. 4 describes the questionnaire items that the system can generate, and Sect. 5 describes the details of the questionnaire items and their data. The questionnaire results are discussed in Sect. 6, and Sect. 7 is a summary of this paper.

2 Related Research

2.1 Automatic Generation of Programming Problems

Kitamura et al. [3] proposed a method for automatically generating programming problems by analyzing and processing example answers with user-defined tags. They demonstrated that this method can be used in conjunction with an existing learning system, MAX/JAVA [1].

Uchida [4] developed "JavaDrill," a system for automatically generating fill-in-the-blank problems in the Java language. This system generates fill-in-the-blank problems by inputting the problem number, problem name, problem text, and source code, and setting blanks for reserved words and operators. JavaDrill is designed for programming beginners, and aims to improve their programming skills by teaching them the grammar and reserved words of the Java language.

Ariyasu et al. [5] created a system that automatically generates fill-in-the-blank questions and their answers in C language. This system accepts as input the program code of the answer and data describing the tendency of the question. The system can place blanks according to the intention of the author by inputting variables, type declarations, functions, and conditional judgments into the question trends. This system aims to improve the efficiency of the process of creating a large number of exercises.

Takeuchi et al. [6] developed a system that generates fill-in-the-blank problems in the Haskell language. This system can automatically generate fill-in-the-blank questions and determine their correctness. They have also proposed an effective method for generating fill-in-the-blank questions that considers the significance of programming elements, such as functions and recursive structures.

2.2 Research on Automatic Grading of Programming Problems

Kogure et al. [7] created a monitoring system for learning programming. This system allows you to track the types of tasks that your students are working on. Furthermore, the system automatically analyzes the learner's program so that the teacher can provide appropriate instructions to the learner.

Ito et al. [8] developed a plug-in for judging the correctness of assignment programs running on Moodle. In this system, a server for judging correct and incorrect answers is prepared separately from the server on which Moodle runs. The system then checks whether there is a difference between the correct answer program prepared on that server and the result of running the assignment program, and returns the result to Moodle. This allows the user to immediately know if the submitted assignment program is correct or not.

Kitaya et al. [9] developed a Web-based system for submitting, grading, and returning the results of Java programming assignments. The system evaluates the correctness of the programs using compiler checks, JUnit tests, and output result tests, and it is distinguished by its extremely high grading accuracy.

Saikkonen et al. [10] developed Scheme-robo, an evaluation system for Scheme programming exercises that evaluate the procedure, structure, execution time and so on. Scheme-robo examines programs from an algorithmic standpoint and determines their correctness.

Aizu Online Judge [11] is a popular online judging system. Aizu Online Judge is public online judging system developed at the University of Aizu. Users can solve problems, submit their source code, and be judged in Aizu Online Judge.

3 Programming Problem Generation System: Waquema

3.1 Overview

Cloud Waquema's website is depicted in Fig. 1. The generated problems in the cloud version can be exported to the teacher's Google Drive as Google Forms. To create a question, click "Generate." To run the program created in the editor, click "Run." Clicking "Settings" brings up the settings screen (Fig. 2), where you can choose the language to be used and the questions to be generated.

Figure 3 shows how this system outputs the questions as a Google Form. The answers and scores are contained in the output Google Form, and the user can edit the questions on the Form and process the results using Google Spreadsheet. Supported programming languages are JavaScript, Python, and C++.

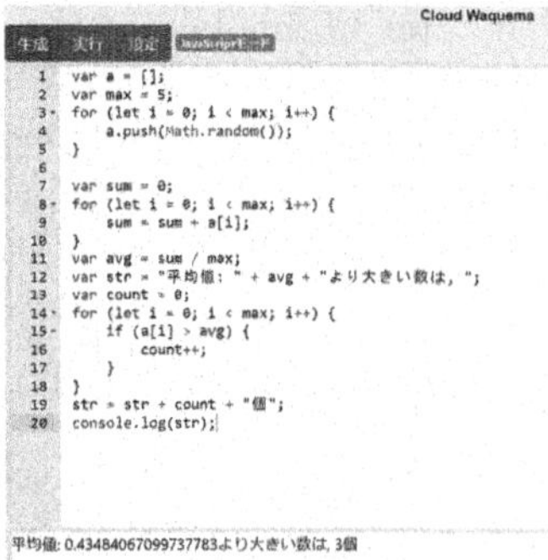

Fig. 1. Programming problem generation system.

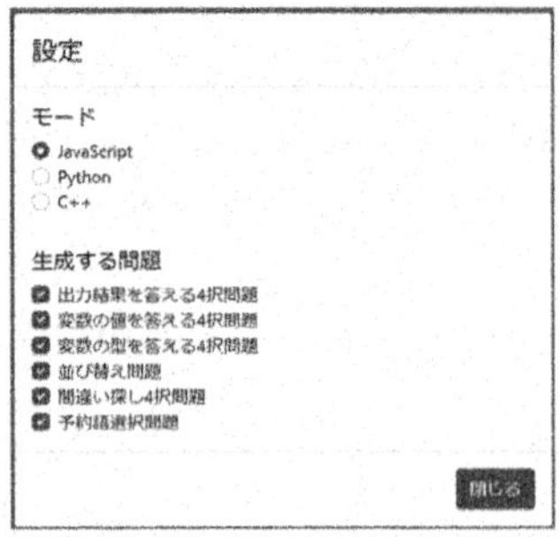

Fig. 2. Configuration.

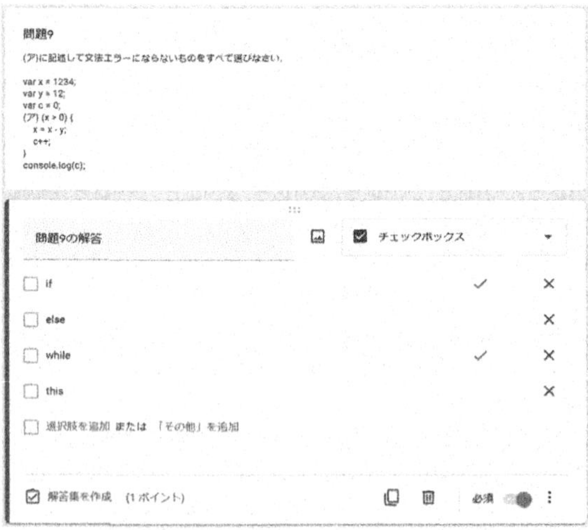

Fig. 3. Problem outputted as Google Form.

3.2 Generable Problems

Questions that Answer the Output Results: Figure 4 depicts a question that answers the output result. This problem requires the user to select one appropriate output result from the options obtained by running the program in the problem statement. It is generated only if the output instruction is included in the input source code. If the output result can be interpreted as a numerical value, then the value closest to the value is selected. If the output result is separated by commas, then choices with different comma separators can be generated as shown in Fig. 4. Otherwise, a choice consisting of a substring of the output result will be generated.

Question to Answer the Value of a Variable: Figure 5 shows a question to determine the value of a variable. In this question, you must select one of the options in the question text as the value of the variable at the specified location in the program.

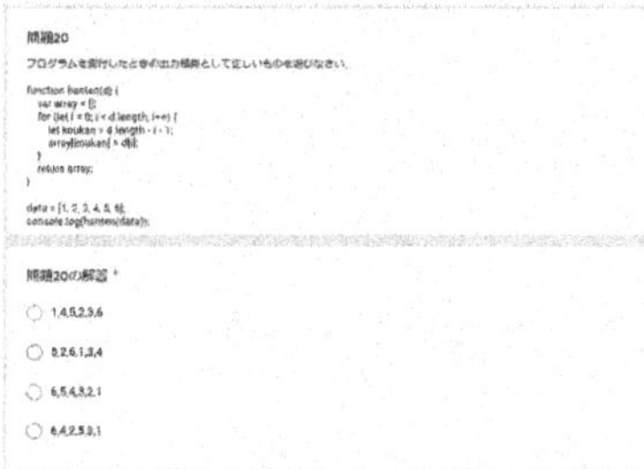

Fig. 4. Questions that answer the output results.

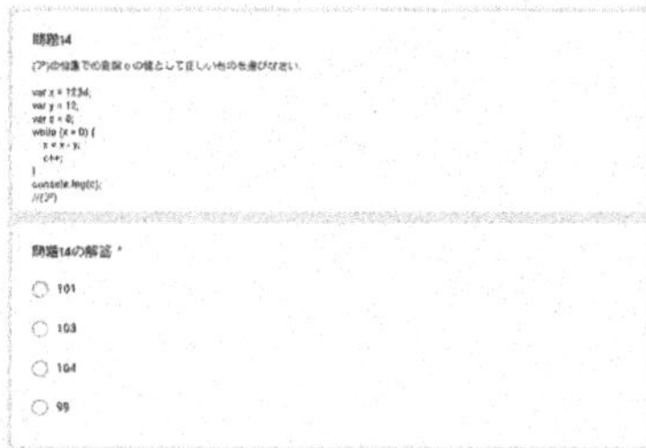

Fig. 5. Question to answer the value of variable.

Questions on the Types of Variables: Figure 6 shows a question that asks about the types of variables. This question requires you to choose one of the options as the appropriate variable type at the indicated location in the program in the question text.

Error Finding Problem: Figure 7 shows an error finding problem. This problem is to choose one line number from the program in the question text that contains a spelling error. The misspelling is associated with one of the reserved words chosen at random from the input source code. The spelling error is assigned to a randomly selected reserved word from the input source code, and the question is generated only if the reserved word is present in the input source code.

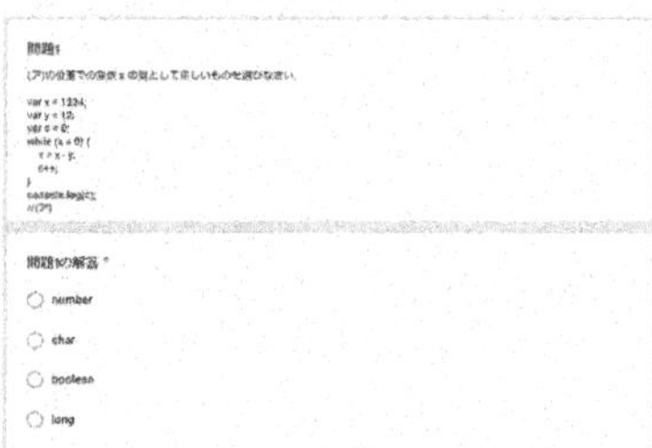

Fig. 6. Questions on the types of variables.

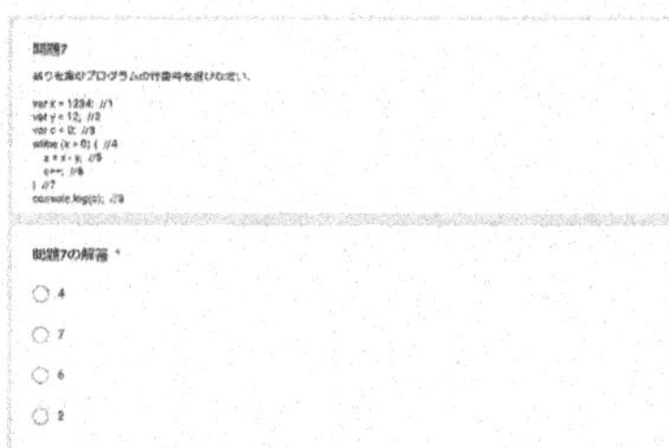

Fig. 7. Error finding problem.

Sorting Problem: Figure 8 shows a sorting issue. The goal of this problem is to select all the program fragments that do not cause errors when shuffled by separating them by one line each and sorting them in the order of the alternatives.

Reserved Word Selection Problem: Figure 9 depicts the problem of reserved word selection. The goal of this problem is to find all the reserved words that do not cause errors when entered into the blank set for the program in the problem statement.

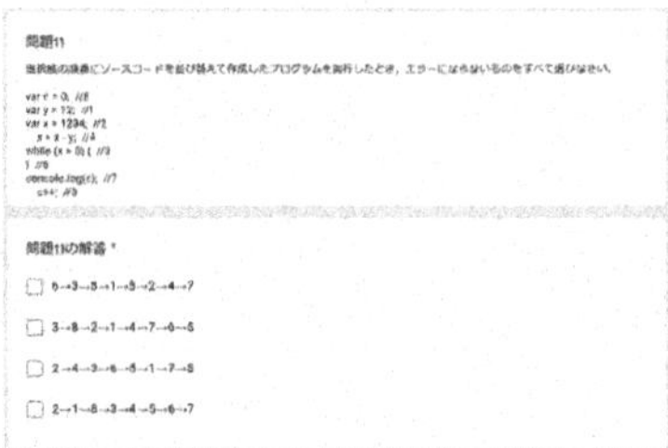

Fig. 8. Sorting problem.

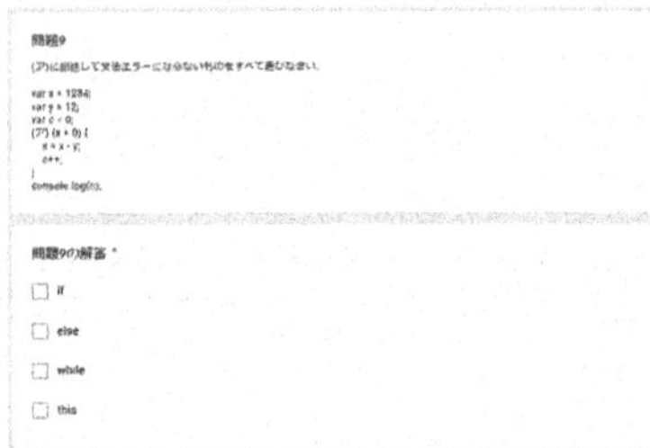

Fig. 9. Reserved word selection problem.

4 Evaluation Experiment

4.1 Evaluation by Students

A questionnaire was distributed to the students to evaluate the exercises and tests developed using the system's generated problems. Students were only asked to complete the questionnaire if they agreed to the data usage policy, which stated that the collected data would only be used for system improvement and paper writing. As a result, 61 of the 75 students who attended the lecture responded. Items and results are shown in Table 1. Table 1 displays the items and results of the 4-point scale, with 4 representing the highest and 1 representing the lowest. The average in Table 1 was calculated by multiplying each rating by the number of respondents in Table 3, then dividing the total by the number of respondents ($N = 61$). The same questionnaire was also distributed for the same lecture given in the fall semester of 2021. The questionnaire included a 4-point evaluation and a free writing section. Sixty-three students responded out of the 94 who attended the lecture. Table 2 summarizes the items and results of the questionnaire.

Table 1. Assessment items and ratings on the problem (2020, $N = 61$).

Item Number	Item	Average	Value / %			
			4	3	2	1
1	Was the difficulty of the question appropriate?	3.27	37.0	54.1	6.6	1.6
2	Were the instructions in the question easy to understand?	3.34	42.6	49.2	8.2	0.0

Table 2. Assessment items and ratings on the problem (2021, $N = 63$).

Item Number	Item	Average	Value / %			
			4	3	2	1
1	Was the difficulty of the question appropriate?	3.12	25.3	65.0	6.3	3.1
2	Were the instructions in the question easy to understand?	3.31	42.8	49.2	4.7	3.1

Table 3. Evaluation value of Table 1 and Table 2.

Item	Value
Very true	4
Fit the bill a little	3
Not very applicable	2
Not applicable at all	1

4.2 Checking Comprehension Using the Output of the System

We used the questions generated by this system in JavaScript lectures for second-year university students to conduct for comprehension checks from November 12 to December 3, 2020. Table 5 displays the results of the comprehension checks for each lecture. The comprehension check was graded on a four-point scale to determine the level of understanding of the lecture material. Students could submit their answers as many times as they wanted. Figure 10 depicts the distribution of scores at the time of the first submission, while Fig. 11 depicts the distribution of scores at the time of the final submission for students who submitted more than once. Figure 12 also displays the frequency with which each response is submitted.

4.3 Evaluation of the System by Teachers

A questionnaire for teachers was used to assess the system. It was explicitly stated that the data gathered would only be used for the dissertation and not for any other purpose. Respondents were only asked to answer the questionnaire if and only if when they agreed with the data usage policy. As a result, we

Table 4. Multiple-choice survey questions and results($N = 61$).

How did you feel after answering the questions?	
Item	Percentage
I was able to monitor my understanding	73.8%
I found it difficult	31.1%
I sensed that the teacher had hand-crafted the problem	14.8%
I felt that the questions presented were not suitable for review	6.6%

Table 5. Results of the comprehension check for each lecture.

Item	11/12	11/19	11/26	12/3
Average score (maximum 4 points)	2.68	2.39	2.16	2.84
Average number of answers	2.22	1.41	1.46	1.38
Correlation between score at first answer and number of answers	−0.13	−0.38	−0.37	−0.26

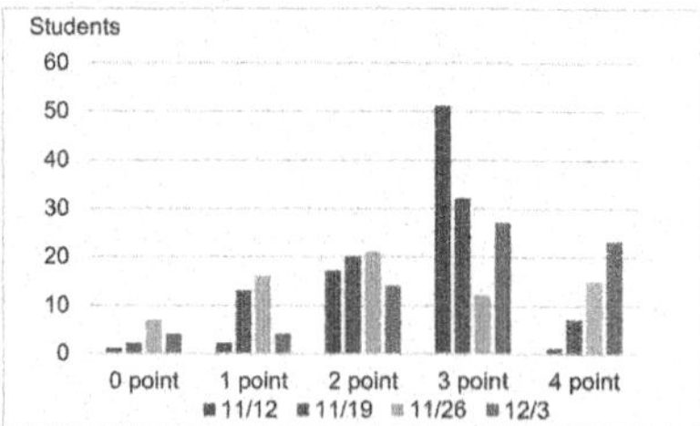

Fig. 10. Distribution of scores when answering for the first time.

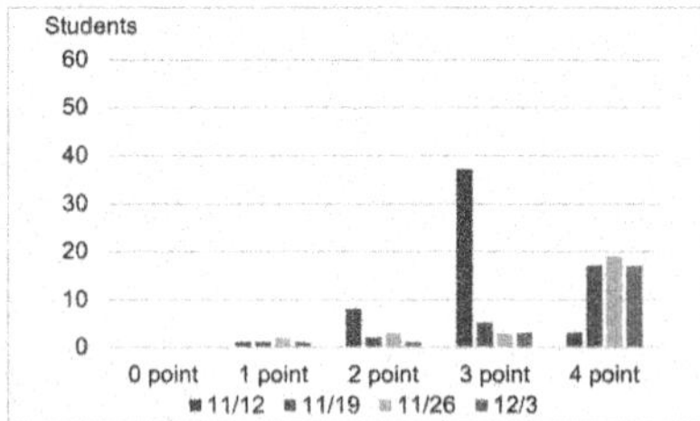

Fig. 11. Distribution of scores at the time of the final answer for students who answered the questionnaire more than once.

were able to obtain questionnaires from five teachers, one for the JavaScript version, three for the Python version, and one for the C++ version of the system, respectively. The questionnaire for the teachers included four options, a multiple-choice question, and a question asking them to describe any other problems or opinions they would like to see resolved. Table 9 shows the results of the multiple-choice questions. Table 6 shows the results of the four-choice questions, and Table 7 shows the choices for the questions in Table 6.

5 Analysis of Evaluation Data

5.1 Analysis of Students Evaluation

Tables 1, 2, and 4 are discussed further below. Item 1 in Table 1 had an average of 3.27. In Table 2, the average for Item 1 was 3.12. More than 90% students

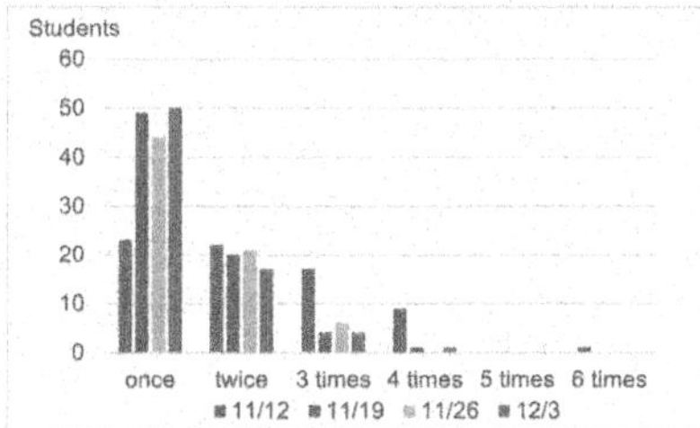

Fig. 12. Distribution of the number of times students answered the questionnaire.

Table 6. Evaluation by teachers. ($N = 1, 3$ and 1 for JavaScript, Python, and C++, respectively).

Item No.	Item	JavaScript				Python				C++			
		A	B	C	D	A	B	C	D	A	B	C	D
1	How easy was it to use the cloud version of Waquema?	0	1	0	0	1	2	0	0	0	1	0	0
2	On an average, how long did it take you to complete the creation of an exercise from the source code?	0	0	0	1	1	1	0	1	0	1	0	0
3	On an average, how long did it take you to complete an exercise creation from the system's output?	0	0	1	0	2	0	1	0	0	0	1	0
4	What percentage of the questions in the system's output were appropriate for practice?	0	0	1	0	0	0	3	0	0	1	0	0
5	On an average, how long did it take you to complete the creation of tests from the source code?	0	0	0	1	2	0	0	1	0	0	0	1
6	On an average, how long did it take you to complete the creation of tests from the system's output?	0	0	0	1	1	1	0	1	0	0	1	0
7	What percentage of the problems in the system's output were appropriate for testing?	0	0	0	1	0	1	1	1	0	0	1	0

indicated that the difficulty level of the problems generated by the system was appropriate, in both questionnaires. Furthermore, Table 4 shows that more than 70% of the students indicated that they were able to use the system to check their understanding. These findings imply that the system-generated questions

Table 7. Question items of Table 6.

Item No.	A	B	C	D
1	I think so very much.	I think so.	I don't think so.	I don't think so at all
2, 3, 5, 6	Less than 10 min	10 to 20 minutes	20 to 30 minutes	More than 30 min
4, 7	80% or more	60% to 80%	40% to 60%	Less than 40%

Table 8. Change in time to generate problems using Waquema.

	Teacher 1	Teacher 2	Teacher 3	Teacher 4	Teacher 5
Language	JavaScript	C++	Python	Python	Python
Exercises	Faster	Later	Faster	Faster	Same
Tests	Same	Faster	Later	Same	Same

Table 9. Multiple-choice questionnaire on the issue.

Which types of questions did you want to use?						
Item	JavaScript		Python		C++	
	Excs.	Tests	Excs.	Tests	Excs.	Tests
1. Questions that answer the output results	1	1	3	3	1	1
2. Question to answer the value of a variable	1	1	3	3	1	1
3. Questions on the types of variables	0	1	1	1	0	0
4. Sorting problem	0	0	2	2	0	0
5. Error finding problem	1	0	2	1	0	0
6. Reserved word selection problem	0	0	0	0	0	0

were appropriate for assessing the students' level of comprehension. This implies that the system-generated questions, as well as the teacher's question selection, were effective. In Table 1, Item 2 had a weighted average of 3.34. More than 90% students said "I think so very much." or "I think so.", with no one saying "I don't think so at all." In Table 2, Item 2 had an average of 3.31. More than 90% students said "I think so very much." or "I think so." while the number of students who said "I don't think so at all" increased from 2020. The percentage of students who said "I don't think so." decreased. Five students had difficulty understanding the meaning of the questions in both questionnaires, but the majority of the other students were able to understand and answer them (Table 8).

5.2 Analysis of Confirmation of Understanding

Table 5 will be discussed. The score of the first answer and the number of answers had a consistent negative correlation (−0.38 to −0.13). This indicates that students who received low scores on their first attempt answered the questions multiple times. The scores of the last answer are concentrated at 4 points in Fig. 11. It can be seen that several students who answered the question more than twice, did so until they received four points. Figure 10 shows the number of students who scored 4 points on the first try as the number of lectures increased. The gradual increase in the number of students who could get full marks in a single attempt can be attributed to students understanding the patterns and methods of answering the questions and becoming accustomed to checking the lecture content. In the first lecture (11/12), the number of answers was distributed over a wide range(Fig. 12). This may be due to the fact that the students were not yet accustomed to checking the lecture contents. A student submitted the questionnaire six times when checking the lecture content in one session (Fig. 12).

5.3 Analysis of Teachers Evaluation

Table 6 will be discussed. For Item 1, one respondent answered "I think so very much", and four answered "I think so." The simple operation method, in which problems are generated by entering the source code and pressing a button, received high marks. There were opinions in the free description column, such as "the policy that problems cannot be generated without entering the program is a problem" and "it would be great if there were templates." As a result, we believe that the difficulty in operating this system stems from the process of writing a program in the editor and testing its functionality. We further discuss about Items 2 and 3 (creating practice problems). The four teachers spent the same amount or less time on writing exercises, while one teacher spent more time. Using this system, however, all of the teachers completed the exercises less than 30 min. We can observe that the time required to create the problems has been reduced, as has the burden placed on the teachers. Concerning the percentage of questions that can be used for practice (Item 4), four teachers said it ranged from 40% to 60%, while one said it ranged from 60% to 80%. Based on these results, we can conclude that our system is capable of generating questions suitable for exercises, although the selection of questions is necessary.

Items 5 and 6 will be discussed in the following section. One teacher needed less time to create test questions, while three teachers needed the same amount of time. Using this system, it took more than 30 min for two teachers and less than 30 min for three teachers to create test questions. It is clear from the preceding data that the time required to create test questions has not changed considerably, nor has the burden on teachers. Concerning the percentage of questions that can be used for the exam (Item 7), one teacher responded "60% - 80%," two responded "40% - 60%," and two responded "less than 40%." Based on these findings, we can conclude that this system's generation of test questions has room for improvement. Furthermore, some of the system's questions were of a type that we had not previously considered. For instance, in a question about reserved words, multiple choices were the correct answer (*let* and *var* in JavaScript). As a result, we can expand the types of questions that can be asked in a problem by searching for appropriate questions in the system output.

We will further discuss Table 9 (Questions to be used for exercises and tests). First, let us discuss the exercise questions. All the teachers said they would use Items 1 and 2. Three faculty members said they would use Item 5 if it were available. Less than two teachers indicated an interest in using the other items. Nobody expressed an interest in using Item 6. The output results of the program, problems related to variable values, and problems finding errors in reserved words are the items that we would like to use as practice problems from the list above. Following that, we will discuss the exam questions. For Items 1 and 2, all the teachers indicated an interest in using the software. Only two or fewer teachers indicated an interest in using the remaining items. No one expressed an interest in using Item 6. Based on the above findings, we would like to use this as a practice exercise for questions about program output and variable values. Because questions about output results and variables values are important factors in assessing students' understanding of programming structures and algorithms, it is safe to assume that all the teachers indicated a desire to use it.

6 Conclusion

The questions generated automatically by the proposed system, Waquema, were used to assess students' comprehension during actual lectures. Following that, we distributed a survey to the students to assess the system. We also distributed a questionnaire to the teachers who used the system and assessed the amount of time required for the exercises and examinations. The results of the student questionnaire revealed that the difficulty level of the system-generated questions as well as the instructions in the questions were appropriate. Based on the results of the questionnaire sent to the teachers who used the system, it was discovered that using the system could reduce the time required to prepare the exercises. The proposed system would not be able to reduce the amount of time needed to prepare examination questions. We hope to use Waquema at more sites in the future to collect knowledge and data with the intent make the system more efficient in preparing examination questions.

References

1. Yamashita, M.: Construction of max/java, a web-based java programming learning support system. In: Bachelor Thesis of the Meiji University Department of Computer Science (2011). in Japanese
2. Daimon, T., Onishi, K.: Development of a system for generating programming problems in a web browser. In: IPSJ Symposium on Information Education, pp. 75–80 (2020). in Japanese
3. Kitamura, K., Tamaki, H.: Automatic generation of programming problem content from tagged sample programs. In: IPSJ Technical Report CE(122), pp. 1–8 (2013). in Japanese
4. Uchida, Y.: An automatic drill-producing system for elementary programming learning. In: IPSJ Technical Report CE(92), pp. 109–113 (2007). in Japanese

5. Ariyasu, K., Ikeda, E., Okamoto, T., Kunishima, T., Yokota, K.: Automatic generation of fill-in-the-blank exercises in adaptive c language learning system. In: DEIM Forum 2009, pp. 1–5 (2009). in Japanese
6. Takeuchi, R., Ohkubo, H., Kasuya, H., Yamamoto, S.: An learning support environment for Haskell programming by automatic generation of cloze question. In: IPSJ Technical Report SE(171), pp. 1–8 (2011). in Japanese
7. Kogure, S., Nakamura, R., Makino, K., Yamashita, K., Konishi, T., Itoh, Y.: Monitoring system for the effective instruction based on the semiautomatic evaluation of programs during programming classroom lectures. Res. Pract. Technol. Enhanced Learn. **10**, 1–12 (2005)
8. Itou, K., Mima, Y., Ohnishi, A.: A linkage mechanism between course-management-system and coursework-checking-functions over web services. IPSJ J. **52**(12), 3121–3134 (2011). in Japanese
9. Kitaya, H., Inoue, U.: An online automated scoring system for java programming assignments. Int. J. Inf. Edu. Technol. **6**, 275–279 (2016)
10. Saikkonen, R., Malmi, L., Korhonen: Fully automatic assessment of programming exercises. In: ACM Sigcse Bulletin, pp. 133–136 (2001)
11. AIZU ONLINE JUDGE. https://judge.u-aizu.ac.jp/onlinejudge/. Accessed 24 Jan 2022

Evaluation of a Data Structure Viewer for Educational Practice

Kensuke Onishi(✉)

Tokai University, 4-1-1, Kitakanme, Hiratsuka, Kanagawa 259-1292, Japan
onishi@tokai-u.jp

Abstract. Data structures and algorithms are fundamental subjects in the curricula of information science faculties and departments. Recently, they were also included in the curriculum as basic subjects of data science and artificial intelligence.

In 2017, we developed a smartphone application, termed Data Structure Viewer(DSV), to promote the understanding of data structures and algorithms. This application has been used in our lectures. In this article, we describe the evaluation of the DSVs used in lectures from 2017 to 2021 through the use of questionnaires. The students' evaluation and confirmation of the lecture content in class, revealed that the DSV contributed to the improvement of students' comprehension. We also discuss important points to be considered when using the DSV in lectures.

Keywords: Data structure · Smartphone application · HyFlex-type lecture

1 Introduction

Data structures and algorithms are taught in numerous universities as the foundation of computer science. For example, Introduction to Algorithms at the Massachusetts Institute of Technology(Cambridge, MA, USA) [1] has been developed as an online courseware, and lecture videos have been uploaded on YouTube. From 2013 to 2022, the first lecture had been viewed more than 4 million times. This course can also be used as basic knowledge for data science and artificial intelligence technology, and the need for this knowledge is increasing.

Algorithms and data structures include arrays, pointers, list structures (including stacks and queues), traversal of trees, binary trees, hashing, and sorting. In general, students learn the concepts of these data structures, understand their functions, and implement them in practice.

In recent years, students from various social and academic backgrounds have been enrolling in universities in Japan. If they only wish to learn the concepts of data structures, it is possible to attend lectures without considerable knowledge as a prerequisite. However, for those wishing to understand the mechanism of data structures, mathematical knowledge (e.g. number sequences and probabilities) will be required in certain situations. For example, to understand that

Published by Springer Nature Switzerland AG 2023
T. Keane et al. (Eds.): WCCE 2022, IFIP AICT 685, pp. 504–516, 2023.
https://doi.org/10.1007/978-3-031-43393-1_46

the number of comparisons in a binary search is proportional to $\log n$ (n is the number of data), knowledge of logarithms and number sequences are necessary. In previous lectures, mathematical knowledge was supplemented within the lectures, but some students rejected them simply because of the presence of mathematical formulas. In addition, the implementation of data structures is a difficult task for students who are not proficient in programming.

Two research questions in this study were as follows: (**Q1**) Does the use of a smartphone applications, termed Data Structure Viewer (DSV) improve students' comprehension when learning data structures? (**Q2**) What factors are necessary to improve comprehension when using the DSV?

The framework of this study is the same as [2]. That is, Budiman et al. [2] examined whether smartphone applications improve the comprehension of lectures on data structures. They used a control group to assess differences in comprehension. Since it was not possible to provide a control group for this study, a questionnaire to students who have been taking "Data Structures and Algorithms" for four years was used to evaluate differences in comprehension. The results showed that the smartphone application (DSV) contributed to lecture satisfaction and comprehension.

In this article, we describe and evaluate the lectures given in 2017, 2019, 2020, and 2021. Section 2 describes a system for displaying data structures and the use of smartphone application in lectures as related works. Section 3 describes DSVs and their evolution. Section 5 describes the details of the lectures, questionnaires, and their results. Section 6 discusses the results of the questionnaires.

2 Related Work

When teaching algorithms and data structures, demonstrating the operation of a program that implements the algorithms and data structures has been used as a method to promote understanding. Around 2000, Java applets were used for this purpose; however, these applets are no longer available.

Recently, a smartphone application for viewing the data structure has becomes available. "Algorithms: Explained and Animated"[1] is an application that allows the viewing of data structures, such as lists and hashes, sorting, list search, graph search, and clustering. A book title "*Algorithm Picture Book: 26 Algorithms in Picture*" [3], describing the data structures included in the Algorithms: Explained and Animated application, is also available. This book and the smartphone application are a good combination for learning the concept of data structures.

In Python tutor [4] [2], when you enter source code, Python tutor visualizes the execution of that code and allows you to see the values of variables. Python Tutor supports the Python language, Java, C/C++, JavaScript, and Ruby. By running the source code of a data structure in Python Tutor, it is possible to observe the function of the data structure. However, the development of some languages has

[1] Algorithms: http://algorithm.wiki/.

[2] Python Tutor: https://pythontutor.com/.

been discontinued. There are some restrictions, such as the inability to run long source codes.

Budiman et al. [5] discussed the contents of an application for learning data structures and the networks required for the application. Budiman et al. [2] conducted an evaluation experiment using the application for learning data structures and a traditional teaching method. The results showed statistically that learning outcomes were higher in the group that used the application. Irmayana et al. [6] also developed a similar application and conducted an evaluation experiment with students. As a result, 75% of the students responded that the learning of data structures and algorithms were optimized. The applications used in these studies differ from ours in that they visualize data structures and do not help students understand the principles of data structures. Note that the applications used in [2,5,6] are all Android OS only.

A review conducted by Kardy and Ghazal [7], surveyed 37 articles on mobile applications for science learning published in the Web of Science and Scopus databases between 2007 and 2014. The study concluded that future research should take advantage of new technologies, individual testing of the usefulness of application features, and develop additional strategies for using mobile applications for collaboration. In recent years, research has also been conducted using mobile applications. Zydnet and Warner [8] developed an application for learning basic mathematics, which was used in lectures. The application has online quizzes and allows students to monitor their understanding. By comparing classes that used the application with those that did not, they concluded that there was a significant difference in the retention of lecture content(75% and 55%, respectively).

3 DSV for Smartphones

The DSV is an application designed to assist students in understanding the principles and the function of data structures. Three versions of DSV (DSV17, DSV19, and DSV20) were developed in 2017, 2019, and 2020, respectively.

Firstly, we will explain the development policies common to all DSVs.

1. DSVs are constructed based on data structures implemented in the language used in the lectures.
2. The data structures used in DSVs are implemented in a simple manner, without using the classes included in the language. The goal of this approach is to present the code of the data structures in the lectures, as well as to promote understanding of the principles and the behavior of data structures.
3. The user can view the inside of the data structure. In the data structure using reference values, the reference values are displayed so that the user can intuitively understand the principles of the data structure.

[DSV17]. DSV17 was the first version of this application written in the Java language for Android smartphones. The data structures supported by this application are stack, queue, lists (array type), list (reference type), ordered list, binary search tree, heap, and hash. DSV17 is available on Google Play; however there is no application for iOS devices.

[DSV19]. DSV19 is an application developed in collaboration with Asial Corporation (Tokyo, Japan). DSV19 was developed on the Monaca platform for smartphones.[3] On this platform, it is possible to develop applications using JavaScript. We implemented the data structure in JavaScript and embedded the data structure to create DSV19. In this version, it is possible to use bubble sort, selection sort, insertion sort, quick sort, and merge sort in addition to the nine data structures available in DSV17. DSV19 was running on a Monaca debugger, so the convenience was not satisfactory.

[DSV20]. DSV20 is a smartphone application of DSV19 and is available on Google Play for Android smartphones[4] and App Store for iOS devices. Therefore, students can download DSV20 to their own smartphones. The data structures available in DSV20 are the same as those in DSV19.

4 Educational Practice

4.1 Details of Educational Practice

This section describes the lecture in which the educational practice was conducted. This lecture take place for 14 weeks in the fall semester and addressed to second-year students at the Department of Mathematical Sciences.

Table 1. Details of the lectures on educational practice.

Course title	Data Structure and Algorithm I			
Eligibility	Second-year students, Fall semester			
Course students	Year	Second-year students	Students in higher grade	Total number
	2017	22 (68%)	10 (31%)	32
	2019	64 (91%)	6 (9%)	70
	2020	71 (89%)	9 (11%)	80
	2021	74 (91%)	7 (9%)	81

The distribution of the number of students in each year is shown in Table 1. In all years, the majority of students were in their second year of study and few were in their third year or above. In particular, after 2019, $\geq 85\%$ of the students were in the second year. Compared with 2017, the number of students enrolled in the course has significantly increased by more than double since 2019.

[3] Monaca, https://monaca.io/.

[4] https://play.google.com/store/apps/details?id=jp.co.asial.algorithm&hl=ja&gl=US.

By the time they attend this class, students would have attended 2 h of lectures on Java language in the spring semester of their first year, 1 h of lecture on Java language and 1 h of lecture on HTML, and JavaScript in the fall semester of their first year, and 2 h of lecture on Processing in the spring semester of their second year. Simultaneously to the aforementioned classes of data structure, they are also attending 2 h graphical user interface programming classes.

The syllabus for this lecture includes the following three objectives:

- students will be able to read and execute various algorithms;
- students will be able to determine which algorithm is appropriate for a given problem;
- students will be able to express the computational complexity of algorithms in mathematical expressions and compare algorithms.

To achieve this goal, the lecture covered general data structures and algorithms such as lists (including stack and queue), binary tree, binary search tree, heap, and hash. Sorting was covered in another lecture due to time constraints.

Each lecture takes place in approximately the following order:

(1) review of the previous lecture;
(2) observation of data structures using DSV (2017);
(2') experience of data structures using DSV(2019, 2020, and 2021);
(3) explaining concepts with pseudo-code;
(4) explaining the source code by the lecturer(2017, 2019);
(4') running and explaining the source code in Python Tutor [4] (2020, 2021);
(5) exercises and Q&A;
(6) confirmation of lecture content (2020, 2021);

Although the content of these lectures has not changed, the applications and the fashion in which they are used in lectures have been altered over the years. Below, we explain the changes which occurred each year.

2017: The lecture was given using DSV17, and the language used was Java. In the lecture, we displayed the screen of the smartphone on the projector. However, since most of the students were using iPhones, they did not use the application themselves.

2019: Students used DSV19 on the Monaca debugger application. However, some students found this application difficult to use. The language used was JavaScript, and the application was produced based on the source code. We have also written a textbook [9] that assumes the use of the DSV.

2020, 2021: Due to the coronavirus disease 2019 (COVID-19) pandemic, the lectures in 2020 and 2021 took *HyFlex-type* lectures, which is a lecture given face-to-face and taken simultaneously by students at a distance. During this period, the lecture content was organized so that only one data structure was covered in each lecture.

The following six learning supports were incorporated: (1) Distribution of lecture materials; (2) Confirmation of lecture contents by Google Forms; (3) Individual questions using the Zoom breakout room; (4) Presentation of URLs for questions during lectures; (5) Demonstration of the execution process of the source code; and (6) Use of DSV20.

Support (2) is the confirmation of the lecture content covered in each lecture. This confirmation is performed via Google Form, and is set up so that students can check their score (0–4 points) as soon as they provide an answer. Students can deepen their understanding of the lectures by repeatedly answering the questions, as if they were practicing calculations. Support (5) was performed using Python Tutor.

Support (6) is an application for smartphones, which is the subject of this article. Since DSV20 is available on Google Play and App Store, students can use them independently at any time. Exercises using the application were conducted in all lectures. The language used was JavaScript.

4.2 Evaluation of the Practice

Evaluation Outline: In this study, we used questionnaires to evaluate the applications and lectures. Three types of questionnaires were used. The first is a questionnaire regarding the DSV and lecture, which was administered after the last lecture. The content of the questionnaire is explained in the next section. The second questionnaire is a confirmation of the lecture contents (support (2)); it measures the level of understanding of the students by confirming the lecture contents from the second lecture to the fourteenth lecture in 2020 and 2021. The last questionnaire is a class evaluation questionnaire conducted by the university, and administered in all courses. Owing to the many items in the questionnaire, we used items which we thought were relevant to the DSVs used.

Questionnaire Concerning the Lecture and DSV: We explained to the students that the questionnaire would be used for the future development of applications and the publication of the article. We instructed the students not to answer if they were not satisfied with the purpose of usage of the questionnaire. As a result, we received responses from 18(2017), 61(2019), 44(2020), and 38(2021) students. Items of the open-ended questionnaire are shown in Table 2; items of the 4-point scale questionnaire and the mean values of the ratings are shown in Table 3. A 4-point scale was used for scoring (4 denoted high satisfaction and 1 denoted low satisfaction).

Table 4 shows the analysis [5] of text mining on the free text of the questionnaires from 2019 to 2021. The three most frequent results of the annual analysis

[5] Analysis by user local text mining tool (https://textmining.userlocal.jp/).

Table 2. Evaluation items for the lecture and Data Structure Viewer (DSV) (open-ended questionnaire).

Item number	Item
1	Please indicate what you think is good about the DSV
2	Please indicate what you think is bad about the DSV

Table 3. Average values of the evaluation of the Data Structure Viewer(DSV) (4-point scale), $N = 18(2017), 61(2019), 44(2020), 38(2021)$.

Item number	Item	2017	2019	2020	2021
1	Did the application help you learn?	3.06	2.44	3.30	3.39
2	Did you want to use the application for yourself?	2.61	2.18	2.68	2.68
3	Did the application help you understand stack behavior better?	3.17	2.48	3.43	3.42
4	" queue behavior better?	3.22	2.49	3.30	3.39
5	" list (array) behavior better?	3.17	2.57	3.32	3.26
6	" list (reference type) behavior better?	3.22	2.42	3.11	3.32
7	" sorted list behavior better?	3.11	2.51	3.09	3.13
8	" binary search tree behavior better?	3.28	2.62	3.18	3.18
9	" heap behavior better?	3.22	2.41	2.98	3.11
10	" hash behavior better?	3.11	2.39	2.89	3.03

regarding the good features (Table 2, item 1) and bad features (item 2) of the application are displayed. The discussion on this data is omitted for the sake of page numbers.

Table 4. Analysis of the free-text questionnaire concerning Data Structure Viewer (DSV).

Category	Year	Word (frequency, term frequency-inverse document frequency[TF-IDF] score)
Good	2019	easy to understand (6, 3.59), understand (6, 0.07), can do (6, 0.05)
	2020	can do (7, 0.06), understand (4, 0.06), visual (3, 3.62)
	2021	understand (12, 2.2), can do (12, 0.18), lecture (7, 1.13)
Bad	2019	update (4, 3), download (3, 0.66), application (3, 0.18)
	2020	understand (3, 0.14), can do (3, 0.01), think (3, 0.01)
	2021	arrays (3, 6.83), number of items (2, 1.61), reset (2,0.49)

In the questionnaire administered to the students, we asked which learning supports should remain in the lecture and which should be removed. The results are shown in Table 5.

Table 5. Percentage of students who would like learning supports in lectures to remain or be removed, $N = 44$ (2020, even numbered row), 38 (2021, odd numbered row).

Learning support		(1)	(2)	(3)	(4)	(5)	(6)
Continue	2020	84.1	52.3	22.7	40.9	47.7	65.9
	2021	89.5	39.5	36.8	50.0	65.8	71.1
Neither	2020	13.6	38.6	75.0	54.5	43.2	29.5
	2021	10.5	47.4	57.8	50.0	31.6	26.3
Discontinue	2020	2.3	9.1	2.3	4.5	9.1	4.5
	2021	0.0	13.2	5.3	0.0	2.6	2.6

Confirmation of Lecture Content: This section explains the methodology used to check the lecture content. The confirmation of lecture content was performed by name to check the level of understanding for each student in 2019, 2020, and 2021. The submitted information was considered attendance to the lecture, but did not affect the student's grade. The items to be checked are shown below; all items were required:

- student's identification number and name;
- ability to use the data;
- student's level of understanding (scale 1 to 4; 4 denotes very well understood and 1 denotes not understood at all);
- what did you understand from the lecture (free description);
- what did you not understand from the lecture (free description);
- questions to confirm the content (4 choices or multiple elections). Each question is worth one point. The maximum score is 4 points and the minimum score is 0 points (only 2020, 2021).

Since students could check the content of the lecture as many times as they wished, they repeatedly answered the same questions to improve their scores.

Table 6. Comprehension of each lecture.

Number of lectures		2	3	4	5	6	7	8	9	10	11	12	13	14
Self-assessment of comprehension	2019	–	2.76	2.56	2.56	2.66	2.86	2.75	1.87	2.47	2.74	2.78	2.49	–
	2020	3.20	3.04	3.06	2.33	2.60	3.01	2.86	2.87	2.58	2.89	2.78	2.66	2.60
	2021	3.22	3.26	3.27	2.91	3.08	3.06	3.25	3.25	2.85	2.97	3.05	2.88	3.00
Difference from 2019	2020	–	0.28	0.30	−0.23	0.04	0.35	0.00	0.12	0.71	0.42	0.00	0.17	–
											0.15			
	2021	–	0.50	0.51	0.35	0.52	0.40	0.39	0.50	0.98	0.50	0.27	0.39	–
											0.23			
Average of confirmation of lecture content	2020	2.95	3.55	2.27	1.37	2.47	2.50	2.49	2.81	2.06	2.82	2.08	2.37	2.07
		3.04	3.79	2.71	3.09	3.18	3.17	3.08	3.39	3.31	3.25	3.05	3.01	2.55
	2021	3.22	3.64	2.49	1.53	2.67	2.51	2.71	2.91	1.87	2.67	2.63	2.51	1.68
		3.43	3.75	3.46	3.46	3.48	3.37	3.33	3.58	3.44	3.62	3.65	3.49	3.24

Table 6 shows aggregate data of students who agreed to participate in the study. In rows 2–4 of Table 6, the mean levels of understanding of students from 2019 to 2021 are displayed. The data for 2020 and 2021 (lines 3 and 4) are the average of the comprehension levels indicated in the last response. Lines 5, 6 and 7, 8 show the difference between the data in 2020 and 2021 and those obtained in 2019, respectively. Because the order of the lectures was slightly changed, the differences are between lectures that covered the same content. For the third, and eleventh through thirteenth lectures, the differences were calculated for the same number of lectures. For the fourth through eleventh lectures in 2020 and 2021, the differences between the third through tenth lectures in 2019 were calculated.

Lines 9 and 11 in Table 6 are the average of the scores of the first confirmation of the lecture content in 2020 and 2021. Lines 10 and 12 are the average of the score of the last confirmation of the lecture contents in 2020 and 2021.

Class Evaluation Conducted by the University: There are approximately 20 questions in this class evaluation questionnaire, and each question is rated using a 5-point scale (5 denotes the best rating and 1 denotes the worst rating). The evaluations of three items related to the DSVs are shown in Table 7.

Table 7. Evaluation items and evaluation of the lecture (5 levels), $N = 25(2017)$, 64(2019), 24(2020), 22(2021).

Item number	Item	2017	2019	2020	2021
1	The explanation was easy to understand.	3.60	2.68	2.92	3.09
2	The writing on the board, audio-visual materials, and handouts were appropriate and easy to understand.	3.80	2.87	3.63	3.41
3	Efforts were made to encourage students' willingness to participate and attend the class.	3.88	2.84	3.71	3.73

5 Discussion

5.1 Questionnaire Concerning the Lecture and DSV

Evaluation of DSV: Firstly, we describe the questionnaire on the DSV (Table 3). Item 1 refers to the usefulness of the DSVs: in 2019 (DV19), the evaluation value of DSVs temporarily and significantly decreased; however, in other years, it was increased an annual basis. This indicates that students consider the DSV to be useful. Item 2 is a question regarding willingness of students to use the DSV themselves. This item showed the same trend as item 1; nevertheless, the mean value was lower than that of item 1.

Items 3 through 10 are questions concerning each data structure. Similar to items 1 and 2, for all data structures, the worst rating was noted in 2019, and the ratings for 2017 (DSV17), 2020, and 2021 (DSV20) were good. The ratings noted in 2020 were better than those recorded in 2019 for all items. In addition, the ratings obtained in 2021 were better than those reported in 2020 for all items, except for item 3 (stack). However, the difference in item 3 was only 0.01. Comparison of the 2021 rating with the 2019 rating, reveled an increase of $\geq$ 0.6 (20%). The largest increase was observed in item 3 (stack), (i.e., 0.94, 32% up). When compared with 2017, five items showed an increase in rating. Item 8 (binary search tree), item 9 (heap), and item 10 (hash) showed a decrease in ratings.

These results suggest that the students who attended the course in 2021 and 2020 thought that the DSV20 helped them to better understand numerous data structures.

Rating for Learning Supports: This section describes the learning supports that students would like to continue using (Table 5). The item related to the DSV in Table 5 is learning support (6), which asks whether or not students wished to continue using the DSV. The percentages of students who wished to continue using the DSV in 2020 (row 2) and 2021 (row 3) are 65.9% and 71.1%, respectively. In contrast, very few students (4.5% and 2.6%, respectively) answered that they did not wish to continue using the DSV. The continue using the DSV was also the second highest among all learning supports, both in 2021 and 2022. This indicate that the students are willing to continue using DSV in the future.

The item for which students expressed the greatest desire to continue using was (1) open access to lecture materials. The percentage of students who did not wish to continue the study support was small for all items, indicating that we would like to continue using learning supports (1) - (6) in the future.

5.2 Confirmation of Lecture Content

In this section, we will discuss the students' own level of understanding and confirmation of the lecture content (Table 6) obtained in each lecture.

Comparison of data from 2020 and 2019 showed that the level of understanding increased for nine lectures, remained unchanged for two lectures, and decreased for one lecture. Comparison of data from 2021 and 2019 revealed that the level of understanding had increased for all lectures. Comparison of 2021 and 2020 data indicated that the level of understanding had also improved.

The average score of the lecture content check is an indicator of the level of understanding of the lecture. Since we proceeded with multiple responses, the final average score revealed improvements for all lectures (2020, 2021). The final average score did not reach 3.0 for only two lectures in 2020. In 2021, all final mean scores were $\geq$3.2. Repeated responses indicate that students' comprehension had improved.

For 2020, the correlation coefficient between the students' own understanding (row 3 of Table 6) and the mean score of the first confirmation of the lecture content (row 9) was 0.754, denoting a strong correlation (p-value: 0.514×10^{-2}). For 2021, the correlation coefficient was 0.741, also indicating a strong correlation (p-value: 0.423×10^{-1}). In other words, by using the students' own level of understanding, we can estimate the level of comprehension of each lecture.

The students' own level of understanding was higher in 2020 versus 2019. Furthermore, the level of comprehension was higher in 2021. Therefore, we can conclude that students' level of comprehension of lectures increased on an annual basis.

5.3 Class Evaluation Conducted by the University

We describe the class evaluation conducted by the university (Table 7). We focused on three items: (1) clarity of the explanations; (2) appropriateness and clarity of the lecture materials; and (3) efforts to encourage students' participation in the lectures. The DSV is a teaching material that supplements the clarity of explanations (items 1 and 2). In addition, the DSV displays data structures on the blackboard and lecture materials, and allows students to experience them at hand (item 3).

The year with the best ratings for all items was 2017, followed by 2021, 2020 and 2019. The number of students who participated was 32(2017), 70(2019) 80(2020), and 81(2021). In general, a small number of students allows us to conduct the lecture while observing the students; this helps the students understand the course better. In 2019, the number of students was very large and the DSV19 had problems with updates and stability, resulting in low ratings in all categories. In 2020 and 2021, the number of students was similar to that of 2019, but the lecture took place as a HyFlex lecture and the DSV20 was used.

As a result, the ratings for items 2 and 3 were the same as those recorded in 2017. Based on the evaluation of the DSV (Table 3) and the students' desire to continue using this tool (Table 5), we can assume that the DSV has a positive impact on comprehension.

5.4 Notes on Using the DSV in Lecture

Important factor to consider when using the application are discussed below. The change from DSV19 to DSV20, significantly improved the students' comprehension. The change in the DSV at that point was due to the release of DSV in the application store. DSV19 and DSV20 have the exact same data structures that DSV can handle. In the 2019 student questionnaire, the responses were related to the stability and download of the application. Since DSV19 runs on the Monaca debugger, it occasionally malfunctions. Moreover, updating DSV19 was cumbersome. These problems were addressed in DSV20. Thus, it is likely that the students were wary of applications that lacked stability, as they are used to stable smartphone applications, and thus rated them poorly.

In 2019, student stated that they would like to have operating instructions within the DSV. Hence, starting in 2020, we allocated time to explain the use of DSV in the first lecture. Firstly, a smartphone screen was displayed as part of the delivery screen to introduce the actual usage of the DSV. Next, as an exercise, we gave students a task using the DSV and asked them to provide the results. In other words, we explained the operability and convenience of the DSV in a step-by-step manner. Additionally, we explained the operation of the first data structure, stack, as carefully as possible. Consequently, in the survey responses after 2020, the opinions on the operation on the DSV were decreased considerably (Table 4, bad futures). Therefore, to create a usable application for students, the application needs to be improved. It is important to carefully explain how to present the application and its results, as well as how to use it.

6 Conclusion

We created an smartphone application, DSV, and its usefulness is presented in this article. In the process, we found out that simply creating an application is not enough to get students to use it. We found that it is necessary to carefully communicate the stability and usefulness of the application.

Unfortunately, the evaluation experiments in this paper have not shown that DSV alone has improved student comprehension. In the future, we intend to verify the effectiveness of DSV by comparing classes in which DSV was introduced with those in which it was not.

Acknowledgments. We express our sincere gratitude to Mr. Yuki Okamoto and Mr. Ryoichi Tsukada of Asial Corporation for their assistance in developing the application and publishing the book.

References

1. Introduction to Algorithms. https://ocw.mit.edu/courses/electrical-engineering-and-computer-science/6-006-introduction-to-algorithms-fall-2011/. Accessed 7 Jan 2022

2. Budiman, E., Pusnitasari, N., Wati, M., Widians, J.A., Tejawati, A., et al.: Mobile learning media for computer science course. In: 2018 International Electronics Symposium on Knowledge Creation and Intelligent Computing (IES-KCIC), pp. 262–267. IEEE (2018)
3. Ishida, M., Miyazaki, S.: Algorithm Picture Book: 26 Algorithms in Pictures. Shoeisha (2017). (in Japanese)
4. Guo, P.J.: Online python tutor: embeddable web-based program visualization for cs education. In: Proceeding of the 44th ACM Technical Symposium on Computer Science Education, pp. 579–584 (2013)
5. Budiman, E., Hairah, U., Haeruddin, H., Saudek, A.: Mobile networks for mobile learning tools. J. Telecommun. Electr. Comput. Eng. (JTEC) **10**(1–4), 47–52 (2018)
6. Irmayana, A., et al.: The implementation of e-learning into mobile-based interactive data structure subject. In: 2017 5th International Conference on Cyber and IT Service Management (CITSM), pp. 1–5. IEEE (2017)
7. Kadry, S., Ghazal, B.: Design and assessment of using smartphone application in the classroom to improve students' learning (2019)
8. Zydney, J.M., Warner, Z.: Mobile apps for science learning: review of research. Comput. Educ. **94**, 1–17 (2016)
9. Onishi, K.: Learning data structures and algorithms with smartphone applications. Asial Corp. (2019). (in Japanese)

Automated Reporting of Code Quality Issues in Student Submissions

Oscar Karnalim[1,2(✉)], Simon[3], William Chivers[1], and Billy Susanto Panca[2]

[1] University of Newcastle, University Drive, Callaghan, NSW 2308, Australia
oscar.karnalim@uon.edu.au, william.chivers@newcastle.edu.au
[2] Maranatha Christian University, Surya Sumantri Street No. 65, Bandung, West Java 40164, Indonesia
billy.sp@it.maranatha.edu
[3] Callaghan, NSW 2259, Australia

Abstract. Despite its importance in industry, code quality is often overlooked in academia. A number of automated tools to report code quality have been developed but many of them are impractical to use. They either are developed as a standalone tool, require the use of a particular IDE, and/or need historical data. This paper presents code quality issues reporter (CQIS), a tool that can be embedded in an assessment submission system; it identifies code quality issues for each student submission via static analysis, and reports those in an HTML page whose link is sent via email. The tool covers 52 code quality issues specifically curated for academia, 32 for Java and 20 for Python. According to four quasi-experiments with a total of 274 students, students with CQIS are likely to have fewer code quality issues so long as the expected solutions are long and complex and code quality is considered as part of the marking. These students are also more aware of code quality, and readability in particular.

Keywords: code quality · static analysis · automation · programming · computing education

1 Introduction

The code written by computing undergraduates is expected not only to function well but also to be of high quality [1]; the code should be understandable by itself without the need to read additional documentation or to conduct functional tests. Writing high-quality code is a desirable skill in industry, but is often overlooked in academia.

A number of automated tools to check the quality of one's code have been developed. Many of them are designed for general use and can be applied in both

Published by Springer Nature Switzerland AG 2023
T. Keane et al. (Eds.): WCCE 2022, IFIP AICT 685, pp. 517–529, 2023.
https://doi.org/10.1007/978-3-031-43393-1_47

industry and academia. Two examples are checkstyle[1], for Java, and Flake8[2], for Python.

General-purpose tools often cover code quality issues that are not relevant for academia, and give explanations that are somewhat too technical for novices. Consequently, a number of dedicated tools for academia have been developed [2]. Integrating such tools into an existing teaching environment may be challenging as they either require the use of a particular integrated development environment (IDE) [3,4], are not readily integrated in both IDE and assessment submission system [2,5], or need both historical data and manual labeling [6].

In response to this gap, this paper proposes an automated tool, code quality issues reporter (CQIS), which can be integrated in many teaching environments. The tool is embedded in an assessment submission system, and reports code quality issues for each student submission via static analysis. Instructors can thus freely choose the IDE for their students, and are not required to provide historical data and do manual labeling.

CQIS currently works for Java and Python submissions. It identifies 32 Java code quality issues: eight concerning comments and identifier names, and the remainder selected from checkstyle by considering their academic relevance and rewording the explanations. For Python, CQIS identifies 20 code quality issues: eight concerning comments and identifier names, and the remainder selected from Flake8 in the same manner as from checkstyle for Java. CQIS, the code, and the documentation are publicly available[3].

Our study has two research questions, following the introduction of CQIS:

- RQ1: Do students with CQIS have fewer code quality issues in their submissions?
- RQ2: Are students with CQIS explicitly aware of various aspects of code quality?

2 Related Work

While educating students to improve the quality of their code, it is important to identify common code quality issues and focus on them first. Three studies have been conducted partly for that purpose. Keuning et al. [7] identify code quality issues relating to algorithms and structure in a large BlueJ data set of Java programs, and find that many of the issues are related to inefficient code and bad design. Aivaloglou & Hermans [8] identify code quality issues in programs collected from a Scratch repository, and find that more than a quarter of the programs contain both unused and reused code. De Ruvo et al. [9] identify 16 code quality issues that relating to program flow in introductory programming, including unnecessary if-else branches, unused variables, and assigning a variable

[1] https://checkstyle.sourceforge.io/.
[2] https://flake8.pycqa.org/en/latest/.
[3] https://github.com/oscarkarnalim/CQS.

to itself. Half of the programs that they examined have at least two distinct issues.

There are some tools that set out to improve student awareness of code quality by automatically reporting code quality issues. FrenchPress [3], an Eclipse plug-in for Java programs, reports four kinds of misuse covering booleans, fields, loop controls, and public modifiers. The study shows that at least a third of students provided with the tool are motivated to look further into their programs.

WebTA [4] is a IDE-like environment that constantly gives students feedback about their Java programs, covering stylistic issues in addition to common errors and failed tests. The stylistic issues themselves concern five anti-patterns: misplaced code, pseudo-implementation, localised instance variables, 'knee-jerk' (pointless use of a recently learnt feature), and repeated resource instantiation. The study does not report the effectiveness of the tool on student perceptions or performance.

Three automated tools are distinct from common IDEs. Refactor Tutor [2] is a web-based tool that specifically educates students about refactoring Python code for better quality. Covered aspects include branching, expressions, loops, and statements. Unique to the tool, the hints are given gradually so that they are not overwhelmed with too much technical detail at once. By analysing student log data [10], the authors show that students with programming background are able to identify and fix code quality issues.

Style++ [5] is a standalone tool to report C++ code quality issues covering comments, identifier names, and code size. Students can voluntarily use the tool before submitting their final programs. The evaluation found that the tool is perceived as beneficial for students. Further, the quality of the submitted programs is somewhat improved.

AutoStyle [6] is an automated tool that is integrated with an assessment submission system. Code quality issues are reported for each submission, and students can resubmit their programs as many times as they wish. To define the set of code quality issues, instructors are expected to provide submissions from a previous offering of the course and to manually label clusters of the submissions.

Some studies consider code quality as part of their analysis. Pettit et al. [11] analyse how students improve the quality of their C++ programs in sequential submissions. Breuker et al. [12] compare code quality of first-year programs with that of second-year programs. Tempero et al. [13] confirm that a count of objects can be useful to assess the quality of student design in object oriented projects.

3 The Tool

This paper proposes CQIS, an automated tool to report code quality issues in student submissions. Unlike existing tools, CQIS allows instructors to choose the IDE for students, and does not require yjrm to provide labeled data from a previous offering of the course.

CQIS is embedded in an assessment submission system, and reports code quality issues for each student submission via static analysis. In total, CQIS covers 32 Java code quality issues and 20 Python code quality issues, and can provide explanations in both English and Indonesian.

CQIS can be embedded in other systems since it is designed as a library with console-based arguments. It accepts a student program and generates an HTML page that reports code quality issues. An example report is shown in Fig. 1.

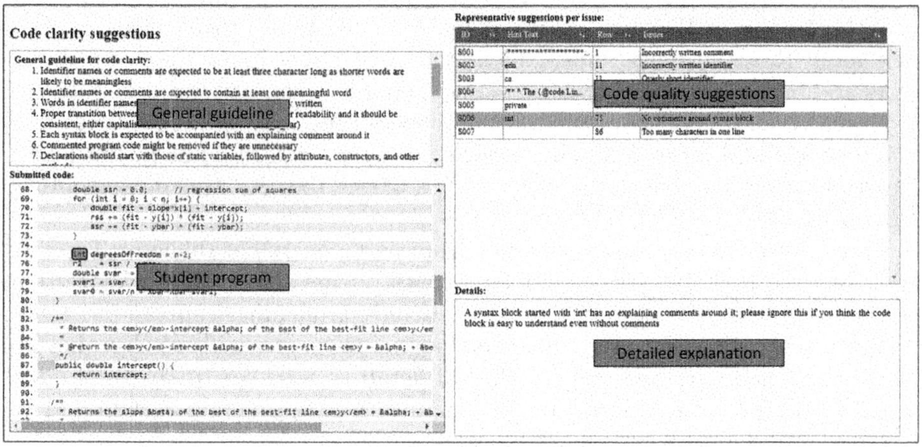

Fig. 1. CQIS generated HTML page; the text is not expected to be readable; the labels in boxes are added for clarity.

A CQIS HTML report contains four panels. The general guideline panel summarises all code quality rules that have been applied. The student program panel shows the input student program displayed with Google Prettify[4]. The code quality suggestions panel lists code quality issues from the student program, including their hint text and position. If a row is clicked, an explanation of the issue and suggestions for fixing it will be displayed in the detailed explanation panel. Further, the student program panel will locate and highlight the hint text.

The selected Java code quality issues can be seen in Table 1. J01-J04 relate to comments. J01 occurs when a comment is empty or has less than three characters; J02 occurs when a comment contains only common words (e.g., conjunction words), which are typically meaningless on their own. The common words are detected with Apache Lucene[5]. J03 occurs when at least one word is misspelled, as checked by Apache Lucene with two English dictionaries (American[6] and British[7]) and one Indonesian[8]. J04 occurs when a syntax block has no explaining comment.

[4] https://github.com/google/code-prettify.
[5] https://lucene.apache.org/.
[6] https://github.com/dwyl/english-words.
[7] https://www.curlewcommunications.uk/wordlist.html.
[8] http://indodic.com/SpellCheckInstall.html.

Table 1. Selected Java code quality issues.

ID	Issue
J01	Overly short comment
J02	Words in comment not meaningful
J03	Misspelled words in comment
J04	No comment before or after the first line of syntax block
J05	Overly short identifier
J06	Words in identifier not meaningful
J07	Misspelled words in identifier
J08	Inconsistent naming style for identifier
J09	Abstract class and prefix 'abstract' in class name inconsistently used
J10	Array declaration: brackets used after variable name
J11	Inline conditionals
J12	Too many boolean operators in expression
J13	Lowercased constant attribute name
J14	Unexpected declaration order expected order: static variables, attributes, constructors, other methods
J15	Empty syntax block
J16	Empty catch block
J17	Only one empty line needed as separator
J18	Empty statement
J19	Too many statements in method
J20	Overly long line
J21	Multiple variable declarations
J22	Missing braces in branching or looping statements
J23	Overly deep nested looping
J24	Overly deep nested branching
J25	Overly deep nested try-catch
J26	Too many statements per line
J27	Non-static attribute access without 'this' keyword
J28	Unnecessarily complex boolean expression (except return)
J29	Unnecessarily complex boolean return statements
J30	String comparison with '=='
J31	Too many parentheses
J32	Unnecessary semicolon

J05-J08 relate to identifiers. The first three are similar to J01-J03 but are now applied to identifier sub-words, tokenised with a module inspired by a software search engine [14]. The module splits sub-words based on two concatenation styles in naming identifiers: camel case (e.g., 'codeQualityIssueReporter') and underscore (e.g., 'code_quality_issue_reporter'). The last issue (J08) occurs when

Table 2. Selected Python code quality issues.

ID	Issu
P01	Overly short comment
P02	Words in comment not meaningful
P03	Misspelled words in comment
P04	No comment before or after the first line of syntax block
P05	Overly short identifier
P06	Words in identifier not meaningful
P07	Misspelled words in identifier
P08	Inconsistent naming style for identifiers
P09	Inappropriate indentation
P10	No space after comment prefix (#)
P11	Overly long line
P12	Multiple statements in one line
P13	Unnecessary semicolon
P14	Compilation error
P15	Unused module
P16	Improper use of 'break' or 'continue'
P17	Improper use of 'return'
P18	Locally undefined identifier
P19	Duplicate function parameter
P20	Unused local variable

both concatenation styles exist in identifiers and one is more common than another.

J09-J32 are adapted from checkstyle, a general-purpose tool to report Java code quality issues. However, these issues are specifically curated for academia, and undergraduate students in particular. According to our analysis of 15,323 program files from seven distinct programming courses [15], all of these issues except J25 (overly deep nested try-catch) occur in student programs. However, we have still included J25 to accompany the similar issues with other syntax constructs (J23 with looping and J24 with branching).

Selected Python code quality issues can be seen in Table 2. P01-P08 are similar to J01-J08, but applied to Python rather than Java. The others (P09-P20) are adapted from flake8, another general-purpose tool dealing with code quality, but this time for Python. P09-P20 are considered relevant for academia; all of them except P16 (improper use of 'break' or 'continue') are found in the student programs from seven distinct programming courses [15]. P16 is still included, for its similarity with P17.

Two important remarks about CQIS. First, CQIS allows instructors to choose which code quality issues the system will reported. Some of them might be subjective and considered acceptable in certain cases. Second, an early version of CQIS that only covers code quality issues in comments and identifier names (J01-J08, P01-P08) has been published elsewhere [16].

4 Evaluation

4.1 Addressing RQ1: Fewer Code Quality Issues

RQ1 asks whether students with CQIS have fewer code quality issues. This is measured by way of four quasi-experiments each of which compares student code quality issues from two academic semesters of a particular course.

Details of the courses used in the experiments can be seen in Table 3; the control group consists of students without CQIS, and the intervention group of students with CQIS. The first course was offered to third-year undergraduates of an information systems degree while the remaining courses were offered to undergraduates of an information technology degree (third-year, second-year, and first-year respectively). A large proportion of the involved students are males aged 17 to 22. While it would be interesting to analyse the findings according student demographics, such analysis is not permitted by our ethics approval.

In the first two experiments, the assessments are about developing GUI applications with Java, and code quality is considered as part of the marking. For the next two experiments, the assessments expect console-based programs, and code quality is encouraged but not considered in the marking. The data structures assessment tasks are about implementing and using various linear data structures, whereas the introductory programming assessments are about basic programming syntax and problem solving. Most of the courses have weekly assessments, except the control group's offering of the second experiment, in which each assessment is to be completed in three or four weeks.

Table 3. Courses involved in the experiments; the control and intervention columns report the number of students, classes, and assessment tasks.

Experiment	Course	Language	Control	Intervention
First	Business application programming	Java	34 stud, 1 cls, 16 asmt	19 stud, 1 cls, 25 asmt
Second	Advanced object oriented programming	Java	27 stud, 1 cls, 3 asmt	47 stud, 2 cls, 21 asmt
Third	Data structures	Python	46 stud, 2 cls, 14 asmt	33 stud, 1 cls, 8 asmt
Fourth	Introductory programming	Java & Python	33 stud, 1 cls 16 asmt	35 stud, 1 cls 25 asmt

In each experiment the comparison is conducted in three stages. First, student submissions are grouped based on their corresponding assessment task. In offerings that have two classes, one assessment offered to both classes is considered as two separate assessments. Second, for each assessment task, its language-specific code quality issues are identified and counted with a modified version of CQIS. J01-J08 and P01-P08 are not reported since their effectiveness have been discussed in our previous study [16]. Third, average numbers of code quality issues from the two offerings are compared for each issue and for all issues combined. The significance is validated with two-tailed unpaired t-test with 95% confidence level.

Table 4 shows that for the first experiment, students with CQIS have fewer code quality issues in their programs. The assessments are about developing GUI applications; Given that the solutions are usually long and complex, student submissions naturally have many code quality issues that can be reminded by CQIS. Further, students are more encouraged to read the report given that code quality is part of the marking.

Table 4. Reported code quality issues with significant and substantial differences for four quasi-experiments; for each experiment, the intervention group used CQIS and the control group did not.

Experiment	Issue	Mean of control	Mean of intervention
First	All	5363	155
	J10	27	0
	J13	12	0
	J14	2345	11
	J16	24	0
	J17	567	79
	J19	43	0
	J20	2141	29
Second	J20	16	39
	J22	2	18
	J31	17	2
Third	All	433	256
	P10	179	93
Fourth	P10	23	6

When analysed per issue, students with CQIS appear to be specifically aware of the expected Java declaration order (J14) where static variables should be declared first, followed by attributes, constructors, and other methods. The number of reported issues is significantly and substantially lowered. They also learn not to put too much code in one line (J20). Students might see both issues reported a lot given that the arise quite frequently.

Five other issues arise less frequently among students using CQIS. They involve brackets after variable name in array declaration (J10), lowercased constant name (J13), empty catch block (J16), missing or unnecessary line separator (J17), and too many statements in one method (J19). All are relatively easy to fix. J19 falls into this category since it occurs mostly in GUI-related methods, where most of the statements do not rely on in-method results.

J09, J23, J25, and J27 do not arise in either the control or intervention groups. Students are already aware that the use of the 'abstract' prefix should be consistent with the use of abstract classes (J09), and that non-static attributes should be accessed with the keyword 'this' (J27). Overly-deep nested looping and try-catch (J23 and J25) are also not expected in these assessment tasks.

For the second experiment, students using CQIS have comparable code quality issues with those not using it: the difference is neither significant nor substantial as it is not reported in Table 4. Although students using CQIS might have greater awareness of code quality, the impact might be diminished by the fact that assessments of the control group have a longer completion period (three or four weeks per assessment), so students in this group have more time to reread and check the quality of their own code prior submission.

Although there is no significant reduction overall, students using CQIS have fewer issues related to unnecessary parentheses (J31). They appear to understand that expressions with unnecessary parentheses are prone to misinterpretation.

It is worth noting that J20 (overly long line) and J22 (missing braces in branching or looping statements) are the other two issues with substantial differences; but these differences are in favor of the control group, students without CQIS. With more limited time in completing assessments, students with CQIS appear not to prioritise fixing these issues; long lines and missing braces do not substantially affect code readability.

Overly-deep nested looping (J23) is the only issue that occurs in neither control nor intervention groups. The assessments do not expect such complex loops as they are mostly about developing business applications.

In the third experiment, students with CQIS generally have fewer code quality issues (see Table 4). This is interesting given that code quality is not specifically considered in the marking of the intervention group. Students with CQIS appear to understand that getting used to writing high quality code might be useful in the future.

When analysed separately, P10 (missing space after comment opening) is the only issue with substantial reduction. This is expected as the issue is common and easy to fix.

In both control and intervention groups from the third experiment, three code quality issues never occur: compilation error (P14), as Python mainly relies on an interpreter; improper use of 'break' and 'continue' (P16), as these keywords are not specifically taught; and duplicate function parameter (P19), as function parameters seldom have similar names.

For the fourth experiment, students using CQIS have comparable code quality issues overall, as Table 4 does not report substantial and significant difference at the general level. The assessments expect short solutions, and code quality is not considered in the marking. P10 (no space after comment prefix) is the only issue with substantial reduction on students with CQIS. The issue can be fixed easily even without programming knowledge.

There are nine code quality issues that do not arise with either the control or the intervention group. Six of them are related to Java: inconsistency in abstract class naming (J09), inline conditional (J11), lowercased constant attribute name (J13), overly deep nested looping (J23), overly deep nested try-catch (J25), and access to non-static attributes without 'this' (J27). The concepts underlying these issues are not covered in the course materials (J09, J11, J13, J25, J27) or the assessment tasks are too simple (J23).

The other three code quality issues that do not arise are related to Python: compilation error (P14), as that kind of error rarely happens; improper use of 'return' (P17), as functions and methods are seldom used in these assessment tasks; and duplicate function parameter (P19), as each function parameter is expected to have a unique name.

4.2 Addressing RQ2: Explicit Awareness of Some Aspects in Code Quality

RQ2 asks whether students are explicitly aware of some aspects of code quality. This is addressed by asking students to list up to three remarkable pieces of information that they learned while using CQIS. The survey was performed at the end of semester in all intervention groups described in Table 3. One hundred and seven students responded to the survey, and together mentioned 18 distinct remarkable pieces of information.

Among the provided information, general knowledge about high quality code is noted by most students (47). This is expected, given that CQIS aims to improve the quality of submitted programs. The second most remarkable piece information is that programmers should use declarative identifier names (34), variable names in particular. Mistyped names sometimes occur, and while CQIS does not always provide good spelling correction, it can at least report the issue.

The next two remarkable pieces of information are not to write too much code in one line (22) and to use white space for readability (17). While completing assessments, many students focus on how to complete the assessments, and they can easily overlook putting appropriate white space (including line breaks) to enhance readability.

Where to put comments (13), more declarative comments (12), and more efficient syntax (11) are three other remarkable pieces of information that were listed. These are mostly noted by students of business application programming and advanced object oriented programming since in these courses, the use of comments is explicitly encouraged and is considered as part of the marking. Further, due to the advanced level of their course materials, it is more likely that some students will begin by writing poor quality code and will then revise it to improve the quality.

The remaining remarkable pieces of information are noted by only a few students. They are about adequate use of braces and/or parentheses (7); removing unused code (4); expected order of declarations in Java (3); adequate use of semicolons (3); clarity in inline conditionals (2); clarity in complex boolean expressions (2); consistent identifier naming style (2); difficulty of expanding code with low quality (1); need for space after comment prefix (1); need for braces in branching or looping statements (1); and writing one statement per line (1).

We have grouped and analysed the responses for each course. However, since the findings are fairly comparable to the general finding described above, we choose not to report those results.

4.3 Discussion

Students using CQIS have fewer code quality issues (RQ1) when the assessments expect long solutions (first and third experiments). The impact can be further improved by designing more advanced assessments and explicitly including code quality in the marking scheme (first experiment). CQIS might be less useful for assessments with long completion periods, given that students have enough time to check the quality of their own code prior to submission (second experiment).

Students who use CQIS observe that their knowledge of code quality is improved (RQ2). They are particularly aware of the need to writing declarative names, to avoid writing too much code in one line, to use white space for readability, to write declarative comments in appropriate locations, and to write more efficient syntax.

5 Conclusion and Future Work

This paper presents CQIS, an automated tool to report a selection of code quality issues. The tool can be integrated in many teaching environments by being embedded in some assessment submission systems. It also does not require students to use a specific IDE, or require instructors to provide historical data. According to our evaluation, students using CQIS are likely to have fewer code quality issues in their submissions if the assessments expect long and complex solutions and code quality is considered as part of the marking. Students using CQIS also become more aware of aspects of code quality, mostly pertaining to readability.

The study has two limitations that can be addressed in the future work. First, the evaluation was performed only at one institution, with a moderate number of students. Replicating the study at other institutions with more students might strengthen the findings. Second, student awareness of code quality was addressed only by asking students to list up to three remarkable pieces of relevant information. Some lessons that they have learned might not be reported as they are not in the top three. Future work might list all knowledge aspects of code quality and ask students which aspects they believe have improved.

From the technical perspective, we plan to improve the quality of spelling checking as some of the suggested words do not make sense for students. We also plan to introduce gamification for further student engagement, especially in courses whose assessments do not consider code quality in the marking.

References

1. Lethbridge, T.C., Leblanc, R.J., Jr., Kelley Sobel, A.E., Hilburn, T.B., Diazherrera, J.L.: SE2004: recommendations for undergraduate software engineering curricula. IEEE Softw. **23**(6), 19–25 (2006)
2. Keuning, H., Heeren, B., Jeuring, J.: A tutoring system to learn code refactoring. In: 52nd ACM Technical Symposium on Computer Science Education, USA, pp. 562–568. ACM (2021)
3. Blau, H., Moss, J.E.B.: FrenchPress gives students automated feedback on Java program flaws. In: ACM Conference on Innovation and Technology in Computer Science Education, Lithuania, pp. 15–20. ACM (2015)
4. Ureel II, L.C., Wallace, C.: Automated critique of early programming antipatterns. In: 50th ACM Technical Symposium on Computer Science Education, USA, pp. 738–744. ACM (2019)
5. Ala-Mutka, K., Uimonen, T., Jarvinen, H.-M.: Supporting students in C++ programming courses with automatic program style assessment. J. Inf. Technol. Educ. **3**, 245–262 (2004)
6. Roy Choudhury, R., Yin, H., Fox, A.: Scale-driven automatic hint generation for coding style. In: Micarelli, A., Stamper, J., Panourgia, K. (eds.) ITS 2016. LNCS, vol. 9684, pp. 122–132. Springer, Cham (2016). https://doi.org/10.1007/978-3-319-39583-8_12
7. Keuning, H., Heeren, B., Jeuring, J.: Code quality issues in student programs. In: ACM Conference on Innovation and Technology in Computer Science Education, Italy, pp. 110–115. ACM (2017)
8. Aivaloglou, E., Hermans, F.: How kids code and how we know: an exploratory study on the Scratch repository. In: ACM Conference on International Computing Education Research, Australia, pp. 53–61. ACM (2016)
9. De Ruvo, G., Tempero, E., Luxton-Reilly, A., Rowe, G.B., Giacaman, N.: Understanding semantic style by analysing student code. In: 20th Australasian Computing Education Conference, Australia, pp. 73–82. ACM (2018)
10. Keuning, H., Heeren, B., Jeuring, J.: Student refactoring behaviour in a programming tutor. In: 20th Koli Calling International Conference on Computing Education Research, Finland, pp. 4:1–4:10. ACM (2020)
11. Pettit, R., Homer, J., Gee, R., Mengel, S., Starbuck, A.: An empirical study of iterative improvement in programming assignments. In: 46th ACM Technical Symposium on Computer Science Education, USA, pp. 410–415. ACM (2015)
12. Breuker, D.M., Derriks, J., Brunekreef, J.: Measuring static quality of student code. In: 16th Annual Joint Conference on Innovation and Technology in Computer Science Education, Germany, pp. 13–17. ACM (2011)
13. Tempero, E., Denny, P., Luxton-Reilly, A., Ralph, P.: Objects count so count objects! In: ACM Conference on International Computing Education Research, Finland, pp. 187–195. ACM (2018)
14. Karnalim, O., Mandala, R.: Java archives search engine using byte code as information source. In: International Conference on Data and Software Engineering, Indonesia, pp. 1–6. IEEE (2014)

15. Karnalim, O., Simon: Work-in-progress: code quality issues of computing undergraduates. In: IEEE Global Engineering Education Conference, Austria, pp. 1734–1736. IEEE (2022)
16. Karnalim, O., Simon: Promoting code quality via automated feedback on student submissions. In: IEEE Frontiers in Education, USA, pp. 1–5. IEEE (2021)

Improvement of Fill-in-the-Blank Questions for Object-Oriented Programming Education

Miyuki Murata[1(✉)], Naoko Kato[2], and Tetsuro Kakeshita[3]

[1] National Institute of Technology, Kumamoto College, Koshi, Japan
m-murata@kumamoto-nct.ac.jp

[2] National Institute of Technology, Ariake College, Omuta, Japan
naoko@ariake-nct.ac.jp

[3] Saga University, Saga, Japan
kake@is.saga-u.ac.jp

Abstract. We have developed a programming education tool, named 'pgtracer', which provides fill-in-the-blank questions in C programming. Pgtracer provides programs and trace tables with blanks. A trace table represents the execution sequence of the target C program. As a result of our research, we could estimate the achievement level of the students and clarify the answering process by analyzing the logs collected by pgtracer. To improve software quality and reusability, object-oriented technology is important from various perspectives, and there is an urgent need to train engineers proficient in object-oriented programming. Thus, we are extending pgtracer to the Java program. Trace tables are extended to represent individual instances and message sending among the instances. In this paper, we create fill-in-the-blank questions for the Java program and attempt to have students solve some of the fill-in-the-blank questions using the "embedded answer (Cloze)" question format of Moodle's question function. The results of the trial are discussed, and improvements are made to the questions and the user interface. We also introduce the notion of ignorable blanks which students do not need to fill. This type of blank is useful to increase the variety of questions.

Keywords: Learning Analytics (LA) · programming education · object-oriented programming · Java · fill-in-the-blank question

1 Introduction

The development of information technology in recent years has led to the provision of IT-based services via many application domains. As these services become more sophisticated and complex, object-oriented programming becomes crucial to improving the quality and efficiency of these services.

Although object-oriented programming education is provided at universities and institutes of technology to software engineering students, insufficient training time and lack of teaching staff hinder sufficient programming training. Considering this situation,

Published by Springer Nature Switzerland AG 2023
T. Keane et al. (Eds.): WCCE 2022, IFIP AICT 685, pp. 530–541, 2023.
https://doi.org/10.1007/978-3-031-43393-1_48

we are developing pgtracer, a programming education support tool that provides fill-in-the-blank questions for Java programming. This project is an extension of pgtracer for C programming [1, 2]. Since the pgtracer log contains every activity of the students, we can obtain valuable knowledge of the student understanding level and characteristic process of the students by analyzing the logs collected by pgtracer using learning analytics (LA) methods [3, 4]. The knowledge obtained from these LA functions can be used to improve the effectiveness of programming education.

In this paper, we developed fill-in-the-blank questions for Java programs. We proposed fill-in-the-blank questions for pgtracer utilizing a Java program and trace tables representing the behavior of the Java program [5]. This is the advantage of our approach. A trace table corresponds to an instance and represents the values of the variables and outputs of the instance as well as the message sending between instances. It is necessary for students to correctly trace changes in variable values and messages sending to understand and write a program. We extended a trace table for the Java program to represent message sending. Furthermore, we introduced a special type of blank that students do not need to fill. This type of blank allows teachers to provide more flexibility in controlling the difficulty level of the questions while hiding hints.

In this paper, we perform a trial using our initial fill-in-the-blank questions in an actual class using a quiz, one of the Moodle activities, to evaluate the validity of the questions. We also analyze the results of the trials and improve the fill-in-the-blank questions and the user interface. These considerations will be useful for the implementation of pgtracer for Java programs.

This paper is organized as follows. In the next section, we describe related research on object-oriented programming education and learning analytics. We introduce pgtracer functions in Sect. 3. In Sects. 4 and 5, we explain fill-in-the-blank questions for a Java program and the creation of the fill-in-the-blank questions respectively. In Sect. 6, we describe the lecture and the trial, and in Sects. 6.2 and 6.3 we analyze the evaluation results. In Sect. 7, we discuss the improvement of the fill-in-the-blank questions and the user interface of pgtracer. We conclude this paper in the last section.

2 Related Works

Hsiao et al. proposed web-based parameterized questions for Java [6]. The questions examined the final value of a variable or predicted the text being printed. Pgtracer allows blanks to be set not only in the final value but also in the variable values during program execution. This is useful to facilitate students' understanding of the program.

Truong et al. introduced a static analysis framework for a Java program [7]. The student answers the entire program for an assigned question. The system uses the model answers and predefined gaps for analysis. In pgtracer, the same kind of problem can be created by defining the entire program as a blank. Furthermore, by analyzing the answer logs of all students, pgtracer can discover trends in errors other than the expected ones.

Hauswirth et al. proposed an Informa clicker system to train Java programming [8]. Informa provides several types of questions related to program code such as multiple-choice questions but does not address the tracing of variables.

Funabiki's research group proposed several programming education systems for Java that utilize fill-in-the-blank problems such as [9]. However, they do not address message sending or variable values for each step of program execution. Our proposed question provides more flexibility because it can also define the blanks for these parts.

There have been studies on the use of LA in programming education. Fu et al. have developed a system that provides a learning dashboard by analyzing error message output at compilation for the C programming language [10]. Carter et al. estimate students' abilities by comprehensively considering the results of analyzing log data in programming activities and students' learning behaviors [11]. The log data used in these studies include programs submitted by students and error messages output at compilation, etc. Grover et al. used logs of submitted programs, students' solution behavior, and operations (execution, insertion, editing, and deletion) for block-based programming to estimate computational thinking estimation [12]. Although research results in C language and block programming have been published, research on object-oriented programming languages, which is the subject of this paper, is new. Pgtracer logs every time each blank is filled in. This allows us to collect candidate answers not only the final answer but also the process leading up to the answer. This makes it possible to analyze the process of students' answers.

3 Programming Education Support Tool Pgtracer Utilizing Fill-in-the-Blank Questions

Pgtracer for the C language provides fill-in-the-blank questions for a student and automatic evaluations of the student's answer [1]. Pgtracer also automatically collects student logs, such as the student's answer, the correct answer, and the required time, immediately after filling in each blank. Pgtracer provides analysis functions for the collected log from various viewpoints such as analysis functions of each student, each question, each blank, and the detailed learning process of a student [2]. The analysis functions are useful for analyzing student achievement and learning processes. Figure 1 shows the programming education process utilizing pgtracer.

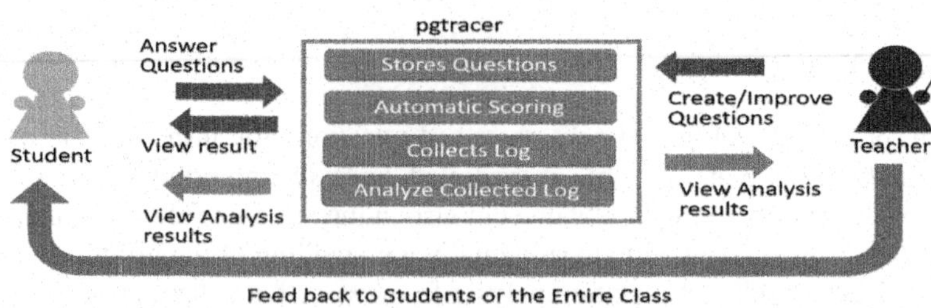

Fig. 1. Programming Education Process utilizing pgtracer.

4 Fill-in-the-Blank Questions of the Java Program

4.1 Blanks Within a Program

In this section, we describe the fill-in-the-blank questions of the Java program. Figure 2 shows an example.

Since the high-level component of a Java program is a class, there is one source file for each class. Thus, the fill-in-the-blank question of a Java program generally contains multiple source files. We also assign a step number to each statement, including the instance variable and local variable definitions, because they may contain initialization statements. Step numbers are assigned according to the following rules and correspond to the step numbers in the trace table described in Sect. 4.2.

- Assign a sequential step number to each statement defined in the Java program, such as assignment statement, method call, and control statement, such as if, else, switch, case, default, and return as well as an instance variable definition.
- The step number starts from 1 in each method definition.
- Assign step numbers such as "x.y" to compound statements having nested structures.

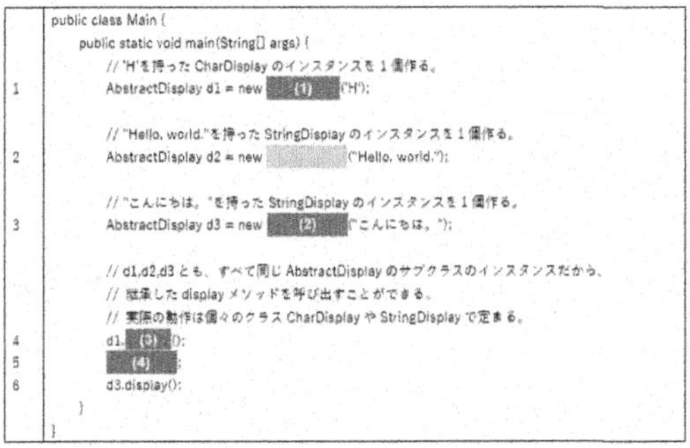

Fig. 2. Example of a Program with Blanks (Template Method, Main Class)

A token is a string that cannot be further subdivided, such as a variable name, class name, operator, or keyword. A comment is defined as a token. Pgtracer allows defining of a blank at an arbitrary sequence of tokens. Thus, part of a statement, an entire statement, and a sequence of consecutive statements can be defined as a blank.

There are two types of blanks. One requires an answer and the other does not. We call a blank of the latter type an ignorable blank. By defining the ignorable brank, it is possible to hide codes and comments that are clues to the blanks that are required answers, such as when there are similar codes before and after the blank. The difficulty level of a blank can be controlled more flexibly by introducing ignorable blanks.

Because it is also possible to hide comments using the ignorable blank, we can also control the difficulty level of a question. To distinguish between the blanks and ignorable blanks, the backgrounds of these blanks are filled with different colors. The blanks without a number represent ignorable blanks in Fig. 2.

4.2 Blanks Within a Trace Table

A Java program is executed through a message sending between the objects. If the trace table is expressed in the order of the execution steps, then the table becomes complicated. Therefore, a trace table was defined for each object. Each instance is expressed as

"ClassName#X" to distinguish between the instances of a class. For example, the identifier of the first generated instance of the class "IDCardFactory" is "idCardFactory#1", which will be the name of the trace table. The proposed trace table is defined as follows. Figure 3 shows a part of this for space limitation.

In the "Caller of the Method" column, the object from which the method is called, the method name, and the step number are displayed. The upper row in the sub-item of the "Argument of the Method", "Instance Value", "Local Variable of the Method" and "External Object" columns shows the data type or class name. The bottom row in the sub-item is the variable name. In each cell, the stored value is displayed as the basic data type. An instance identifier is displayed for a class. If no area is allocated to the variable in the program, nothing is displayed. When the instance creates another instance or sends a message to an instance, all instances are listed as sub-items in the "External objects" column.

Caller of the Method			Step of Called the Method			Argument of the Method		Instarnce Value	Local Variable of the Method	External Object			Output/Return Value of the Method
Caller of			Class	method	step	String	Product	List	Product	IDCard	IDCard	IDCard	戻り値
object	method	step				owner	product	owners	p	idCard#1	idCard#2	idCard#3	
Main	main	1	IDCardFactory	IDCardFactory									
Main	main	2	Factory	create	1	結城浩							
			(1)	(2)	1	結城浩				IDCard			
						結城浩							idCard#1
			(3)	(4)	1	結城浩			idCard#1				
					2				idCard#1				
			(5)	(6)	1		idCard#1		idCard#1	getOwner			
								{idCard#1}	idCard#1				
			Factory	create	2			{idCard#1}	idCard#1				
			Factory	create	3			{idCard#1}	idCard#1				(7)
Omitted													

Fig. 3. Example of a Trace Table with Blanks (Factory Method, Instance ID = idCardFactory#1)

An object can be called multiple times. A double line is drawn in the trace table to distinguish the series of processes in each method call. Specifically, a double line is drawn under the row that corresponds to the return statement.

A single line of code can contain multiple operations, such as assigning the result of a function call to a variable. The purpose is to represent the order in which each operation is performed in a trace table. This allows the student to trace the program completely. In this case, the steps of the two operations are identical. The operation represented by a row in the trace table can be recognized by referring to the column of instance variables and external objects.

In a trace table, the value of each cell is defined as a blank. Specifically, a blank can be defined on a variable value, output value, step number, object identifier, class name, and method name. Moreover, a blank can also be defined for a data type, class name, variable name, or object name. As in the case of the program, it is possible to define ignorable blanks that do not require answers in a trace table.

5 Creation of Fill-in-the-Blank Questions

In this section, we propose a development strategy for the fill-in-the-blank questions. We plan to provide the created problems in "Exercise in Programming III" in the first semester of the 2021 academic year. The class was conducted in the third academic year of computing courses at our university.

5.1 Proving Fill-in-a-Blank Questions

The students learned Python and C++ in their first and second years, respectively. They began learning object-oriented programming using Java in the target class. The class intends to learn the purpose and use of various tools used in the practical field of software development using the Java language. The textbook [13] explains the 23 design patterns introduced by Gamma et al. [14]. In the lecture, detailed explanations of the language were not provided to the students. To support them in mastering Java programming, we provide the fill-in-the-blank questions proposed in this study.

The fill-in-the-blank questions were created by selecting 12 topics from the textbook and using sample programs. The topics were selected in consideration of the contents to be covered in the class, and the levels of the problems were set as beginner, intermediate, and advanced according to the contents of the topics and the order in which they were taught (Table 1).

Table 1. The Topic of the Providing Fill-in-the-Blank Questions

Level	Beginner	Intermediate	Advanced
Design Pattern (The section in the Textbook)	TemplateMethod (3)	Decorator (12)	Adapter (2)
	FactoryMethod (4)	Strategy (10)	Builder (7)
	Iterator (1)	AbstractFactory (8)	Command (22)

5.2 Development Policy of the Fill-in-the-Blank Questions

Since the students had already learned the basics of programming through the previous classes, we designed questions for the students to learn the basics of object-oriented programming and design patterns.

The blanks within the program are defined mainly to check the understanding of Java-specific grammar such as class definitions and to check the execution flow of message sending. Furthermore, the blanks within the trace table are mainly defined for topics related to the caller objects, such as classes, method names, step numbers; items related to the called object; and values that change as messages are transmitted.

Considering these factors, we developed the following policies to create questions at appropriate levels on the topic.

1. Define approximately ten blanks that required an answer per question.
2. Create two problems for one topic with different difficulty levels.
3. Clarify the educational objective of each question.
4. Clarify the intent for each blank.
5. To define blanks within a program, we used individual tokens as the basis at the beginner level. We used a longer sequence of tokens for intermediate and advanced levels.

6. To define blanks within a trace table, we mainly used variable values at the beginner level. At the intermediate level, we used more blanks, such as instance identifiers and methods.

According to our previous experience [3, 4], we found that if the number of blanks in the question was too many, students' motivation would decrease, which would prevent them from continuously using pgtracer. In our previous experiment, five blanks were defined per question because the target students were beginners in the C language and the total number of lines of the program was approximately 20. In this study, however, approximately ten blanks are defined for each question because the level of programming proficiency of the students is expected to be higher than that of the previous students. The total number of lines in the program is larger for the same reason.

The second policy is defined to investigate the difference in difficulty between the types of questions. Furthermore, the educational objective of the questions and the intention of each blank, clarified by Policies 3 and 4, are used to analyze the learning logs. Policies 5 and 6 are defined to clarify the differences among beginner, intermediate, and advanced levels.

6 Primary Trials of the Questions at Lecture

6.1 Trial Using Moodle

Because the Java version of pgtracer is still under development, we used the embedded answer (cloze) feature of Moodle to represent the answer field. The programs and trace tables for the fill-in-the-blank questions were manually created and displayed as images. Since a fill-in-the-blank question contains several Java programs and trace tables, each was displayed in a separate tab on the browser. Representative screenshots of a question are available on the web due to space limitations.[1]

Each week, we conducted trials with the following problems, as indicated in Table 2. Suffixes such as PR and TR in the problem ID indicate that the problem type is a program or trace table, respectively. The column on the right shows the number of examinees on the first attempt. Ex01_PR, Ex01_TR, and Ex08_SP are sample problems that explain how to answer or the concept of a trace table. Therefore, we have excluded these problems from the discussion.

6.2 Answer Result

Table 3 represents the number of blanks and the average of correct answer ratio for each of the fill-in-the-blank questions whose problem type is "program", categorizing the blanks into two types that are composed of one or more tokens. At both beginner and intermediate levels, the average of correct answer ratio for the blanks containing multiple tokens was lower than for the blanks containing a token. This indicates that it is more difficult for students to answer a blank containing multiple tokens. For both blanks containing one or more tokens, the average of correct answer ratio is lower

[1] http://y-page.y.kumamoto-nct.ac.jp/u/m-murata/WCCE2022/.

Table 2. Problems and Number of Examinees

Week	Design Pattern	level	Problem Type	Problem ID	# of Blanks	# of Examinees
1	Exercise to understand fill-in-the-blank questions and trace tables		Program	Ex01_PR	6	67
			Trace table	Ex01_TR	4	
6	Template Method	Beginner	Trace table	Ex06_PR	12	71
		Beginner	Program	Ex06_TR	12	
7	Factory Method	Beginner	Trace table	Ex07_PR	9	58
8	Simple Example	Beginner	Program	Ex08_SP	2	67
	Iterator pattern	Beginner	Trace table	Ex08_TR	10	
10	Factory Method	Beginner	Trace table	Ex10_TR	9	61
11	Composite	Beginner	Trace table	Ex11_PR	11	69
13	Strategy	Intermediate	Program	Ex13_PR	6	66
14	Observer	Intermediate	Program	Ex14_PR	10	65

at the intermediate level than at the beginner level. At the intermediate level, we set blanks that required an understanding of the processing flow of the program to derive the correct answer. Therefore, we were able to reflect on the difficulty level intended by the contestants, even if it was a blank containing a token.

Table 3. Number of blanks and right answer correct for problems whose type is "program"

Level of Problem	# of problem	Blanks containing a Token		Blanks containing Multiple Tokens	
		# of Blanks	Average of Correct Answer Ratio (%)	# of Blanks	Average of Correct Answer Ratio (%)
Beginner	3	22	76.5	10	57.7
Intermediate	2	11	67.2	9	41.9

Table 4 represents the number of blanks and the average correct answer ratio for the fill-in-the-blank questions whose problem type is "Trace table" categorized by the type of blanks. Table 4 indicates that the average correct answer ratio for the step number of the method caller and the variable value that answers the instance is low. This suggests that problems related to object-oriented specific method invocations and instances are difficult for students.

Table 4. Number of blanks and correct answer ratio for problems which type is "Trace table"

Type of Blanks	# of Blanks	Average of Correct Answer Ratio (%)
Call for constructor or method	16	72.5
Step number of the calling method	3	46.0
Called Class	2	61.7
Return value (Instance)	5	64.0
Variable value (Instance)	1	38.8
Variable value (Basic type)	4	71.1

6.3 Questionnaire Result

On the last day of the lecture, we administered a questionnaire regarding the trial. The total number of responses received was 69. Regarding fill-in-the-blank questions, 63.8% answered that they were rather difficult. This suggests that the level of difficulty of the problem is appropriate. The number of fill-in-the-blank questions was appropriate for 87.0% of the respondents. We consider that ignorable blanks allowed us to set an appropriate number of blanks to be answered while hiding codes and variable values that could be used as hints.

Furthermore, we obtained 14 comments from the students. There are five responses regarding the method of displaying the programs and trace tables. In this experiment, the programs and trace tables were presented as images in multiple tabs, but it was necessary to switch tabs when understanding the program and trace messages sent and received, which may hinder students' understanding. In addition, three responses are related to writing answers. They complained about incorrect answers because of differences in capitalization and lowercase letters when typing. However, in actual programming, the difference between lowercase and uppercase letters can be fatal; therefore, we should consider it educationally reasonable and require the correct input.

7 Improvement of Fill-in-the-Blank Questions

In this section, we describe the improvement of the fill-in-the-blank questions. The programs and trace tables for the fill-in-the-blank questions described in Sect. 4 are referred to as old programs or old trace tables.

7.1 Improvement of Programs

In the old programs, step numbers were also added to the instance variable-definition statements. However, in Java, instance variables are initialized with default values when the constructor is called and values are assigned by the statements written in the constructor. This default value is implicitly set and not explicitly stated in the program. For this reason, we decided against assigning a step number to the statement of an instance variable definition and describing the default value in the trace table because they would confuse students. In addition, explicitly stating the value of the instance variable in the first-instance variable assignment statement is consistent with the policy of Java programs that there is no indefinite state, such as variable values.

The sample programs referenced to create the old programs were from a textbook published in 2004 and did not correspond to the evolution of the Java language, such as support for generic terms. The third edition of the textbook was published in 2021, and the sample programs have been updated since 2004 to reflect the evolution of the Java language. Using the sample programs in the third edition, it is now possible to provide problems that correspond to the latest evolution of Java.

When the incorrect answers were carefully examined, we found that there were other answers in addition to the set of correct answers and that there were answers that were incorrect because they filled the blank with other correct answers. For example, when “i < 5” was the correct answer, students answered “5 > i” or “i ≤ 4”, resulting in an incorrect answer. To avoid this, we adjusted the location of the blanks so that the correct answer was unique. As an improvement on the previous example, we can eliminate another correct answer by not setting a blank in part “i <”. Instead, we set it in “5”.

In addition, many answers were incorrect because of the presence or absence of whitespace, such as “i < 5” when “i < 5” was correct. According to Java coding conventions [15], a space should be inserted before and after the comparison operator. In system development, the reusability of programs is required, and it is important to be able to code according to the guidelines, not just to have a program that works correctly. Therefore, we decided to treat this as an incorrect answer.

7.2 Improvement of Trace Tables

The trace tables were created by manually tracing the program; however, now that the automatic trace table generation function has been completed with a few minor adjustments [16], we are using the trace tables created by this function. This function outputs a trace table in an Excel file format by providing a Java program and input data. Each sheet corresponds to each instance in the output Excel file. With the completion of this function, the development cost of a trace table is significantly reduced.

In the old trace table, the definitions of instance variables are also shown in the trace table, and the values were assumed to be indefinite; however, for the reasons mentioned in Sect. 7.1, we decided not to include them in the trace table as well.

7.3 User Interface

In the old fill-in-the-blank questions, programs and trace tables were presented as images. The images were displayed in a new browser tab. According to the questionnaires from the students, several answers were including that the switching tabs were troublesome and made it difficult to understand.

Therefore, as shown in Fig. 4, when asking fill-in-the-blank questions, the frame function of the browser is used to display a list of programs and trace tables. By selecting an item from the list, the program or trace table concerned is displayed. In addition, for instance, the collapsing function is used to switch between showing and hiding instances of the same class. This user interface can also be applied to pgtracer.

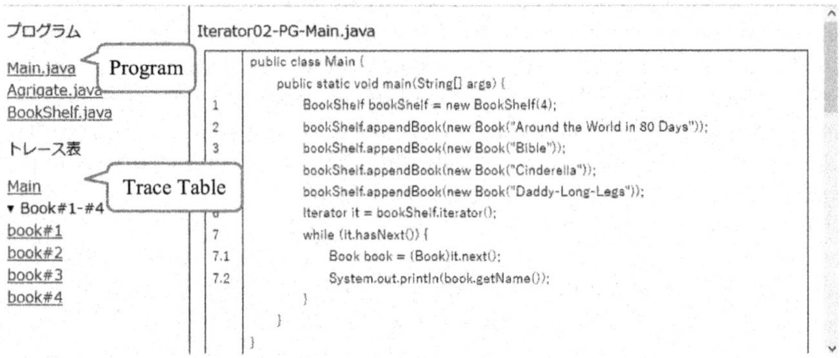

Fig. 4. Improvement of the User Interface

8 Conclusions and Future Works

In this paper, we improve the fill-in-the-blank questions for pgtracer, a Java programming education support tool using fill-in-the-blank questions. The improvement is made based on the results of the trial. We also improve pgtracer user interface to reduce the difficulty of solving problems for students. These improvements are expected to help students understand the program and trace tables, and promote continuous learning. In pgtracer for the C language, the program answered by the student is compiled and executed, and if the output is the same, it is judged to be the correct answer. By incorporating this module into the Java language pgtracer, we believe that it will be possible to control the difficulty level of the problem by making the setting of blank removal more flexible. In this study, we did not analyze the required time as analytical data, but we believe that an analysis including the required time is necessary to estimate students' programming ability. The analysis of response time is an issue to be addressed in the future.

In the future, we plan to complete pgtracer and conduct experiments using the problems we created. Using the collected data, we will be able to extract the tendency of students' answers and the tendency of questions that are prone to mistakes using LA techniques, and we believe that the obtained knowledge will contribute to Java programming education.

Acknowledgment. This research is supported by JSPS KAKENHI under grant numbers #20K03265 and #20K03233.

References

1. Murata, M., Kato, N., Kakeshita, T.: Development and evaluation of programming education support tool pgtracer utilizing fill-in-the-blank question. IPSJ Trans. Comput. Educ. **2**(2), 20–36 (2016). (in Japanese)
2. Kakeshita, T., Ohta, K.: Student log analysis functions for web-based programming education support tool pgtracer. IPSJ Trans. Comput. Educ. **5**(2), 456–468 (2019)
3. Kakeshita, T., Murata, M.: Application of programming education support tool pgtracer for homework assignment. Int. J. Learn. Technol. Learn. Environ. **1**(1), 40–61 (2018)
4. Murata, M., Kakeshita, T.: Analysis method of student achievement level utilizing web-based programming education support tool pgtracer. In: 5th International Conference on Learning Technologies and Learning Environment (LTLE 2016), Kumamoto, Japan, pp. 316–321 (2016)
5. Murata, M., Kato, N., Kakeshita, T.: Fill-in-the-blank questions for objected-oriented programming education. In: 10th International Congress on Advanced Applied Informatics (IIAI-AAI), pp. 116–122 (2021)
6. Hsiao, I., Brusilovsky, P., Sosnovsky, S.: Web-based parameterized questions for object-oriented programming. In: E-Learn'2008: World Conference on E-Learning (2008)
7. Truong, N., Roe, P., Bancroft, P.: Static analysis of students' Java programs. In: Sixth Australasian Computing Education Conference (ACE 2004) (2004)
8. Hauswirth, M., Adamoli, A.: Teaching Java programming with the Informa clicker system. Sci. Comput. Program. **78**(5), 499–520 (2013)
9. Funabiki, N., Matsushima, Y., Nakanishi, T., et al.: A Java programming learning assistant system using test-driven development method. IAENG Int. J. Comput. Sci. **40**(1), 38–46 (2013)
10. Fu, X., Shimada, A., Ogata, H., Taniguchi, Y., Suehiro, D.: Real-time learning analytics for C programming language courses. In: 7th International Conference on Learning Analytics and Knowledge (LAK 2017), pp. 280–288 (2017)
11. Carter, A.S., Hundhausen, C.D., Adesope, O.: The normalized programming state model: predicting student performance in computing courses based on programming behavior. In: ICER 2015 - Proceedings of the 2015 ACM Conference on International Computing Education Research, pp. 141–150 (2015)
12. Grover, S., Basu, S., Bienkowski, M., Eagle, M., Diana, N., Stamper, J.: A framework for using hypothesis-driven approaches to support data-driven learning analytics in measuring computational thinking in block-based programming environments. ACM Trans. Comput. Educ. **17**(3), Article no. 12 (2017)
13. Yuki, H.: An Introduction to Design Patterns using Java Programming Language, 3rd edn. SoftBank Creative, Tokyo (2021). (in Japanese)
14. Gamma, J., Helm, E., Johnson, R., Vlissides, R.: Design Patterns Elements of Reusable Object Oriented Software. Addison-Wesley Professional, Boston (1994)
15. Code Conventions for the Java Programming Language. https://www.oracle.com/java/technologies/javase/codeconventions-contents.html. Accessed 25 Feb 2021
16. Kishikawa, M., Ohtsuki, M., Kakeshita, T.: Generating trace table for Java programs. In: Proceedings of the 11th International Congress on Advanced Applied Informatics (IIAI-AAI), pp. 200–207 (2022)

Cycles in State Transition as Trial-and-Errors in Solving Programming Exercises

Taku Yamaguchi[1](✉), Yoshiaki Matsuzawa[2], Ayahiko Niimi[3], and Michiko Oba[3]

[1] Graduate School of Future University Hakodate, Hakodate, Hokkaido, Japan
g3221002@fun.ac.jp

[2] Aoyama Gakuin University, Sagamihara, Kanagawa, Japan
matsuzawa@si.aoyama.ac.jp

[3] Future University Hakodate, Hakodate, Hokkaido, Japan
niimi@fun.ac.jp, oba@tachibana-u.ac.jp

Abstract. In recent years, Japan's education system has started regarding trial-and-error favorably and is accordingly evaluating its strategy. Evaluation of trial-and-error has become crucial to learning analytics. Jigsaw Code is a programming exercise that gives students shuffled code blocks of a solution program, including fake ones, and asks them to rearrange the blocks in the correct order. It logs the solving actions of each student. This paper shows that the cycles in the state transition of the solution indicate the students' trial-and-error process. Two hundred and thirty undergraduates solved 11 puzzles (problems) of Jigsaw Code. We analyzed the transition of the solution sequence at each solving action and found cycles in the state transition. For 97% of the plays, including the frequently appearing cycles, the first state of each cycle was the subsequence of the final solution. A cycle in the solution state transition shows that the student returned to the cycle's first state after searching for other solutions, as they probably regarded the cycle's first state as leading to the correct final solution.

Keywords: Trial-and-error · Programming Exercises · Cycles in the State Transition

1 Introduction

The education system in Japan regards trial-and-error favorably and evaluates the strategy of trial-and-error. It is a human advantage to find a satisfactory solution to a problem that seemingly has no correct solution. Accordingly, trial-and-error evaluation is becoming crucial in learning analytics.

However, there have been few mechanical ways to estimate students' trial-and-error processes other than to find backtracking. Some researchers are evaluating the solving processes of programming exercises where students rearrange the shuffled code fragments of a solution program into the correct form instead of writing codes from scratch.

Published by Springer Nature Switzerland AG 2023
T. Keane et al. (Eds.): WCCE 2022, IFIP AICT 685, pp. 542–553, 2023.
https://doi.org/10.1007/978-3-031-43393-1_49

However, those researchers exclude trial-and-error or depend on the existence of the correct solution.

In this paper, we propose estimating students' trial-and-error processes in solving such exercises independently from the existence of the correct solution by detecting cycles in the state transition of the process.

1.1 Trial-and-Errors in Education

In recent years, the education system of Japan has started regarding trial-and-error favorably and is evaluating its strategy (described in the next paragraph); in other words, trial-and-error processes can have strategies. The Central Council for Education of Japan has stated that, "unlike Artificial Intelligence, humans can set their own goals and find satisfactory solutions to *problems which have no solutions* [emphasis added], even in a complex environment of diverse contexts. Humans develop these abilities through learning." [1, p. 10]. The Council remarked that it is necessary to help children "go beyond the efficiency of solving problems with predetermined solutions and the efficiency of completing predetermined procedures" toward engaging in trial-and-error [1, p. 10]. Hence, the solving process of problems with no solution can be considered the subject of learning analytics.

The Curriculum Research Center in the National Institute for Educational Policy Research published reference materials explaining learning assessment [2]. In these materials, as examples of trial-and-error strategies, they mentioned that, while determining the parameters of a mathematical expression, "trial-and-error without perspective" is defined as "inputting a randomly selected number and then making adjustments"; additionally, "trial-and-error with perspective" is defined as "making adjustments after obtaining a rough estimate." [2, p. 59]. Moreover, they explained that trial-and-error processes with and without perspective are "fully satisfied" and "generally satisfied," [2, p. 59] respectively. Therefore, there are different types of trial-and-errors, which they evaluate positively.

Evaluation of trial-and-error is becoming increasingly crucial in learning analytics. It may not necessarily be similar to evaluating the edit distance from the optimal process of the correct solution, or analyzing the correlation with the percentage of correct solutions, because sometimes there are no correct solutions.

1.2 Research Ignoring Trial-and-Error

Parsons problems (also referred to such as Parson's problem and Parsons puzzles) are a programming exercise [3–5] that shuffles the code blocks and asks students to rearrange them in the correct position. They are similar to our Jigsaw Code described in Sect. 3.1 (see Fig. 1). As a representation of students' puzzle-solving behavior, Kumar [3] proposed a solution sequence, defined as a sequence of blocks in the temporal order when placed in the correct position. The block's temporal order is when it is finally placed in that position by the student, even though the block may be placed in the correct position (and removed from there) multiple times in the solving process.

If a student moves blocks in the order s3 (the ID of a code block), s5, s4, s2, s1, s5, s2, s4, and those blocks are in the correct position, the solution sequence will be [s3, s1, s5, s2, s4]. In this case, the solution sequence does not show that the student moved s5 a second time, s4 a third time, and s2 a fourth time.

As Kumar stated, this approach loses trial-and-error information. He regarded trial-and-error—such as backtracking and looping behavior—as unproductive and as a sign of students' misconception, not as part of a problem-solving strategy. The concept of "misconception" implies that a correct solution exists. This view of trial-and-error may be due to the usage of the Parsons puzzle for rote learning the syntax of a programming language.

1.3 Research Identifying Backtracking as an Intentional Trial-and-Error

Helminen et al. [8] proposed representing the solving processes in Parsons problems as state transitions of the solution and visualized them as diagrams (defined later in the Method section). In individual transitions, there were loops (we call these "cycles" in this paper) returning to states visited earlier in the same transition path. They identified different kinds of loops. Backtracking is a kind of loop returning to "an earlier state by undoing the operations exactly in the reverse order." A circular loop is a kind of loop "returning to an earlier state via different intermediate states." Helminen et al. stated that it is difficult to say whether a circular loop is an intentional trial-and-error or an accident, while one might assume backtracking is intentional.

This paper reveals that also a circular loop points out intentional trial-and-error.

1.4 Research Depending on the Correct Solution

Through split-paper testing [6], Kuno [7] proposed evaluating thinking, judgment, and expression abilities, not rote learning. For example, he proposed to evaluate the ability to argue in a well-reasoned order. Split-paper ("*Tanzaku*" in Japanese) testing belongs to the same type of programming exercise as Parsons problems and our Jigsaw Code (described in Sect. 3.1).

Ueno et al. [9] proposed representing the solving processes in split-paper testing as state transitions of the solution and visualizing them as diagrams (defined later in the Method section). They represent the solution as a sequence of split papers. Unlike the process described in the Method section, their method aggregates all of the students' transitions into a single diagram. Using such a diagram, they have found, for example, that students tend to construct a program from outer parts, such as def and end. However, they pointed out that the diagram contains too much information to identify the stumbling points (trial-and-errors). They defined trial-and-error depending on the transitions of students providing both correct and incorrect solutions. Hence, it may be challenging to apply their method to problems with no solutions.

2 Objective

This paper aims to show how cycles in the state transition of the solution indicate the students' trial-and-errors process. A cycle refers to a clue to a student's knowledge rather than their misconception. The students who formed the cycle believed that the first state would help them reach the correct solution, and used it as a branch point.

3 Method

This paper defines the state transition of the solution and the cycle (described in Sect. 3.2) in the solving process of Jigsaw Code puzzles (described in Sect. 3.1) and elucidates how a cycle can help infer a player's trial-and-error process (described in Sect. 3.3). Subsequently, we verify this by confirming that the first state in the cycle is a subsequence of the player's final solution (described in Sect. 3.4). We analyze data from 11 Jigsaw Code puzzles, played by 230 undergraduates in an introductory programming course for first-year undergraduate students (described in Sect. 3.5).

3.1 Jigsaw Code

We developed and used the Jigsaw Code—a programming exercise—in class, which gives students shuffled code blocks of a solution program, including fake ones, and asks them to rearrange these blocks in the correct order. Accordingly, it logs the solving actions taken by each student [10].

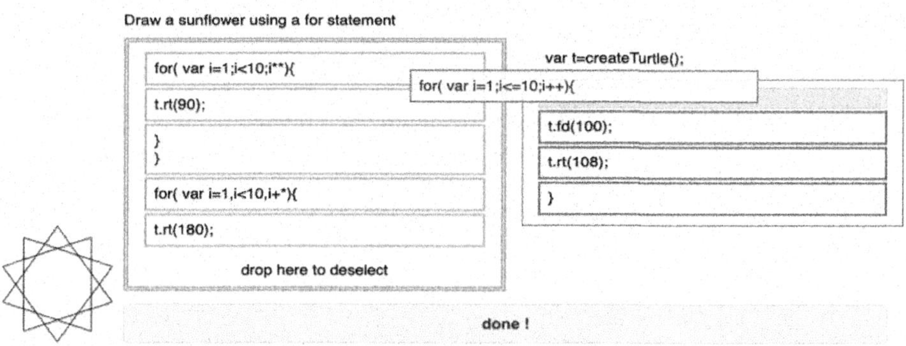

Fig. 1. "2-2 Drawing Sunflower": A sunflower drawing (left) and puzzle on a programming exercise Jigsaw Code (right). Students select pieces from the left side, deselect and sort pieces on the right side, and complete the correct pieces on the right side to draw a sunflower. "var t = createTurtle();" is placed above the right side box in advance and could not be moved.

Figure 1 illustrates Jigsaw Code on the screen. Similar to a jigsaw puzzle, Jigsaw Code breaks the whole code into code fragments or *pieces*. When a student, *player*, starts solving a puzzle, it shuffles some pieces and places them in the choice box, the frame on the left. Sometimes, it places some correct pieces above, inside, or below the solution box at the beginning, which is the frame on the right. Unlike the original jigsaw puzzle, there may be *fake pieces* mixed in. A player then drags a correct piece from the choice box and drops it into the solution box. When a piece turns out to be incorrect, the player can drag and drop it back into the choice box. A player can sort pieces by dragging and dropping pieces inside both boxes. By repeating these actions, the player completes the puzzle. As well as the jigsaw classroom [11], Jigsaw Code was named after a jigsaw puzzle because students are processing pieces (portions of a picture) of their answer—the complete picture—.

Jigsaw Code collects the player's actions in the solving process:

- type of the action
- piece ID of the target of the action
- sequence of IDs of the pieces in the solution box
- a timestamp.

Jigsaw Code collects these actions associated with a Document ID generated uniquely for the play.

3.2 State Transition of Solution Sequence and Cycles

State of the Solution. The state of the solution refers to the sequence of the pieces in the solution box. Jigsaw Code records the state when a player makes an action in the solving process. A piece has an ID that is usually hidden from the players. We represent the state as a sequence of IDs of the pieces. Figure 2 illustrates a state in the process of solving the puzzle "2-2 Sunflower." S1, s2, and ... are the pieces' IDs, respectively. The instruction "Draw a sunflower using a for statement" is a piece and has an ID as well. The sequence of IDs "s8, s3, s5, s6" in the solution box is the state of the solution at the point.

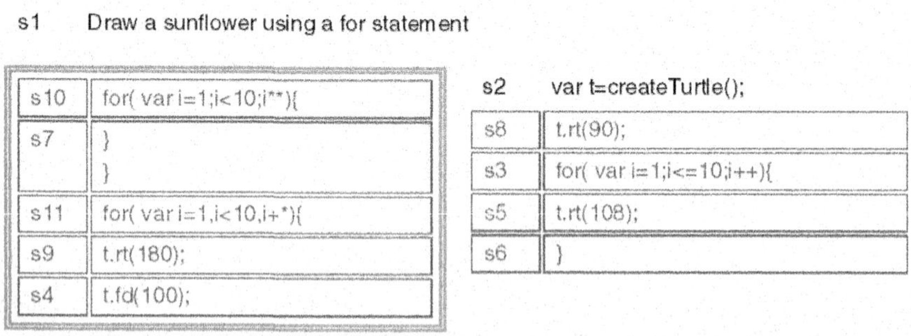

Fig. 2. In the middle of the solution process. The sequence of the piece IDs "s8, s3, s5, s6" is the state at this time and is not correct as a final solution.

State Transition and Diagram. The state of the solution will change with progression. We represent the state transition in the diagram shown in Fig. 3. In the diagram, a circle represents a state. A label in the circle is the sequence of the pieces representing the state. An arrow represents a transition from one state to another state. In this paper, the state diagram represents the real-life transition, while the state diagram used in software engineering represents possible transitions. The diagram does not aggregate all students' transitions, but corresponds to a single one. Figure 3 includes three examples of the state transitions diagram. A number on the arrow counts the times the player has transitioned. In the state transition diagram on the right, the player transitioned from state "s2, s3" to "s2, s3, s10" twice in one solution process. We draw these diagrams by "d3-graphviz"[1] (and D3.js) on a web browser.

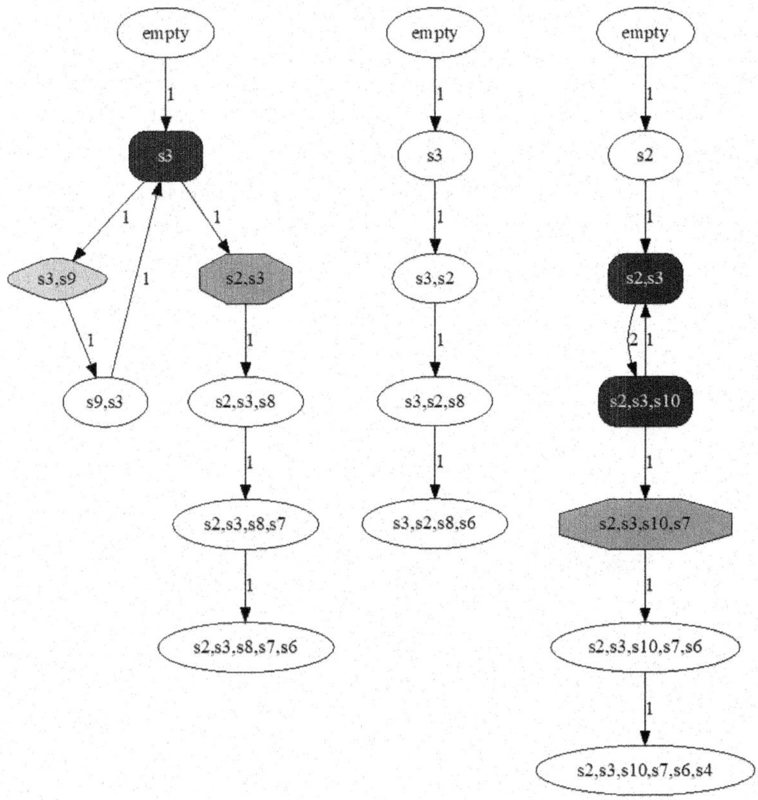

Fig. 3. Examples of state transition diagrams. The left includes one cycle, the middle includes no cycles, and the right includes two cycles. The ellipses are the normal states, the rounded box is the first and the last state in the cycle, the diamond is the following state of the first in the cycle, and the octagon is the following state of the last state out of the cycle.

Cycle. A cycle in a state transition graph is a non-empty closed sequence of states in which all states (vertices), except the first and the last state, are distinct. In Fig. 3, the left diagram has one cycle (Helminen et al. called it a circular loop [8]), and the middle has none. The right has two cycles: ("s2, s3," "s2, s3, s10," "s2, s3") and ("s2, s3, s10," "s2, s3," "s2, s3, s10") (Helminen et al. called them backtracking [8]). The shape indicates the type of state. The rounded box represents the cycle's first and last state; the diamond represents the following state of the first state; the octagon represents the next state of the last one out of the cycle. A state is not precisely shape-coded because it sometimes belongs to more than one of these three types (rounded box, diamond, and octagon.) Fig. 4 extracts three cycles from Fig. 3: the left cycle is from the left state transition diagram, and the rest two are from the right.

[1] GitHub - magjac/d3-graphviz: Graphviz DOT rendering and animated transitions using D3 https://github.com/magjac/d3-graphviz.

The First Piece Moved in the Cycle. The piece moved first in the cycle represents the difference between the first state (rounded box) and the next state (diamond). In the left cycle in Fig. 4, s9 is the first piece moved. In the righthand cycle, the first action is a removal: s10 is removed from the solution box and is the first piece moved in the cycle.

The First Piece Moved After the Escape from the Cycle. The first piece moved after the escape from the cycle represents the difference between the last state (the first state, too, rounded box) and the next state of the last state (octagon). In the left cycle in Fig. 4, s2 is moved right after the escape. When the last state (rounded box) is the final solution of the player, no piece is moved after the escape from the cycle.

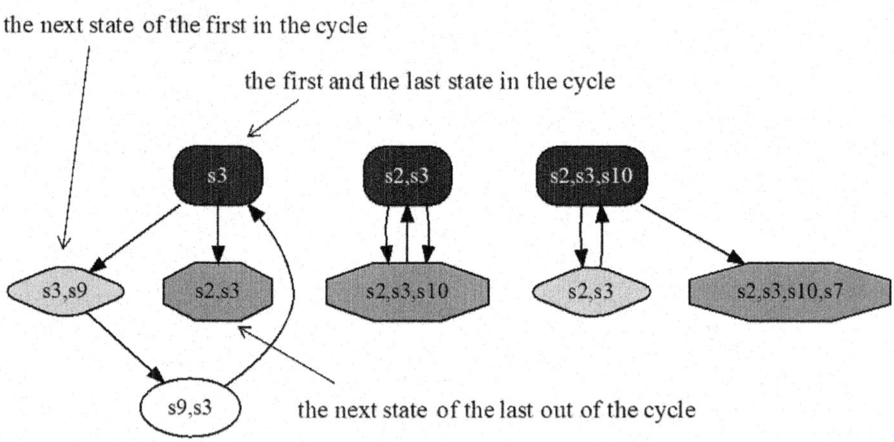

Fig. 4. Start and endpoint of the cycle, the first state after the start, the first state after escape from the cycle.

3.3 Trial-and-Error

Cycles in a state transition provide a clue to inferring a player's trial-and-error. A cycle indicates that the player has returned to the first state in the cycle. They moved from the first state to explore the correct solution (trial), reached some state and realized it is a wrong state (error), returned to the first state (the last state); this state transition forms a cycle. At the time, the player must have regarded the cycle's first state, their current state, as leading to the correct final solution, which is why they returned to the first state.

In the state transition on the left in Fig. 5, the player reached "s3, s4." Then, they took a detour to "s3, s4, s8," instead of going straight to "s3, s4, s5" from "s3, s4." They tried "s3, s4, s8", realized that it was wrong, and returned to "s3, s4."

3.4 Verification

If the cycle's first state is the subsequence of the player's final solution, it is more likely that the player regarded the first state as leading to the correct final solution (Fig. 5).

It does not matter whether the player's final solution is correct. Here, a subsequence of a given state (sequence of pieces) is one that can be derived from the given state by deleting some or no pieces, without changing the order of the remaining pieces.

In the transition diagram on the left in Fig. 5, the player did not go from "s3, s4, s8" back to "s4, s3" possibly because they did not regard "s4, s3" as leading to the correct solution. In other words, it was not a coincidence that the player did not go back to "s4, s3" because it was not the subsequence of their final solution "s3, s4, s5, s6."

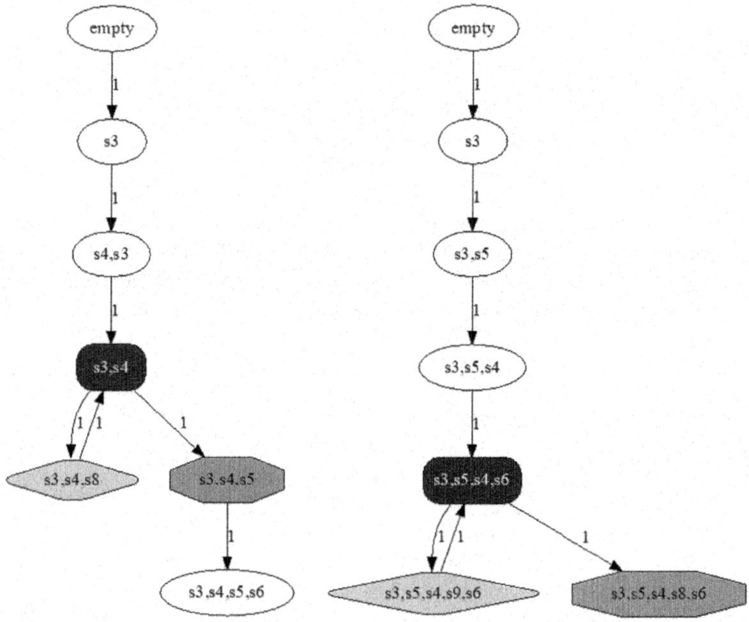

Fig. 5. State transitions include cycles whose first state (rounded box) is the subsequence of the final solution. "S3, s5, s4, s6" is the subsequence of "s3, s5, s4, s8, s6" in the right hand diagram.

We now evaluate the data collected by Jigsaw Code to verify our estimation method for trial-and-error. We take the frequently appearing cycles and examine if the first state in the cycle is the subsequence of the final solution. Here, "frequently appearing" means that the cycle appears over average + two standard deviation times. If a cycle appears frequently, it is not a coincidence; there must be a reason. Furthermore, if the frequently appearing cycle's first state is frequently the subsequence of the final solution, that is not a coincidence either.

3.5 Data

We evaluate the data collected by Jigsaw Code used in short tests in an introductory programming course for first-year undergraduate students. Two hundred and thirty students took the course online and solved eleven puzzles in total in 2020. The course covers variables, conditional branch, loop, and function with JavaScript, HTML, and Turtle Graphics Library.

The students solved the short tests at the beginning of the class. The purpose of the puzzles was to review the previous lesson. The teacher designed the puzzles to include fake pieces to let students (players) carefully select and deselected correct/fake pieces. The puzzles covered various topics, such as drawing a sunflower using the Turtle Graphics Library (Fig. 1), drawing an hourglass, and calculating the discounted rate for travel.

4 Result

For 97% of the plays that include the frequently appearing cycles, their first states of the cycles are the subsequence of their final solution (Table 1).

Table 1. The last column is the ratio of plays whose cycle's first state is the subsequence of their final solution. A: frequently appearing cycles, B: plays (state transitions) that include the frequently appearing cycles (A), C: plays that include frequently appearing cycles (A), and the first state of the cycle is the subsequence of the final solution.

puzzle	No. of A	No. of B	No. of C	C/B (%)
1-1 Drawing hourglass	3	69	68	99
1-2 Determining concentration	2	20	20	100
1-3 Replacing digits	4	52	45	87
2-1 PCR	4	30	29	97
2-2 Drawing sunflower	2	8	8	100
3-2 Calculating the square	1	9	9	100
3-3 Multiplication table	2	31	31	100
4-1 Drawing donut	2	27	23	85
4-2 Determining leap year	1	11	11	100
5-1 Go To Travel discount rate #1	1	22	22	100
5-2 Go To Travel discount rate #2	4	22	22	100
Average				97

5 Discussion

97% is high. For example, "S3, s5, s4, s6" is the subsequence of "s3, s5, s4, s8, s6" and has $4! - 1 = 23$ different anagrams that are not the subsequence. It is not an accident but intentional that the cycle's first state is the subsequence of the final solution.

What happened in the process, according to the cycle in Fig. 5? Let us observe the pairs of the first piece moved in the cycle (diamond) and the first piece moved after the escape from the cycle (octagon). Figure 6 shows the final solution of the player for "2-2 Drawing Sunflower". Half of the pairs derived from the data were (s8, s5). The state transition diagram on the left of Fig. 5 is an example for the pair (s8, s5).

The piece s5 "t.rt(108);" commands the turtle to turn right by 108°, whereas s8 "t.rt(90);" commands it to turn right by 90°. The diagram on the left of Fig. 5 shows that the players selected s8 at first (trial) but deselected it later (after realizing their error); they went back to "s3, s4," and this time, selected s5 instead of s8. They figured out the angle of turning to the right through trial-and-error. The teacher mixed the fake piece s8 to test students' comprehension.

They did not go back to "s4, s3" further because they believed "s3, s4" to be correct. We infer their belief because "s3, s4" is a subsequence of their final solution "s3, s4, s5, s8," shown in Fig. 6.

Furthermore, it seems that s5 and s8 were the players' alternatives [12]. We will leave that verification to future research.

A cycle in the solution state transition shows that the student returned to the cycle's first state after searching other solutions, possibly because they regarded the cycle's first state as leading to the correct final solution. When they returned to the cycle's first state exactly in the reverse order—backtracking—it seemed that they thought computationally [13]. When they did not return exactly in the reverse order, it is unclear whether they thought computationally; for example, the entire cycle may be one step in backtracking. We will leave it to future research.

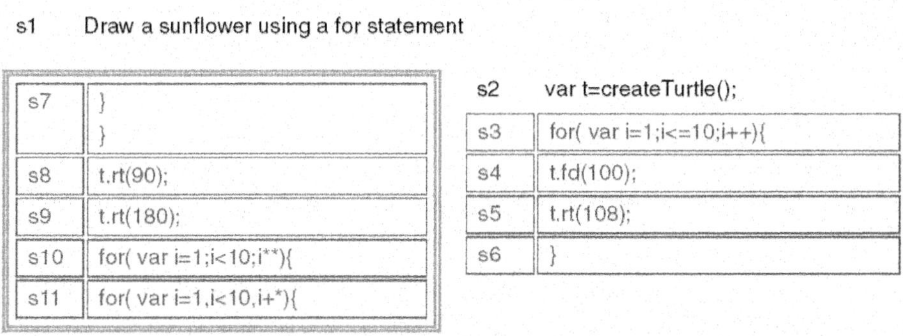

Fig. 6. The final solution for the "2-2 Drawing Sunflower" example

Trial-and-error does not always begin with selecting a new piece. Some cycles begin with the removal of pieces. In Fig. 7, the player probably thought s5 unnecessary in the rounded box state, removed it, and transitioned to diamond state; however, they retrieved it later and transitioned to the rounded box state again.

There may be a trial-and-error process that does not form a cycle. In Fig. 8, the player added s6 to the state "s10, s4, s5," removed s10 from the state "s10, s4, s5, s6," and added s3 to the state "s4, s5, s6." This process does not form a cycle. The state "s10, s4, s5, s6" may be an error for the player, but it is unclear when their trial began. We will leave this type of trial-and-error for future research.

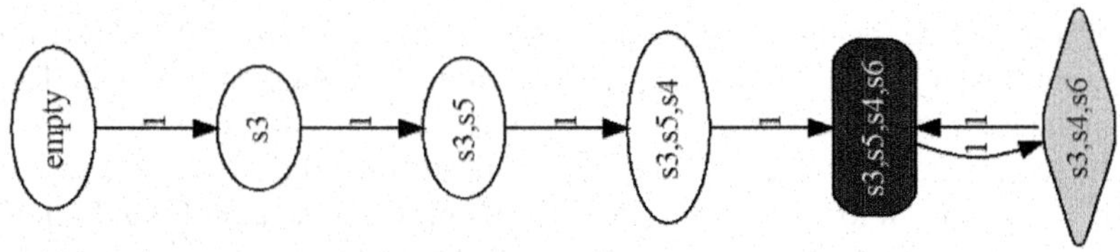

Fig. 7. A state transition diagram (inverted counterclockwise) for "2-2 Drawing Sunflower." It contains a cycle that begins with deselecting of a piece s5.

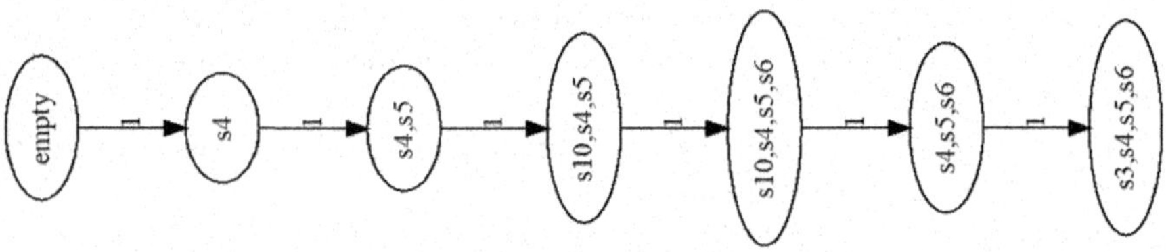

Fig. 8. A state transition diagram (inverted counterclockwise) for "2-2 Drawing Sunflower." It does not contain any cycles but may represent trial-and-error because of selecting and deselecting piece s10.

6 Conclusions

The cycle is a clue to the player's knowledge, rather than their misconception. It mechanically points out more trial-and-errors than backtracking does. This finding meets the demands of Japanese education regarding trial-and-error favorably and evaluates trial-and-error strategy.

In future research, we expect cycles to provide a clue as to what the players are trying to do, such as their alternatives they attempt. We expect to apply this method to problems that have no solutions because the above-discussed results and discussions are independent of whether the player's final solution is correct.

A limitation of this study is that the trial-and-error process does not always form a cycle. Furthermore, we elucidated that cycles in state transitions indicate trial-and-errors only with regard to programming exercises. It is not clear whether this is true for other problem-solving processes.

Acknowledgments. This work was supported by JSPS KAKENHI Grant Number 20H01728.

References

1. Central Council for Education: Youchi-en, Shou-gakkou, Chuu-gakkou, Koutou-gakkou oyobi Tokubetsu-Shien-gakkou no Gakushu-shidou-youryou tou no Kaizen oyobi Hitsuyou-na Housaku ni tsuite (Japanese) [Improvement of the Curriculum Guideline for Kindergartens, Elementary Schools, Junior High Schools, High Schools, and Special Needs Schools and Necessary Measures (Report)]. https://www.mext.go.jp/b_menu/shingi/chukyo/chukyo0/toushin/1380731.htm

2. National Institute for Educational Policy Research: Shidou to Hyouka no Ipponka no tameno Gakushu Hyouka ni kansuru Sankou Shiryou (Koutou-gakkou hen) Jouhou (Japanese) [Reference Materials on Learning Evaluation for the "Integration of Teaching and Evaluation" (High School Part), Information]. https://www.nier.go.jp/kaihatsu/shidousiryou.html
3. Kumar, A.: Representing and evaluating strategies for solving parsons puzzles. In: Coy, A., Hayashi, Y., Chang, M. (eds.) ITS 2019. LNCS, vol. 11528, pp. 193–203. Springer, Cham (2019). https://doi.org/10.1007/978-3-030-22244-4_24
4. Du, Y., Luxton-Reilly, A., Denny, P.: A review of research on parsons problems. In: Proceedings of ACE 2020: Twenty-Second Australasian Computing Education Conference, pp. 195–202 (2020)
5. Maharjan, S., Kumar, A.: Using edit distance trails to analyze path solutions of parsons puzzles. In: Rafferty, A.N., Whitehill, J., Cavalli-Sforza, V., Romero, C. (eds.) The 13th International Conference on Educational Data Mining (EDM 2020), pp. 638–642 (2020)
6. Nakayama, Y., Kuno, Y., Kakuda, H.: Split-paper testing: a novel approach to evaluate programming performance. J. Inf. Process. **28**, 733–743 (2020)
7. Kuno, Y.: Examination questions construction manual for evaluating thinking/judgement/expression abilities (Japanese). In: Jouhou Kyouiku Symposium (Japanese) [Information Education Symposium], vol. 2018, no. 1, pp. 1–8 (2018)
8. Helminen, J., Ihantola, P., Karavirta, V., Malmi, L.: How do students solve parsons programming problems?: an analysis of interaction traces. In: Proceedings of the Ninth Annual International Conference on International Computing Education Research (ICER 2012), pp. 119–126. Association for Computing Machinery, New York, NY, USA (2012)
9. Ueno, S., Terui, Y., Imamura, R., Kuno, Y., Egi, H.: Analysis of the answering processes in split-paper testing to promote instruction. In: Rodrigo, M.M.T., et al. (eds.) Proceedings of the 29th International Conference on Computers in Education. Asia-Pacific Society for Computers in Education (2021)
10. Yamaguchi, T., Oba, M.: Measurable interactive application to find out user recognition and strategy when problem solving. J. Softw. **15**(1), 12–22 (2020)
11. Aronson, E.: Jigsaw Basics (n.d.). https://www.jigsaw.org/pdf/JigsawBasics.pdf
12. Yamaguchi, T., Matsuzawa, Y., Niimi A., Oba M.: Detecting hesitation in a programming process by analyzing temporal co-occurrence of selection and discard operations. Computer in Education Technical reports, 2021-CE-160(8), pp. 1–6 (2021). (in Japanese)
13. Jeannette, W.: Computational thinking. Commun. ACM **49**(3), 33–35 (2006)

Web Application Development Achievement: Clarifying the Relationship Between Visual GUI Design and Textual Programming

Djordje M. Kadijevich(✉)

Institute for Educational Research, Belgrade, Serbia
djkadijevic@ipi.ac.rs

Abstract. To develop web applications, the design of a graphical user interface (GUI design) is combined with textual programming. As these two practices are inevitably interconnected, the relationship between students' achievements in GUI design and textual programming should be a positive one. In order to improve instruction in web application development, this relationship should be clarified. This clarification is relevant because different kinds of GUI controls are available (e.g., standard input/output controls, data validation controls). These controls differ with respect to the nature and complexity of their properties, which need to be specified, possibly resulting in positive relationships of different strengths. To this end, this study used a sample of 74 second-year undergraduate students, who developed simple web applications through combining visual GUI design in the ASP.NET language and textual programming in C# language. By considering the students' web development achievements regarding this design and that programming, a positive relationship between them was found. In one group of 36 students, whose achievements in a 3-variable task were modest (almost 65% correct), this relationship was very strong (Spearman's $rho = 0.868, df = 34, p < 0.01$); the correlation between visual GUI design using validation controls and textual programming was also very strong ($r_S = 0.872, df = 34, p < 0.01$), whereas the correlation between visual GUI design using standard controls and textual programming was moderate ($r_S = 0.555, df = 34, p < 0.01$). In the other group of 38 students, whose achievements in a 5-variable task were quite good (about 90% correct), this relationship was moderate ($r_S = 0.564, df = 36, p < 0.01$); the correlation between visual GUI design using standard controls and textual programming was also moderate ($r_S = 0.540, df = 36, p < 0.01$), whereas the correlation between visual GUI design using validation controls and textual programming was rather weak ($r_S = 0.348, df = 36, p < 0.05$). Suggestions for practice and research are included.

Keywords: ASP.NET · C# · Standard Controls · Textual Programming · Undergraduate Students · Validation Controls · Visual GUI Design · Web Applications

Published by Springer Nature Switzerland AG 2023
T. Keane et al. (Eds.): WCCE 2022, IFIP AICT 685, pp. 554–566, 2023.
https://doi.org/10.1007/978-3-031-43393-1_50

1 Introduction

Initially, programming was mainly practiced through developing console applications, which enabled limited human-computer interaction by using strings of text that were entered in computers and displayed by them in a line-by-line fashion. With the wider implementation of graphical user interfaces (GUIs) at the end of the twentieth century – first done in operating systems, then in various application software – this interaction was greatly simplified by using graphical elements, such as input boxes, buttons, menus, icons, and windows (e.g., [1]). As a result, the development of console applications has been coupled with and gradually replaced by developing emergent windows and web applications. Bearing in mind the increasing relevance of web applications to today's work and life, some elements of web programming are even included in introductory programming courses (e.g., [2,3]); this programming may be an ideal vehicle for teaching students a range of important computer science topics [4].

To practice web programming (i.e. to develop web applications), the design of a graphical user interface (GUI design) is combined with programming; the two practices can be accomplished in visual and textual modes, respectively (e.g., [5]). These practices belong to core programming knowledge areas, especially regarding components and relations [6]. They are also inevitably interconnected because, in practical terms, the outcome of one practice cannot be made live without the outcome of the other. To this end, the two practices require students to apply a range of related cognitive processes successfully (e.g., analysis and application in data manipulation and calculation; evaluation and synthesis in binding variables to GUI components; adapted from [7]). It is thus reasonable to expect that the relationship between students' achievements in visual GUI design and textual programming should be a positive one.

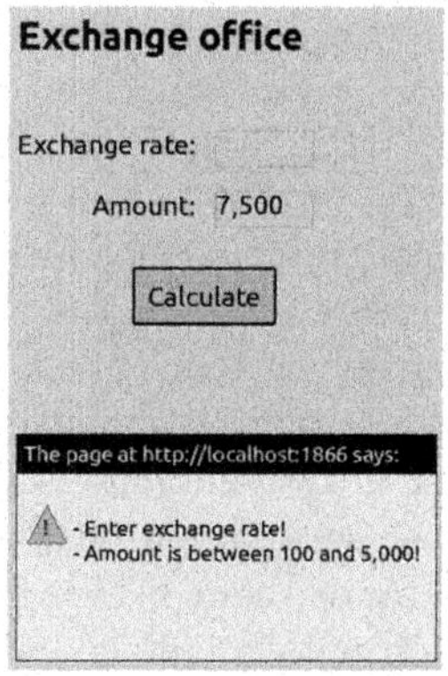

Fig. 1. Examples of GUI controls; messages concern data validation controls (taken from Fig. 1 in [3])

In order to improve instruction in web application development (e.g., to support students' better connection between visual GUI design and the work with its components in the underlying program), this relationship should be clarified. This clarification is relevant because different kinds of GUI controls can be applied. These are primarily standard input/output controls (e.g., labels and text-boxes) and data validation controls (e.g., required field validators and range validators); see Fig. 1. These kinds of controls differ with respect to the nature and complexity of their properties, which need to be specified, possibly resulting in positive relationships of different strengths. Despite this relevance, the relationship in question has not (to the author's knowledge) been studied in the literature so far. (A Google Scholar search with the phrase "visual GUI design", performed in May 2023 among papers published in the last five years, returned just 9 hits, none of which was relevant to the research summarized in this paper.) Hence, this study applied empirical research that examined the following research questions:

1. Was there a positive relationship between visual GUI design and textual programming? If so, could its strength be related to the complexity of tasks assigned to students or to their success in solving them?
2. If this positive relationship applied, did it differ in strength for different kinds of GUI controls? If so, what might the possible reasons for this be?

These questions were answered by a sample of second-year undergraduate students pursuing business studies at a private faculty.

The next, second section describes the method used in this empirical research. Its main findings are summarized in the third section, whereas the fourth section discusses these findings in detail. The final, closing section critically examines this empirical research and gives suggestions for practice and further research.

2 Method

2.1 Sample

This study used a convenience sample of seventy-four second-year undergraduate students attending a "Basics of programming" course as part of their business studies at a private faculty. Forty-seven of them (63.5%) were female. There were two groups of students attending this course in two academic years. About half of the students registered for the second year participated in this study. As most second-year students did not have any prior experience in programming, many of them decided to postpone their obligation regarding this course. Such an approach reduced the size of the potential sample to be used.

2.2 Programming Course

The content of the course "Basics of programming" focused on developing simple web applications, paying special attention to data validation. Students were taught both visual GUI design and textual programming, and this design included detailed work with standard input/output controls and data validation controls [3].

This course lasted for fifteen weeks, each week comprising five 45-min lessons with lectures and practical work. Students' programming achievements during the course were evaluated using three examinations and one optional project. The first examination in week 4 dealt with developing a web application with linear structure. The second examination in week 8 assessed the development of a web application that involved branch and/or loop structure(s). The third, last examination in week 12 dealt with creating a simple database and developing a web application that showed and updated its content. An optional project, completed at the end of the course, required students to create a database and develop a web application that processed its content. As web applications with data validation are highly relevant to today's businesses, developing such applications should be included in modern business studies. Although most future business executives would not develop these applications, many of them would be involved in projects concerning their development (e.g., [4]).

2.3 Software

Developing web applications was realized in Visual Web Developer, a component of Microsoft Visual Studio (https://visualstudio.microsoft.com/). The edition of the Developer was 2010 Express, which could be downloaded from the Internet for free. This environment was found to be suitable for introducing programming to undergraduate students engaged in business studies because, even with modest visual GUI design and only a little textual programming (with just 5–10 lines of code), interesting, business-relevant web applications could be developed. Consider, for example, a web calculator for a break-even analysis that determines the volume of production needed to produce zero profit.

2.4 Design and Variables

This study utilized a correlative design involving four variables. These variables were: Visual GUI design using standard controls; Visual GUI design using validation controls; Overall visual GUI design; and Textual programming.

There were three variables regarding visual GUI design because two types of GUI controls were used. These controls were standard controls (including labels, text-boxes, and buttons) and validation controls (including required field validators, range validators, and validation summaries). The controls differed with respect to the nature and complexity of their properties, which needed to be specified. Contrary to the standard controls that required at most one property to be specified (e.g., label text for labels), validation controls had two or more properties that needed to be specified. For range validators, for example, these properties were: control to validate, error message, minimum value, maximum value, and data type. Furthermore, their display property had to be set to "None" as summary validators were used.

2.5 Instrument and Procedure

The values of the four applied variables were determined using a programming assignment given on the first examination mentioned above concerning simple web applications with linear structures, covering data validation. As this examination was part of regular assessments during the academic year, participants were not told that their solutions and achievements might be used as data in subsequent research.

The variables applied were measured in the following way:

- visual GUI design using standard controls was measured by the student's success in designing web pages using labels, text-boxes, and a button;

- visual GUI design using validation controls was measured by the student's success in designing web pages using a required field validator, a range validator, and a validation summary;
- overall visual GUI design concerned the success in applying all these six controls;
- textual programming was measured by the student's success in declaring variables, assigning values to them, and calculating these values.

The reliability of these measures (Cronbach's alpha) are reported in Table 1. For scoring students' solutions, see the appendix.

In each academic year (recall that there were two groups of students in two academic years), the students completed the assignment working in three groups. All students were taught both types of control and were required to use them to solve the task given. Although these groups solved different programming tasks, the structures of these tasks could be considered as isomorphic because they required the students to use the same number of variables, connected straightforwardly. In one group, the 3-variable task group, the relations to apply were: $c = a - b, c = a/b$, or $c = a * b$. In another group, the 5-variable task group, these relations were: $e = a * (b + c + d), e = a * b + c * d$, or $e = a + b * c + d$. An example of a 3-variable task and its solution with scoring are given in the Appendix. An example of the 5-variable tasks can be found elsewhere (e.g., [3], Exam 1 in Appendix 2). Note that in each academic year the achievements of these three student groups were not different, statistically, according to the Kruskal-Wallis test. Hence, in each academic year, all students could be considered as being members of one programming group.

2.6 Data Transformation and Statistical Analysis

The values of each variable were first rescaled to interval [0, 1]. Apart from calculating descriptive statistics, correlative analyses were undertaken. Because the assumption of normality was violated for all variables applied (see the values of *K-S z* listed in Table 1), the relationship between pairs of variables was measured by Spearman's correlation. Instead of the values of variables in question, this correlation deals with the ranks of these values by variable. Note that because of this violation, instead of one-way ANOVA, the Kruskal-Wallis test was used. This test examined whether there were different achievements from students who solved tasks using the same number of variables as already mentioned in the previous paragraph.

3 Results

Table 1 summarizes the means and standard deviations of the measured variables (in terms of percentage correct) and reports Spearman's correlations among them. For each variable, the first row contains data regarding students who solved 3-variable tasks ($N_1 = 36$), whereas the second row lists data concerning students who solved 5-variable tasks ($N_2 = 38$).

Table 1. Descriptive and correlative statistics for measured variables

Variable	M (SD); α; *K-S z*	Correlations		
		2	3	4
1. VGUID (SCs)	73 (32); 0.86; 2.197**	0.554**	0.739**	0.555**
	86 (12); 0.66; 1.581*	0.314+	0.854**	0.540**
2. VGUID (VCs)	56 (44); 0.86; 1.596*		0.959**	0.872**
	94 (12); 0.80; 1.908**		0.708**	0.348*
3. VGUID	63 (36); 0.85; 1.732**			0.868**
	90 (11); 0.78; 1.581*			0.564**
4. TP	64 (40); 0.95; 1.352+			
	87 (15); 0.89; 2.058**			

VGUID (SCs) – Visual GUI design using standard controls;
VGUID (VCs) – Visual GUI design using validation controls;
VGUID – Overall visual GUI design; TP – Textual programming;
$+ \ p < 0.06$, $* \ p < 0.05$, $** \ p < 0.01$

Programming achievements of students who solved 3-variable tasks were modest (almost 65% correct), and the relationship between visual GUI design and textual programming was very strong ($r_S = 0.868, df = 34, p < 0.01$). It was very strong due to a very strong correlation between visual GUI design using validation controls and textual programming ($r_S = 0.872, df = 34, p < 0.01$). On the other hand, programming achievements of students who solved 5-variable tasks were quite good (about 90% correct), but the relationship between visual GUI design and textual programming was moderate ($r_S = 0.564, df = 36, p < 0.01$). It was moderate due to a weak correlation between visual GUI design using validation controls and textual programming ($r_S = 0.348, df = 36, p < 0.05$). The correlation between visual GUI design using standard controls and textual programming did not differ from group to group (0.555 vs. 0.540; $p < 0.01$).

4 Discussion

Three important findings emerged from this study. Firstly, for students with lower achievements who solved 3-variable tasks, the relationship between visual GUI design and textual programming was very strong due to a very strong correlation between visual GUI design using validation controls and textual programming. Secondly, for students with higher achievements, who solved 5-variable tasks, the relationship between visual GUI design and textual programming was moderate due to a weak correlation between visual GUI design using validation controls and textual programming. Thirdly, for both groups of students, there was a moderate, almost identical correlation between visual GUI design using standard controls and textual programming. The following paragraphs examine these findings in more detail.

4.1 First Research Question

The first research question asked whether there was a positive relationship between visual GUI design and textual programming, and if so, could its strength be related to the complexity of tasks assigned to students or to their success in solving them. It was found that this relationship was indeed positive, also being of different strength for different programming tasks solved (0.868 for 3-variable tasks vs 0.564 for 5-variable tasks). As shown below, instead of the complexity of these tasks in terms of the number of variables applied, this difference in strength could be attributed to the students' success in solving them (almost 65% vs. about 90%), with a stronger correlation for students with lower achievements.

That there was a positive relationship between visual GUI design and textual programming was expected. Visual GUI design and textual programming influence each other in a positive way. This is because the two practices, which belong to core programming knowledge areas, especially regarding components and relations, require students to apply a range of related cognitive processes successfully (e.g., [6,7]). A detailed argumentation that considers two kinds of controls applied in this design may go as follows.

- Standard controls used by a web application hold, as their values, data processed by a program implementing web application. In other words, to have these visually-managed controls live, a program written in the textual mode was needed, and vice versa.
- Validation controls required a number of their properties to be set properly, making the work with validation controls beyond the drag-and-drop actions similar (albeit small in scope) to the work required by textual programming in general. In particular, to make a web application workable, visual GUI design using these controls and textual programming were mutually dependent. These practices link with each other through entities and their properties used at both web application development sides (e.g., specify input/output entity, choose entity data type, do entity value assignment, choose entity value constraint(s)).

That this positive relationship between visual GUI design and textual programming might be of different strength for different groups of students might also hold true. A stronger correlation was found for students with lower achievements, who solved simpler tasks applying three variables only. Additional correlative analysis showed why a stronger correlation was found for those students. In each group of students, visual GUI design and textual programming were not related for students whose achievements in both GUI design and textual programming were higher than 80%. There were many more such students who solved 5-variable than 3-variable tasks with that success (32 of 38 vs. 18 of 36; $\chi^2 = 9.873, df = 1, p = 0.002$). Hence, it was this wider absence of relationship that might primarily contribute to a lower correlation for the group of students with higher achievements. To realize the impact of zero or low correlation in a subsample on the correlation in the whole sample, see [8], for example.

As already underlined in the Introduction, the relationship between visual GUI design and textual programming has not been examined in earlier studies according to the author's readings. However, there is a study that examined the relationship between design skills and programming skills in an advanced programming class [9]. These skills were related to (1) writing a Unified Modeling Language (UML) class diagram for a solution (program) of the problem given and (2) implementing in Java several methods applied in this diagram. There was a strong, positive correlation between these skills ($r = 0.797, df = 35, p < 0.001$). According to the scatterplot of the students' scores, the examined relationship was missing for students with high achievements in both design and programming skills as found in our study.

4.2 Second Research Question

Provided that a positive relationship between visual GUI design and textual programming applied, the second research question asked whether this relationship differed in strength for different kinds of GUI controls, and if so, what might be the possible reasons for such a state. It was found that for students with lower achievement who solved 3-variable tasks, this relationship did differ in strength for different kinds of GUI controls; textual programming correlated much higher with visual GUI design using validation controls than with visual GUI design using standard controls ($0.872 > 0.555, Z = 3.524, p = 0.000$). Although the opposite seemed to apply for students with higher achievement who solved 5-variable tasks ($0.348 < 0.540$), the relationship did not differ for different kinds of GUI controls, statistically ($Z = 0.951, p = 0.341$). Being aware of the fact that, in both groups of students, there was a moderate, almost identical correlation between visual GUI design using standard controls and textual programming (0.555 vs. 0.540; $p < 0.01$), possible reasons for the existence/non-existence of differences in strength might be found in the specificity of the relationship between visual GUI design using validation controls and textual programming.

That the relationship between visual GUI design and textual programming applied could differ in strength for different kinds of GUI controls favoring standard controls was suggested by the fact that the use of standard controls is vital to program execution. On the other hand, the use of validation controls is optional, provided that input data are correctly given. However, the work with validation controls beyond the drag-and-drop actions requires a number of properties to be specified. Hence, this work is, as already underlined, similar (albeit small in scope) to the work required by textual programming in general. This similarity might cause a much higher correlation of textual programming with visual GUI design using validation controls than with visual GUI design using standard controls in the group of students with lower achievements who solved 3-variable tasks. The similarity was always there, but this pattern was not present in the group of students with higher achievements who solved 5-variable tasks. What could the reasons for that be?

Possible reasons for the existence/non-existence of differences in strength might be found in another specificity of the relationship between visual GUI design using validation controls and textual programming observed in students' achievement scores. Recall that we already considered students whose achievements on both visual GUI design and textual programming were higher than 80% and underlined that there were many more such students among those who solved 5-variable than 3-variable tasks with that success (84% vs. 50%). As in each group of students, visual GUI design using validation controls and textual programming was not related ($r_S = 0.112, df = 30, p = 0.543$ vs. $r_S = 0.330, df = 16, p = 0.181$), this absence limited the strength of the relationship in question, especially in the 5-variable task group.

It is important to underline that the missing dependency between visual GUI design using validation controls and textual programming for high achieving students was a result of a somewhat careless approach to one kind of practice of many students. For example, inappropriate or missing assignments for some properties of validation controls used; inappropriate declarations of variables and thus inappropriate conversions of data in programs developed. The same careless approach might be applied by some Java programmers in the above–mentioned study on the relationship between design skills and programming skills [9]. Future studies may confirm the implication that some students with high levels of achievement for both kinds of practice nevertheless need special support regarding these shortcomings in order to develop a positive relationship between visual GUI design and textual programming. Note that the dependency between visual GUI design using standard controls and textual programming was missing among best solvers of 3-variable tasks due to a missing label or unclear/unsuitable label text, for example.

5 Closing Remarks

The relationship between visual GUI design and textual programming was found to be positive, being of different strength for different programming tasks solved. Instead of the complexity of these tasks in terms of the number of variables applied, this difference in strength could be attributed to the students' success in solving them, with a stronger correlation for lower-achieving students. Furthermore, the relationship could differ in strength for different kinds of GUI controls as found for lower-achieving students who solved 3-variable tasks. The existence/non-existence of differences in strength might be attributed to the missing dependency for high-achieving students between visual GUI design using validation controls and textual programming, which was a result of a somewhat careless approach of many high achievers to this design or that programming.

Bearing in mind that modern approaches to introductory programming start with applying control flow from the very beginning (e.g., [10]), the programming tasks used in this study (applying linear structures only) may appear very simple because they do not call for the application of a full range of the cognitive skills required for successful programming. As already mentioned, the participants in this study were novice programmers. Novice programmers can only successfully deal with programs with linear and branch structures; programs with loop structures are usually hard for most of them (e.g., [11,12]). Hence, focusing first on the tasks used in this study might be found appropriate. Furthermore, visual GUI design, as a design activity that calls for the demanding learning activity of problem structuring and articulation [13], involved (although indirectly) some sort of algorithmization.

It is important to underline that the positive relationship between visual GUI design and textual programming found in this study should not imply that requiring students to create web pages with validation controls would help them learn some programming logic. It should rather imply that, as already emphasized, a workable web application calls for a mutual interdependence between visual GUI design and textual programming. These practices link with each other through entities and their properties used at both web application development types (e.g., input/output entities, entity data type, entity value assignment, entity value constraint(s); validation summary controls make use of branch and loop structures). The finding that a positive relationship between visual GUI design and textual programming only applies at lower achievement levels for both kinds of practice might be a signal that, in order to develop a positive relationship between these kinds of practice, some high-achieving students may need special support to make this linkage more explicit to them.

To summarize: Although this study used a relatively small sample and a simple programming task that might be characterized as preliminary research, it revealed valuable findings. To improve textual programming, educators may invest in visual GUI design, and vice versa. In doing that, certain aspects of web controls used (especially validation ones) should be connected to the corresponding aspects of textual programming. Despite its educational relevance, a positive relationship between visual GUI design and textual programming has not been clarified in the literature so far. In order to improve instruction in web application development (e.g., to support students' better connection between visual GUI design and work with its components in the underlying program), further research may focus on this clarification using more complex programming tasks (including also other kinds of controls) solved by students of different programming experience. Although visual GUI design may not be considered as visual programming, the outcome of this research may suggest promising directions to follow in clarifying the relationship between visual and textual programming. This clarification, which has not been done so far as well, would help educators better arrange programming practice in so-called hybrid programming environments, which support both kinds of programming, aiming at attaining competent textual programming (e.g., [14]).

Acknowledgement. This contribution resulted from the author's research funded by the Ministry of Education, Science and Technological Development of the Republic of Serbia (Contract No. 451-03-47/2023-01/200018). The author dedicates the contribution to his son Aleksandar.

Appendix

– One exam task and its solution with scoring

Exam Task
The total value of issued bonds is calculated in the following way:
Total value of bonds = Value of one bond * Number of bond issued.
Create a web application that calculates the total value of issued bonds for the given value of one bond and the number of bonds issued. (When this value and that number are 50,000 val and 10,000 respectively, the total value of bonds is 500,000,000 val). To validate input data, use three different validation controls.

Ten controls needed are underlined in Fig. 2 on the next page. If correctly applied, one point was given for each shaded assignment. One point was given for each text-box used. Eighteen points (4-labels, 2-text-boxes, 1-button, 3-required field validator, 6-range validator, 2-validation summary) could be earned in total.

```
<form id="form1" runat="server">
  <div>
    <asp:Label ID="Label1" runat="server" Height="9px" Style="z-index: 100; left: 112px;
      position: absolute; top: 59px" Text="Total value of bonds" Width="120px"></asp:Label>
    <asp:Label ID="Label2" runat="server" Style="z-index: 101; left: 50px; position: absolute;
      top: 120px" Text="Value of one bond"></asp:Label>
    <asp:Label ID="Label3" runat="server" Style="z-index: 102; left: 45px; position: absolute;
      top: 173px" Text="Number of bonds issued"></asp:Label>
    <asp:TextBox ID="TextBox1" runat="server" Style="z-index: 103; left: 109px; position: absolute;
      top: 117px"></asp:TextBox>
    <asp:TextBox ID="TextBox2" runat="server" Style="z-index: 104; left: 128px; position: absolute;
      top: 172px"></asp:TextBox>
    <asp:Button ID="Button1" runat="server" Style="z-index: 105; left: 108px; position: absolute;
      top: 227px" Text="Calculate" OnClick="Button1_Click" />
    <asp:Label ID="Label4" runat="server" Style="z-index: 106; left: 52px; position: absolute;
      top: 286px" Text=""></asp:Label>
    <asp:RequiredFieldValidator ID="RequiredFieldValidator1" runat="server"
      ControlToValidate="TextBox1" Display="None" ErrorMessage="Enter bond value!" Style="z-
      index: 107; left: 356px; position: absolute; top: 42px"></asp:RequiredFieldValidator>
    <asp:RangeValidator ID="RangeValidator1" runat="server" ControlToValidate="TextBox2"
      Display="None" ErrorMessage="Number of bonds is between 100 and 1000!" MaximumValue="1000"
      MinimumValue="100" Style="z-index: 108; left: 370px; position: absolute; top: 97px"
      Type="Integer"></asp:RangeValidator>
    <asp:ValidationSummary ID="ValidationSummary1" runat="server" Style="z-index: 109;
      left: 375px; position: absolute; top: 179px" ShowMessageBox="True" ShowSummary="False"
      Style="z-index: 110; left: 383px; position: absolute; top: 168px"></asp: ValidationSummary>
  </div>
  </form>
```

Fig. 2. Code generated with visual GUI design

```
protected void Button1_Click(object sender, EventArgs e)
  {
    decimal value = Convert.ToDecimal(TextBox1.Text);
    int number = Convert.ToInt32(TextBox2.Text);
    decimal totalValue = number * value;
    Label4.Text = "Total value of bonds: " + Convert.ToString(totalValue) + " val";
  }
```

Fig. 3. Code produced by textual programming

Code Produced by Textual Programming
The code is given in Fig. 3 between {}. Three points could be earned for declaring variables (one point for each variable needed); four points for assigning values to these variables and a label (one point for each assignment required); and five points for calculating these values (one arithmetic operation, three data conversions, and one string operation needed); twelve points in total.

About Partial Credit
For an inappropriate variable declaration (e.g., decimal instead of int) or an inappropriate data conversion (e.g., Convert.ToDecimal instead of Convert.ToInt32), only half a point could be earned. Inappropriate assignments of some properties of the web control used (e.g., an unclear error message or label text) were assigned 0.75 point each.

References

1. Martinez, W.L.: Graphical user interfaces. WIREs Comput. Stat. **3**(2), 119–133 (2011)
2. Xiong, X., Ning, A.: Exploration and research on web programming course in higher vocational college. In: 10th International Conference on Computer Science & Education (ICCSE), New York, pp. 824–828. IEEE (2015)
3. Kadijevich, D.M.: First programming course in business studies: content, approach, and achievement. In: Barendsen, E., Chytas, C. (eds.) ISSEP 2021. LNCS, vol. 13057, pp. 45–56. Springer, Cham (2021). https://doi.org/10.1007/978-3-030-90228-5_4
4. Taylor, T.: Web competencies for IT students. In: Braun, R. (ed.) Proceedings of 7th International Conference on Information Technology Based Higher Education and Training, New York, pp. 297–304. IEEE (2006)
5. Delamater, M., Boehm, A.: Murach's ASP.NET 4.6 Web Programming with C# 2015. Mike Murach & Associates, Fresno (2016)
6. Wang, W., Bromall, N.: Knowledge and skill gaps in programming. In: Proceedings of the EDSIG Conference, Norfolk, VA, pp. 1–10. Information Systems & Computing Academic Professionals, Wrightsville Beach (2018)
7. Sobral, S.R.: Bloom's taxonomy to improve teaching-learning in introduction to programming. Int. J. Inf. Educ. Technol. **11**(3), 148–153 (2021)
8. Charter, R.A., Alexander, R.A.: A note on combining correlations. Bull. Psychon. Soc. **31**(2), 123–124 (1993). https://doi.org/10.3758/BF03334158
9. Coffey, J.W.: Relationship between design and programming skills in an advanced computer programming class. J. Comput. Sci. Coll. **30**(5), 39–45 (2015)
10. Robins, A.V.: Novice programmers and introductory programming. In: Fincher, S.A., Robins, A.V. (eds.) The Cambridge Handbook of Computing Education Research, pp. 327–376. Cambridge University Press, Cambridge (2019)
11. Hofuku, Y., Cho, S., Nishida, T., Kanemune, S.: Why is programming difficult? Proposal for learning programming in "small steps" and a prototype tool for detecting "gap". In: Diethelm, I., Arndt, J., Dnnebier, M., Syrbe, J. (eds.) Informatics in Schools: Local Proceedings of the 6th International Conference ISSEP 2013 - Selected Papers, pp. 13–24. Universittsverlag Potsdam, Potsdam (2013)

12. Lahtinen, E., Ala-Mutka, K., Jrvinen, H.-M.: A study of the difficulties of novice programmers. In: Proceedings of the 10th Annual SIGCSE Conference on Innovation and Technology in Computer Science Education (ITiCSE 2005), pp. 14–18. ACM, New York (2005)
13. Jonassen, D.H.: Toward a design theory of problem solving. Educ. Tech. Res. Dev. **48**, 63–85 (2000). https://doi.org/10.1007/BF02300500
14. Noone, M., Mooney, A.: Visual and textual programming languages: a systematic review of the literature. J. Comput. Educ. **5**(2), 149–174 (2018). https://doi.org/10.1007/s40692-018-0101-5

Improving a Model-Based Software Engineering Capstone Course

Michael J. May(✉) and Amir Tomer

Kinneret College on the Sea of Galilee, Jordan Valley, 15132 Zemach, Israel
{mjmay,tomera}@mx.kinneret.ac.il

Abstract. Capstone projects are a common feature of software engineering bachelor's degrees. We report on the experience and lessons learned from a decade of capstone projects at a small regional Israeli college. We first created a capstone process adapted to the department's model-based software design philosophy, cultural aspects of the student body, and the sparse industrial environment surrounding the college. After several years, we improved the process through the introduction of mandatory fill-in report templates. Analyses of ten years of project statistics and outcomes led us to an understanding of what capstone features led to better outcomes and how the report templates affected grading outcomes. Our templates are released under the Creative Commons Attribution-ShareAlike 4.0 International License.

Keywords: Software design engineering · Student assessment · Software engineering education · Capstone projects

1 Introduction

The Israeli Council for Higher Education (CHE) requires that all certified four-year software engineering degree programs include a capstone project, but leaves management details up to the institution [1]. Having managed software engineering capstone projects at a regional Israeli college for ten years and received numerous outstanding project awards at the national level, we amassed an archive of project reports, project metadata, and institutional knowledge of how to produce successful capstones. We performed a reflective qualitative and statistical analysis of our results, summarized here. We sought to answer three research questions about our capstone process:

1. What factors in the project team, customer, or topic can lead to improved evaluation (*i.e.,* grades) from academic and industrial advisors?
2. Did the introduction of the fill-in document templates improve project outcome and grades?
3. What did students think about their advisor, team, and project documents (with or without templates)?

Published by Springer Nature Switzerland AG 2023
T. Keane et al. (Eds.): WCCE 2022, IFIP AICT 685, pp. 567–578, 2023.
https://doi.org/10.1007/978-3-031-43393-1_51

We present two contributions related to our experience that ought to be of interest to the community. First, we share our conclusions from the research questions and the process we used to reach them. They give guidance about what led to project success using our capstone process. Second, we detail the design and motivation behind the set of fill-in templates for capstone project documentation that helped improve our process. All of the templates we describe can be accessed at the projects URL listed at the end of the paper and are released under the Creative Commons Attribution-ShareAlike 4.0 International License.

While the use of templates for software engineering is well known (see MIL-STD-498 DIDs (Data Item Descriptions) [2] and the IEEE Software Developers Toolkit), our templates improve on previous work in two major aspects:

1. They are tailor-made, *i.e.*, generated specifically to our institution's capstone process.
2. Unlike other templates that only describe the content of the documents and give guidelines, we provide color-coded text, detailed instructions, and formatting styles.

2 Methods

Our method to answer the research questions was influenced by the history of the capstone process in our department.

2.1 Initial Capstone Project Process

The capstone course began to operate in the 2009–10 academic year. It was a full year course (2 semesters) performed in the final year of the degree program.

We primarily sought projects at industrial customers, preferably high tech or software companies. We also allowed research-supporting capstones in which the customer was a researcher who needed software for research purposes. We did not allow theoretical or exploratory capstone projects that do not produce a concrete deliverable system.

Whether industrial or research-supporting, we required an active industrial advisor who met with the students weekly or biweekly (without the academic advisor). For research-supporting topics, the researcher took the role of the industrial advisor. The industrial advisor's job was to decide the requirements, guide planning and design, and ensure that development proceeded. Each customer chose the development methodology to be used (*e.g.,* agile methods, scrum, waterfall) and managed the team accordingly. We did not allow topics without an advisor who is the customer of or a significant stakeholder in the project's results. That decision was meant to ensure that projects were guided steadily and that the advisor had a stake in the project's success.

Each capstone project was assigned an academic advisor whose job was to offer guidance on theoretical and technical matters, resolve team member conflicts, and ensure projects proceed in a timely manner.

Table 1. Project document contents and due dates.

Document	Chapter	Contents
Charter (Due: 31 Dec)	Project background	customer information, overview
	Project properties	goals, deliverables, lifecycle, test plan, Gantt chart, stakeholders, risks
	Theoretical background	existing state, similar systems
	Technical attributes	high level requirements, implementation and solution constraints, interfaces, development and implementation tools
Specification and Design (Due Partial: 1 Apr, Final: 1 Aug)	Background	overview of project goals, background
	Organizational environment and business processes	customer organization, existing software state
	Glossary	problem domain object model, term list
	Software/system requirements	stakeholders, actors, sources, detailed requirements, use case specifications
	Architectural specification	physical architecture, logical architecture, composite model, sequence diagrams
	Software specification	class diagrams, database diagram
	Implementation and build	developers guide
	Testing specification	tests and expected results
	Installation, use, validation	installation and maintenance manual, user manual, validation tests
Final Report (Due: 1 Aug)	Introduction	background, problems and challenges, solution approach, results, solution environment
	Theoretical background	sources, potential external customers
	Technical summary	design and implementation considerations, logical planning and execution, logical changes, screen shots, physical implementation and deployment
	Project execution	actual Gantt chart, hardware changes, integration and operation, test results, maintenance, support
	Self-evaluation, reflection	personal thoughts
	Conclusion	personal thoughts
	Second language project brief	brief in an alternate language (usually English in Hebrew documents)
	Appendices	code snippets, meeting summaries, extra tables

The students' primary task was to create the working capstone deliverables. The deliverables were typically software systems that the project customer could use as part of its business needs.

Since a system without documentation is not maintainable, we also required them to create a set of documents that support the deliverables. To fulfill the model based design philosophy, we designed a set of three documents: the project charter, the specification and design, and the final report. Their contents and due dates[1] are summarized in Table 1. To ensure nothing was forgotten, we prepared a checklist of elements for all documents with required sections, technical required figures (*e.g.*, use case diagram), and typographic specifications.

Table 2. Selection of capstone projects 2010–2020.

Customer	Capstone Topics
Industrial	Airline web services interface customer sandbox
	Remote fault management dashboard
	Water meter testing tracking tool
	Custom Wireshark file analyzer
	Water desalination plant energy optimization
	Flight recommender for travel agency website
Academic	Automated attendance and class participation app
	Conference management system
	Cemetery digitization system
	Life long learning knowledge discovery website
	Interactive co-op social game
	Tutor scheduling and hours reporting website

The **charter document** is a managerial and planning document. It reflects the original plans for the system and is submitted early in the project lifecycle, after the topic and basic requirements are decided.

The **specification and design** is a technical document. It was designed to be built incrementally or in accordance with the chosen development methodology (*e.g.*, as user stories are reached or as modules are designed). It reflected the system as delivered.

The **final report** is a summary and reflective document. It summarized the project as performed from managerial and technical perspectives. Students wrote about the problems they faced in execution, what changes were made during the course of the project, and provided an after-the-fact timeline (Gantt chart).

Evaluation. Capstone projects were evaluated by the industrial advisor and the academic advisor by filling in advisor-specific grading forms. The final grade was calculated as the average of the two grades. The forms can be found at the projects URL listed at the end of the paper.

The grading criteria for the industrial advisor are divided into three parts. Part A (60%) covered planning and performance in creating the deliverables. Since personal behavior and topics were covered, each student on the team was

[1] The academic year for our institution runs from late October to the end of June. July and August are the spring semester final exam period.

given a separate grade. Part B (30%) covered documentation, including elements for all required documents. Part C (10%) covered the capstone presentation defense.

The grading criteria for the academic advisor were similar. Part A (60%) was an overall grade per student for the capstone's planning, complexity, execution, and integration. Parts B (30%) and C (10%) for the academic advisor grade were identical to the industrial advisor's.

2.2 Process Update: Introduction of Fill-In Templates

In 2014, we decided to improve the course by introducing the use of fill-in Microsoft Word document templates for the project reports. The templates gave the students a clear framework for their requirements, design, models, and tests, removing uncertainty about how to structure their first long documentary task. Initially, the templates were optional, but following positive feedback from students we made them mandatory in 2016.

The templates included in-place instructions with color-coded boilerplate, examples, instructions, and fields. A sample of the templates is shown in Fig. 1.

To manage student progress and detect personnel issues, we introduced the requirement for each team to submit a monthly one-page progress report (also a Microsoft Word fill-in template). The report must be signed by the industrial advisor and submitted to the academic advisor. It can also be found at the projects URL listed below.

2.3 Data Collection and Analysis Methodology

Throughout the history of the capstone course, we gathered yearly performance data. At the end of each year, we collected statistics about the course's performance, including basic information on the student team, the type of topic (industrial or research supporting), the customer, the industrial advisor, and the evaluation scores. At the end of 2020, having collected ten years of data, we performed an internal review of the capstone process and the gathered data.

We analyzed the data to search for answers to the research questions. For the first question, we used Pearson's and Spearman's correlation tests to find factors that correlated numerically with grades. For categorical data, we compared the distributions using the Kolmogorov-Smirnov test. For the second question, we examined distribution of grades for projects submitted without the templates and those submitted with (again using Kolmogorov-Smirnov). For the third question, we reviewed a reflection sections from final reports submitted before and after the introduction of the templates and noted comments and sentiments expressed about the process and templates.

The data analysis was performed by the capstone course staff with the help of a data analyst within our institution who was only given access to capstone statistics, removing student identifiers and other personal information. To preserve student and advisor privacy, only group statistics are reported in this work.

4.4 Software/System Requirements Specification

This section includes a specification of the software/system requirements in the form of Use Cases. The Use Case diagram of the entire system is shown in Figure 2 below. The Use Cases in the diagram are detailed in the following subsections.

Use Case Diagram

Figure 2 : Use Case Diagram for <Software/System Name> Software/System

Use the correct format for Use Cases, including a clear division between primary actors/initiators and supporting actors.

4.4.1 <Use Case Name> Use the exact name of the use case shown in the figure!

Actors	*List the actors involved in the use case in the following manner:* • <Actor name>: Primary actor *Detail what the actor wants to achieve* • <Actor name>: Supporting actor *Detail what the system needs from him* • Spontaneous Use Case *(If the use case is initiated by some event within the system and there is no primary actor)*
Other Stakeholders	• <Stakeholder name>: *Give the interests the stakeholder has in the use case. What is its influence on the operation of the use case and how is it influenced by the use case?*
Pre-Conditions	• *One or more assumptions that must hold for the use case to operate. Example: The system is online*
Post-Conditions	• *One or more results whose fulfilment is necessary for the* ***successful completion*** *of the use case (from the perspective of the actors and stakeholders)*
Trigger	*The event that causes the use case to begin. It can be one (or more) of the following:* • *An action by the primary actor* • *An internal system event*

9

Fig. 1. Specification and Design template snippet. The use case specification continues on the page following the one shown. Upright text is boilerplate to be left in. Italics (blue) text is instructions to be removed. Text between triangle brackets (red) is to be replaced with appropriate values. (Color figure online)

3 Results

For background, we first assembled a series of population statistics of the 2010–2020 projects and student teams, which we present first. We then present the results from the statistics analyses that we use to answer the research questions.

3.1 Capstone Project Population and Topics

A total of 148 students completed 80 capstone projects. Team size (Fig. 2(a)) was predominantly two, but about one third were lone students or teams of three.

Capstones were done for 38 distinct customers (Fig. 2(b)), with the majority done for industries. Customers were about evenly distributed between small ($\leq$ 10 employees), medium (11 to 99 employees), and large ($\geq$ 100 employees) (Fig. 2(c)).

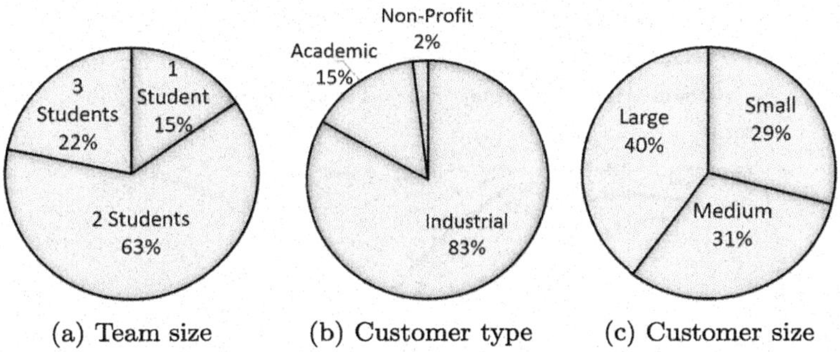

Fig. 2. Capstone project population distribution. Percentages reflect the number of students who performed a capstone in the team size, customer type, or customer size shown.

Topics varied widely (see Table 2 for example topics), but two themes dominated. For industrial topics, most were development projects not on the customer's product critical development path. Instead, they were productivity tools, simulators, or proofs-of-concept the customer wanted, but was unable to develop due to manpower or time limitations. The results echo ones reported by [3] at a Finnish institution who reported that industries sponsored capstones for recruitment, technological exploration, and getting the software developed. For research supporting topics, capstones developed rough but useful tools to advance research efforts. They were usually standalone tools that achieved some concrete research goal.

Table 3. Capstone grade statistics 2010–2020

	Final Grade	Industrial Grade	Academic Grade
Mean	91.47	93.04	89.85
Median	93.00	95.00	91.00
Max	100.00	100.00	100.00
Min	70.00	60.40	65.50
Std Dev	6.08	6.95	8.03
Confidence ($p<0.05$)	0.98	1.12	1.29

3.2 Question 1: Factors Influencing Evaluation

Grades include per-student evaluation, so team members may receive different final scores. Analysis showed grades to be high on the whole across all years, team sizes, and customer sizes (see Table 3). There were no statistically significant differences based on student sex or advisor.

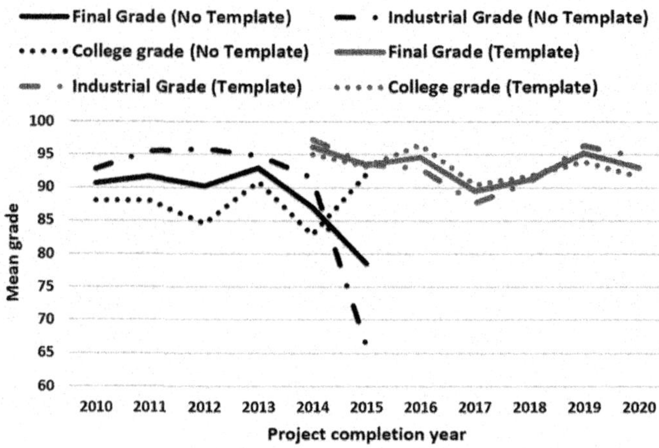

Fig. 3. Mean final capstone project grades with and without the fill-in template.

Small, but significant positive correlations were found between the academic advisor grade and team size[2] (*i.e.*, larger teams got slightly higher academic advisor grades) and between academic advisor grade and customer size[3] (*i.e.*, teams at larger customers got higher academic advisor grades). This points to the college being slightly more satisfied with work performed by larger teams at larger companies. This also gives support to the departments' discouraging of single-person capstone project teams, which are more likely to work at smaller organizations with simpler requirements.

Another positive predictive correlation was found between final grades and repeat industrial customers[4]. The implication is that capstones that receive higher grades are more likely to lead to a customer returning in following years for additional capstone projects. This points to the positive reinforcement effect a good result can have on the relationship between a customer and the college. Given the small number of industrial customers geographically near our institution, each such multi-year relationship is valuable and must be maintained.

3.3 Question 2: Impact of Fill-In Templates

The capstone course staff agreed that the introduction of the fill-in templates led to fewer student questions about how to prepare the report and to greater uniformity of report quality.

[2] Pearson correlation test, $[Rp = 0.213, p < 0.05]$.

[3] Spearman correlation test, $[Rs = 0.204, p < 0.05]$.

[4] We used binary logistic regression. The regression model was found to be statistically significant ($X^2(3) = 27.288, p < 0.001$). The predictor variables (independent variables, *i.e.*, grades) explain 28.6% of the variance in the dependent variable (*i.e.*, repeat customers). Prediction success overall was 66.7%.

We analyzed whether the introduction of the capstone template had an effect on grades. Figure 3 graphs the average capstone project grades per year. The template was introduced in 2014, but was not mandatory until 2016, so we plot the average grades per year before the introduction of the template, during the overlap, and after the template became mandatory. In 2015, only one student team chose to not use the template, so the data point is an outlier. Statistical analysis and the graphs show that the introduction of the templates led to an increase in the academic advisor grade, had no statistically significant impact on industrial grades, and closed the gap between the academic advisor and industrial advisor grades. This suggests that the templates led to the academic advisors being more satisfied with the capstone, but that the industrial advisor was more interested in the project deliverables than the reports' formatting.

3.4 Question 3: Student Attitudes

We reviewed a sample of 40 student project reflections (part of the final report), 20 from projects that used the templates and 20 from those that did not. We marked the reflections for mentions of 3 aspects - the advisors, team dynamics, project documents - and whether the mention implied a positive, neutral, or critical attitude.

Of the 40 reflections, 36 mentioned the advisors. The majority (31, 86%) expressed a positive attitude, mostly gratitude for the energy and time they spent helping the team. A few (5, 14%) expressed critical attitudes, mostly about communication issues with the students (*e.g., "the advisors were disconnected from what was going on with the project"*). There was no significant difference in the advisor grades between the projects with positive and critical attitudes (mean 92% positive, 91% critical, null hypothesis not rejected).

Of the 40 reflections, 20 mentioned the team. We cross referenced attitudes about the team with team size. As shown in Table 4a, the majority of reflections showed a positive or neutral attitude toward the team, but some were critical. The results clearly showed that students of larger teams tended to have more positive attitudes about the team (χ^2 test $p < 0.01$). Positive mentions tended to be about how the students learned to divide up work (*e.g., "Cleanly dividing up*

Table 4. Attitudes in student reflections.

(a) Team Attitude vs Size

Team Size	Team Attitude		
	Critical	Neutral	Positive
1	3	0	0
2	2	5	9
3	0	0	1

(b) Document Attitude vs Template Use

Used Template?	Document Attitude		
	Critical	Neutral	Positive
Yes	3	0	17
No	1	0	11

work and planning meetings between the team make the work more efficient.") and give each other feedback (*e.g.*, *"We were surprised to find that two minds working together as one made the work richer in information and reduced the chances of errors."*). Critical attitudes toward the team reflected poor team chemistry (*e.g.*, *"For future project developers we warmly recommend choosing an appropriate partner for doing the project."*). For lone students, they were generally regret at working alone (*e.g.*, *"It's better to work in pairs, the work is then divided in half and thinking will be more developed."*).

Most of the reflections mentioned the documents (32). We cross referenced attitudes about the documents with template use. As shown in Table 4b, the majority of students (28, 87.5%) expressed positive attitudes, primarily about how the documents helped them remain organized and on track (*e.g.*, *"Building the Charter document helped a lot to understand what the customer requires"*, *"The Design document helped me stay organized during implementation (I implemented one use case at a time)"*). Those with critical attitudes (4, 12.5%) criticized the documents as being inappropriate for agile development. In 3 of the critical reflections, the teams had received a detailed design document from the customer before the project began, so they felt the college documents were superfluous. Analysis did not show a conclusive dependency between document attitude and template use (χ^2 test $p > 0.05$, null hypothesis not rejected), so the templates may not have affected student attitudes toward the documentation.

4 Related Work

Capstone projects are common requirements in engineering departments. [4] give a taxonomy of engineering capstone courses, including a survey of common practices and a literature review relating to them. [5] present a model for evaluating the inclusion of external stakeholders in project courses in general and [6] describe results from industrial capstone projects, issues central to our model since we directed the majority of capstone projects to external industrial customers. [7] describe two different capstone processes and their outcomes.

Software engineering capstones have been researched by many institutions. [8] and [9] describe project processes in computer science and software engineering at their institutions. [10] present a multi-institutional study of capstone projects in computing departments. They survey five institutions and the methodologies that they use in the capstone project courses. The emphasis of their work is on the integration of open source or free software in capstone projects and on the use of community-oriented topics in motivating student interest. [11] presents an industrial internship model for capstone projects used in the software engineering department of a large American institution. [12] discuss capstone project models in the computing departments in six universities on multiple continents. Each university summarizes the technical basics of the capstone course(s) at their institutions. Some of the institutions mention the use of large project teams, with one using globally distributed teams that must coordinate across time zones and continents. The context of the project (industrial or academic) and the documentation methods that each institution uses are not mentioned.

[13] presents a course in the spirit of our capstone project's process. It makes the jump from undergraduate software engineering courses to applied software management.

5 Conclusions

Capstone projects are the final step in a software engineering student's academic path at our institution. We encourage students to take on challenging projects in industrial settings that force them to work as a team, use the knowledge they acquired during their course work, and learn new technologies. Gathering data from ten years of capstones has given us insight into how project teams form, how their work progresses, and where process improvements are needed.

Our analyses found that most students preferred to work in teams and were satisfied with their project's software product and its documentation. Most students were happy with their industrial advisor's help during the project. Expressions of critical attitudes about the advisor and advisor grade were not shown to be dependent, so even students who were less than satisfied with their industrial advisor received grades similar to those who were satisfied with them. This points to the students successfully fulfilling their project obligations despite a less than ideal advisor relationship.

While the introduction of document templates for project reports was not associated with improved industrial grades or changes in student reflections, they led to improved academic outcomes and reduced headaches for students and academic advisors. We recommend their use at other institutions to formalize their documentation procedures and increase reporting uniformity and completeness.

Since Hebrew is our institution's language of instruction, the templates were created in Hebrew. Due to their success, we have translated the templates to English to make them usable by the wider community. They can be accessed at http://www2.kinneret.ac.il/mjmay/finalprojects.html.

References

1. Council for Higher Education: Kavim mankhim vi'hagdarot li'tokhniot limudim ba'tkhumim handasat makhshavim, handasat khashmal vi'elektronika, handasat tokhna u'mada'ey ha-makhshev - hakhlatat malag mi'yom 27.09.2016. Council for Higher Education, Jerusalem (2016). (Feitelson committee report)
2. United States Department of Defense: MIL-STD-498. United States Department of Defense Standard (1994)
3. Paasivaara, M., Vanhanen, J., Lassenius, C.: Collaborating with industrial customers in a capstone project course: the customers' perspective. In: 2019 IEEE/ACM 41st International Conference on Software Engineering: Software Engineering Education and Training (ICSE-SEET), pp. 12–22 (2019)
4. Dutson, A.J., Todd, R.H., Magleby, S.P., Sorensen, C.D.: A review of literature on teaching engineering design through project-oriented capstone courses. J. Eng. Educ. **86**(1), 17–28 (1997)

5. Steghöfer, J.P., et al.: Involving external stakeholders in project courses. ACM Trans. Comput. Educ. **18**(2), 8:1–8:32 (2018)
6. Gorka, S., Miller, J.R., Howe, B.J.: Developing realistic capstone projects in conjunction with industry. In: Proceedings of the 8th ACM SIGITE Conference on Information Technology Education. Association for Computing Machinery, New York (2007)
7. Davis, H.G., Zilora, S.J.: A tale of two capstones. In: Proceedings of the 17th Annual Conference on Information Technology Education, SIGITE 2016, pp. 130–135. Association for Computing Machinery, New York (2016)
8. Mohan, S., Chenoweth, S., Bohner, S.: Towards a better capstone experience. In: Proceedings of the 43rd ACM Technical Symposium on Computer Science Education, pp. 111–116. Association for Computing Machinery, New York (2012)
9. Conn, R.: A reusable, academic-strength, metrics-based software engineering process for capstone courses and projects. In: Proceedings of the 35th SIGCSE Technical Symposium on Computer Science Education, pp. 492–496. Association for Computing Machinery, New York (2004)
10. Braught, G., et al.: A multi-institutional perspective on H/FOSS projects in the computing curriculum. ACM Trans. Comput. Educ. **18**(2), 7:1–7:31 (2018)
11. Reichlmay, T.J.: Collaborating with industry: strategies for an undergraduate software engineering program. In: Proceedings of the 2006 International Workshop on Summit on Software Engineering Education, pp. 13–16. Association for Computing Machinery, New York (2006)
12. Adams, L., Daniels, M., Goold, A., Hazzan, O., Lynch, K., Newman, I.: Challenges in teaching capstone courses. In: Proceedings of the 8th Annual Conference on Innovation and Technology in Computer Science Education, pp. 219–220. Association for Computing Machinery, New York (2003)
13. Tomer, A.: Software mangineeringment: teaching project management from software engineering perspective. In: 2015 IEEE Global Engineering Education Conference (EDUCON), pp. 5–11 (2015)

A Feasibility Study on Learning of Object-Oriented Programming Based on Fairy Tales

Motoki Miura(✉)

Chiba Institute of Technology, Tsudanuma, Narashino, Chiba, Japan
motoki.miura@p.chibakoudai.jp

Abstract. In learning object-oriented programming (OOP), it is necessary to understand the concept of OOP and apply it to actual development. However, acquiring such skills is not easy for novice programmers. We propose a learning method based on fairy tales in order to make it easier for learners to work by assuming a specific situation, and to make it easier for other learners to share the situation. In the proposed method, the learners select one fairy tale as the subject themselves, and express the flow of the story by interaction between characters, changing attributes, exchanging objects, and outputting narrations. Finally, the learners design the classes and methods necessary for expressing them, and actually realize as an executable program. We applied the proposed method in a lecture at the graduate school and confirmed the feasibility.

Keywords: Object-Oriented Programming · Software Analysis and Design · Software Engineering

1 Introduction

Object-oriented programming (OOP) is a basic programming paradigm, and its importance and need are high. The best feature of OOP is that it can naturally express real-world relationships and events in a practical way. In order to express the real-world relationships and events in an object-oriented (OO) paradigm, OO software analysis is necessary. There are several approaches for OO software analysis that have been developed: (1) the object model approach, (2) the dynamic model approach, and (3) the functional model approach. The difference between these approaches is the model that the developer works with first. However, during the analysis and design, it is expected that the developer considers these approaches while going back and forth.

Generally, it is difficult to understand the concepts of OOP for novice learners [7,9,13]. Therefore, there are many hurdles to master the model approaches in addition to the concepts. We thought that these hurdles can be lowered by considering small situations based on the principle of small steps.

In this paper, we propose a practical OOP learning method that employs fairy tales. In this learning method, the learner selects a specific fairy tale, and defines

Published by Springer Nature Switzerland AG 2023
T. Keane et al. (Eds.): WCCE 2022, IFIP AICT 685, pp. 579–590, 2023.
https://doi.org/10.1007/978-3-031-43393-1_52

the classes and interfaces that are appropriate and necessary for expressing the story. In addition, by describing and implementing it as OOP source code, the relationships and interactions between the characters can be expressed.

2 Related Work

There are much research on learning OOP languages and concepts. Dwarika et al. [3] used a visual programming environment called *Alice* for novice programmers to learn OOP concepts, whilst creating animated movies and video games. Using Alice addressed challenges faced by inexperienced learners within the object-oriented domain and increased their motivation to learn OOP. Kanemune and Kuno introduced an object-oriented programming (OOP) language suitable for K12 education named *Dolittle* [5]. Dolittle adopts a prototype-based OOP language such as Javascript for simplicity. Therefore, the users are not required to understand class and abstraction concepts. Although the simple prototype-based language design is appropriate for elementary school education, learning abstract concepts such as class and inheritance is not covered. Miura et al. [8] proposed an interactive workbench software for learning fundamentals of data structures with the concepts of type, variable, object, and their relations in OOP language. When the learner manipulates graphical models, the system immediately generates corresponding codes. Tanielu et al. [12] utilize virtual reality (VR) and analogies of "houses" and its blueprint for OOP concepts learning. VR is used to promote immersiveness and deep involvement. Method calls are represented by entering and exiting the room, and arguments are represented by placing a box on a window sill. This research employs visual elements and its interactions to help the learner understand the OOP language and concepts. Our method also expects the learners to understand OOP, but we focus on the activities of the learners themselves modeling the situation through the story.

Sasaki et al. [11] proposed OOP education using learning content based on stories. In this research, some situations are given by the stories, which facilitate the students to perform tasks. Teachers carefully design and prepare learning content with scenarios. Our proposed method that employs "fairy tales" differs in that the learners themselves freely select the story and then design and implements it to express the story.

Akayama et al. [2] proposed an effective use of Model-driven development (MDD) tools in UML modeling education. By using the MDD tool, the learner can generate the code and check the operation immediately after drawing the class diagram and the state machine diagram. Comparing the case with and without the MDD tool, the group using the MDD tool tends to develop from the bottom up because the operation can be confirmed for each function, and the group without the MDD tool tends to perform top-down development.

Knuth proposed a programming style named "literate programming" [6]. In this programming style, programs and explanatory documents are mixed and described in one literary file, and development can be performed while maintaining the consistency between the two. Although there are similarities in terms of literary description of the program, the method proposed in this study aims to understand and establish the learner's knowledge by expressing the story using the paradigm of OOP.

A web article "Let's write storytelling code" [10] introduced merits and its importance of OOP with "sense of story" while showing two types of different codes. The author emphasizes the sense of story in the second section that "the class naturally becomes the subject, the method naturally becomes the predicate, and the argument naturally becomes the object," which is consistent with the basic idea of our proposed method. In our study, as a learning method of OO software design, the learners themself recall a concrete fairy tale, and think about how to express the story with OOP.

3 Method

The proposed OOP learning method based on a story is a learner-centric approach. Firstly, the leaners themselves decide a specific "fairy tale" and express the story through OOP. In this process, the learners should consider both class hierarchy and dynamic aspects of OOP. After expressing the story, the learners organize presentation by composing resources such as figures, source code, and execution results. Finally, the learners explain their work and ingenuity along with the chosen fairy tale.

3.1 Characteristic

In a fairy tale, characters appear in the story and act along the time axis while interacting with each other. The characters can be categorized into specific types, such as humans and animals, and include attributes such as age, gender, height and weight. Some characters own items, and perform with their emotions. In addition, relationships and responses are dynamically changed. These changes in the story can be expressed by analysis, design, and implementation of an OOP approach. The preconditions and situation settings of a specific "story" become appropriate constraints, and common recognition and understanding are promoted, which facilitates communication. The experience of thinking with a specific story can be applied to the real-world analysis.

3.2 Expected Benefits

The following points can be mentioned as the merits assumed by "adopting a fairy tale as a subject" in the proposed method.

- **The charm of the story:** Existing fairy tale is known over many years, and the story itself is highly attractive.
- **Diversity and degree of freedom:** Since there are many stories in the world, the degree of freedom in selecting a story is high.
- **Concreteness:** After selecting a story and a scene, the characters and events are determined concretely, so it is easy to analyze, design, and implement.

- **Ingenuity and arrangement are possible:** In addition to expressing the story as it is, the learners can arrange some parts such as "what if."
- **A gap between story and program expression:** There is a gap that expresses a classic story in a modern program notation. The gap creates fun and novelty.
- **Easy to share intentions with other learners:** If the story itself is well known, it is easy to share the meaning and intention when explaining it to other learners.

By expressing the story, it is possible to handle not only the static relationships contained in the story but also the analysis, design, and implementation of dynamic aspects along the time axis. Also, by using an integrated development environment (IDE), the learners can easily check the syntax of implementation while coding.

3.3 Issues of Concern

The problems of concern in the proposed method are listed below.

- **Difficult to select a story:** Since the degree of freedom in story selection is high, the learner may stumble at the time of story selection. It may take too much time to select a story.
- **Cannot apply OOP concepts:** We believe that most of fairy tales and stories can be represented by OOP. However, there might be some stories not suitable for the OOP paradigm.
- **Using uncommon stories may reduce effectiveness:** If the selected fairy tale is not well known, mutual understanding between learners is hindered. In such case, the effect of "easy to share intentions with other learners" mentioned in the above merit will be reduced.

4 Feasibility Study

In order to investigate the effect of the proposed learning method, we conducted a feasibility study in the lecture.

4.1 Course Contents and Assignment

We chose the course "Advanced System Software" for graduate students. The course was held online for 13 weeks, 120 min per week. Seven students took the course. The first half of the course contains object-oriented and design patterns [4] through Java programming. As a summary of the first half, the following assignment was given to the students at the beginning of the 5th course on October 19th, 2021. We explained the detail of the assignment for about 40 min.

Assignment

> Select one specific story (old story or fairy tale), define multiple classes required to express that story, and then express the flow of the story as well as the behavior of the characters in Java program.

The purposes of the assignment were (1) to check the knowledge and concepts of OOP learned in the first half of the course, and (2) to confirm if the class can be designed properly by applying the story.

The students were asked to work on this task individually or in groups. As a result, five students worked individually, and two students composed a pair. The students selected a story and created a program while thinking about how to express it in the class. In addition, we asked them to create Web pages containing figures, source code, execution results, etc. as presentation material. The expected time for presentation was 5 min per theme. The presentation was held at the time of the 8th course (November 9th, 2021). There was a three-week period for the assignment.

When presenting the assignment, the teacher explained to the students the following source code example based on "*Momotaro*." Momotaro (Peach Boy) [1] is one of the famous and popular Japanese folklore.

Figure 1 defines the main method of code example. It represents the beginning of Momotaro. Figure 2 and Fig. 3 show class definitions of "Things" and "Creatures" and its subclasses that appear in Momotaro respectively. Figure 4 is the output of the code example. Note that the name of classes and variables of the following code examples were translated to English.

While showing the code example, we explained the following notes in the course.

- The "story" should be something that everyone is familiar with.
- First, create a class to represent characters and things that appear as objects. At that time, if there is a hierarchical relationship, it is expressed by inheritance, and common members and methods are defined in the parent class.
- The exchanges between characters and the delivery of things are expressed by method calls. We will add the methods necessary for that.
- We recommend adopting the "subject.action(predicate)" format for readability.

Although the design tools and development environment were not particularly specified, many students might use Visual Studio Code and its Extension Pack for Java introduced in the course.

After the presentation, we administered a questionnaire to the students, which consisted of the following questions.

1. How long did it take to decide on the story that explains object-oriented programming?
   (1) About 1 h (2) About 2 h (3) About 3 h (4) About 4 h (5) More time

```
public class MyApp {
    Run | Debug
    public static void main(String[] args) throws Exception {
        // Once upon a time, an old man and an old woman lived in a certain place.
        Grandpa granpa = new Grandpa();
        Grandma grandma = new Grandma();
        // Grandma picked up a peach in the river
        Peach momo = new Peach();
        // Momotaro was born from peach
        Momotaro taro = momo.bornMomotaro();
        // The grandmother gave Momotaro a bag of kibi dumplings.
        grandma.makeDumplings();
        grandma.handOverBag(taro);

        // There was a dog. Momotaro gave the dog a kibi dumpling
        Dog dog = new Dog();
        taro.watasuKibi(dog);
        // There was a monkey. Momotaro gave the monkey a kibi dumpling
        Monkey monkey = new Monkey();
        taro.watasuKibi(monkey);
        // There was a pheasant. Momotaro gave the pheasant a kibi dumpling
        Pheasant pheasant = new Pheasant();
        taro.watasuKibi(pheasant);
    }
}
```

Fig. 1. Main method of Momotaro.

2. How long did it take to design the classes that express the chosen story? (Excluding the time to create UML diagrams, etc.)
   (1) About 1 h (2) About 2 h (3) About 3 h (4) About 4 h (5) More time
3. After designing the class, how long did it take to create a program to express the story?
   (1) About 1 h (2) About 2 h (3) About 3 h (4) About 4 h (5) More time
4. Please say what is challenging when creating a program that expresses a story. If possible, answer separately for the class definition and the coding.
5. What kind of knowledge and skills do you think you could acquire by creating a program that expresses the chosen story with object-oriented thinking?
6. If you have any ideas for learning object-oriented programming other than using a story, please tell us.
7. If you have any other suggestions for improving the assignment, please tell us.

4.2 Student Work

Table 1 shows the characteristics of student work with the title of the fairy tale, number of classes, lines of the program and the explanation time at the presentation. Except for "The Straw Millionaire," the explanation was based

```
import java.util.ArrayDeque;
public class Item {
    String name = "";
    public Item(String name){
        this.name = name;
    }
    @Override
    public String toString(){
        return name;
    }
}
class Peach extends Item {
    Peach(){
        super("Peach");
    }
    Momotaro bornMomotaro(){
        return new Momotaro(); //Momotaro was born
    }
}
class Kibidango extends Item {
    Kibidango(){
        super("Kibidango");
    }
}
class Bag extends Item {
    ArrayDeque<Item> fukuro;
    Bag(){
        super("a bag containing kibidango");
        fukuro = new ArrayDeque<Item>();
    }
    public void add(Item mono){
        fukuro.add(mono);
    }
    public Item pop(){
        return fukuro.pop();
    }
    public int size(){
        return fukuro.size();
    }
}
```

Fig. 2. Class definition regarding "things" in Momotaro.

on valid and executable Java programs. For "The Straw Millionaire," the concept codes that contain item bartering and class definition of characters were submitted, but concrete codes for representing story were not shown. At least 5 classes (9 on average) including inheritance were defined. In addition, some

```
public class Creatures {
    String name = "";
    void printName(){  System.out.println(name);  }
    void get(Item mono){
        System.out.println(name + " got "+mono.toString()+".");
    }
}
class Momotaro extends Creatures {
    Bag kibiBukuro;
    Momotaro(){    name = "Momotaro";    }
    void get(Item mono){
        super.get(mono);
        if (mono instanceof Bag) kibiBukuro = (Bag)mono;
    }
    void watasuKibi(Creatures dareka){
        Kibidango oneKibi = (Kibidango)kibiBukuro.pop();
        dareka.get(oneKibi);
        System.out.println("  "+kibiBukuro.size()+" kibidango(s) left");
    }
}
class Grandpa extends Creatures {
    Grandpa(){  name = "Grandpa";    }
}
class Grandma extends Creatures {
    Bag bag;
    Grandma(){
        name = "Grandma";
        bag = new Bag();
    }
    void makeDumplings(){
        bag.add(new Kibidango());
        bag.add(new Kibidango());
        bag.add(new Kibidango());
    }
    void handOverBag(Creatures dareka){
        dareka.get(bag);
        bag = null;
    }
}
class Dog extends Creatures {
    Dog(){    name = "Dog";     }
}
class Monkey extends Creatures {
    Monkey(){  name = "Monkey";     }
}
class Pheasant extends Creatures {
    Pheasant(){  name = "Pheasant";    }
}
```

Fig. 3. Class definition regarding "creatures" in Momotaro.

work adopted design patterns and students mentioned this at the presentation. "Princess Kaguya" used the Singleton pattern not to generate more than two princesses. "The Three Axes" adopted the Template Method pattern for the series of similar events. "The Giant Turnip" utilized recursive function calls to represent the story. "Little One-Inch" adopted the setting that the height is

```
Momotaro got a bag containing kibidango.
Dog got Kibidango.
   2 kibidango(s) left
Monkey got Kibidango.
   1 kibidango(s) left
Pheasant got Kibidango.
   0 kibidango(s) left
```

Fig. 4. Output of Momotaro example program.

doubled when using a gavel. Almost all students could clearly explain the intent in both class design and implementations.

Table 1. Characteristics of student works.

Fairy Tale	Num of Classes	Lines	Time to explain
The Three Axes	8	162	5 m 36 s
The three little pigs	11	110	3 m 27 s
The Giant Turnip	9	138	5 m 58 s
The Straw Millionaire	14	117	3 m 55 s
Princess Kaguya	7	238	4 m 37 s
Little One-Inch	5	76	3 m 58 s
Average	9.0	140.2	4 m 35 s
Std. Dev.	3.2	55.9	60 s

4.3 Result of Questionnaire

Based on the answers of questionnaire items (1) to (3), Fig. 5 shows how much time the students spent on story selection and decision, class design, and programming. From the results, most of the students chose a story in about one hour, and spent more time on class design and program creation. Note that the order of the student ID and the story titles shown in Table 1 does not correspond.

The students' answers to question item (4) is shown below.

- I had a certain idea in my head, but when I actually started writing, I learned that I could express it in various ways, so it was difficult to complete the program as I expected.
- I was a little confused about how much generalization and specialization should be done when defining a class.
- I was wondering what to define for the method of the parent class.
- Conditional branch is not suitable for representing similar stories because the statement becomes too complicated.

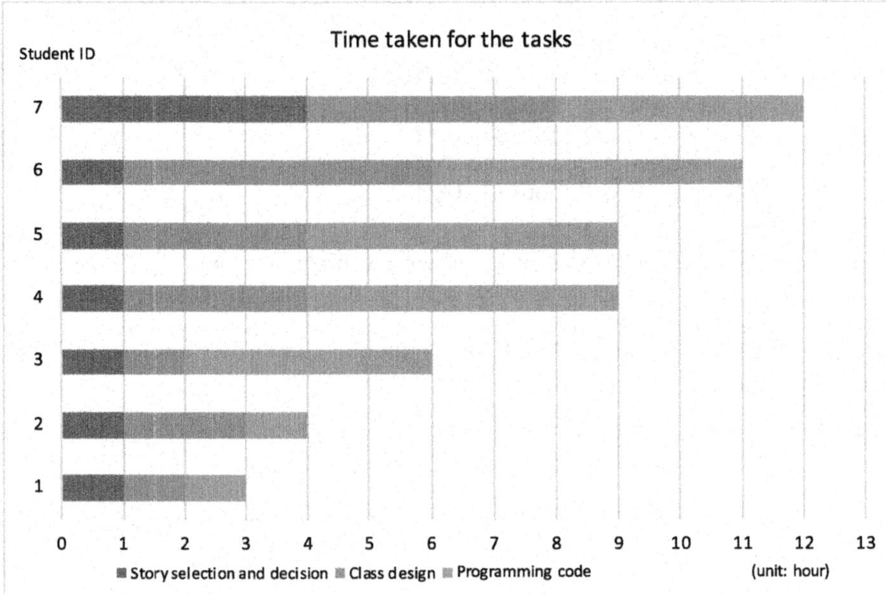

Fig. 5. Result of questionnaire (1) to (3) for 7 students.

The students' answers to question item (5) is shown below.

- By writing while actually thinking, I think I was able to use the knowledge I learned, saying, "If you have this knowledge, you can improve this part by changing it like this." Also, I think that I have become able to look up the information accurately when there is something I do not understand with my ability to think.
- I made a story without using design patterns, but after investigating, I understood that design patterns can be used in such cases.
- I haven't learned this yet, but I got a better understanding by actually making something using object-oriented programming.
- The whole structure can be determined to some extent by using a design pattern.

The students' answers to question item (6) is shown below.

- I wanted to express a famous scene from the game.
- Organizations such as companies
- I thought that the idea of expressing a story in a program would be very educational. I can't think of anything else.

4.4 Discussion

As a result of presenting the task based on the proposed method in this experimental course, it can be said that all the learners understood the intention of the task and were able to apply the idea of object-oriented design to the story. In addition, the ratio of story selection time to the total task execution time was at most one third. From this result, it was found that even if the method of making the learner think from the selection of the story is adopted, the graduate students can carry out the task without any problem. Most students noticed that there is not only one answer for design and implementation, and that appropriate design and implementation differ depending on the situation and purpose.

Since the course explained the design pattern from the 5th week to the 7th week, there were some implementations and presentations related to the design pattern. The results of the questionnaire also showed references to design patterns. By listening to the course while thinking about how to tackle the task of expressing the story, it is possible that the consciousness of utilizing knowledge was strengthened.

5 Conclusion

We have proposed a method of using fairy tales as an assignment for learners learning object-oriented programming to work on each phase of analysis, design, and implementation while considering each phase simultaneously and across aspects. In the proposed learning method, the learners select one fairy tale as the subject themselves, and express the flow of the story by interaction between characters, changing attributes, exchanging objects, and outputting narrations. The learners design the classes and methods necessary for expressing them, and implement as an executable program.

Although fairy tales are fiction, they have been popular for a long time and are well known. Therefore, the learner can freely arrange the detailed settings for a part of the fairy tale while following the basic plot. In addition, by carefully examining the program execution results, it is possible to confirm the correctness of the design and implementation. Learners can be trained to analyze fairy tale stories and plots and select the appropriate level of abstraction from a meta perspective.

As a result of applying the proposed method in the lecture at the graduate school, the learner was able to understand the intention and select an appropriate fairy tale. In addition, based on the characteristics of the selected fairy tale, the learner created a program consisting of multiple classes while demonstrating abundant creativity. From these facts, it is considered that the proposed method is highly feasible and has a high learning effect.

Acknowledgement. The part of this research was supported by the fund of KAKENHI Grant-in-Aid for Scientific Research (C): Grant Number 22K12319 and 19K03056.

References

1. Momotaro. https://en.wikipedia.org/wiki/Momotar%C5%8D. Accessed 26 Feb 2022

2. Akayama, S., Hisazumi, K., Hiya, S., Fukuda, A.: Using model-driven development tools for object-oriented modeling education. In: EduSymp@ MoDELS (2013)
3. Dwarika, J., de Villiers, M.R.R.: Use of the Alice visual environment in teaching and learning object-oriented programming. In: Proceedings of the 2015 Annual Research Conference on South African Institute of Computer Scientists and Information Technologists, SAICSIT 2015. Association for Computing Machinery, New York (2015). https://doi.org/10.1145/2815782.2815815
4. Gamma, E., Helm, R., Johnson, R., Vlissides, J.: Design Patterns: Elements of Reusable Object-Oriented Software (1994)
5. Kanemune, S., Kuno, Y.: Dolittle: an object-oriented language for K12 education. In: EuroLogo, pp. 144–153 (2005)
6. Knuth, D.E.: Literate programming. Comput. J. **27**(2), 97–111 (1984)
7. Liberman, N., Beeri, C., Ben-David Kolikant, Y.: Difficulties in learning inheritance and polymorphism. ACM Trans. Comput. Educ. (TOCE) **11**(1), 1–23 (2011)
8. Miura, M., Sugihara, T., Kunifuji, S.: Anchor garden: an interactive workbench for basic data concept learning in object oriented programming languages. In: Proceedings of the 14th Annual ACM SIGCSE Conference on Innovation and Technology in Computer Science Education, pp. 141–145 (2009)
9. Ragonis, N., Ben-Ari, M.: A long-term investigation of the comprehension of OOP concepts by novices (2005)
10. Roku: Let's write storytelling code (2020). https://zenn.dev/ad5/articles/6780d514ed8cda6bdf0f. (in Japanese, Accessed 2 Feb 2022)
11. Sasaki, S., Watanabe, H., Takai, K., Arai, M., Takei, S.: A practice example of object-oriented programming education using WebCT. In: Proceedings of the 2005 Conference on Towards Sustainable and Scalable Educational Innovations Informed by the Learning Sciences: Sharing Good Practices of Research, Experimentation and Innovation, pp. 871–874 (2005)
12. Tanielu, T., 'Akau'ola, R., Varoy, E., Giacaman, N.: Combining analogies and virtual reality for active and visual object-oriented programming. In: Proceedings of the ACM Conference on Global Computing Education, pp. 92–98 (2019)
13. Xinogalos, S., Sartatzemi, M., Dagdilelis, V.: Studying students' difficulties in an OOP course based on BlueJ. In: IASTED International Conference on Computers and Advanced technology in Education, pp. 82–87 (2006)

Scaffolding Task Planning Using Abstract Parsons Problems

James Prather[1], John Homer[1], Paul Denny[2], Brett A. Becker[3](✉), John Marsden[4], and Garrett Powell[1]

[1] Abilene Christian University, Abilene, TX, USA
james.prather@ucd.ie

[2] The University of Auckland, Auckland, New Zealand
paul@cs.auckland.ac.nz

[3] University College Dublin, Belfield, Dublin 4, Ireland
brett.becker@ucd.ie

[4] North Carolina State University, Raleigh, NC, USA
jmmarsde@ncsu.edu

Abstract. Interest is growing in the role of metacognition in computing education. Most work to-date has examined metacognitive approaches of novices learning to code. It has been shown that novices navigate through discernible stages of a problem-solving process when working through programming problems, and that scaffolding can be beneficial. In this paper, we describe a novel scaffolding task aimed at guiding novices through a crucial stage of developing and evaluating a problem-solving plan. We presented novices with a problem statement before working through an Abstract Parsons Problem, where the blocks present structural elements rather than complete code, to aid high-level planning before writing code. Comparing groups who experienced this approach with those that did not, revealed that novices who worked on an Abstract Parsons Problem before coding were more successful in solving the task and demonstrated improved metacognitive knowledge related to task planning when asked to identify useful future problem-solving strategies. Our observations from two courses over two years suggest that scaffolding students through a planning step prior to coding can be beneficial for students. We provide directions for future work in exploring strategies for providing this type of guidance, including the use of different types of planning activities, and studying these effects at scale.

Keywords: Automated assessment tools · CS1 · Introductory programming · Novice programmers · Metacognition · Metacognitive awareness · Parsons problems

1 Introduction

Metacognition, or thinking about thinking, is an increasingly important topic in computing education [1]. It is an essential set of skills necessary for efficient

Published by Springer Nature Switzerland AG 2023
T. Keane et al. (Eds.): WCCE 2022, IFIP AICT 685, pp. 591–602, 2023.
https://doi.org/10.1007/978-3-031-43393-1_53

and elegant programming problem-solving [2], and most successful novice students tend to display more metacognitive behaviors than their less successful peers [3]. However, many novices lack metacognitive insight [4] making problem-solving laborious and difficult, particularly in programming which is inherently complex [5,6] and could be made easier to learn [7]. Without the ability to step back and think through one's progress (or lack thereof) during problem-solving, novices may waste time on incorrect approaches or become lost and frustrated [8]. Applying metacognitive scaffolds in the context of novices learning to program, holds promise but is under-investigated [9].

We present a novel classroom activity for scaffolding novice programmers' metacognition through a specific stage of problem-solving as they envision their solution *before writing code*. We utilize a variation on Parsons Problems [18] for students to explicitly engage in planning out the structure of solutions after reading a problem prompt. Unlike other forms of Parsons Problems, we used abstract code statements (e.g. "while loop", "assignment", generic input/output, etc.) rather than syntactically complete lines of code. This novel use of the Parsons Problem framework, which we call "Abstract Parsons Problems", served two purposes. First, it removed syntactic clues from the blocks which researchers have previously observed being used to construct solutions without having a full understanding of the problem [20]. Second, these abstract statements aim to get students to plan the general structure of solutions before jumping into code – supported by prior research showing that prematurely writing code often inhibits success [13]. We hypothesize that this approach will: (1) assist students in successfully solving the corresponding programming task; and (2) encourage them to plan solutions to future programming tasks once the scaffolding is removed.

We explored the use of Abstract Parsons Problems in two introductory courses taught over two years, and have observed students solving programming problems both with and without their use. We frame our evaluation around two high-level goals: **Goal 1:** Explore whether students are more likely to successfully solve a programming task when they first work through a related Abstract Parsons Problem. **Goal 2:** Discover in what ways the Abstract Parsons Problem step affects students' perceptions of task difficulty and their identification of future problem-solving strategies. We address the first by comparing task completion rates when students work through an Abstract Parsons Problem beforehand with a control group. To address the second, we analyze student comments from treatment group surveys for evidence of metacognitive thoughts and behaviors related to task difficulty and strategies students plan to use in the future.

2 Background

Metacognition describes knowledge about a person's own cognitive control, including identifying past strategies that have been successful (or not), monitoring emotions and self-efficacy, and evaluating the validity of metacognitive knowledge based on feedback [1]. It has been used in psychology-based research for decades but has only begun to be researched in the context of computing education [1]. Regardless of discipline, metacognitive skills are accepted as aiding learning, but such skills do not necessarily transfer easily across different pursuits [10]. It is likely that the development of metacognitive skills needs to take place within the context of a student's learning in order to be effective.

Few studies have tried to explicitly attempt this. VanDeGrift et al. reported helping students think through their design process, arguing that programming courses should not only teach language/syntax but also metacognitive skills associated with programming [11]. More recent work has required students to solve a test case problem (i.e. converting input to output) after reading the problem prompt before they began coding [12]. Their results indicate that students who first solved the test case problem were more successful at solving the subsequent programming problem, avoided early misunderstandings that could potentially derail their problem-solving process, and verbalized more metacognitive behaviors than those in a control group. Their findings were confirmed in two separate replications [13,14]. Another recent study found that both high- and low-performers can exhibit weak metacognitive accuracy, illuminating the potential for metacognitive interventions to benefit students of all skill levels [15].

2.1 Loksa's Problem-Solving Framework

Loksa et al. proposed a six-stage programming problem-solving process based on psychology of programming literature [16,17] which serves as a theoretical framework for novice metacognition while solving programming problems. Although nominally sequential, these stages are in practice revisited frequently as programmers refine a solution iteratively. The six stages are: (1) Reinterpret problem prompt; (2) Search for analogous problems; (3) Search for new solutions or adapt existing solutions; (4) Evaluate a potential solution; (5) Implement a solution; and (6) Evaluate implemented solution.

When solving programming problems, beginners are often not aware of where they are in the problem-solving process – demonstrating a lack of metacognition. In the present work, we focus on stage 4 of Loksa's framework *Evaluate a potential solution*, described as [17]: "With a solution in mind, programmers must evaluate how well this solution will address the problem. ... Without evaluating potential solutions, programmers may waste time writing code and integrating it into their program only to find that it does not actually solve their problem".

One way to scaffold novice programmer metacognition during stage 4 of the problem-solving process is with Abstract Parsons Problems (see Sect. 3). Loksa suggested that novice programmers could benefit from some sort of explicit scaffolding during the murky middle of the problem-solving process [17], and it has been suggested that Parsons Problems could be used for this purpose [8].

2.2 Parsons Problems

Parsons & Haden first introduced Parsons Programming Puzzles, a kind of drag-and-drop exercise involving code fragments, in 2006 [18]. Since then "Parsons

Problems" have received much attention, appearing in dozens of computing education research papers [19]. Parsons Problems have been used as a scaffolding step before students learn to code as they remove the requirement for constructing syntactically correct statements at the character level. However, this can oversimplify the problem-solving process. Weinman et al. observed that some students use syntactic clues in the blocks to find solutions without necessarily understanding the problem, and thus introduced Faded Parsons Problems in which parts of the provided code are incomplete [20]. Garcia et al. used Parsons Problems to scaffold the programming design process [21]. However, they defined blocks at a coarser level of granularity than what we propose, and did not seek to discuss the intervention in the context of novice programmer metacognition.

3 Methodology

Our observations were made during two consecutive years (referred to as Year 1 and Year 2) of a typical introductory programming or "CS1" [22] course using C++ taught at a small US university. The Abstract Parsons Problems were introduced approximately half-way through the course. Figure 1 shows a schematic view of the evaluations where students completed a survey after attempting a programming problem. In each year, students solved the same programming problem both with and without the Abstract Parsons Problem step. The Year 1 evaluation used a between-subjects design, where each student was assigned to one of two groups, with only one prompted to solve the Abstract Parsons Problem after reading the problem statement. When presenting and discussing our results, we will refer to these two groups for Year 1 as the "Parsons" group and the "non-Parsons" group. The Year 2 evaluation used a within-subjects design where all students initially solved a programming problem (problem #1) without the Abstract Parsons Problem step, and then approximately one week later solved a problem of similar complexity (problem #2) that included the Abstract Parsons Problem step. In both years, students had a whole class period (50 min) to complete each programming task and the survey.

The programming problem in Year 1 asked students to write a program to display the set of distinct values coming from standard input until encountering −1. This problem prompt can be seen in Fig. 2. In Year 2, programming problem #1 asked students to print out a table of exponential numbers, and programming problem #2 (presented to students one week later) asked students to sequentially search for a value in an array. The difficulty of the two problems in Year 2 was roughly similar for where students were in the course when they encountered them, and commensurate with the topics covered in the two weeks.

The survey that students were prompted to complete after each programming problem was designed to help us address Goal 2 (see Sect. 1). In both years, the survey was identical and consisted of the following two reflective questions: 1) What did you find most difficult about this programming task? 2) What strategies do you think might be useful for solving similar problems in the future?

The Abstract Parsons Problem was delivered via a web-based interface, using js-parsons [23] integrated into Canvas, illustrated in Fig. 2. Students

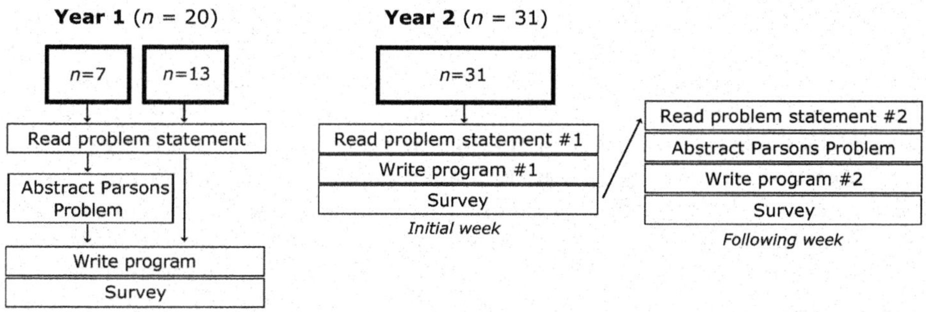

Fig. 1. Overview of the use of Abstract Parsons Problems to scaffold programming tasks and student surveys.

could drag individual blocks, corresponding to structural, data assignment, and input/output statements, from the left side of the screen (where they were initially presented in a random order) to the right side of the screen. We included more blocks than students would need since there are multiple solutions using sequential loops or nested loops, one array or two arrays, etc. Most of these blocks are not visible in Fig. 2. As described earlier, this "Parsons step" was designed to focus students on planning their solution prior to writing code. The Parsons interface did not provide students with feedback on the correctness of their plans, and students were free to end the planning step and begin coding at any time. Thus, it was acting as a supporting scaffold, and not feedback or otherwise explicit guidance towards a correct answer.

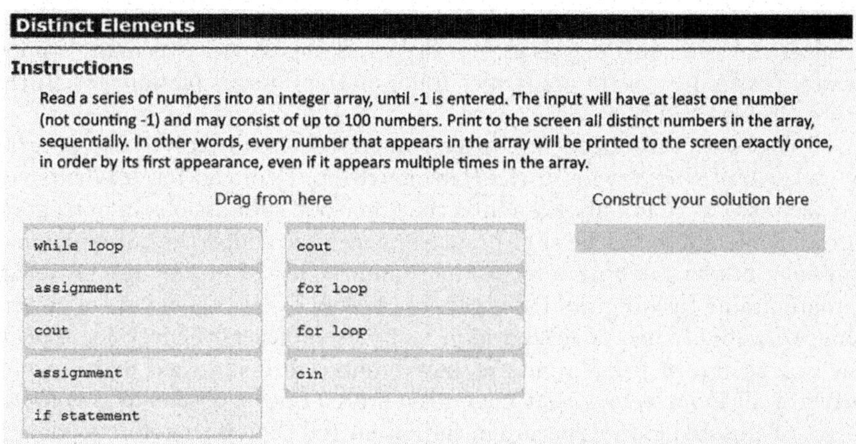

Fig. 2. Screenshot of the Abstract Parsons Problem shown to students in the Parsons group prior to coding.

4 Results

In Year 1, the 33 students (4 women, 29 men) enrolled in the course were originally assigned to the non-Parsons ($n = 16$) and Parsons ($n = 17$) groups alphabetically by surname, resulting in the four women being divided evenly across the two groups. We include in our data analysis all students who responded to the survey and who attempted the coding task. In total, we have complete data for 13 students in the non-Parsons group and 7 students in the Parsons group (as illustrated in Fig. 1). In Year 2, there were 40 students (8 women and 32 men) enrolled in the course. We include in our data analysis all students who responded to both surveys as well as attempted programming problems #1 and #2. In total, we have complete data for 31 students.

4.1 Task Success (Goal 1)

A key measure of success for a programming task is solution correctness. Our first goal explores if the Parsons planning step helped students produce successful solutions. Two observations suggest that this step may have been helpful: in Year 1 data, the only students to successfully complete the programming task were in the Parsons group. In Year 2 data, a greater proportion of students solved the programming task when it followed the Abstract Parsons Problem step. We now explore these results in more detail.

Most Year 1 students made just a single submission to the grading system, towards the end of the timed task. All except one student made their first submission within 10 min of the session's end, with 65% of students making their first submission in the final 5 min. This pattern is consistent with the fact that many students were unable to complete the problem in the time allowed – a theme that emerged from our analysis of the survey responses (see Sect. 4.2), particularly for the non-Parsons group. In Year 2, nearly twice as many students successfully solved Problem #2 (which followed the Parsons planning step) compared to Problem #1.

In Year 1, only three students in the course successfully solved the programming task, all of whom were in the Parsons group. Given so few students completed the task, we manually examined the final code submissions in both groups to further understand the level of progress made. We coded the submissions for the presence of two patterns: a *nested loop*, and the use of *two arrays*. Given that the programming task required students to identify distinct elements in an input stream, we would expect a nested loop to be used either to check for repeated values in a record of prior inputs as new inputs are being read or to examine an array of all input values that have been stored once the stream is complete. Presence of a nested loop structure in the submitted code is therefore evidence of progress towards a viable solution. Although an elegant solution to the problem requires just a single array (either to store all values, or to keep track of only unique values), some students introduced two arrays – one to store all input values from the stream and the second to store the distinct values. Although use of a second array is not necessary, it is evidence of students executing a plan to store the distinct values separately for printing the solution. In addition to manually coding the submissions for these two patterns, we also computed the number of lines of code and the number of variables that were used. Table 1 compares the final submissions across students in Year 1 with respect to these metrics, and shows the rate of success for students in Year 2.

Table 1. Comparison of metrics across the final code submissions made by students in each group. Where counts are given, percentages are shown (in brackets).

Year 1	non-Parsons ($n = 13$)	Parsons ($n = 7$)
Solved task (count)	0 (0.0%)	3 (42.9%)
Nested loop (count)	2 (15.4%)	5 (71.4%)
Two arrays (count)	3 (23.1%)	4 (57.1%)
Lines of code (mean)	33.38	38.66
Number of variables (mean)	3.15	4.22
Year 2	**Problem #1**	**Problem #2**
Solved task (count)	8 (25.8%)	13 (41.9%)

In addition to their greater success at solving the task in Year 1, we also found that a larger proportion of students in the Parsons group produced code that was closer to a working solution – particularly in terms of employing a nested loop – as well as producing more lines of code, and making more use of variables, on average. The number of students in each group is relatively small, and so we are cautious about drawing any conclusions regarding the generalizability of this result. Additionally we are not assuming that more lines and more variables are good without taking context into account. However here, given that most students did not submit a working solution, we see this as positive. Regardless, students in the Parsons group had to divide their time between the planning step and the coding step, and so we view it as promising that they achieved greater success on the coding task in this study.

4.2 Difficulties and Future Strategies (Goal 2)

Our second goal was to understand how the Abstract Parsons Problem, when used as a scaffolding step, might affect student perceptions of the programming task. In particular, we were interested in what students found most *difficult* about the task, and how the scaffolding might impact these perceived challenges. We were also interested in understanding how the planning step might influence the ways that students approach future programming problems, and in particular the *strategies* they choose to adopt. Our post-survey targeted both of these ideas. To analyze qualitative responses, we undertook a thematic analysis to identify the main patterns of meaning. We followed guidelines described by Braun &

Clarke [24], beginning with data familiarisation. After reading all responses, we assigned codes to each response and synthesized these into main themes.

4.3 Year 1

All students responded to both questions, with the exception of one student in the non-Parsons group who did not respond to the second, yielding 39 qualitative responses. We found two clear themes, one of which was prominent in the non-Parsons group and the other prominent in the Parsons group.

The first theme related to *time pressure*, which was reported as a difficulty of the task. This theme was very common in responses from students in the non-Parsons group, but *not* from students in the Parsons group. This is surprising, because both groups had an identical time limit for the programming task, yet students in the Parsons group also had to engage with the Parsons Problem step prior to coding, leaving less time for the coding itself. In other words, the students in the Parsons group were asked to do more in the same time, yet they raised time pressure as a challenge less frequently. Time pressure was mentioned as the most difficult aspect of the programming task by 6 of 13 students in the non-Parsons group (46%), compared with just 2 of the 7 students in the Parsons group (29%). As an example, one student in the non-Parsons group expressed feeling time pressure as: *"I felt like the most difficult part was the time constraint. The entire time I was working I could feel the pressure of the time running out. I feel like if I had more time to work and debug I could have solved the problem"*.

The second theme related to *task planning* emerged from responses about strategies identified as being useful for solving similar problems in the future. In this case, students in the Parsons group were more likely to identify that some form of planning would be useful to them in the future. Of the 7 students in the Parsons group, 4 identified task planning as being an important future strategy (57%), compared with just 2 of the 13 students in the non-Parsons group (15%). A student from the Parsons group expressed the importance of task planning as: *"I think planning out what I am going to do before I actually write the code will help. It allows for me to think out the problem and I might even be able to figure out the problem without even writing code first"*.

4.4 Year 2

All students responded to both questions for problems #1 and #2, for a total of 62 qualitative responses. In addition to the same themes from Year 1, we saw some new themes which we present below.

Problem #1. The first theme for Problem #1 was about *domain knowledge*. Fourteen of the 31 students wrote something that indicated they did not have enough domain knowledge to complete the task. Interestingly, none of these students completed the program within the time limit. From understanding nested loops to proper formatting using the `setw()` function (a function used in programs since week 2 of the course), almost half of students verbalized a lack of course content understanding. One student exemplified this as: *"Having more experience and practicing more. If I had more practice with nested for loops I might've been able to figure it out"*.

Although there was no metacognitive intervention in Problem #1, the second theme that emerged was related to *task planning* as vague metacognitive statements. Six of the 31 students wrote about breaking the problem down or ensuring they understood the prompt. Five completed the program within the time limits; one did not. We labeled these as vague because there were no specific examples of what to do, only evidence that they understood some kind of strategy was necessary as exemplified by this response: *"Understanding how to put multiple different ideas into a complex idea. I was able to understand the basic concepts, but had trouble combining those concepts to solve the problem"*.

Problem #2. The first theme to emerge from Problem #2 was also about a lack of *domain knowledge.* Thirteen of the 31 students wrote about their lack of understanding of course content, such as arrays. This is similar to what we saw in Problem #1. Similarly, the second theme for Problem #2 was about *task planning.* In contrast to the vague statements from Problem #1 a week earlier, 10 of 31 students responded with concrete ideas about how to aid their problem-solving process in the future. One example was: *"Writing down the goals of the code with pen/paper, and structuring where you might need a loop using Parson's is something I will try to practice in future coding projects as well"*.

We also tagged all student statements with one of three codes in Problems #1 and #2: non-cognitive, cognitive, and metacognitive. A statement was *non-cognitive* if students wrote things like "I don't know."; *cognitive* if the student mentioned needing to better understand course concepts or other domain knowledge; and *metacognitive* if the student showed a reflective stance toward their own mental problem-solving process. We then mapped the change from Problem #1 to #2. We believe that non-cognitive is the least desired response type, followed by cognitive, then metacognitive. Therefore, a positive change is movement towards metacognitive (non-cognitive to cognitive, non-cognitive to metacognitive, or cognitive to metacognitive). A negative change is movement toward non-cognitive. Neutral change is where the student gave the same type of response both times. In total we recorded 12 positives, 7 negatives, and 13 neutrals.

5 Limitations and Future Work

In Year 1, the COVID-19 pandemic proved highly disruptive due to a switch to a hybrid mode of teaching in the middle of the semester. Originally, we envisaged running the task as an in-class, supervised activity, however due to the switch some students attended class on campus while others studied remotely. We found that the students studying remotely, and thus unsupervised, were generally less likely to engage with course activities and abandoned some more readily. During the session in which we ran this study, around 40% of the class either did not engage or did not complete the tasks, resulting in less data than originally envisioned. Nevertheless, our allocation of students into the two groups was such that a similar percentage of students in each group were studying remotely. In Year 2, students were supervised in-class for both of the programming problems.

In Year 1, we did not randomly assign our original participant pool to the two groups, but allocated students to them based on surname. A post-hoc analysis indicated no significant differences in the course marks of students in these groups prior to the study commencing. Additionally, we have no data regarding interactions between students and the interactive Parsons Problem tool. Thus, we do not know how long students in this group spent with the Parsons Problem, or how sophisticated their planning was prior to programming.

One avenue of future work focuses on metacognitive strategies. This involves further investigating the use of Parsons Problems to scaffold the problem-solving process. We introduced Abstract Parsons Problems to do this, but as discussed in Sect. 2, there are many different variations of Parsons Problems. Possible questions include: *Do other types of Parsons Problems cause an increase in verbalization of metacognitive strategies when used as a pre-coding scaffold?* and *Is there a similar effect with other types of planning activities or is there something specific about Parsons Problems causing the effect?* Additionally, our findings warrant a deeper, qualitative, exploration into the types of metacognitive strategies that design activities like Parsons Problems elicit.

Another avenue of future work involves scale, invigilation, and complexity. As noted in Sect. 5, our sample size was constrained by the limitations of running a live classroom study during the COVID-19 pandemic. Future work should replicate this study at scale. This experiment could also be run as a non-invigilated homework activity with a multi-day time window. Finally, increasing the complexity of the study itself, including crossover designs or conducting it longitudinally, could help establish related factors and what types of programming problems benefit from this kind of activity [14].

6 Implications and Conclusions

Our original hypothesis was that novice programmers would benefit from explicit scaffolding during the problem-solving process with higher task completion and an increase in metacognitive behaviors. Using a Parsons Problem to provide this metacognitive scaffolding is a novel contribution of our work. Our findings not only support our hypothesis, but they are somewhat surprising – despite having more time for writing code, when not presented with the Parsons Problem students tended to be less successful at completing the programming task, and were more likely to report being under time pressure. These findings could positively contribute to student learning in several ways. First and foremost it provides evidence that scaffolding learning during explicit metacognitive problem-solving stages can benefit students.

Recent research has shown metacognition to be a critical skill for novice programmers to develop alongside their domain knowledge. These results suggest that inserting a planning step with an interactive tool, in this case Abstract Parsons Problems, to guide students through this stage of the problem-solving process could help to scaffold metacognitive skills in novices. Due to the limitations of our study, we interpreted these findings as positive indicators that warrant future work in metacognitive strategies, non-invigilated assignments, and increasing the scale and complexity of future investigations.

References

1. Prather, J., Becker, B.A., Craig, M., Denny, P., Loksa, D., Margulieux, L.: What do we think we think we are doing? Metacognition and self-regulation in programming. In: Proceedings of the 2020 ACM Conference on International Computing Education Research, ICER 2020, pp. 2–13. ACM, New York (2020)
2. Loksa, D., Ko, A.J.: The role of self-regulation in programming problem solving process and success. In: Proceedings of the 2016 ACM Conference on International Computing Education Research, ICER 2016, pp. 83–91. ACM, New York (2016)
3. Bergin, S., Reilly, R., Traynor, D.: Examining the role of self-regulated learning on introductory programming performance. In: Proceedings of the 1st International Workshop on Computing Education Research, ICER 2005, pp. 81–86. ACM, New York (2005)
4. Roll, I., Holmes, N.G., Day, J., Bonn, D.: Evaluating metacognitive scaffolding in guided invention activities. Instr. Sci. **40**(4), 691–710 (2012)
5. Luxton-Reilly, A., et al.: Introductory programming: a systematic literature review. In: Proceedings of the Companion of the 23rd Annual ACM Conference on Innovation and Technology in Computer Science Education, ITiCSE 2018 Companion, pp. 55–106. ACM, New York (2018)
6. Becker, B.A.: What does saying that 'programming is hard' really say, and about whom? Commun. ACM **64**(8), 27–29 (2021)
7. Karvelas, I., Li, A., Becker, B.A.: The effects of compilation mechanisms and error message presentation on novice programmer behavior. In: Proceedings of the 51st ACM Technical Symposium on Computer Science Education, SIGCSE 2020, pp. 759–765. ACM, New York (2020)
8. Prather, J., Pettit, R., McMurry, K., Peters, A., Homer, J., Cohen, M.: Metacognitive difficulties faced by novice programmers in automated assessment tools. In: Proceedings of the 2018 ACM Conference on International Computing Education Research, ICER 2018, pp. 41–50. ACM, New York (2018)
9. Loksa, D., et al.: Metacognition and self-regulation in programming education: theories and exemplars of use. ACM Trans. Comput. Educ. **22**(4), 1–31 (2022)
10. Bandura, A.: Perceived self-efficacy in cognitive development and functioning. Educ. Psychol. **28**(2), 117–148 (1993)
11. VanDeGrift, T., Caruso, T., Hill, N., Simon, B.: Experience report: getting novice programmers to THINK about improving their software development process. In: Proceedings of the 42nd ACM Technical Symposium on Computer Science Education, SIGCSE 2011, pp. 493–498. ACM, New York (2011)
12. Prather, J., et al.: First things first: providing metacognitive scaffolding for interpreting problem prompts. In: Proceedings of the 50th ACM Technical Symposium on Computer Science Education, SIGCSE 2019, pp. 531–537. ACM, New York (2019)
13. Denny, P., Prather, J., Becker, B.A., Albrecht, Z., Loksa, D., Pettit, R.: A closer look at metacognitive scaffolding: solving test cases before programming. In: Proceedings of the 19th Koli Calling International Conference on Computing Education Research, Koli Calling 2019. ACM, New York (2019)

14. Craig, M., Petersen, A., Campbell, J.: Answering the correct question. In: Proceedings of the ACM Conference on Global Computing Education, CompEd 2019, pp. 72–77. ACM, New York (2019)
15. Lee, P., Liao, S.N.: Targeting metacognition by incorporating student-reported confidence estimates on self-assessment quizzes. In: Proceedings of the 52nd ACM Technical Symposium on Computer Science Education, SIGCSE 2021, pp. 431–437. ACM, New York (2021)
16. Loksa, D., Ko, A.J., Jernigan, W., Oleson, A., Mendez, C.J., Burnett, M.M.: Programming, problem solving, and self-awareness: effects of explicit guidance. In: Proceedings of the 2016 CHI Conference on Human Factors in Computing Systems, pp. 1449–1461. ACM (2016)
17. Loksa, D.: Explicitly training metacognition and self-regulation for computer programming. Ph.D. thesis, University of Washington (2020)
18. Parsons, D., Haden, P.: Parson's programming puzzles: a fun and effective learning tool for first programming courses. In: Proceedings of the 8th Australasian Conference on Computing Education, ACE 2006, vol. 52, p. 157–163. Australian Computer Society Inc., Australia (2006)
19. Du, Y., Luxton-Reilly, A., Denny, P.: A review of research on Parsons problems. In: Proceedings of the 22nd Australasian Computing Education Conference, ACE 2020, pp. 195–202. ACM, New York (2020)
20. Weinman, N., Fox, A., Hearst, M.: Exploring challenging variations of Parsons problems. In: Proceedings of the 51st ACM Technical Symposium on Computer Science Education, SIGCSE 2020, p. 1349. ACM, New York (2020)
21. Garcia, R., Falkner, K., Vivian, R.: Scaffolding the design process using Parsons problems. In: Proceedings of the 18th Koli Calling International Conference on Computing Education Research, Koli Calling 2018. ACM, New York (2018)
22. Becker, B.A., Quille, K.: 50 years of CS1 at SIGCSE: a review of the evolution of introductory programming education research. In: Proceedings of the 50th ACM Technical Symposium on Computer Science Education, SIGCSE 2019, pp. 338–344. ACM, New York (2019)
23. Ihantola, P., Karavirta, V.: Open source widget for Parson's puzzles. In: Proceedings of the 15th Annual Conference on Innovation and Technology in Computer Science Education, ITiCSE 2010, p. 302. ACM, New York (2010)
24. Braun, V., Clarke, V.: Using thematic analysis in psychology. Qual. Res. Psychol. **3**(2), 77–101 (2006)

IDE Interactions of Novices Transitioning Between Programming Environments

Ioannis Karvelas, Joe Dillane, and Brett A. Becker(✉)

University College Dublin, Dublin, Ireland
joe.dillane@itcarlow.ie, brett.becker@ucd.ie

Abstract. Novices in introductory programming courses typically learn the fundamentals of programming using one of a wide of programming environments. These vary greatly in terms of the mechanisms they employ to assist programmers, including their approaches to compilation and error message presentation. It is yet to be established which, if any, of these mechanisms are more beneficial for learning. In this study, we utilize Java programming process data to investigate the interaction between novices and two different versions of the BlueJ pedagogical IDE, which differ substantially in terms of compilation mechanism and error message presentation. Specifically, we compare novices that used both BlueJ 3 and BlueJ 4 with those who exclusively used either and the effects of the order in which they transition between BlueJ versions. We find substantial differences between different cohorts in terms of error messages and compilation which provides evidence that programming environments play an important part in influencing the programming practices of novices. This work supports the hypothesis that the choice of programming environment significantly affects user behavior with respect to specific programming interactions and therefore it is reasonable to expect a difference in how these environments affect learning.

Keywords: Compiler error messages · CS1 · Java · Programming environments · Programming process data

1 Introduction

Novices enrolled in introductory programming courses - commonly called CS1 [1] - face substantial challenges [2] as they learn the theoretical aspects of programming and familiarize themselves with the software development process [3]. This is usually accomplished through programming assignments which aim not only to enable students to put theory into practice, but also to expose them to the often strenuous task of debugging and testing their code.

Students usually engage with programming while following small cycles of editing, compiling, and executing code [4] using a programming environment, ranging from simple text editors used to write source code files which they later compile manually at a command line, to complex industry-focused Integrated

Published by Springer Nature Switzerland AG 2023
T. Keane et al. (Eds.): WCCE 2022, IFIP AICT 685, pp. 603–614, 2023.
https://doi.org/10.1007/978-3-031-43393-1_54

Development Environments (IDEs). In the middle of this range are pedagogical environments designed for learning. All of these environments vary in terms of the tools they provide and mechanisms they employ. Two of the most commonly varied mechanisms are the compilation mechanism and feedback presentation, the latter of which normally involves error messages as a core facet.

Since environments act as a medium through which users create and interact with programs, it is important that this interaction is appropriate for student learning and efficient in assisting them in improving skills such as syntax mastery in order to overcome issues that may disrupt the core learning experience. Most instructors would agree that learning to program should not be complicated with learning the intricacies of an elaborate environment, or tools that otherwise hinder the learning of programming concepts. At a minimum, more advanced environments would likely impart a higher extraneous cognitive load on the student. For novices, there is also a particularly important feature that all environments should provide: constructive and informative (ideally formative) feedback on the code written by the student. This puts error messages, their mechanisms, and their presentation in the spotlight. However, little progress has been made on investigating the effectiveness of such mechanisms on achieving optimal outcomes [5]. Although some educators may encourage their students to use a pedagogical environment, this is not always the case and students may end up using IDEs designed for experienced programmers. The benefit of such environments for novices is not established [6].

In order for developers to include effective functionalities and feedback mechanisms when designing environments (pedagogical or professional), they should ideally be basing decisions on empirical evidence. To achieve this, more studies should focus on establishing evidence, frameworks and guidelines for designing these tools. This would ideally result in environments that benefit users in terms of programming patterns, compilation habits and the usefulness of information that users receive from the environment.

This research investigates student interaction with two versions of the BlueJ pedagogical environment [7], that differ in compilation and error message presentation. Through this, we aim to provide a more transparent view of how programming environments can influence novice programmer behavior and ultimately, learning.

1.1 BlueJ and Blackbox

BlueJ [7] is a popular introductory programming environment for text-based Java programming used by millions of novices over more than two decades. BlueJ logs the programming process data of opted-in users in the Blackbox database [8,9]. BlueJ versions up to and including version 3 (2010–2017) featured only manual (click to compile) compilation. If errors were present in the code, only the line(s) corresponding to the first error were highlighted and only the first error message was displayed at the bottom of the window. BlueJ has a relatively long version cycle, and in 2017, BlueJ 4 was released and included substantial changes in the compilation mechanism and error message presentation. Specifically, automatic background compilation was added. This is triggered every time users change lines in the source code, load the source code, and create class instances. In addition, standard manual compilation was retained. By default, if errors are present in the code, no error messages are presented automatically, but all offending code is underlined in red. In order to see (truncated) error messages, users must hover over the specified area in the code with the keyboard or mouse, or click the compile button. If multiple errors are present, clicking the compile button more than once causes the full (non-truncated) error messages to appear one at a time, from first to last (and from there re-presents the error messages in round-robin fashion upon continued clicks).

Thus, these two BlueJ versions employ drastically different mechanisms for compilation and feedback presentation, while keeping the rest of the features in the environment largely unchanged. This enables us to infer that changes in programming behavior between the two versions are largely due to these feature changes.

1.2 Research Questions

Previous findings [10] showed that novice programming interaction with BlueJ shows substantial differences between BlueJ 3 and BlueJ 4. In BlueJ 4, users get exposed to more compiler error messages in the same amount of time, they compile manually less frequently and their manual compilations are more often successful. However, the cohort involved in that analysis consisted of users with substantial time spent using both BlueJ versions. Thus, any conclusions regarding the differences in the interaction of users with BlueJ 3 and 4 were not based on users who used exclusively one of the two versions, and did not take into account any effects on novice programming behavior imposed by the order of transitioning between versions. In this work, we investigate the differences between versions, and the effect of transitioning between versions by focusing on distinct user cohorts, compared to just one: users that used BlueJ 3 exclusively, users that used BlueJ 4 exclusively, and those that transitioned between BlueJ versions. For the latter, we study various subcohorts further, depending on the transition order ($3 \rightarrow 4$), ($3 \leftarrow 4$) and ($3 \leftrightarrow 4$). Our research questions are:

RQ1: How does transitioning between environments affect novice interaction regarding compilation and error messages as opposed to being exposed to a single environment?

RQ2: How does the order of transition between environments affect this interaction? Possibilities include: (BlueJ $3 \rightarrow$ BlueJ 4), (BlueJ $3 \leftarrow$ BlueJ 4) and (BlueJ $3 \leftrightarrow$ BlueJ 4).

2 Methodology

We initially selected two cohorts from the Blackbox database:

1. Transition Users (TR): Users who switched between BlueJ 3 and BlueJ 4 versions between October 2017 and February 2018. We chose these dates as this coincides with the introduction of BlueJ 4. This cohort includes users regardless of their transition status (e.g. a user in this cohort could be switching from BlueJ 3 to BlueJ 4 or vice versa). All users in this cohort had programming activity in BlueJ 3 and BlueJ 4. We break these users down further later.

2. Exclusive Users (X): These users were selected randomly from users who had only a single BlueJ version (either BlueJ 3 or BlueJ 4) installed on their machine during the period their data were logged by Blackbox. All users in this cohort had programming activity only in one of these two versions. We study these separately later (we refer to users who only used BlueJ 3 as X3 and BlueJ 4 as X4).

Only programming events that were associated with Java version 8 were retrieved (which is also the most common version in Blackbox for the dates studied)[1]. In addition, the programming activity of both cohorts was expanded to the range of the 14th of January 2016 and the 24th of May 2019[2].

2.1 Compilation and Error Message Presentation Metrics

After retrieving the programming events of the users as described in Sect. 2, the programming time (H) in hours that every user spent programming in BlueJ was calculated. This was done by summing all time differences between the first and the last programming events of every session[3] for each user. This methodology presents a complication: sometimes, connection interruptions cause Blackbox to stop logging events requiring a manual means of calculating session duration. We discuss this further in Sect. 4.

We used the following metrics for describing the interaction regarding compilation and error message presentation for every user: (1) Displayed Compiler Error Messages per Hour (DCEMpH), (2) Manual Compilations per Hour (CpH), and (3) Percentage of Success of manual Compilations (PSC). This approach of quantifying the BlueJ users' interaction is consistent with previous work [10].

2.2 Removing Outliers

When dealing with large repositories of programming process data like that in Blackbox, it is expected that there will be many cases of irregular activity. In our

[1] This was done as compiler error messages are known to differ across Java versions [8].

[2] The range limits are equidistant from the first day that transition to BlueJ 4 was observed.

[3] A session is bounded by two distinct events sent from the user to the Blackbox database, indicating the launch and termination of BlueJ.

case, there were users with unrealistically high programming time (for instance, tens of thousands of hours) or displayed compiler error messages over time (for instance, several hundred per hour). Extremely high programming times can be a result of idle activity in BlueJ, whereas many compiler error messages could be triggered by stuck keyboard keys or similar hardware failures or even a book falling on a keyboard – with hundreds of thousands of users total and millions of events per day, strange things happen. Although these users were few in number, such extreme values could distort results. In order to mitigate against this, we excluded users in all TR and X cohorts independently, based on the following procedure as used in [10]: **Step 1:** Removal of users whose programming time in BlueJ 3 was greater than the maximum programming time in BlueJ 4. This was done to eliminate few cases where programming time was exceptionally high in BlueJ 3, something not observed for BlueJ 4. **Step 2:** Recalculation of the means and standard deviations after Step 1 and removal of users whose programming time (H) was greater than the mean increased by three standard deviations. **Step 3:** Removal of users whose DCEMpH was greater than the mean increased by three standard deviations.

2.3 Categorizing Transition Users

In this stage of analysis, we classified transition users (see Sect. 2) based on all three possible transition possibilities: transitions from BlueJ 3 to BlueJ 4 (we will use the acronym 3t4 later for these), transitions from BlueJ 4 to BlueJ 3 (4t3), and transitioning repeatedly between the two versions (Overlap).

2.4 Metric Restriction in BlueJ 3

In BlueJ 3, each compilation causes at most one error message to be displayed. In other words, users see a maximum number of error messages equal to the number of compilations they invoke (if all compilations involve an error). Based on this, we can define a relationship between the three metrics that are examined in this work (DCEMpH, CpH, PSC) using the formula described in Eq. 1[4]. We will refer to this equation in later sections as the *BlueJ 3 equation.*

$$DCEMpH = (1 - PSC) \times CpH \tag{1}$$

2.5 Similarity Calculation

To gain a high-level view of differences between the BlueJ 3 and BlueJ 4 distributions, we quantified the differences between versions regarding our metrics for each cohort using three approaches:

[4] This equation can be used to describe every user's interaction with BlueJ 3 (or similar environment). Values that do not satisfy the equation are a result of missing data in Blackbox.

Method 1 (M1) – Average minimum distance from BlueJ 3: Figure 1 represents the surface defined by Eq. 1. This involves the calculation of the shortest Euclidean distance between the BlueJ 4 interaction of a user and this surface. Specifically, we defined a new function describing the distance between user interaction in BlueJ 4 and BlueJ 3. For every user, we used the Nelder-Mead downhill simplex algorithm [11] to obtain the minimized function value. This can be viewed as a process of answering the question: "What is the closest possible BlueJ 3 behavior to this particular BlueJ 4 user's behavior?".

Method 2 (M2) – Distance between BlueJ 3 and BlueJ 4 mean coordinate values: In this method, we created a hypothetical "average user" using the mean values of DCEMpH, CpH, and PSC of all users for each BlueJ version, and calculated the Euclidean distance between them.

Method 3 (M3) – Minimum distance between BlueJ 4 mean coordinate values and BlueJ 3: In this method, we used the mean coordinate values of BlueJ 4 (in the respective user cohort) to come up with one "average" BlueJ 4 user profile, and calculated its minimum Euclidean distance from the surface represented by the BlueJ 3 equation.

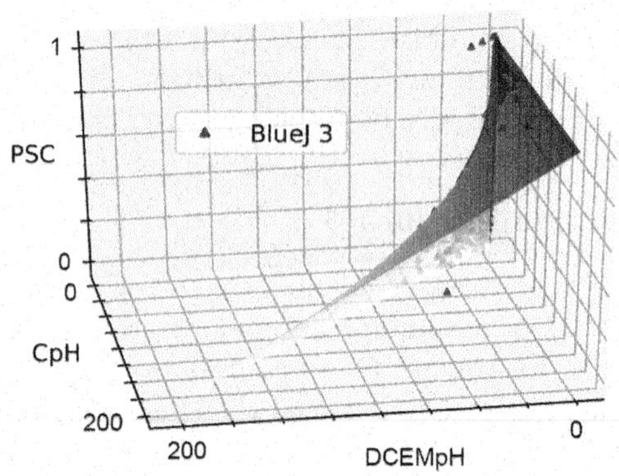

Fig. 1. Surface representing Eq. 1 and each BlueJ 3 user mapped by their metric coordinates (blue triangles). (Color figure online)

3 Results

Table 1 summarizes results discussed in this section. Statistical tests were performed for each individual cohort to reveal the statistical significance in the difference between the metrics in BlueJ 3 and BlueJ 4. We carried out a Shapiro-Wilk test for normality [12] and after the null hypothesis for normality was rejected for all distributions, a Mann-Whitney U test for statistical significance [13] was performed along with a calculation of Cohen's d as a measure of effect size (ES) [14]. Cohen's d was calculated using BlueJ 4 as the experimental group and BlueJ 3 as the control group in all cases. Since the effect direction was consistent for every metric in all user cohorts (increase in DCEMpH, decrease in CpH, increase in PSC), only absolute values are displayed in Table 1. All tests revealed statistical significance with $p < 0.05$ and the effect sizes support our results in Table 1 and Sects. 3.1 and 3.2. As there are two results (Mann-Whitney and Cohen's d), three metrics (DCEMpH, CpH, PSC) and four data cohorts (3t4, 4t3, Overlap and X), there are 24 independent results. For space, we present the complete set of the statistical results along with the processed data in a Zenodo open source repository[5].

Table 1. Mean values of programming time in Hours (H), Displayed Compiler Error Messages per Hour (DCEMpH), manual Compilations per Hour (CpH) and Percentage of Successful manual Compilations (PSC) for BlueJ 3 and BlueJ 4 of all user cohorts. Effect sizes (ES) using Cohen's d are displayed alongside each pair of metrics. The direction of effect is omitted in ES since it is consistent in all metrics across all cohorts. ES Sum refers to the cumulative effect size derived by summing all ES values in that row. The last three columns display the values of distance between BlueJ 3 and BlueJ 4 using the methods described in Sect. 2.5. In the first row, n_3 and n_4 refer to the number of users in cohorts X3 and X4 respectively.

User Cohort (n)	H		DCEMpH			CpH			PSC			ES Sum	M1	M2	M3
	V3	V4	V3	V4	ES	V3	V4	ES	V3	V4	ES				
X ($n_3 = 727, n_4 = 536$)	19	30	11	17	.36	22	12	.59	.52	.76	1.2	2.15	1.39	12.11	1.22
3t4 ($n = 1008$)	101	41	7	9	.32	15	10	.34	.53	.74	1.2	1.86	.8	5.16	.66
4t3 ($n = 190$)	62	9	7	12	.55	17	15	.15	.58	.73	.74	1.44	.78	5.68	.54
Overlap ($n = 463$)	125	44	6	10	.48	14	11	.23	.54	.73	1.06	1.77	.76	4.92	.64

3.1 RQ1: Exclusive vs Transition Use

Our first research question was: *How does transitioning between environments affect novice interaction regarding compilation and error messages as opposed to being exposed to a single environment?*

Displayed Compiler Error Messages per Hour (DCEMpH) are greater in BlueJ 4 than in BlueJ 3 for all cohorts. The mean values in BlueJ 3 and BlueJ 4 for each cohort are: 11 and 17 for cohort X, 7 and 9 for cohort 3t4, 7 and 12 for cohort 4t3, and 6 and 10 for cohort Overlap. Manual Compilations per Hour (CpH) are lower in BlueJ 4 than in BlueJ 3 in all cohorts. The mean values in BlueJ 3 and BlueJ 4 for each cohort are: 22 and 12 for cohort X, 15 and 10 for cohort 3t4, 17 and 15 for cohort 4t3, and 14 and 11 for cohort Overlap. Regarding Percentage of Success of manual Compilations (PSC), the differences between BlueJ 3 and BlueJ 4 are very similar for all user cohorts, with more successful manual compilations in BlueJ 4. Manual compilations in BlueJ 4 are 73–76% successful compared to BlueJ 3, in which they are 52–58% successful.

[5] Zenodo repository url: https://doi.org/10.5281/zenodo.7509557.

All three methods discussed in Sect. 2.5 show a larger difference between X4 and X3 interactions for users in cohort X than for the rest of the cohorts. Specifically: (1) the average minimum distance between cohorts and the BlueJ 3 equation is 1.39 for X4 and around 0.76–0.8 for the transition cohorts, (2) the distance between the means of the metrics for users in X3 and X4 is 12.11, while for the transition cohorts, the distances are between 4.92 and 5.68, and (3) the minimum distance between X4 mean coordinate values and the BlueJ 3 equation is 1.22, whereas for the rest of the cohorts it is between 0.54 and 0.66. The results of these three methods align with the cumulative ES reported in Table 1. This is expected since all discussed methods and the sum of the absolute values of the ES incorporate all three metrics in their calculation.

Based on these findings we conclude that the difference in programming behavior between using BlueJ 3 and using BlueJ 4 is substantially greater for users that used one of the two versions exclusively than for those who program using both versions. This is primarily the result of changes in numbers of displayed compiler error messages and manual compilations, as the difference in successful manual compilations between BlueJ versions remains relatively stable across different cohorts of users.

3.2 RQ2: Order of Transition

Our second research question was: *How does the order of transitioning between environments affect this interaction?*

Regarding DCEMpH, the difference between the means in BlueJ 3 and BlueJ 4 for the each of the transition cohorts from highest to lowest are: (1) 71% for cohort 4t3, (2) 67% for cohort Overlap, (3) 29% for cohort 3t4. Regarding CpH, the differences between the means in BlueJ 3 and BlueJ 4 for the each of transition cohorts from highest to lowest are: (1) 33% for cohort 3t4, (2) 21% for cohort Overlap, (3) 12% for cohort 4t3. Regarding PSC, the differences between the means in BlueJ 3 and BlueJ 4 are very similar for all user cohorts.

Methods 1–3 (discussed in Sect. 2.5) present similar numbers for the interaction difference between BlueJ 3 and BlueJ 4 for the users in cohorts 3t4, 4t3, and Overlap. Although there are minor differences, they are not on the same order of magnitude as those for the X cohort (which is around twice as high for all three methods). Cumulative effect sizes using Cohen's d also align with this as they range between 1.44 and 1.86 for all transition cohorts.

Based on these findings, we conclude that the order in which users transition from one BlueJ version to the other does not play a substantial role in the programming behavior change between BlueJ 3 and BlueJ 4 and the interaction regarding DCEMpH, CpH and PSC is not significantly altered.

4 Threats to Validity

Blackbox data are anonymous, and do not contain any information about the programming level of BlueJ users. Although BlueJ is not practical for experienced programmers, some users could be educators trying out the environment or making sure that the environment can execute certain exercises without issues. Additionally, one Blackbox user could in fact be several users working on the same machine, which is very common in institutional labs. This limitation is inherent to all studies that use these data [9].

The metrics involved in the current work incorporate the time spent on BlueJ. However, network interruptions can cause Blackbox to stop logging events for a session. In our analysis we treat the last event logged in the session as the true final event. This approach inevitably results in some missing data – if a user's connection is disrupted, the last logged activity for that session may not be complete. We regard this as a minor threat, since we are comparing two different BlueJ versions and the probability of an incomplete session should be the same for both versions, potentially mitigating this otherwise unavoidable issue to some degree.

Finally, one of the metrics we used (Displayed Compiler Error Messages per Hour) involves counting the numbers of shown compiler error messages that are logged in Blackbox. These logged events can sometimes be triggered by users inadvertently in BlueJ 4. Since these events are triggered by moving the cursor to the area of the code responsible for the error, if users accidentally move their cursor or if they click the offending code area to fix the error, this counts as a shown error message in the current analysis. We will work towards isolating these instances in the future.

5 Discussion

In this study, we explored the programming interaction between novices and two versions of the BlueJ pedagogical environment that differ fundamentally in compilation and error message presentation. BlueJ 3 features a click-to-compile mechanism and enforced first error message presentation. BlueJ 4 features automatic error checking and on-demand error message presentation. The aims of our research were: (1) to investigate how exposure to a single BlueJ version affects the interaction between novices and the environment regarding compilation and error messages compared to being exposed to multiple BlueJ versions, and (2) to what extent the order in which this exposure takes place affects the interaction.

The analysis was conducted using programming process data from four distinct user cohorts using two different BlueJ versions. The cohorts included users who exclusively used only one of the two BlueJ versions, users who transitioned from BlueJ 3 to BlueJ 4, users who transitioned from BlueJ 4 to BlueJ 3, and users who switched multiple times between the two. In order to answer our research questions, we utilized three metrics that describe user interaction with the environment regarding compilation and error message presentation: displayed compiler error messages per hour, manual compilations per hour, and percentage of successful manual compilations. Including these metrics in our study could allow researchers to generalize our findings outside of the BlueJ context, as the interaction they measure is common to almost all programming environments.

By quantifying the cumulative interaction comprised by the three metrics, we conclude that programming interaction difference between programming in BlueJ 3 and BlueJ 4 is higher for users who only used one of the two versions exclusively than for users who transitioned between versions, primarily due to the numbers of displayed compiler error messages and manual compilations. The order of transitioning between versions does not seem to play a role of similar magnitude in this difference however. It is reasonable for novices who learn programming while using a single environment to adapt their interaction habits according to how the environment operates while displaying substantially diverging behavior from those using another environment. In contrast, novices who transition between programming environments (regardless of the reason behind such transitions) could be influenced by mechanisms present in both versions and display a moderated behavior.

In terms of differences in displayed compiler error messages over time, the cohort of users who moved from BlueJ 4 to BlueJ 3 exhibited the largest variation, followed by those who kept switching repeatedly between versions, those who used exclusively one BlueJ version, and those who moved from BlueJ 3 to BlueJ 4. All cohorts showed changes situated between the small to large spectrum of effect size interpretations [15].

In terms of differences in manual compilations over time, the cohort of users who exclusively used only one BlueJ version exhibited the largest variation between versions, followed sequentially by those who moved from BlueJ 3 to BlueJ 4, those who kept switching between versions and those who moved from BlueJ 4 to BlueJ 3. All cohorts showed changes situated between the very small to large spectrum of effect size interpretations.

In terms of successful manual compilations, differences between versions are very high in all cohorts of users, and the magnitude of the differences is relatively stable. All cohorts showed changes situated between the medium (users who moved from BlueJ 4 to BlueJ 3) to very large spectrum (users who exclusively used one BlueJ version and users who moved from BlueJ 3 BlueJ 4) of effect size interpretations.

Regardless of whether users were exposed to a single BlueJ version or multiple versions, we made a common observation: in BlueJ 4, users see significantly more error messages, compile manually less frequently and have higher manual compilation success. This is in accord with previous findings that took a more holistic approach to analyzing programming activity in BlueJ 3 and BlueJ 4 [16], and without comparing transitioning users with those who programmed only in one of the two [10].

A further observation is that users exposed only to a single environment generated more error messages and compiled manually more frequently in both BlueJ versions than users exposed to both. An exception to this are novices that moved from BlueJ 4 to BlueJ 3, who seem to compile more frequently than users who programmed only in BlueJ 4. This requires further investigation.

Due to the nature of Blackbox data, we have no access to the reasons why users transition between environments. A survey targeting the reasons behind this could reveal important insights into the motivations for such behavior. We can speculate that some novices who used only one environment felt comfortable while programming in it, therefore not attempting to switch to another version. Others may be constrained by institutional or other factors. Users who moved from one version to another may have had trouble with the manner in which the environment operated. For example, those who moved from version 3 to 4 could feel restricted by the need to compile manually or by only having access to the first error message. On the other hand, users who moved from 4 to 3 could feel overwhelmed by the constant red underlining of errors triggered by automatic compilations [17] and desired a more simple approach. Again, institutional and other factors beyond student control could also be at play.

Our research indicates that programming behavior is largely determined by the mechanisms of the programming environment, and that the transfer of behavior from one environment to another, if it occurs, is affected substantially by the restrictions of the environment. This is evidence that the choices of environment designers heavily affect novice programmer behavior and likely their learning opportunities. Programming educators should be aware of these effects on novices, but also of how the featured mechanisms of the chosen environments in their courses operate. It could be beneficial if educators are encouraged to facilitate short tutorials during which they explain the functionalities of the chosen programming environment and address students' questions on their use. These tutorials could be taking place in the beginning of the term, which is when students are just starting to get exposed to many new variables and concepts that introductory programming courses introduce, and serve as a proactive step against frustration and confusion, emotions that commonly emerge among CS1 students [18].

Acknowledgements. The work presented in this paper is funded by the Irish Research Council under grant agreement GOIPG/2020/1660.

References

1. Hertz, M.: What do "CS1" and "CS2" mean? Investigating differences in the early courses. In: Proceedings of the 41st ACM Technical Symposium on Computer Science Education, SIGCSE 2010, pp. 199–203. ACM, New York (2010)
2. Becker, B.A.: What does saying that 'programming is hard' really say, and about whom? Commun. ACM **64**(8), 27–29 (2021)
3. Luxton-Reilly, A., et al.: Introductory programming: a systematic literature review. In: Proceedings Companion of the 23rd Annual ACM Conference on Innovation and Technology in Computer Science Education, ITiCSE 2018 Companion, pp. 55–106. Association for Computing Machinery, New York (2018)
4. Jadud, M.C.: Methods and tools for exploring novice compilation behaviour. In: Proceedings of the 2nd International Workshop on Computing Education Research, ICER 2006, pp. 73–84. ACM, New York (2006)
5. Denny, P., Prather, J., Becker, B.A.: Error message readability and novice debugging performance. In: Proceedings of the 2020 ACM Conference on Innovation

and Technology in Computer Science Education, ITiCSE 2020, pp. 480–486. International Foundation for Autonomous Agents and Multiagent Systems, Richland (2020)
6. Reis, C., Cartwright, R.: Taming a professional IDE for the classroom. In: Proceedings of the 35th SIGCSE Technical Symposium on Computer Science Education, SIGCSE 2004, pp. 156–160. ACM, New York (2004)
7. Kölling, M., Quig, B., Patterson, A., Rosenberg, J.: The BlueJ system and its pedagogy. Comput. Sci. Educ. **13**(4), 249–268 (2003)
8. Brown, N.C.C., Kölling, M., McCall, D., Utting, I.: Blackbox: a large scale repository of novice programmers' activity. In: Proceedings of the 45th ACM Technical Symposium on Computer Science Education, SIGCSE 2014, pp. 223–228. ACM, New York (2014)
9. Brown, N.C.C., Altadmri, A., Sentance, S., Kölling, M.: Blackbox, five years on: an evaluation of a large-scale programming data collection project. In: Proceedings of the 2018 ACM Conference on International Computing Education Research, ICER 2018, pp. 196–204. ACM, New York (2018)
10. Karvelas, I., Li, A., Becker, B.A.: The effects of compilation mechanisms and error message presentation on novice programmer behavior. In: Proceedings of the 51st ACM Technical Symposium on Computer Science Education, SIGCSE 2020, pp. 759–765. Association for Computing Machinery, New York (2020)
11. Nelder, J.A., Mead, R.: A simplex method for function minimization. Comput. J. **7**(4), 308–313 (1965)
12. Shapiro, S.S., Wilk, M.B.: An analysis of variance test for normality (complete samples). Biometrika **52**(3/4), 591–611 (1965). http://www.jstor.org/stable/2333709
13. Mann, H.B., Whitney, D.R.: On a test of whether one of two random variables is stochastically larger than the other. Ann. Math. Stat. **18**(1), 50–60 (1947). http://www.jstor.org/stable/2236101
14. Cohen, J.: Statistical Power Analysis for the Behavioral Sciences. Routledge (2013)
15. Sawilowsky, S.S.: New effect size rules of thumb. J. Mod. Appl. Stat. Methods **8**(2), 26 (2009)
16. Karvelas, I., Dillane, J., Becker, B.A.: Compile much? A closer look at the programming behavior of novices in different compilation and error message presentation contexts. In: United Kingdom & Ireland Computing Education Research Conference, UKICER 2020, pp. 59–65. Association for Computing Machinery, New York (2020)
17. Karvelas, I., Becker, B.A.: Sympathy for the (novice) developer: programming activity when compilation mechanism varies. In: Proceedings of the 53rd ACM Technical Symposium on Computer Science Education, SIGCSE 2022, vol. 1, pp. 962–968. Association for Computing Machinery, New York (2022)
18. Lishinski, A., Rosenberg, J.: All the pieces matter: the relationship of momentary self-efficacy and affective experiences with cs1 achievement and interest in computing. In: Proceedings of the 17th ACM Conference on International Computing Education Research, ICER 2021, pp. 252–265. Association for Computing Machinery, New York (2021)

Mitigating Accidental Code Plagiarism in a Programming Course Through Code Referencing

Muftah Afrizal Pangestu[1(✉)], Simon[2], and Oscar Karnalim[1,3]

[1] University of Newcastle, University Dr Callaghan, Newcastle, NSW 2308, Australia
{muftah.pangestu,oscar.karnalim}@uon.edu.au

[2] Newcastle, Australia

[3] Maranatha Christian University, Bandung, Jawa Barat 40164, Indonesia

Abstract. Code plagiarism – taking code from external sources and using it without reference in one's own programs – can be a serious issue for programming students, depending on the policies being applied by their instructors. However, plagiarism can be inadvertent, due to a lack of knowledge among students. Our research shows varied understandings of correct code reuse, suggesting that students are not provided with appropriate guidelines. Our goal is to introduce good code referencing practice to students, to help raise students' awareness of academic integrity and reduce the possibility of accidental plagiarism. We present Corona, a code referencing system that can assist students in creating references for their code while simultaneously educating them about ethical code reuse. Technical evaluation of the system shows that Corona can successfully generate references for code taken from 20 of 24 distinct programming assistance websites, and that it can find matches between students' code and instructors' example code and generate appropriate references. Our research in a small-scale environment suggests that the use of Corona as a demonstration tool in a lecture about code referencing increases student awareness of correct referencing practice. To improve our intervention, we also show steps that lecturers can take to further elevate students' engagement in code referencing.

Keywords: code referencing · code similarity detection · comment generation · academic integrity · programming · computing education

1 Introduction

Much research has been conducted into detecting similarities in programming students' code [1], with the intention that human checking will then evaluate the similarities and determine whether it constitutes plagiarism [2].

Code reuse is an important aspect of programming education. Lecturers may actively encourage students to find and reuse appropriate code as this is a practice that is both common [3] and helpful [4] in software development. However,

Published by Springer Nature Switzerland AG 2023
T. Keane et al. (Eds.): WCCE 2022, IFIP AICT 685, pp. 615–626, 2023.
https://doi.org/10.1007/978-3-031-43393-1_55

the legitimacy of code reuse in the learning process may not carry over to the assessment process: unacknowledged code reuse in an assessment task may constitute plagiarism [5]. Simply finding and copying the code of others can actually impede the student's learning process [6], and when marking an assessment task, educators are required to assess the students' own work.

Preventing plagiarism is a step beyond detecting it [2]. Just as with written assignments in other disciplines of study, some plagiarism can be averted by teaching students correct referencing practice and asking them to implement it. But what is a correct referencing standard for program code? We have found two proposed standards, but neither appears to be in broad use [7].

Both of the referencing standards we have found take the form of inline code comments; they include several fields of information, making them error-prone and tedious to apply. This process can potentially be eased by automating the comment creation process.

This research proposes an approach that helps to raise students' awareness of accidental plagiarism through the explicit introduction of code referencing practice. We introduce Corona (COde Reference autONomous Assistance), a largely automated referencing system for programming students to help them avoid accidental plagiarism and adopt good code referencing habits following the standard proposed by Simon et al. [7]. We also explain how to help to build code referencing habits by encouraging students to participate in code reuse practice in a way that requires them to create references for externally sourced code and for collaborative assistance.

Corona can help students by creating a standardised reference for any assistance received on their assignments, thus reducing the likelihood of accidental plagiarism. Furthermore, information included by Corona in the reference, such as the purpose, modifications to copied code, and type of assistance given, can also help to make clear the students' own contribution and understanding when completing their assignments.

2 Related Work

Despite the wide acceptance of code reuse in programming, there are no generally accepted standards for referencing the sources of reused code, and there are calls for that to change [7]. One code referencing standard is proposed by Massachusetts Institute of Technology in its academic integrity handbook [8] and has been adopted by several other universities. The guideline specifies when and how to reference externally sourced code, making use of inline comments in the code. Another standard, proposed by Simon et al. [7], addresses not only references for external code (such as from websites or books) but also other forms of assistance received while programming. Again, the information is to be included in an inline comment. When referencing external code, it requires the programmer to specify purpose, date, source, author, URL and modifications made to the reused code, if any.

Various works have addressed the automatic generation of comments for code [9], mainly because of the importance of code comments and the effort required to make complete and helpful comments. Yang et al. [10] have classified a number of approaches to achieving this goal, one of which, template based methods, generally involves two instances of code: the user's code and the template code. A code similarity detection method is employed to match the user's code with the relevant part of the template code, and a predefined comment in the template code is then applied to its paired user code.

Rahman et al. [11] and Wong et al. [12] use code from the answers in Stack Overflow[1] as the template code, and the description and title given by the code's author as the comment. This information is mined in advance from Stack Overflow and stored in a repository, and a code similarity detection approach is used to compare the user's code with the code in the repository.

In academic computing, code similarity detection is geared toward detecting collusion among students by finding similar code passages in their assignments. One approach is text and token matching, which compares the structures of code segments in either raw or tokenised form. Cordy and Roy [13] apply this approach, using code normalisation as a preprocessing step and longest common subsequences (LCS) for similarity counting.

3 Corona

We present Corona, a system that helps users to create references for externally sourced code or assistance. Corona uses the code referencing standard of Simon et al. [7] because it provides more detailed information than that of MIT [8] and because it includes a standard for referencing assistance received. Corona provides two different ways to generate a reference in the form of an inline comment: manually, by providing a form that gathers all the required information; and automatically, by using a template based code similarity detection approach on the code at a URL provided by the user. By introducing Corona to students, we can facilitate the code referencing process for them and also help them to learn correct ethical practice for using externally sourced code or assistance, thus helping to reduce plagiarism.

Corona is built as a standalone web app, so it can be used by all students regardless of the IDE that they use. However, it also provides a web service, which will enable future improvements such as a desktop app or IDE plugins. Both the user website and the web service are built using the Python Flask framework[2]. The way the system works can be divided into three cases, which will be explained in following paragraphs.

When creating a reference for externally sourced code, users first input their own code, either as raw text or as a file upload. They are then asked to indicate the external 'target' code. They can copy and paste the target code – for example, if it comes from a book or their previous assignments – or they can input the URL of the website where they found the target code. If they provide a URL, Corona will gather all code from the website, along with further selected information,

[1] www.stackoverflow.com.

[2] https://flask.palletsprojects.com/en/2.0.x/.

using either web scraping or an API request. API requests are employed for particular websites that are popular sources for code reuse, such as Github and Stack Overflow [14], while web scraping is a generalised approach that aims to extract code and supporting information from any website. At the next step, Corona shows a number of snippets from the target code, ranked by how similar they are to the user's code. The user can then choose which code snippet they want to use as the target code. This selection process is helpful when creating a reference for code found on a site such as Stack Overflow, where a single page usually has many code snippets provided by different authors.

Next, users are asked to indicate which part of their own code they copied from the target. Code similarity detection is used again, this time to rank the user's code snippets according to how similar they are to the selected target code. We adapted the approach of NiCad [13], which employs longest common subsequences (LCS). After both user's and target code have been selected, the system generates a reference based on the information taken from the target website. Users can fine-tune the reference by modifying it or adding further information. For example, users will need to add information such as the reason for copying the code and any modifications they have made to the code. Finally, Corona displays the complete reference, which the user can copy and paste into their code.

When creating a reference for code that is not drawn from a website, users manually input the information in a form provided by Corona. There is still some benefit, in that Corona makes it clear what information is required, and forms that information into a valid inline code comment.

Using a similar form, users can also create a reference for any assistance they have received in their work.

If users want to quickly create a reference for external code without going through the process of selecting the most appropriate matching code segments, there is also an option for them to manually complete all required fields, after which Corona generates the reference for them to copy and paste into their code.

Because it uses a text-based method to compare code, Corona is not limited to code written in a specific programming language, and has been tested on several commonly used languages. Figure 1 shows an example of a Python reference produced by the system and ready for copying to the user's code.

4 Educating Students in Use of the System

One of the biggest problems of code referencing is that it generally has to be done voluntarily, at the students' own initiative, so students' participation can be minimal. In this section, we suggest steps to actively encourage students to participate in code referencing practice.

The lecturer can point out that code reuse is a common practice in professional software development [3] and proven to be helpful [4]. The same applies to collaborative work, which is common in software development. These are therefore good habits for programming students to acquire. Lecturers can also argue

```
# ######################################
# Reference: externally sourced code
# Purpose: Find a way to list all filename in a given folder path and combine it with its extension
# Date: 16 October 2021
# Source: Stack Overflow
# Author: pycruft (https://stackoverflow.com/users/346573/pycruft)
# url: https://stackoverflow.com/questions/3207219/how-do-i-list-all-files-of-a-directory
# Adaptation: Changing variable name and adding variable for pathname
# ######################################
from os import listdir
from os.path import isfile, join
mypath = "documents/assignments"
onlyfiles = [f for f in listdir(mypath) if isfile(join(mypath, f))]
# ######################################
# End reference
# ######################################
```

Fig. 1. An example of a reference generated by Corona and ready for copying to the user's code

for the importance of code referencing as it helps students to create good documentation for their code, which is a necessary skill for a programmer. With this in mind, the lecturer can design an assignment where students are required to adapt a set amount of external code to solve a certain problem. The lecturer can even provide the external code – perhaps for a standard algorithm such as sorting or searching. Students should quickly come to see that the reference helps both them and the lecturer remain aware of which code they have adapted from elsewhere and which code they have written themselves.

To stimulate the creation of references for assistance given in students' coding, we can encourage students to interact with one another in limited and clearly specified ways when working on an assignment. References for this activity will clearly indicate the nature and extent of assistance given by other students.

It is important to give students a clear guideline of acceptable code reuse practice in each course. This may include such topics as: what are acceptable sources of external code; when is a reference required; how much modification is required to the copied code; and how much assistance is allowed to be accepted from another person. Our initial evaluation shows that students are still confused about these questions, as seen in Sect. 5.

5 Evaluation

This section explains how Corona has been and will continue to be evaluated, and presents the findings of the evaluation that has so far been conducted. It is separated into several sections based on different aspects of the functionality. These sections will include evaluation methods that we have already applied and those that we plan to apply in the future.

5.1 Evaluating the Web Scraping

To evaluate our web scraping method, we selected several websites that we have confirmed to contain programming code. We used Google to search for "code tutorial" along with other words such as Python, Java, Javascript, C#, and C++. These searches led us to 24 freely accessible code tutorial websites. We then used our system to scrape all code from a page of each website and manually compared the scraped result with our own inspection of the page in question. We found that our web scraping system successfully scraped all code snippets from 20 of the 24 websites, a success rate of 83%. Table 1 shows the 24 sites, along with an indication of which were successfully scraped. We conclude that our system works well with most tutorial websites that students may use, but that there are a few websites that use distinct ways of displaying program code that are not covered by our generalised web scraping approach.

Table 1. Websites on which we tested our web scraping approach, with an indication of whether the approach was successful

Website		Website		Website	
pypi.org	✓	javatpoint.com	✕	developer.mozilla.org	✓
w3schools.com	✓	codecademy.com	✓	javascripttutorial.net	✓
docs.python.org	✓	docs.microsoft.com	✓	datacamp.com	✕
learnpython.org	✓	csharp.net-turorials.com	✕	kaggle.com	✕
tutorialspoint.com	✓	cplusplus.com	✓	flask.palletsproject.com	✓
programiz.com	✓	learncpp.com	✓	realpython.com	✓
guru99.com	✓	beginnersbook.com	✓	fullstackpython.com	✓
docs.oracle.com	✓	javascript.info	✓	laravel.com	✓

5.2 Evaluating the Code Similarity Detection

To evaluate the code similarity detection we checked for similarities between students' code assignments and the code examples given by lecturers. We chose an Algorithms and Data Structures course, in which students are taught how to implement data structures such as queues and stacks using Python lists. The learning materials provided by lecturers include code for creating and working with those data structures. Students are then given assignments that require them to extend those methods to fulfil a specified requirement. We evaluate our LCS similarity detection approach by looking for code blocks in the students' code that match examples in the lecturer's code.

Our first step was to copy the lecturer's example code from the provided lecture slides, and to group the students' submitted programs according to the examples they are expected to be based upon. Next, we defined 'blocks' in the students' code as sequences of lines of code separated by blank lines. For each of the lecturer's examples, we then used LCS to measure the similarity between each block of the student's code and the lecturer's example. If the similarity percentage exceeds a predetermined threshold, we count that code block as similar to the example. We then calculate an average similarity for the assignment, being the total number of similar blocks divided by the number of student submissions. These assignments are quite tightly constrained, so we would expect the average similarity to be close to 100%, indicating that every student had copied the lecturer's example reasonably closely.

For this evaluation we selected three related assignments, all dealing with stacks. The first was based on a lecturer's example showing how to implement a stack; the second, how to push to the stack; the third, how to pop from the stack. The results can be seen in Table 2. The code similarity detector works relatively well at a similarity threshold of 50%. Higher thresholds do not come close to finding the expected level of similarity. However, the 134% value for code example 1 shows that our method is being overly sensitive in detecting similarity: effectively, it detects more than one match with the example code in some students' assignments even though the nature of the assignment suggests that it should only detect one copy. Based on our observations, the length of the code and the uniqueness of the code greatly affect the result. As Corona permits and expects users to select the appropriate piece of code from all segments found to match the target, this is not a problem: users will simply not select any incorrect matches that are found.

Table 2. Average of student similarities to lecturer's example code for three different code examples; the percentage greater than 100 is explained in the text

Similarity threshold	Example 1: implement	Example 2: push	Example 3: pop
50%	134%	93%	93%
60%	69%	38%	52%
70%	24%	14%	17%
80%	3%	7%	7%
90%	3%	7%	7%
100%	3%	0%	3%

We also compared LCS with other commonly used character-level similarity detection approaches (string alignment and RKRGST (running Karp-Rabin greedy string tiling) [15]) and several token-level approaches (surface, syntactic and pseudo-semantic token) adapted from the similarity detection method accuracy comparison conducted by Karnalim et al. [16]. The IR-Plag dataset [17] was employed for the comparison, and the results are shown in Table 3. The top-K precision of each approach was calculated on IR-Plag's six different groups of code, which correspond to differing amounts of disguise that were applied to an original program. The execution time of each approach was also calculated, by embedding a time-calculating program in the code for each approach, and running all tests on the same computer. The comparison of execution times of the code similarity detection approaches can be found in Table 4. This is not necessarily a reliable measure, but it is sufficient to show that this method does not impose an unreasonable time burden.

Table 3. Top-K precision of several code similarity detection approaches at different levels of disguise

Disguise level	LCS	String alignment	RKRGST	Surface	Syntatic token	Pseudo-semantic token
L1	16%	5%	3%	8%	13%	12%
L2	6%	3%	0%	9%	15%	14%
L3	8%	0%	0%	12%	21%	13%
L4	0%	0%	0%	3%	3%	2%
L5	0%	0%	0%	2%	0%	0%
L6	5%	1%	1%	6%	9%	7%
Overall	5%	1%	1%	6%	9%	7%

As seen in Table 3, LCS generally outperforms other character-level approaches with a significant gap ($p = 0.01$ when compared with string alignment and $p < 0.01$ when compared with RKRGST). When observed for each disguise level, LCS results in higher top-K precision than string alignment and RKRGST at the first three levels. However, the differences are statistically significant only on level 3 disguises ($p = 0.03$), showing that LCS performs especially better on component declaration relocation disguises. As shown in Table 4, LCS also outperforms other character-level approaches in execution time, being 28 s faster than string alignment and 27 s faster than RKRGST.

When compared with token-level approaches, LCS appears to have a lower top-K precision; however, a two-tailed t-test with 95% confidence rate shows that the differences are not statistically significant. This illustrates that LCS is comparable to token-level approaches despite not requiring any language-specific tokenization when dealing with cross-language code similarity detection. However, LCS is slower than token-level approaches, given that LCS conducts the comparison on smaller code segments. For the pseudo-semantic token approach we used a web-based code similarity detection tool, JPlag [18], which made it appear slower as JPlag requires time to generate similarity reports.

5.3 Evaluating Student Learning

Evaluation of student learning entails conducting student surveys at the start and end of each semester in question. This shows us students' initial knowledge of acceptable code reuse practice, and the impact of our system after it is introduced to them through the semester. For the pilot experiment we selected a course that has not yet been optimized for adapting code referencing (as opposed to

Table 4. Execution time comparison of several code similarity detection approaches

Similarity detection approach	Execution time (seconds)
LCS	83
String alignment	112
RKRGST	111
Surface token	60
Syntatic token	65
Pseudo-semantic token	90

the approach that we propose in Sect. 4) as we wanted to see how effective our system is in a course that has not been tailored to its use. For the survey we have adapted the scenarios of Simon et al. [19], as shown in Table 5. Those scenarios were designed to find respondents' opinions on whether certain actions are acceptable and on whether they constitute plagiarism or collusion. As used in our survey, they are used to ask whether students believe that the actions require a reference.

For each scenario, students are asked to choose one of three options: a reference is required; a reference is not required; I don't know whether a reference is required. The answers to these questions are not set in stone, and are likely to vary across institutions and indeed across courses within the same institution. In Table 5 we show the pre-intervention results from 24 respondents, along with the answers selected by their lecturers. We can see that the students have varying knowledge of when a code reference is required, showing confusion in selecting the appropriate response for several scenarios. We hoped to see this improve following introduction to the students of our system and the corresponding code referencing guidelines.

We then conducted a similar survey with students at the end of semester to see how our system and the lecture on code referencing affected their knowledge regarding correct code reuse practices (Table 5).

In scenario C1, we can see a decrease in the number of students who think that references are necessary when reusing code from the internet, which is not an ideal result. This may be due to the fact that in the project course we selected, students are under the supervision of different lecturers, each of whom has their own acceptable code reuse expectations due to varying complexity of their projects: the type of system they are building, and their research topics, will affect the code reuse tolerance level. We believe that when students think that a scenario is unacceptable behaviour, they will not indicate that it requires a reference. They may think that code reuse should not take place, and that if it does, it should be hidden. The same also seems to apply to scenarios C4 (modifying another student's code to make it look different from the original) and C9 (asking another student to fix your code), which in most cases will be considered as collusion. Students will clearly be uncertain whether a reference is needed for an action if they are not sure whether that action is acceptable, as we

Table 5. Knowledge of students before (N = 24) and after (N = 22) introduction of our system as to whether references are required; lecturers' expected answers are shown in bold; answer columns are Required, Don't know, and Not required

Scenario	Before			After		
	Rqd	DKn	Not	Rqd	DKn	Not
C1: Using a freely available internet source as the basis for your work	**96%**	0%	4%	**91%**	9%	4%
C2: Basing an assessment largely on work that you wrote and submitted for a previous course	**50%**	25%	25%	**55%**	18%	27%
C3: Posting a question to an online help board (e.g. stack overflow) and using the answer in your work	**37%**	21%	42%	**63%**	5%	32%
C4: Using another student's code and changing it so that it looks different from the original	**25%**	25%	50%	**23%**	18%	59%
C5: Copying an early draft of another student's work and developing it into your own	**63%**	17%	21%	**54%**	41%	5%
C6: Discussing with another student how to approach a task and what resources to use, then developing the solution independently	79%	0%	**21%**	64%	4%	**32%**
C7: Discussing the detail of your code with another student while working on it	71%	8%	**21%**	68%	9%	**23%**
C8: Showing your code to another student and asking them for advice about a coding problem	**71%**	4%	25%	**68%**	9%	23%
C9: Asking another student to fix your code so that it runs correctly	**50%**	17%	33%	**27%**	23%	50%
C10: After completing an assessment, adding features that you noticed when looking at another student's work	46%	12%	**42%**	45%	14%	**41%**

can see in scenario C5 (using another student's early draft) where the number of students who answered "Don't know" increased post-intervention. The same may also apply for scenarios C6 (discussing the approach with another student) and C7 (discussing your code with another student while working on it), as in both cases more students respond post-intervention that a reference is not required.

There is also a slight increase in the number of students who think that a reference is required when they are reusing a previously submitted code assignment (C2), which is a desirable result but still leaves room for improvement. Scenario

C3 shows a substantial increase (37% to 63%) in the number of students who think that a reference is needed when using an answer to a question they post on an online help board. This may be due to the fact that referencing code from an online help board is a substantial part of Corona's functionality.

Very minor changes can be observed in C8 (showing code to another student for advice) and C10 (adding features after looking at another student's code), but these may due to the difference in numbers of participants for the pre and post surveys, both of which were fully voluntary.

6 Conclusion

We have presented Corona, an automated code referencing system to assist students in creating references for externally sourced code or assistance, which is part of our initiative to raise students' awareness of correct code reuse practice through code referencing and thus to help mitigate inadvertent code plagiarism. A pre-intervention survey with a small pilot class shows that students have varying knowledge regarding acceptable code reuse practice and would benefit from a standardised baseline. By introducing Corona through a code referencing lecture and demonstration, and making the system available to students, we introduced a referencing standard to students and helped them to implement it. We employ a template based automatic code comment generator to assist students in creating references. Our evaluations of two components of our automatic code comment generation system, the web scraping method and the code similarity detection method, demonstrate that our system performs well in automatically generating code references. A post-intervention repeat of the pre-intervention survey suggests that Corona has had some positive impact on students' knowledge of correct code reuse practice. Further, we have suggested steps for lecturers to further improve students' participation in code referencing and help to raise their awareness of unintentional code plagiarism.

References

1. Novak, M., Joy, M., Kermek, D.: Source-code similarity detection and detection tools used in academia: a systematic review. ACM Trans. Comput. Educ. **19**(3), 1–37 (2019)
2. Lukashenko, R., Graudina, V., Grundspenkis, J.: Computer-based plagiarism detection methods and tools: an overview. In: International Conference on Computer Systems and Technologies, pp. 1–6. CompSysTech 2007 (2007)
3. Haefliger, S., von Krogh, G., Spaeth, S.: Code reuse in open source software. Manag. Sci. **54**(1), 180–193 (2008)
4. Huang, H., Youssef, A.M., Debbabi, M.: Binsequence: fast, accurate and scalable binary code reuse detection. In: ACM on Asia Conference on Computer and Communications Security, pp. 155–166. ASIA CCS '17 (2017)
5. Flores, E., Barrón-Cedeño, A., Rosso, P., Moreno, L.: Towards the detection of cross-language source code reuse. In: Muñoz, R., Montoyo, A., Métais, E. (eds.) NLDB 2011. LNCS, vol. 6716, pp. 250–253. Springer, Heidelberg (2011). https://doi.org/10.1007/978-3-642-22327-3_31

6. Zander, C., Eckerdal, A., McCartney, R., Mostrom, J.E., Sanders, K., Thomas, L.: Copying can be good: how instructors use imitation in teaching programming. In: 24th Conference on Innovation and Technology in Computer Science Education, pp. 450–456. ITiCSE 2019 (2019)
7. Simon, Sheard, J., Morgan, M., Petersen, A., Settle, A., Sinclair, J.: Informing students about academic integrity in programming. In: 20th Australasian Computing Education Conference, pp. 113–122. ACM Press, New York, New York, USA (2018)
8. Academic integrity at MIT. https://integrity.mit.edu/handbook/writing-code. Accessed 20 Aug 2020
9. Zhao, L., Zhang, L., Yan, S.: A survey on research of code comment auto generation. J. Phys. Conf. Ser. **1345**(3), 250–253 (2019)
10. Yang, B., Liping, Z., Fengrong, Z.: A survey on research of code comment. In: Third International Conference on Management Engineering, Software Engineering and Service Sciences, pp. 45–51 (2019)
11. Rahman, M.M., Roy, C.K., Keivanloo, I.: Recommending insightful comments for source code using crowdsourced knowledge. In: 15th International Working Conference on Source Code Analysis and Manipulation (SCAM), pp. 81–90. IEEE (2015)
12. Wong, E., Yang, J., Tan, L.: Autocomment: mining question and answer sites for automatic comment generation. In: 28th International Conference on Automated Software Engineering (ASE), pp. 562–567. IEEE (2013)
13. Cordy, J.R., Roy, C.K.: The NiCad clone detector. In: 2011 IEEE 19th International Conference on Program Comprehension, pp. 219–220. IEEE (2011)
14. Hata, H., Treude, C., Kula, R.G., Ishio, T.: 9.6 million links in source code comments: purpose, evolution, and decay. In: 41st International Conference on Software Engineering, pp. 1211–1221. ICSE '19, IEEE Press (2019)
15. Wise, M.J.: YAP3: improved detection of similarities in computer program and other texts. In: 27th SIGCSE Technical Symposium on Computer Science Education, pp. 130–134. SIGCSE 1996 (1996)
16. Karnalim, O., Simon, Chivers, W.: Layered similarity detection for programming plagiarism and collusion on weekly assessments. Comput. Appl. Eng. Educ. **30**(6), 1739–1752 (2022)
17. Karnalim, O.: Source code plagiarism detection with low-level structural representation and information retrieval. Int. J. Comput. Appl. 566–576 (2019)
18. Prechelt, L., Malpohl, G.: Finding plagiarisms among a set of programs with JPlag. J Univers. Comput. Sci. **8**, 1016–1038 (2003)
19. Simon, Cook, B., Sheard, J., Carbone, A., Johnson, C.: Academic integrity perceptions regarding computing assessments and essays. In: 10th Annual Conference on International Computing Education Research, pp. 107–114. ACM Press, New York, New York, USA (2014)

National Policies and Plans for Digital Competence

Senior Computing Subjects Taught Across Australian States and Territories

Therese Keane(✉) and Milorad Cerovac

La Trobe University, Melbourne, VIC 3086, Australia
{t.keane,m.cerovac}@latrobe.edu.au

Abstract. The ever-changing nature of technology in a globally inter-connected world has placed our educational institutions at the forefront of ensuring a future-ready workforce. More than ever before, the regular revisions, refreshes and re-designs of school curricula, especially in the domain of computer science education, need to ensure that the knowledge and skills that students acquire will adequately prepare them for progressing into either university, a vocational pathway, or directly into the workforce. School computer science courses are therefore uniquely positioned with multiple opportunities to immerse students in authentic real-world problem-solving challenges, that will encourage the development of a collection of key skills. When faced with a complex problem to solve, students need to be able to demonstrate the resilience and ability to work collaboratively, creatively and to think critically. One other fundamental set of skills that is gaining much-needed traction around the world, are the computational thinking skills of decomposition, pattern recognition, abstraction, and algorithm design. This paper will provide a brief overview of the teaching of the Digital Technologies curriculum from the Foundation Year to Year 10, before sharing a deeper insight into the current aims, rationale, knowledge and skills as they manifest across each Australian State and Territory.

Keywords: Digital Technologies Curriculum · Computer Science · Senior Secondary

1 Introduction

Even though Australia has a national mandatory curriculum that encompasses Foundation (students commencing primary school aged 5) to Year 8 and then optional in Years 9 and 10, this however is not the case at senior secondary school (Years 11 & 12). Each State and Territory devise their own curriculum, and this is reviewed periodically to maintain academic standards and the relevancy of the content. Given the rapidly changing nature of the computing discipline, coupled with the availability and accessibility to an enormous amount of data and information, the curriculum can very rapidly lose relevance. Therefore, it is imperative that the curriculum is often reviewed and updated to maintain currency.

Published by Springer Nature Switzerland AG 2023
T. Keane et al. (Eds.): WCCE 2022, IFIP AICT 685, pp. 629–640, 2023.
https://doi.org/10.1007/978-3-031-43393-1_56

The computing field, particularly in the area of software design and development, offers opportunities for creativity and problem-solving and a collaborative environment where working with people and exploring issues is an integral part of the real world. Data Science is experiencing unprecedented growth, with IT professionals in this specialty in high demand. Many of the benchmarked curricula have either recently been revised or are in the process of revision; driven by a fast changing technological and information landscape.

This paper will examine the final two years of secondary school computing curriculum across the six States and two Territories in Australia and explore the common themes and directions that each jurisdiction has deemed important for their students.

2 Literature Review

In a rapidly changing technological landscape, where digital devices and digital technologies are omnipresent, the importance of computer science education has never been more important and relevant [1, 2]. Bruno and Lewis [3] as part of their analysis acknowledged the recent dramatic shift to promote computer science education across Foundation to Year 12, citing the argument that the knowledge and skills fostered through computer science education would provide students with "access to high-paying and high-status jobs" (p. 2).

In the 2020 Emerging Jobs Report [4], careers in artificial intelligence, robotics (includes software engineering), and data science, were identified as the top three emerging jobs in the US. Associated with these three disciplines are the unique set of skills referred to as computational thinking, made popular by Wing [5], in her seminal paper. Computational thinking consists of a range of mental tools, such as abstraction and decomposition, that are considered essential for solving complex problems, across a broad spectrum of disciplines. As such, computational thinking has drawn increasing levels of attention from researchers, educators, and policy makers [6].

Buitrago Flórez et al. [7] recognized the significance and broad application of computational thinking, and accordingly argued for computer science courses to be built around the computational thinking skillset. Furthermore, they contend that computational thinking be offered across all levels of education as part of a Computer Science curriculum, from the primary year levels through to university. Bocconi et al. [6] as part of supporting the European Commission's policy making process acknowledge that countries have been introducing computational thinking across their education systems to "foster the 21st century skills necessary to fully participate in the digital world" (p. 8). In Malaysia, computational thinking skills have been recently and deliberately integrated in an effort to address the global trend towards developing and strengthening digital literacy among its students [8].

However, the explicit embedding of computational thinking is not without its challenges. For instance, Ung et al. [8] as part of their preliminary work have identified an "apparent lack of understanding of computational thinking skills in general among teachers" (p. 1). The authors also share the same concerns when they have undertaken field work, and have noted that this is most apparent when teachers do not have adequate training in this specialized discipline. Nonetheless, it is anticipated that as the emphasis on 21st century skills, such as computational thinking, continues to gain prominence in the curriculum, subsequent teacher professional development will inevitably address these challenges.

3 Teaching Computing from Foundation – Year 12

3.1 Digital Technologies Curriculum Foundation – Year 10

The Digital Technologies curriculum that is part of the Australian Curriculum is taught across all of Australia in each of the six States and two Territories. The curriculum is compulsory from Foundation (age 5 years and this is the first-year students begin formal primary schooling in Australia) – Year 8 (age 14 years). In Years 9 and 10, the Digital Technologies curriculum is optional, even though there is formalized curriculum for those States and Territories that want to offer the subject. The Digital Technologies curriculum focuses on Digital Systems, Data and Information, and Creating Digital Solutions. The key concepts underpinning the curriculum include:

- designing, creating, managing and evaluating digital solutions;
- developing computational thinking skills (abstraction; data collection, representation and interpretation; specification, algorithms and implementation to create digital solutions);
- using digital systems to automate the transformation of data into information and to creatively communicate ideas in a range of settings;
- understanding and applying protocols and legal practices to support safe, ethical and respectful communications and collaboration with known and unknown audiences; and
- applying systems thinking to monitor, analyze, predict and shape the interactions within and between information systems and the impact of these systems on individuals, societies, economies and environments [9].

Additionally, students are introduced to programming throughout the curriculum, starting with visual programming in the younger years using colored blocks and shapes (Years 3–6), then as students' progress to high school, they undertake general-purpose programming (Years 7–8) and at Years 9 and 10 where Digital Technologies is optional, students use object orientated programming languages. As part of the course, there are activities that are also "unplugged" where they do not require a computer or the internet.

3.2 Curriculum in Years 11 and 12

Unlike the national Digital Technologies curriculum, the Computing discipline in the final two years of secondary school (Years 11 & 12) is not uniform across Australia. The Computing curriculum is optional and varies in each State and Territory. Whilst all students must study Digital Technologies from Foundation until Year 8, Computing as a subject is optional from Years 9–12. However, in Years 11 and 12 each State and Territory has jurisdiction over what is included and taught in the curriculum. The authors have reviewed the senior Computing curriculum in all states and territories in Australia. These included Victoria, New South Wales, Queensland, Western Australia, South Australia, Tasmania and Northern Territory and Australian Capital Territory. There is an assortment of naming conventions for courses that are in use by the various educational jurisdictions, across Australia.

Senior Secondary Curriculum Victoria

The focus on the Computing curriculum taught in Victoria varies depending on the unit taught. The Year 11 unit *Applied Computing* focuses on how data can be used in databases and spreadsheets to create visualizations; the use of programming languages to develop working software solutions; the development of innovative solutions through a collaborative effort; and security risks to data/information in a networked environment. The *Data Analytics* subject in Year 12 focuses on applying a devised problem-solving methodology; data and information; and the creation of infographics or dynamic data visualizations based on large complex data sets. The second Year 12 subject on offer is *Software Development* where the focus is on applying the problem-solving methodology; developing underlying skills to develop working software modules; and an exploration of risks to software and data during the development process. The distinctive feature of the curriculum in Victoria is the over-arching problem-solving methodology which is central to all three courses.

The subjects offered aim to have students:

- understand how digital systems and solutions can be used by individuals and organizations;
- develop an understanding of the roles and applications of cybersecurity, data analytics and programming;
- apply the problem-solving methodology to analyze needs and opportunities, design and develop solutions to problems and evaluate how effectively solutions meet needs and opportunities;
- apply project management techniques to assist with the development of digital solutions;
- develop an informed perspective on current and emerging digital technologies and disseminate findings;
- identify and evaluate innovative and emerging opportunities for digital solutions and technologies; and
- develop critical and creative thinking, communication, and collaboration, and personal, social and ICT skills [10].

Some of the concepts include an introduction to data analysis, networking security, cybersecurity and programming. The curriculum endeavors to address Australia's future job needs, with an emphasis on data (including collection, management, analysis, and visualization), programming, networks and security.

Senior Secondary Curriculum New South Wales

The New South Wales curriculum in Years 11 & 12 *Information Processes and Technology* focuses on teaching students about information-based systems. It covers the processes of collecting, organizing, analyzing, storing/retrieving, processing, transmitting/receiving, and displaying data and information, as well as the technologies that support them. With this background, students will be well placed to adapt to new technologies as they emerge [11]. The second offering in Years 11 & 12, *Software Design and Development* refers to the creativity, knowledge, values and communication skills required to develop computer programs [12]. *Software Design and Development* provides students with a systematic approach to problem-solving and an opportunity to be creative. The subjects offered aim to have students:

- become confident, competent, discriminating, and ethical users of information technologies, to possess an understanding of information processes and to appreciate the effect of information systems on society; and
- develop the knowledge, understanding, skills and values to solve problems through the creation of software solutions [12].

Some of the concepts taught include project management, social and ethical issues, databases, software development approaches, defining and understanding problems and programming.

Senior Secondary Curriculum Queensland

The focus on the Queensland curriculum in *Digital Solutions* is to enable students to learn about algorithms, computer languages and user interfaces through generating digital solutions to problems. They engage with data, information, and applications to create digital solutions while understanding the need to encrypt and protect data. Moreover, students are encouraged to explore the impact of computing at a local and global level and the issues associated with the ethical integration of technology. The focus on *Information & Communication Technology* is on the knowledge, understanding and skills related to engagement with information and communication technology in a variety of contexts such as work, study and leisure.

The aims of the Digital Solutions subject are to have students:

- recognize and describe elements, components, principles and processes;
- symbolize and explain information, ideas and interrelationships;
- analyze problems and information;
- determine solution requirements and criteria;
- synthesize information and ideas to determine possible digital solutions;
- generate components of the digital solution;
- evaluate impacts, components and solutions against criteria to make refinements and justified recommendations; and
- make decisions about and use mode-appropriate features, language and conventions for particular purposes and contexts.

The aims of the Information & Communication Technology subject are to have students:

- identify and explain hardware and software requirements related to ICT problems;
- identify and explain the use of ICT in society;
- analyze ICT problems to identify solutions;
- communicate ICT information to audiences using visual representations and language conventions and features;

- apply software and hardware concepts, ideas and skills to complete tasks in ICT contexts;
- synthesize ICT concepts and ideas to plan solutions to given ICT problems;
- produce solutions that address ICT problems; and
- evaluate problem-solving processes and solutions, and make recommendations [13].

Senior Secondary Curriculum Western Australia

The Western Australian curriculum offers two streams of courses: *Applied Information Technology* (AIT); and *Computer Science* (CS). The Computer Science stream of subjects focuses on fundamental principles, concepts and skills within the field of computing. Students learn how to diagnose and solve problems and explore principles related to the analysis and creation of computer and information systems; software development; the connectivity between computers; the management of data; the development of database systems; and the moral and ethical considerations for the development and use of computer systems. The Applied Information Technology stream of subjects focuses on the development of knowledge and skills using a range of computer hardware and software to create, manipulate and communicate information in an effective, responsible and informed manner. Students develop an understanding of computer systems; the management of data; and the use of a variety of software applications to investigate, design, construct and evaluate digital products and digital solutions. Students investigate client-driven issues and challenges, devise solutions, produce models or prototypes and then evaluate and refine the developed digital product and solution.

The aims of the Applied Information Technology subject are to have students:

- devise solutions, produce models or prototypes and then evaluate and refine the design solution in collaboration with the client;
- develop digital solutions for real situations;
- solve information problems (practical application of skills);
- gain an understanding of computer systems and networks; and
- evaluate the legal, ethical and social issues associated with each solution.

The aims of the Computer Science subject are to have students:

- develop problem-solving abilities and technical skills as they learn how to diagnose and solve problems in the course of understanding the building blocks of computing;
- investigate the impact of technological developments on the personal, social and professional lives of individuals, businesses and communities; and
- recognize the consequences of decisions made by developers and users in respect to the development and use of technology [14].

Senior Secondary Curriculum South Australia

The South Australian senior secondary curriculum offers two streams of computing: *Information Processing and Publishing* and *Digital Technologies*. Information Processing and Publishing focuses on the use of technology to design and implement information-processing solutions. The subject emphasizes the acquisition and development of practical skills in identifying, choosing, and using the appropriate computer hardware and software for communicating in a range of contexts. It focuses on the application of practical skills to provide creative solutions to text-based communication tasks. Students create both hard copy and electronic text-based publications, and critically evaluate the development process. They choose and use appropriate hardware and software to process, manage, and communicate information. They develop problem-solving, critical-thinking, and decision-making skills which they then can apply to meet the needs of the audience. Throughout their learning, students are provided with opportunities to develop an appreciation of the current social, legal, and ethical issues that relate to the processing, management, and communication of text-based information, and to assess their impact on individuals, organizations, and society.

The Digital Technologies subject focuses on the application of digital technologies, which can lead to discoveries, new learning, and innovative approaches to understanding and solving problems. Students make connections with innovation in other fields and across other learning areas. In Digital Technologies students create practical, innovative solutions to problems of interest. By extracting, interpreting, and modelling real-world data sets, students identify trends and examine sustainable solutions to problems in, for example, business, industry, the environment, and the community. They investigate how potential solutions are influenced by current and projected social, economic, environmental, scientific, and ethical considerations, including relevance, originality, appropriateness, and sustainability. Students use computational thinking skills and strategies to identify, deconstruct, and solve problems that are of interest to them. They analyze and evaluate data, test hypotheses, make decisions based on evidence, and create solutions. Through the study of Digital Technologies, students are encouraged to take ownership of problems and design, code, validate, and evaluate their solutions. In doing so, they develop and extend their understanding of designing and programming, including the basic constructs involved in coding, array processing, and modularization.

The Information Processing and Publishing course aims to have students:

- create both hard copy and electronic text-based publications, and critically evaluate the development process;
- develop solutions to text-based problems in information processing and publishing;
- use the design process to apply problem-solving, critical-thinking, and decision-making skills;
- communicate their thinking and design proposals;
- analyze the impacts and consequences of the use of publishing technologies; and
- develop an appreciation of the current social, legal, and ethical issues and the impact on individuals, organizations, and society.

  – The aim of the Digital Technologies course is to have students:

- identify, deconstruct, and solve problems, with an emphasis on creating practical and innovative solutions;
- analyze data sets to identify patterns and/or trends, draw conclusions, and make predictions;
- investigate how potential solutions are influenced by current and projected social, economic, environmental, scientific, and ethical considerations;

- experiment and learn from what does not work as planned, as well as from what does work; and
- apply their programming skills to develop, test and evaluate a digital solution (product, prototype, and/or proof of concept) that is appropriate to the context of the problem and meets the needs of the intended user [15].

It needs to be noted that the Northern Territory curriculum in Years 11 and 12 is similar to the South Australian Curriculum given they have a service agreement. Senior secondary schools in the Northern Territory must follow the policies, guidelines and procedures and assessment as set out by the South Australian Certificate of Education (SACE).

Senior Secondary Curriculum Tasmania

The Tasmanian jurisdiction assigns senior secondary courses with a complexity level ranging from Level 1 (lowest difficulty) to Level 4 (highest difficulty). The two Level 3 courses (equivalent to Year 12) which form the basis for analysis of the Tasmanian system are: *Computer Science* and *Information Systems and Digital Technologies.*

Computer Science is considered a starting point for students wanting to move onto further studies in ICT or engineering, as well as a preparation for a broad range of careers. A key component of this course is algorithmic thinking, where students develop formal stepwise algorithms for solving problems. Information Systems and Digital Technologies provides students with an opportunity to develop an understanding of how organizations manage, use and organize complex data to solve a range of information problems. This course will help prepare students for further education and study in a wide range of disciplines, such as IT, business, health, commerce, and engineering. Both courses offer a mix of theory and practical skills development.

Basic Computing (Level 1) is designed for students who have little or no background in computing. The Essential Skills – Using Computers and the Internet (Level 2) course provides students with 'everyday' computer and internet skills (e.g. use of common software tools/applications, file management, website navigation/search strategies). These courses lead on to the Level 2 Computer Applications subject, which provides students with an opportunity to undertake a focused learning in one specific applied area. Some examples include: Information Processing; Information Management; Publishing; Multimedia; Programming and Control. The pathways provided from Computer Applications include: Computer Science (Level 3); Information Systems & Digital Technologies (Level 3); and Computer Graphics & Design (Level 3).

The focus of the Computer Science curriculum is to have students:

- develop the ability to identify, analyze and design algorithms;
- gain an understanding of programming concepts;
- acquire skills in the design, documentation, analysis, testing and evaluation of computer programs
- develop an understanding of Boolean logic, binary data, representation of data types and their relationship to underlying digital hardware;
- gain familiarity with high-level and low-level programming languages; and
- develop an awareness of the social, ethical and professional aspects of computer science.

The focus of the Information Systems and Digital Technologies curriculum is to have students:

- identify, analyze and solve real world information problems;
- describe, explain and analyze the components of an information system, and the inter-relationships between these components;
- describe, explain and analyze social issues associated with information systems;
- design, develop, use and evaluate an information system;
- plan, organize, and complete activities, using a project management approach; and
- communicate ideas and information in a variety of forms [16].

Senior Secondary Curriculum Australian Capital Territory

The ACT curriculum has adopted a novel approach in offering the following three courses across Years 11 and 12: *Data Science*; *Digital Technologies*; and *Networking and Security*. Data Science is designed to develop in students the knowledge, understanding and skills to identify, analyze and solve problems, through the use of data as evidence to form compelling and persuasive arguments for change and innovation [17]. Digital Technologies focuses on students developing and extending their understanding of designing and programming to solving problems which they have identified and analyzed [18]. In creating their solution, students can either engage in a single technology deeply or consider many different technologies in pursuit of their solution. Networking and Security focuses on network technologies and architecture, and the devices, media and services and operations in different types of networks [19]. Identifying, analysing and solving problems is central to this course.

There are three distinctive features of the ACT curriculum. These are: (1) Courses and units are not specifically labelled as being a Year 11 or Year 12 course/unit, which allows both Year 11 and Year 12 students to enroll in the same subjects and units at the same time, but be assessed against different achievement standards; (2) there are no external subject-based examinations with flexibility for teachers to design assessments that are rigorous and take into account student interest, background knowledge and experience; and (3) use of university terminology when referring to students as completing a course either as a minor, major, or a combination of these.

The subjects offered aim to have students:

- analyze problems or challenges to determine needs for solutions or products;
- apply the process of design (investigate, design, plan, manage, create, evaluate solutions);
- use critical and creative thinking to design innovative solutions;
- produce or create solutions or products to address a need, problem or challenge;
- evaluate and use technologies in a range of contexts;
- demonstrate problem solving skills;
- communicate to different audiences using a range of methods; and
- engage confidently with and responsibly select and manipulate appropriate technologies – materials, data, systems, tools and equipment.

Each of the above objectives is achieved through the context of the specific course (Data Science; Digital Technologies; and Networking and Security) that students are enrolled.

4 Discussion

The commonalities and significant differences that were observed are formulated and described below.

4.1 Commonalities

The following commonalities were observed between all the offerings:

Problem-Solving Methodology
Use of an over-arching problem-solving methodology or an equivalent approach (e.g. Software Development Life Cycle) featured in almost all jurisdictions. It is seen as an important method to help students systematically identify problems, needs or opportunities, and then develop their solutions.

Networks
All jurisdictions cover the basics of networks as a minimum.

Programming/Algorithms
Most jurisdictions allow teachers/schools to select the programming language that students will use. Pseudocode and/or flowcharts were common ways of teaching students algorithms. Tasmania makes specific reference to Java.

Web Development/Authoring Tools
Specific tools for students to learn and use are not explicitly mentioned.

Spreadsheets
Widely used in the commercial world for storing and presenting data; thus provides a useful set of skills for students. No distinction is made between using Excel or other applications (e.g. Google Sheets). Some jurisdictions specifically mention the macros that students are expected to know and use.

Data Management/Databases/Big Data
The importance of students learning to analyze data is covered in nearly all jurisdictions, but some place a greater emphasis on providing students with an opportunity to work with 'big' data. There is a compelling argument for students to learn through use of authentic problems, such as the analysis of complex data provided by the likes of the Australian Bureau of Statistics or Bureau of Meteorology.

Testing and Evaluation
Seen as key stages within the systematic problem-solving methodology (or its equivalent in other jurisdictions). It appears almost universally.

Documentation
Internal documentation (within programs) is covered almost universally; with a few making specific references to students needing the ability to create other document forms (e.g. Quick Start guide).

4.2 Differences

The following differences were observed between all the offerings:

Computer Architecture
This covers the internals of computers (e.g. CPUs, RAM, graphics cards) as well as peripheral devices that are connected to computers; and which form a part of a home or business network.

HTML
Very few jurisdictions explicitly mention HTML coding. One can only surmise that the presence of numerous web authoring tools has reduced the need for students to learn HTML, though counter-arguments to this point do exist.

Logic Gates/Circuits/Truth Tables
Tasmania is one jurisdiction that delves more deeply into logic gates, with students also learning about Truth Tables, and basic flip-flop circuits.

Context/Data Flow Diagrams
Context and data flow diagrams are common tools used by businesses to provide a graphical visualization of the flow of data in an organization.

Disaster Recovery
While all jurisdictions cover security and threats to data in varying degrees, only Victoria and Western Australia Make specific reference to disaster recovery.

Legal, Social and Ethical Issues
ICT has given rise to a host of legal and ethical issues that students need to be aware of (e.g. sensitivity/privacy of data, software piracy) in our technology-rich world where data and information is easily accessible.

Some areas identified as differences tend to align with the teaching of Computer Science. However, most Australian states have moved away from teaching Computer Science with the exception of Western Australia and Tasmania.

5 Conclusion

The rapid changes in the information technology landscape, as has been cited on several occasions, has been a catalyst for school boards to review their courses. All jurisdictions refer to either skills shortages, or the need to ensure that their respective countries are competitive in the global environment. There is great deal of similarity between these jurisdictions, as the governing bodies seek to make learning relevant and authentic. The knowledge and skills that students acquire provide pathways for students to progress to further studies or if they choose, proceed directly into the workforce; as well as making them 'informed' citizens. Hence, programming, web development, data analysis and management (including database technology), ethics and law are commonly observed topics across each jurisdiction.

References

1. Code.org, CSTA, ECEP Alliance: 2020 State of Computer Science Education: Illuminating disparities (2020). https://advocacy.code.org/stateofcs. Accessed 12 Apr 2023
2. Lodi, M., Martini, S.: Computational thinking, between Papert and Wing. Sci. Educ. **30**(4), 883–908 (2021)
3. Bruno, P., Lewis, C.M.: Computer science trends and trade-offs in California high schools. Educ. Adm. Q. **58**(3), 386–418 (2022)
4. LinkedIn 2020 emerging jobs report. https://business.linkedin.com/content/dam/me/business/en-us/talent-solutions/emerging-jobs-report/Emerging_Jobs_Report_U.S._FINAL.pdf. Accessed 12 Apr 2023
5. Wing, J.M.: Computational thinking. Commun. ACM **49**(3), 3–35 (2006)
6. Bocconi, S., Chioccariello, A., Dettori, G., Ferrari, A., Engelhardt, K.: Developing computational thinking in compulsory education: implications for policy and practice. European Commission, Joint Research Centre, Spain (2016)
7. Flórez, F.B., Casallas, R., Hernández, M., Reyes, A., Restrepo, S., Danies, G.: Changing a generation's way of thinking: teaching computational thinking through programming. Rev. Educ. Res. **87**(4), 834–860 (2017)
8. Ung, L.L., Labadin, J., Mohamad, F.S.: Computational thinking for teachers: development of a localised e-learning system. Comput. Educ. **177**, 104379 (2022)
9. Australian Curriculum Assessment and Reporting Authority (ACARA), Aims of Digital Technologies. https://www.australiancurriculum.edu.au/f-10-curriculum/technologies/digital-technologies/aims/. Accessed 12 Apr 2023
10. Victorian Curriculum and Assessment Authority (VCAA): Victorian Certificate of Education Applied Computing Study Design. VCAA, Melbourne (2019)
11. Board of Studies NSW Information Processes and Technology Stage 6 Syllabus (2009). https://educationstandards.nsw.edu.au/wps/portal/nesa/11-12/stage-6-learning-areas/technologies/information-processes-technology-syllabus. Accessed 12 Apr 2023
12. Board of Studies NSW Technological and Applied Studies Stage 6. https://educationstandards.nsw.edu.au/wps/portal/nesa/11-12/stage-6-learning-areas/technologies. Accessed 12 Apr 2023
13. Queensland Curriculum & Assessment Authority Technologies senior subjects. https://www.qcaa.qld.edu.au/senior/senior-subjects/technologies
14. School Curriculum and Standards Authority Western Australia. Technologies, 26 February 2022 (2014). https://senior-secondary.scsa.wa.edu.au/syllabus-and-support-materials/technologies. Accessed 12 Apr 2023
15. South Australian Certificate of Education Digital Technologies. https://www.sace.sa.edu.au/web/digital-technologies. Accessed 12 Apr 2023
16. Office of Tasmanian Assessment, Standards & Certification Technologies. https://www.tasc.tas.gov.au/students/courses/technologies/. Accessed 12 Apr 2023
17. The ACT Board of Senior Secondary Studies (ACT BSSS): Data Science. ACT BSSS, Canberra (2020). https://www.bsss.act.edu.au/__data/assets/pdf_file/0003/549552/Data_Science_A-T-V_20-24.pdf. Accessed 12 Apr 2023
18. The ACT Board of Senior Secondary Studies (ACT BSSS): Digital Technologies. ACT BSSS, Canberra (2020). https://www.bsss.act.edu.au/__data/assets/pdf_file/0011/549560/Digital_Technologies_A-T-M-V_20-24.pdf. Accessed 12 Apr 2023
19. The ACT Board of Senior Secondary Studies (ACT BSSS): Networking and Security. ACT BSSS, Canberra (2020). https://www.bsss.act.edu.au/__data/assets/pdf_file/0007/544804/Networking_and_Security_A-T-V_20-24.pdf. Accessed 12 Apr 2023

Implications for Computer Science Curricula in Primary School: A Comparative Study of Sequences in England, South Korea, and New Zealand

Michiyo Oda[1(✉)], Yoko Noborimoto[2], and Tatsuya Horita[1]

[1] Tohoku University, Sendai, Japan
oda.michiyo.r4@alumni.tohoku.ac.jp, horita@horilab.info
[2] Tokyo Gakugei University, Tokyo, Japan
noborimt@u-gakugei.ac.jp

Abstract. This study aimed to gain insights into the design of computer science curricula in primary schools in Japan by analyzing K–12 computer science curriculum sequences in England, South Korea, and New Zealand. This study focuses on the progression of key areas of computer science learning in K–12 education. This study identified trends in the sequence of computer science concepts and practices in K–12 education in the three countries. The trends were classified into three categories: (1) learning the concept itself is limited below Grade 6 and learning related to advanced concepts becomes extensive above Grade 7, (2) learning about the concepts becomes progressively more advanced and extensive throughout K–12 education, and (3) learning about the concepts becomes more advanced in scope and complexity throughout K–12 education as the context in which concepts are applied becomes more advanced. These implications can be applied to K–12 computer science curriculum design in Japan and also in other countries around the world.

Keywords: Computer science education · curricula · K–12 education

1 Introduction

1.1 Background

The rapid advancement of information technology in the last few decades has significantly impacted society. Upon recognizing the impact, academics and policymakers in Europe and America focused on K–12 computer science education and published several reports in which they advocate for transforming computer science education from ICT application or computer use into a rigorous academic subject. Bocconi et al. [1] reported that based on a combination of desk research and information from ministries of education surveys, 24 countries in Europe either renewed curricula to introduce computer science, planned to introduce computer science, or had built a long-standing computer science tradition in their compulsory education.

Published by Springer Nature Switzerland AG 2023
T. Keane et al. (Eds.): WCCE 2022, IFIP AICT 685, pp. 641–652, 2023.
https://doi.org/10.1007/978-3-031-43393-1_57

Given the growing interest around introducing computer science into K–12 education, research efforts have been made in this area to examine and promote development of the K–12 computer science curricula. These efforts include but are not limited to the following: (a) situation analysis on the introduction of K–12 computer science curriculum (e.g., [2, 3]); (b) policy recommendations on the introduction of K–12 computer science curriculum (e.g., [4]), and (c) K–12 computer science curriculum analysis (e.g., [5]). These studies provide insight about the scope of skills and understanding that students should acquire in computer science at K–12 levels. For example, Oda et al. [6] summarized the trends of the similarities and differences of the K–12 computer science curriculum in England, South Korea, and New Zealand. However, there is still room for further research in terms of sequencing, such as when and in what order computer science should be taught based on grade level. In this regard, the Association for Computing Machinery et al. [7] acknowledge that students need explicit support to connect new ideas to previously learned ideas, and therefore they recommend that curricula be organized in a coherent way to support student progress across multiple grade levels. However, Webb et al. [3] referred to the limited empirical evidence available for designing K–12 computer science curricula and suggested epistemological considerations followed by empirical evidence should be used to design the curricula. Therefore, examining the computer science curricula of countries that have introduced and established computer science curricula ahead of other countries may contribute to existing research on how to structure the curriculum.

1.2 Computer Science Education in Japan

The Japanese school system includes six years of primary school, three years of middle school, and three years of high school. The nine years of primary and middle school education is compulsory, but more than 97% of students go on to complete the additional three years of high school. In Japan, computer science has been integrated as a part of compulsory technology and home economics in middle school since 2000 and as part of the individual compulsory information in high school since 2001. The revised curriculum guidelines (announced in 2017 for primary and middle schools and in 2018 for high schools), which were sequentially executed from the primary level in 2020, enhanced computer science education, covering approximately 6.2 million primary school students, 3.2 million middle school students, and 3 million high school students (2021).

The general provision of the primary school curriculum guidelines shows that computer science education at the primary level includes "learning activities to foster logical reasoning skills for children through experiencing programming" [8: p. 22]. The programming activities include drawing regular polygons in fifth-grade mathematics, learning efficient use of electricity through contorting conditions in sixth-grade science, and conducting an integrated study as a part of project-based learning [8]. In middle schools, computer science education was incorporated into the information technology unit of the technology and home economics subject. The previous curriculum already included computer science concepts in the unit, but the new curriculum, which began in 2021, became more rigorous, increasing teaching hours and incorporating more complex programming activities into the unit. The previous curriculum of the high school information subject included two subjects: Information Study for Participating Community, focusing on the effects of information technology on society without programming, and Information Study by Scientific Approach, focusing on computer science. Although 80% of high schools chose the former subject, the new compulsory Information I, implemented in 2022, incorporated rigorous computer science, meaning all high school students will learn to program. Schools can add Information II, which is more challenging than Information I and includes data science and designing information systems.

Under these guidelines, computer science subjects differ across school stages. Since different subjects have different learning goals and the curriculum is organized according to learning goals, consistency across school levels from primary to high school is challenging for computer science education in Japan. In primary schools, computer science education is not an independent subject, so the teaching concepts and skills for computer science tend to be particularly unclear.

As Webb et al. [9] explained, the terminology for computer science as a curriculum subject differs from country to country. This study defined computer science as the scientific discipline encompassing principles such as algorithms, data structures, programming, and problem-solving [3, 4]. The length of the school year also varies between countries, so K–12 referred to primary and secondary education in this study. Furthermore, although the school year is referred to as a student's year in England and New Zealand and a student's grade to denote grade levels in South Korea uses, this study applied universal term grades in a unified manner.

1.3 Research Purpose

This study aims to gain insights to inform the computer science curriculum in primary education in Japan by finding sequence trends on computer science curricula in K–12 education in countries with existing K–12 computer science education. To this end, this research focuses on the progression of key areas of computer science learning through K–12 to draw meaningful implications for elementary education.

2 Related Work

2.1 Curriculum Research

Print [10: p. xvii] defined curriculum as "all the planned learning opportunities offered to learners by the educational institution and the experiences learners encounter when the curriculum is implemented". Curriculum has been perceived as a multi-layered learning experience provided to learners. This multi-layered structure includes the intended curriculum established by the state and district, the taught curriculum that is taught in classrooms and in schools, and the learned curriculum, which is what students actually learn [11]. Cuban [11] argued that there is a gap between the three. This study examines the intended curriculum to identify the scope of skills and understanding that each nation expects students to acquire. Therefore, one of this study's limitations is that it does not explore the information that is conveyed in the taught curriculum or learned curriculum.

2.2 Curriculum Design Research

Curriculum design organizes a curriculum's components along two basic organizational dimensions: horizontal and vertical [12]. The horizontal dimension is called the scope and is usually represented by units [12]. The vertical dimension is known as the sequence, and it represents how content and experiences build on and deepen previous learned content and experiences [12]. Therefore, this study focused on the sequence of computer science curricula to assess how content and experiences are deepened throughout students' K–12 education.

3 Research Method

3.1 Analytical Framework

Analyzing the national curriculum in multiple countries requires a high-level, globally applicable, and evidence-informed framework that illustrates literacy foundations to be gained in K–12 computer science education. The K–12 Computer Science Framework [7] was used for the curriculum analysis to address these aspects. The framework provides a baseline literacy in computer science that all students should possess. The framework is organized into computer science concepts (five core concepts further divided into 17 sub-concepts) that represent "major content areas in the field of computer science" (p. 3) and practices (seven core practices divided into 23 achievement levels by the end of Grade 12) that represent "the behaviors that computationally literate students use to fully engage with the core concepts of computer science" [7: p. 3].

The reasons for applying this framework in light of the criteria are as follows. First, the concept and practice statements are big ideas [7] that are intellectual priorities and the basis for the transfer of learning [13]. In this regard, the framework is unique in providing a high-level guide for teaching K–12 computer science based on structural knowledge that identifies key areas of computer science learning in the curriculum. Second, this framework is applicable globally. For example, although the framework was developed in the U.S., it benchmarked against the curricula in other advanced countries, such as the United Kingdom, Germany, Poland, and New Zealand, referencing multiple countries' perspectives [7]. In addition, the framework is broadly applied both in the U.S. and other countries. For example, computer science standards exist in 43 of the 50 U.S. states, many of which refer to CSTA's K–12 Computer Science Standards developed based on this framework [14]. The framework has also been introduced in primary schools in Japan [15]. Third, it is evidence-informed. According to the Association for Computing Machinery [7], the framework was designed based on the existing research, interview with experts in the field, and the collective expertise of the computer science education and research communities.

Computer science concepts that are essential to the K–12 Computer Science Framework include the following:

- Computing Systems (*Devices, Hardware and Software, Troubleshooting*)
- Networks and the Internet (*Network Communication and Organization, Cybersecurity*)

- Data and Analysis (*Collection, Storage, Visualization and Transformation, Inference and Models*)
- Algorithms and Programming (*Algorithms, Variables, Control, Modularity, Program Development*)
- Impact of Computing (*Culture, Social Interactions, Safety, Law, and Ethics*)

The K–12 Computer Science Framework also identifies seven core practices that should be included in computer science curricula:

- Practice 1: Fostering an Inclusive Computing Culture
- Practice 2: Collaborating Around Computing
- Practice 3: Recognizing and Defining Computational Problems
- Practice 4: Developing and Using Abstractions
- Practice 5: Creating Computational Artifacts
- Practice 6: Testing and Refining Computational Artifacts
- Practice 7: Communicating About Computing

3.2 Country Selection

This study covered England, South Korea, and New Zealand. To gain meaningful findings useful not only in Japan but also internationally, this study set the following criteria in addition to the introduction of computer science into their K–12 education: (1) unbiased inclusion of computer science concepts and practices in the curriculum [16], and (2) introduction of curricula countrywide. The first criterion was established since designing a computer science curriculum requires facilitating meaningful learning experiences that include concepts and practices, according to the Association for Computing Machinery [7]. The second criterion was established to align the Japanese education system with this study's purpose. Because the Japanese curriculum requirements are legally obligatory, this study focused on countries that implement the curriculum at the national level rather than the state level, which is as close to the Japanese educational system as possible. The study examined 10 countries implementing computer science curricula in K–12 education [16] to identify whether they meet the two criteria. Geographic diversity, such as Europe, Oceania, and Asia, were also considered while selecting from 10 nations, some of which were in the same region. For example, England, France, Poland, and Portugal met the two criteria in Europe. England was selected over the other countries because England has advanced in this area, having been one of the first to implement computer science education in primary schools and to publish a comprehensive report on its implementation [17]. South Korea and Hong Kong met the criteria in Asia. South Korea was chosen because its educational system is more aligned with that of Japan.

3.3 Curricula Selection

This study examined the computer science curricula that has been introduced in England, South Korea, and New Zealand. Print [10] suggested four essential components of curriculum: (1) aims, goals, and objectives; (2) subject matter or content; (3) learning activities; and (4) evaluation. Since this study aimed to gain insights into designing the computer science curriculum for primary education in Japan, it focused on the first three components: (1) aims, goals, and objectives; (2) subject matter or content; and (3) learning activities. Curriculum evaluation was not included as part of this study. The collection of national curricula was conducted from May to September 2019.

In England, computer science has been introduced in Grades 1–12 as Computing, a compulsory subject. This study investigated *subject content* in *Computing programmes of study: key stages 1 and 2 National curriculum in England* [18] and *Computing programmes of study: key stages 3 and 4 National curriculum in England* [19]. The grade levels within the curriculum are divided into Key Stage 1 (Grades 1–2), Key Stage 2 (Grades 3–6), Key Stage 3 (Grades 7–9) and Key Stage 4 (Grades 10 and 11).

In South Korea, computer science has been introduced in Grades 5 and 6 as a compulsory subject in Practical Arts; in Grade 7–9 as the compulsory subject Informatics; and in Grade 10–12 as the elective subject Informatics. This study investigated *performance standard* of the target subjects in *Elementary School Curriculum and Education Notice No. 2015-74* [20], *Middle School Curriculum and Education Notice No. 2015-74* [21], and *High School Curriculum (I, II, III)* [22]. The grade levels within the curriculum are divided into elementary school (Grades 1–6), middle school (Grades 7–9), and high school (Grades 10–12).

In New Zealand, computer science has been introduced as a compulsory subject within Technology for Grade 1–10 and an elective subject for Grades 11–13. This study investigated *progress outcomes* (POs) in *Technology in the New Zealand Curriculum* [23]. The grade levels of the technological area "computational thinking for digital technologies" are divided into PO1 (Grades 1–3), PO2 (Grades 4–6), PO3 (Grades 7, 8), PO4 · 5 (Grades 9, 10), PO6 (Grade 11), PO7 (Grade 12), and PO8 (Grade 13). The grade levels of the technological area "designing and developing digital outcomes" are divided into PO1 (Grades 1–4), PO2 (Grades 5–8), PO3 (Grades 9, 10), PO4 (Grade 11), PO5 (Grade 12), and PO6 (Grade 13).

3.4 Curriculum Analysis

This study adopted the curriculum analysis methodology by the previous works [6, 16], which references content analysis methodology by Cohen et al. [24]. Since the South Korean curriculum was written in Korean, Google Translate was used to translate the curriculum from Korean to English. In sections where the translation was not clear, an education researcher who is a native Korean speaker verified the translation.

First, the text in the curriculum was separated into individual sentences. Next, the divided sentences were further subdivided into units that retained their meaning. For example, in New Zealand PO2 (Grades 4–6) [23], the sentence was subdivided into two units by shading, as in "In authentic contexts and taking account of end-users, / students give, follow and debug simple algorithms in computerised and non-computerised contexts." Finally, the units were coded into computer science concepts (17 sub-concepts) and practices (23 achievement levels) according to the K–12 Computer Science Framework. For example, the definition of concepts and practices in the K–12 Computer Science Framework was used as a reference and compared with the units. As a result, when the unit was applicable to the definitions of concepts and practices, concepts (17 subconcepts) and practices (23 achievement levels) were tagged. Coding was not applied to units whose meanings did not correspond to the definitions of concepts and practices in the K–12 Computer Science Framework. In cases where more than one concept or practice was included in a unit, multiple coding was performed. The coding was conducted by the first author, and the accuracy of the coding was reviewed by the second author, who has experience teaching high school computer science. If there were any disagreements regarding coding, the authors discussed until they reached a consensus.

4 Results and Findings

4.1 Sequence Trends on Computer Science Curricula in K–12 Education

Tables 1 and 2 display the trends in the sequence of curriculum descriptions of computer science concepts (five core concepts, which are divided into 17 sub-concepts) and practices (seven core practices, which are divided into 23 achievement levels), with trends shown for concepts or practices found both below Grade 6 and above Grade 7. Based on the results presented in Tables 1 and 2, the main features of the sequence of concepts in relation to practice were classified into the three types. These three classifications are not exclusive; all concepts and practices have more or less of these three characteristics: (1) learning the concept itself is limited below Grade 6 and learning related to advanced concepts becomes extensive above Grade 7, (2) learning about the concepts becomes progressively more advanced and extensive throughout K–12 education, and (3) learning about the concepts becomes more advanced in scope and complexity throughout K–12 education as the context in which concepts are applied becomes more advanced. Classifications are based on the concept or practice's most prominent features.

Regarding the first classification, while learning about hardware and software, algorithms, and program development concepts was limited to Grade 6 and below, learning related to advanced concepts became extensive in Grade 7 and above. Oda et al. [25] analyzed K–12 computer science curricula in seven countries, including England, South Korea, and New Zealand, and reported that computer science concepts and practices tend to be described together. The computer science concepts in this classification tended to be described together with multiple practices below Grade 6 and above Grade 7. For example, hardware and software descriptions are described together with Practice 3, Practice 5, and Practice 6 below Grade 6 and Practice 5, Practice 6, and Practice 7 above Grade 7 [25]. *Algorithms* are described together with Practice 3, Practice 5, and Practice 6 below Grade 6 and Practice 3, Practice 4, Practice 5, Practice 6, and Practice 7 above Grade 7 [25]. Therefore, in this classification, learning activities that combine multiple practices with limited concepts are the primary focus below Grade 6, whereas learning related to advanced concepts, combined with practices, becomes extensive above Grade 7.

In the countries examined in this study, for the second classification, learning about *variables* and *control* became more advanced throughout K–12 education, with students learning about and then building on the sequence, selection, iteration, and variables to acquire knowledge of nested control and data structures. Therefore, it is likely that in this classification, students gradually learn advanced concepts through K–12 education. In addition, *variables* and *control* tended to be described together with limited computer science practices below Grade 6 and an increased number of practices above Grade 7. For example, *variables* and *control* were described together with Practice 5 below

Table 1. Sequence trends of computer science concepts in curriculum descriptions.

	Below Grade 6	Above Grade 7
Hardware and software	The curricula descriptions were combined with practices, such as controlling physical systems, in England and South Korea. However, in New Zealand, the content is mainly related to understanding the underlying mechanism, including identifying the inputs and outputs of a system	Beginning with the characteristics of digital information and the roles of hardware and software, understanding of operating systems and resource management increased with grade level
Network Communication and Organization	The focus was on recognizing and understanding the basic concepts of the internet	Understanding the characteristics of networks and setting up network environments were also covered
Collection and *visualization and transformation*	The curriculum included collecting, analyzing, evaluating, and presenting data and information to achieve goals	The curriculum included collecting, analyzing, and presenting data and information to achieve challenging goals
Storage	All grade levels focused on an understanding of storing content on digital devices	
Algorithms	The curriculum began with the definition of algorithms and their characteristics. As the grade level increased, the curriculum descriptions were combined with practices, such as designing and debugging algorithms	The curriculum included advanced algorithms, such as sorting and searching, understanding the existence of alternative algorithms for the same problem, and comparing and evaluating their effectiveness
Variables and Control	The curriculum included sequence, selection, iteration, and variables combined with *program development*	The curriculum included nested control structures and data structures
Program development	Education started by creating simple programs, and as the grade level increased, the curriculum descriptions became more advanced and combined with other sub-concepts	The curriculum included multiple programming languages, understanding the development environment of programming languages, and programming with advanced variables and control structures

(*continued*)

Table 1. (*continued*)

	Below Grade 6	Above Grade 7
Culture	Beginning with an understanding that humans make digital devices, followed by describing how people use information technology, and as the grade level increased, clarifying the effects of digital devices and software on people's lives	Beginning with how information technology affects individuals and society, and as the grade level increased, understanding of the effects of data and advanced technology on society
Social interactions	The curriculum included information technology's role in society, such as providing opportunities for communication and collaboration	Beginning with the influence of information technology on work, and as the grade level increased, materials also included identifying social effects and career paths in the field of information science
Safety, law, and ethics	The curriculum included safe use of technology and understanding of personal information	Beginning with the protection of personal information and copyright, and as the grade level increased, the materials focused on using personal information

Grade 6 and Practices 4, 5, 6, and 7 above Grade 7 [25]. Therefore, it is assumed that students learn these concepts gradually, become more advanced over time, and deepen their knowledge by combining limited practices below Grade 6 and broad practices above Grade 7.

For the third classification, the application of *collection, visualization and transformation, storage, culture, social interactions, safety, law, and ethics* concepts changed in K–12 education. Different trends in the association of these concepts with the practice were identified. For example, *collection, visualization and transformation* were described together with limited practices below Grade 6 and above Grade 7 [25]. Therefore, it is assumed that these concepts are learned by themselves rather than in connection with practices. As in the first classification, *storage* tended to be described with multiple practices below Grade 6 and above Grade 7 [25]. Since *storage* descriptions were found only in New Zealand among the three countries, more curricula descriptions should be investigated to understand the trends in the concept. *Culture, social interactions, safety, law, and ethics* tended to be described with limited practices below Grade 6 and more practices above Grade 7 [25], similar to the second classification. Thus, learning activities, such as *collection, visualization and transformation*, changed in the contexts that excluded practices, whereas *storage, culture, social interactions, safety, law, and ethics* changed in the contexts that included practices.

Table 2. Sequence trends of computer science practices in curriculum descriptions.

		Below Grade 6	Above Grade 7
Practice 1	*Practice 1.2*	All grade levels considered end-users in authentic contexts.	
Practice 3	*Practice 3.1*	The curriculum descriptions were related to the application of problem-solving procedures.	Beginning with an understanding of the status and goals of the problem, and as the grade level increased, the materials included the status and goals of complex problems.
	Practice 3.2	The curriculum included decomposing problems and tasks.	The curriculum included problem decomposition and classification of necessary and unnecessary elements for problem-solving.
Practice 4	*Practice 4.2*	The curriculum included selecting necessary technologies according to their purpose.	Beginning with identifying the key features of the software and selecting software to develop digital content, and as the grade level increased, educational materials incorporated the analysis and evaluation of digital technologies.
Practice 5	*Practice 5.1*	The curriculum included designing simple programs.	The curriculum included the design of programs and algorithms.
	Practice 5.2	The curriculum included creating simple programs.	The curriculum included creating complex programs.
Practice 6	*Practice 6.1*	All grade levels included digital content testing.	
	Practice 6.2	Debugging was included to find and fix errors in programs and algorithms, both with and without computers.	The curriculum included debugging and modifying programs and algorithms and being able to express their cause and solution.
	Practice 6.3	The curriculum included the evaluation of information to achieve objectives.	Beginning with the evaluation of digital content, and as the grade level increased, evaluation expanded to include social and ethical considerations and the intended purpose.
Practice 7	*Practice 7.3*	The curriculum included the meaning of intellectual property and its application in daily life.	The curriculum included respecting technology and applying personal information and copyright knowledge to the real world.

4.2 Suggestions for Designing Computer Science Curricula for Primary Level

Two suggestions for designing computer science curricula for primary education are outlined.

First, this study classified the computer science curriculum sequence in K–12 education into the three categories described above. The trends of these three computer science concepts could be applied to the Grade 6 and below curriculum while considering curriculum coherence above Grade 7. Second, rather than changing the computer science practices throughout K–12 education, they were changing in combination with computer science concepts. Since the above analysis also showed trends in the computer science practices described together with the computer science concepts, these trends could be incorporated into the curriculum design of computer science in primary education.

In addition, using the K–12 Computer Science Framework, Oda et al. [26] examined the Japanese curriculum and indicated that the computer science concepts or practices had not changed coherently in primary education. The findings of this study can be used to consider coherence when examining the computer science curriculum in Japanese primary schools.

5 Conclusion

To gain information for designing the computer science curriculum in primary education in Japan, this study analyzed the trends of computer science curricula sequences in K–12 education in England, South Korea, and New Zealand, because these three countries have established computer science curricula. The main trends of the sequences were classified into three categories: (1) learning the concept itself is limited below Grade 6 and learning related to advanced concepts becomes extensive above Grade 7, (2) learning about the concepts becomes progressively more advanced and extensive throughout K–12 education, and (3) learning about the concepts becomes more advanced in scope and complexity throughout K–12 education as the context in which concepts are applied becomes more advanced. The implications from this study can be applied to K–12 computer science curriculum design in Japan and also in other countries around the world. This study focused on the intended curriculum and did not include the taught curriculum or learned curriculum. Since there is a gap between these curricula, further research on taught curriculum and learned curriculum is necessary.

References

1. Bocconi, S., et al.: Developing computational thinking in compulsory education – implications for policy and practice. EUR 28295 EN (2016)
2. Heintz, F., Mannila, L., Nordén, L.-Å., Parnes, P., Regnell, B.: Introducing programming and digital competence in Swedish K-9 education. In: Dagienė, V., Hellas, A. (eds.) ISSEP 2017. LNCS, vol. 10696, pp. 117–128. Springer, Cham (2017). https://doi.org/10.1007/978-3-319-71483-7_10
3. Webb, M., et al.: Computer science in K-12 school curricula of the 2lst century: why, what and when? Educ. Inf. Technol. **22**(2), 445–468 (2017)
4. The Royal Society: Shut Down Or Restart?: The Way Forward for Computing in UK Schools. The Royal Society, London (2012). https://royalsociety.org/topics-policy/projects/computing-in-schools/report/. Accessed 25 Dec 2022
5. Falkner, K., et al.: An international comparison of K-12 computer science education intended and enacted curricula. In: Proceedings of the 19th Koli Calling International Conference on Computing Education Research, pp. 1–10. Association for Computing Machinery, New York, NY, USA (2019)
6. Oda, M., Noborimoto, Y., Horita, T.: 英国・韓国・ニュージーランドの初等中等教育におけるコンピュータサイエンス教育のカリキュラムの体系に関する整理. IPSJ SIG Technical report, 2021-CE-158(11), pp. 1–8 (2021)
7. Association for Computing Machinery, Code.org, Computer Science Teachers Association, Cyber Innovation Center, Math and Science Initiative: K–12 Computer Science Framework (2016). http://www.k12cs.org. Accessed 2 Oct 2022
8. Ministry of Education, Culture, Sports, Science and Technology: 小学校学習指導要領 (平成29年告示) (2017)
9. Webb, M., et al.: Computer science in the school curriculum: issues and challenges. In: Tatnall, A., Webb, M. (eds.) WCCE 2017. IFIP AICT, vol. 515, pp. 421–431. Springer, Cham (2017). https://doi.org/10.1007/978-3-319-74310-3_43
10. Print, M.: Curriculum Development and Design, 2nd edn. Routledge, Abingdon (1993)
11. Cuban, L.: Curriculum stability and change. In: Jackson, P.W. (ed.) Handbook of Research on Curriculum: A Project of the American Educational Research Association, pp. 216–247 (1992)

12. Ornstein, A., Hunkins, F.: Curriculum: Foundations, Principles, and Issues, Global Edition, 7th edn. Pearson Education Limited, London (2017)
13. Wiggins, G., McTighe, J.: Understanding by Design, 2nd edn. Association for Supervision & Curriculum Development, Alexandria (2005)
14. Code.org: K–12 Computer Science Policy and Implementation in States (n.d.)
15. Code.or.jp: 2021年度「コンピュータサイエンス教育」のカリキュラム開発に向けての実証研究. https://code.or.jp/news/10704/. Accessed 2 Oct 2022
16. Oda, M., Noborimoto, Y., Horita, T.: International trends in K–12 computer science curricula through comparative analysis: implications for the primary curricula. Int. J. Comput. Sci. Educ. Sch. **4**(4), 24–58 (2021)
17. The Royal Society: Computing Education. https://royalsociety.org/topics-policy/projects/computing-education/. Accessed 2 Oct 2022
18. Department for Education: Computing programmes of study: Key stages 1 and 2 National curriculum in England. Department for Education, London (2013)
19. Department for Education: Computing programmes of study: Key stages 3 and 4 National curriculum in England. Department for Education, London (2013)
20. Ministry of Education: 초등학교 교육과정 교육부 고시 제2015-74호 (2015)
21. Ministry of Education: 중학교 교육과정 교육부 고시 제2015-74호 [별책 3] (2015)
22. Ministry of Education: 고등학교 교육과정 (I, II, III) (2015)
23. Ministry of Education: Technology in the New Zealand Curriculum (2017)
24. Cohen, L., Manion, L., Morrison, K.: Research Methods in Education, 6th edn. Routledge, Abingdon (2007)
25. Oda, M., Noborimoto, Y., Horita, T.: Analysis of K–12 computer science curricula from the perspective of a competency-based approach. In: Langran, E. (ed.) Proceedings of Society for Information Technology & Teacher Education International Conference, pp. 75–79. Association for the Advancement of Computing in Education, San Diego, CA, United States (2022)
26. Oda, M., Noborimoto, Y., Horita, T.:小学校から大学・社会人までのコンピュータサイエンスの体系的な指導に向けての考察. Educ. Inf. Res. **36**(2), 15–28 (2020)

Where is Technology in the 'Golden Thread' of Teacher Professional Development?

Chris Shelton(✉) and Mike Lansley

University of Chichester, Chichester, UK
c.shelton@chi.ac.uk

Abstract. Researchers and policy makers have consistently agreed that the quality of teachers is one of the most important factors in determining the quality of an educational system and that teachers need to be supported and developed through rigorous initial teacher education and continuous professional development. In the specific case of teachers' ability to make effective use of technology, it has been noted that teachers require both technological and pedagogical training and education that equips them with the knowledge, confidence and skills they need. Given this broad, international consensus about the importance of teacher education for effective technology use, this paper explores the 'golden thread' of teacher development proposed by the UK government for teachers in England. This sets out a detailed curriculum for teacher development with very little reference to educational technology. The paper considers some of the potential missed opportunities to develop teacher expertise and practice with technology.

Keywords: Teacher Education · Education Technology · Teacher Training · Professional Development

1 Introduction

The use of educational technology has become an important part of many teachers' classroom practice. This was particularly highlighted during the Covid-19 pandemic when teachers throughout the world were suddenly expected to teach online even if they had never done this before [1].

Research into technology adoption over the past 40 years has consistently identified teacher knowledge as a key driver for effective technology use. Teacher professional development is "critically important" for effective use of technology [2], it should empower teachers to use technology to match educational activities to learners' needs [3], develop skills and confidence with technology [4] and prepare teachers to use pedagogic approaches that make the best use of digital technologies [5].

However, in England, despite a very detailed set of curriculum documents (referred to as 'frameworks') that set out what teachers need to learn during their initial training, in the early stages of their career, and as they develop into specialist or leadership roles, there is little acknowledgement of technology. This is in spite of a clear governmental 'EdTech' strategy that recognises the value of educational technology and aims to develop it [6].

Published by Springer Nature Switzerland AG 2023
T. Keane et al. (Eds.): WCCE 2022, IFIP AICT 685, pp. 653–662, 2023.
https://doi.org/10.1007/978-3-031-43393-1_58

2 Learning to Teach with Technology

Research into the adoption of technology has highlighted that technology is used within a multifaceted environment and affected by many complex factors [7]. For example, in responding to the need to teach online during the Covid-19 pandemic, teachers displayed varying degrees of readiness reflecting both individual and institutional factors [1].

To adopt and use a particular technology effectively, teachers need to have knowledge of the technology, the skills and confidence to use it and the pedagogic expertise to ensure this is effective. However, a lack of teacher professional development has been a "perennial barrier" [8], p. 179] to the adoption of educational technology. While it might be thought that this would have improved over time, recent survey data from the UK indicates that:

> *Staff barriers, including teachers' skills, confidence and appetite for using EdTech also represented a substantial barrier. Almost nine out of ten headteachers (88%) and three-fifths of teachers (58%) cited teacher skills and confidence as a barrier to the increased uptake of EdTech* [4, p. 20].

While this quotation highlights the need for teachers to be confident and skilled to use technology, this alone is not sufficient. Webb and Cox [5] note that using technology for learning and teaching requires that teacher undertake "more complex pedagogical reasoning than before" (p. 235) and that the need for teacher professional development to support this is clear. Albion and Tondeur [3] go further and suggest that many teachers only make routine rather than transformational use of technology unless their professionalism and teacher agency are recognized and supported.

The professional development required to develop teachers' skills, pedagogy and agency needs to be available throughout a teachers' career and not just as part of their initial teacher preparation. In fact, the DfE EdTech survey [4] suggested that "teachers who have been in the profession longer would benefit from additional CPD" (p. 19). This ongoing development is vital if the use of technology is to have a positive impact on pupil learning. As the Education Endowment Foundation (EEF) guidance on using digital technology to improve learning makes clear, training in the use of a new technology should be planned, delivered and reinforced as part of a planned implementation process [9]. Professional development also needs to ensure that teachers are aware of new technological developments throughout their career, for example, new opportunities and risks posed by technologies and new ethical concerns (such as artificial intelligence, cybersecurity scams, etc.).

There are many different models and approaches to teacher development in the use of technology [2]. These include traditional expert-led pre-service or in-service courses, online programmes, and school-led workshops. However, it has been argued that such programmes have had limited impact on teachers' adoption of technology because they fail to address teachers' authentic contexts [10]. More recently, research has explored alternative approaches that aim to address this, for example through mentoring [10], professional learning communities [11] and teacher inquiry or design-based research [12].

The need for professional development is clearly identified in the 2019 EdTech Strategy for England [6] where the Secretary of State for Education stated his belief that "technology can be an effective tool to help reduce workload, increase efficiencies, engage students and communities, and provide tools to support excellent teaching and raise student attainment" (p. 2). The third section of this strategy is devoted to developing digital capability and skills and states that "ensuring teachers have adequate training available is often the biggest challenge" (p. 16). The strategy suggests a number of actions that the government will take to address this including launching online training courses for teachers and leaders (for example: https://www.futurelearn.com/courses/technology-teaching-learning) and introducing a network of EdTech demonstrator schools to share best practice and offer support to other schools. The strategy focuses on partnering with other organizations and technology companies to encourage innovation and to "reap the benefits that technology can bring" (p. 3).

3 England's 'Golden Thread' of Teacher Development

Responsibility for education in the UK is devolved to the four nations of England, Scotland, Wales and Northern Ireland and there are significant and longstanding differences between the four nations in terms of curriculum, examinations, methods of accountability and teacher education policy. In 2019, the Department for Education, the ministerial department of the UK government with responsibility for children's services and education in England, published a strategy for teacher recruitment and retention [13]. This strategy acknowledged that a lack of support for teachers at the start and throughout their careers can be a barrier to retaining teachers in the profession and action was needed to address this.

Therefore, alongside this strategy, the DfE launched the 'Early Career Framework' (ECF) [14] which was intended to provide a 'fully-funded, 2-year package of structured support for all early career teachers' [13, p. 19]. This induction support would be underpinned by a framework of content 'linked to the best available evidence' [14, p. 4]. This content is divided into two types: 'Learn that…' evidence statements and 'Learn how to…' practice statements. These statements are structured into five core areas: behaviour management, pedagogy, curriculum, assessment and professional behaviours but presented in eight sections mirroring the eight Teachers' Standards that English teachers are required to meet.

Shortly after the publication of the Early Career Framework for teachers in their first two years of the profession, the DfE published a new framework for Initial Teacher Training (ITT) that set out what student teachers needed to learn in order to qualify and begin employment. This ITT Core Content Framework (CCF) was designed to mirror the ECF [15, p. 4]. Using the same structure as the ECF, the 'Learn that…' statements of the CCF were:

> *"deliberately the same as the 'Learn that…' statements in the ECF because the full entitlement – across both initial teacher training and early career development – for new entrants to the profession is underpinned by the evidence of what makes great teaching"* [15, p. 4].

The "Learn how to…" practice statements from the ECF were slightly adapted for the CCF by being sorted into two categories – those statements that student teachers would require expert support with and those that they would require practice in. But the content and focus of each statement remained identical for both student and early career teachers.

In 2021, the DfE also reformed the content of the National Professional Qualifications (NPQs) - a set of training programmes for serving teachers. Together, these reforms were intended to establish "a 'golden-thread' of high-quality evidence underpinning the support, training and development available through the entirety of a teacher's career" [16, p. 5]. These new qualifications were divided into specialist qualifications for classroom teachers and leadership qualifications (see Table 1).

Table 1. The 'Golden Thread' - Teacher Development System (adapted from [16]).

Who?	What?	Basis
Trainee Teacher	Initial Teacher Training (ITT)	ITT Core Content Framework (CCF)
Early Career Teacher (first 2 years)	Early Career Support	Early Career Framework (ECF)
Experienced teachers and middle leaders	Specialist Development	*Specialist NPQs* - Leading Teacher Development (NPQLTD) [17] - Leading Teaching (NPQLT) [18] - Leading Behaviour and Culture (NPQLBC) [19] - Leading Literacy (NPQLL) [20]
Senior leaders, headteachers and executive leaders	Leadership Development	*Leadership NPQs* - Senior Leadership (NPQSL) [21] - Early Years Leadership (NPQEYL) [22] - Headship (NPQH) [23] - Executive Leadership (NPQEL) [24]

As for the CCF and ECF, the NPQ framework documents are divided into 'Learn that…' and 'Learn how to…' statements. In some cases, evidence statements are used across several qualification frameworks. For example, the NPQ Leading Behaviour and Culture consists of six sections. The first 'Teaching' is just a statement that participants will have met the requirements of the ECF but the second 'School Culture' contains 7 'Learn that..' statement all of which are repeated from the ECF, which in turn are identical to the statements in the CCF. These 7 statements are then also repeated in the

NPQs for Leading Teaching, Senior Leadership, Headship and Executive Leadership. These statements include such insights as:

> *"Teachers have the ability to affect and improve the wellbeing, motivation and behaviour of their pupils."*

Thus, over their career, a teacher experiencing the 'golden thread' of teacher development might be expected to learn this statement seven times. (The 'Learn how to...' statements for the NPQs are generally different and more advanced than those of the CCF and ECF to reflect the participants' different roles).

4 Technology in the Golden Thread

In the DfE EdTech survey, 42% of teachers who responded "indicated that more information on what good technology use looks like in the early careers framework would help" [4, p. 108]. But that survey does not address the question of how much information about technology is currently included in the ECF and exactly what additional content should be added. Similar questions should be asked about the other ITT and NPQ frameworks.

To address this question, each of the framework documents that make up the 'golden thread' from CCF to NPQ were analysed by the authors. During the analysis, three specific research questions were considered:

1. Does this framework make any explicit mention of technology?
2. Does this framework make any implicit reference to technology?
3. Are there any additional opportunities to refer to technology evident within this framework?

ITT Core Content Framework (CCF)
The CCF contains no explicit mention of technology in the content statements either in terms of the use of technology to support learning or the use of technology to support teachers' professional responsibilities (e.g. planning, assessment, etc.).

There is one reference to the use of technology (video clips) to support teacher learning and development in the introduction to the framework where the phrase (frequently used in the CCF statements) "Observing how expert colleagues ... and deconstructing this approach" is defined as:

> *"Working with expert colleagues – using the best available evidence – to critique a particular approach – whether using in-class observation, modelling or* ***analysis of video*** *– to understand what might make it successful or unsuccessful"* [15, p. 5, our emphasis]

It could also be argued that some statements of the CCF do have an implicit reference to technology in that it might be expected that teachers would need to use technology to achieve them. For example, statements about the use of data for assessment including recording data (p. 24) or "looking at patterns of performance over a number of assessments" (p. 23) might imply the use of digital assessment records although it is not clear that a novice teacher would recognize this.

It should also be noted that the CCF is explicitly intended as a minimum requirement: "The ITT Core Content Framework does not set out the full ITT curriculum for trainee teachers" (p. 4) and "It will be crucial for providers to ensure trainees have adequately covered any foundational knowledge and skill that is pre-requisite for the content defined in this framework." (p. 4). It could be argued that understanding of technology should be considered part of this 'foundational knowledge and skill' although none of this foundational material is defined or signposted.

Given that the CCF sets out a minimum requirement, there are many possible opportunities to extend the content of the CCF with reference to technology. For example, *'Seeking opportunities to engage parents and carers in the education of their children'* could be exemplified with reference to digital communication systems.

Early Career Framework (ECF)
As the content and focus of the ECF is identical to the CCF, with variation only in the degree of independence expected by the practice statements, there is no explicit mention of technology in the framework.

Similar to the CCF, there are a few statements within the ECF that might be considered to imply the use of technology. For example, there is reference to freely available training materials which will be shared online.

However, there are also some places where technology could usefully have been explicitly mentioned. For example, new teachers are expected to learn how to provide high-quality feedback including by sharing model work with pupils and highlighting key details (ECF 6.17 [14]). This might be achieved through using visualisers or other technologies for sharing pupil work.

Specialist National Professional Qualifications (NPQs)
The four Specialist NPQs (Leading Teacher Development; Leading Teaching; Leading Behaviour and Culture; and Leading Literacy) each contain identical content on 'Implementation' and 'Professional Development' (although this is structured differently and extended in the NPQLTD). Throughout these four frameworks, there is only one explicit reference to technology – this comes in the shared 'Professional Development' content where there is a single reference to teacher learning through viewing and discussing videos of teaching.

These shared sections also contain some statements that might be considered to imply the use of technology. These are references to using evidence (which will probably be most freely available online), interpreting data (which will most likely be collected and stored electronically); networking or sharing knowledge amongst staff (which may be through digital media) and making reasonable adjustments for staff with disabilities (which may include using assistive technologies).

There is, however, no mention of online approaches to professional development (e.g. those proposed by the EdTech Strategy) which may have been usefully discussed and evaluated and might be considered essential content for the NPQLTD. There are also multiple opportunities to include specialist uses of technology in these frameworks, for example, communication with parents or understanding cyber-bullying (NPQLBC); understanding digital texts or using digital tools when writing or editing (NPQLL); or using technology to support effective planning, teaching and assessment (NPQLT).

Leadership National Professional Qualifications (NPQs)
The four Leadership NPQs (Senior Leadership; Early Years Leadership; Headship; Executive Leadership) cover similar (and in many cases identical) content but with increasing scope and complexity to reflect the differing roles. These frameworks all contain an explicit reference to technology under resource management, for example:

> *Learn how to... manage resources... by: Developing and implementing a technology infrastructure that is good value for money, supports school operations and teaching, and is safe and secure.* (NPQH [23], p. 28]).

However, there are no references in any framework that will support participants to be able to know what uses of technology might support teaching to enable this statement to be achieved.

There is also an explicit mention of engagement with social media as a public advocate within three of these frameworks.

Similar to the specialist NPQs, there are references to communication with parents and carers and to the use of data or systems that might be considered to imply an understanding of the role of technology in education. There are also references to networks and communications with external organisations that are likely to involve digital communication tools. And there are opportunities across the leadership NPQs to incorporate discussion and evaluation of uses of technology in teaching, inclusion, professional development and collaborative working practices.

Summary
In summary, the only specific technology explicitly referred to in any of the frameworks for professional development is video and this is in the context of teachers developing their practice through watching videos rather than any use of the technology with pupils.

There are also statements that imply or possibly assume the use of technology, for example, for recording and analysing data, and in the case of the leadership NPQs there is an explicit reference to school leaders' use of social media. However, these are focused on teachers' professional use of technology rather than developing teacher expertise in the use of technology for learning and teaching. The frameworks set out no expectations that teachers need to learn how to use technology effectively with pupils.

In comparing the professional development frameworks with the aims of the UK EdTech strategy, there is one direct link – school leaders are expected to learn how to manage an efficient and effective technology infrastructure. However, the broader focus of the strategy on supporting teaching and raising pupil attainment are not addressed.

5 Conclusions

The system of teacher development created by the DfE represents a major investment in supporting teacher learning. It is envisioned that teachers will move through the different stages of their career using each framework and qualification to deepen their knowledge and effectiveness from student teacher to becoming an executive leader of a chain of schools.

Such frameworks send a clear message to teachers about what is considered to be important to the government and the aspects of professional practice that they consider to be "evidence-based" and worthy of dissemination throughout the profession. The omission of educational technology is therefore notable because the official DfE position, as stated in the 2019 EdTech Strategy, is that digital technology is very important. It is difficult to explain why, if teachers need "greater skills and confidence to use technology effectively" [6, p. 7], the frameworks that set out what teachers should learn in their initial training [15] and first two years of teaching [14] make no mention of this.

Similarly, if the EdTech strategy identifies specific potential opportunities for making better use of technology (to help reduce workload, increase efficiencies, engage students and communities, support excellent teaching and raise student attainment), it is unclear why these are not all reflected in the frameworks for teacher specialist and leadership development. A single statement about ensuring value for money of technology is unlikely to fully reflect the knowledge and skills leaders need to develop. In particular, if the government is supporting the development of online courses for teachers, it would seem appropriate for those taking a qualification on Leading Teacher Development to develop some understanding of how to use and evaluate online professional development.

Each of the frameworks contains a sentence noting that they have all been independently reviewed by the Education Endowment Foundation (EEF) to ensure that they draw on the "best available evidence and that this evidence has been interpreted with fidelity" (e.g. NPQLBC, [19, p. 7]). However, the EEF have published several reports about digital technology (e.g. [9]) so it is unclear why the EEF's independent review missed or decided not to acknowledge these.

However, it is acknowledged that the content of each of these frameworks must "be kept under review as the evidence base evolves. As in any profession, the evidence base is not static and research insights develop and progress." (NPQLL [20, p. 8]). As is clear from the previous section, there are lots of opportunities to integrate technology into the English 'golden thread' of professional development and a good starting point might be to look at potential synergies between the aspirations of the EdTech strategy and the 'golden thread' of professional development. There are many examples of successful professional development practices for educational technology (see, for example, [2, 3, 8], etc.) that could be used to inform the content and delivery of the professional development frameworks.

If a future review of England's 'golden thread' frameworks can reflect this current research into educational technology practice and professional development, then, in the future, England's teachers can be better prepared to use technology in the classroom and to meet the aspirations of the DfE EdTech Strategy.

References

1. Howard, S., Tondeur, J., Siddiq, F., Scherer, R.: Ready, set, go! Profiling teachers' readiness for online teaching in secondary education. Technol. Pedagogy Educ. **30**, 1 (2021)
2. McDougall, A.: Models and practices in teacher education programs for teaching with and about IT. In: Voogt, J., Knezek, G. (eds.) International Handbook of Information Technology

in Primary and Secondary Education. SIHE, vol. 20, pp. 461–474. Springer, Boston (2008). https://doi.org/10.1007/978-0-387-73315-9_28

3. Albion, P., Tondeur, J.: Information and communication technology and education: meaningful change through teacher agency. In: Voogt, J., Knezek, G., Christensen, R., Lai, K. (eds.) Second Handbook of Information Technology in Primary and Secondary Education. SIHE, pp. 381–396. Springer, Cham (2018). https://doi.org/10.1007/978-3-319-71054-9_25
4. Department for Education (DfE). Education Technology (EdTech) Survey 2020–21 Research report. DfE, London (2021). https://www.gov.uk/government/publications/education-technology-edtech-survey-2020-to-2021. Accessed 25 Feb 2022
5. Webb, M., Cox, M.: A review of pedagogy related to information and communications technology. Technol. Pedagogy Educ. **13**(3), 235–286 (2004)
6. Department for Education (DfE). Realising the potential of technology in education: a strategy for education providers and the technology industry. DfE, London (2019). https://www.gov.uk/government/publications/realising-the-potential-of-technology-in-education. Accessed 25 Feb 2022
7. Davis, N.: Digital Technologies and Change in Education: The Arena Framework. Routledge, New York (2017)
8. Watson, G.: Models of information technology teacher professional development that engage with teachers' hearts and minds. J. Inf. Technol. Teach. Educ. **10**, 1–2 (2001)
9. Stringer, E., Lewin, C., Coleman, R.: Using Digital Technology to Improve Learning: Guidance Report. EEF, London (2019)
10. Baran, E.: Professional development for online and mobile learning: promoting teachers' pedagogical inquiry. In: Voogt, J., Knezek, G., Christensen, R., Lai, K. (eds.) Second Handbook of Information Technology in Primary and Secondary Education. SIHE, pp. 463–478. Springer, Cham (2018). https://doi.org/10.1007/978-3-319-71054-9_31
11. Prestridge, S., Main, K.: Teachers as drivers of their professional learning through design teams, communities, and networks. In: Voogt, J., Knezek, G., Christensen, R., Lai, K. (eds.) Second Handbook of Information Technology in Primary and Secondary Education. SIHE, pp. 433–447. Springer, Cham (2018). https://doi.org/10.1007/978-3-319-71054-9_29
12. McKenny, S., Roblin, N.: Connecting research and practice: teacher inquiry and design-based research. In: Voogt, J., Knezek, G., Christensen, R., Lai, K. (eds.) Second Handbook of Information Technology in Primary and Secondary Education. SIHE, pp. 449–462. Springer, Cham (2018). https://doi.org/10.1007/978-3-319-71054-9_30
13. Department for Education (DfE). Teacher Recruitment and Retention Strategy. DfE, London (2019). https://www.gov.uk/government/publications/teacher-recruitment-and-retention-strategy. Accessed 25 Feb 2022
14. Department for Education (DfE). Early Career Framework. DfE, London (2019). https://www.gov.uk/government/publications/early-career-framework. Accessed 25 Feb 2022
15. Department for Education (DfE). Initial teacher training (ITT) Core Content Framework. DfE, London (2019). https://www.gov.uk/government/publications/initial-teacher-training-itt-core-content-framework. Accessed 25 Feb 2022
16. Department for Education (DfE). Delivering World-Class Teacher Development. DfE, London (2021). https://assets.publishing.service.gov.uk/government/uploads/system/uploads/attachment_data/file/991390/Delivering_World-Class_Teacher_Development.pdf. Accessed 25 Feb 2022
17. Department for Education (DfE). National Professional Qualification (NPQ): Leading Teacher Development Framework. DfE, London (2020). https://assets.publishing.service.gov.uk/government/uploads/system/uploads/attachment_data/file/925511/NPQ_Leading_Teacher_Development.pdf. Accessed 25 Feb 2022

18. Department for Education (DfE). National Professional Qualification (NPQ): Leading Teaching Framework. DfE, London (2020). https://assets.publishing.service.gov.uk/government/uploads/system/uploads/attachment_data/file/925513/NPQ_Leading_Teaching.pdf. Accessed 25 Feb 2022
19. Department for Education (DfE). National Professional Qualification (NPQ): Leading Behaviour and Culture Framework. DfE, London (2020). https://assets.publishing.service.gov.uk/government/uploads/system/uploads/attachment_data/file/925508/NPQ_Leading_Behaviour_and_Culture.pdf. Accessed 25 Feb 2022
20. Department for Education (DfE). National Professional Qualification (NPQ): Leading Literacy Framework. DfE, London (2021). https://assets.publishing.service.gov.uk/government/uploads/system/uploads/attachment_data/file/1025652/NPQ_Leading_Literacy_Framework.pdf. Accessed 25 Feb 2022
21. Department for Education (DfE). National Professional Qualification (NPQ): Senior Leadership Framework. DfE, London (2020). https://assets.publishing.service.gov.uk/government/uploads/system/uploads/attachment_data/file/925512/NPQ_Senior_Leadership.pdf. Accessed 25 Feb 2022
22. Department for Education (DfE). National Professional Qualification (NPQ): Early Years Leadership Framework. DfE, London (2021). https://assets.publishing.service.gov.uk/government/uploads/system/uploads/attachment_data/file/1024896/National_Professional_Qualification_for_Early_Years_Leadership.pdf. Accessed 25 Feb 2022
23. Department for Education (DfE). National Professional Qualification (NPQ): Headship Framework. DfE, London (2020). https://assets.publishing.service.gov.uk/government/uploads/system/uploads/attachment_data/file/925507/NPQ_Headship.pdf. Accessed 25 Feb 2022
24. Department for Education (DfE). National Professional Qualification (NPQ): Executive Leadership Framework. DfE, London (2020). https://assets.publishing.service.gov.uk/government/uploads/system/uploads/attachment_data/file/925506/NPQ_Executive_Leadership.pdf. Accessed 25 Feb 2022

Understanding the Stakeholder Perspectives on Assessing Educators' Digital Competence

Linda Helene Sillat(✉), Kairit Tammets, and Mart Laanpere

Tallinn University, 10120 Tallinn, Estonia
{sillat,kairit,martl}@tlu.ee

Abstract. Digital competence of educators is one of the key factors affecting wide-scale digital transformation of education and is considered as one of the major aims in the European Digital Education Action Plan (2021–2027). To plan, conduct and report progress in digital competence development requires the ability to measure this competence. Hence, the importance of valid, reliable and usable digital competence assessment has been increasing among researchers, policy makers and teacher educators in recent years. While there exist a number of different instruments for assessing digital competence, there are not many comparative studies that would inform different stakeholders how to choose a suitable instrument to match specifically their context and goals. Furthermore, there is a lack of understanding of needs and expectations of various stakeholders when they consider assessment of educators' digital competence. This paper summarizes a study that explored the stakeholder perspectives in digital competence assessment and related trade-offs.

Keywords: Digital Competence · Assessment · Teacher Education · Instrument Validation

1 Introduction

Digital transformation in schools and teacher education is necessary to prepare children and young people to act in the future knowledge society [1]. One of the key skills of knowledge society citizens is adaptation to fast technological change, rapidly growing knowledge, as well as global competition. Knowledge society development is closely related to the strategies that guide the embedding of information and communication technology in schools [2]. This means that the educators and school leaders need to be digitally competent to provide quality education while implementing digital technologies. To analyze the level and context of digital competence of educators we need valid and reliable assessment instruments. While there exists a multitude of tests, self-assessment scales, rubrics, portfolios and other instruments for measuring teachers' digital competence, only a few of these have been properly validated by researchers [3]. Furthermore, there are no comparative studies that contrast the quality and suitability of various alternative assessment instruments, considering different needs of various stakeholders. We may safely assume that one instrument, even a scientifically validated one, is not equally suitable for all potential user groups.

Published by Springer Nature Switzerland AG 2023
T. Keane et al. (Eds.): WCCE 2022, IFIP AICT 685, pp. 663–674, 2023.
https://doi.org/10.1007/978-3-031-43393-1_59

This paper introduces the results of a mixed method study which focused on deepening the understanding of stakeholder needs and perspectives in implementing digital competence assessment instruments. The instruments described in the study were based on the European framework of digital competence of educators DigCompEdu [4] and the aim of the research was to understand the characteristics of the instruments based on the stakeholder experiences and how they support the digital competence assessment process. Based on the variety of stakeholders involved in the study we aim to determine the relevance and meaningfulness of different assessment methods for the different actors involved in the assessment of teachers' digital competence. The study was guided by a single research question: What are the main characteristics of assessment instruments that increase the perceived usefulness of the teachers' digital competence assessment process for different stakeholder groups?

2 Theoretical Implications

The concept of competence has been defined as an ability to use the knowledge, skills and attitudes in the context of professional practice which are presented in the appropriate level of generality [5]. In this paper, the concept of competence is narrowed down to 'digital competence'. Based on the European Commission [6] description, digital competence is the ability to confidently and critically use Information Society Technologies for work, leisure and communication. The same definition is used as a base level when designing DigCompEdu, the European Framework for Digital Competence of Educator. This framework defines teachers' digital competence as a construct with six dimensions: the use of digital technology in professional engagement, learning resources, teaching and learning, assessment, empowering learners, and facilitating learners' digital competence [4]. However, despite the efforts to design frameworks and instruments for assessing teachers' digital competence, it has been described in research as a hard-to-measure construct. Hard-to-measure constructs mean that the interaction and dependencies with other types of skills and knowledge not intended to be investigated in the construct influence the assessment [7]. Constructs can be hard to measure due to different reasons: there might be a lack of clear definition of the construct, subjectivity of assessment and scores, multidimensionality of the construct etc. Although there are some constructs which are hard-to-measure because of their complex nature and theoretical background, it is still possible to draw conclusions about an individual's level of certain competence based on what they say or how they act in certain situations [8].

It is widely accepted that a survey is the method applied the most for measuring digital skills and competence, which might be useful for studying large samples and their self-perceived skills, but it is also known that self-reported measures face issues with validity due to the misalignment between perceived and actual skills [9]. Pinto et al. [10] explain that digital competence includes mixed perspectives that combine both perceptions and evidence, meaning that during the assessment process both subjective (attitudes and motivations) and objective (knowledge and skills) values are evaluated. Although it can be argued that attitudes and motivations should not drive the assessment process itself, they are still necessary to understand and consider when choosing the suitable assessment instrument. Digital competence is often defined as a multidimensional construct or latent variable that reflects a complex relationship between general cognitive and technical skills [11]. Law et al. [12] explain that multidimensional constructs often exist at a deeper level than their dimensions and thus need to be considered as a latent trait. Also, Cartelli et al. [13] have pointed out that digital competence is a complex multidimensional construct that integrates cognitive, relational and social abilities and skills. They claim that it cannot be measured by a single test, it is tightly connected with other competences like reading, problem-solving etc. And finally - it is sensitive to the socio-cultural context, because the meaning of digital competence can change over time depending on the context where individual operates and develops daily (ibid). Clearly different approaches for assessing digital competence need to be argued.

There are different ways to assess hard-to-measure constructs and three major trends are knowledge-based testing, self-assessment and portfolio-based formative assessment approaches. Often all these approaches are built on common frameworks and models. One such approach highly accepted by the community is the DigCompEdu framework, which models' teachers' digital competence as a multidimensional construct into six dimensions or factors. The framework proposes six proficiency levels: newcomer, explorer, integrator, expert, leader and pioneer. There are many ways to develop assessment instruments based on the same competence model. As for any other latent variable, the digital competence is inferred indirectly from observed variables that are measured by a specifically designed instrument, such as an online self-rating scale or multiple-choice test that consists of many test items. Traditionally, researchers have preferred the latter type of measurement to any other, as it allows unbiased and objective data collection in a controlled environment. However, what is preferable for researchers, does not have to be so for teachers or school leaders. Next, we describe a few alternative assessment instruments that were both designed in line with the DigCompEdu framework.

2.1 DigCompEduSAT: Knowledge-Based Online Test

The DigCompEduSAT instrument was developed in collaboration with the European Commission Joint Research Centre (JRC) in 2019 and was the first instrument designed and developed based on the DigCompEdu framework. Although the questionnaire is presented as a self-assessment instrument, it was designed as a diagnostic knowledge-based test, which included 47 items divided into six competence dimensions and in three difficulty levels – easy, medium, hard. During the design stage it was agreed that each of the item inputs to the overall score or the competence area equally, meaning if Area 1 – professional development consisted of 4 items each of the items was valued at 25% of the total area score. Thus, it was considered that the construct of digital competence could indirectly be derived from a single item reliability. Based on the results, calculated by percentages, the test divides participants into 6 different proficiency levels: newcomer (A1), explorer (A2), integrator (B1), expert (B2), leader (C1), pioneer (C2). As a restriction of the online survey platform used for implementing the test, the test consisted of multiple-choice items that had one correct response out of four options (see Fig. 1 below).

2.2 SELFIE for Teachers: Online Self-reflection Scale

The next assessment instrument, DigCompEduSELF or alternatively branded as SELFIE for Teachers was developed by JRC and a group of international experts in 2021. This self-reflection questionnaire includes 32 statements that cover six dimensions of the DigCompEdu framework and it was piloted with more than 3200 teachers in Estonia, Italy, Lithuania and Portugal. The instrument is designed for use by individual teachers as well as groups, providing both individual and group-based reports that were highly appreciated by a large majority of participants in the pilot study. The self-reflection scale includes six statements that correspond to six digital competence proficiency levels suggested by the DigCompEdu framework and are also used in the DigCompEduSAT instrument.

2.3 Portfolio-Based Assessment Instruments

In addition to the self-assessment and diagnostic testing approaches, the community has widely accepted the portfolio-based assessment of digital competence as one of the alternatives and more formative approaches. For decades portfolios have been considered as a potential tool for the development and assessment of teachers' competence [14] and also as a tool that could make teachers' competence transparent for the teacher and the wider audience [15]. Different competence models can be used in portfolio-based assessment, however, the research in this sense is rather scarce and often based on localized frameworks. A study involving student teachers indicated that using portfolios for competence development and assessment helps them to accomplish personal growth [16]. However, it was also emphasized that such an assessment approach needs scaffolding: examples of good practices to illustrate competence and clear assessment criteria are needed.

Based on the above, we can see that there are a variety of approaches developed for assessing teachers' digital competence and also ways to make it meaningful for the teachers.

3 Research Design and Methods

The research was carried out in the two phases. First, a large-scale national web-based self-assessment study of teachers' digital competence was carried out, with the aim to understand how teachers perceive the experience of assessing their digital competence. In this phase, the self-assessment methodologically enabled engagement with a large number of teachers in authentic assessment situations. In the second phase, semi-structured interviews with typical representatives of four of the most common stakeholder groups were carried out to collect a deeper understanding on the stakeholder perspective, motivation, experiences and needs in the digital competence assessment process.

3.1 Sampling

In the first phase of the study, 1125 Estonian primary and secondary school teachers were recruited in the national level study to assess their own digital competence. 92%

of the teachers were female and 8% of the teachers were male. 8% of the respondents were younger than 30 years, 19% of them were aged between 31–40 years, 25% were 41–50 years old, and 48% were older than 51.

In the second phase of the study, four representatives of the key stakeholders were chosen to be interviewed. Based on our previous studies on identifying stakeholders in teachers' digital competence assessment, we came up with four personas to guide our research design and sampling. Personas are fictional characters that are used to inform the empathic design process mainly for two purposes: (1) for writing contextualized narrative scenarios, and (2) sampling the relevant and representative participants for interviews or participatory design sessions. We created a purposive sample based on the four personas, inviting one interviewee per each persona. The stakeholders included:

1. A teacher with a low digital experience (T1) – 26 years of work experience with the main focus on teaching music and natural sciences.
2. A teacher with a rich and deep digital experience (T2) – 4 years of work experience with additional training in implementing technology in teaching and student learning.
3. An educational technologist (ET) – 7 years of experience in supporting schools and kindergartens in supporting teachers in implementing technology in student learning and facilitating digital competence development.
4. A teacher educator in a university (TT) – 15 years of experience in teaching courses related to technology enhanced learning with the focus on supporting teacher students' digital competence and professional development.

3.2 Data Collection and Analysis

In the first phase, teachers were asked to self-assess their digital competence through a web-based questionnaire, which was designed based on the DigCompEdu Framework, localized by an Estonian expert working group and validated in 2019. Questionnaire items were based on six competence dimensions: Professional Engagement, Digital Learning Resources, Teaching and Learning, Assessment, Empowering Students and Developing Students' Digital Competence. The questionnaire consisted of 25 items and teachers were asked to assess themselves on the scale of 0 (not applicable) to 5 (leader). Additionally, teachers were asked to provide open answers regarding the perceived usefulness of self-assessing their digital competence. In this study we report only the results of the open answers, due to the scope of this research. Content analysis was carried out to analyze teachers' responses regarding the usefulness of assessing their digital competence. Answers were categorized as: self-assessment was not useful; self-assessment was useful; feedback about the instrument and 'other' - when respondents provided answers which were not relevant for the self-assessment process.

In the second phase, the data was collected through a semi-structured interview which was guided by five broad questions. Questions were focused on understanding stakeholder motivation behind digital competence assessment, their previous experience with the DigCompEdu questionnaires and needs for digital competence assessment. The questions also elaborated on the process of digital competence assessment and the outcome of the questionnaires. We used an inductive content analysis approach to understand the differences in stakeholder perspectives, meaning we coded the data based on the leading interview questions and highlighted the commonalities. Based on the analysis we propose trade-off scales in digital competence assessment.

4 Results

By analyzing the stakeholder responses to understand the perceptions towards the digital competence assessment we produced an initial trade-off model to describe the constructs related to motivation and needs. We also described the commonalities between the stakeholders.

4.1 Teachers' Experiences with the Self-assessment Process

During the first phase of the study 523 teachers (46% of the respondents) filled in the open question where we asked them to reflect on how relevant and useful the digital competence self-assessment process was. 68% out of 523 teachers reported that the process was useful for them, 17% considered the process not useful, 8% were not sure and 7% provided irrelevant answers for this question.

Close to 90 teachers who considered the process useful did not provide any explanations for their response but the rest - almost 300 teachers - provided different justifications. The majority of teachers admitted that the self-assessment process made them think about their professional development gaps and needs ("*The questions made me understand my own level more clearly*"; "*I learned that I am not a digitally competent person*"; "*made me think about how I can develop myself as a teacher and a learner and about what my students need*"). Teachers also pointed out some more concrete gaps in their practice ("*I realized that I don't focus enough on ethical aspects in my teaching*"). Regarding the instrument, teachers valued the concrete examples that were provided ("*The examples were thought-provoking*"). 17% of teachers who considered the self-assessment process as not useful pointed out the following main reasons: instrument design and the culture of self-reflection. About 30 teachers argued that the instrument was too long ("*it was too long a process*"), items were complicated ("*statements need to be more explained*"), the scale was not appropriate ("*I missed the option "can but don't use"*"). A significant number of teachers however reported that the process of self-assessment was not useful for them, because they already knew their level of competence ("*It did not help much, I already know what I can do and what I can't*"). Few teachers mentioned that focusing only on assessment of digital competence is not meaningful for them ("*Not helpful, in our school we analyze our development as a whole picture*"). Finally, about 30 teachers also pointed out that such self-assessment needs to provide feedback for the teachers ("*After such a questionnaire, you might get an idea if there is room for improvement. But not very much in terms of what should change*").

Such results clearly indicate that the self-assessment process makes teachers think about their professional development gaps and needs, but there is a need to think how to embed self-assessment in the other processes of professional development. We learnt that a significant number of teachers think that they don't need self-assessment, because they already know their level of competence, however it might not always be the most subjective feeling. And finally, it is important to think about the feedback loops that self-assessment would be more forward-looking and it helps teachers to understand how to fill in the gaps in their level of competence.

4.2 Stakeholder Motivation for Digital Competence Assessment

During the second phase of the study we focused on getting a deeper understanding of the teachers' feedback on digital competence self-assessment. During this phase we involved four stakeholders representing different personas to get a wider view on the digital competence assessment needs. This meant that to understand their perceptions towards digital competence assessment we first needed to understand their motivation behind the processes. All participants emphasized that digital competence assessment is highly important due to the focus on continuous professional development. Both teachers stated that it is becoming quite difficult to prepare teaching and learning materials without using digital technologies and they need to understand their own digital competence before facilitating the students. They also brought out that digital competence assessment provides them with an overview of their digital competence and helps to plan additional training (T1: "*I need to assess my digital competence to understand what are my weakest areas and plan additional training based on that*"). Similarly, the educational technologist stated that motivating and supporting all teachers in the school to evaluate their digital competence helps to get an overview of the state of competence and plan future training, infrastructure updates and collaboration between teachers. The teacher trainer brought out that having student teachers assess their digital competence gives an opportunity for personalized learning paths and also engages student teachers in setting their professional development goals. She also considered digital competence assessment results as means for learning analytics and getting feedback from the students (TT: "*I ask the students to analyze their digital competence so they plan their personal goals in the long run and plan activities accordingly*").

The participating teachers both stated that they would need external motivation to carry out digital competence assessment meaning they would prefer for the school leader or educational technologist to guide the process. At the same time, they pointed out that it is important for them to be aware where the assessment data and results are stored and who has access to it. Still both agreed that they would prefer if the assessment results are used as input for teaching staff training and the school leader is aware of their competence level (T1 & T2: "*I wouldn't mind if my school leader sees the results if they plan or send me to trainings based on the results*"). The teachers also stated that external motivation in the form of higher income or new technologies, i.e. updated school computers or robotics tools, would motivate them. The beginner teacher deemed important that the school leader is aware of the level of digital competence for providing support and limiting expectations meaning that the responsibilities would be appropriate based on the competence level (T1: "*I think it's important my school leader sees the results. I don't want him to give me job assignments that I'm not able to perform*").

While teachers pointed out that trust towards the data collecting – human access or safe storage was a weighing aspect the teacher trainer and educational technologist also stated that gaining trust of the assessment participants is an important factor. They stated that without the participant's trust it is close to impossible to get reliable results (ET: "*Before I ask the student teachers to assess their competence I need to explain the use and access of the data and results. I don't expect them to freely give out their results – although that would already reflect their digital competence"*). Because digital competence is a central competence in teacher qualification standards, the teacher trainer and educational technologist believed that regular self-assessment and development goal setting is important. They stated that not only self-assessment is needed but also giving evidence on the digital competence is necessary which would explain the weak-spots of educators digital competence (TT: *"They might assess themselves as an advanced technology user but when the evidence is just a link to an online website it tells me opposite information. Thus, it's not only necessary to carry out regular self-assessment but we also need to inform educators on what is applicable evidence"*). All participants suggested that digital competence assessment should be a means for structured evidence-based decision making and centrally monitored process with clear outcomes like updated infrastructure, additional teacher training, continuous professional development or personalized learning paths.

During the study all participants had access to the DigCompEduSAT and DigCompEduSELF instruments prior to the interviews. Both teachers had previous experience in assessing their digital competence with the DigCompEduSELF questionnaire and a standardized self-assessment survey based on the DigCompEdu Framework. They stated that DigCompEduSELF provided them with a clear overview of the framework and its dimensions making it easy to follow the questionnaire. It was also important that the instrument provided examples and terminology explanations where necessary (T2: *"Some other surveys that I have used rarely give me examples of technology use and also don't include explanations on foreign words or specific terminology"*). Because the DigCompEduSELF was easy to follow the teachers agreed that giving evidence on their digital competence would be easy as the questionnaire items explain real-life situations in schools (T1: *"The question about creating digital learning resources would be easy to provide evidence because while reading the question statement I right away started thinking about the digital worksheets I created on Live Worksheet platform"*). Teachers also thought that the questionnaire influenced them to think about digital competence in a wider sense and realized that they are actually doing a lot more than they previously believed. They also brought out that although DigCompEduSELF took them longer to finish it was more informative and reflective. Meaning that although time plays an important factor for the teachers they consider quality feedback more important than the survey length or completion time. The item length was also noted as a positive factor in DigCompEduSELF as all stakeholders believed that lengthy item statements are confusing and often reflect on the participant's motivation. However, the teacher trainer believed that a longer item statement which includes real-life examples could provide the educators with a learning possibility. The teacher trainer and educational technologist brought out that the DigCompEduSELF reflects well on the framework and also that the items reflect the educational reality well. It was also important for them that the technical solution allows raw data to be downloaded and to get a holistic view on their participant group results (TT: *"I think the best thing about DigCompEduSELF is that I can create my own participant group and although the platform gives me a really good overall report and visuals it also allows me to download raw data. The raw data format however needs some work"*).

DigCompEduSAT was mainly redeemed unusable as it didn't reflect the educational reality and the assessment scale was difficult to follow. The teachers stated that although it would be interesting to see which competence level they fit into it is difficult to assess themselves as many questions do not relate to their everyday work experience. Advanced teachers also believed that assessments based on testing make it easier for school leaders to compare teachers' results which often reflects back on their attitude towards teachers with lower digital competence. Teachers also stated that although some of the test items did not relate their daily work or experiences it was easy to guess the right answer (T2 *"I'm not sure what the right answer is based on my own work but I can guess the right one because all other possibilities seem completely unbelievable"*). Educational technologists thought that although it would be convenient to use an instrument which divides educators based on the competence level it was still difficult to relate some of the DigCompEduSAT items to teachers' daily work. It was also clear that the test design was based on an average sized (500–1000+ students) general school (1–12 grades) and does not consider small schools (under 200 students) or basic schools (grades 1–6(9)), thus making some of the questions redundant. Because DigCompEduSAT does not require participants to give evidence or always reflect on the educational reality, the teacher trainer felt that it was not usable among the student teachers as the test items might give a distorted overview of digital competence. It was also stated by the teacher trainer and educational technologist that because DigCompEduSAT does not provide access to the overall report it is nearly impossible to support participants in goal setting or reflection.

4.3 Stakeholders' Needs for Purposeful Digital Competence Assessment

During the data analysis of both research phases we realized that the stakeholders' needs presented repetition meaning that there are characteristics that relate back to each stakeholder and digital competence assessment method (Fig. 1). We first focused on understanding the stakeholder teacher (T1) needs which indicated that the teachers evaluate the usefulness of the assessment instrument and tool based on the transparency, time demand, anonymity, feedback quality and accessibility. It was also evident that the decision making while choosing a self-assessment instrument came mainly from external motivators which included compulsory self-assessment administered by the school leader. Although the teacher with rich experience (T2) in implementing digital technologies mainly valued the same aspects it was also clear that they understood the need for self-assessment and thus can be considered as internally motivated. They also regarded both personalized and generalized feedback important as it would help them to understand their development needs in comparison of other teachers.

Opposite ends of the scale points reflect the needs indicated by the educational technologist (ET) and teacher trainer (TT). They stated the decision making when choosing a digital competence assessment instrument is strongly guided by the evidence and data which can be used to support teachers' professional development but also improve their teaching practices. Additionally, the question of instrument sustainability was considered as important as based on the stakeholder experiences there is a constant change in the assessment instruments which makes it difficult to focus on repeatability and comparison the assessment results.

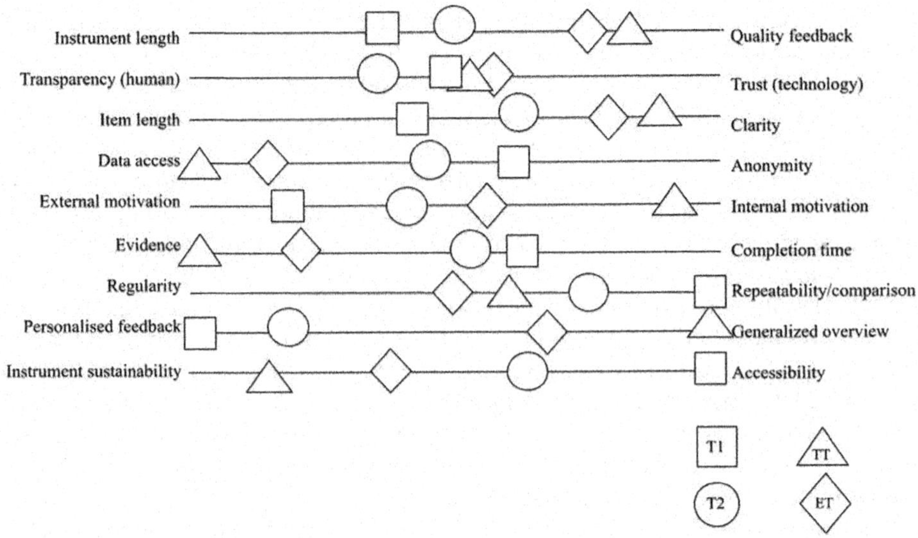

Fig. 1. Trade-off model for teachers' digital competence assessment instrument design.

Based on the teachers experiences and explanations of the self-assessment usefulness and stakeholder needs for digital competence assessment we described the trade-off scales (Fig. 1).

The trade-off model visualizes the differences between perspectives of four stakeholder groups regarding nine opposite value pairs that can be considered when designing or choosing a suitable assessment instrument, or combining two or more different instruments. The opposite ends of each scale depict user values that are incompatible and suggest a need for trade-off.

5 Discussion and Conclusions

A noteworthy result of our national self-assessment process indicates that teachers actually consider the self-assessment of their digital competence to be a rather useful experience, because it helps them to understand their professional development gaps and needs. However, there are some implications that need to be considered: self-assessment should be embedded into other assessment processes, the instrument needs to be simplified and most importantly, feedback loops are needed.

Additionally, one of the main outcomes of the study was the overview of contrasting stakeholder needs regarding teachers' digital competence assessment in the future. Based on the inductive content analysis of the differences in stakeholder needs gave a clear indication towards understanding the scope and dimension of different preferences that can be represented in a form of trade-off scales (Fig. 1). This first version of the trade-off model and the scales help us understand the need for different assessment instrument depending on its usage contexts and users. While a scientifically valid and reliable test might be a preferable option for a researcher, it will not be as helpful for a single teacher struggling with motivation to develop her basic digital competence. Figure 1 gives an overview of the digital competence trade-off model and describes the relations and importance of the scales based on stakeholder needs which gives us a way for structured decision making in the digital competence assessment process.

This study explored the differences in stakeholder perspectives regarding teachers' stakeholders, we identified nine aspects that can be used as binary, contrasting value pairs forming a trade-off model for designing, selecting or combining different digital competence assessment instruments depending on the prioritized target groups and goals of assessment. The current study suggests an initial version trade-off model and we consider that it has to be validated with a larger sample of participants and also a larger set of instruments in the future.

Acknowledgements. The research presented in the article has received partial funding from the European Union's Horizon 2020 research and innovation programme under grant agreement No. 856954.

References

1. Ahonen, A.K., Kankaanranta, M.: Introducing assessment tools for 21st century skills in Finland. In: Griffin, P., Care, E. (eds.) Assessment and Teaching of 21st Century Skills. EAIA, pp. 213–225. Springer, Dordrecht (2015). https://doi.org/10.1007/978-94-017-9395-7_10
2. Ilomäki, L., Kankaanranta, M.: The information and communication technology (ICT) competence of the young. In: Tan Wee Hin, L., Subramaniam, R. (eds.) Handbook of Research on New Media Literacy at the K-12 Level: Issues and Challenges, pp. 101–118. IGI Global (2009)
3. Lucas, M., Bem-Haja, P., Siddiq, F., Moreira, A., Redecker, C.: The relation between in-service teachers' digital competence and personal and contextual factors: what matters most? Comput. Educ. **160**(3), 104052 (2021)
4. Redecker, C., Punie, Y.: Digital Competence of Educators DigCompEdu. EUR 28775 EN. Publications Office of the European Union, Luxembourg (2017). https://doi.org/10.2760/178382
5. Biggs, J.: Enhancing teaching through constructive alignment. High. Educ. **32**, 347–364 (1996). https://doi.org/10.1007/BF00138871
6. Brande, L., Carretero, S., Vuorikari, R.: DigComp 2.0: the digital competence framework for citizens. Publications Office. Joint Research Centre (European Commission) (2017)
7. Barton, K., Schultz, G.: Using technology to assess hard-to-measure constructs in the common core state standards and to expand accessibility: English language arts. In: Invitational Research Symposium on Technology Enhanced Assessments, pp. 1–17 (2012)
8. Shute, V., Ke, F., Wang, L.: Assessment and adaptation in games. In: Wouters, P., van Oostendorp, H. (eds.) Instructional Techniques to Facilitate Learning and Motivation of Serious Games. AGL, pp. 59–78. Springer, Cham (2017). https://doi.org/10.1007/978-3-319-39298-1_4
9. van Laar, E., van Deursen, A.J., van Dijk, J.A., de Haan, J.: Measuring the levels of 21st-century digital skills among professionals working within the creative industries: a performance-based approach. Poetics **81**, 101434 (2020)

10. Pinto, M., Fernandez-Pascual, R., Puertas, S.: Undergraduates' information literacy competency: a pilot study of assessment tools based on a latent trait model. Libr. Inf. Sci. Res. **38**(2), 180–189 (2016)
11. Markauskaite, L.: Exploring the structure of trainee teachers' ICT literacy: the main components of, and relationships between, general cognitive and technical capabilities. Educ. Technol. Res. Dev. **55**, 547–572 (2007). https://doi.org/10.1007/s11423-007-9043-8
12. Law, K.S., Wong, C.-S., Mobley, W.H.: Toward a taxonomy of multidimensional constructs. Acad. Manag. Rev. **23**(4), 741–755 (1998)
13. Cartelli, A., Dagienė, V., Futschek, G.: Bebras contest and digital competence assessment: analysis of frameworks. Int. J. Digit. Lit. Digit. Competence **1**, 24–39 (2010)
14. Struyven, K., Blieck, Y., De Roeck, V.: The electronic portfolio as a tool to develop and assess pre-service student teaching competences: challenges for quality. Stud. Educ. Eval. **43**, 40–54 (2014)
15. Korhonen, A.-M., Lakkala, M., Veermans, M.: Identifying vocational student teachers' competence using an ePortfolio. Eur. J. Workplace Innov. **5**(1), 41–60 (2019)
16. Korhonen, A.-M., Ruhalahti, S., Lakkala, M., Veermans, M.: Vocational student teachers' self-reported experiences in creating ePortfolios. Int. J. Res. Vocat. Educ. Training **7**(3), 278–301 (2020)

National Policies and Services for Digital Competence Advancement in Estonia

Mart Laanpere[1](✉), Linda Helene Sillat[1], Piret Luik[2], Piret Lehiste[3], and Kerli Pozhogina[4]

[1] Tallinn University, 10120 Tallinn, Estonia
{martl,sillat}@tlu.ee
[2] University of Tartu, Tartu, Estonia
piret.luik@ut.ee
[3] Järveküla School, 75312 Peetri, Estonia
[4] Agency of Education and Youth, 10119 Tallinn, Estonia
kerli.pozogina@harno.ee

Abstract. Just like the rest of the EU, Estonia has prepared a national strategy for the next 15 years and this strategy focuses on a smarter, digitally transformed and sustainable economy and society. Digital competence of citizens is an important prerequisite for wide-scale digital transformation in industry and society at large. This paper describes and analyzes the coordinated activities at the national level to create a coherent system of services for assessing, developing and making use of digital competence among learners and teachers on different levels of education.

Keywords: Digital competence · competence frameworks · education policy · digital innovation

1 Introduction

Estonia is a tiny North-European country that was eager to realign its governance and education systems to democratic Western values as soon as it escaped from the ruins of Soviet Union in 1991. Being close to Finland regarding geography, economy, culture and language helped us to learn from the best, as the Finnish educational system has been considered an exemplary one since the turn of the century. Within last 25 years, systematic educational reforms have resulted with a success story in relation to the Estonian school system. In 2018, the OECD PISA study ranked Estonian 8-graders the best across Europe in all three categories: reading, math and science skills. In 2019, the Centre for European Policy Studies introduced a new index for Readiness for Digital Lifelong Learning, where Estonia ranked on top among EU member countries. Whether there is any causal relationship between excellent academic achievements and the digital competence of Estonian students, remains to be demonstrated by future research. One contributing factor might also be the general advancement in digitalization of the society and governance across all levels and sectors. According to the European Commission's

Published by Springer Nature Switzerland AG 2023
T. Keane et al. (Eds.): WCCE 2022, IFIP AICT 685, pp. 675–686, 2023.
https://doi.org/10.1007/978-3-031-43393-1_60

Digital Economy and Society Index [1], Estonia has ranked 1st place in the EU on Digital public services for several years in a row, while being in 5th place when it comes to digital skills of the whole population. This paper explores the potential impact to this success story of the recent policies, actions and results in teachers' and learners' digital competence development in Estonia.

2 Background

Estonia's efforts to leverage technology for teaching and learning began in 1997 with an ambitious national program called Tiger Leap, which resulted with equipping all schools with modern computer labs and Internet access by 2001 [2]. The program was coordinated by a small foundation that was established through a public-private partnership, it succeeded in engaging various actors on macro (national), meso (regional) and micro (local) level in joint efforts of digitalization of schools. Local municipalities made significant contributions to funding the technology procurements, hiring IT specialists to schools and building connectivity. The follow-up strategy called Tiger Leap Plus 2001–2005 shifted the focus on upscaling the digital innovation in education through integrating educational technologies to all levels and sectors of primary and secondary school curricula. The main action was massive teacher education: almost 80% of Estonian teachers attended 80-h ICT training based on Intel's Teach to the Future program. The first national framework for teachers' ICT skills was drafted by a group of local experts in 2001, but it was never legitimized or recognized by the Ministry of Education. The third national strategy Learning Tiger [2] focused on developing e-learning platforms, resources and competences in 2006–2009. A representative expert group was formed to design a modern framework for teachers' educational technology competence, inspired by the National Educational Technology Standard for Teachers (NETS-T) issued by the International Society for Technology in Education in 2008 [3]. This framework served as a basis for designing the new massive in-service teacher education program DigiTiger jointly with 20 + trainers who gained their experience during the previous program. This community of trainers covered geographically the whole territory of Estonia, all of them had to get the formal qualification of adult educators on level 5 of the Estonian Qualification Framework. Within the next 4 years, more than 70% of all primary and secondary teachers in the country passed the DigiTiger training program that included development of didactically sound e-learning resources [4]. These open online learning resources were shared through the new national repository Koolielu, becoming inspiration for other teachers.

In parallel, the reforms of the national curricula for primary and secondary education aligned with the digitalisation strategies. First, ICT as a cross-curricular theme was introduced in curricula in 2001, followed by introduction of the national test of students' ICT skills between 2003 and 2005 [5]. In 2011, the new concept of school informatics was announced, bringing to curricula digital communication and content production skills, but also geoinformatics, robotics, mechatronics, software engineering and data analysis. In 2014, digital competence was introduced in national curricula as one of the eight key competences. It is defined as "*the ability to use developing digital technology for coping in a quickly changing society for learning, acting as a citizen as well as communicating in communities; to use digital means for finding and preserving information and to evaluate the relevance and trustworthiness of the information; to participate in creating digital content; including creation and use of texts, images, multimedia; to use suitable digital tools and methods for solving problems, to communicate and cooperate in different digital environments; to be aware of the dangers of the digital environment and know how to protect one's privacy, personal information and digital identity; to follow the same moral and value principles as in everyday life*" [6]. It is easy to notice the full compliance of this definition with the European digital competence standard for citizens, DigComp [7].

While the first three digitalization strategies were separate from any other strategic planning instruments, the situation changed in 2012 when the civic initiative for creating the first overarching education strategy included digital goals in more generic framework. The Estonian Lifelong Learning Strategy 2020 [8] comprised the most important priorities of further development of Estonian educational system until the year 2020, reaching from primary and basic education to professional education and adult in-service training. One of its five strategic goals was the Digital Turn in lifelong learning, across all levels and forms of education. The objective was to apply modern digital technology in learning and teaching in a more efficient way and to improve the digital skills of the general population. The implementation of Digital Turn was delayed for one year due to the COVID19 pandemic, which is why the final analysis of its effectiveness is not yet completed. However, the studies on coping strategies of Estonian schools during the pandemic have demonstrated that availability of modern interactive textbooks and Open Educational Resources helped our schools to continue effective teaching in online distance mode [9].

The next national education strategy foresees development of digital competence, content and platforms that help improve the accessibility, diversity and efficiency of education by 2035. There will be significant investment in developing digital infrastructure for next-generation ecosystem of educational services, including digitized curricula, automatized Learning Analytics, Artificial Intelligence applications for flexible Learning Paths supporting self-regulated learning and formative assessment.

Digital competence is an important target also on societal level at large. Estonia's Digital Society Development Plan for 2030 emphasizes the need for large-scale in-service and retraining initiatives that aim to lessen the digital skills gap among employees in all sectors of our economy. It also highlights the importance of a rapid increase in the number of professionals having advanced IT skills that should help to create new jobs with higher added value in IT sector.

Digital competence development in Estonia is coordinated by the Digital Competence Task Force Group (DCTF Group) established by the National Education & Youth Board of Estonia (HARNO), which is a government agency of the Estonian Ministry of Education and Research. The DCTF Group involves experts from the HARNO agency, Tallinn University, University of Tartu and schools. The group meets monthly and it aims to adapt, validate and pilot digital competence frameworks and respective assessment instruments on the national level. The DCTF Group reports twice a year on the results and developments of its work to the Digital Competence Advisory Board, which includes 30 + representatives from the following strategically important organizations:

Estonian Association of Educational Technologists, Estonian Association for Advancement of Vocational Education, Estonian Teachers' Association, University of Tartu, Estonian Informatics Teachers' Association, Estonian Association of Kindergarten Teachers, Tallinn University, Estonian Qualifications Authority, Estonian Association of Heads of Schools, and Ministry of Education and Research. The Advisory Board evaluates the deliverables of the DCTF Group, then outlines and confirms the detailed action plan for the next period. Below we will introduce the main achievements of the DCTF Group over the last three years.

3 Digital Competence Definition and Underlying Conceptual Frameworks

Digital competence is considered an important 21st century skill. However, there are different definitions of digital competence and it has changed over the years. Already in 2006, the European Commission included digital competence in the list of eight key competences for lifelong learning and the importance of this competence has been only growing since then. As the universally accepted definition of digital competence was missing until 2013 in Europe, the meaning and scope of this concept has been varying. While some authors interpret digital competence as a synonym of information and communication technology (ICT) literacy [10], others expand it by adding the use of digital technologies for problem-solving [11]. However, some definitions of digital competence seem to be closer to the concept of critical media literacy [12].

In parallel with national curriculum development in Estonia emerged the need to define the students' digital competence in the local educational context. The national framework for learners' digital competence was created in line with the European Commission's framework DigComp 2.1, which includes five dimensions of digital competence: information and data literacy, communication and collaboration, digital content creation, digital safety, and digital problem-solving [7].

In addition to the translated and localized competence model we developed a publicly accessible set of detailed assessment criteria for each key stage of education, linked to the five dimensions of the learners' digital competence framework. There is also an adapted version of the assessment criteria for learners with special needs which is included in the curriculum, published on the national portal of digital competence[1]. Teachers can use these to assess student progress in building digital competence within their taught courses.

4 Instruments

This chapter describes the main instruments for self-assessment of digital competence created and/or promoted nationwide by DCTF Group.

[1] https://digipadevus.ee.

4.1 Digital Mirror: Self-assessment of School's Digital Maturity

DigitalMirror[2] is a web-based tool that allows any school team to self-assess the digital maturity of their organization as whole, then to use this data for benchmarking yourself with other schools. The tool also allows planning a whole-school digital strategy, as well as aggregated strategy for all schools in the city or district. The Digital Maturity framework was inspired by ideas of Michael Fullan [13], who claims that knowledge from three domains (technology, pedagogy and change management) should be combined for successful whole-school policy on digital innovation. Pedagogical innovation indicators of Digital Mirror were drawn from Estonian national strategy for lifelong learning. The Digital Maturity scale was taken from EduVista framework, that was created within iTEC project [14] and inspired by the Capability Maturity Model [15]. The Digital Maturity model of Digital Mirror has 15 indicators in total, distributed between 3 domains: (1) pedagogical innovation, (2) change management and (3) digital infrastructure. Each indicator is evaluated on a 5-point scale, which is inspired by the EduVista framework [14]:

A. **Exchange**: Innovation has no impact on core processes, technology is used only by a small group of innovators, school leaders are not involved.
B. **Enrich**: School leaders support innovation on wider scale, they coordinate uptake of innovative practices on the school level.
C. **Enhance**: School begins to redesign and digitally transform the core processes so, impact goes beyond immediate use of technology in classroom.
D. **Extend**: Digital transformation has taken place and technology is used ubiquitously.
E. **Empower**: Innovation extends beyond institutional boundaries, school uses learners as co-authors etc.

Schools' digital maturity assessment process in Digital Mirror starts with creating the **Self-assessment report** which describes the current level of a school's digital maturity. For the initial **Individual** assessment phase, the school principal or other knowledgeable staff member fills in a quick evaluation form. In the next phase (**Group** assessment) a digital task force group consisting of 3–8 active staff members validates the initial evaluation report by providing comments and evidence (links or uploaded resources) for each indicator level making the decision more grounded. Online group discussion and argumentation is strongly encouraged next to each indicator, to reach consensus. Optionally, schools have the possibility to re-validate their group assessment by inviting external experts or a group of teachers from other schools to visit their school for lesson observations, interviews and confirmation (**Peer** assessment phase). Finally, the school principal confirms the validated report and decides whether to make the report public or just share it with selected persons (e.g. local government) (Fig. 1).

DigitalMirror has been used by more than 80% of Estonian schools, first in 2016 and then in 2019. School teams did set target levels for each of the 15 indicators and then described specific actions that would help to achieve these targets. For better cooperation between school owners and schools, school owners can see drafts of school digital strategies and contribute during the planning process. After adding an action plan to school's digital strategy, the strategy can be confirmed and published by the principal.

[2] https://digipeegel.ee.

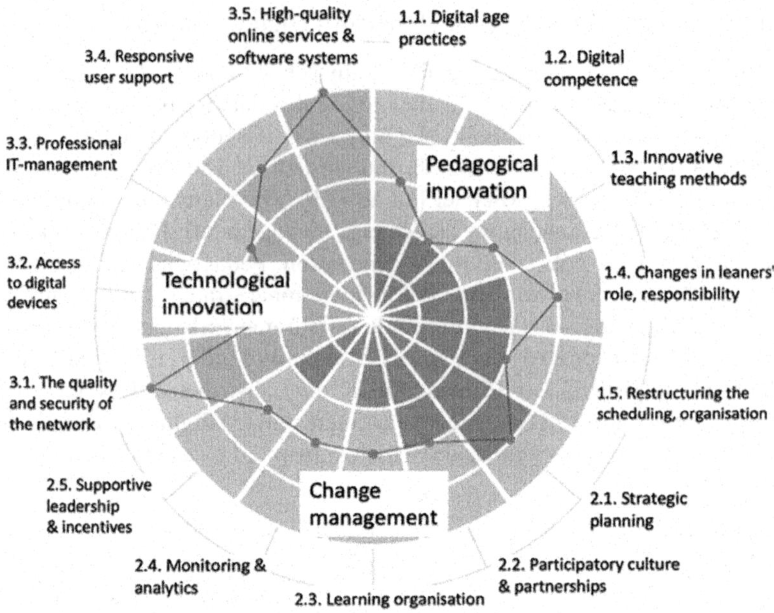

Fig. 1. A school's self-assessment report in DigitalMirror, green dots indicate strategic goals.

The results of Estonian schools' (n = 499) self-assessment with DigitalMirror were analyzed in [16], K-means cluster analysis identified three categories of schools located on different stages of digital transformation:

1. **Schools in the early stage of transition**, where digital transformation is not yet guided by well-defined organizational goals, leadership and change management practices, while some teachers have already started to implement innovative teaching and learning practices;
2. **Schools focused on digital innovation** (the largest group, more than half of all schools nationwide), where the digital transformation process has resulted in some structural changes, but change management is not participatory and digitally enhanced teaching and learning practices not yet adopted by the majority of teachers. These schools often report issues with their digital infrastructure, including limited access to WIFI and digital devices.
3. **Digitally mature schools** are learning organizations that have adopted participatory and evidence-based change management practices to redesign teaching and learning, resulting with wide-scale adoption of digital pedagogy and changes in teachers' and students' roles.

Digital competence of teachers and students is one indicator of school's digital maturity in DigitalMirror, but in order to rank the school on level 3, the team has to provide evidence that a majority of the teachers and students have reached the expected level. In order to collect such evidence, additional assessment tools are needed. Below we will describe the available instruments for assessing the digital competence of teachers and learners.

4.2 Digital Competence of Educators

As mentioned above, the initial digital competence framework for Estonian teachers was based on ISTE NETS-T model and it was distributed as an annex to the teachers' qualification standard in a format of 5-page PDF file presenting a self-assessment rubric with five levels of proficiency. This rubric was rarely used by anyone, as it was perceived by teachers as too complex and long. Although there was an initiative to develop a more user-friendly online instrument for self- and peer-assessment of teachers' digital competence [17], it was not adopted on the wide scale. The next attempt to model and standardize the educators' digital competence was associated with the renewal of the national qualification standard for teachers in 2017, which integrated in teachers' core competences the ability to enhance the teaching activities and learning environment with technology. The new version of the teachers' qualification standard was released in 2019, redefining the digital competence of educators in line with the new European standard DigCompEdu [18]. This time the DCTF Group decided to integrate or embed the digital competence within the main professional competences required from all teachers. Notice the similarity with national strategies for school digitalization that used to be separated from other macro-level planning instruments until 2014 when digital innovation was included in the national strategy for lifelong learning. There is still also a localized Estonian teachers' digital competence framework, an adaptation of DigCompEdu which defines educators' digital competence through 6-dimensions: professional development and engagement, digital resources, teaching and learning, assessment, empowering learners, and facilitating learners' digital competence. This framework is published online and is used mostly as design guidelines by teacher trainers, course designers and developers of self-assessment tools for teachers.

DCTF Group members have contributed to European R&D projects aiming at new digital competence self-assessment instruments for teachers. The first of such instruments was developed in collaboration with the European Commission's Joint Research Center (JRC Seville) and it comprised an online knowledge-based test with multiple-choice items on six proficiency levels: newcomer, explorer, integrator, expert, leader and pioneer [18]. After the initial piloting of the test and interviews with participants we concluded that using a knowledge-based test for assessing teachers' digital competence was not suitable in the Estonian context. On one hand, the test itself had some serious issues regarding content validity. Second, the Estonian teachers refused the idea of being tested, as they usually never take any tests after graduating from university. After that we focused on designing a localized self-assessment instrument catered towards the needs of educators. The DCTF Group created then self-assessment instruments for educators in both general schools and higher education, in Estonian and Russian, in various formats that can be easily copied and modified by anyone: Google Form survey, LimeSurvey XML import file, MS Excel spreadsheet file and QTI-compliant TAO import file. This self-assessment instrument includes 25 statements (e.g. '*I use digital technology to support learners with different needs and abilities*') with response options on a 6-point proficiency scale (including level 0). The previous bad experience with the too extensive CNETS self-assessment rubric inspired the DCTF group to engage 20 expert teachers in participatory design research to re-designed the teachers' self-assessment scale. The new scale is more compact and describes only three main proficiency levels in a uniform manner for all indicators, while allowing teachers to place themselves between two levels:

0) I am not aware of it,
1) **Beginner**: I know what it is, but don't apply it yet
2) Interim level: beyond beginner level, but not an expert yet,
3) **Expert**: I am quite knowledgeable and skilled regarding it, applying it regularly
4) Interim level: beyond expert level, but nor a pioneer yet,
5) **Pioneer**: I am evaluating and designing strategies and leading implementation regarding it.

The instrument was piloted by the DCTF Group in 2019 with Estonian educators in primary, secondary and higher education, its reliability and validity was confirmed [19].

In 2021 the DCTF Group members from Tallinn University were contracted by EC JRC to coordinate piloting and validation of a new all-European self-reflection tool SELFIE for Teachers, which is based on the DigCompEdu model. The instrument includes 32 self-reflection items and a 6-point proficiency scale that describes desired performance in detail for each level. The items and the user interface of this online tool was translated into Estonian, Lithuanian, Italian and Portuguese languages and piloted in four countries with more than 3200 primary and secondary school teachers. After successful piloting and confirming both the reliability and validity of the instrument, the tool was translated to all official languages of European Union and made accessible to all teachers in Europe [20].

While we now have two competing instruments for self-assessment of teachers' digital competence (SELFIE for Teachers and locally developed questionnaires), both have their uses and can easily complement each other. SELFIE is a preferred tool for single teachers who are interested in self-reflection. However, it would be very difficult for schools or the Ministry to use SELFIE for informing themselves about progress or integrating the self-assessment results in some other information system - e.g. DigitalMirror or the database of teacher training courses. So, there is still a need for our locally developed, more flexible, simplified self-assessment tool. For instance, the DCTF Group has cooperated with a large group of teacher trainers who have designed a large number of in-service training courses to raise various aspects of teachers' digital competence. This cooperation resulted with a clear mapping of all available courses to DigCompEdu competence indicators and also to proficiency levels.

The community of teacher trainers involves more than 80 experienced and qualified adult educators, who work mostly as teachers in primary and secondary schools (61 of them), in vocational school (3) or preschool (7), trainers in private companies (3) or lecturers in university (9). To initiate this process, the DCTF Group created a detailed guidelines for trainers on the mapping process that involved six stages:

- familiarize the trainers' team with the structure of DigCompEdu,
- annotate your course content with skill-based keywords from DigCompEdu,
- review the learning outcomes of your course using the skill-based keywords from DigCompEdu,
- analyse your new learning outcomes and map each of these to one of the six proficiency levels,

- define the prerequisite level of skills for your course in accordance with DigCompEdu and its proficiency levels,
- plan the further adaptation of your course to avoid overlaps with other courses and to address the "empty areas" that are not covered by courses yet.

The next step will be to build a recommender system that automatically suggests some relevant courses to a teacher who has just completed her self-assessment of her digital competence. Such functionality has already been implemented in the Belgian DigiSnap service [21] that served as an inspiring example for us.

4.3 Digital Competence of Students

The national agency responsible for quality assurance in education has been developing an online platform for electronic tests since 2012. In many school subjects, the level tests are conducted online at the end of the school year for a random sample of students in primary and lower-secondary schools. The students do not receive a grade for this test, only aggregated feedback is made available for teacher, school leader and ministry. The national test on digital competence was piloted in 2018 using automatically graded tasks in the national web-based Examination Information System (EIS). The test was designed for students in grades 9 and 12 and it has been repeated also in 2019 and 2021. The test was designed by a group of experts representing three main universities and association of computer science teachers. The test contains 24 multiple choice items in five groups related to European digital competence model DigComp 2.1:

- Information and data literacy – 5 tasks
- Digital communication and collaboration – 6 tasks
- Digital content creation – 6 tasks
- Digital safety – 5 tasks
- Digital problem solving – 2 tasks.

Figure 2 below demonstrates two items from the test, the first one belongs to information and data literacy category, the second to digital safety category. A psychometric analysis of the students' digital competence test was conducted in 2022 by members of the DCTF Group together with an external psychometry expert, using the responses of 200 students from grades 8 and 11 who took the test in 2021. Confirmatory Factor Analysis showed satisfactory factor loadings and values for the main fit indices ($\chi 2 = 9174$, $df = 4554$, $p < .001$, RMSEA = 0.02, CFI = 0,87). Item Analysis with IRT confirmed suitable difficulty levels and discrimination for majority of test items, only one item was an outlier and had to be removed.

An alternative online self-assessment tool was created in 2020 for lower- and upper-secondary students. This tool consists of 45 descriptions of digital activities representing the competence indicators and assessment criteria described in the learners' digital competence model. The learner does not have to solve the tasks given in the self-evaluation tool but evaluates on the basis of the given 6-point scale whether they can solve the tasks given in the self-evaluation tool. The tool was piloted in 2020 using the think aloud method with two students and after the revisions were made 324 students from three secondary schools filled in the self-evaluation tool in 2021 and wrote comments

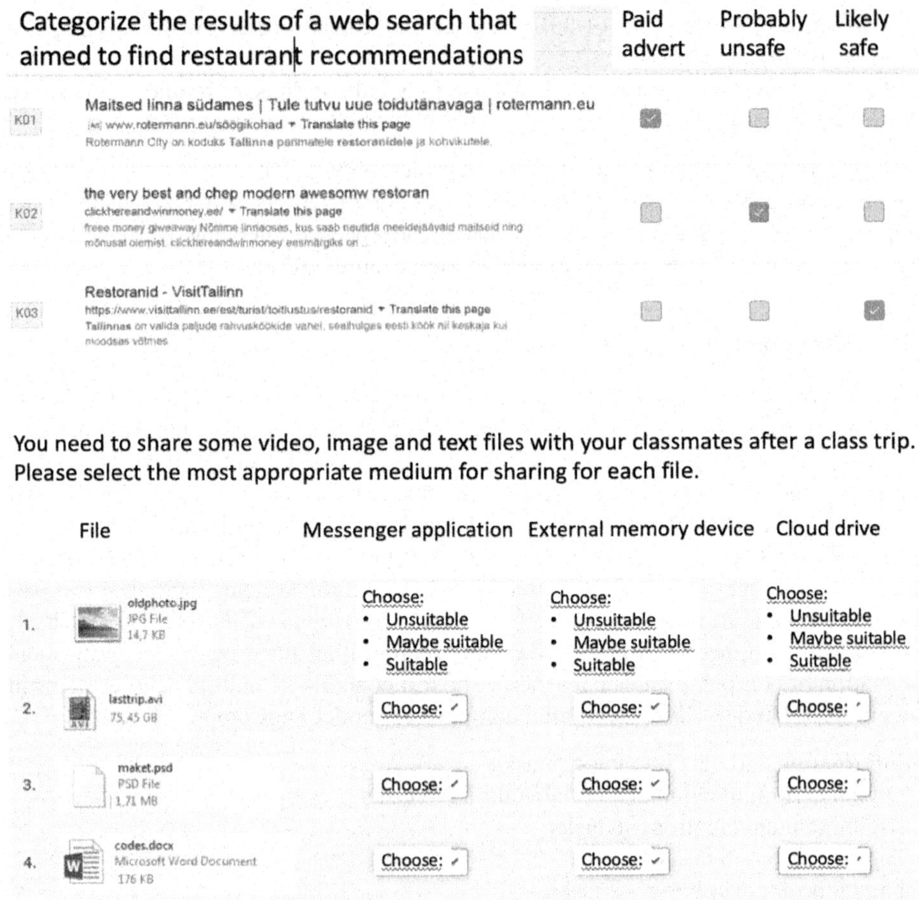

Fig. 2. Two examples of digital competence test items.

suggesting ideas for improving the wording of the scale. After the second piloting round the tool was revised again and is now publicly accessible for schools to use in different digital, editable formats[3]: Google Form, TAO, MS Excel and Limesurvey [22].

To standardize this large variety of assessment instruments, a set of detailed digital competence assessment criteria for key stage 1, 2 and 3 were developed by the DCTF group and published on the Digital Competence portal. In addition, a simplified version of this assessment rubric was created for learners with special educational needs. Having a variety of assessment instruments available was an important first step, but the schools needed also DigComp-compliant learning resources that would help the teachers to develop learners' digital skills. DCTF group along with two invited experts designed a guiding implementation framework and related online course on Moodle platform that schools can download, modify and re-use with their students in grades 4–9.

[3] https://digipadevus.ee/oppija-digipadevusmudel/enesehindamise-kusimustik/.

5 Conclusions

This paper describes the systemic work on analyzing, modelling and raising the digital competence of teachers and learners in Estonia, a small Northern European country that has demonstrated success in educational reforms, academic achievements of students, readiness for digital education and also digital public services. The experience of long-term collaboration between experts from academia, practitioners "from the field", specialists from the national agency of education and high-level educational policy makers in Estonia might serve as an inspiring case study for other countries which are still struggling with wide scale uptake of digital innovations in education.

References

1. EuroStat: Digital Economy and Society Index (2021). https://digital-strategy.ec.europa.eu/en/library/digital-economy-and-society-index-desi-2021. Accessed 20 Apr 2022
2. Toots, A., Plakk, M., Idnurm, T.: National policies and practices on ICT in education: Estonia. In: Plomp, T., Anderson, R.E., Law, N., Quale, A. (eds.) Cross-National ICT Policies and Practices in Education. Information Age Publishing, Charlotte NC (2009)
3. Thomas, L.G., Knezek, D.G.: Information, Communications, and Educational Technology Standards for Students, Teachers, and School Leaders. In: Voogt, J., Knezek, G. (eds.) International Handbook of Information Technology in Primary and Secondary Education. Springer International Handbook of Information Technology in Primary and Secondary Education, vol. 20. Springer, Boston (2008). https://doi.org/10.1007/978-0-387-73315-9_20
4. Peenema, K.: Designing a Knowledge Environment for Teachers in the Context of Professional Development Programme DigiTiger. Master thesis. Tallinn University (2010)
5. Villems, A., Tooding, L.-M.: Study on ICT Competency of Estonian Pupils. In: V. Dagiene, R. Mittermeir (eds.). Information Technologies at School, pp. 436–446. TEV, Vilnius (2006)
6. Teataja, R.: National Curriculum for Basic Schools. https://www.riigiteataja.ee/akt/129082014020. Accessed 28 Mar 2022
7. Carretero Gomez, S., Vuorikari, R., Punie, Y.: DigComp 2.1 - The digital competence framework for Citizens with eight proficiency levels and examples of use. Publications Office of the European Union, Luxembourg (2017)
8. Ministry of Education & Research: National Strategy of Education 2021–2035. https://www.hm.ee/en/activities/strategic-planning-2021-2035. Accessed 28 Mar 2022
9. Tammets, K., et al.: Eriolukorrast tingitud distantsõppe kogemused ja mõju Eesti üldharidussüsteemile. Vaheraport. Tallinna Ülikool, Tallinn (2021)
10. Ilomäki, L.,Kankaanranta, M.: The information and communication technology (ICT) competence of the young. In: Tan Wee Hin, L., Subramaniam, R. (eds.), Handbook of Research on New Media Literacy at the K-12 Level, pp. 101–118. IGI Global, Hershey (2009)
11. Simović, V.M., Domazet, I.S..: An overview of the frameworks for measuring the digital competencies of college students: a European perspective. In: edited by Neimann, T., Felix, J.J., Reeves, S., Shliakhovchuk, E. (eds) Stagnancy Issues and Change Initiatives for Global Education in the Digital Age, 259–282. IGI Global, Hershey, PA (2021)
12. Calvani, A., Fini, A., Ranieri, M.: Assessing digital competence in secondary education. In: Leaning, M. (ed.) Issues in Information and Media Literacy: Education, Practice and Pedagogy, pp. 153–172. Informing Science Press, Santa Rosa, CA (2009)
13. Fullan, M.: Stratosphere: Integrating Technology, Pedagogy, and Change Knowledge. Pearson, Canada (2013)

14. Toikkanen, T., Keune, A., Leinonen, T.: Designing edukata, a participatory design model for creating learning activities. In: Van Assche, F., Anido, L., Griffiths, D., Lewin, C., McNicol, S. (eds.) Re-engineering the Uptake of ICT in Schools. Springer, Cham (2015). https://doi.org/10.1007/978-3-319-19366-3_3
15. Paulk, M.C., Curtis, B., Chrissis, M.B., Weber, C.V.: Capability maturity model, version 1.1. IEEE Softw. **10**, 18–27 (1993)
16. Pata, K., Tammets, K., Väljataga, T., Kori, K., Laanpere, M., Rõbtsenkov, R.: The patterns of school improvement in digitally innovative schools. Technol. Knowl. Learn. **27**, 823–841 (2021)
17. Põldoja, H., Väljataga, T., Tammets, K., Laanpere, M.: Web-based self- and peer-assessment of teachers' educational technology competencies. In: Lau, R., Nejdl, W. (eds.) Advances in Web-based Learning, pp. 122–131. Springer LNCS, Berlin (2011). https://doi.org/10.1007/978-3-642-25813-8_13
18. Punie, Y., Redecker, C.: European Framework for the Digital Competence of Educators: DigCompEdu. Publications Office of the European Union, Luxembourg (2017)
19. Sillat, L.H., Sillat, P.J., Vares, M., Tammets, K.: Providing meaningful digital competence assessment feedback for supporting teachers professional development. In: González-González, C.S., et al. (eds.) Learning Technologies and Systems for Education, ICWL SETE 2022 2022, vol. 13869, pp. 180–189. Springer, Berlin (2022). https://doi.org/10.1007/978-3-031-33023-0_16
20. Educators Go Digital: SELFIE for Teachers home page. https://educators-go-digital.jrc.ec.europa.eu. Accessed 28 Mar 2022
21. Bernaerts, K.: DigiSprong, SELFIE for Teachers and DigiSnap, presentation at SELFIE workshop in JRC Seville. https://www.klascement.net/articles/144237/what-is-digisnap/. Accessed 28 Mar 2022
22. HARNO: National Framework and Instruments for Digital Competence Advancement. https://digipadevus.ee. Accessed 28 Mar 2022

Digital Technologies for Learning, Teaching and Assessment: Tackling the Perennial Problem of Policy and Practice

Deirdre Butler and Margaret Leahy(✉)

Institute of Education, Dublin City University, Dublin, Ireland
{deirdre.butler,margaret.leah}@dcu.ie

Abstract. Education policy implementation is a complex, evolving process that involves many stakeholders often with seemingly conflicting and opposing visions. This paper presents an account of work in progress in which the authors are conducting an analysis of the enactment of a strategy for digital learning in schools in Ireland. The aim of the study is both to analyse and theorise the extent to which the policy has achieved its aims but also to identify a means of tackling the perennial challenge of policy development and enactment at the school and classroom level. This paper presents the findings of the first phase of analysis.

Keywords: policy · practice · digital technologies for learning

1 Introduction

As we engage in developing the next iteration of a Digital Strategy for Schools (DSS) to 2027 in Ireland, consideration needs to be taken of what has happened since the launch of the DSS in 2015 [1] and in particular if and how all the parts of an education system worked together to support the type of learning envisioned in the DSS, 2015–2020.

2 Context

The publication of the Digital Strategy for Schools 2015–2020 [1] in Ireland was perceived as the glue that would not only leverage existing educational policies but would also be the catalyst for enabling the move towards systemic transformation of Irish schools [2]. Underpinned by the vision "to realise the potential of digital technologies to enhance teaching, learning and assessment so that Ireland's young people become engaged thinkers, active learners, knowledge constructors and global citizens to participate fully in society and the economy" (1, p. 5), the strategy defines embedding digital technology as 'Moving beyond ICT integration, where digital technology is seamlessly used in all aspects of teaching, learning and assessment to enhance the learning experiences of all students' [1, p. 15]. Four themes underpin the Digital Strategy, which specifies a set of actions under each theme:

Published by Springer Nature Switzerland AG 2023
T. Keane et al. (Eds.): WCCE 2022, IFIP AICT 685, pp. 687–696, 2023.
https://doi.org/10.1007/978-3-031-43393-1_61

- Theme 1: Teaching, learning and assessment using ICT
- Theme 2: Teacher professional learning
- Theme 3: Leadership, research and policy
- Theme 4: ICT infrastructure.

A Digital Learning Framework (DLF) for primary and post-primary schools was subsequently published by the Department of Education and Skills [3, 4] followed by Digital Planning Guidelines and a Planning Template. The DLF is designed as an instrument to enable schools engage with and implement elements of the DSS [1]. It aims to guide educators to (i) reflect on their current understanding and use of digital technologies in their practice and (ii) on how to use digital technologies effectively to transform their teaching, learning and assessment practices. The DLF was adapted from the UNESCO ICT Competency Framework for Teaching [5–8], DigComp Org [9] and DigComp Edu [10], for the Irish context and is intended to be used in tandem with the Looking at Our Schools school self-evaluation framework [11, 12] which is a process that all schools are expected to engage in.

The DLF is articulated as a set of domains and standard statements across two dimensions: Teaching and Learning, and Leadership and Management. Each standard is illustrated by at least one example of effective and highly effective practice [13]. In using the DLF, schools are encouraged to engage in a process of reflection as part of the School Self-Evaluation Process [14] that culminates in action, i.e. the creation of a Digital Learning Plan (DLP) that outlines how they will enhance their existing digital learning practices over a defined period of time.

3 Methodology

The authors carried out an in-depth review of the implementation of the Digital Strategy for Schools (2015–2020) from multiple perspectives. It included analysis of (i) Department of Education (DE) Digital Strategy Actions Plans (2017–2019) and the draft Action Plan (2020), (ii) research evidence from published reports including those which focused on the experiences of schools in Ireland during the school closures brought about by the Covid-19 pandemic and (iii) the findings from the public consultation carried out by the DE in relation to the implementation of the DSS [1]. This included reports from the open call for submissions, the DE survey of principals, teachers and students, the DE focus group interviews with key stakeholders in education and the National Parents Council's survey of parents. As part of the analysis, we extracted the key findings from each data source before carrying out further analysis across the three sets of findings. This led to a final set of conclusions that serve both to highlight the progress that has been made across the four themes of the DSS (2015–2020) (Teaching, Learning and Assessment using ICT; Teacher Professional Learning; Leadership, Research and Policy and ICT Infrastructure) [1] as well as to identify a number of aspects of each theme that requires further attention and development.

4 What We Have Learned

Findings indicate that overall, teachers are now using a wider range of digital technologies and using them more frequently in their practice [15]. Digital technologies are found to be used by teachers in lessons to creatively engage learners although they are sometimes only used by teachers [16]. A prominent use is by the teacher for lesson preparation, presenting information or giving class instruction to students although post primary teachers also use technologies to communicate with students, to support peer-to-peer assessment and learner collaboration [15, 16]. Across all levels however, digitally supported assessment remains underdeveloped; 45% of post primary teachers report no change in assessment practices while the figure was between 65% and 77% at primary level [15]. These figures are not surprising given the focus on ePortfolios for assessment at post primary level but overall, they indicate a need for a greater focus on digitally supported assessment.

Some progress has also been achieved as a result of the necessity to engage with the use of digital technologies during the two periods of school closure and remote teaching due to the Covid 19 pandemic. It has resulted in an increase in the level of collaboration, collegiality and teamwork among teachers as well as an increase in professional learning relating to the use of digital technologies for teaching and learning [17, 18]. However, it has been a challenge for many teachers, particularly for those who felt they did not have the skills required.

While these findings are encouraging in many respects, it is significant that in 45% of primary schools and 38% of post-primary schools, digital technologies were not a feature of teaching and learning [16]. In addition, many schools were and still are unaware of what (i) dimension of the DLF their school is focusing on; (ii) the supporting resources available e.g. Scoilnet/Webwise; (iii) unsure on how to access external professional learning support; and (iv) require help with procurement [15, 16, 19]. It is also the case that, although the DL planning website, while widely praised as a useful resource, is widely under-utilised [15] Indeed, as experienced worldwide the Covid crisis in Ireland exposed more keenly the weaknesses and inequities already in the education system, it also lead to an increase in the level of collaboration, collegiality and teamwork among teachers as well as an increase in professional learning relating to the use of digital technologies for teaching and learning [17, 18]. However, for the most part it did not lead to any innovative practices across the system which could be considered as central to the next iteration of the DSS to 2027. In reality, the majority of the schools are still at the Knowledge Acquisition stage with some in the Knowledge Deepening stage [8].

Policy enactment takes time and realistically the timeframe for the implementation of the DLF in schools to date has been less than three years as Covid interrupted the normal running of school systems globally. Despite this short implementation phase some interesting trends have emerged which we believe are significant "sticking points" which need to be considered when designing the next iteration of the DSS to 2027.

- Although, 60% of schools rated themselves as being mostly at levels of effective practice or higher on their chosen domain, there is a lack of understanding of what constitutes effective practice and schools tend to use multiple and mainly informal approaches to assess the level of practice within a chosen domain. This points to a need for further guidance to promote a more uniform understanding of levels of effective and highly effective practice for monitoring purposes. In fact, a key theme emanating from the consultative process is the need for reporting on schools DLPs to ensure impact of the DLF is monitored and measured to help inform future policy, and allow for best practice to be identified, shared and supported

- The lack of awareness and underutilisation of the DL Planning website and other resources such as Webwise and Scoilnet needs to explored in order to establish why that is the case. Nonetheless, it would appear that there is a need for all resources and supports relating to all things digital in teaching, learning and assessment, and associated issues, to be made more accessible and readily available.
- The focus in schools has generally been on dimensions of Teaching and Learning rather than Leadership and Management and that to date, the focus has generally been on providing awareness sessions for school leaders rather than on the provision of focused professional learning programmes for leaders [15, 20].
- Challenges reported in implementing the DLF related to time for staff to implement the DLP, issues concerning the fit between the aims of the DLF and the structure of the standardised assessments, and infrastructure [15, 19].

5 Leveraging the Key Sticking Points to Move Towards Translating Policy to Practice

As we emerge from the period of emergency remote teaching and adapt to life back in schools, policy makers need to critically reflect on the critical sticking points of translating policy into practice at the school level in Ireland. While efforts to address alignment had taken place (e.g. development of DLF, in particular the alignment with the SSE process; development of supporting resources; curriculum specifications to include the use of digital technologies), this did not appear to result in practice at the classroom level that exemplified what is characterised as "Knowledge Deepening" [5–8], which had been the original intention of the DSS of 2015.

The problem is complex and there is a need for policy makers to visualise the system as a whole in order to pinpoint what part/s of the system need particular attention in the next iteration of the DSS in order to enable alignment and move beyond "Knowledge Acquisition". Butler et al. [2] explored the issue of alignment (c.f. Fig. 1), noting that this required alignment of purpose, policy (including curriculum, assessment, accountability and teacher professional learning), and practice at three levels (macro/national, meso/school, and micro/ teacher).

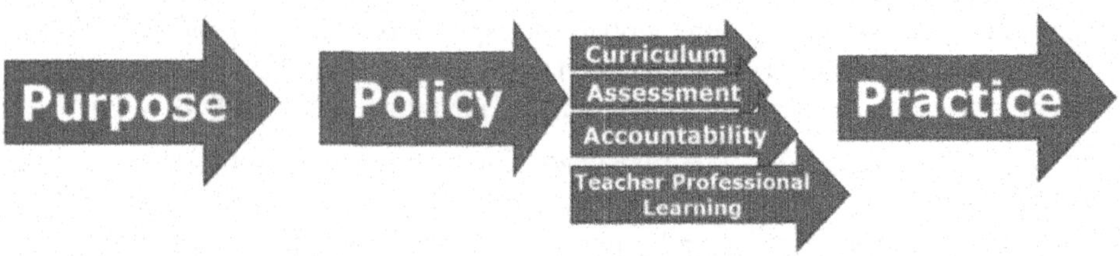

Fig. 1. Alignment of purpose, policy and practice

Twining [21] extended this analysis using a sociocultural framework and the model proposed in Twining et al. [22] provides a possible starting point for examining this problem of alignment and enabling the translation of policy into action at the school and classroom level (c.f. Fig. 2). This framework has three levels,

- The constitutive order – the broader context, including cultural norms, values and beliefs, as well as more explicit policies, rules and regulations.
- The arena – the enduring elements of the school context which are taken up from the constitutive order. For example, how policies and expectations at the national level are interpreted and enshrined in the school expectations, policies and facilities. The arena provides opportunities for action.
- The setting – the local context (e.g. the classroom) in which practice is implemented. At this level of analysis, the actors (e.g. teacher and students) perceive what is possible within the context of the school arena in the light of their identities. As illustrated by the shaded box within the setting in Fig. 2 actors 'take up' some of those perceived possibilities in their iterative interactions with the other people in their setting.

Achieving alignment between and within each of these levels (Constitutive Order, School Arena, and Setting) is complex.

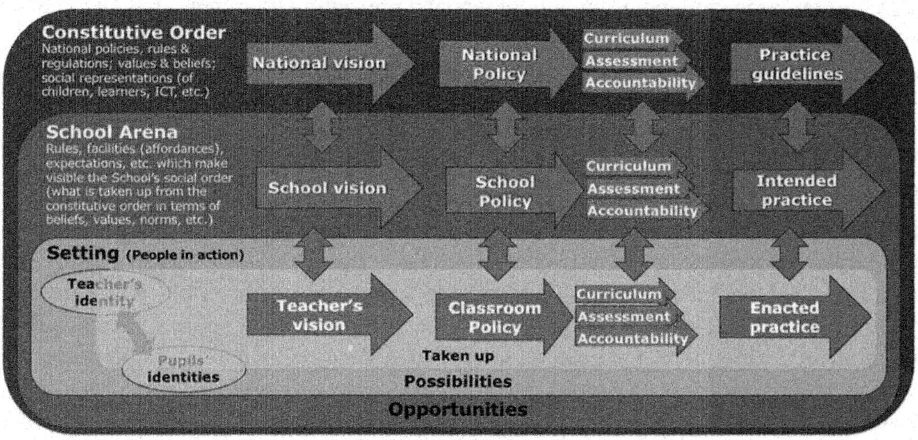

Fig. 2. System Alignment

Against this backdrop, it is essential to acknowledge that digital technologies do not have an independent existence and cannot be considered separately from the values that people bestow on them. Indeed, the ways digital technologies may or may not be used reflect these understandings. Research has consistently demonstrated that digital technology per se is not necessarily a driver or catalyst for change and that the introduction of digital technology into schools does not in and of itself lead to the development of innovative teaching practices or the transformation of education [e.g., 21, 23–28]. In order for digital technologies to be effectively used in teaching and learning at school level, their use has to be part of the school vision and must be supported by specific national policies [27–29].

So looking across the three levels; we can say that there are national policies which in accordance with the DSS [1], articulate a vision towards embedding the use of digital technologies in teaching, learning and assessment. What we need to consider is first, if this vision is consistent across all policy documentation related to school curriculum and assessment and second if this vision permeates and is enshrined in individual school and teacher visions (i.e. shared at the School Arena and Setting level). For example, is there consistency across the learning principles underpinning Primary and Post-Primary levels? Is there consistency in how digital technologies are used across Primary and Post-Primary schools?

Primary level - The view of learning as presented in the Draft Primary Curriculum Framework [30] is one where learning is viewed as an active process of enquiry, reflection and dialogue, and children are considered co-constructors of knowledge in collaboration with their peers, teachers and the wider community. This view of learning is mirrored in the DSS (2015–2020) [1] and the DLF [3, 4].

Post-Primary level – Eight Key Skills set out in the Framework for Junior Cycle focus on the four 'C's of communication, collaboration, creativity and critical thinking. These key skills are embedded into all subject specifications and are developed on an ongoing basis throughout the Junior Cycle. Students have opportunities to use these skills in their engagement with classroom-based assessments (CBAs) through conducting and analysing research, collaborating with others and presenting their work. CBAs in junior cycle also offer opportunities for the use of digital technologies for collaboration, presentations and so on as well as providing the basis for the development of digital media literacy skills particularly in relation to the safe, critical and ethical use of information found online. In addition, ePortfolios can form part of the student assessment process.

A framework of key skills has also been developed at senior cycle. These five key skills, (information processing, being personally effective, communicating, critical and creative thinking and working with others), are integrated across the current senior cycle curriculum supporting the development of digital skills in a variety of ways. Since the launch of the DSS (2015–2020) [1] significant emphasis has been placed on the use of ePortfolios inTransition Year. Moreover, recently developed subject specifications and those in development for Leaving Certificate, place an increased emphasis on the development of digital skills. As an example, Economics students have an opportunity to explore how technology impacts on the economy and also use technology to discuss, explain and communicate research findings and analyse data. Digital technology also forms part of assessment in a number of new subject specifications with 50% of the assessment component in the new Leaving Certificate PE specification involving the use of digital technologies to record student progress. Computer Science has also been introduced as an optional subject since 2020 with the subject being made available to all interested schools. Despite this, the primary mode of assessment at Senior Cycle is the high stakes Leaving Certificate examination.

Within these contexts, we need to ask the following questions: is there an inconsistency with what is advocated at Primary level and what is considered as effective or highly effective practice as outlined in the DLF? Do the uses of digital technologies identified at Junior and Senior cycle align with the development of the key skills that are identified at Junior and Senior cycle? Can they be considered effective or highly effective practice? Are the key skills that are identified at Junior and Senior cycle valued and assessed in any way in the current Leaving Certificate examination process. These are some of the questions that must be addressed if we are to achieve greater consistency of vision across and between the various levels in the learning eco-system.

Of paramount importance is the recognition that there is a need to work towards understanding what everyone values and what their beliefs about learning are, as this directly impacts what technologies are valued and how they are used. Taking this approach will be the starting point to moving towards a consistency of vision across and between the various levels in the learning eco-system but this will need to be supported with robust contextually and culturally relevant models of professional learning for teachers and school leaders. This approach will require a well-funded coherent, flexible and sustainable model of professional learning for teachers, that will enable continued and progressive implementation of the DLF as school work toward developing their DLP, specific to subjects, class levels, and teacher knowledge [15, 19]. In addition, as advocated by the DSS 2015–2020 [1], teacher professional learning programmes need to focus on student-centred, creative pedagogies, employ interdisciplinary approaches and project tasks to engage learners in real-world problem solving as well as how to create meaningful student-teacher connections using digital technologies [16]. In order for this to happen, teachers will need to be supported within a learning culture that encourages them to work with others to critically and purposefully use a range of digital technologies for teaching, learning and assessment.

Effective school leadership is key in enabling staff engage in a process to identify specific actions for changes in teaching, learning and assessment linked to the School Self Evaluation process (SSE) and the DLF. The focus to date, has generally been on providing awareness sessions for school leaders rather than on the provision of focused professional learning programmes for leaders [15, 20] to build capacity to develop, lead and support a learning culture which leverages critical and purposeful uses of digital technologies for teaching, learning and assessment in school communities.

Moving forward, it is vital that an emphasis on supporting school leadership to engage in developing this type of learning culture is included in the DSS to 2027. It is imperative that effective professional learning for school leaders acknowledges that schools are at different levels in embedding digital technologies into their learning eco-systems. A one size fits all approach will not suffice and a range of appropriate supports must be put in place to enable them build this learning culture. Depending on the context, school leaders may be able to develop and leverage expertise within the school community. However, this may not always be possible and school leaders need to be empowered to recognise when help is needed and be supported to draw on a range of supports, both internal and external, as required. Supporting school leadership in this way will enable effective school planning which combines school self-evaluation priorities and actions in tandem with the DLF [3, 4]. It will develop the processes required to leverage critical and purposeful uses of digital technologies for teaching, learning and assessment in school communities. Of critical importance is that teacher professional learning should then be linked to these actions. In addition, consideration of how to develop teacher competences and how to embed development of digital competences in curricula specifications also needs to be addressed [16]. It has been suggested that digital competence frameworks for teachers/students across each level of the system should be developed [16, 19] and appropriate professional learning opportunities put in place to support such development. In addition, the inclusion of the development of digital skills as a core element of Initial Teacher Education programmes [31] will contribute to a more holistic model of teacher professional learning.

6 Conclusion

To conclude, it is only when we engage the whole system that educational transformation can occur [32] and this involves the complex interaction of a range of contextual factors including national and regional policy, cultural norms and values, leadership, teacher attitudes and skills, and student characteristics [33]. Fullan [34] refers to this connectedness of factors as 'permeable connectivity' and stresses the need to pursue "strategies that promote mutual interaction and influence within and across the three levels" (p. 11) (Macro/Meso/Micro). In summary; national goals, approaches, and priorities must align with the contexts and values of local school communities. However, alignment cannot be achieved unilaterally; it requires careful consideration and engagement by groups and individuals who influence education policy, resources, and decisions within the school community [35].

Finally, while the introduction and use of the UNESCO framework [7] for the conceptualisation and design of DSS [1] and DLF [3, 4], enabled policy makers to identify the interconnectedness of the aspects of the learning eco-system, and helped them to understand the deliberate links that needed to be made between policy and practice in order for systemic change to emerge, this was only the first step. An understanding of the interconnectedness between the three levels of the system (Constitutive Order, School Arena, and Setting) (See Fig. 2) and the importance of ensuring a consistency of shared vision is required. The appreciation and understanding of the importance of context at the school and classroom levels cannot be emphasised enough as policy is translated into different school and classroom settings.

References

1. Department of Education and Skills (DES). The digital strategy for schools 2015–2020 (2015). https://www.education.ie/en/Publications/Policy-Reports/Digital-Strategy-for-Schools-2015-2020.pdf. Accessed 08 June 2023
2. Butler, D., et al.: Education systems in the digital age: the need for alignment. Technol. Knowl. Learn. **23**(3), 473–494 (2018). https://doi.org/10.1007/s10758-018-9388-6
3. Department of Education and Skills (DES). Digital learning framework for primary schools. Department of Education and Skills, Dublin (2017). https://www.education.ie/en/Schools-Colleges/Information/Information-Communications-Technology-ICT-in-Schools/digital-learning-framework-primary.pdf. Accessed 08 June 2023
4. Department of Education and Skills (DES). Digital learning framework for post-primary schools. Department of Education and Skills, Dublin (2017). https://www.education.ie/en/Schools-Colleges/Information/Information-Communications-Technology-ICT-in-Schools/digital-learning-framework-post-primary.pdf. Accessed 08 June 2023

5. UNESCO. ICT competency standards for teachers: competency standards modules. UNESCO, Paris (2008). http://unesdoc.unesco.org/images/0015/001562/156207e.pdf. Accessed 08 June 2023
6. UNESCO. ICT competency standards for teachers: policy framework. UNESCO, Paris (2008). http://unesdoc.unesco.org/images/0015/001562/156210E.pdf. Accessed 08 June 2023
7. UNESCO. ICT competency standards for teachers: policy framework. UNESCO, Paris (2011). http://iite.unesco.org/pics/publications/en/files/3214694.pdf. Accessed 08 June 2023
8. UNESCO. ICT competency standards for teachers: policy framework. UNESCO, Paris (2018)
9. Carretero, S., Vuorikari, R., Punie, Y.: The digital competence framework for citizens. Publications Office of the European Union (2017)
10. Redecker, C.: European framework for the digital competence of educators: DigCompEdu (No. JRC107466). Joint Research Centre (Seville site) (2017)
11. Department of Education and Skills (DES). Looking at Our School 2016 A Quality Framework for Primary Schools. Inspectorate, Department of Education and Skills, Dublin (2016). https://assets.gov.ie/25260/4a47d32bf7194c9987ed42cd898e612d.pdf. Accessed 08 June 2023
12. Department of Education and Skills (DES). Looking at Our School 2016 A Quality Framework for Post-Primary Schools. Inspectorate, Department of Education and Skills, Dublin (2016). https://assets.gov.ie/25261/c97d1cc531f249c9a050a9b3b4a0f62b.pdf. Accessed 08 June 2023
13. Butler, D., Hallissy, M., Hurley, J.: The digital learning framework: what digital learning can look like in practice, an Irish perspective. In: Society for Information Technology & Teacher Education International Conference, pp. 1339–1346. Association for the Advancement of Computing in Education (AACE) (2018)
14. Department of Education and Skills. An introduction to school self-evaluation of teaching and learning in primary schools. Inspectorate guidelines for schools. Inspectorate, Department of Education and Skills, Dublin (2012). https://www.education.ie/en/Publications/Inspection-Reports-Publications/Evaluation-Reports-Guidelines/School-Self-Evaluation-Guidelines-2016-2020-Primary.pdf. Accessed 08 June 2023
15. Feerick, E., Cosgrove, J., Moran, E.: Digital Learning Framework (DLF) national evaluation: one year on – wave 1 report. Educational Research Centre, Dublin (2021). https://www.erc.ie/2018/05/16/publications-2020/. Accessed 08 June 2023
16. DE Inspectorate. Digital learning 2020: reporting on practice in early learning and care, primary and post-primary contexts. Inspectorate, Department of Education and Skills, Dublin (2020). https://www.education.ie/en/Publications/Inspection-Reports-Publications/Evaluation-Reports-Guidelines/digital-learning-2020.pdf. Accessed 08 June 2023
17. Devitt, A., Bray, A., Banks, J., Ni Chorcora, E.: Teaching and learning during school closures: lessons learned. Irish second-level teacher perspective. Trinity, Dublin (2020). https://www.tcd.ie/Education/research/covid19/teaching-and-learning-resources/. Accessed 08 June 2023
18. Burke, J., Dempsey, M.: COVID-19 practice in primary schools in Ireland report, Maynooth, Ireland (2020)
19. Department of Education. Reports on consultation process. https://www.gov.ie/en/publication/69fb88-digital-strategy-for-schools/#reports-on-consultation-process. Accessed 08 June 2023
20. Cosgrove, J., Moran, E., Feerick, E., Duggan, A.: Digital Learning Framework (DLF) national evaluation: starting off – baseline report. Educational Research Centre, Dublin (2019). https://www.erc.ie/2019/02/20/publications-2019/. Accessed 08 June 2023
21. Twining, P.: Educational alignment (and sociocultural theory). Halfbaked Education Blog (2018). https://halfbaked.education/educational-alignment-and-sociocultural-theory/. Accessed 08 June 2023

22. Twining, P., et al.: Developing a quality curriculum in a technological era. Educ. Technol. Res. Dev. **69**, 2285–2308 (2020). https://doi.org/10.1007/s11423-020-09857-3
23. European Schoolnet and University of Liège. Survey of schools: ICT in education. Benchmarking access, use and attitudes to technology in Europe's schools. Final report (ESSIE). European Union, Brussels (2013). http://ec.europa.eu/digital-agenda/sites/digital-agenda/files/KK-31-13-401-EN-N.pdf. Accessed 08 June 2023
24. Kozma, R. (ed.): Technology, Innovation, and Educational Change: A Global Perspective. International Society for Educational Technology, Eugene (2003)
25. Law, N., Pelgrum, J., Plomp, T.: Pedagogy and ICT use in schools around the world: findings from the IEA SITES 2006 study. The Comparative Education Research Centre, Hong Kong (2008)
26. OECD. Students, computers and learning: making the connection. OECD Publishing, Paris (2015). https://doi.org/10.1787/9789264239555-en. Accessed 08 June 2023
27. Shear, L., et al.: The Microsoft innovative schools program year 2 evaluation report. Microsoft, Redmond (2010). http://www.microsoft.com/en-us/download/details.aspx?id=9791. Accessed 08 June 2023
28. Shear, L., Gallagher, L., Patel, D.: ITL research 2011 findings: evolving educational ecosystems. Microsoft, Redmond (2011)
29. Plomp, T., Law, N., Pelgrum, J. (eds.): Cross-National Information and Communication Technology. Policies and Practices in Education. Information Age, Charlotte (2009)
30. National Council for Curriculum and Assessment. Draft primary curriculum framework: for consultation (2020). https://ncca.ie/media/4456/ncca-primary-curriculum-framework-2020.pdf. Accessed 08 June 2023
31. Teaching Council (TE) Céim: Standards for Initial Teacher Education (2020). https://www.teachingcouncil.ie/en/news-events/latest-news/ceim-standards-for-initial-teacher-education.pdf. Accessed 08 June 2023
32. Fullan, M.: Stratosphere: integrating technology, pedagogy, and change knowledge. Pearson, Canada (2013)
33. Owston, R.: School context, sustainability, and transferability of innovation. In: Kozma, R. (ed.) Technology, Innovation, and Educational Change: A Global Perspective. International Society for Educational Technology, Eugene (2003)
34. Fullan, M.: Change theory. In: Seminar Series. A Force for School Improvement (2006)
35. Russell, C.: System supports for 21st century competencies. Asia Society: Centre for Global Studies (2016). https://asiasociety.org/files/system-supports-for-21st-century-competencies-2016_0.pdf

Author Index

Published by Springer Nature Switzerland AG 2023
T. Keane et al. (Eds.): WCCE 2022, IFIP AICT 685, pp. 697–699, 2023.
https://doi.org/10.1007/978-3-031-43393-1

Printed by Printforce, United Kingdom